Berlin

Andrea Schulte-Peevers

LONELY PLANET PUBLICATIONS
Melbourne • Oakland • London • Paris

Berlin
2nd edition – April 2000
First published – August 1998

Published by
Lonely Planet Publications Pty Ltd ABN 36 005 607 983
90 Maribyrnong St, Footscray, Victoria 3011, Australia

Lonely Planet Offices
Australia Locked Bag 1, Footscray, Victoria 3011
USA 150 Linden St, Oakland, CA 94607
UK 10a Spring Place, London NW5 3BH
France 1 rue du Dahomey, 75011 Paris

Photographs
Many of the images in this guide are available for licensing from
Lonely Planet Images.
email: lpi@lonelyplanet.com.au

Front cover photograph
Section of the Wall, East Side Gallery (Andrea Schulte-Peevers)

ISBN 0 86442 790 5

text & maps © Lonely Planet 2000
photos © photographers as indicated 2000

Printed by SNP SPrint (M) Sdn Bhd
Printed in Malaysia

Although the authors
and Lonely Planet try
to make the informa-
tion as accurate as
possible, we accept
no responsibility for
any loss, injury or
inconvenience sus-
tained by anyone
using this book.

Contents – Text

THE AUTHOR — 4

THIS BOOK — 5

FOREWORD — 6

INTRODUCTION — 9

FACTS ABOUT BERLIN — 11

History 11
Geography 24
Climate 24
Ecology & Environment 24
Flora & Fauna 25
Government & Politics 25
Economy 26
Population & People 26
Education 27
Science & Philosophy 27
Arts 28
Society & Conduct 40
Religion 41
Language 41
Berlin's Architecture 43

FACTS FOR THE VISITOR — 56

When to Go 56
Orientation 56
Maps 58
Tourist Offices 58
Documents 59
Embassies & Consulates 61
Customs 62
Money 62
Post & Communications 67
Internet Resources 69
Books 70
Newspapers & Magazines 71
Radio 72
Television 72
Video Systems 73
Photography & Video 73
Time 74
Electricity 74
Weights & Measures 74
Laundry 74
Toilets 74
Health 75
Women Travellers 76
Gay & Lesbian Travellers 77
Disabled Travellers 78
Senior Travellers 78
Berlin for Children 79
Libraries 80
Universities 80
International Centres 80
Dangers & Annoyances 81
Legal Matters 82
Business Hours 82
Public Holidays & Special Events 83
Doing Business 84
Work 85

GETTING THERE & AWAY — 87

Air 87
Train 92
Bus 95
Car & Motorcycle 96
Hitching 96
Organised Tours 96
Travel Agents 96
Warning 97

GETTING AROUND — 98

The Airports 98
To/From the Airports 98
Public Transport 99
Car & Motorcycle 101
Taxi 102
Bicycle 103
Walking 103
Organised Tours 103

THINGS TO SEE & DO — 106

Mitte 106
Unter den Linden 107
Museumsinsel 111
Schlossplatz Area 114
Friedrichstrasse 115
Oranienburger Tor Area 116
Gendarmenmarkt Area 117
Potsdamer Platz Area 118
Third Reich Government Quarter 120
Alexanderplatz Area 123
Nikolaiviertel 124
Molkenmarkt Area 125
Märkisches Ufer 125
Spandauer Vorstadt 126
Charlottenburg 129
Walking Tour 130
Schloss Charlottenburg 132
Schloss Area Museums 134
Funkturm Area 136
Olympic Stadium Area 136

2 Contents – Text

Tiergarten **136**
Moabit 137
Tiergarten Park 138
Kulturforum Area 139
Schöneberg **142**
Nollendorfplatz Area 143
Kleistpark Area 143
Rathaus Schöneberg 144
Kreuzberg **144**
North-West Kreuzberg 145
Kreuzberg Walking Tour 147
Friedrichshain **150**
East Side Gallery 151
Karl-Marx-Allee 151

Volkspark Friedrichshain 152
Prenzlauer Berg **153**
Walking Tour 153
Northern Prenzlauer Berg ..154
Northern Districts **155**
Pankow 155
Weissensee 155
Eastern Districts **157**
Lichtenberg 157
Marzahn 159
Hellersdorf 159
Hohenschönhausen 159
Southern Districts **160**
Neukölln 160

Treptow 161
Köpenick 163
Western Districts **165**
Wilmersdorf 167
Zehlendorf 168
Activities **172**
Fitness Centres 172
Swimming 172
Saunas 175
Cycling 175
Running 176
Tennis & Squash 176
Casino 176
Courses 176

PLACES TO STAY   177

Camping 177
Hostels 178

Private Rooms 181
Hotels 181

Long-Term Rentals 188

PLACES TO EAT   190

Food 190
Drinks 191
Restaurants 192

Cafes 202
Snacks & Fast Food 206
Food Courts 207

Student Cafeterias 208
Kantinen 208
Self-Catering 208

ENTERTAINMENT   209

Cinemas 210
Pubs & Bars 210
Clubs 215
Cultural Centres 218

Live Music 219
Opera & Musicals 220
Cabaret 220
Theatre 222

Dance 224
Gay & Lesbian Berlin 224
Spectator Sports 226

SHOPPING   228

What to Buy 228
Where to Shop 233

Department Stores 234
Markets 235

EXCURSIONS   237

Brandenburg **237**
Potsdam 237
Brandenburg an der Havel 244
Spreewald 245
Buckow 247

Sachsenhausen Memorial &
Museum 248
Rheinsberg 249
Chorin 250
Niederfinow 250

Beyond Brandenburg **251**
Lutherstadt-Wittenberg 251
Dresden 252
Leipzig 257

LANGUAGE   263

Food & Drink 267

GLOSSARY   269

INDEX   282

Text 282

Boxed Text 288

METRIC CONVERSION   inside back cover

Contents – Maps

FACTS ABOUT BERLIN

Tour I – Age of Schinkel 50   Tour III – DaimlerCity 53
Tour II – Modernist Visions in
Tiergarten 51

FACTS FOR THE VISITOR

Districts of Berlin 57

GETTING THERE & AWAY

Transport Routes 93

THINGS TO SEE & DO

Potsdamer Platz   Spandau Map 9 166
Development 120

EXCURSIONS

Berlin Excursions 238   Dresden 254
Potsdam 240   Leipzig 258

COLOUR MAPS   back of book

Tarifbereiche   Charlottenburg ....Map 7
(Berlin Railways) ....Map 1   Mitte ....Map 8
Berlin ....Map 2-6

MAP LEGEND   back page

The Author

Andrea Schulte-Peevers

Andrea is a Los Angeles-based writer, editor and translator who owes her love of languages and travel to her mother who lugged her off to foreign lands when she was still a toothless toddler. After completing high school in Germany, Andrea left for London and stints as an au-pair, market researcher and foreign language correspondent. In the mid-'80s she swapped England for Southern California and the hallowed halls of UCLA. She then hit the job market armed with a degree in English literature and charted a course in travel journalism. Assignments have taken her to all continents but Antarctica and her work has been published in several countries. Andrea joined the fleet of Lonely Planet writers in 1995 and has updated and authored the *Los Angeles*, *California & Nevada*, *Germany* and *Western Europe* guides.

FROM THE AUTHOR

Books like these don't get written without the help, encouragement and ideas of many wonderful people. Topping the list is my husband David without whom this kind of itinerant career would be impossible. Thank you, David, for tolerating the separations and the recurrent borderline madness that strikes around deadline times.

In Berlin, big fat kudos go to Jörg Thelen and Kerstin and Marco Göllrich for their unsurpassed hospitality and friendship: I couldn't do it without you! A round of applause to Bernd Buhmann and Natasha Kompatzki of Berlin Tourismus Marketing for supplying lots of useful information and for getting me in touch with the right people. Heaps of thanks to Peter and Sven at the Odyssee Hostel for sharing beers, laughs and insights; and to Francis, Mickey and Chris of Insider Tours for pointing me to the hottest Berlin restaurant and nightlife spots. A special mention goes to my fellow author Jeremy Gray for use of his research and information for the Excursions chapter.

Finally, a heartfelt *Danke Schön* to the dream team of editors, cartographers and designers at LP Melbourne – including Kate Kiely, Chris Wyness and Birgit Jordan – who once again worked their magic to put this 2nd edition into readers' hands.

This Book

Andrea Schulte-Peevers and David Peevers researched and wrote the 1st edition of *Berlin*. Andrea updated this 2nd edition.

From the Publisher

The editing of this 2nd edition of *Berlin* was coordinated in the Lonely Planet head office in Melbourne by Kate Kiely. She was assisted by editors Yvonne Byron and Susannah Farfor. Mapping and design was coordinated by Birgit Jordan, who was assisted by Mark Germanchis. Tim Uden advised on layout, Quentin Frayne produced the Language chapter, and Jocelyn Harewood created the index. Jamieson Ross designed the cover, Lonely Planet Images (LPI) supplied the images and Matt King advised on illustrations. Many thanks to the Berliner Verkehrsbetriebe (BVG) for supply of the Tarifbereiche (Berlin Railways) map.

Thanks

Many thanks to the following travellers who used the last edition and wrote to us with helpful hints, useful advice and interesting anecdotes:

Ray Baker, Noel Boutin, Alicia Burton, Kendall Crowe, Michelle Doty, Jessica Egyhazi, Jenny Elsby, Scott Finlay, John Goring, Grace Hawley, Francis Hayward, Justin Hendriks, Dionneau Herve, J H Higgs, Meryl Ibis, Inge Kimenai, Maree Loader, Bill McLaughlin, Emily MacWilliams, Peter Marshman, Derek Mason, Kelsey Merrow, Hilary Naavi, Joel Northcott, Valerie Parkinson, Claudia Pastorino, Bob Quick, Amanda Schell, Angel Simpson, Cara Sottak, Melissa Sutton, Acb Tyson, Remko Vermeulen, Maximilian Wagner, Jorg Wenckowski, Ton Wortman.

Foreword

ABOUT LONELY PLANET GUIDEBOOKS

The story begins with a classic travel adventure: Tony and Maureen Wheeler's 1972 journey across Europe and Asia to Australia. Useful information about the overland trail did not exist at that time, so Tony and Maureen published the first Lonely Planet guidebook to meet a growing need.

From a kitchen table, then from a tiny office in Melbourne (Australia), Lonely Planet has become the largest independent travel publisher in the world, an international company with offices in Melbourne, Oakland (USA), London (UK) and Paris (France).

Today Lonely Planet guidebooks cover the globe. There is an ever-growing list of books and there's information in a variety of forms and media. Some things haven't changed. The main aim is still to help make it possible for adventurous travellers to get out there – to explore and better understand the world.

At Lonely Planet we believe travellers can make a positive contribution to the countries they visit – if they respect their host communities and spend their money wisely. Since 1986 a percentage of the income from each book has been donated to aid projects and human rights campaigns.

Updates Lonely Planet thoroughly updates each guidebook as often as possible. This usually means there are around two years between editions, although for more unusual or more stable destinations the gap can be longer. Check the imprint page (following the colour map at the beginning of the book) for publication dates.

Between editions up-to-date information is available in two free newsletters – the paper *Planet Talk* and email *Comet* (to subscribe, contact any Lonely Planet office) – and on our Web site at www.lonelyplanet.com. The *Upgrades* section of the Web site covers a number of important and volatile destinations and is regularly updated by Lonely Planet authors. *Scoop* covers news and current affairs relevant to travellers. And, lastly, the *Thorn Tree* bulletin board and *Postcards* section of the site carry unverified, but fascinating, reports from travellers.

Correspondence The process of creating new editions begins with the letters, postcards and emails received from travellers. This correspondence often includes suggestions, criticisms and comments about the current editions. Interesting excerpts are immediately passed on via newsletters and the Web site, and everything goes to our authors to be verified when they're researching on the road. We're keen to get more feedback from organisations or individuals who represent communities visited by travellers.

Lonely Planet gathers information for everyone who's curious about the planet – and especially for those who explore it first-hand. Through guidebooks, phrasebooks, activity guides, maps, literature, newsletters, image library, TV series and Web site we act as an information exchange for a worldwide community of travellers.

Research Authors aim to gather sufficient practical information to enable travellers to make informed choices and to make the mechanics of a journey run smoothly. They also research historical and cultural background to help enrich the travel experience and allow travellers to understand and respond appropriately to cultural and environmental issues.

Authors don't stay in every hotel because that would mean spending a couple of months in each medium-sized city and, no, they don't eat at every restaurant because that would mean stretching belts beyond capacity. They do visit hotels and restaurants to check standards and prices, but feedback based on readers' direct experiences can be very helpful.

Many of our authors work undercover, others aren't so secretive. None of them accept freebies in exchange for positive write-ups. And none of our guidebooks contain any advertising.

Production Authors submit their raw manuscripts and maps to offices in Australia, USA, UK or France. Editors and cartographers – all experienced travellers themselves – then begin the process of assembling the pieces. When the book finally hits the shops, some things are already out of date, we start getting feedback from readers and the process begins again ...

WARNING & REQUEST

Things change – prices go up, schedules change, good places go bad and bad places go bankrupt – nothing stays the same. So, if you find things better or worse, recently opened or long since closed, please tell us and help make the next edition even more accurate and useful. We genuinely value all the feedback we receive. Julie Young coordinates a well travelled team that reads and acknowledges every letter, postcard and email and ensures that every morsel of information finds its way to the appropriate authors, editors and cartographers for verification.

Everyone who writes to us will find their name in the next edition of the appropriate guidebook. They will also receive the latest issue of *Planet Talk*, our quarterly printed newsletter, or *Comet*, our monthly email newsletter. Subscriptions to both newsletters are free. The very best contributions will be rewarded with a free guidebook.

Excerpts from your correspondence may appear in new editions of Lonely Planet guidebooks, the Lonely Planet Web site, *Planet Talk* or *Comet*, so please let us know if you *don't* want your letter published or your name acknowledged.

Send all correspondence to the Lonely Planet office closest to you:

Australia: Locked Bag 1, Footscray, Victoria 3011
USA: 150 Linden St, Oakland, CA 94607
UK: 10a Spring Place, London NW5 3BH
France: 1 rue du Dahomey, 75011 Paris

Or email us at: talk2us@lonelyplanet.com.au

For news, views and updates see our Web site: www.lonelyplanet.com

HOW TO USE A LONELY PLANET GUIDEBOOK

The best way to use a Lonely Planet guidebook is any way you choose. At Lonely Planet we believe the most memorable travel experiences are often those that are unexpected, and the finest discoveries are those you make yourself. Guidebooks are not intended to be used as if they provide a detailed set of infallible instructions!

Contents All Lonely Planet guidebooks follow roughly the same format. The Facts about the Destination chapters or sections give background information ranging from history to weather. Facts for the Visitor gives practical information on issues like visas and health. Getting There & Away gives a brief starting point for researching travel to and from the destination. Getting Around gives an overview of the transport options when you arrive.

The peculiar demands of each destination determine how subsequent chapters are broken up, but some things remain constant. We always start with background, then proceed to sights, places to stay, places to eat, entertainment, getting there and away, and getting around information – in that order.

Heading Hierarchy Lonely Planet headings are used in a strict hierarchical structure that can be visualised as a set of Russian dolls. Each heading (and its following text) is encompassed by any preceding heading that is higher on the hierarchical ladder.

Entry Points We do not assume guidebooks will be read from beginning to end, but that people will dip into them. The traditional entry points are the list of contents and the index. In addition, however, some books have a complete list of maps and an index map illustrating map coverage.

There may also be a colour map that shows highlights. These highlights are dealt with in greater detail in the Facts for the Visitor chapter, along with planning questions and suggested itineraries. Each chapter covering a geographical region usually begins with a locator map and another list of highlights. Once you find something of interest in a list of highlights, turn to the index.

Maps Maps play a crucial role in Lonely Planet guidebooks and include a huge amount of information. A legend is printed on the back page. We seek to have complete consistency between maps and text, and to have every important place in the text captured on a map. Map key numbers usually start in the top left corner.

Although inclusion in a guidebook usually implies a recommendation we cannot list every good place. Exclusion does not necessarily imply criticism. In fact there are a number of reasons why we might exclude a place – sometimes it is simply inappropriate to encourage an influx of travellers.

Introduction

The one thing constant about Berlin is perpetual change. It's always 'becoming' something; it never simply 'is'. Energetic, individualistic, self-confident, decadent, tolerant, cutting edge and edgy, Berlin and its people share happily in a refusal to settle down. City planners may dream of stability but here the status is never quo for long.

With reunification, Berlin, like no other metropolis in history, has been given the chance – and the challenge – to remake itself in its own modern perception of what it should be. By comparison, other global hubs like Paris, London and Tokyo, are finished products, whereas Berlin is a work in progress. As the corps de ballet of cranes still pivots and sways above the emerging skyline – performing its dance of innovation and creation – a fresh chapter begins for a city that is at once vibrant and moody, but also maddeningly complex.

The German capital presents visitors with a cornucopia of diversions. Like New York,

Berlin is a city that never sleeps. Bustling bars and thumping nightclubs teem with restless energy. In fine weather, life assumes an almost Mediterranean insouciance with people sprawling in street cafes, beer gardens and parks. The wealth and quality of Berlin cultural life is peerless, with world-class museums, opera and theatre, music – from classical to countercultural – and a spirited art and gallery scene. Despite the ravages of war and neglect, surviving palaces, monuments and historic structures spur the imagination and lift the spirit. The vast green belt of forests, parks and lakes that fringe the city makes escape from the urban grit and velocity a simple matter of an S-Bahn ride.

In history, Berlin occupies a unique position. No other city has ever undergone the kind of peacetime trauma visited on Berlin. Brutally sliced in half by an impenetrable wall, its people were physically and ideologically separated for 40 years. But now,

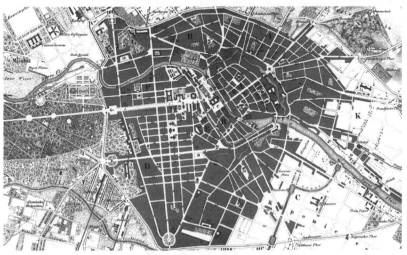

This copy of an original engraving appeared in an 1851 edition of *The Iconographic Encyclopaedia of Science, Literature and Art*. Just 20 years on, the city's population had tripled and change was afoot.

the former epicentre of the Cold War – and a symbol of the division of Germany – is poised to be the bridge between east and west in the 21st century.

While Berlin's physical scars are healing, its people have not easily rejoined. The wall that lingers in the minds and hearts of residents has proven more difficult to bring down than the one they looked across with such longing for four decades. But Berlin demands that its people get on with their lives, and they will undoubtedly rise to the challenge. Divisions among Berliners may persist, but they're united in their resilience.

Another facet of the Berlin character is its people's directness and refusal to mince words. While this brashness can be both refreshing and unsettling, it's really rooted in an attitude of tolerance, a willingness to accept differences among people. They may not like what you do or how you look, but the vast majority still follow the motto 'live and let live.' It's no coincidence that one in eight residents in Berlin is an immigrant or

that Europe's largest gay and lesbian scene flourishes here.

All these factors make Berlin a most 'un-German' city. The rigid social structure so entrenched in much of Germany has been replaced by cosmopolitan largesse and a distinctly laissez-faire attitude. Where you come from doesn't matter so much as what you can do. Nowhere else in the country is it easier for young entrepreneurs to realise their ambitions or for cultural and political movements to develop at a grassroots level. A trendsetter by nature and necessity, Berlin feeds on fledgling moods, trends and appetites and processes them into the new *Zeitgeist*, which is then exported to the rest of the country and beyond.

The world has always looked to Berlin, this most dramatic city – sometimes in fascination, sometimes in horror and sometimes even in deep sympathy. At once repellent and seductive, light-hearted and brooding, Berlin continues to be a city of fascinating extremes.

Facts about Berlin

HISTORY
Early Settlements

The area now occupied by Berlin has been settled since the Stone Age, as numerous archaeological findings show. About 3000 BC, early forms of agriculture and animal husbandry took place, and the oldest pottery also dates from this period. Weapons, tools and jewellery from the early Bronze Age were found at digs in Spandau and Lichtenrade. From the later Bronze Age are the urn cemeteries and remains of settlements attributed to the Lausitz society.

In the first centuries AD, several tribes settled along the Havel and Spree rivers, including the Burgundians and the Germanic Semnones. After the 6th century AD, they competed for territory with the Slavic tribes called Heveller and Sprewanen. The Heveller tribe built fortresses in Spandau and Köpenick.

After the German king Heinrich I conquered Brandenburg in 928 his son, Otto the Great, tried in vain to Christianise the Slavs. In 1134, Albrecht der Bär (Albrecht the Bear) of the House of the Askanians became margrave of the Nordmark (Northern March), a territory which included Brandenburg. Albrecht managed to increasingly suppress and squeeze out the Slavs, resettling the land with immigrants from west of the Elbe River.

Medieval Berlin

Berlin's 'modern' history began in the 13th century with the founding of the trading posts of Cölln and Berlin by itinerant merchants in the area of today's Nikolaiviertel in the Mitte district. Thanks to their strategic location at the crossroads of medieval trading routes, the two settlements soon developed into *Handelsstädte* (trade centres). In 1307, they merged into the double city of Berlin-Cölln, thus formalising the loose cooperation that had existed since their establishment.

A self-confident merchant class managed to keep the city – which was a member of the Hanseatic League in the 14th and 15th centuries – largely independent. But even they could not prevent it from being absorbed into the sphere of power of the Hohenzollern dynasty eventually. After lengthy squabbling between rival factions, it was this family who managed to establish itself as the rulers of the Mark (March) of Brandenburg, a role it would hold until 1918.

In the 1440s, under Elector Friedrich II (ruled 1440-70), Berlin and Cölln gradually lost their independence as the ruler dissolved their administrative council and laid the foundation for a city palace, the future Berliner Schloss. By the time his nephew Johann inherited the title in 1486, Berlin-Cölln had become a residential city and the capital of the March of Brandenburg.

Under the electors, Berlin grew into a powerful and civilised city. It would take the Thirty Years' War (1618-48) to, at least temporarily, put an end to this expansion. An outgrowth of the Reformation, the war had begun as a religious conflict between Protestant and Catholic leagues and soon degenerated into one of Europe's bloodiest dynastic wars. Over the period of hostilities the entire Holy Roman Empire, including Berlin, was ravaged.

The Phoenix Rises

As a result of the war, Berlin's population had been decimated to a mere 6000 people and more than one third of the city's houses lay in ruins. Replenishing the population was foremost in the mind of Elector Friedrich Wilhelm (called the Great Elector, ruled 1640-88), which he shrewdly accomplished by inviting foreigners to settle in Berlin. In 1671, for instance, he asked 50 wealthy Jewish families, who had been expelled from Vienna, to come to the city with the proviso that they bring their enormous fortunes with them.

The bulk of new settlers, though, were Huguenot refugees from France. Some 6000 arrived after King Louis XIV, in

1685, revoked the Edict of Nantes, which had granted the Protestants religious freedom. Berlin's population swelled by 25%, and the French language superseded German in some districts. By 1700, one in five inhabitants was of French descent. Some French words – or corruptions thereof – can still be heard in Berlinisch: *Feez* for *fête*; *Budiker* for *boutiquier*; *Milljöh* for *milieu*; and of course *Boulette*, a Berlin version of the meatball. The French Cathedral on Gendarmenmarkt serves as a tangible reminder of the Huguenots' influence to this day.

Berlin continued to grow in leaps and bounds throughout the 18th century, in no small part because it was known for its religious tolerance and thus remained a haven for Protestants from around Europe. The population catapulted from a mere 29,000 in 1700 to 172,000 one hundred years later, making Berlin the second-largest city in the Holy Roman Empire behind Vienna.

The Age of Prussia

The Great Elector's son, Elector Friedrich III, was a man with great ambition and a penchant for the arts and sciences. Joined by his beloved wife, Sophie Charlotte, he presided over a lively and intellectual court, founding the Academy of Arts in 1696 and the Academy of Sciences in 1700. One year later, Friedrich advanced his career by promoting himself to King Friedrich I (ruling 1688-1701 as elector, 1701-13 as king) of Prussia, making Berlin a royal residence and the capital of the new state of Brandenburg-Prussia.

His son, Friedrich Wilhelm I (ruled 1713-40), was quite a different leader. Frugal and militaristic minded, his obsession was to build an army of 80,000, which is why he was called *Soldatenkönig* (Soldier King). In the early years of his reign, some 17,000 males – including about 7000 craftsmen – left Berlin to avoid being drafted. Friedrich Wilhelm responded by enclosing the city with a wall in 1734, officially for customs-collection purposes but actually to prevent further desertions. (Isn't it ironic that, some 230 years later, a different government

would use his idea to keep its own people from leaving?)

Everyone breathed a sigh of relief when his son Friedrich II (ruled 1740-86) – better known to English speakers as Frederick the Great and to his subjects as 'der alte Fritz' (Old Freddy) – came to the throne. He sought greatness through developing the city architecturally and was known for his political and military savvy. Berlin flourished as a great cultural centre and became known as *Spree-Athen* ('Athens on the Spree').

Friedrich's cultural side, though, was counterbalanced by a thirst for military exploits and a particular desire for the territory of Silesia in today's Poland. After a series of battles stretching over a period of about two decades, victory was his. With the signing of the Peace of Hubertusburg in 1763, Austria and Saxony agreed to put Silesia officially into the Prussian camp.

The Enlightenment & Napoleonic Occupation

During Friedrich II's reign, the Enlightenment arrived with some authority. The playwright Gotthold Ephraim Lessing, the thinker and publisher Christophe Friedrich Nicolai and the philosopher Moses Mendelssohn (grandfather of composer Felix Mendelssohn-Bartholdy) all helped make Berlin a truly international city. After 1780, intellectual salons, organised by women such as Henriette Herz and Rahel Levin, provided an open forum for discussion for anybody regardless of social standing or religious background.

After 1800, another wave of scientists, philosophers and literary greats descended on the capital. The group included Heinrich von Kleist, Clemens von Brentano, Achim von Arnim, Novalis, Johann Gottlieb Fichte and the brothers Alexander and Wilhelm Humboldt. Many of them taught at the new university the latter founded in 1810.

Politically, Prussia went into a downward spiral after the death of Friedrich II, culminating in the defeat of the Prussian army by Napoleon's forces at Jena, some 400km south-west of Berlin, in 1806. On 27 October of the same year, Napoleon marched through the Brandenburg Gate, beginning a seven-year occupation of Berlin. The French troops finally left in exchange for a handy sum in reparation payments, leaving behind a humiliated city mired in debt so deep that it would take 53 years to climb out of it. In the end, though, Napoleon didn't fare so well either, with his empire shattered by the combined forces of Austria, Russia and Prussia at the Battle of Leipzig in 1813.

Reforms & Nationalism

The first half of the 19th century was a crucial period in the development of both Germany and Europe, when a self-made class of public servants, academics, theologians and merchants – stressing individual achievement – questioned the right of the nobility to rule. Brandenburg-Prussia was caught up in the maelstrom of reforms brought on by this movement. Restrictive guild regulations were lifted, allowing anyone to take up any profession. Agricultural reforms abolished bonded labour, providing the basis for industrialisation. Jews won civic equality in 1812.

The decay of feudal structures, the redistribution of wealth and the rise of industry changed the socio-economic ground rules, eventually leading to nationalist calls for a centralised state. At the Academy of Sciences in Berlin, philosopher Johann Gottlieb Fichte gave a series of speeches, the so-called *Reden an die deutsche Nation* (Speeches to the German Nation) in which he called for a new national consciousness.

All this ferment brought relatively little change from the top, however, and so in March 1848 Berlin joined with other German cities in a bourgeois revolution demanding freedom of the press, formation of a parliament, withdrawal of the military from the political sphere and other basic democratic rights. Government troops quickly suppressed the riots, in the process sounding the death knell for 250 people and for political development spurred by the Enlightenment. Stagnation set in for the next eight years as the reactionary Friedrich Wilhelm IV (ruled 1840-61) ascended the throne.

The Industrial Age

With the manufacturing trades already well established since the 18th century, Berlin developed into a centre of technology and industry right from the dawn of the Industrial Age. The building of the German railway system (the first track from Berlin to Potsdam opened in 1838) led to the foundation of more than 1000 factories, including electrical giants AEG and Siemens and other companies in the machine, chemical, textile and food production sectors.

The abundance of jobs created a new class in Berlin – the proletariat – as workers flocked to the city from throughout Germany; from 1850 to 1870 the population more than tripled to about 870,000. Putting a roof over the heads of the masses became a problem that was solved by building countless *Mietskasernen* (literally 'rental barracks'). These were labyrinthine tenements built around successive courtyards; entire families subsisted in poorly ventilated, tiny flats without indoor plumbing.

New political parties formed to give a voice to the proletariat, including the Sozialdemokratische Partei Deutschland (SPD, or Social Democratic Party). Founded in 1875 as the Socialist Workers' Party, it took its present name in 1890. In response to the party's growing influence, in 1878 Prussian prime minister Otto von Bismarck passed the *Sozialistengesetze* (Socialist Laws) that prohibited socialist organisations and allowed censorship of socialist writings. However, this did nothing to curb support for the SPD; in the 1890 elections it received about 50% of the votes, forcing Bismarck to repeal the laws. At the height of its popularity in 1912, the SPD garnered 75% of the votes in Berlin.

Road to the German Empire

After Friedrich Wilhelm IV suffered a stroke in 1857, his brother Wilhelm became regent and, in 1861, King Wilhelm I. Unlike his brother, Wilhelm was a man who recognised more clearly the signs of the times and was not averse to progress. Besides appointing a number of liberal ministers, he made Bismarck Prussian prime minister in 1862.

Bismarck's grand ambition was to create a Prussian-led unified Germany. His methods would be old-fashioned and effective: through manipulation and war. Bismarck began by winning the province of Schleswig-Holstein in a war with Denmark in 1864 (with Austria as his ally), then fought and beat Austria itself in 1866 and formed the North German Confederation the following year.

With northern Germany under his control, Bismarck turned his attention to the south. Through skilful diplomacy, he isolated France and manoeuvred it into declaring war on Prussia in 1870. He then surprised Napoleon III by winning the backing of most southern German states. That war ended with Prussia's annexation of Alsace-Lorraine. But more importantly, with the southern German princes no longer opposed to him, Bismarck's grand plan finally came to fruition: Germany was unified with Berlin as its capital. On 18 January 1871, King Wilhelm I was crowned Kaiser Wilhelm I at Versailles (an ultimate humiliation of the French), with Bismarck as his 'Iron Chancellor'. The German Empire was born.

MICK WELDON

Otto von Bismarck: used manipulation and war to create a unified Germany.

Gründerzeit

Gründerzeit (Foundation Era) refers to the early years of the German Empire following the defeat of France in 1871. Reparations from that country, and the increased magnetism of Berlin as the centre of the new empire, engendered another wave of company foundings.

Germany was now a wealthy, unified country thanks in large part to the force and vision of Bismarck. He had painted himself in liberal colours to buy inches and stop socialist demands for miles, providing health and accident benefits and retirement pensions. But the reform issue was to be his downfall. When Wilhelm II became Kaiser in 1888 (Friedrich, the son of Wilhelm I, was sick and ruled for only 99 days), divisions arose between the Kaiser, who wanted to extend the social-security system, and Bismarck, who enacted stricter anti-socialist laws. In 1890 the Kaiser finally excised Bismarck from the political scene.

The period leading up to the outbreak of war in 1914 – called the 'New Direction' – was in fact an aimless one under the personal rule of Wilhelm II, who brought his weak chancellors to heel. Although industrially advanced (especially in the chemical and electrical industries) and having produced some of the best social-revolutionary minds, Germany paddled into the new century with incompetent leaders at its helm.

WWI & Revolution

On 28 June 1914, the heir to the Austrian throne, Archduke Franz-Ferdinand and his wife were assassinated in Sarajevo, which triggered a war between Austria-Hungary and Serbia. Russia mobilised as part of its alliance with Serbia. Germany, allied with Austria-Hungary since 1879, declared war on Russia, followed two days later by a declaration of war on France (which had taken the Russian side). The Reichstag (German parliament) immediately granted the necessary war credits. Among the general population initial euphoria and belief in a quick victory soon gave way to disillusionment, exacerbated by the increasing hardship of food shortages in Berlin and elsewhere.

When peace came with Germany's defeat in 1918, it meant an end to fighting but it didn't create stability at home. Germany paid dearly for the war. The Treaty of Versailles forced it to relinquish its colonies in Africa, to cede Alsace-Lorraine and territory in western Poland, and to pay cripplingly high reparations.The treaty made Germany responsible for all losses incurred by its enemies. The humiliation was huge.

The loss of the war also brought the collapse of the monarchy. Kaiser Wilhelm II abdicated on 9 November 1918, ending more than 500 years of Hohenzollern rule and paving the way for a power struggle between socialist and democratic parties. In the early afternoon of the same day, from a window of the Reichstag, Philipp Scheidemann of the SPD proclaimed the birth of the German Republic with party leader Friedrich Ebert as its head. Hours later Karl Liebknecht, founder of the German Communist Party (then known as the Spartacus League) proclaimed the Free Socialist Republic of Germany from a balcony of the Berliner Schloss.

Founded by Rosa Luxemburg and Liebknecht, the Spartacus League sought to establish a republic based on Karl Marx's theories of proletarian revolution. Opposed by moderate socialists, it merged with other groups to form the Kommunistische Partei Deutschland (KPD, or German Communist Party) in the final days of 1918. Rivalry between the SPD and the Spartacus League led to a period of instability which culminated in the so-called Spartacus Revolt in Berlin from 6 to 15 January 1919. Following the bloody quashing of this uprising, Luxemburg and Liebknecht were arrested and murdered by right-wing *Freikorps* soldiers and their bodies dumped in Berlin's Landwehrkanal.

The Weimar Republic

The federalist constitution of the fledgling republic, Germany's first experiment with democracy, was adopted in July 1919 in the town of Weimar, where the constituent assembly had sought refuge from the chaos of Berlin. It gave women the vote and established basic human rights, but it was also unwieldy and gave too much power to the president, who could rule by decree in times of emergency. This was a clause that would later be abused by Paul von Hindenburg, Germany's second president.

A broad coalition government of left and centre parties formed, led by president Friedrich Ebert of the SPD which, until 1932, remained Germany's largest party. Too many forces in Germany rejected the republic, however, and the government satisfied neither communists nor monarchists.

More trouble erupted in 1920 when the right-wing military circle staged the so-called Kapp Putsch, occupying the government quarter. Called on by the government to act (it had fled to Dresden), workers and unions went on strike, and the military putsch collapsed.

The year 1920 also saw the amalgamation of seven cities and countless communities into Gross-Berlin (Greater Berlin), making it one of the largest cities in the world with an area of 87,000 hectares and a population of nearly 4 million. It was divided into 20 *Bezirke* (administrative districts), essentially the same set-up that exists today. (The three districts of Hohenschönhausen, Marzahn

MICK WELDON

Rosa Luxemburg: co-founder with Carl Liebknecht of the German Communist Party.

and Hellersdorf were added in the 1980s, bringing the total to 23 districts.)

The 'Golden' Twenties The 1920s began as anything but golden, marked as they were by the humiliation of a lost war, social and political instability, hyperinflation, hunger and illness. Some 235,000 Berliners were unemployed and strikes, demonstrations and riots had become commonplace. The introduction of a new currency, the *Rentenmark*, brought some relief but things really started to turn around only after cash, in the form of loans under the Dawes Plan, flowed into Germany after 1924. Berlin was on the rise once again.

For the next few years, the city launched into a cultural heyday that exceeded anything that had come before. It gained a reputation as a centre for both tolerance and indulgence, and outsiders flocked to a city of cabaret, dada and jazz. Theatres, opera houses and concert halls did a brisk trade, and the film company UFA was established. Almost 150 daily newspapers competed with each other.

In 1923, Germany's first radio broadcast hit the airwaves over Berlin and, in 1931, TV had its world premiere here. In the field of science, Berliners Albert Einstein, Carl Bosch and Werner Heisenberg were awarded Nobel Prizes. A Who's Who of architecture (including Bruno Taut, Martin Wagner, Hans Scharoun and Walter Gropius), the fine arts (George Grosz, Max Beckmann, Lovis Corinth) and literature (Bertolt Brecht, Kurt Tucholsky, WH Auden, Christopher Isherwood) contributed to Berlin's reputation as the artistic centre of the world.

Karl Marx had long ago met his maker when the stock market crashed on his birthday, 25 October 1929. The so-called Black Friday cast an instant pall over the Golden Twenties. Within weeks, about half a million Berliners were jobless, and riots and demonstrations once again ruled the streets. The ensuing Depression undermined an already fragile German democracy and bred support for extremist parties.

In response to the chaos, Field Marshal Paul von Hindenburg, who had succeeded Ebert as president in 1925, used Article 48 of the constitution – the emergency powers – to circumvent parliament and appoint the Catholic Centre Party's Heinrich Brüning as chancellor. Brüning deflated the economy, forced down wages and destroyed whatever savings – and faith – the middle classes had built up since the last economic debacle. It earned him the epitaph 'the hunger chancellor'.

The volatile, increasingly polarised political climate became characterised by frequent confrontations between communists and members of a party that had just begun to gain momentum – the Nationalsozialistische Deutsche Arbeiterpartei (National Socialist German Workers' Party, or NSDAP).

Hitler's Rise to Power

In 1930 Hitler's NSDAP made astounding gains, winning 18% of the vote. Hitler set his sights on the presidency in 1932, running against Hindenburg; he received 37% of the second-round vote. In the ensuing national elections, the Nazis became the largest party in the Reichstag with 230 seats. Berliners, though, had remained comparatively sceptical; only one in four had voted for Hitler.

Shortly thereafter, Brüning was replaced as chancellor by Franz von Papen, a hardcore monarchist associated with a rightwing club for industrialists and gentry in Berlin. Papen called two Reichstag elections, hoping to build a parliamentary base, but Hindenburg soon replaced him with Kurt von Schleicher, a military old boy.

Schleicher's attempt to pump-prime the economy with public money – a policy begun by Papen – alienated industrialists and landowners. Finally on 30 January 1933, won over by the right and following Papen's advice, Hindenburg dismissed Schleicher and appointed Hitler as chancellor, with a coalition cabinet consisting of National Socialists (Nazis) and Papen's Nationalists. The Nazis were by far the largest single party but were still short of an absolute majority.

In March 1933, without a clear majority, Hitler called Germany's last 'officially' free prewar election. With the help of his intimidating party militia, the *Sturmabteilung* or SA, and the staged Reichstag fire, which gave him an excuse to use emergency laws to arrest communist and liberal opponents, he won 43% of the vote (31% in Berlin) – still not an absolute majority. The turning point was reached with the Enabling Law, which gave Hitler the power to decree laws and change the constitution without consulting parliament. As a result of this law, by June 1933 the SPD had been banned and other parties disbanded. Hitler's NSDAP governed alone.

The Road to WWII
The totalitarian Nazi regime brought immediate far-reaching consequences for the entire population. Unions were banned. Propaganda minister Joseph Goebbels' crack-down on intellectuals and artists sent many of them into exile. On 10 May 1933, students burned 'un-German' books on Bebelplatz. Freedom of the press was nonexistent as the NSDAP took over publishing houses. Membership in the *Hitlerjugend* (Hitler Youth) became compulsory for boys aged 10 to 18; girls had to join the Bund Deutscher Mädchen (BDM, League of German Girls). The 1936 Berlin Olympics only served to legitimise the Nazi government and to distract the world from the everyday terror perpetrated in Germany – apparently with success.

The Röhm Putsch Originally formed to guard public meetings, by 1934 the SA had become a powerful force of 4.5 million men, capable of challenging and undermining Hitler's authority. With rumours of revolt circulating, on 30 June 1934 elite SS troops (Hitler's personal guard) rounded up and executed high-ranking SA officers, including leader Ernst Röhm, in what came to be known as the 'Night of the Long Knives'. More than 1000 people were killed that night.

In Berlin, Hermann Göring led the death squads, with executions taking place in the SS barracks in the district of Lichtenberg. Göring and his lieutenants also exploited

the occasion to settle old (sometimes homophobic) scores with some of Hitler's opponents. In the same year, the death of Hindenburg allowed Hitler to merge the positions of president and chancellor.

Plight of the Jews As has been thoroughly documented, Jews became the main target in Nazi Germany. In April 1933 Goebbels organised the boycott of Jewish businesses and medical and legal practices. Jews were expelled from public service and prohibited from engaging in many professions, trades and industries. The Nuremberg Laws of 1935 deprived all non-Aryans (ie Jews, Gypsies, blacks etc) of German citizenship and prohibited their marriage with Aryans. On the night of 9 November 1938 the terror escalated with the Reichspogromnacht (also known as Kristallnacht or 'Night of Broken Glass'). On this single night the windows of thousands of Jewish businesses and shops throughout Berlin and indeed all of Germany were shattered, the premises looted and set alight. Jews had started to emigrate after 1933, but this terror set off a new wave. Very few of those who remained in Berlin – about 60,000 – were still alive in 1945.

WWII
On 1 September 1939, Hitler attacked Poland, a move not greeted with euphoria in Berlin, whose people still remembered the hunger years of WWI and the early 1920s. Again, war brought food shortages and even greater political oppression.

Belgium and the Netherlands fell quickly, as did France. In June 1941 Hitler attacked the USSR, opening up a new front. Delays in staging what was called 'Operation Barbarossa' – caused by problems in the Mediterranean – would contribute to Germany's downfall as lines of supply were overextended. Hitler's troops, bogged down and ill-prepared for the bitter winter of 1941-42, were forced into retreat. With the defeat of the German 6th Army at Stalingrad (then called Volgograd) the following winter, morale flagged both at home and on the fronts.

In 1941, the USA signed the Lend-Lease Agreement with Britain to provide and finance badly needed military equipment. In December of the same year the Japanese attacked the American fleet at Pearl Harbor, prompting the USA to formally enter the war.

The 'Final Solution' The fate of Jews deteriorated after the outbreak of war. Heinrich Himmler's SS troops systematically terrorised and executed local populations in occupied areas, and war with the USSR was portrayed as a fight against 'subhuman' Jews and Bolsheviks.

At Hitler's behest, Göring commissioned his functionaries to find an *Endlösung* (Final Solution) to the 'Jewish question'. A conference, held in January 1942 on the shores of Berlin's Wannsee lake, laid the basis for the Holocaust: the efficient, systematic and bureaucratic murder of millions.

Concentration camps, though not a Nazi invention, now reached a new level of efficiency. Besides Jews, the main target groups were Gypsies, political opponents, priests (especially Jesuits), homosexuals and resistance fighters. In the end there were 22 camps, mostly in Eastern Europe, and another 165 work camps. Altogether, about 7 million people were sent to concentration camps. Only 500,000 survived to be freed by Soviet and Allied soldiers.

Resistance Resistance to the Nazis from socialist, social-democratic and workers' groups had been effectively quashed during the 1930s, with opponents either sent to camps or forced underground or abroad. The most famous case of resistance was that

The Mystery of Hitler's Body

The ultimate fate of Adolf Hitler and Eva Braun, whom he married the day before their dual suicide, is one of the more perplexing and enduring Nazi myths. More ill-informed fantasy has been written on the subject than about the supposed whereabouts of Elvis, Amelia Earhart and Bigfoot combined. However, the facts as we now know them should lay any speculation to rest.

At 4 pm on Monday 30 April 1945, as the Soviet flag was already waving atop the Reichstag, Hitler and Braun bit down on cyanide capsules while sitting on a couch in his bunker on Vosstrasse (Map 8). For good measure, he also shot himself through the head. Henchmen then carried the bodies outside, drenched them in petrol and set them alight. The remains ended up in a shallow grave in the garden.

Shortly after the fighting ended, the Soviets discovered the graves and identified the bones as Hitler's with the help of a dental worker apparently familiar with his extremely bad teeth. It was then that the Soviet penchant for secrecy came into play, doing much to obscure the actual history.

The bones of Hitler and Braun travelled around eastern Germany in the hands of the Soviet Smersh counterintelligence agency before being reburied at Smersh headquarters in Magdeburg. Delighted with the obfuscation that it was causing, Smersh even refused to divulge the true sequence of events to its own government. It wasn't until 1970, under the orders of Yuri Andropov, then chief of the KGB, that the bones were exhumed one last time and incinerated thoroughly.

In 1945 a young British intelligence officer, Hugh Trevor-Roper, compiled the defining document on the suicide/cremation which became the book *The Last Days of Hitler*. It has never been successfully refuted and the testimony of two eyewitnesses released by the Russians in 1956 fully corroborated his account. Even in death, Hitler managed to write another chapter of twisted deeds. But the book on the subject should now finally be closed.

involving Claus Graf Schenk von Stauffenberg and other high-ranking army officers who set out to assassinate Hitler and seize power from the SS on 20 July 1944. The attempt failed and over 200 women and men from the underground were immediately arrested and executed. Over 7000 people were arrested directly or indirectly as a result of the plot, several thousand of whom were executed.

The Battle of Berlin With the Normandy invasion of June 1944, Allied troops arrived in formidable force on the European mainland, supported by systematic air raids on Berlin and most other German cities. In the last days of the war Hitler, broken and paranoid, ordered the destruction of all remaining German industry and infrastructure, a decree that was largely ignored.

The final Battle of Berlin began on 16 April 1945. More than 1.5 million Soviet soldiers approached the capital from the east, reaching Berlin on 21 April and fully encircling it on 25 April. Two days later, they were in the city centre. On 30 April, the fighting reached the government quarter where Hitler was ensconced in his bunker behind the chancellery (Map 8), along with his wife Eva Braun whom he'd married just a day earlier. In the afternoon, they committed suicide. Goebbels and his wife, who were in the bunker too, poisoned their six children, then killed themselves as well.

The capital fell two days later, and on 7 May 1945 Germany capitulated. The signing of the armistice took place at the US military headquarters in Reims (France) and at the Soviet military headquarters in Berlin-Karlshorst. (See the Lichtenberg section in the Things to See & Do chapter).

The Aftermath The war took an enormous toll on Berlin and its people. The civilian population had borne the brunt of the bombings. Entire neighbourhoods lay reduced to rubble, with more than half of all buildings and one-third of industry destroyed or damaged. With some 1 million women and children evacuated, only 2.4 million people were left in the city in May

1945 (4.3 million in 1939), two-thirds of them women. About 125,000 Berliners had lost their lives.

In Soviet-occupied Berlin, it was the women who did much of the initial cleanup, earning them the name *Trümmerfrauen* (literally 'rubble women'). Over the following months, enormous amounts of debris were piled up into so-called *Trümmerberge*, artificial hills such as the Teufelsberg in the Grunewald.

Small recoveries came quickly: the first U-Bahn train ran on 14 May, the first newspaper was published on 15 May, and on 26 May the Berliner Philharmonisches Orchester gave its first postwar concert. The first crosstown phone connection succeeded on 5 June.

The Politics of Provocation

In line with agreements reached at the Yalta Conference (February 1945), Germany was divided into four zones of occupation. Berlin was carved up into 12 administrative areas under British, French and US control and another eight under Soviet control. At the Potsdam Conference in July and August 1945, regions east of the Oder and Neisse rivers were transferred to Poland as compensation for earlier territorial losses to the Soviet Union.

Soviet demands for high reparations, a bone of contention that soon led to a breakdown in cooperation with the Allies, were ultimately met by brutalising their own zone of occupation. In practice this meant that factory production was requisitioned and able-bodied men and POWs were marched away and put to work in forced-labour camps in the Soviet Union. Due to foot-dragging by the Soviets, American and British troops didn't actually occupy their respective Berlin sectors until 4 July; the French arriving on 12 August. The Soviets also forcibly fused the communist KPD party and the SPD into the Sozialistische Einheitspartei Deutschland (Socialist Unity Party of Germany, or SED) on 22 April 1946 with Walter Ulbricht as general secretary.

The coalition of the western Allies and the USSR eventually collapsed in June

The Berlin Airlift

The ruined city of Berlin was still digging itself out from the rubble of WWII when the Soviet hammer fell on its people on 24 June 1948. The military leadership ordered a complete block-ade of all rail and road traffic into the city. Berlin would be completely cut off and it was as-sumed that it would only be a matter of days before the city submitted to the Soviets.

Faced with such provocation, many in the Allied camp urged responses that would have been the opening barrages of WWIII. In the end, wiser heads prevailed. A mere day after the blockade began, the US Air Force launched 'Operation Vittles'. The British followed suit on the 28th with 'Operation Planefair'. (France did not participate in the Airlift because its planes were tied up in Indochina.)

Until May 12 of the following year only an act of astonishing determination and technical expertise kept Berlin alive. For about 11 months, the entire city was supplied exclusively from the air by Allied planes bringing in coal, food and machinery. Every day, around the clock, de-termined pilots made the treacherous landings at Berlin's airports – sometimes as frequently as one per minute. On one day alone – the 'Easter Parade' of 16 April 1949 – they flew 1400 sorties delivering 13,000 tons. By the end of the Airlift they had flown a combined 125 mil-lion miles in 278,000 flights and delivered 2.5 million tons of supplies. The operation cost 79 lives, which are commemorated by the Airlift Memorial at Tempelhof airport.

Given the ever-escalating Allied effort – and the universal scorn of the world – the Soviets backed down and Berlin's western sectors were free once again. The heroic resolve of the pi-lots, the Allies and Berlin's people had caused the Kremlin to stumble.

Had Berlin fallen into the Soviet realm, we would most likely be looking at a vastly differ-ent Europe today, perhaps a vastly different world. The Berlin Airlift thus marks a historical event of incalculable significance. In a very real sense, the Berlin Wall never stood a chance of standing forever, built as it was in a city whose people had defiantly said 'We will never submit'.

1948 with the Berlin Blockade. Proposed currency reform in the Allied zones prompted the USSR not only to issue its own currency but to also use it as a pretext for beginning an economic blockade of West Berlin (of course, with the intent of bringing the entire city under its complete control). The Allies responded with the Berlin Airlift which would last almost a year and see 278,000 flights supply the city.

The relationship between the Allies and the Germans changed as a result of the Air-lift. No longer did Berliners regard them as occupational forces but as *Schutzmächte* (protective powers). For more details see the boxed text 'The Berlin Airlift'.

Two German States

In this dawn of the Cold War between East and West, the Allies went ahead with their establishment of government institutions and, in 1949, the Federal Republic of Ger-many (FRG, or BRD by its German initials) was founded. Konrad Adenauer, a 73-year-old former mayor of Cologne during the Weimar years, became West Germany's first chancellor. Bonn was chosen as the provisional capital.

Berlin remained an isolated island in the sea of the Soviet sector and was dependent on help from the west. In 1950, 300,000 Berliners were unemployed. Thanks to as-sistance from the FRG and the US, that number had shrunk to practically zero a mere 10 years later.

Meanwhile, the Soviet zone evolved in 1949 into the German Democratic Republic (GDR, or DDR by its German initials) with Berlin as its capital. Although nominally a parliamentary democracy, the dominance of the SED was such that party boss Walter Ulbricht called all shots. The early years saw a party takeover of economic, judicial and security functions, including the establishment of the Ministry for State Security – or Stasi – which set about neutralising opposition to the SED.

In 1952, the GDR began to cut off relations with the West. West Berliners were no longer allowed to travel to East Germany. Real estate and property owned by West Berliners was expropriated. At the same time, political and moral pressure was exerted on East Berliners to participate in the *Nationale Aufbauwerk* (National Reconstruction Project) which meant rebuilding the country in their spare time – for no pay. On 27 May 1952, all phone connections between East and West Berlin and between the GDR and West Germany were cut.

Uprising in East Berlin

By 1953 the first signs of discontent appeared in the GDR. Production bottlenecks stifled industrial output, heavy industry was given priority over consumer goods and increased demands on industrial workers bred bitterness. Furthermore, the death of Stalin had raised hopes of reform but brought little in the way of real change. Under pressure from Moscow, the government backed down on a decision to raise prices, but it refused to budge on tougher production goals.

Strikes and calls for reform turned to unrest in the urban and industrial centres, culminating in demonstrations and riots on 17 June 1953. Triggered by construction workers on Berlin's Karl-Marx-Allee, the unrest soon involved about 10% of the country's workers. When the GDR government proved incapable of containing the situation, Soviet troops stationed on East German soil quashed the uprising, with scores of deaths and the arrest of about 4000 people.

The Building of the Wall

As the GDR government continued to restrict the freedom of its citizens, the flow of refugees to the west increased. In 1953 alone about 330,000 East Germans fled to the west, most of them young and well-educated, thus amplifying the strain on an already brittle economy. The exodus reached such a level that on the night of 12 August 1961, with the approval of Warsaw Pact countries, fences and ditches were erected between East and West Berlin. On the 15th, construction of the Wall began, thus creating one of the Cold War's most potent symbols.

Formal protests from the western Allies as well as demonstrations by more than half a million people in West Berlin went unheeded. Tension rose further on 25 October 1961 as US and Soviet tanks faced off at Checkpoint Charlie. The incident was sparked by the GDR's refusal to grant free passage to some members of the US forces. Soon, the entire FRG/GDR border was fenced off and mined, the guards given the order to shoot to kill anybody trying to escape. By the time the Wall collapsed on 9 November 1989, over 80 people had died in such attempts in Berlin alone. (For more on the Wall, see the boxed text 'The Berlin Wall' in the Things to See and Do chapter.)

Rapprochement

Restrictions that had prevented anybody from entering East Berlin and the GDR eased temporarily in 1963 with the *Passagierscheinabkommen* (Pass Agreement). It permitted westerners to visit relatives in East Berlin between 19 December 1963 and 5 January 1964. About 1.2 million visits were recorded in this period. From 1964-66, the GDR opened up its borders three more times for such short periods.

In 1971, after Erich Honecker replaced Walter Ulbricht as SED party head, the *Vier-Mächte-Abkommen* (Four Powers Agreement) between the four victorious Allies set up permanent regulations for visits from west to east, including a transit route to Berlin from West Germany through GDR territory. Except for senior citizens, however, it was still the case that no-one else was allowed to leave the GDR. Visitors to East Berlin were saddled with a compulsory exchange from Deutschmarks to the weak Ostmarks (based on a 1:1 exchange rate).

In December 1972 the two Germanys signed the Basic Treaty. This guaranteed sovereignty in international and domestic affairs, normalised East Germany-West Germany relations and paved the way for both countries to join the United Nations.

Economic Developments

During a period of economic stabilisation in the 1960s, the standard of living in the GDR rose to the highest in the Eastern bloc and the country became its second-largest industrial power (behind the USSR).

Meanwhile, West Germany strengthened its ties to the US and Western Europe and embarked on a policy of welfare-state capitalism. An economic boom called *Wirtschaftswunder* (economic miracle) lasted throughout the 1950s and most of the 1960s. Its architect, Ludwig Erhard, oversaw policies that encouraged investment and capital formation, aided by the Marshall Plan and a trend towards European economic integration. *Gastarbeiter* (guest workers) were called in from southern Europe (mainly Turkey, Yugoslavia and Italy) to solve a labour shortage. In 1958, West Germany was one of the original five countries to sign the Treaty of Rome which created the European Economic Community, now the expanded European Union.

Student Unrest & Terrorism in the West

In West Germany, the two major parties CDU (Christliche Demokratische Union or Christian Democratic Union) and SPD formed a broad coalition in 1966. The absence of parliamentary opposition fuelled an increasingly radical student movement with Berlin at its centre. At sit-ins and protests, students demanded an end to the Vietnam War and reform of Germany's dated university system and teaching programs.

By 1970 the student movement had fizzled, but not without having shaken up the country and brought about some changes, including women's emancipation, university reforms, and a politicisation of the student body.

A few radicals, though, didn't think that enough had been achieved and went underground. Berlin thus became the germ cell of the terrorist Red Army Faction (RAF), led by Ulrike Meinhof, Andreas Baader and Gudrun Ensslin. Throughout the 1970s, the RAF abducted and assassinated prominent business and political figures. By 1976, however, Meinhof and Baader had committed suicide (both in prison). Remaining members found themselves in prison, in hiding or taking refuge across the border in East Germany.

Collapse of the GDR

Erich Honecker's rise to the position of state secretary in 1971 rang in an era of changes to the East German constitution. Hopeful reunification clauses were struck out in 1974 and replaced by one declaring East Germany's irrevocable alliance with the USSR. Honecker fell comfortably in line with Soviet policies, rode out a world recession and an oil crisis in the early 1970s, and oversaw a period of housing construction, pension increases and help for working mothers.

In the mid-1980s, however, prices for consumer goods rose sharply and, with East Germany struggling to keep pace with technological innovations elsewhere in the world, stagnation set in. Reforms in Poland and Hungary, and especially Mikhail Gorbachev's new course in the USSR, put pressure on an increasingly recalcitrant SED leadership to introduce reforms.

The *Wende* (turning point) began in May 1989, when Hungary announced it would suspend its Travel Agreement, which had once prevented East Germans from entering the west via Hungary. The SED responded by tightening travel restrictions. Meanwhile, more and more East Germans filled West German consulates and embassies in East Berlin, Warsaw, Prague and Budapest, seeking to emigrate. The breakthrough came on 10 September 1989 when Hungary's foreign minister, Gyula Horn, officially opened the Hungarian border to Austria, allowing refugees to cross legally to the west.

A wave of opposition groups, notably the Neues Forum (New Forum), which were supported by church leaders emerged and led calls for human rights and an end to the

The Rise & Fall of Erich Honecker

A miner's son, Erich Honecker was born in Neunkirchen, Saarland, on 25 August 1912. He worked as a roof tiler, joined the central committee of the communist youth organisation in the 1920s, and led the group's underground activities in southern Germany after Hitler took power. He was imprisoned for 10 years from 1935, and on his release became president of the youth organisation Freie Deutsche Jugend (Free German Youth).

One of the SED's promising talents, in 1958 he was appointed Politbüro member and secretary of the central committee, handling state security matters. A diligent if unspectacular functionary, in 1971 he succeeded Walter Ulricht as state secretary and by 1976 he rose to party general secretary and head of East Germany.

Honecker continued the policy of limiting relations with West Germany, and made himself unpopular in the west by raising the minimum sum of money West Germans had to exchange when visiting the GDR. Like West German chancellor Helmut Schmidt, he tried to prevent international tensions from flowing over into friction between the two German states.

Honecker's period of leadership was one of lethargy and disillusionment in East Germany. He was made to step down as leader of the SED in October 1989 and was stripped of all party and political functions shortly afterwards. In December of the same year he was investigated for treason, corruption and abuse of public office, and put under house arrest. He was jailed in 1990, released shortly afterwards due to bad health and transferred to a Soviet military hospital.

With an arrest order hanging over him, Honecker fled to the USSR in March 1991. He was soon returned to Germany and placed on trial for manslaughter (for his role in giving the order to shoot fleeing East Germans), but Honecker's ill health meant that the case was abandoned.

In 1993 Honecker went to Chile and died of liver cancer the following year.

SED political monopoly. This in turn sparked a leadership crisis in the SED, which resulted in the replacement of Honecker by Egon Krenz. On 4 November 1989, about 500,000 demonstrators gathered on Berlin's Alexanderplatz. By this time, East Germany was losing its citizens at a rate of about 10,000 per day.

Five days later, on 9 November 1989, the floodgates opened when Günther Schabowski, a member of the Politbüro of the GDR, announced – surprisingly and clearly not in any coordinated fashion – that travel to the west was now possible. Tens of thousands passed through border points in Berlin as perplexed guards looked on. Amid scenes of wild partying and worldwide media attention, the Wall had fallen.

Reunification

Opposition groups and government representatives soon met in so-called 'round table talks' to hammer out a course of action. In March 1990, the first free elections in East Germany since 1949 took place and an alliance, headed by Lothar de Maizière of the CDU, won convincingly. The SPD, which took an equivocal view of reunification, was punished by voters accordingly. The old SED administrative regions were abolished and the Länder (states) revived. Currency and economic union became a reality in July 1990.

In September 1990 the two Germanys, the USSR and the Allied powers signed the Two-Plus-Four Treaty, ending postwar occupation zones. One month later the East German state was dissolved and Germany's first unified post-WWII elections were held. Berlin once again became the German capital. In 1991, a small majority (338 to 320) of members in the Bundestag (German Parliament) voted in favour of moving the federal government to Berlin as well.

The Berlin Republic

Federal elections in 1998 spelled an end to the era of Helmut Kohl, who'd governed for 16 years, and put Gerhard Schröder of the SPD at Germany's helm in a coalition with the Greens. This is the first time a Green party has co-governed at the federal level.

In 1999 the German parliament moved from Bonn to Berlin, and now convenes in the restored Reichstag building. Most ministries followed, including the foreign ministry, though some, like defence and education, remain in Bonn (with secondary offices in Berlin) for now. The move, ultimately costing an expected DM20 billion, has produced a flurry of logistical activity in Berlin. New homes and offices are being built for parliamentarians, and older structures are being renovated to accommodate ministries.

Germany, restored to its position as 'the land in the middle', now juggles its inward-looking reunification process with an outward-looking commitment to European integration, while gaining new confidence on the international stage.

GEOGRAPHY

Berlin is Germany's largest city, both in terms of population (around 3.4 million) and area. Its north-south extent measures 38km, while from east to west it stretches for 45km, and covers a total of 889 sq km. Apart from rivers and lakes, Berlin is completely lacking in geographical distinction, the result of its location in the vast plains of the north German flatlands. Several hills, like the Teufelsberg in the Grunewald forest, are actually *Trümmerberge* made from rubble piles gathered during the post-WWII clean-up.

Berlin is crisscrossed by two rivers that are important for inland navigation. These are the 343km-long Havel, which has its headwaters in the Mecklenburg Lake District about 110km north-west of Berlin, and its tributary the Spree, which joins it in Spandau. On its course, the Havel travels through several canals and lakes, including the Wannsee.

CLIMATE

Berlin has a moderately cool and humid climate determined by a mixing of air masses

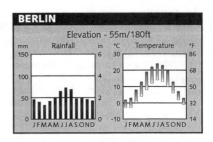

BERLIN
Elevation - 55m/180ft

from the Atlantic Ocean and the continental climate of Eastern Europe. Predictably, December to February are the coldest months. When the winds blow from Russia it can get mighty chilly, with temperatures dropping to below freezing. Generally, though, winters are relatively mild. More than half of the city's annual inversion days (when stagnant cold air traps warmer air below, bringing about smog) occur in these months.

July and August are warmest, though usually not chokingly hot. The nicest months are September and October which deliver the added bonus of autumn foliage. May and June, when the trees are in bloom and the outdoor cafe season kicks off, are popular months too, though rain is more likely at this time.

ECOLOGY & ENVIRONMENT

Berlin has some of the highest air pollution levels in Germany, higher than any other big city in the former West Germany, though still lower than in some eastern cities like Dresden, Halle or Chemnitz. In 1991, Berlin joined the International Climate Convention, pledging to halve CO_2 emissions by 2010.

Pollution and acid rain have done major damage to Berlin's forests. In 1997, less than one in three trees remained healthy, with 52% displaying minor damage and 20% being either heavily damaged or dead.

Berlin's drinking water is fine, though its lakes and rivers are not. The Havel lakes, including the Wannsee, are prone to excessive algae growth; the Spree River and the Landwehr Canal that flow right through the city are badly polluted. Only the lakes in the Grunewald forest are slightly cleaner.

The most tangible sign of pollution, however, is the massive amount of dog shit (40 tons daily) in parks and on the pavement. Regulations require dog owners to clean up after their pooch, but this is widely ignored. Berliners sure love their canines; there's one dog for every 35 people.

Despite all these problems Berlin is, in many ways, a very ecologically minded city. In order to stave off further destruction of plant and animal life, the state government has devised the ambitious Programme for the Protection of Land and Endangered Species which seeks to balance the objectives of nature and conservation with urban development.

Awareness also happens on a smaller scale. Bicycle lanes abound, there are solar-powered parking voucher dispensers and even U/S-Bahn stations have recycling bins. The city has a comprehensive and efficient public transport system; by the same token, it tries to discourage drivers through restricted parking and expensive parking meters and garages.

Greenpeace is very active in Germany. Its Berlin branch (Map 4, ☎ 28 39 15 50, fax 28 39 15 51) is at Chausseestrasse 131 in Mitte and is open from 4 to 6.30 pm weekdays. Its Web site address is www.green peace-berlin.de (in German). An important local environmental lobby group is the Grüne Liga (Green League, ☎ 44 33 910, fax 44 33 91 33), whose head office is at Prenzlauer Allee 230. Its opening hours are from 9 am to 6 pm Monday to Thursday, to 3 pm Friday. Its (bilingual) Web site can be found at www.berlin@grueneliga.de.

FLORA & FAUNA

Berlin is a relatively green city. Parks, forests, lakes and rivers take up about one third of its space. Nearly every neighbourhood has its own park, and a ring of forests encircles the urban sprawl.

During the years of division – when West Berlin was essentially an 'island' in the GDR 'sea' – the improvement and maintenance of these natural features was imperative in order to give residents access to recreational areas. As Berliners used to say,

'No matter whether you go north, south, east or west from Berlin, you're still going East.'

Berlin considers itself Europe's tree capital, a result of a successful tree-planting campaign undertaken during the past couple of decades. Of the city's 400,000 trees most are linden (lime) trees (36%) and maple trees (18%); others are oak (8%), plane (6%) and chestnut (4%). The eastern district of Hohenschönhausen has the most trees per kilometre of road (134) compared to the city average of 78 per kilometre.

Animal life has declined dramatically since WWII. Construction and a growing population have displaced more than half of all previously existing species from their natural habitats. Low ground-water levels have dried up biotopes, threatening the survival of reptiles, amphibians and fish. Only about 33 fish species still inhabit the city's rivers and lakes, the most common being perch, pike, roach and bream. Sparrows and pigeons are the most prevalent bird species. In the green belt surrounding Berlin, you might still find deer, rabbits and even wild boar.

GOVERNMENT & POLITICS

Along with Hamburg and Bremen, Berlin is a German city-state. Its government consists of the *Abgeordnetenhaus* (parliament, or legislative body) and the *Senat* (Senate, or executive body). Members of parliament are elected directly by the people for a four-year term. Their primary function is to pass legislation and to elect and supervise the Senate.

The Senate is made up of the *Regierender Bürgermeister* (governing mayor), the deputy mayor and up to nine senators. The governing mayor sets policy with the agreement of senators and represents Berlin nationally and internationally. Senators have similar roles as cabinet members, with each in charge of a particular department.

The seat of government of both the governing mayor and the Senate is the *Rotes Rathaus* (Red Town Hall). Parliament meets in the Abgeordnetenhaus on Niederkirchnerstrasse, just across from the Martin-Gropius-Bau (Map 8).

Though Berlin has historically been an SPD stronghold, in recent decades the CDU has been the dominant party with governing mayor Eberhard Diepgen at the helm since 1984. Elections held in October 1999 once again confirmed its leading role; 40.8% of votes were cast for the CDU, up from 37.4% in 1995. The SPD experienced a moderate 1.2% loss, coming in with 22.4% of the vote. Support for the Greens plunged to 9.9% from 14.6% in 1995. The PDS, the successor party to the SED, gained 3.1% and now stands at 17.7%. Support for this party, however, is uneven; in the eastern districts, reaching 39.5%, while only receiving 4.2% in the west.

In 1920, Berlin was divided into *Bezirke* (districts), each with its own local administration. There are currently 23 districts but, in an effort to streamline government and to cut down on bureaucracy, the city parliament voted in 1999 to reduce that number to 12, effective in 2001. In all but three cases (Neukölln, Reinickendorf and Spandau), this will be accomplished by merging two or three existing districts into one. This is really a behind-the-scenes administrative change only; the districts will continue to be referred to by their old name.

ECONOMY

Germany is the world's third largest economic power (behind the USA and Japan), a committed member of the EU, and a member of the expanded G8 group of industrial nations since 1974.

The German economy is under strong pressure from foreign competition, and many of its companies have moved production abroad, especially to Eastern Europe, where wages and social-security overheads are lower (Germany's are the highest in the world). Political figures have tried to reverse the trend by appealing to business leaders' loyalty, but the decisions are financial, not sentimental, and it is unlikely a change will occur in the near future.

Berlin has felt the full brunt of this overall trend despite experiencing an economic boom in the years following reunification. Unemployment figures are at record highs, especially among young people, foreigners and older workers. In June 1999, there were about 262,000 unemployed Berliners, an increase of 60,000 in just five years (concurrent with a population drop of over 100,000). Figures would probably be even worse if entrepreneurship – especially in the service sector and among young people – hadn't picked up some of the slack after having been aggressively promoted by politicians and employers' associations. The other side of the coin, however, is the high bankruptcy rate among such start-up companies.

For the time being, Berlin is undergoing painful restructuring, moving away from manufacturing and towards service industries. East Berlin was one of the GDR's manufacturing capitals, but after the Wende most of its outdated and unprofitable factories were closed. West Berlin, on the other hand, had not been an important location for industry and manufacturing after WWII because of its island status.

The shift of government to Berlin did not draw as many corporations in its wake as had been expected; of the 500 largest corporations active in Germany, only 11 are based in the capital, whereas 50 are based in Hamburg and 30 in Munich. More than half of Berlin's 1.6 million workers are employed in the service sector, though mostly with state and federal government agencies. In fact, Berlin has more than twice as many civil servants as any other big city in Germany. In eastern Berlin, one in 10 people holds a government job; in the western districts it's 6.8%. These figures are expected to increase now that the federal government has moved to Berlin. Other growth areas in the service sector are tourism, software development, marketing, advertising, law and financial services.

In 1997, Berlin's gross domestic product was DM156.2 billion, only DM2.4 billion higher than the previous year but still greater than that of countries like Ireland and Greece.

POPULATION & PEOPLE

In April 1999, Berlin had 3.39 million inhabitants, making it Germany's largest city; about 2.11 million people live in former West Berlin and 1.28 million in the eastern districts. Oddly, a post-unification population boom has been offset by the exodus of young families from the capital to the surrounding countryside. This has resulted in an actual population drop of almost 100,000 since April 1994. During the same five-year period, though, the number of non-ethnic Germans in Berlin increased by 33,000 to 432,675.

There's no doubt that Berlin is Germany's most multicultural city, with an amazing patchwork of people from 184 nations. The vast majority (83%) live in the western districts with Kreuzberg having the highest concentration (33.6%), followed by Wedding with 28.8% and Tiergarten with 26.4%. In 1997, one in three immigrants was of Turkish descent and people from the former states of Yugoslavia accounted for 16.5%. Other large groups are Poles (6.4%) and immigrants from the former Soviet republics (5.4%). There are also about 13,000 Italians and 10,800 Greeks.

On the whole, Berlin is becoming a younger city. The percentage of people over 65 dropped from 16.3% in 1985 to 13.8% in 1997. Almost 70% of Berliners are between 18 and 65 years of age.

EDUCATION

Berlin's public school system is the same as throughout the rest of Germany. Education is compulsory for 12 years and financed by the state. Most students attend free state schools which, overall, are excellent.

Following an optional two or three years at kindergarten, children start attending the Grundschule (primary school), usually at six years of age. After four years, they transfer to one of three traditional secondary high school types: Hauptschule (vocational emphasis, five years), Realschule (commercial emphasis, six years), and Gymnasium (academic emphasis, nine years). The Gymnasium culminates with the Abitur, an extremely rigorous multiday examination which must be passed in order to obtain university admission. Graduates of the Hauptschule and Realschule usually take up a two or three-year apprenticeship taught in a system called 'dual education'

where students divide their time between on-the-job training and the Berufsschule (vocational school).

Berlin also has a number of specialist schools, many of them catering for students from other countries. The John F Kennedy School in Zehlendorf has an equal proportion of German and American students taught in German and English. There's also the French Grammar School, the Swedish School, the Japanese School, and others. More such schools are expected to open because of the government's move and the resultant growth in the diplomatic corps.

Berlin is Germany's largest university town with about 145,000 students studying at three universities, four arts colleges and nine technical colleges. The largest are the Freie Universität (48,000 students), the Technische Universität (35,000 students) and the Humboldt Universität (29,000 students). Berlin also has some 250 research institutes, including the famous Max Planck Institute.

SCIENCE & PHILOSOPHY

Germany, with its rigorous education system based on the ideas of the Berlin-born philologist and statesman Wilhelm von Humboldt (1767-1835), has made enormous contributions to the disciplines of philosophy and the natural sciences. The importance of Germans in the social sciences and physics in particular is inestimable. Up to 1939, 10 out of 45 Nobel Prizes in physics had gone to Germans.

In philosophy, it was Immanuel Kant (1724-1804) who, as a founder of German idealism, paved the way for Georg Wilhelm Friedrich Hegel (1770-1831). In *The Phenomenology of the Spirit* (1807), Hegel developed a theory of dialectics, or opposites, that culminated idealistically in pure consciousness. From 1818, he taught at the Humboldt University and actively participated in the literary salons in vogue at the time. He died in Berlin in 1831. His influence extended to Arthur Schopenhauer (1788-1860), an idealist with pessimistic predilections, who was associated with Goethe and Schiller in Weimar.

If Schopenhauer drove German idealism to its subjective limits, the Trier-born Karl Marx (1818-83) injected it with a historical basis and re-interpreted Hegel's pure consciousness as proletarian revolution. As an economist and the author of *Das Kapital*, Marx occupies a place alongside his British predecessor, David Ricardo (1772-1823). As a social theorist, his brilliance was in describing the change from feudalism to modern capitalism. As a revolutionary, he laid the groundwork for 20th century political developments.

Friedrich Nietzsche (1844-1900) shared Schopenhauer's idealism but saw subjectivity as a positive condition. Much of his work focuses on power and the human will. His ideas on an Übermensch (superman), however, were distorted by Hitler and used to justify racial abuses.

Germany's achievements in the natural sciences are no less impressive. Geographer and naturalist Alexander von Humboldt (1769-1859), the younger brother of Wilhelm, stands out as an important figure for his study of flora and species distribution, physical geography and meteorology.

Physics, however, is the field in which Germany has particularly excelled. Born in Kiel, Max Planck (1858-1947) came to Berlin in 1889 where he concentrated his work and research on theoretical thermodynamics. He is considered the founder of quantum physics, a theory for which he was awarded the Nobel Prize in 1918. Planck served as president of the Kaiser-Wilhelm-Society from 1930 to 1937. First dissolved by the Allies after the war, it was refounded in 1947 and renamed the Max Planck Institute.

A close ally of Planck, Albert Einstein (1879-1955) was born in Ulm and moved to Berlin in 1913 where he became director of the Kaiser-Wilhelm-Institut for Physics and a member of the Prussian Academy of Sciences. His theories on the atomic structure of matter were followed by the publication of his theory of relativity in 1914/15. In 1921, he too received the Nobel Prize for his contributions to the field of quantum physics. A Jew and Zionist, he left Germany in 1933 for the USA, eventually becoming an American citizen in 1940.

The German tradition of excellence in the social and natural sciences continues to this day, with Berlin's Max Planck Institute being one of the leading research facilities in the world.

ARTS
Painting & Sculpture

Beginnings When merchants founded Berlin in the 13th century, the fine arts were not a priority. Time, wars and the iconoclastic zeal of church reformers in the 16th century destroyed much of what little medieval art there was in the first place. Among the few surviving objects are a Romanesque goblet, late-Gothic altar paintings and the faded 15th century *Totentanz* (Dance of Death) fresco, all of which are on view in the Marienkirche in Mitte.

The arts scene continued to slumber until the reign of Elector Joachim II (ruled 1535-71) who enlarged the city palace in the German Renaissance style and invited the era's leading artists – including Saxon painters Lucas Cranach the Elder (1472-1553) and his son, Lucas Cranach the Younger (1515-86) – to his court.

Whatever artistic spirit had developed under Joachim was quashed by the mayhem of the Thirty Years' War (1618-48). When it was over, the Great Elector Friedrich Wilhelm looked to Holland for inspiration for his two new palaces at Oranienburg and Köpenick. The painters Willem van Honthorst and Hendrik de Fromantious briefly worked on site, aided by German artists like Michael Willmann and Michael Conrad Hirt.

Baroque & Rococo In the late 17th and early 18th century the arts finally began to flourish in Berlin, partly because self-crowned King Friedrich I felt the need to surround himself with more grandeur. At the instigation of the sculptor Andreas Schlüter (1660-1714), he founded the Academy of the Arts in 1696.

Meanwhile, Schlüter enhanced Berlin's artistic landscape with several outstanding sculptures, including the *Great Elector on Horseback* (1699), now in front of Schloss Charlottenburg. The haunting *Masks of Dying Warriors* in the courtyard of the German Historical Museum (closed until at least 2001) are his as well.

During this period the allegorical fresco re-emerged as an established art form and frequently decorated the ceilings of various palaces. This endeavour kept busy German painters like Johann Friedrich Wentzel and Friedrich Wilhelm Weidemann, but especially the skilled Antoine Pesne (1683-1757) who satisfied Friedrich I's taste for the French rococo style.

The arts languished under his successor, Soldier King Friedrich Wilhelm I, then took a turn towards greatness when his son, Friedrich II, ascended the throne in 1740. Friedrich drew heavily on the artistic, architectural and decorative expertise of Georg Wenzeslaus von Knobelsdorff (1699-1753), a student of Pesne. Knobelsdorff gave the world Schloss Rheinsberg (see the Excursions chapter), though he's most famous for designing the German State Opera and Sanssouci Palais.

19th Century The 19th century saw a proliferation of styles which in some ways reflected the socio-political undercurrents rumbling through Europe at this time. New political and economic ideas coming to Germany from England and France especially resonated with the educated middle classes. This new self-confidence found expression in neoclassicism, a style which brought a formal shift to line and body and an emphasis on Roman and Greek mythology.

A major artist of the period was Johann Gottfried Schadow (1764-1850), whose most famous work is the *Quadriga*, the horse-drawn chariot which crowns the landmark Brandenburg Gate. While basing his work on classic Greek sculpture, Schadow also imbued it with great naturalness and sensuousness.

Another important neoclassical sculptor was Christian Daniel Rauch (1777-1857), a Schadow student. Rauch had a talent for representing idealised, classical beauty in a realistic fashion. He created the sarcophagi of Friedrich Wilhelm III and Queen Luise – both on view at the Mausoleum in the gardens of Schloss Charlottenburg. His most famous work, though, is the monument of Friedrich II on horseback (1851), which normally stands on Unter den Linden outside Humboldt University but which has been under restoration for several years.

A student of Rauch, the sculptor Reinhold Begas (1831-1911) developed a neo-baroque, theatrical style full of pathos that was so ostentatiously counter-neoclassical that he met with a fair amount of controversy, even in his lifetime. The Neptune fountain (1891) outside the Marienkirche is a Begas work, as is the Schiller monument on Gendarmenmarkt.

In painting, Romanticism began to overtake neoclassicism in popularity. A reason for this was the awakening of a nationalist spirit in Germany – spurred by the Napoleonic Wars – during the reign of Friedrich Wilhelm III (1797-1840). Romanticism was the perfect form of expression for the idealism, emotion and dreams that characterised the period.

Top billing among Romantic painters goes to Caspar David Friedrich whose works are on display at the Gallery of the Romantics. Also here are paintings by Karl Friedrich Schinkel, Berlin's dominant neoclassical architect (see the Architecture section in this chapter) who, early in his career, created a series of romantic, moody landscapes and fantastic depictions of Gothic architecture. The frescoes in the vestibule of his Altes Museum are by him too.

A parallel development during the period of 1815-48 was the so-called Berliner Biedermeier. The most successful and famous artist of this period was Franz Krüger (1797-1857) whose best-known works are meticulous depictions of public parades such as *Parade auf dem Opernplatz* (Parade on the Opera Square, 1829).

There was also an interest in paintings that chronicled Berlin's constantly evolving cityscape. Important artists of the genre include Eduard Gaertner and Wilhelm Brücke. These paintings sold especially well among the middle classes, as did still lifes and those of flowers. Other Romantic painters, like Wilhelm Schadow and Karl Wilhelm Wach, represented a group of intensely religious artists called the *Nazarener* (Nazareths).

The Berliner Sezession In 1892, an exhibit of paintings by Norwegian artist Edvard Munch shook up Berlin's art establishment. After conservative forces opposed to such nontraditional 'modern' art had the show closed, a group of young artists banded together in protest. Initially calling themselves the Gruppe der XI (Group of 11), they became better known under the name Berliner Sezession, adopted in 1898.

Led by Max Liebermann (1847-1935) and Walter Leistikow (1865-1908), member artists were not linked by a common artistic style, but by a rejection of reactionary attitudes towards the arts which stifled new forms of expression. They preferred scenes from daily life to historical and religious themes. They shunned the studio in favour of painting in natural outdoor light. The artists of the Berliner Sezession were hugely successful and influential and provided inspiration for the emergence of new styles.

Liebermann himself evolved from a painter of gloomy naturalist scenes to one of the most important representatives of 'Berlin impressionism'. In the early 1900s, Lovis Corinth (1858-1925) and Max Slevogt (1868-1932) joined the group, as did Käthe Kollwitz (1867-1945). Kollwitz was a veritable 'Renaissance woman', active in virtually all fields of visual art. In her long life, much of it spent in working-class Prenzlauer Berg, she worked her way through naturalist and expressionist movements to arrive at agitprop (short for 'agitation' and 'propaganda' and meaning left-leaning propagandist art) and socialist realism. An excellent place to see her works is the Käthe Kollwitz Museum in Charlottenburg.

The 1920s If Berlin before WWI had emerged as a dynamic place where modern art could develop freely, it evolved into *the* centre of contemporary German and inter-

national art in the 1920s. Movements proliferated as a veritable Who's Who of artists flocked to Berlin. Dadaism, co-founded by George Grosz (1893-1959), emerged as a prevalent form. Dadaists rejected traditional art and considered chance and spontaneity as determining artistic elements. Collages and photo montages were art forms that grew out of dada. The works were outrageous, provocative and *everybody* was talking about them.

Parallel movements had expressionist artists like Max Beckmann (1884-1950) and Otto Dix (1891-1969) examining in their works the threats posed to humanity by urbanisation. Constructivists like El Lissitzky and László Moholy-Nagy explored the relationship between art and technology. Wassily Kandinsky, Paul Klee, Lyonel Feininger and Alexej Jawlensky formed the 'Group of the Blue Four' in 1924 and went on to work and teach at the Bauhaus art school, which moved to Berlin from Dessau in 1932, only to be closed down by the Nazis in 1933.

The impact on the Berlin arts scene after the Nazis took power was devastating. Many artists had to leave the country or ended up in prison or concentration camps, their works classified as 'degenerate' and often confiscated and destroyed. Only a few artists – Käthe Kollwitz, Gerhard Marcks and Otto Nagel – remained in Berlin, largely managing to avoid the artistic evisceration enforced by the Nazis.

Post-1945 After WWII, Berlin's art scene was as fragmented as the city itself. In the east, artists were forced to toe the 'socialist -realist' line, which Otto Nagel and Max Lingner frequently managed to leap over. In the late 60s, East Berlin established itself as an arts centre in the GDR with the formation of the Berliner Schule (Berlin School). Main members like Manfred Böttcher and Harald Metzkes succeeded at freeing themselves from the confines of officially sanctioned socialist art in order to embrace a more multifaceted realism. In the 70s, when conflicts of the individual in society became a prominent theme, underground galleries flourished in Prenzlauer Berg and the creation of art became a collective endeavour.

In postwar West Berlin, artists eagerly soaked up new abstract influences from France and the USA. Leading the movement was a group called Zone 5 (a play on the four zones into which Berlin was now divided) around Hans Thiemann, Heinz Trökes and Mac Zimmermann. At the same time, returning veteran expressionists Max Pechstein and Karl Schmidt-Rottluff provided a more 'traditional' counterweight.

In the 1960s, major new impulses were inspired by the politicisation of art. A new style called 'critical realism' emerged, propagated primarily by artists like Ulrich Baehr, Hans-Jürgen Diehl and Wolfgang Petrick. The 1973 movement called Schule der Neuen Prächtigkeit (School of New Magnificence) had a similar approach and involved artists like Manfred Bluth, Matthias Koeppel and Johannes Grützke. In the 1980s, expressionism found its way back onto the canvasses of painters like Salomé, Helmut Middendorf and Rainer Fetting who were members of a group called Junge Wilde (Young Wild Ones).

Post-Wende Since reunification, the arts scene has been as fickle, energetic and in constant flux. Too unruly for a particular aesthetic style to crystallise, it is more characterised by the process of creation than by final results. More than anything, art has moved into the public and has been popularised, sometimes even becoming an 'event'. Christo's *Wrapped Reichstag* project of 1995 is perhaps the best example, though others are the East Side Gallery and the artistic cauldron that is the Tacheles cultural centre.

Film

Until 1945, German movie making was inextricably tied to Berlin, where studios and production companies had clustered. Today, Hamburg and especially Munich have stolen Berlin's limelight, though there have been recent efforts to gain at least some of it back. The capital still hosts the most important event in Germany's annual film calendar, the International Film Festival. Better known as Berlinale, it was founded in 1951 on the initiative of the western Allies. Held every February, it features screenings of around 750 films, with some of them competing for the Golden and Silver Bear trophies awarded by an international panel of judges. Since 1971, the International Forum of New Cinema, which showcases more radical and alternative films, has taken place alongside the more traditional competition.

The Early Days Berlin's pioneering role in movie history is undeniable. While America had Edison and France had the Lumiére brothers, Berlin had Max Skladanowsky. A former fairground showman, his 1895 invention – the bioscope, a prototype film projector – paved the way for others to develop and improve on his technological achievement and to ring in the era of film making in Germany.

One of those to pick up the baton was the Berlin mechanic Oskar Messter who made, patented and sold some 17 projector types between 1896 and 1913. By 1910, Berlin had 139 *Kinematographentheater* (hence the German word for cinema, Kino), though most flicks in those days didn't go much beyond slapstick, melodramas and short documentaries.

It wasn't until after WWI that movies blossomed as an artistic genre. In 1917, the Universum Film AG (UFA) was founded on the initiative of General Field Marshal Ludendorff to produce pro-war propaganda movies. The first was *Die Schuldigen des Weltkrieges* (The Culprits of the World War), which depicted the Allies as responsible for starting WWI. After the war, UFA began making a name for itself with Ernst Lubitsch's hugely successful but hopelessly silly monster movies. By 1922, Germany had produced 474 movies, making it the second-largest film producer after the USA. Almost all those films came out of Berlin.

The Silent Era Silent films were heavily influenced by expressionism, often adopting morbid, pathological themes and using disjointed images and clever cutting to create the warped psychology of their characters. The influence of Sigmund Freud is clear in Stellan Rye's 1913 classic *Der Student von Prag* (The Student of Prague), which tells the story of a student who sells his mirror image to a stranger and ends up fleeing his own self. *Das Kabinett des Dr Caligari* (The Cabinet of Dr Caligari, 1919) by Robert Wiene, about a hypnotist who causes his patients to commit murder, also shows expressionist influences and deals with tyranny. The world it created through bizarre visual effects was almost unthinkable, given the primitive nature of film making at the time. This style would later resonate powerfully in the works of Alfred Hitchcock.

Another *Gruselfilm* (horror, or Gothic, film) is FW Murnau's *Nosferatu* (1922), a seminal Dracula work in which the plague is brought to a northern German town. It hints broadly at collective fear in the early days of the Weimar Republic.

Fritz Lang's *Metropolis* (1926), about the dangers of totalitarianism, stands out as an ambitious cinema classic. It depicts the revolt of a proletarian class – manipulated by a mechanical temptress and living underground – as it strikes at its dehumanising masters. In the theatres, though, it flopped. Also by Lang is *M* (1931) with Peter Lorre as a child killer chased by police, and other criminals with their own ideas about justice.

The next phase of Berlin cinema belonged to film makers of the Neue Sachlichkeit (New Objectivity). Representatives included Georg Wilhelm Papst who made *Die freudlose Gasse* (The Joyless Street, 1925) and *Die Büchse der Pandora* (Pandora's Box, 1929). Pabst, who worked in New York theatre before WWI, dominated the film scene in the 1920s and 1930s, using montage to elucidate character and create stirring visual sequences. In *Die freudlose Gasse* he takes two women – one a society lady, the other a prostitute – to illustrate a perceived loss of values. The most important documentary of the era was Walter Ruttmann's *Berlin – Die Sinfonie einer Grossstadt* (Berlin – Symphony of a Big City, 1927), which portrays the diversity of Berlin over the course of a 24-hour spring day.

Sound Films of the 1930s Berlin film makers were late in recognising the importance of talkies, despite the fact that sound had been invented in Berlin. Supported by UFA, three engineers – Hans Vogt, Joseph Massolle and Jo Engel – set up a sound studio called Tri-Ergon. They developed and produced the first talkie in 1925 called *Das Mädchen mit den Schwefelhölzern* (The Girl with the Matchsticks) which premiered – and bombed – at the Metropol Theatre on Nollendorfplatz. Talkie production didn't make inroads in Berlin until 1930.

In 1927 UFA passed into the hands of the Hugenberg group, which was sympathetic to the burgeoning right-wing movement. The new film era resulted in the Marlene Dietrich classic *Der blaue Engel* (The Blue Angel, 1930), directed by Joseph von Sternberg and loosely based on Heinrich Mann's novella *Professor Unrat*. It tells the story of a pedantic professor who is hopelessly infatuated with a sexy cabaret singer, played by Dietrich. For Marlene, it created the vamp image she enjoyed all her life.

Pabst's *Dreigroschenoper* (Threepenny Opera, 1931), based on the play by Bertolt Brecht (music by Kurt Weill), was set in the gangster milieu around Mackie Messer (Mack the Knife). *Das Testament des Dr Mabuse* (The Testament of Dr Mabuse, 1932) was Fritz Lang's first talkie. It is about a psychiatric patient who devises plans to take over the world. If that rings ironic, it's worth noting that the Nazis prevented the German premiere, forcing Lang to shift it to Austria.

Third Reich Hitler's power grab ripped through German cultural life, and the world of film was not spared. Financial trouble at UFA between 1933 and 1937 allowed the Nazis to anonymously buy out Hugenberg and step up control over the industry.

Films now required approval from Goebbels' Reichskulturkammer (Chamber of Culture). Censorship laws and bans drove over 500 actors and directors into

Dubbed 'the Pope's revenge', when hit by sunlight the TV tower's sphere reflects a huge cross.

Wannsee Memorial Museum.

Checkpoint Charlie museum commemorates the Berlin Wall.

Berlin isn't all cranes and buildings ...

In summer Berlin's cafes spill out onto the pavements.

A memento?

Marlene Dietrich

Marlene Dietrich, whose real name was Marie Magdalena von Losch, was born in Berlin into a good middle-class family on 27 December 1901. After attending acting school, she worked in the fledgling German silent-film industry in the 1920s, stereotyped as a hard living, libertine flapper. In the 1927 film *Wenn ein Weib den Weg verliert* (When a Girl Loses Her Way) she played a well-mannered young woman who falls into the clutches of a gigolo. She soon carved a niche in the film fantasies of lower middle-class men as the dangerously seductive *femme fatale*, best typified by her 1930 talkie *Der blaue Engel* (The Blue Angel), which also made her a Hollywood star.

Dietrich landed the role only through the insistence of Josef von Sternberg, the film's director, who had previously watched her perform. Nevertheless, he still had to convince Heinrich Mann, on whose novel, *Professor Unrat*, the movie was based and who wanted to give the part to his lover, Trude Hesterberg, a cabaret artist. Meanwhile, the film's scriptwriter was doing his best to get his own lover into the role. Dietrich won the part and Mann lost his lover.

Working closely with Sternberg, Dietrich built on her image of erotic opulence – dominant, severe, always with a touch of self-irony. When she put on men's suits for *Marocco* in 1930, she lent her 'sexuality is power' attitude bisexual tones, winning a new audience overnight.

Marlene stayed in Hollywood after the Nazi rise to power, though Hitler, no less immune to her charms, reportedly promised perks and the red-carpet treatment if she moved back to Germany. She responded with an empty offer to return if she could bring Sternberg, who was a Jew and no Nazi favourite.

When Allied GIs rolled into Paris in 1944, Marlene was there too. Asked once whether there was any truth to the rumour that she had slept with General Eisenhower, she reportedly replied, 'How could I have? He was never at the front'.

After the war, Dietrich made only occasional appearances in films, choosing instead to cut records and perform live. Discreet, uncompromising and, contrary to the film image, always the well-bred woman from Berlin, Dietrich retreated from the public eye as age and illness slowly caught up with her.

She died in 1992, aged 90. The Deutsche Bahn named one of its ICE trains to Berlin after her – *Der blaue Engel*. Selections from her estate will soon be on display at the new Filmhaus on Potsdamer Platz.

MICK WELDON

exile. Many went to Hollywood and ended up playing parts as stereotypical Nazis. Some directors and actors were successful, but the majority struck a language barrier and sank into oblivion.

Most films produced in Berlin under the Nazis are either histories glorifying famous Germans, such as Wolfgang Liebeneiner's *Bismarck* (1940), or outright propaganda flicks like the anti-Semitic *Jud Süss* (Jew Süss, 1940) by Veit Harlan.

A tempestuous woman was to place her stamp – creatively, infamously and forever – on the capability of film to tell a story and to sway opinion and events. Leni Riefenstahl made brilliant documentaries about the Olympic Games of 1936 as well as her famous propaganda film *Triumph of the Will*, which gave an emotional boost to Hitler's psychotic Third Reich programs. Escapist comedies like Willi Forst's *Allotria* (1936) rounded out the cinematic fare.

Post-1945 After the war, the Allies confiscated all film material and archives, about 70% of which was in the Soviet zone at the Babelsberg studios. These studios quickly became the main production site for DEFA (Deutsche Film AG), founded in 1946.

The same year, Wolfgang Staudte made the first postwar film, *Die Mörder sind unter uns* (The Murderers Are Among Us). Set in 1945 at Christmas, it tells the story of a guilt-ridden army doctor who encounters a commanding officer responsible for the execution of women and children in Russia. He threatens the officer with a pistol as the latter is celebrating with his wife and children.

The founding of the GDR in 1949 interrupted the artistic development of film making in the Soviet sector as the SED party prevented the production of movies not in line with party doctrine. DEFA became East Germany's film and TV production centre. Important movies of this early period include Falk Harnacks' *Das Beil von Wandsbek* (The Axe of Wandsbeck, 1951).

In West Germany, movie making comprised mostly escapist and inane entertainment. Exceptions were Robert Siodmaks *Die Ratten* (The Rats, 1955) with Maria Schell, and Billy Wilder's *Eins, Zwei, Drei* (One, Two, Three), filmed days before the Wall went up in 1961. Wilder's film was a commercial flop because its ironic portrayal of the east-west conflict was largely lost in the maelstrom of actual events. A boost to the film industry came with the first Berlinale in 1950.

1960 to 1990 Television presented major competition to film making, and the industry in West Berlin was particularly hard hit. Many artists and directors had already left the city because the infrastructure lagged far behind international standards. In addition, the city's 'island' status confined outdoor shoots to an urban environment, thereby limiting creative expression. The Junge Deutsche Film (Young German Film), a movement centred around directors like Volker Schlöndorf, Wim Wenders, Werner Herzog and Rainer Werner Fassbinder, took roots in Munich and only had an indirect effect on the development of the Berlin film scene. Off-beat directors like Rosa von Praunheim, who remained in Berlin, focused largely on movies portraying the city's alternative and underground culture.

In East Berlin, the government's censorship grip loosened a little in 1971 after Erich Honecker replaced Walter Ulbricht as head of state. The most important director was Frank Beyer who made *Jakob der Lügner* (Jacob the Liar, 1974), based on the book by Jurek Becker and set in a ghetto in Poland. The 1999 Hollywood remake starred Robin Williams.

The late 70s brought significant change when an ambitious program of film subsidies launched by the Berlin Senate attracted important directors like Volker Schlöndorff, Margarethe von Trotta and Rainer Werner Fassbinder back to West Berlin. Terrorism increasingly became a theme, as in Schlöndorff's *Die verlorene Ehre der Katharina Blum* (The Lost Honour of Katharina Blum, 1975), an adaptation of a Heinrich Böll short novel. Trotta, who collaborated with Schlöndorff on the film, later dealt with the theme again in *Das zweite Erwachen der Christa Klages* (The Second Awakening of Christa Klages, 1978) and in *Die Bleierne Zeit* (Leaden Time, 1981).

Huge international box-office successes were Schlöndorff's *Die Blechtrommel* (The Tin Drum, 1979), based on the Günter Grass novel, and Fassbinder's *Querelle* (1982). One of the last great movies to emerge out of pre-Wende Berlin was Wim Wenders' *Der Himmel über Berlin* (Wings of Desire, 1987), starring Americans Peter Falk and Peter Coyote, which features two angels who move through divided Berlin. The movie was remade by Hollywood in

1999. Called *City of Angels*, it starred Nicholas Cage and Meg Ryan.

Post-Wende In recent years, Berlin has experienced a small renaissance with directors like Wenders and Jutta Brückner joining Volker Schlöndorff, who's trying to drag the Filmstadt Babelsberg, the legendary UFA studios, back from obscurity. (Also see the boxed text 'Hollywood on the Havel' in the Potsdam section of the Excursions chapter). One of Schlöndorff's recent productions was *Der Unhold* (The Monster) with John Malkovich. Other international successes include Dani Levy's *Stille Nacht* (Silent Night, 1995), the underground smash hit *Lola Rennt* (Run Lola Run, 1997/98) by Tom Tykwer, and *Die Comedian Harmonists* (The Harmonists, 1998) about a famed group of a cappella singers whose career was cut short when their Jewish members had to flee the Nazis.

Upcoming film-related developments include the opening of the Filmhaus am Potsdamer Platz in the new Sony Center. For the first time the public will be able to view the extensive archives and collections of the Deutsche Kinemathek, including the estate of Marlene Dietrich. The Berlinale is also set to move to Potsdamer Platz from its historic Zoo Palast headquarters.

Theatre

Berlin's theatre scene had rather modest beginnings; it wasn't until the middle of the 18th century and the emergence of such thespian luminaries as Gotthold Ephraim Lessing and Johann Wolfgang von Goethe that high-quality productions were staged in the city. In 1796, August Wilhelm Iffland (1759-1814), one of the great early impresarios, took over the helm of the Royal National Theatre. Iffland was noted for his natural yet sophisticated productions (especially those of Schiller plays) and for cultivating a talented ensemble.

Iffland's act proved hard to follow and when he died in 1814, Berlin theatre languished for 80 years until Otto Brahm became director of the Deutsches Theater in 1894. Dedicated to the naturalistic style,

Brahm must be considered a pioneer of modern dramatic theatre. He coaxed psychological dimensions out of the characters and sought to make their language and situations mirror real life. The critical works of Gerhart Hauptmann and Henrik Ibsen were staples on his stage throughout the 1890s.

In 1894, Brahm hired a young actor by the name of Max Reinhardt (1873-1943), who became perhaps the most famous and influential director in the history of German theatre (also see the boxed text 'Max Reinhardt – Impresario Extraordinaire' in the Things to See and Do chapter). Reinhardt's path crossed that of another seminal theatre figure, Bertolt Brecht (1898-1956), who moved to Berlin in 1924 and began working with Reinhardt at the Deutsches Theater. Their collaboration was short-lived after Brecht developed his own unique style, the so-called 'epic theatre' (see the boxed text 'Bertolt Brecht').

After WWII, artistic stagnation spread across German theatre for more than two decades. In West Berlin, a new period of greatness would not begin until 1970 with the opening of the Schaubühne am Halleschen Ufer under Peter Stein. The theatre, which later moved to the Ku'damm and was renamed Schaubühne am Lehniner Platz, became one of Germany's leading stages.

In East Berlin, the Volksbühne became one of the most innovative venues, along with the Deutsches Theater. Taking advantage of the relative political and artistic freedom granted to these stages by the government, they provided platforms for political exchange and renewal and indirectly fomented the peaceful revolution of 1989. One of the driving forces was the prolific and outspoken dramatist Heiner Müller.

After the Wende, Berlin's theatre landscape – both in the east and west – was swept by major artistic, structural and personnel changes. Several government-subsidised stages closed for lack of funding, most notably the Schiller Theater in West Berlin. Now integrated into the western system, the eastern stages underwent a significant reorientation in form and content. At the Berliner Ensemble, Heiner Müller was

Bertolt Brecht

Bertolt Brecht (1898-1956), the controversial poet and playwright who spent the last seven years of his life in East Berlin, wrote his first play, *Baal*, while studying medicine in Munich in 1918. His first play to reach the stage, *Trommeln in der Nacht* (Drums in the Night, 1922), won the coveted Kleist Prize, and two years later he moved to the Deutsches Theater in Berlin to work with the Austrian director Max Reinhardt.

Over the next decade, in plays like *Die Dreigroschenoper* (The Threepenny Opera, 1928), he developed his theory of 'epic theatre' which, unlike 'dramatic theatre', forces its audience to detach themselves emotionally from the play and its characters and to reason intellectually.

A staunch Marxist, Brecht went into exile during the Nazi years, surfaced in Hollywood as a scriptwriter, then left the USA after being called in to explain himself during the communist witch hunts of the McCarthy era. He wrote most of his best plays during his years in exile: *Mutter Courage und ihre Kinder* (Mother Courage and Her Children, 1941), *Leben des Galilei* (The Life of Galileo, 1943), *Der gute Mensch von Sezuan* (The Good Woman of Sezuan, 1943) and *Der kaukasische Kreidekreis* (The Caucasian Chalk Circle, 1948).

Brecht returned to East Berlin in 1949 where he founded the Berliner Ensemble with his wife, Helene Weigel, who directed it until her death in 1971. His *Mother Courage and her Children* premiered in 1949 at the Deutsches Theater. In 1954, the troupe moved into the Theater am Schiffbauerdamm.

During his lifetime Brecht was both suspected in the east for his unorthodox aesthetic theories and scorned (and often boycotted) in much of the west for his communist principles. A staple of left-wing directors throughout the 1960s and 1970s, Brecht's plays are now under reassessment, though his influence in freeing the theatre from the constraints of a 'well made play in three acts' is undeniable. The superiority of Brecht's poetry, so little known in English, remains undisputed.

MICK WELDON

among those who shook the dust off this venerable troupe, while *enfant terrible* Frank Castorf ignited a creative firestorm at the Volksbühne. Though city planners' dreams of making Berlin Germany's musical metropolis have fizzled, other art forms – most notably variété and cabaret – have experienced a meteoric renaissance in recent years.

Meanwhile, a flock of both young and established theatrical directors is poised to spark new inspirations and to take Berlin's thespian scene into the new millennium.

After 13 years at the famous Burg Theater in Vienna, Claus Peymann will take over the reins at the Berliner Ensemble. His focus will be on modern drama and works by contemporary authors like George Tabori and Elfriede Jelinek.

In 2001 Bernard Wilms, currently garnering accolades as director of the Maxim Gorki Theater, will take the helm of the legendary Deutsches Theater. A new generation of theatre directors is led by Thomas Ostermeier, under whose guidance the Baracke emerged as one of the foremost experimental stages in

Germany. In 2000, he will move to the Schaubühne am Lehniner Platz where he'll be joined as director by noted choreographer Sasha Waltz.

Dance

Dance as an art form has always taken a back seat to theatre in Berlin. This is true of both modern dance as well as ballet, despite the fact that all three opera houses (Deutsche Oper, Staatsoper and Komische Oper) maintain their own dance companies (though this may change soon as plans are under way to merge them into a single troupe, the BerlinBallet).

The popularity of modern/free dance especially has gained momentum since the Wende with new and innovative troupes attracting a growing audience. Leading venues are the TanzWerkstatt Berlin and the Hebbel Theater, which organise the annual Tanz im August dance festival that draws international attention. One of the people giving new impetus to the scene is the choreographer and dancer Sasha Waltz.

Historically, Berlin has made several contributions to the evolution of free and expressive, ie modern, dance. The eccentric American dancer Isadora Duncan opened her own school (the Duncanschule) in Berlin in 1904. Duncan banished the ballet shoe – which she considered 'an instrument of torture' – and flitted across the stage barefoot and in her trademark flowing white gowns.

In the artistically fecund 1920s, Berlin gave birth to a new dance form, the so-called grotesque dance. Influenced by dadaism, it was characterised by excessive, and often comical, expressiveness. One of its prime practitioners was Valeska Gert. Even more influential in the long run was the vision of Mary Wigman who regarded body and movement as tools to express the universal experience of life in all its complexity. Her style inspired some of today's leading German choreographers (including Pina Bausch and Reinhild Hoffmann).

Berlin's first encounter with ballet came under the reign of Friedrich II who brought Italian star Barberina to the city in 1744. The first royal ballet company formed in

1811 but, in the absence of home-grown talent, it had to rely on imported dancers and choreographers. Ballet went commercial in the 1920s with the emergence of the glitzy revues featuring rows of leg-kicking showgirls, a tradition that's lately been revived at the Friedrichstadtpalast which maintains its own 80-member dance troupe.

After WWII, ballet experienced a renaissance under the Russian immigrant Tatjana Gsovsky. Working within a very limited infrastructure (at least initially with no permanent stage), she nevertheless managed to choreograph a number of notable productions, including *Hamlet* (1953) and *The Idiot* (1954) at the Theater des Westens. Gsovsky was later director of the ballet of the Deutsche Oper, a position held until 1962. Later she founded the Berliner Tanzakademie.

Gsovsky was succeeded by her solo dancer, Gert Reinholm, who produced few highlights during his 28-year tenure. One rather scandalous work was *Suzi Creamcheese* (1970), which was based on a song of the same name and featured the music of Frank Zappa. Today's ballet troupes concentrate on audience-pleasing, classical repertoires including such well-known pieces as *Swan Lake* and *The Nutcracker*.

Music

For centuries, Berlin was largely eclipsed by Vienna, Leipzig and other European cities when it came to music. The few musical styles generated here were the *Lieder* (songs), hymns and ballads produced during the reign of the culture-loving Friedrich II by a trio of composers: Friedrich Wilhelm Marpurg, Johann Abraham Peter Schulz and Carl Friedrich Zelter (1758-1832). Carl Zelter served as director of the Berlin Singing Academy from 1800 to 1832, whose student body included later composers Felix Mendelssohn-Bartholdy (1809-1847) and Giacomo Meyerbeer (1791-1864).

In 1882, the Berliner Philharmonisches Orchester was founded and went on to gain international stature under the leadership of Hans von Bülow and Arthur Nikisch. In

1923, Wilhelm Furtwängler became artistic director, a post he would hold, with interruptions, until 1954. His successor, Herbert von Karajan, was an autocratic figure who took the orchestra to a position of real dominance on the world stage and remained its director until 1989. Current artistic director (until at least 2001) is Claudio Abbado.

The pulsating 1920s drew numerous musicians to Berlin, including Arnold Schönberg and Paul Hindemith who taught at the Arts Academy and the Berliner Hochschule (Berlin College) respectively. Schönberg's atonal compositions found a following here, as did his experimentation with noise and sound effects. Hindemith explored the new medium of radio broadcast and taught a seminar on film music.

The era also generated the Berlin *Schlager*, silly but entertaining songs with titles like *Mein Papagei frisst keine harten Eier* (My Parrot Doesn't Eat Hard-boiled Eggs) and *Veronika, der Lenz ist da* (Veronica, Spring is Here). Singing groups like the Comedian Harmonists built their success on this music.

New expressionistic approaches to musical theatre came from such classically trained composers as Hanns Eisler and Kurt Weill who collaborated with Brecht on *The Threepenny Opera* and *The Rise and Fall of the City of Mahagonny*. Mischa Spoliansky was among the leading lights of the cabaret stages.

Contemporary Music Berlin continues to be a fertile breeding ground for new musical trends and it is estimated that in the late 90s the scene consisted of nearly 2000 bands. But even before the Wende, numerous homegrown performers managed to leap onto the national and even international stage.

In the late 60s, Tangerine Dream hit the airwaves with its electronically charged, psychedelic sound. A decade later, East Berlin-born Nina Hagen followed her adopted father, writer Wolf Biermann, to West Germany and soon became the diva of German punk. Her laconic Berlin style blended well enough with English-American punk for the

New Musical Express to describe her as an epileptic Edith Piaf and a cross between Johnny Rotten, Maria Callas and Bette Midler. Hagen also laid the groundwork for the major musical movement of the 80s, the Neue Deutsche Welle (New German Wave) which gave the stage to Berlin bands like Ideal, the Neonbabies and UKW.

Back in the GDR, bands like Die Puhdys and Rockhaus kept alive a vibrant underground scene; both continue to perform today.

West Berlin also drew a slew of international talent. David Bowie and Iggy Pop both spent stints here, living at Hauptstrasse 152. Nick Cave owned a club, and U2's Zoo album was inspired by Zoo station.

Coinciding with the Wende, another essentially homespun music form – techno – took over Berlin. Techno may have its roots in Detroit-based house music and the synthetic sounds of bands like Kraftwerk, but it was from Berlin that it conquered Germany and Europe. Reflecting the apolitical and almost nihilist *Zeitgeist*, these aggressive, urban sounds have influenced the fashion and tastes of an entire generation. Pioneering clubs included Ufo, Planet and the extant Tresor. The scene went commercial in the mid-90s with the opening of the now-defunct E-werk, a converted power station with space for thousands of ravers.

Berlin also gave birth to the annual Love Parade which takes over city streets every July. What began as a three-car procession with 150 ravers has turned into a weekend-long phenomenon that attracted 1.5 million in 1999. (Also see the boxed text 'Techno Town' in the Entertainment chapter.)

Despite techno's dominance, other sounds continue to be produced in Berlin. Since 1992, the two-day Metrobeat Festival has been a major showcase for emerging talent. It's been a launch pad for groups as diverse as the retro-band Rosenstolz and the female Turkish hiphop singer Aziza-A.

Literature

Since its beginnings, Berlin's literary scene has reflected a peculiar blend of provincialism and worldliness. As with the other arts,

Berlin didn't emerge as a centre of literature until relatively late, reaching its zenith during the dynamic 1920s. Overall, the city was not so much a place that generated influential writers – or where they came to write – as it was one where they came to meet each other, exchange ideas and be intellectually stimulated.

Berlin's literary history only begins with the Enlightenment at the end of the 18th century, a period dominated by humanistic ideals. One of the main authors of the period was Gotthold Ephraim Lessing (1729-81) who is noted for his critical works, fables and tragedies. In Berlin he wrote the play *Minna von Barnhelm*, though his best-known dramatic works are *Miss Sara Samson*, *Emilia Galotti* and especially *Nathan der Weise* (Nathan the Wise). He also wrote extensively about the theory of drama, drawing on the elements of Greek tragedy, which employs empathy and fear to arouse the audience's passion.

The Romantic period, which grew out of the Enlightenment, was marked by a proliferation of literary salons, usually sponsored by women, such as Rahel Levin (later Rahel Varnhagen). At these gatherings, men and women from all walks of life came together to discuss philosophy, politics, art and other subjects. Literary greats working in Berlin in this era included Friedrich and August Wilhelm von Schlegel (the latter made a mark with his translations of Shakespeare) and the Romantic poets Achim von Arnim, Clemens Brentano and Heinrich von Kleist.

The realist movement, which emerged in the middle of the 19th century, saw the popularisation of novels and novellas. Much interest in these forms came from the newly established middle class, who wanted to read realistic depictions of their daily lives. Historical novels and work critical of society also caught on, such as those by Wilhelm Raabe (1831-1910) who, in his *Chronik der Sperlingsgasse* (Chronicle of Sperling Lane, 1857), examines various aspects of urban life in Berlin. It was Theodor Fontane (1819-98) who raised the Berlin society novel to an art form. Most of his works are set around the March of Brandenburg and in Berlin and show both the nobility and the middle class mired in their societal confinements.

Naturalism, a spin-off of realism, took things a step further after 1880. It aimed at painstakingly re-creating the milieu of entire social classes, down to the local dialect. In Berlin, Gerhart Hauptmann (1862-1946) was the main representative of the genre. Many of his plays and novels focus on social injustice and the harsh life of workers – subjects so provocative that several of his premieres ended in riots and scandals. As a result of the staging of *Die Weber* (The Weavers) at the Deutsches Theater in 1892, which depicted the misery of Silesian weavers, the Kaiser cancelled his subscription to the royal box. The play, however, was a smashing success. In 1912, Hauptmann won the Nobel Prize for Literature.

In the 1920s, Berlin's reputation as an intellectual, cultural and artistic centre made it a magnet for writers from around the world. The period was characterised by great experimentation and innovation as various literary approaches developed simultaneously. Alfred Döblin (1878-1957) wrote the first major 'Berlin novel' called *Berlin Alexanderplatz*, which provides a dose of big-city lights and the underworld during the Weimar Republic. Other notables from the era were the political satirists Kurt Tucholsky (1890-1935) and Erich Kästner (1899-1974), as well as Egon Erwin Kisch, a newspaper journalist and author of critical essays.

One of the dominant artists working in the 1920s, primarily in drama, was Bertolt Brecht (also see the boxed text 'Bertolt Brecht' earlier in this chapter). Brecht was among the artists who left Germany after the Nazis came to power. Many of those who stayed went into inner emigration, which essentially meant keeping their mouths shut and working underground, if at all.

After the war, different developments took hold in the two Berlins. In East Berlin, government censorship stifled author creativity and freedom of expression. The SED party organised regular cultural conferences and author congresses to hammer in the official line. Safe themes were postwar reconstruction and the historical evolution of the socialist state.

In the mid-70s, a segment of the literary scene began to detach itself slowly from the party grip. Authors like Christa Wolf (1929-) and Heiner Müller (1929-95) belonged to loose literary circles that regularly met in private houses. Wolf is one of the best and most controversial East German writers. *Der geteilte Himmel* (Divided Heaven) has an industrial backdrop and tells the story of a woman's love for a man who fled to the west.

Müller had the distinction of being unpalatable in both Germanys. It is said that he worked for the Stasi, but that his messages were so ambiguous as to be worthless. His works, which are dense and difficult, include *Der Lohndrücker* (The Man Who Kept Down Wages) and the *Germania* trilogy of plays.

In West Berlin, the postwar literary scene didn't revive until the arrival of Günter Grass in the late 1950s. His famous *Die Blechtrommel* (The Tin Drum) humorously traces recent German history through the eyes of Oskar, a child who refuses to grow up. The book made Grass a household name, and he has followed up with an impressive body of novels, plays and poetry. In Berlin he lived and worked as part of a writers' colony which also included Hans-Magnus Enzensberger, Ingeborg Bachmann and the Swiss writer Max Frisch. Together they paved the way for the political and critical literature that has been dominant since the 1960s. In 1999, Grass became the ninth German to win the Nobel Prize for Literature.

Literary achievement stagnated at first after the Wende as writers from the east and west began a process of self-examination and self-absorbed analysis. Rather than working together on coming to terms with their separate pasts, the creative chasm resulting from the years of division was emphasised. Only Heiner Müller and Botho Strauss stood out amid the creative void. In the late 90s Berlin's literary scene finally picked up steam. New books dealing with the past are characterised not by analytical introspection but by emotionally distanced,

nearly grotesque, imagery. Examples here are Thomas Brussig's *Helden wie wir* (Heroes like us, 1995) and Ingo Schulze's *Simple Stories* (1998). On the more populist end of the spectrum is a revitalisation of the genre of the 'Berlin detective story' which features Pieke Biermann and Horst Bosetzky as prime practitioners.

SOCIETY & CONDUCT

Berlin is a very casual city. Except for formal gourmet restaurants, there's no need to dress up for dinner or a theatre or opera performance (though you're certainly free to do so). Some nightclubs may have dress codes, though originality and creativity are usually what matters here.

We found Berliners to be accommodating and fairly helpful towards visitors, although there are reports that things can be different if you 'look foreign', for instance because of your skin colour. In general, though, people are quite likely to volunteer help if you look lost and will occasionally even accompany you to make sure you get to your destination.

If you're invited to someone's home, ask if there's anything you could bring. Even if the answer is no, it's still nice to arrive clutching some flowers or a bottle of wine. After a dinner party, call the next day or send a little thankyou note.

Berliners tend to be quite opinionated and the conversation may touch on many subjects, from politics to the weather in Spain. It *is* OK to mention 'the war', if done with tact and relevance. After all, a lot of the people you will meet have grown up demanding explanations. What causes offence, however, is a 'victor' mentality, which is perceived as righteous and gloating, or the idea that fascist ideas are intrinsically German.

Shaking hands is common among both men and women, as is a hug or a kiss on the cheek, especially among young people. When making a phone call, give your name at the start. Germans consider it impolite or simply get annoyed when no name is given. If you don't want to give your name (when dealing with bureaucracy, for instance), make one up.

Like elsewhere in Germany, great importance is placed on the formal 'Sie' form of address, though young people and eastern Germans are much more relaxed about 'Sie' and 'du'. In bars, where a lot of young people gather, 'du' is often used, but saying 'du' to a shop assistant or to staff in a restaurant/bar is likely to result in bad service.

Academic titles (Herr or Frau Doktor) are important. If someone introduces herself as Dr Schmidt, that's what she wants to be called. If you have a title yourself, you may of course insist on it as well; this can be useful in situations where you want the extra respect.

RELIGION

Berlin's astonishing religious diversity is largely a result of the constant influx of people from all parts of the world over the course of its history. Since the Reformation in the 16th century, Berlin has been predominantly Protestant. After 1685 it became a haven for Huguenots who fled France in droves after King Louis XIV revoked the Edict of Nantes which had granted them religious freedom. About 6000 of them settled in Berlin at the invitation of the Great Elector, Friedrich Wilhelm, accounting for about 20% of the population by 1700. Even today, Protestants greatly outnumber Roman Catholics. The latest figures show about 900,000 Lutherans and 345,000 Roman Catholics.

Small though it is, Berlin has one of Germany's largest Jewish communities, its number (about 12,000) bolstered in recent years by the immigration of Russian Jews (there were 160,000 Jews in Berlin before WWII). The community maintains a hospital, schools, six synagogues, and the Centrum Judaicum museum and community centre on Oranienburger Strasse. In 1986, a chapter of Adass Jisroel, a conservative Jewish congregation, formed as well. It currently has about 1000 members.

With 200,000 followers, Islam has a significant place in Berlin's religious landscape, its number largely coming from the city's vast Turkish population. Nearly 40 other religious affiliations are represented –

some, like the Unitarian Church, with fewer than 100 members.

Germans who belong to a recognised denomination have to pay a church tax amounting to 10% of their income tax. Once considered a social taboo, more and more people have left their churches in recent years for financial reasons. Agnosticism and atheism, however, are the main reasons why nearly one in two Berliners claims not to have any religion at all.

LANGUAGE

German belongs to the Indo-European language group and is spoken by over 100 million people throughout the world, including Austria and part of Switzerland. There are also ethnic German communities in neighbouring Eastern European countries such as Poland and the Czech Republic, although expulsion after 1945 reduced their numbers dramatically.

High German is the official and proper form of the language, though most people also speak a local or regional dialect. The same is true of Berlin, though only a small number of Berliners speak pure Berlinisch.

It was the reformer Martin Luther who laid the groundwork for a unified written German language through his translation of the New Testament from the Greek in 1521/22. Until that time, nearly every German state had its own dialect, which was not necessarily understood elsewhere.

In the 19th century Jacob Grimm, who is considered the founder of German philology, co-wrote the first German grammar with his brother Wilhelm.

Regional dialects still thrive throughout Germany, especially in Cologne, rural Bavaria, Swabia and parts of Saxony. The Sorb minority in eastern Germany has its own language. In northern Germany it's common to hear Plattdeutsch (Low German) spoken. Both High and Low German are distant relatives of English, and the fact that many German words survive in the English vocabulary today makes things easier for native English speakers.

For useful phrases in German, see the Language chapter.

BERLIN'S ARCHITECTURE

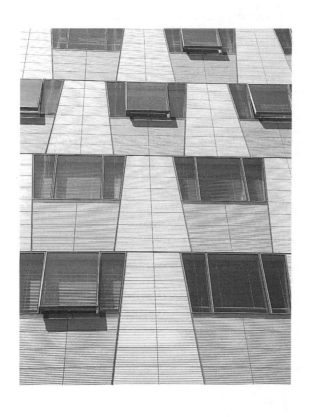

The fact that Berlin is more than 750 years old is certainly not reflected in its appearance. Even in the 1920s, contemporary observers noted that the city is 'essentially a creation of modern times'. While this doesn't make it any less interesting a city, it means that in terms of architectural aesthetics, the German capital will never be on a par with Prague, Paris or other European cities.

Surviving structures from the Middle Ages are scarce, with the Marienkirche and the reconstructed Nikolaikirche in Mitte being the most noteworthy examples. The Renaissance period is even more poorly represented with the ornately gabled Ribbeckhaus (1624), nearby at Breite Strasse 35-36, the only remaining residential building from that era.

Berlin's first architectural heyday came in the late baroque period, propelled by self-crowned King Friedrich I's growing representational needs. The arrival of master architect Karl Friedrich Schinkel marked the beginning of a veritable building boom during the reign of Friedrich Wilhelm II (1786-97) when neoclassicism ruled the day.

The founding of the German Empire in 1871, with Berlin as its capital, launched a population explosion and the need for mass housing. Industrial architecture emerged as a new field led by Peter Behrens, who was a trailblazer for Modernism. This first flourished in the 1920s as the International Style (under people like Walter Gropius and Ludwig Mies van der Rohe) only to be eradicated by the Nazis who loathed anything modern and favoured architecture that was essentially a caricature of neoclassicism.

After WWII, the wrecking ball destroyed much of what the bombs had left standing. A 'de-construction' boom preceded reconstruction and resulted in different architectural visions of the divided city.

East Berlin architects followed the 'bigger is better' maxim as best exemplified by Karl-Marx-Allee who built the *Zuckerbäckerstil* (wedding cake style), a deceptively pleasant term for monumental structures with Stalinist charm. At the same time, soulless high-rise blocks – the so-called *Plattenbauten* made from pre-fab building elements – provided much needed housing.

In West Berlin, putting a roof over people's heads was also a postwar priority and it took a long time before an architectural style was consolidated. In Berlin this mostly took the form of a continuation and perfecting of the International Style with much the same cast of practitioners.

After the Wende, Berlin's struggle to redefine itself extended to architecture as well. This has resulted in a timid approach called critical reconstruction that has met with tepid approval from critics and the general public. For now, though, Berlin remains a work in progress, its constantly evolving cityscape offering ever new angles of discovery and aesthetics.

Previous page: Isozaki's Volksbank (photograph by Andrea Schulte-Peevers).

Inset: Debis building by Renzo Piano (photograph by Andrea Schulte-Peevers).

ARCHITECTS

The following are some of the most important people associated with Berlin architecture. Their work can be seen in various parts of the city.

Georg Wenzeslaus von Knobelsdorff (1699-1753)

Georg Knobelsdorff was the leading light of what became known as the 'Frederician Rococo', a particular fusion of that late baroque style with neoclassical elements, which flourished under King Friedrich II. A student of court painter Antoine Pesne, Knobelsdorff drew much inspiration from his journeys to France and Italy where he picked up early neoclassical influences. A friend of the king, he was tapped for work at the court as soon as Friedrich ascended the throne. His greatest claims to fame are Sanssouci Palace in Potsdam (1747), the new wing of Charlottenburg Palace (1747) and the State Opera Unter den Linden (1742).

Carl Gotthard Langhans (1732-1808)

Originally trained as a baroque architect, Carl Langhans made his mark as a pioneer of pure neoclassicism in Germany and especially in Berlin. His landmark Brandenburg Gate (1791), based on an ancient Greek design, was the first major structure in this style on German soil. Other major works of his include the Belvedere in the park of Charlottenburg Palace and an early version of the Schauspielhaus (theatre) on Gendarmenmarkt.

Karl Friedrich Schinkel (1781-1841)

No single architect has determined the face of Berlin more than Karl Friedrich Schinkel. Regarded as the most prominent and mature architect of German neoclassicism, Schinkel studied classical architecture in Italy but at first was unable to practise his art when he returned to a Berlin stifled by Napoleonic occupation. Instead he earned a living as a romantic painter, furniture and set designer before becoming a senior assessor with the Royal Building Authority in 1810. Five years later he was promoted to royal building master, a position that allowed him to put his stamp on the cityscape.

Besides his major accomplishments (detailed in Tour I later in this section), Schinkel also gave the world the Mausoleum (1810) for Queen Luise and the Schinkel Pavilion (1824) in the park of Charlottenburg Palace; the neo-Gothic war memorial in Viktoriapark atop the Kreuzberg (1821); the Schloss Charlottenhof (1827), and the Nikolaikirche (1837) in Potsdam. For details on any of these, see the Things to See & Do chapter and the Excursions chapter, respectively.

In his spare time, Schinkel also developed the underlying principles for the protection and preservation of historical monuments.

Peter Behrens (1868-1940)

Often called the 'father of modern architecture', Behrens actually started out as a painter and spent some time in Darmstadt, the centre of Art Nouveau in the early 20th century. In 1907, he joined the artistic council of the Berlin-based electricity giant AEG, an unusual position that put him in charge of a wide array of tasks, from designing the corporate letterhead to factory buildings. Behrens is best known for his industrial cathedrals, in particular the AEG Turbine Hall (1909) in Wedding. An airy and light-flooded factory with high ceilings and exposed structural beams, it is considered a milestone in modern architecture. Behrens also paved the way for the upcoming generation of avant-garde designers like Bruno Taut, Le Corbusier, Walter Gropius and Ludwig Mies van der Rohe.

Bruno Taut (1880-1938) & Contemporaries

Berlin's late 19th century population explosion generated an urgent need for cheap housing, which resulted in the mushrooming of *Mietskasernen* – warren-like, claustrophobic tenements built around successive courtyards. In the 1920s, several architects started applying Peter Behrens' approach to humanising the workplace to residential living quarters. Their housing colonies are an unlikely marriage of functionality, organic design and symbolism. A maximum height of four storeys, integration of open and pleasant green spaces, and geometric simplicity were among the hallmarks of this new approach. Examples include Hufeisensiedlung (Horseshoe Colony, 1924-26) in Britz by Bruno Taut (see Neukölln in Things to See & Do); Waldsiedlung Onkel-Toms-Hütte (Forest Colony Uncle Tom's Cabin, 1926) in Zehlendorf by Otto Rudolf Salvisberg and Hugo Häring; and Siemensstadt (1931) between Charlottenburg and Spandau by Hans Scharoun, Walter Gropius and others.

Hans Scharoun (1893-1972)

Hans Scharoun had already designed apartment buildings in Charlottenburg and supervised the construction of the Siemensstadt colony (1929-31) before Hitler hit the world stage. After the war, he helped re-establish the Berlin Arts Academy and became a prime representative of a Modernist subgenre called 'organic architecture'. It was characterised by asymmetry, dynamic, round and flowing shapes and a general attempt to integrate architecture with the sensory needs of humans. One of his basic tenets was to adapt the shape of the building to its stated purpose and function. Though Scharoun's work was critically acclaimed in architectural circles and frequently honoured in competitions, few of his designs ever made it off the drawing board. When they did, as for example in the Philharmonie (see Tour III), the results are quite dramatic.

STYLES

The following are some of the main styles of architecture that have flourished in Berlin throughout the centuries. You'll find examples of each scattered throughout the city.

Baroque/Rococo

The baroque, which blossomed in Germany from the early 17th century to the mid-18th century, merges structures, sculpture, ornamentation and painting into a single *Gesamtkunstwerk* (complete work of art). Not nearly as frilly and flamboyant as southern German examples of the style, Berlin baroque remained subdued with a formal and precise bent. Rococo is a derivation of late baroque and coincided with the Enlightenment. The period's most famous practitioners in Berlin were Knobelsdorff (see Architects earlier this section), but also Johann Arnold Nering (1659-95), best known for designing the oldest part of Schloss Charlottenburg.

Neoclassicism

Neoclassical architecture, which emerged in the late 18th century, has had the most lastingly effect on Berlin's cityscape and in fact most surviving historical buildings date back to this era. A reaction against baroque exuberance, the style brought a return to classical forms and traditional design elements like columns, pediments, domes and restrained ornamentation as had been typical of the Graeco-Roman period.

Neoclassicism peaked under Friedrich Wilhelm II (ruled 1786-97) who tried to turn Berlin into a European centre of culture by linking Prussian nationalism with the greatness of ancient Greece (which is what later gave the city the moniker 'Athens on the Spree'.) The most prolific architects of the age were Langhans and Schinkel (see Architects).

Historism

The western world at large changed dramatically during the second half of the 19th century as industrialisation altered the basic structure of society, and scientific discoveries undermined people's fundamental belief systems.

This time of progress – but also of insecurity – gave birth to Historism, sometimes also called Revivalism, which clings to an entire palette of earlier styles, often blending them together in an aesthetic hotchpotch. Good examples of this type of architecture are the Theater des Westens (1896) in Charlottenburg, the Rotes Rathaus (1869) in Mitte and, of course, the Reichstag (1894) and Berliner Dom (1905), both in the neo-Renaissance style.

International Style

The industrialisation, mechanisation and rationalisation of the outgoing 19th century fed into a new aesthetic that was a wholesale rejection of all that preceded it: the International Style, more descriptively known as 'Functionalism' or 'New Objectivity'. Its main characteristics are boxlike shapes, flat roofs, plain and unadorned facades and interior walls, and the abundant use of glass.

Begun in the early 20th century by Peter Behrens, Bauhaus founder Walter Gropius, Mies van der Rohe and Le Corbusier, this type of modern architecture was suppressed in the Third Reich but re-emerged in a more mature form after WWII. Echoes of it are still with us today, both in its residential and 'corporate' forms. (For examples turn to Tour III later in this section).

Monumentalism

Nazi architecture, like Nazism itself, revelled in pomposity. In 1937, Hitler appointed Albert Speer as his main architect and charged him with redesigning Berlin into Germania, the capital of Nazi Germany.

Unfortunately for Speer, classicism had two 'neo' prefixes by the time he got his hands on it, which perhaps explains why Nazi monumentality often seems absurd. The never-realised Great Hall, for example, boasted a 250m-diameter dome and was planned to accommodate 150,000 people. (For Nazi-era projects that did make it off the drawing board see Tour II later in this section.)

Critical Reconstruction

After the Wende, city planners were faced with the challenge and opportunity of rebuilding the New Berlin to reflect the Zeitgeist at the dawn of the third millennium. Rejecting anything too bold, avant-garde or monumental, the powers that be turned instead to 'critical reconstruction', an approach that seeks to forge a link with history

KELLI HAMBLET

Left: The never realised Great Hall, an example of Nazi monumentalism with a 250m dome, would have dwarfed the famous Brandenburg Gate (1791), one of Berlin's major landmarks

JONATHAN SMITH

ANDREA SCHULTE-PEEVERS

ANDREA SCHULTE-PEEVERS

Top: Marble statues on the Schlossbrücke bridge trace the training of a Greek warrior (Tour I).

Middle: Weinhaus Huth, surrounded by modern architecture, is all that remains from Potsdamer Platz's heyday (Tour III).

Bottom: At 22-floors high, the Debis Building is DaimlerCity's largest structure (Tour III).

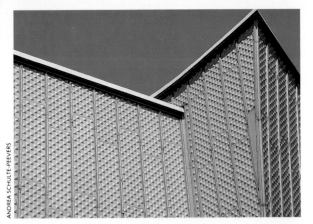

ANDREA SCHULTE-PEEVERS

DAVID PEEVERS

Top: The Philharmonie concert hall, where every seat has perfect views (Tour II).

Bottom: Designed by Renzo Piano, the IMAX is the latest addition to Berlin's movie scene (Tour III).

without creating replicas of earlier landmarks. Tight building regulations – extending to cornice height and construction materials used – stifled architects' creativity from the onset of this formidable project. The goal of avoiding anything too bold has certainly been met so far, with the notable exception of Daniel Libeskind's Jewish Museum (see the Kreuzberg section in Things to See & Do). For an overview of other construction projects of the new Berlin, see Tour IV.

TOUR I – THE AGE OF SCHINKEL

Prussian master builder Schinkel has left his mark all over the city and Potsdam as well. But nowhere is his prolific output more concentrated than in the city's historic core along Unter den Linden and its side streets.

Neue Wache (1818)

The Neue Wache (New Guardhouse) was Schinkel's first major architectural project. Looking a bit like a miniature-military-fortress-meets-Greek-temple, the dignified structure is fronted by a double-row of Doric columns supporting a tympanum embellished with allegorical war scenes. Built to accommodate the palace guard, it now serves as united Germany's central memorial, harbouring the tombs of an unknown soldier, a resistance fighter and a concentration-camp victim, as well as an enlarged Käthe Kollwitz sculpture *Mother and Her Dead Son*. It's open from 10 am to 6 pm daily and admission is free.

Schauspielhaus/Konzerthaus (1821)

The Schauspielhaus acts as the unifying element of Gendarmenmarkt, which is anchored by the French and the German Dom on its north and south end, respectively.

When the original structure by Langhans (1801) burned down in 1817, Schinkel received the commission to rebuild it with the proviso that he integrate the former structure's remaining outside walls and columns. Schinkel did so but added a massive open staircase leading up to the raised Ionic portico. This entrance section is lorded over by a much taller central structure crowned by a phalanx of statues. Badly mauled during WWII, the exterior was reconstructed according to Schinkel's plans. In 1994, it was renamed Konzerthaus (also see the Entertainment chapter).

Friedrichswerdersche Kirche (1830)

In the Friedrichswerdersche Kirche, Schinkel unites neoclassical strict symmetry with neo-Gothic elements, like the use of red bricks, the building blocks of choice in medieval northern Germany. The church is easily recognised by its characteristic roofline punctuated by a row of slender, square turrets. The same turrets crown the pair of square towers. Inside, the single nave construction is supported by a series of pillars buttressing a gallery which contains the Schinkelmuseum (see the Mitte section in the Things to See & Do chapter).

Altes Museum (1830)

The imposing edifice on the northern flank of the Lustgarten is Schinkel's Altes Museum (Old Museum), Berlin's first purpose-built museum. A phalanx of 18 Ionic columns holds up an 87m-long portico reached via an open staircase flanked by sculptures of an amazon and a lion tamer. Inside the rectangular structure are two inner courtyards and the famed central rotunda, modelled after the Pantheon in Rome, with its Roman statues of Greek gods. For museum exhibits, see Things to See & Do – Mitte. Schinkel also designed the lovely **Schlossbrücke** (Palace Bridge) nearby, with its eight clusters of white marble statues tracing the training and development of a Greek warrior.

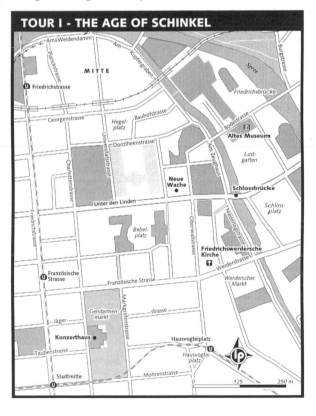

TOUR I - THE AGE OF SCHINKEL

TOUR II – MODERNIST VISIONS IN TIERGARTEN

After WWII, the district of Tiergarten became the experimental stage for new city planning, anchored by the Hansaviertel on the park's northern edge and the Kulturforum on its southern. Both developments allow for a quick survey of the architectural acumen of that day's best-known international modernists.

Hansaviertel (1953-57)

The Hansaviertel (Hansa Quarter) on the north-western perimeter of the Tiergarten is a loosely structured residential community for 3500 people. A mix of high-rises and single-family homes – plus a commercial centre with shops, two churches, a school and library – it escapes sterility thanks to a reasonable amount of open areas and green spaces.

The Hansaviertel was the result of an architectural competition in 1953 and represents the cutting edge of architectural vision in the 1950s. More than 50 renowned architects from 13 countries, including Walter Gropius, Luciano Baldessari, Alvar Aalto and Werner Düttmann, participated in the building of the Hansaviertel. (Take the U9 to Hansaplatz.)

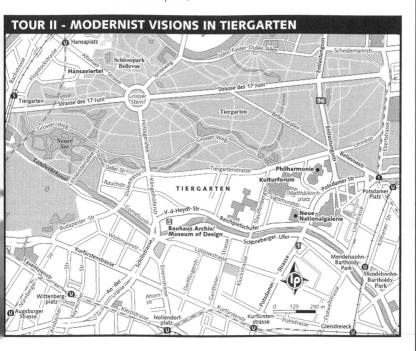

TOUR II - MODERNIST VISIONS IN TIERGARTEN

Neue Nationalgalerie (1965-68)

Completed shortly before his death in 1969, Ludwig Mies van der Rohe's New National Gallery at Potsdamer Strasse 50 epitomises the 'less is more' approach that made him one of the 20th century's leading architects. His structures are simple shapes in solitary settings that make no attempt at blending with their surroundings. This museum of contemporary art is a 50m by 50m glass and steel cube perching on a raised granite platform reached via two large open staircases. The flat steel roof defies gravity with the help of eight steel pillars and a floor to ceiling glass front. For details on the collection, see Things to See & Do – Kulturforum Area. (Take the U2 to Mendelssohn-Bartholdy-Park.)

Bauhaus Archiv/Museum of Design (1976-79)

Founded in Darmstadt in 1960, the Bauhaus Archiv moved to Berlin in 1971 and into its current home at Klingelhöferstrasse 13/14 in 1979. It was designed by Walter Gropius but was built, after Gropius' death, by Alexander Cvijanovic. Sharply structured, the complex consists of two gleaming white two-storey wings arranged in parallel fashion and connected by an undulating ramp and lower central edifice. The most distinctive – and attractive – design element is the angled shed roofs which give the museum its unmistakable silhouette. For more on the exhibit itself, see Things to See & Do – Kulturforum Area. (Take the U2/4 to Nollendorfplatz, Bus Nos 100 and 129.)

Philharmonie (1960-63)

Hans Scharoun's design principle 'Form follows Function' is given perfect expression in this glorious concert hall at Herbert-von-Karajan-Strasse 1. Scharoun ditched the traditional stage in favour of a complicated layout of three pentagonal sections twisted and angled around a central orchestra pit. The audience is seated in terraced blocks with every seat offering perfect views and acoustics. It's all covered by a tent-like roof that gives the building its unique shape. The gold-coloured aluminum facade was added in 1981. For details about concerts, see the Entertainment chapter. (Take the U2 to Mendelssohn-Bartholdy-Park.)

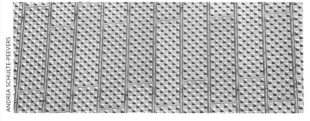

ANDREA SCHULTE-PEEVERS

Left: Facade detail of the Philharmonie by Hans Scharoun.

TOUR III – THE NEW BERLIN: DAIMLERCITY

DaimlerCity gets its name from DaimlerChrysler, the main investor in a 68,000 sq metre area of real estate on Potsdamer Platz. The new quarter, roughly pie-shaped, ballooned out in only four years (1994-98) and consists of 19 buildings of varying heights arranged in an irregular grid of 10 new streets — some new, some revived like the Alte Potsdamer Strasse. Three high-rises mark the edges of the development. About 50% of the space is taken up by offices, 20% by flats and 30% by mixed-use facilities (hotels, theatres etc).

An international team of the finest and brightest minds in contemporary architecture was tapped to design the various structures based on a masterplan conceived by Renzo Piano and Christoph Kohlbecker. Design criteria included wide sidewalks, ground floor arcading and

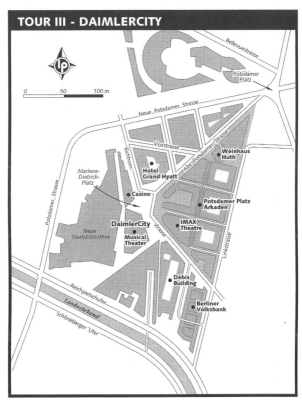

TOUR III - DAIMLERCITY

facades made from natural materials like terra-cotta, sandstone or clinker. Renzo Piano himself designed six of the 19 structures, including the entertainment ensemble of **Musical Theater**, **IMAX** and **Casino**, all orbiting a central plaza called Marlene-Dietrich-Platz.

Some of the complex's main buildings include the following.

Debis Building – Renzo Piano

The Debis Building is the single largest structure in DaimlerCity and appropriately home to a subsidiary of the DaimlerChrysler corporation. Its most arresting feature is its dramatic atrium with dimensions of a postmodern basilica that force an upward gaze and it's anchored by Jean Tinguely's bizarre *Méta-Maxi* sculpture. Rising skyward for 22 floors, the building also draws attention with its 83m-tall tower topped by an all-green 'Rubic's cube', the company's logo. It doubles as a chimney for the exhaust from the underground tunnel snaking beneath the structure.

Hotel Grand Hyatt – Rafael Moneo

The famed Spanish architect didn't strain his imagination on the exterior of this luxury hotel: it has all the charm of an airport facility, despite its shiny sleek facade. However the interior projects sophistication with Zen-like minimalism, while the rooftop fitness center Club Olympus provides fitting environs for a thorough indulgence of the senses.

Potsdamer Platz Arkaden – Richard Rogers

This stylish three-story interior mall is sheltered by a glass canopy and enlivened by marble and leafy plants, and thoughtfully placed benches allow you to take it all in.

Berliner Volksbank – Arata Isozaki

The Japanese postmodern master architect has created one of the most interesting and appealing structures in DaimlerCity. Two rectangular

ANDREA SCHULTE-PEEVERS

Left: Hotel Grand Hyatt by Rafael Moneo.

parallel office blocks are connected via several glass-covered bridges, while the waffle-patterned mocha-coloured facade boasts subtle wave-like curves.

Weinhaus Huth

This majestic structure, dwarfed by its postmodern neighbours, is the only eyewitness to the Potsdamer Platz heyday. Aside from the wine shop that was already here in the 1920s, it contains a gourmet restaurant. The upper floors have been turned into flats.

NAZI MONUMENTALISM

Thankfully most of the legacy of the Third Reich has disappeared from the cityscape of Berlin. The following are among the few remaining relics, all of them visual metaphors of the preposterous Nazi sense of grandeur and self-importance.

Air Force Ministry (1935-36)

The most prominent relic of Nazi architecture is Göring's Reichsluftfahrtsministerium (Air Force Ministry) on Leipziger Strasse 5-7, corner of Wilhelmstrasse, the heart of the traditional government centre. (It's strangely ironic that the administrative center of the Luftwaffe somehow survived the predations of Allied bombers.)

Designed by Ernst Sagebiel, it took a giant fleet of workers less than a year to build this beehive-like complex honeycombed with more than 2000 offices. The concrete and steel structure, up to seven storeys tall, wraps around three inner courtyards and opens to a park at its rear. A facade of crushed shells hides the concrete and steel skeleton. The building is being reconfigured to house the Federal Ministry of Economics. (Take the U2, S1 or S2 to Potsdamer Platz.)

Tempelhof Airport (1936-41)

Sagebiel is also responsible for expanding Tempelhof into an airport of truly bombastic proportions; it is one of the largest building complexes in continental Europe. Behind the Platz der Luftbrücke, anchored by the monument to the Berlin Airlift, opens up a huge central courtyard which leads to the 100m-long terminal and a 400m-long building with numerous gates. A succession of hangars extends from both sides of this structure in a semicircular arrangement that measures a total of 1200m. (Take the U7 to Platz der Luftbrücke.)

Olympic Stadium (1936)

The Olympic Stadium as we still see it today was built by Werner March and his brother Walter, replacing an earlier stadium completed by their father Otto in 1913. The colosseum-like structure boasts a sunken field and seating for 90,000. Also part of the gigantic complex are the Maifeld, used for mass parades by the Nazis, a hockey stadium and a swimming and diving pool. (Take the U2 to Olympiastadion-Ost.)

Facts for the Visitor

WHEN TO GO

Berlin is a fascinating city year round, with the bulk of visitors arriving in May and September when the weather is most reliable. Naturally, this is also when museums and tourist sights are the most crowded and room rates are highest.

Summer can be great because temperatures tend to remain tolerable and much of life moves outdoors. Some activities, like swimming in the lakes or sitting in outdoor cafes and beer gardens, can only be enjoyed at this time. Though some theatres and orchestras are on summer hiatus, there is a rich menu of cultural events and festivals to be enjoyed.

From November to early March, skies tend to be gloomy and the mercury often drops to below freezing. On the plus side, this is accompanied by plummeting visitor numbers, leaving museums and other attractions devoid of long lines. Just pack the right clothes and remember that there are only six to eight hours of daylight. In December, the sun (if there is any) sets around 3.30 pm.

Avoid major holidays like Easter, Christmas and New Year and special events like the Love Parade when the city bursts at the seams (unless, of course, that's the reason you're visiting Berlin in the first place).

ORIENTATION

Berlin sits in the middle of the region known from medieval times as the Mark (March) of Brandenburg, now the *Bundesland* (federal state) of Brandenburg. The state of Berlin measures some 892 sq km while the municipal boundaries encompass 234 sq km.

Roughly one third is made up of parks, forests, lakes and rivers. There are more trees here than in Paris and more bridges than in Venice. Much of the natural beauty of rolling hills and quiet shorelines is in the south-east and south-west of the city.

The Spree River wends its way across the city for over 30km, from Grosser Müggelsee, the city's largest lake, in the east to Spandau in the west. North and south of Spandau, the Havel River widens into a series of lakes, from Tegel to below Potsdam. A network of canals links the waterways to each other and to the Oder River on the Polish border, and there are beautiful walks along some of them.

Berlin has 23 districts *(Bezirke)*, although most travellers will end up visiting only the eight 'core' ones. They are (clockwise from the west): Charlottenburg, Tiergarten, Mitte, Prenzlauer Berg (locals say Prenz'lberg), Friedrichshain, Kreuzberg, Schöneberg and Wilmersdorf. Kreuzberg is quite different in its eastern and western sections, and in this book it is split into Kreuzberg 36 and Kreuzberg 61 for clarity. These numbers refer to the old postal codes.

Berlin continues to have two centres that reflect its 40-year division. The western centre is in the area around Zoo station and Kurfürstendamm in Charlottenburg (Map 7); the eastern centre is along Unter den Linden and around Alexanderplatz in Mitte (Map 8).

You can't really get lost within sight of the monstrous TV Tower (Map 8) on Alexanderplatz in Mitte. Unter den Linden, the fashionable avenue of aristocratic old Berlin, and its continuation, Karl-Liebknecht-Strasse, extend east from the Brandenburg Gate to Alexanderplatz, once the heart of socialist East Germany. Some of Berlin's finest museums are nearby on Museumsinsel in the Spree River (though most are currently closed for renovation). One of several epicentres of nightlife has sprung up around the Hackesche Höfe and along Oranienburger Strasse north-west of Alexanderplatz.

South of the Brandenburg Gate, in areas once occupied by the Wall, Berlin's newest quarter is emerging around Potsdamer Platz. East of here, office buildings now occupy the former site of Checkpoint Charlie, the infamous border crossing. The Wall itself, Berlin's grim erstwhile landmark, has not been forgotten altogether; sections of it remain on public view around the city (see

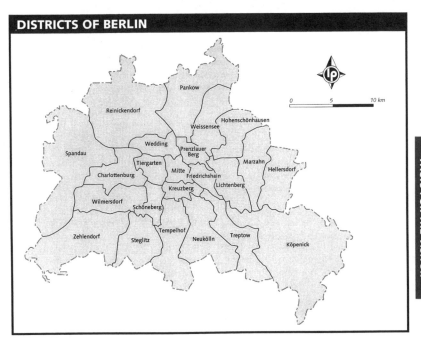

DISTRICTS OF BERLIN

the boxed text 'The Berlin Wall' in the Things to See & Do chapter).

Back in former West Berlin, the ruin of the Kaiser Wilhelm Memorial Church (Map 7), on Breitscheidplatz near Zoo station, is the most visible landmark. The Europa-Center, a tacky shopping centre which anchors the square's eastern end, is also home to the tourist office. The Kurfürstendamm (known as the 'Ku'damm'), Berlin's main shopping street, runs for 3.5km south-west from Breitscheidplatz to Halensee.

To the north-east, between Breitscheidplatz and the Brandenburg Gate, is Tiergarten (Maps 3, 5 & 7), a district named after the vast city park that was once a royal hunting domain. The new government and diplomatic quarter is being built along the northern edge of the park. The Lehrter Stadtbahnhof, off Franz-Liszt-Ufer, will eventually become the capital's main train station. For what Berlin will look like in the future, visit the Infobox

(open at least until December 2000) on Potsdamer Platz.

While in central Berlin, keep in mind that the street numbers usually run sequentially up one side of the street and down the other (important exceptions are Unter den Linden and, in Schöneberg, Martin-Luther-Strasse and Lietzenburger Strasse). Although number guides appear on most corner street signs, this is not always the case in eastern Berlin. Be aware, too, that a continuous street may change names several times along its length, and that on some streets (eg Kurfürstendamm, Kantstrasse, Knesebeckstrasse etc) numbering sequences continue after interruptions caused by squares.

After the Wende (the 'turning point' of 1989), several streets and landmarks in former East Berlin, which was renamed during the communist era, were given back their old names. Prominent examples include Dimitroffstrasse (now Danziger Strasse) in

Prenzlauer Berg and Marx-Engels-Platz (now Schlossplatz) in Mitte.

MAPS

The maps in this book should suffice in most cases. However, if you plan to travel extensively in the outer suburbs, or want to look up specific streets, you may need to buy a more detailed map. Lonely Planet's Berlin city map has three scales (Berlin & Vicinity 1:60,000; Central Berlin 1:34,500; and Zoo, Tiergarten, Mitte 1:20,000) and an index to all streets and sights. It includes an S-bahn and U-bahn network map, essential information, an English-German glossary, and the unique Lonely Planet walking tour. The laminated map costs AUS $7.95 (UK £3.99).

Other good choices include those published by Falkplan (either the standard sheet map or the Falk Megaplan with a patented folding system), ADAC's 1:25,000 map, or the RV Verlag Euro City 1:27,500 version. The latter is very user-friendly with an additional 14 1:10,000 and 1:20,000 maps of the centre, suburbs and Potsdam, along with an up-to-date street index. Maps cost from DM7 to DM15.

If you plan to stay in Berlin for several months, a street atlas, such as the one published by RV Verlag (DM24.80), might come in handy. It has more than 150 detailed maps (1:20,000) of the city, suburbs and Potsdam, a street name index, public transport routes, plus descriptive information and listings (in German).

Newsagents, most bookshops and the tourist offices stock a decent supply of city and area maps. See Bookshops in the Shopping chapter for suggestions on where to go.

TOURIST OFFICES
Local Tourist Offices

The main office of Berlin Tourismus Marketing (BTM, Map 7) is on the ground floor of the Europa-Center at Budapester Strasse 45 in Charlottenburg. It is open from 8.30 am to 8.30 pm Monday to Saturday and 10 am to 6.30 pm Sunday. A second branch (Map 8) is in the south wing of the Brandenburg Gate and is open from 9.30 am to

The bear has been the symbol of Berlin for centuries. Some say the city's name comes from the German word *Bärlein*, meaning 'Little Bear'.

6 pm daily. Both offices handle in-person hotel (but not private room) reservations at no charge.

Smaller tourist offices with fewer services, called Info Points, are in the main hall of Tegel airport at the left-luggage office opposite Gate O (open from 5 am to 10.30 pm daily); and in the Reisecenter on the ground floor of the KaDeWe department store (Map 7) at Tauentzienstrasse 21 (open 9.30 am to 8 pm weekdays, 9 am to 4 pm Saturday).

For telephone information or reservations, call the new BTM Hotline on ☎ 0190-75 40 40. This number is valid from within Germany only and calls are charged at an exorbitant rate of DM2.42 per minute. The number to call from outside of Germany is ☎ 49-30-1805-75 40 40. The cheapest method to access information or to book rooms or tickets to events is via the tourist office's Web site at www.btm.de.

All tourist offices sell maps, books and the heavily touted Berlin WelcomeCard (DM32). The WelcomeCard entitles one adult and up to three children (under 14 years of age) to 72 hours of public transport within the Berlin-Potsdam area and to minor discounts on museums, shows, attractions, sightseeing tours and boat cruises. The WelcomeCard is also available at hotels and public-transport ticket offices.

Tourist Offices Abroad

Germany's national tourist office (Deutsche Zentrale für Tourismus, DZT) has its headquarters (☎ 069-97 46 40, fax 069-75 19 03) at Beethovenstrasse 69, 60325 Frankfurt/Main. Staff can answer questions over the phone or send promotional brochures of Berlin and most destinations within Germany. Their Web page is at www.germany-tourism.de. Branch offices around the world include the following:

Australia
   (☎ 02-92 67 81 48, fax 92 67 90 35),
   PO Box A980, Sydney South, NSW 1235
Austria
   (☎ 01-513 27 92, fax 513 27 92 22,
   email dztwien@compuserve.com), Schubertring 12, 1010 Vienna
Canada
   (☎ 416-968 1570, fax 968 1986, email germanto@idirect.com),
   175 Bloor St East, North Tower, Suite 604, Toronto, Ont M4W 3R8
France
   (☎ 01 40 20 01 88, fax 40 20 17 00,
   email gnto.par@compuserve.com),
   47 Avenue de l'Opéra, 75002 Paris
Japan
   (☎ 03-3586 5046, fax 3586 5079,
   email dzt.tokyo@compuserve.com),
   7-5-56 Akasaka, Minato-ku, Tokyo 107-0052
Netherlands
   (☎ 020-697 8066, fax 691 2972,
   email duitsland@compuserve.com), Hoogoorddreef 76, 1101 BG Amsterdam ZO
Russia
   (☎ 095-975 3001, fax 975 2383), c/o Lufthansa German Airlines, Hotel Olympic Penta, Olimpiski prospekt 18/1, 129 110 Moscow
South Africa
   (☎ 011-643 1615, fax 484 2750),
   c/o Lufthansa German Airlines, 22 Girton Rd, Parktown, PO Box 10883, Johannesburg 2000
Switzerland
   (☎ 01-213 22 00, fax 212 0175,
   email gnto.zrh@compuserve.com),
   Talstrasse 62, 8001 Zürich
UK
   (☎ 0891-60 01 00, costs 50 pence/minute, fax 020-7495 6129, email 106167.3216@compuserve.com),
   PO Box 2695, London W1A 3TN

USA
   (☎ 212-661 7200, fax 661 7174,
   email gntony@aol.com),
   Chanin Building, 122 East 42nd St, 52nd Floor, New York, NY 10168-0072
   (☎ 312-644 0723, fax 644 0724),
   401 North Michigan Ave, Suite 2525, Chicago, IL 60611

Additional offices exist in Brussels, Budapest, Copenhagen, Helsinki, Hong Kong, Madrid, Mexico City, Milan, Oslo, Prague, São Paulo, Seoul, Stockholm, Tel Aviv and Warsaw.

DOCUMENTS
Visas

European Union (EU) nationals and those from certain other European countries, including Switzerland and Poland, require only a passport or their national identity card to enter and stay in Germany. Citizens of Australia, Canada, Israel, Japan, New Zealand, Singapore and the US do not need a visa (passport only) if entering as tourists for up to three months.

Nationals from most other countries need a so-called Schengen Visa, named after the Schengen Agreement that abolished passport controls between the Netherlands, Belgium, Luxembourg, Germany, France, Spain, Portugal, Italy, Austria, Greece, Denmark, Sweden and Finland. Residency status in any of the Schengen countries negates the need for a visa, regardless of your nationality.

Three-month tourist visas are issued by German embassies or consulates. They can take a while to be processed, so leave enough time before departure to apply. You'll need a valid passport and sufficient funds to finance your stay. Fees vary depending on the country.

Travel Insurance

No matter how you're travelling to Berlin, be sure to take out travel insurance. Depending on the scope of your coverage, this will protect you against sudden medical or legal expenses, luggage theft or loss, personal liability and the cancellation of or delays in your travel arrangements. Before taking out any insurance, be certain that you understand all the small print and know what to do in case you need to file a claim.

Some policies specifically exclude 'dangerous activities', which can include scuba diving, motorcycling, even trekking. A locally acquired motorcycle licence is not valid under some policies.

You may prefer a policy which pays doctors or hospitals directly rather than you having to pay on the spot and claim later. If you have to claim later make sure you keep all documentation. Some policies ask you to call back (reverse charges) to a centre in your home country where an immediate assessment of your problem is made. Check that the policy covers ambulances or an emergency flight home.

Also check your medical policy at home, since some policies already provide coverage worldwide, in which case you only need to protect yourself against other problems (see Health later in this chapter).

Buy travel insurance as early as possible. If you buy it the week before you leave you may, for example, not be covered for delays to your trip caused by strikes or other industrial action. Some policies also cover ticket loss, so be sure to keep a photocopy of your ticket in a separate place. Also make a copy of your policy, in case the original is lost.

Paying for your airline ticket with a credit card often provides you with limited travel-accident insurance, and you may be able to reclaim the payment if the operator doesn't deliver. Ask your credit card company what it's prepared to cover.

Driving Licence

If you plan to drive in Germany, you need to carry a driving licence. Although you are not required by law to have an International Driving Permit (IDP), having one helps Germans make sense of your unfamiliar local licence (make sure you take that with you, too) and simplifies the car and motorcycle rental process. IDPs are valid for one year and may be obtained for a small fee from your local automobile association – bring a passport photo and a valid licence.

Hostel Cards

You must be a member of a Hostelling International-affiliated organisation in order to stay at hostels run by the Deutsches Jugendherbergswerk (DJH). Non-Germans who don't have an HI card may obtain a so-called International Guest Card (IGC) at any hostel. It costs DM30 and is valid for one year. If you don't want it, DM6 per night will be added to your regular hostel rate; you'll be given a pass which is stamped once for each night and after six nights you automatically get the IGC. If you're German or have residency status in Germany, you can buy a DJH/HI card at the hostel when checking in (DM21 for juniors and DM34 for seniors). Independent hostels don't require a card, but in some cases you will be charged less if you have one.

Student & Youth Cards

The International Student Identity Card (ISIC), a plastic ID-style card with your photograph, provides discounts on many forms of transport (including airlines and local public transport) and on admission to museums and sights, as well as cheaper meals in some university cafeterias. If you're under 26 but not a student, you can apply for a FIYTO (Federation of International Youth Travel Organisations) card or the Euro 26 card (known in the UK as the Under 26 card) which give much the same discounts and benefits as an ISIC. All these cards are issued by student unions, hostelling organisations and youth-oriented travel agencies.

Photocopies

The hassles brought on by losing your passport can be considerably reduced if you have a photocopy of the relevant data pages. It's also sensible to photocopy your airline ticket and credit cards. Also record the serial numbers of your travellers cheques (cross them off as you cash them).

Keep all this emergency material separate from the original documents, along with a small amount of emergency cash. Leave extra copies with someone reliable at home. If your passport is stolen or lost, notify the police immediately and obtain a statement, then contact your nearest embassy or consulate. It's also a good idea to store details of your vital travel documents in Lonely Planet's free online Travel Vault. Your password-protected Travel Vault is accessible online anywhere in the world – you can easily create it at www.ekno.lonely planet.com.

EMBASSIES & CONSULATES
Your Own Embassy
Generally speaking your own embassy – the embassy of the country of which you are a citizen – won't be much help in emergencies if the trouble you're in is remotely your own fault. Remember you are bound by the laws of the country you're visiting. Your embassy will not be sympathetic if you end up in jail after committing a crime locally, even if such actions are legal in your own country. In genuine emergencies you might get some assistance, but only if other channels have been exhausted. For example, if you need to get home urgently, a free ticket home is exceedingly unlikely – the embassy would expect you to have insurance. If you have all your money and documents stolen, the embassy might assist in getting a new passport, but a loan for onward travel is out of the question.

German Embassies Abroad
German embassies around the world include the following:

Australia
 (☎ 02-6270 1911),
 119 Empire Circuit, Yarralumla, ACT 2600
Austria
 (☎ 01-711 54)
 Metternichgasse 3, Vienna 3
Canada
 (☎ 613-232 1101)
 1 Waverley St, Ottawa, Ont K2P 0T8
France
 (☎ 01-53 83 45 00)
 13-15 Ave Franklin Roosevelt, 75008 Paris
Ireland
 (☎ 01-269 3011), 31 Trimleston Ave, Booterstown, Blackrock/Co, Dublin
Japan
 (☎ 03-3473 0151)
 5-10, 4-chome, Minami-Azabu, Minato-ki, Tokyo 106

Netherlands
 (☎ 070-342 0600),
 Groot Hertoginnelaan 18-20, 2517 EG The Hague
New Zealand
 (☎ 04-473 6063)
 90-92 Hobson St, Wellington
Russia
 (☎ 095-956 1080)
 Ul Mosfilmovskaya 56, 119285 Moscow
South Africa
 (☎ 012-427 89 00)
 180 Blackwood St, Arcadia, Pretoria 0083
Switzerland
 (☎ 031-359 4111),
 Willadingweg 83, 3006 Bern
UK
 (☎ 020-7824 1300)
 23 Belgrave Square, London SW1X 8PZ
USA
 (☎ 202-298 8141)
 4645 Reservoir Rd NW, Washington, DC 20007-1998

Foreign Consulates & Embassy Branches in Berlin
Since the transfer of Parliament from Bonn, numerous diplomatic missions, including those listed below, have also moved to Berlin. For a complete list, check the phone book under 'Botschaften' or 'Konsulate'.

Australia
 Embassy:
 (Map 7, ☎ 880 08 80)
 Uhlandstrasse 181-183
Austria
 Embassy:
 (☎ 229 05 65)
 Friedrichstrasse 60
Belgium
 Embassy:
 (Map 8, ☎ 20 35 20)
 Friedrichstrasse 95
Canada
 Embassy:
 (Map 8, ☎ 20 31 20)
 Friedrichstrasse 95, 23rd floor
Czech Republic
 Embassy:
 (Map 8, ☎ 22 63 80)
 Wilhelmstrasse 44
Denmark
 Consulate:
 (☎ 25 00 10)
 Wichmannstrasse 5

France
  Embassy:
  (Map 8, ☎ 204 39 90)
  Französische Strasse 23
  Consulate:
  (Map 7, ☎ 88 59 02 43)
  Kurfürstendamm 211
Hungary
  Consulate:
  (Map 8, ☎ 220 25 61)
  Wilhelmstrasse 61
Ireland
  Honorary Consulate:
  (Map 3, ☎ 34 80 08 22)
  Ernst-Reuter-Platz 10
Israel
  Consulate:
  (☎ 89 32 203)
  Schinkelstrasse 10
Italy
  Consulate:
  (Map 5, ☎ 25 44 00)
  Hiroshimastrasse 1
Japan
  Consulate:
  (Map 7, ☎ 21 09 40)
  Kleiststrasse 23
Netherlands
  Embassy:
  (☎ 201 20 23)
  Friedrichstrasse 95
Poland
  Embassy:
  (Map 8, ☎ 220 25 51)
  Unter den Linden 72-74
Russia
  Embassy:
  (Map 8, ☎ 226 63 20)
  Unter den Linden 63-65
  Consulate:
  (☎ 229 12 07)
  Behrenstrasse 66
Slovakia
  Embassy:
  (☎ 204 45 38)
  Leipziger Strasse 36
South Africa
  Embassy:
  (☎ 825 27 11)
  Douglasstrasse 9
UK
  Embassy:
  (Map 8, ☎ 20 18 40)
  Unter den Linden 32-34
USA
  Embassy:
  (Map 8, ☎ 238 51 74)
  Neustädtische Kirchstrasse 4-5

Consulate:
(☎ 832 92 33)
Clayallee 170
Visa Information Service: ☎ 0190-91 50 00
(DM2.42/minute)

CUSTOMS

Articles that you take to Germany for your personal use may be imported free of duty and tax with some conditions. The following allowances apply to *duty-free goods* purchased at the airport: 200 cigarettes or 100 cigarillos or 50 cigars or 250g of loose tobacco; 1L of strong liquor or 2L of less than 22% alcohol by volume *and* 2L of wine; 500g of coffee or 200g of extracts *and* 100g of tea or 40g tea extracts; 50g of perfume or scent *and* 0.25L of eau de toilette; and additional goods up to a value of DM350.

You must be 17 years or over to bring in tobacco products and alcohol; and the importation of duty-free coffee is, oddly, barred to those under 15. There are no currency import restrictions.

Do not confuse these with *duty-paid* items (including alcohol and tobacco) bought at normal shops and supermarkets in another EU country and brought into Germany, where certain goods might be more expensive. Then the allowances are more generous: 800 cigarettes, 200 cigars, or 1kg of loose tobacco; 10L of spirits (more than 22% alcohol by volume), 20L of fortified wine or aperitif, 90L of wine or 110L of beer.

Note that duty-free shopping within the EU was abolished in mid-1999. This means that you can still take duty-free goods into an EU country, like Germany, from, say the US or Australia, but you can't buy duty-free goods within Europe unless you're headed for a non-EU country.

MONEY
Currency

The German Mark, or Deutschmark (DM), usually just called the Mark or D-Mark, is made up of 100 Pfennig. Coins include one, two, five, 10 and 50 Pfennig, as well as DM1, DM2 and DM5. There are banknotes of DM5, DM10, DM20, DM50, DM100, DM200, DM500 and DM1000.

Exchange Rates

country	unit		DM
Australia	A$1	=	1.2230DM
Austria	AS1	=	0.1421DM
Canada	C$1	=	1.3126DM
Denmark	Dkr1	=	0.2631DM
euro	€1	=	1.9558DM
France	1FF	=	0.2982DM
Japan	¥100	=	1.8682DM
Netherlands	NLG1	=	0.0188DM
New Zealand	NZ$1	=	0.9856DM
South Africa	R1	=	0.3148DM
Switzerland	Sfr1	=	1.2203DM
UK	UK£1	=	3.0949DM
USA	US$1	=	1.9265DM

Exchanging Money

The easiest places to change money are banks or foreign-exchange counters at airports and train stations. Post offices often have money-changing facilities as well, and their rates for cash – though not for travellers cheques – are sometimes better than at banks. Commissions here are DM2 for cash transactions if the exchanged amount is under DM200, and free if it's higher. Converting travellers cheques to Deutschmarks costs a flat DM6 each regardless of the face value.

At banks and exchange offices, the charge usually comes to between DM5 and DM10 per transaction. Occasionally you'll see currency exchange machines but they almost never give good rates.

There are a number of reliable exchange centres in Berlin, including:

AGW Exchange (Map 7, ☎ 882 10 86), Joachimstaler Strasse 1-3, open from 8 am to 8 pm weekdays, from 9 am to 3 pm Saturday.

American Express Friedrichstrasse 172 in Mitte (Map 8, ☎ 20 45 57 21); and at Bayreuther Strasse 23 (Map 7, ☎ 21 47 62 92). They charge no commission on their own travellers cheques, open from 9 am to 6 pm weekdays, 10 am to 1 pm Saturday.

Euro-Change (Map 7, ☎ 261 14 84), on the street level of the Europa-Center facing Breitscheidplatz, open from 9 am to 6 pm weekdays, to 4 pm Saturday. There are branches at Friedrichstrasse 80 in Mitte, on Alexanderplatz and at Tempelhof airport.

Reisebank (Map 7, ☎ 881 71 17), Hardenbergplatz 1 outside Zoo station, open from 7.30 am to 10 pm daily. Other branches are at Ostbahnhof (Map 6, ☎ 296 43 93) and at Bahnhof Friedrichstrasse (Map 8, ☎ 20 45 50 96), Opening hours are from 7 am to 7.30 pm weekdays and 8 am to noon and 12.30 to 4 pm weekends.

Thomas Cook (Map 8, ☎ 20 16 59 16), Friedrichstrasse 56, open 9.30 am to 6 pm weekdays, from 10 am to 1 pm Saturday. They charge no commission on their own cheques.

Cash Nothing beats cash for convenience ... or risk. If you lose it, it's gone forever and few travel insurers will come to your rescue. Those that will, limit the amount to about US$300. But since Germany is still a cash-based society, you can't avoid having at least some cash, say DM200 or so, in your pocket at all times. Plan to pay in cash almost everywhere (see Credit Cards below for likely exceptions). Remember that banks only exchange foreign paper money not coins.

Travellers Cheques & Eurocheques The main idea of carrying travellers cheques rather than cash is the protection they offer from theft, though their popularity is waning as more travellers – including those on tight budgets – deposit their money in their bank at home and withdraw it as they need it through ATMs.

In Germany, travellers cheques are *not* commonly used to pay for store-bought goods, at restaurants or hotels, especially if they are not issued in Deutschmarks. Cheques issued in any other currency must be exchanged into local currency at a bank, exchange office or post office (bring your passport). American Express and Thomas Cook cheques are most widely recognised. Both have efficient replacement policies and neither charges commission for exchanges at their own offices.

Eurocheques, available to those with a European bank account, are guaranteed up to DM400. It takes at least two weeks after applying for the bank to issue the card and the cheques. Until recently Eurocheques have been widely accepted in Germany, but their popularity is decreasing because of the high commission (DM4 to DM6 per cheque) charged by banks.

euro currency converter DM1 = €.51

Introducing the Euro

On 1 January 1999 a new currency, the euro, was introduced in Europe. As part of the har-monisation of the European Union (EU) countries. Along with national border controls, the cur-rencies of various EU members are being phased out. Not all EU members have agreed to adopt the euro, however: Denmark, Greece, Sweden and the UK rejected or postponed participation. The 11 countries which have participated from the beginning of the process are Austria, Belgium, Finland, France, Germany, Ireland, Italy, Luxembourg, the Netherlands, Portugal and Spain.

The timetable for the introduction of the euro runs as follows:

• On 1 January 1999 the exchange rates of the participating countries were irrevocably fixed to the euro. The euro came into force for 'paper' accounting and prices could be displayed in local currency and in euros.

• On 1 January 2002 euro banknotes and coins will be introduced. This ushers in a period of dual use of euros and existing local notes and coins (which will, in effect, simply be tempo-rary denominations of the euro).

• By July 2002 local currencies in the 11 countries will be withdrawn. Only euro notes and coins will remain in circulation and prices will be displayed in euros only.

The €5 note in France is the same €5 note you will use in Italy and Portugal. There will be seven euro notes in different colours and sizes, in denominations of five, 10, 20, 50, 100, 200, and 500 euros. There are eight euro coins, in denominations of one, two, five, 10, 20 and 50 cents, and also one and two euros. Each participating state will be able to decorate the coins with their own designs on the reverse side, but all euro coins can be used anywhere that accepts euros.

So, what does all this mean for the traveller? It is somewhat uncertain exactly what prac-tices will be adopted between 1999 and 2002, and travellers will probably find differences in 'euro-readiness' between different countries, between different towns in the same country, or between different establishments in the same town. It is certain, however, that euro cheque

ATMs Automatic teller machines are com-mon in central Berlin, though occasionally you may have to swipe your card through a slot to gain entry to a secure area. Most ma-chines take Visa and MasterCard, and if your bank at home is part of the Cirrus, Star or Maestro systems, you'll be able to use your ATM card to withdraw money directly from your home account. Check the fees and availability of services with your bank before you leave. Always keep handy the number of where to report lost or stolen cards.

Credit Cards All the major international cards – eg MasterCard, Visa and American Express – are recognised but still not widely accepted, except at major hotels, petrol sta-tions and large shops and department stores. It's best not to assume that you'll be able to

pay for your meal, room, ticket or purchase with a card.

Some stores may require a minimum pur-chase, others may refuse to accept a credit card even if that credit-card company's logo is displayed in the window. In the eastern districts and outside Berlin, even fewer places accept payment in this way. Never-theless, it can't hurt to take your card along, if only for emergencies or for renting a car.

Check with your credit card issuer about fees and interest rates for cash withdrawals through ATMs. Make a note of where to call in case your card is lost or stolen.

International Transfers Money sent by wire transfer from your bank to a bank in Berlin should reach you within a week. Note that some banks charge an exorbitant amount just for receiving the money (fees

Introducing the Euro

accounts and travellers cheques will be available. Credit card companies can bill in euros, and shops, hotels and restaurants might list prices in both local currency and euros. Travellers should check bills carefully to make sure that any conversion from local currency to euros has been calculated correctly. The most confusing period will probably be between January 2002 and July 2002 when there will be two sets of notes and coins.

Luckily for travellers, the euro should eventually make everything easier. One of the main benefits will be that prices in the 11 countries will be immediately comparable, avoiding all those tedious calculations.

Also, once euro notes and coins are issued in 2002, you won't need to change money at all when travelling to other single-currency EU members. Banks may still charge a handling fee (yet to be decided) for travellers cheques but they won't be able to profit by buying the currency from you at one rate and selling it back to you at another, as they do at the moment. However, even EU countries not participating may price goods in euros and accept euros over shop counters.

There are many Web sites dealing with the introduction of the euro but most are devoted to the legal implications and the processes by which businesses may adapt to the single currency and are not particularly interesting or informative for the traveller. The Lonely Planet Web site at www.lonelyplanet.com has a link to a currency converter and up-to-date news on the integration process.

Australia	A$1	=	€0.6253	Canada	C$1	=	€0.6711
France	1FF	=	€0.1524	Germany	DM1	=	€0.5113
Japan	¥100	=	€0.9552	New Zealand	NZ$1	=	€0.5039
Spain	100pta	=	€0.6010	UK	UK£1	=	€1.5824
USA	US$1	=	€0.9850				

FACTS FOR THE VISITOR

of up to DM50 are common), unless you have an account with them. Opening an account, however, may well be impractical or even impossible to do.

Western Union offers ready and fast international cash transfers through agent banks such as Postbank (branches at many post offices) or Reisebank (see Exchanging Money earlier this chapter). MoneyGram money orders, offered through American Express and Thomas Cook (see the Changing Money section for addresses), are much the same. Cash sent becomes available as soon as the order has been entered into the computer system, ie instantly.

Since commissions can be costly, you should use this service in emergencies only. Commissions are paid by the person making the transfer; the amount varies from country to country.

Costs

Naturally, it's easy to spend lots of money in Berlin. But you can save money by careful choice of accommodation and food. Hostels or simple pensions can cost DM50 or less per person per night. Staying in a room with shared bathroom will save at least 30% off fully equipped ones.

Preparing your own meal or getting food from an *Imbiss* (snack bar) can save you a bundle, and many cafes and restaurants have small, inexpensive dishes that are tasty and filling. At restaurants, cut down on drinks since even non-alcoholic beverages are quite expensive.

Buying passes keeps public transport costs way down (see the Getting Around chapter). If you're a student, bring along your ID. If you're very economical, you can expect to survive on DM80 a day. If you can

Making an Art of Discounts

There are many ways to cut costs while exploring Berlin, though savings are particularly large if you happen to be a student, senior, child or are unemployed (if so, bring along ID). At museums, sights and attractions, you can expect to save about 50% off the regular admission price. Reduced rates are also available for public transport, and admission to public pools, ice rinks and other such facilities. Students also qualify for unsold or returned tickets which are available at box offices immediately before curtain, usually at half price.

Anyone can save on theatre and musical tickets by buying them from Hekticket, a last-minute booking agency (see the Entertainment chapter). During the off season, you can negotiate discounted room rates at some hotels or ask for a reduction for stays of over three nights. The concept of Happy Hour – when you can get cheaper or half-price drinks – is also catching on fast in Berlin's pubs and bars.

afford to spend twice that, you can live quite comfortably.

Tipping & Bargaining

The service charge *(Bedienung)* is always included in bills and tipping is not compulsory. If you're satisfied with the service, simply round up the amount by 5 to 10%. Rather than leaving the money on the table, tip as you're handing over the money by announcing the amount you intend to pay. For example say '60, bitte', if your bill comes to DM57 and you want to give a DM3 tip. If you have the exact amount, just say 'Stimmt so' (roughly 'that's fine'). Taxi drivers, too, expect a small tip. In general, a tip of 10% is considered generous and is gratefully received.

Bargaining rarely occurs in Germany, certainly not in shops or restaurants. At hotels, you can sometimes ask for a lower rate which you may get if business is slow. Haggling is commonplace at flea markets, however, and you should be able to get at least 10 to 25% off the asking price so long as you appear confident. Prices at produce markets are usually not negotiable, though vendors may throw in an extra tomato or two towards the end of the day.

Taxes & Refunds

Most German goods and services include a value-added tax (VAT) called *Mehrwertsteuer* (or MwSt) of 16%. Non-EU residents leaving the EU can have this tax (minus processing fee) refunded for goods (not services) bought, which is definitely worth it for large purchases.

Check that the shop where you're buying has the necessary Tax-Free Shopping Cheque forms. The shop will issue you a cheque for the amount of VAT to be refunded, which you can cash in at VAT Cash Refund offices when leaving the country. Before you can get your money, the Tax-Free Shopping Cheque, together with the invoices or receipts, must be stamped by German customs as you leave the country. You're not allowed to use the items purchased until you have left Germany.

If you're flying out of Germany, have the paperwork stamped at the airport *before* you check in for your flight (with the exception of Frankfurt airport, where you check in first and then proceed to customs with your luggage). Note that you will have to show the goods. Refunds are made directly at VAT Cash Refund desks at the airports. There are customs offices at all three Berlin airports.

If you're travelling via another EU country, you must go through this procedure at the EU airport from which you depart for your non-EU destination.

If you want to avoid the lines at the VAT Cash Refund office, you can mail the customs-stamped forms and receipts to them after you return home and ask that the refund be issued to your credit card or mailed as a cheque.

Those unable to obtain the necessary seal or stamp before leaving Germany may obtain it at a German embassy or consulate back home. The items purchased must be shown to a mission official and sales slips, tax forms and passport must be presented.

Some 17,000 shops, including Germany's biggest department stores, are affiliated with the Tax-Free Shopping Cheque service; they can be identified by a special label on their window reading 'Tax-Free for Tourists'. Printed information is available at affiliated shops, some tourist offices, major hotels, airports and harbours.

POST & COMMUNICATIONS

There are dozens of post offices in Berlin, but most have restricted opening hours (usually from 8 am to 6 pm weekdays, until noon on Saturday). An exception is the main post office at Budapester Strasse 42 (Map 7), opposite the tourist office, which is open from 8 am to midnight Monday to Saturday, from 10 am on Sunday and holidays. Stamps and phone cards are also available in the Lotto shop on Kantstrasse beneath the railway bridge next to Zoo station. There's also a small post office at the Infobox (Map 8). Most post offices exchange currency and travellers cheques and are a good place to fall back on when the banks are closed.

Postal Rates Within Germany and the EU, normal-sized postcards cost DM1, a 20g letter is DM1.10 and a 50g letter is DM2.20. Postcards to North America and Australasia cost DM2, a 20g airmail letter is DM3 and a 50g airmail letter is DM4. If the postcard or letter is oversized, there is a significant surcharge, sometimes up to triple the base rate. German postal workers can be very finicky about this and are bound to measure any piece of mail that looks even remotely like it might not be standard sized. A parcel up to 2kg within Germany costs DM6.90. Surface-mail parcels up to 2kg within Europe are DM12 and to destinations elsewhere DM15. Fees for airmail parcels depend on weight and destination. For instance, a 2kg parcel sent somewhere within Europe is DM38; to the USA it costs DM71; and to Australia DM91.

Sending & Receiving Mail Stamps are sold at post offices only, though some branches have stamp machines outside the main entrance. Occasionally souvenir and postcard shops also carry stamps.

Letters sent within Germany usually take only one day for delivery; those addressed to destinations within Europe or to North America take four to six days and to Australasia five to seven days.

Mail can be sent poste restante to any post office. Select one, then inquire about the address, which usually consists of the postal code only (the main post office at Budapester Strasse is 10612 Berlin). Ask those sending you mail to mark the letter or package *Postlagernd* and to write your name clearly, followed by the postal code. German post offices will hold mail for two weeks. Bring your passport or other photo ID when picking up mail. There is no fee for this service.

American Express (see Exchanging Money earlier this chapter for Berlin branches) offers a free client-mail service to those with an American Express card or travellers cheques (DM2 per item otherwise). The sender should make sure that the words 'Client Mail' appear somewhere on the envelope. Branches will hold mail for 30 days but won't accept registered post or parcels.

Telephone

Making phone calls in Germany is best done from pay phones using phone cards which allow you to make calls of any length to anywhere in the world. If you're calling abroad, look for a pay phone marked 'International,' dial 00 followed by the country code, local area codes and number. If you're calling Germany from abroad, the country code is 49.

Most pay phones in Berlin accept only phone cards, though it's a good idea to carry a few coins as well. Cards – available in denominations of DM12 and DM50 – are sold at post offices and occasionally at tourist offices, news kiosks and public transport offices.

A reverse-charge call (or *R-Gespräch)* from Germany is only possible to a limited number of countries. For calls through the German operator, dial ☎ 0010. To reach the operator direct in the USA and Canada dial ☎ 0130 followed by ☎ 0010 (AT&T), ☎ 0012 (MCI), ☎ 0013 (Sprint) or ☎ 0014 (Canada). To Australia, dial ☎ 0130-80 06 61 for the Optus operator and ☎ 0130-80 00 61 for Telstra.

For directory assistance within Germany, dial ☎ 11833; for numbers abroad it's ☎ 11834.

Telephone Rates Since the lifting of Deutsche Telecom's (DT) monopoly status on 1 January 1998, a bewildering number of private long-distance providers offering lower rates has entered the market (DT continues its grip on local calls). In most cases, getting the low rates means dialling a five-digit access number before the number you're trying to reach. This only works from private lines and *not* from pay phones which still are all owned by DT.

Faced with the competition, DT has lowered its rates also, though again *not* for calls made from pay phones! Since most travellers don't have access to a private phone line and are thus dependent on pay phones, they will also continue to contend with DT and its expensive and incredibly confusing rate plan.

Rates are divided into call units, zones and time periods. How long you can talk per phone unit depends on where and when you are calling. At pay phones, call units cost DM0.20 when using coins or the DM12 phone card, and DM0.19 per unit with the DM50 card. (By comparison, DT call units using private phones are just DM0.12) Assuming a DM0.20 per unit charge, a three-minute call from, for example, Berlin to Munich made at 3 pm on a weekday costs DM3; the same call after 9 pm costs just DM1.60.

International calls are also subject to zones and time periods. Reduced rates are available after 6 pm and before 8 am to EU countries and between 3 am and 2 pm to the USA and Canada. Calls to Australia and New Zealand cost the same all day.

A three minute call to the USA will cost you DM7.20 (DM6.60 reduced), to an EU country DM5 (DM4 reduced) and to Australia DM12.

While calls made from private phone lines are considerably cheaper, those made from your hotel room are not. In fact, here you'll often be charged as much as DM0.60 or even DM0.80 per call unit. One way to save is to ask the person you're contacting to call you back. Just place a short call to relay your hotel and room number and tell whoever is calling you back to dial their international access code plus 4930 (Germany code plus Berlin area code) and that number.

The cellular phone craze has spread through Germany as everywhere else. Note that calls made *to* cellular phones cost a lot more than those to a stationary number, though how much more depends on the service used by the cellular-phone owner.

Numbers starting with 0130 or 0800 are toll-free, but rates are astronomical for numbers starting with 0190 (usually sex lines, but also Berlin tourism's hotline).

International   Phonecards Lonely Planet's eKno Communication Card (see the insert at the back of this book) is aimed specifically at travellers and provides cheap international calls, a range of messaging services and free email. (Note that for local calls, you're usually better off with a German phonecard.) You can join online at www.ekno.lonelyplanet.com, or toll-free by phone from Germany by dialling 0800-000-7138. Once you have joined, simply dial 0800-000-7139 to use eKno from within Germany.

Check the eKno Web site for joining and access numbers from other countries and updates on super budget local access numbers and new features.

Fax

If you're staying at upmarket hotels, fax transmissions are generally not a problem. There's usually no fee for receiving faxes, though sending them can cost a bundle, so it pays to check in advance. If you carry a laptop with a fax modem, you only pay for the cost of the telephone call (keep in mind that hotel phone rates are exorbitant).

Cheaper, in most cases, is the use of public fax-phones now in place at larger post offices. These operate with a phone card from which the regular cost of the call, plus a DM2 service charge, is deducted if the connection succeeds. Occasionally you can also find public fax-phones in train stations. Full-service copy shops will also let you send faxes (see Doing Business later this chapter for addresses).

Email & Internet Access

Those travelling with their own laptop and modem, can get online by dialling their home country service provider or by taking out a local account. Reliable local providers include ComBox (☎ 59 00 69 00, email info@combox.de, www.combox.de) at Potsdamer Strasse 96 and Interactive Networkx (☎ 01802-52 42, email info@snafu.de, www.snafu.de) at Hardenbergplatz 2. Both offer various packages, but going rates are DM30 to DM40 for set up and DM40 for unlimited monthly access.

Getting your modem to work with German phone lines can be quite frustrating. German phone plugs are rather unique and you're quite likely to need an adaptor to get online. If you haven't brought one with you, check with an electronics store.

There are usually no problems getting connected from a line in a private home. At some hotels, however, you'll find that the phone cable is wired right into the wall and/or the phone itself. Larger hotels sometimes have digital (ISDN) lines or complex internal phone systems that require you to make changes to your modem string in order to get an outside line. Finding competent help is almost impossible. Contact your service provider before leaving home to see if they can offer any specific advice about Germany.

Internet Cafes The easiest way to surf the Web and to send and receive email is at a cybercafe. Expect to pay from DM5 to DM7 for 30 minutes. Café Website (Map 7, ☎ 88 67 96 30), at Jochimsthaler Strasse 41 near Zoo station, has 40 PCs and stays open until 2 am. Across the street, on the top floor of the

Karstadt Sporthaus, is Cyberb@r (Map 7, ☎ 88 02 40), open during regular shop hours, where you can surf and also take out six-month email accounts (DM15).

The Alpha Internet Café (Map 4, ☎ 447 90 67), Dunckerstrasse 72 in Prenzlauer Berg (S8 or S10 to Prenzlauer Allee), is a fun place with 10 computers, AOL, Netscape, printers, scanners and other office equipment. It's open from 3 pm to midnight daily.

Internet Café Hai Täck (Map 5, ☎ 85 96 14 13 at Brünnhildestrasse 8 in Schöneberg (U9 and S4/45/46 to Bundesplatz) has AOL and CompuServe, fax service and good food. It's open from 11 am to 1 am daily.

INTERNET RESOURCES

The World Wide Web is a rich resource for travellers. You can research your trip, hunt down bargain air fares, book hotels, check on weather conditions or chat with locals and other travellers about the best places to visit (or avoid!).

One place to start your Web explorations is the Lonely Planet Web site (www.lonelyplanet.com). Here you'll find succinct summaries on travelling to most places on earth, postcards from other travellers and the Thorn Tree bulletin board, where you can ask questions before you go, or dispense advice when you get back. You can also find travel news and updates to many of our most popular guidebooks, and the sub-WWWay section links you to the most useful travel resources elsewhere on the Web.

There are dozens of Internet Web sites dedicated to Berlin, its culture, institutions, events etc. American Online has put together a very useful page with lots of hot links (keyword: Berlin). Most of the sites listed here also provide useful hot links.

www.berlin.de
   Official Web site of the Berlin Senate. Basic city information on culture, transport, the economy, politics etc. In English and German.
www.berlinonline.de
   Comprehensive site maintained by Gruner + Jahr, the big nationwide magazine and newspaper publisher (including *tip* magazine and *Berliner Zeitung*). Current information: news, travel, culture etc. Searchable.

euro currency converter DM1 = €.51

FACTS FOR THE VISITOR

www.btm.de
> Web site maintained by the tourist office with information, hotel reservation system, links and historical information. In German and English.

www.chemie.fu-berlin.de
> Web site maintained by the Chemistry Institute of the Free University, with lots of info and links. (To get to the right page, switch to the English version at the bottom of the home page, then click on the User Pages link, and then on About Berlin.) In English and German.

www.dhm.de
> Web site of the Museum of German History, but best for its hot links to other museums in Berlin and Brandenburg. In English and German.

BOOKS

Most books are published in different editions by different publishers in different countries. As a result, a book might be a hardcover rarity in one country while it's readily available in paperback in another. Fortunately, bookshops and libraries search by title or author, so your local bookshop or library should be able to advise you on the availability of any of the books recommended in this guide.

Lonely Planet

Lonely Planet's *Germany* is an excellent source for those planning to travel around the country extensively. It contains up-to-date information on all popular mainstream travel spots, as well as eye-opening destinations that are off the beaten track. Lonely Planet's *Central Europe*, *Western Europe* and *Europe* all include a big Germany chapter for those on a grand 'shoestring' tour, in which case the *Central Europe Phrasebook* might also come in handy. Lonely Planet also publishes a *German Phrasebook* so you can chat with the locals. All books are available at good bookstores or may be ordered from the Lonely Planet Web site at www.lonelyplanet.com.

Guidebooks

Berlin for Young People, which is published by Herden Studienreisen Berlin, gives a quick overview of clubs, museums, hangouts, tours, restaurants and other information. Published in English and German, it sells for around DM10 at the tourist office and major bookstores.

History

Berlin, Then and Now by Tony Le Tissier is a fascinating record of the modern history of Berlin told largely in black and white photographs. The accompanying text is heavy sledding, perhaps because the author was the warden of Spandau prison, a time he has chronicled in *Farewell to Spandau*. It was actually on his watch that Prisoner No 7 committed suicide; a man by the name of Rudolf Hess.

The Biography of a City by Anthony Read and David Fisher is an excellent social history tracing the life of the city from its beginnings to post-Wall times. The *very* expensive *Berlin and its Culture* by Ronald Taylor is lavishly illustrated and traces the cultural history of Berlin from medieval beginnings through to the 1990s.

A wide body of work deals with the years between WWI and WWII and the artistic brilliance and moral decadence that marked the city in the 1920s. The list includes *Before the Deluge* by Otto Friedrich, but a more engaging read is *A Dame Between Flames* by Anton Gill.

There's a plethora of English-language books about Nazi Germany and Berlin's role during those 12 years. *The Rise and Fall of the Third Reich* by William Shirer, a one-time Berlin correspondent, remains one of the most powerful works of reportage ever written. His portrait of the Berlin of those times – a city which he loved, grew to fear and eventually fled – is considered a giant of the genre.

Inside the Third Reich by Albert Speer is one of the best books about the day-to-day operations of Hitler's inner clique. It was written by the brilliant architect who stood at the Führer's elbow and built much of the Berlin that would be bombed into rubble. For another take on the same troubling subject there's *Albert Speer: His Battle With Truth* by Gitta Sereny. In over 700 pages, you'll learn of the life and times of one of the more controversial – and somehow oddly tragic – Nazi figures.

The Fall of Berlin, another co-production by Anthony Read and David Fisher, is considered one of the standards on the subject of the apocalyptic last days of the war and the Wagnerian death of Adolf Hitler. Still the defining work on the subject is *The Last Days of Hitler* by Hugh Trevor-Roper, in which much idle speculation about Hitler's ultimate fate is firmly laid to rest. The writing style is atrocious but the content makes it forgivable: it was written by a young intelligence officer in 1947. *The Road to Berlin* by John Erickson is an exhaustive military chronicle of the Soviet prosecution of the war against the Nazis.

Jews in Germany: After the Holocaust by Lynn Rapaport is based on interviews with nearly 100 Jews who continue to live in Germany and deals with how the memory of the Holocaust has affected their lives. There are many touching passages about the love/hate aspects of the German/Jewish relationship and much insight into how difficult it is to develop real friendships between Jews and Germans.

Books dealing with the life and times of the GDR include *Man Without a Face: The Memoirs of a Spymaster* by Markus Wolf and Anne McElvoy. It is the autobiography of Wolf himself who was the enormously successful chief of East Germany's intelligence services, the hated Stasi and – like Albert Speer – sort of an admirable monster. For a more withering portrait of Wolf, seek out *Spymaster: The Real Life Karla* by Leslie Colitt, who concludes that there's absolutely nothing admirable about the man who ruined lives with such perverse joy and then prospered from the agony and destruction he engineered.

Berlin and The Wall by Ann Tusa is a saga of the events, trials and triumphs of the Cold War, the building of the Wall and its effects on the people and the city of Berlin. For a chilling read about the days after the fall of the Wall there's *The File* by Timothy Garton Ash, an author who discovered his own Stasi files while doing research in Berlin. The book is full of personal accounts of the confrontations between the author and those who stalked him.

General

Christopher Isherwood will always be synonymous with Berlin because of the film *Cabaret*, based on his semi-autobiographical work *Goodbye to Berlin*. It remains a must read because of its often hilarious descriptions of a young man lost in the Berlin of the 1920s, an anarchic and lurid age. It should be read for its wonderful descriptions of the people and events of the time.

Aimée & Jaguar by Erica Fischer is the true story of two women in Berlin who fell in love during the warped and dangerous days of 1942. It's all the more remarkable a tale in that one of the women was a mother of four married to a German soldier while the other was Jewish. The photographs are poignant, to say the least. It was made into a movie in 1999.

Billing herself as 'Berlin's most distinguished transvestite', Charlotte von Mahlsdorf has written a rollicking account of her outlaw life as celebrated crackpot, museum owner and GDR cultural fixture in the ironically titled *I Am My Own Woman*.

Architecture students and professionals will love *Bauwelt Berlin Annual: Chronology of Building Events 1996-2001*, a series of annual volumes chronicling the new face of Berlin as it emerges. *Berlin/Brandenburg*, published by Ernst & Sohn, is a good general primer on the subject, in English and German, with copious photographs.

NEWSPAPERS & MAGAZINES
German

The newspaper with the largest circulation in Berlin is the *BZ,* which is borderline sensationalist and practically devoid of meaningful content. It is, believe it or not, a step up from *Bild,* which woos readers with headlines like 'Sex Waves From Space' and photographs of scantily clad young women. *BZ* is not to be confused with the respected *Berliner Zeitung*, a left-leaning daily newspaper that is most widely read among the eastern districts.

The *Berliner Morgenpost* is especially noted for its vast classified section; its Sunday edition is where to look first for cars, flats, second-hand appliances etc.

euro currency converter DM1 = €.51

Der Tagesspiegel has a centre-right political orientation, a solid news and foreign section and decent cultural coverage. At the left end of the spectrum is the alternative *taz* which appeals to an intellectual crowd with its news analysis and thorough reporting.

Early editions of some dailies are available after 9 pm from newspaper vendors passing through pubs and restaurants or positioned outside theatres and U-Bahn stations.

Der Spiegel and *Focus*, both popular weekly magazines, offer hard-hitting investigative journalism, a certain degree of government criticism, and other deep thoughts between covers often featuring scantily clad models. *Stern* used to be similar but has become more light-weight and trivial in its coverage. *Die Zeit* is an excellent weekly newspaper with in-depth reporting on everything from politics to fashion.

Zitty and *tip* are Berlin's best bi-weekly what's-on magazines. See Listings in the Entertainment chapter for details.

English

English-language newspapers and magazines – most from the UK and the USA – are readily available. Look for them in larger bookstores and at international newsagents (try the train stations).

The *International Herald Tribune*, edited in Paris with wire stories from the *New York Times* and *Washington Post*, is the most commonly available English-language daily paper; it sells for DM3.50.

The biggies on offer from the UK include *The Guardian* (DM3.80), the *Financial Times* (DM4.30) and *The London Times* (DM5). From the USA, *USA Today* (DM3.50) has made huge inroads, and the *Wall Street Journal* (DM4.20) is also available.

As for magazines, *The Economist* (DM8) is on sale widely as are the international editions of *Time* (DM6.80) and *Newsweek* (DM6.90). In addition, practically the whole gamut of women's, car, lifestyle and speciality magazines are available as well. *Spotlight* (DM9) is a monthly English-language magazine for Germans who want

to learn English, with good feature articles and travel pieces.

RADIO

Berlin has a bewildering choice of radio stations, many increasingly modelled on US-style contemporary music shows interspersed with inane talk and advertisement. If you like that kind of thing, check out the youth-oriented Fritz at 102.6, the techno-driven Kiss at 98.8 or Radio Energy at 103.4. The BBC broadcasts at 90.2. Among the more sophisticated stations is Radio Eins (95.8) which has lots of high-quality programming with topical information and political and social themes. SFB4, aka Radio Multikulti (106.8), is an excellent multicultural station with music and event information about various ethnic groups. It occasionally broadcasts in the respective languages. Jazz fiends should check out Jazzradio at 101.9, while classical music rules Klassik-Radio at 101.3. InfoRadio at 93.1 has an all-news format, including live interviews.

TELEVISION

Most mid-range and better hotel rooms have a television set and most will be hooked up to a cable connection or a satellite dish, providing access to at least 15 channels. English-language channels broadcast within Germany include CNN, BBC World, the Sky Channel and NBC Europe. The quality of the reception, though, depends on the location, on whether the TV is hooked up to cable or to a satellite dish and on the quality of the television set.

Germany has two national public channels, the ARD (Erstes Deutsches Fernsehen) and the ZDF (Zweites Deutsches Fernsehen). The Berlin channels B1 and ORB (Ostdeutscher Rundfunk Brandenburg) are regional public stations. Generally, programming is comparatively highbrow featuring political coverage, discussion forums and foreign films. Advertising is limited to the two hours between 6 and 8 pm.

Private cable TV has proliferated in Germany since the 1980s. It offers the familiar array of sit-coms and soap operas (usually dubbed US shows), chat and game shows and, of course, feature films of all stripes. DSF and EuroSport are dedicated sports channels, and MTV and its German equivalent VIVA can also be received. Commercial breaks are frequent on these stations.

A recent development are several Turkish-language channels which cater for Germany's large population with roots in that country. Don't expect religious programming, though! Scantily clad women and explicit subjects are just as commonplace here as they are on German-language TV.

VIDEO SYSTEMS

German video and television operates on the PAL (Phase Alternative Line) system that predominates in most of Europe and Australia. It is not compatible with the American and Japanese NTSC or French SECAM standards; pre-recorded video tapes bought in countries using those standards won't play in Germany and vice versa.

PHOTOGRAPHY & VIDEO
Film & Equipment

German photographic equipment is among the best in the world. All makes and types are readily available, as are those manufactured in other countries, though bargains are rare. Print film is sold at supermarkets and chemists, but for B&W and slide film you'll have to go to a photographic store. The latter two are hard to find (or sold at inflated prices) outside the city, so if you're taking a day trip from Berlin, stock up.

For general-purpose shooting – either prints or slides – 100 ASA film is the most useful and versatile as it gives you good colour and enough speed to capture most situations on film. For shooting in dark areas or in brightly lit night scenes without a tripod, switch to 400 ASA.

The best and most widely available films are made by Fuji, Kodak and Agfa. Fuji Velvia and Kodak Elite are easy to process and provide good slide images. Stay away from Kodachrome: it's difficult to process quickly and creates major headaches if not handled properly. For print film you can't beat Kodak Gold, though Fuji and Agfa have just about perfected their films for print as well.

Film of any type is rather inexpensive in Germany, so there's no need to stock up at home. A roll of 36-exposure standard print film costs around DM6; slide film costs DM10 to DM13. The cost drops significantly if you buy multipacks of three, five or 10 rolls, so shop around. Occasionally, processing is included with purchase, though slides will come back unmounted unless you specify that you want them mounted (gerahmt), in which case an extra charge applies.

Chemists and supermarkets are cheap places to get your film processed, provided you don't need professional quality. Standard developing for print film is about DM4, plus DM0.40 for each 10 x 15cm print (allow about four days), and about DM0.60 per print for overnight service. Processing slide film costs about DM3.50 in these shops; if you want mounts your total comes to about DM7. Prices quoted are for rolls of 36.

Professional developers include the full-service Jacobs & Schulz (Map 5, ☎ 261 80 20) at Potsdamer Strasse 98 in Tiergarten. It's open from 8 am to 10 pm weekdays and (almost unheard of in Germany!) from 2 to 6 pm weekends. Many of the staff speak English.

Another professional developer is PPS (☎ 28 52 84 00) at Rosenthaler Strasse 28-31 in Spandauer Vorstadt.

Video recorders bought in North America or Japan can record with German-bought tapes and then play back with no problems. The size of the tapes is the same, only the method of recording and playback differs between PAL and NTSC standards. A standard VHS tape costs about DM6 to DM10.

Airport Security

In general, airport X-ray technology isn't supposed to jeopardise lower-speed film (under 1600 ASA). Recently, however, new high-powered machines designed to inspect checked luggage have been installed at major airports around the world.

FACTS FOR THE VISITOR

These machines are capable of conducting high-energy scans that may damage unprocessed film. Be sure to carry film and loaded cameras in your hand-luggage and ask airport security people to inspect them manually. Pack all your film into a clear plastic bag that you can quickly whip out of your luggage. This can save you time at the inspection points and will help minimise confrontations with security staff. In this age of terrorism, their job is tough but they can also add to your pre-flight hell, big time.

TIME

Throughout Germany clocks are set to Central European Time (GMT/UTC plus one hour), the same time zone as Madrid and Warsaw. Daylight-saving time comes into effect on the last Sunday in March, when clocks are turned forward one hour. On the last Sunday in October they are turned back an hour. Without taking daylight-saving times into account, when it's noon in Berlin, it's 11 am in London, 6 am in New York, 3 am in San Francisco, 8 pm in Tokyo, 9 pm in Sydney and 11 pm in Auckland. Official times (eg shop hours, train schedules, film screenings etc) are usually indicated by the 24-hour clock, eg 6.30 pm is 18.30.

ELECTRICITY

Electricity is 220V, 50 Hz AC. Plugs are the European type with two round pins. Your 220V appliances may be plugged into a German outlet with an adaptor, though their 110V cousins (eg from North America) require a transformer.

WEIGHTS & MEASURES

Germany uses the metric system – there's a conversion table on the inside back cover of this book. Like other Continental Europeans, Germans indicate decimals with commas and thousands with points (ie 10,000.00 is 10.000,00). Cheese, vegetables and other food items are often sold by the *Pfund* (pound), which means 500 grams.

Clothing sizes – especially for women's clothing – are quite different from those in North America (NA) and Great Britain.

Women's size 8 in NA (size 10 in the UK) equals size 36 in Germany. Sizes then increase in increments of two, making German size 38 an NA 10 (UK 12) and so on.

Shoes are another matter altogether. NA size 5 (UK 3) is size 36 in Germany. It continues in increments of one, so that NA 6 (UK 4) equals size 37. Just to make things more complicated, men's sizes are a bit different. A men's 41 equates to an NA 8 (UK 7). A men's 42 would be an NA 9 (UK 8) etc.

LAUNDRY

Coin-operated laundrettes *(Münzwäscherei)* are normally open from 6 am to 9 or 10 pm. A load of washing costs DM6 to DM7 including soap powder; the dryer is DM1 per 10 minutes. In most laundrettes you select your machine and deposit the coin(s) in a central machine with numbers corresponding to the washers and dryers. The panel also distributes soap powder, so have at the ready one of the plastic cups you'll find strewn around the laundrette.

The Schnell und Sauber chain has outlets across Berlin, eg in Charlottenburg at Uhlandstrasse 53 (Map 7) and Leibnizstrasse 72 (Map 7) and in Kreuzberg at Karl-Marx-Strasse 19 (Map 6) and on Mehringdamm on the corner of Gneisenaustrasse (Map 6). Other chains include Waschcenter with a branch at Bergmannstrasse 109 in Kreuzberg 61 (Map 6, U6 and U7 to Mehringdamm) and Öko-Express at Rosenthaler Strasse 71 (Map 4, U8 to Rosenthaler Platz) in Mitte.

TOILETS

Public toilets are not ubiquitous in Berlin and you may have to pay DM0.20 to DM1.50 for the privilege. Sneaking into a bar or restaurant is an easy alternative, though it's best to pick a busy place to avoid withering stares from the staff. The public facilities in department stores are usually a better choice. If there's an attendant, it's nice to tip DM0.50, at least if the toilet was clean. All train stations have toilets; Zoo station even has a spic-and-span establishment called McWash where you can take a shower for DM10, soap and towel included.

Overall, the standard of hygiene is high, although toilets in some pubs and nightclubs can get outright disgusting.

Occasionally you'll also see self-cleaning toilet pods (DM0.50), which are sometimes gay hang-outs, as is the public toilet below Alexanderplatz near the World Time Clock.

Largely a thing of the past are the green Wilhelminian *pissoirs*, commonly called Café Achteck (Café Octagonal) in reference to their shape. They're for men only, and there's a still-functioning one (Map 6) on Chamissoplatz in Kreuzberg 61. Another sits outside the Senefelderplatz U-Bahn station in Prenz'lberg.

HEALTH
Medical Services
Berlin has about 6000 doctors and 2600 dentists, so you're quite likely to find one nearby by checking under *Ärzte* in the phonebook. If you need a referral or have an emergency, call ☎ 31 00 31 (24 hours). Hotel staff can usually make recommendations as well.

For after-hour referrals to a dentist *(Zahnarzt)* phone ☎ 89 00 43 33. The Zahnklinik Medeco has some English-speaking doctors. It's at Königin-Louise - Platz 1 (☎ 841 91 00) in Dahlem and open from 6 am to midnight daily.

Everyday Health

Normal body temperature is up to 37°C (98.6°F); more than 2°C (4°F) higher indicates a high fever. The normal adult pulse rate is 60 to 100 per minute (children 80 to 100, babies 100 to 140). As a general rule the pulse increases about 20 beats per minute for each 1°C (2°F) rise in fever.

Respiration (breathing) rate is also an indicator of illness. Count the number of breaths per minute: Between 12 and 20 is normal for adults and older children (up to 30 for younger children, 40 for babies). People with a high fever or serious respiratory illness breathe more quickly than normal. More than 40 shallow breaths a minute may indicate pneumonia.

First aid and emergency health care is free for EU citizens with an E111 form. Any other form of treatment can be very expensive, so make sure that you have travel insurance (see the earlier section Documents).

No vaccinations are required to visit Germany, except if you're coming from an infected area – a jab against yellow fever is the most likely requirement. If you're going to Berlin with stopovers in Asia, Africa or Latin America, check with your travel agent or with the German embassy or consulate nearest you.

Tap water is safe to drink. If you're travelling on to a country where vaccinations are required, you can get them at the Tropen- und Reisemedizinisches Institut (☎ 395 10 42) at Wiclefstrasse 2 in Tiergarten (U9 to Birkenstrasse).

Hospitals There are hospitals all over Berlin but the following are university-affiliated and have large, 24-hour emergency rooms. If you need an ambulance, call ☎ 112.

Uniklinikum Benjamin Franklin (☎ 844 50, emergencies ☎ 84 45 30 15/25) is at Hindenburgdamm 30 in Steglitz.
Uniklinikum Charité (Map 4, ☎ 282 00, emergencies ☎ 28 02 47 66) is at Schumannstrasse 20-21, just off Luisenstrasse in Mitte (U6 to Oranienburger Tor).
Uniklinikum Rudolf Virchow (Map 3, ☎ 450 50, emergencies ☎ 45 05 20 00) is at Augustenburger Platz 1 in Wedding.

Pharmacies The only places where you can obtain over-the-counter *(rezeptfrei)* medications for minor health concerns, like flu or a stomach upset, are pharmacies *(Apotheke)*. For more serious conditions, you will need to bring a prescription *(Rezept)* from a licensed physician. If you need medication after hours, call ☎ 31 00 31 or ☎ 01141 for the address of the nearest open pharmacy. The following organisations may be of use if you need support:

Berliner AIDS-Hilfe (Berlin AIDS Help, Map 7, ☎ 885 64 00), at Meinekestrasse 12, is dedicated to prevention, counselling and support for those infected with HIV. Counselling is by telephone from 10 am to midnight daily.

Deutsche AIDS-Hilfe (German AIDS Help, ☎ 690 08 70), at Dieffenbachstrasse 33 in Kreuzberg, is a political interest group fighting for the rights of the HIV-positive.

Medical Kit Check List

Following is a list of items you should consider including in your medical kit – consult your pharmacist for brands available in your country.

☐ **Aspirin or paracetamol (acetaminophen in the USA)** – for pain or fever
☐ **Antihistamine** – for allergies, eg, hay fever; to ease the itch from insect bites or stings; and to prevent motion sickness
☐ **Cold and flu tablets, throat lozenges and nasal decongestant**
☐ **Multivitamins** – consider for long trips, when dietary vitamin intake may be inadequate
☐ **Antibiotics** – consider including these if you're travelling well off the beaten track; see your doctor, as they must be prescribed, and carry the prescription with you
☐ **Loperamide or diphenoxylate** –'blockers' for diarrhoea
☐ **Prochlorperazine or metaclopramide** – for nausea and vomiting
☐ **Rehydration mixture** – to prevent dehydration, which may occur, for example, during bouts of diarrhoea; particularly important when travelling with children
☐ **Insect repellent, sunscreen, lip balm and eye drops**
☐ **Calamine lotion, sting relief spray or aloe vera** – to ease irritation from sunburn and insect bites or stings
☐ **Antifungal cream or powder** – for fungal skin infections and thrush
☐ **Antiseptic (such as povidone-iodine)** – for cuts and grazes
☐ **Bandages, Band-Aids (plasters) and other wound dressings**
☐ **Water purification tablets or iodine**
☐ **Scissors, tweezers and a thermometer** – note that mercury thermometers are prohibited by airlines

Infectious Diseases

HIV & AIDS Infection with the human immunodeficiency virus (HIV) may lead to acquired immune deficiency syndrome (AIDS), which is a fatal disease. Any exposure to blood, blood products or body fluids may put the individual at risk. The disease is often transmitted through unprotected sex or dirty needles, including those used for vaccinations, acupuncture, tattooing and body piercing. Fear of HIV infection should never preclude treatment for serious medical conditions.

The following organisations may be of use if you need support:

Berliner AIDS-Hilfe (Berlin AIDS Help, Map 7, ☎ 885 64 00), at Meinekestrasse 12, is dedicated to prevention, counselling and support for those infected with HIV. Counselling by phone is from 10 am to midnight daily.
Deutsche AIDS-Hilfe (German AIDS Help, ☎ 690 08 70), at Dieffenbachstrasse 33 in Kreuzberg, is a political interest group fighting for the rights of the HIV-positive.

Sexually Transmitted Diseases Gonorrhoea, herpes and syphilis are among these diseases; sores, blisters or rashes around the genitals and discharges or pain when urinating are common symptoms. In some STDs, such as wart virus or chlamydia, symptoms may be less marked or not observed at all, especially in women. Syphilis symptoms eventually disappear completely but the disease continues and can cause severe problems in later years. While sexual abstinence is the only 100% effective prevention, using condoms is also effective. The treatment of gonorrhoea and syphilis is with antibiotics. Different sexually transmitted diseases require specific antibiotics. There is no cure for herpes or AIDS, though only AIDS will ultimately lead to death.

WOMEN TRAVELLERS

Women shouldn't encounter too many difficulties or harassment in Berlin, though naturally it pays to use common sense. Getting hassled in the streets is rare and most common when walking past a bunch of construction guys on their break. Cat whistles and hollering are best ignored as any response will be interpreted as encouragement.

Younger German women are quite emancipated and just as likely to initiate contact with the opposite sex as men are. Such confidence, however, hasn't yet translated into equality in the workplace where sexual harassment is more commonplace and tolerated than in countries like the USA and Australia.

Many women juggle jobs and children but there's an extensive network of public, church-run and private kindergartens and daycare centres to fall back on.

The women's movement is very active in Germany and women's centres abound. A central clearing house for information of any kind is the *Fraueninfothek* (Map 8, ☎ 282 39 80, Dircksenstrasse 47) in Mitte. It's open from 10 am to 6 pm weekdays. Others are *EWA* (Map 4, ☎ 442 55 42 or ☎ 442 72 57, Prenzlauer Allee 6) in Prenzlauer Berg; *Frieda* (☎ 422 42 76, Proskauer Strasse 7) in Friedrichshain; and *Paula Panke* (☎ 485 47 02, Schulstrasse 6) in Pankow.

Those who can read German may find Christiane Theiselmann's *Berliner Frauen Handbuch* (Berlin Women's Handbook, DM29.80) of great use. Topics covered include leisure, jobs, children, self-help and more.

Organisations

The following organisations may prove useful in times of crisis:

Frauenkrisentelefon (Women's Crisis Hotline, ☎ 615 42 43 and ☎ 615 75 96) is a listening and referral service for anyone wanting to talk about any kind of problem. It's staffed from 10 am to noon Monday and Thursday; from 7 to 9 pm Tuesday, Wednesday and Friday; and from 5 to 7 pm weekends.

Frauennotdienst (Women's Emergency Service, ☎ 851 10 18) is a 24-hour counselling and assistance service.

LARA: Krisen- und Beratungszentrum für vergewaltigte Frauen (Crisis and Counselling Centre for Raped Women, ☎ 216 88 88), at Tempelhofer Ufer 14, provides free and anonymous help regardless of when the act of violence occurred. If necessary, they can also arrange for therapy and medical and legal information. It is staffed from 9 am to midnight Monday to Thursday, 24 hours on weekends.

GAY & LESBIAN TRAVELLERS

Germans are generally fairly tolerant of homosexuality and Berlin is certainly the country's most progressive city. It's estimated that up to 500,000 gays and lesbians call Berlin their home. These numbers were augmented mostly by Ossies (a nickname for East Germans) since the Wende, as East Berlin was the only place in the GDR where one could have any semblance of a lifestyle.

Today, the sight of homosexual couples holding hands is not uncommon and kissing in public is becoming more practised and accepted. Gays are known as *Schwule* (formerly a pejorative term equivalent to 'queer' but now a moniker worn with pride and dignity), lesbians are *Lesben*.

Information

The first port of call for lesbian and gay visitors to Berlin wanting to connect with the local scene should be an information centre. Among the best is *Mann-O-Meter* (Map 5, ☎ 216 80 08, Motzstrasse 5, email info@mann-o-meter.de) in Schöneberg. The savvy staff will provide information on just about everything you may want to know and can also help you find inexpensive, gay-friendly accommodation. Free publications and pamphlets are available here, as are referrals to other information and support centres. Mann-O-Meter is open from 5 to 10 pm Monday to Saturday and to 9 pm on Sunday. Their Web site is at www.mann-o-meter.de.

Another good centre is *aha* (Map 6, ☎ 692 36 00, Mehringdamm 61) in Kreuzberg 61.

The best and most up-to-date publication is the free monthly *Siegessäule* which also has a Web site at www.siegessaeule.de. This, the *Gay Express* and *Sergej* can be found at bars, clubs and information centres. Another option is the slick monthly *Männer Aktuell* (DM14.80), available at newsagents.

Another source (in German only) is *Homopolis* (DM28) by Micha Schulze and published by the people from *Siegessäule* magazine. A thorough guide (in English and German) to Berlin's gay scene is the piquantly named *Berlin von Hinten* (Berlin from Behind, DM22.80) by Bruno Gmünder, available at mainstream and gay bookshops (see the Shopping chapter). There's little information for lesbians in either of these books.

Organisations

The following organisations may be of use if you need support:

Lesbenberatung (Lesbian Advice Centre, Map 5, ☎ 215 20 00), at Kulmer Strasse 20a in Schöneberg, offers help with coming to terms with being lesbian and runs discussion groups on issues like discrimination and safe sex. Hours are from 4 to 7 pm Monday, Tuesday and Thursday, 2 to 5 pm Friday.

Schwulenberatung (Map 7, Gay Counselling Centre, ☎ 32 70 30 40) is just what it says. It's located at Mommsenstrasse 45, on the corner of Wilmersdorfer Strasse.

Schwules Überfalltelefon (Gay Attack Hotline, ☎ 216 33 36) is a phone service that provides support to victims of violence and also documents the number of violent attacks against gays. It's staffed from 6 to 9 pm daily, to 4 am Saturday.

Sonntagsclub (Map 4, ☎ 449 75 90), at Greifenhagener Strasse 28 in Prenzlauer Berg, is an informal gathering place and information exchange for gays, lesbians, bisexuals and transsexuals.

See the Health section earlier in this chapter for AIDS organisations.

DISABLED TRAVELLERS

Overall, Germany caters well for the needs of disabled people *(Behinderte)*, especially the wheelchair-bound. You'll find access ramps and/or lifts in many public buildings, including toilets, train stations, museums, theatres and cinemas. Other disabilities, like blindness or deafness, aren't as well catered for but the German organisations for disabled people are continuing to lobby for improvements.

Getting around Berlin on public transport while confined to a wheelchair is possible but requires some planning. Buses with a blue wheelchair symbol have special ramps which can be pulled out. This works fine as long as the driver knows how to do it or the equipment isn't broken. Getting onto U-Bahn or S-Bahn trains isn't as much of a problem as getting onto the platform itself. Many stations have lifts (marked on route maps with the blue symbol), but these don't always work. To find out which are working, you can call Berlin public transport (BVG) at ☎ 25 62 92 12. They also put out a brochure with helpful hints on how to use their system with a wheelchair. As a last resort you can always call a taxi company and ask for a *Behindertentaxi*.

Information for disabled people is available from the Berliner Behindertenverband (☎ 204 38 47), Jägerstrasse 63d in Mitte, from 8 am to 6 pm weekdays; Movado (☎ 471 30 22) from 8am to 8pm weekdays; Service-Ring-Berlin (☎ 859 40 10), from 10 am to 6 pm weekdays; and the Verband Geburts-und anderer Behinderter (Disabled Persons' Association, ☎ 341 17 97). The last two also have a wheelchair-hire service, the latter for free.

An especially useful service is provided by Telebus (☎ 47 88 20), Esplanade 17, in Pankow which operates buses for the disabled, including tourists. Contact the office as early as possible to obtain a pass that entitles you to use these special buses. A similar service is provided by Notrufdienst Berlin (☎ 84 31 09 10).

SENIOR TRAVELLERS

Museums and other sights, public swimming pools, spas and some forms of transport such as Deutsche Bahn (DB) usually offer discounts to retired people, old-age pensioners and those over 60. Since there are no international seniors' cards, bring along your passport in case you're asked for proof of age.

Occasionally discounts are not posted, in which case simply ask *'Gibt es Ermässigungen für Senioren?'* If you're on a tight budget, keep in mind that there's no age limit for stays at most of Berlin's independent and DJH hostels, and that student cafeterias at universities, which offer cheap meals, are open to anyone.

BERLIN FOR CHILDREN

Successful travel with young children requires planning and effort. Don't try to overdo things; even for adults, packing too much into a day can cause fatigue and frustration. And make sure the activities include the kids as well – balance that day at the Kulturforum museums with a visit to the zoo or a park. Include the kids in the planning; if they've helped to work out where you are going, they will be much more interested when they get there. Lonely Planet's *Travel with Children* by Maureen Wheeler is a good source of information on this subject.

Most car-rental firms in Germany have children's safety seats for hire at a nominal cost, but it is essential to book them in advance. The same goes for highchairs and cots (cribs); they're common in restaurants and hotels, but numbers are limited. The choice of baby food, infant formulas, soy and cow's milk, disposable nappies (diapers) and the like is great in Berlin supermarkets, but keep in mind store-trading hours – run out of nappies on Saturday afternoon and you're facing a very long and messy weekend. Nappy-changing stations can be found in many public toilets at train stations and department stores as well as family-oriented restaurants.

It's perfectly fine to bring your kids, even toddlers, along to casual restaurants (though not to upmarket ones), cafes and events. They're even allowed in bars and pubs, although the cigarette smoke may be uncomfortable for them.

For kids in crisis, the Kindernotdienst (☎ 61 00 61) provides free and anonymous 24-hour counselling, help and referrals to those under 14. For teens, there's the Jugendnotdienst (toll-free ☎ 0130-86 52 52).

Most of the larger hotels offer a baby-sitting service and others may be able to help you make arrangements. Alternatively, there are a number of agencies you could contact. KidsCare (☎ 854 81 88) is geared specifically towards travellers. Sitters come to your hotel or home, lugging a bag of supplies customised to your child's age. It's quite expensive at DM20 per hour.

Hekticket (☎ 24 31 24 31 or ☎ 230 99 30), the last-minute theatre ticket service, arranges for teaching students to take care of your children for around DM10 per hour. You may use this service even if you haven't bought any tickets.

The Heinzelmännchen (☎ 831 60 71) can arrange for students from the Free University to come at short notice for an hourly rate of DM15 to DM20. Another one is Aufgepasst (☎ 851 37 23), which has 200 registered and background-checked babysitters and charges DM12 to DM15 per hour.

Museums

Most of Berlin's museums are not particularly kid-friendly. In fact, the security staff's penetrating stares are unpleasant to most adults, let alone to little ones. Sucking on a bottle or eating a banana are out of the question in most places and don't even think about letting your tots run around – their movement may set off the sensitive alarms. Following is a list of museums where kids – and you – don't have to feel like social outcasts. Most are mentioned in greater detail in the Things to See & Do chapter.

Domäne Dahlem (☎ 832 50 00) in Zehlendorf is centred around a farmhouse from 1680 and illustrates the daily workings of a large Berlin farm at that time (see Western Districts – Zehlendorf in Things to See & Do chapter).

Juniormuseum (☎ 20 90 55 55), part of the Museum of Ethnology in Dahlem, has changing kid-oriented exhibits and events intended to awaken tolerance and teach understanding for other cultures (see Western Districts – Zehlendorf in Things to See & Do chapter).

Museum für Naturkunde (Museum of Natural History, Map 4, ☎ 20 93 85 40) is a sure winner with dinosaur fans (see Mitte section in Things to See & Do chapter).

Museum Kindheit & Jugend (Museum of Childhood & Adolescence, Map 8, ☎ 275 03 83) at Wallstrasse 32 in Mitte traces the history of education from the late 19th century to the 1950s. You can see textbooks and notebooks, ink pots, grade reports and chalkboards, plus pick up fascinating tidbits like the purpose of the *Eselskappe* (donkey hat) which had to be worn by undisciplined kids. Open from 9 am to 5 pm Tuesday to Friday. Admission is DM3/1.50.

FACTS FOR THE VISITOR

Museumsdorf Düppel (Düppel Museum Village, ☎ 802 66 71), a recreated medieval village with demonstrations of old-time crafts on Sundays (see Western Districts – Zehlendorf in Things to See & Do chapter).

Puppentheater-Museum Berlin (Map 6, ☎ 687 81 32) is in the rear building at Karl-Marx-Strasse 135 in Neukölln (U7 to Karl-Marx-Strasse). Changing exhibits tell the history of puppet theatre while displaying a wealth of hand puppets, marionettes, stick figures and other dolls from around the world. Open from 9 am to 5 pm weekdays, from 11 am weekends. Adults/children admission is DM5/4.

Spectrum at Deutsches Technikmuseum (German Technical Museum, Map 6, ☎ 25 48 40) has 250 or so experiment stations where kids can discover why the sky is blue or how a battery works (see Kreuzberg section in Things to See & Do chapter).

Theatre

For children's and youth-oriented theatre, see the Entertainment chapter.

LIBRARIES

Berlin has a comprehensive network of about 350 public libraries with a total of 5 million tomes. Most libraries also have international periodicals, videos, CD-Roms, photocopiers and games. Internet access is becoming more common. As a visitor you may go to any library and browse for as long as you want for free, but only Berlin residents may obtain a library card needed to borrow materials. What follows is a short list of Berlin's main libraries.

Amerika-Gedenkbibliothek (American Memorial Library, Map 6, ☎ 20 28 61 05), built to commemorate the Berlin Airlift of 1948-49, is the largest circulating library in Germany (850,000 items). It is at Blücherplatz 1 (U6 or U15 to Hallesches Tor) and is open from 3 to 7 pm Monday and from 11 am to 7 pm Tuesday to Saturday.

Berliner Stadtbibliothek (Berlin City Library, Map 8, ☎ 20 28 64 01), next door at Breite Strasse 32-34, has 800,000 volumes and is open from 10 am to 9 pm weekdays, to 6 pm Saturday.

Staatsbibliothek (State Library) has two branches. Haus 1 (House 1, Map 8, ☎ 201 50) at Unter den Linden 8 in Mitte is open from 9 am to 9 pm weekdays, to 5 pm Saturday and has books

published until 1955. There's a free tour in German at 10.30 am every first Saturday of the month. Books published after 1955 are at Haus 2 (Map 5, ☎ 26 60), across from the Kulturforum at Potsdamer Strasse 33 in Tiergarten, open from 10 am to 9 pm weekdays and to 5 pm Saturday. Free guided tours are offered at 10.30 am on the third Saturday of every month. The Staatsbibliothek is not part of the public library system. You will need ID to enter, so bring your passport. To understand how to read or borrow books, pick up the leaflet 'Notes for First-Time Users' by the entrance.

Zentrum für Berlin-Studien (Centre for Berlin Studies, Map 8, ☎ 90 22 64 85), at Breite Strasse 35-36 in Mitte, has a comprehensive collection on anything you ever wanted to know about Berlin (350,000 items). Hours are from 10 am to 7 pm weekdays and from 1 to 6 pm Saturday.

UNIVERSITIES

Berlin has the largest student body in Germany with a total of 145,000 students of which 17% are foreigners. There are three universities: the Humboldt Universität (Map 8, ☎ 209 30) at Unter den Linden 6 in Mitte; the Freie Universität Berlin (☎ 83 81) at Kaiserwertherstrasse 16-18 in Zehlendorf; and the Technische Universität (☎ 31 40) at Hardenbergstrasse and Strasse des 17 Juni in Charlottenburg. (Also see Education in the Facts about Berlin chapter.)

INTERNATIONAL CENTRES

Cosmopolitan Berlin has a number of international cultural institutes. Most have an active events schedule as well as a library with books, videos and periodicals from the country they represent. Other offerings include a message board, information about exchange programs, language courses and exhibitions.

Amerika Haus (Map 7, ☎ 31 10 73 and ☎ 31 50 55 70), at Hardenbergstrasse 22-24 in Charlottenburg, is open from 1 to 5 pm Wednesday, Thursday and Friday.

British Council (Map 7, ☎ 311 09 90), at Hardenbergstrasse 20 in Charlottenburg, is open from 2 to 6 pm weekdays (to 7 pm on Tuesday and Thursday).

Finnland-Institut (Finland Institute, Map 3, ☎ 399 41 41), at Alt Moabit 98 in Tiergarten, is open from 11 am to 7 pm Tuesday to Sunday.

Haus Ungarn (Hungary House, Map 8, ☎ 240 91 46), at Karl-Liebknecht-Strasse 9 in Mitte, is open from 10 am to 6 pm weekdays, the cafe is open from noon to 9 pm daily.

Institut Français (Map 7, ☎ 885 90 20), at Kurfürstendamm 211 in Charlottenburg, is open from 9 am to 1 pm and 2 to 6 pm weekdays (to 5 pm Friday).

Italienisches Kulturinstitut (Italian Cultural Institute, ☎ 261 78 75), at Hildebrandstrasse 1 in Tiergarten, is open from 10 am to 5 pm on weekdays.

Polnisches Kultur-Institut (Polish Cultural Institute, Map 8, ☎ 242 30 60 and ☎ 247 58 10), at Karl-Liebknecht-Strasse 7 in Mitte, open from 10 am to 6 pm Tuesday to Friday. The library is open from 10 am to 6 pm on Tuesday, and to 4 pm Thursday and Friday.

Tschechisches Zentrum (Czech Centre, Map 8, ☎ 208 25 92), at Leipziger Strasse 60 in Mitte, is open from 1 to 6 pm weekdays.

DANGERS & ANNOYANCES

By all accounts, Berlin is among the safest and most tolerant of European cities. Walking alone at night on city streets isn't usually dangerous for anyone, bearing in mind the caveat that there is always safety in numbers in any urban environment.

Despite some bad press, racial attacks are quite infrequent in Germany and in Berlin. Having said that, while people of any skin colour are usually safe in the central districts, prejudice towards foreigners and gays is more likely to rear its ugly head in the outlying eastern districts like Marzahn and Lichtenberg, where unemployment and a general dissatisfaction with post-Wende society are rampant. In order to report a racially motivated attack, telephone the SOS-Rassismus hotline at ☎ 200 25 40 or ☎ 251 2277. No matter what skin colour you are, if you see any 'white skins' (skinheads wearing jackboots with white boot laces) run the other way – and fast.

Berlin has an estimated 5000 prostitutes who are harmless but annoying with their solicitations. On Friday and Saturday nights the Ku'damm is crawling with day-tripping Polish whores. Other stomping grounds after dark include Oranienburger Strasse, Kurfürstenstrasse, Lietzenburger Strasse, Strasse des 17 Juni and Stuttgarter Platz.

What To Do In An Emergency

If there is an emergency which requires police attention, call ☎ 110. Otherwise, there are police stations all over the city, including the City-Wache (Map 7) at Joachimstaler Strasse 14-19 just south of Zoo station, and the station at Jägerstrasse 48 in Mitte (Map 8). For mishaps on trains, your first recourse should be the *Bahnpolizei* with offices at all major stations.

The general emergency number for the fire brigade *(Feuerwehr)* throughout Berlin is ☎ 112.

Police headquarters (Map 6, ☎ 69 90) and the municipal lost & found office (Map 6, ☎ 69 95) are at Platz der Luftbrücke 6 beside Tempelhof airport. The latter is open from 7.30 am to 2 pm Monday and Tuesday, noon to 6.30 pm Wednesday and 7.30 am till noon on Friday. If you've lost something on public transport, contact the BVG (Map 3, ☎ 25 62 30 40) at Fraunhofer Strasse 33-36 (9th floor, room No 119) from 9 am to 6 pm Monday to Thursday, until 2 pm Friday. The Deutsche Bahn lost & found office (☎ 29 72 96) is at Mittelstrasse 20 at Schönefeld S-Bahn station and is open from 10 am to 4 pm Monday to Wednesday, until 6 pm Thursday, and 8 am to noon Friday.

The German auto club ADAC (☎ 868 60) has an office at Bundesallee 29 in Wilmersdorf. Their emergency helpline is on ☎ 01802-22 22 22; assistance is free to members of ADAC or any of its foreign affiliates.

A fairly new service is the American Hotline (mobile ☎ 0177-814 15 10) which provides free referrals for people in need of psychological, medical, social or legal help. You don't have to be American to use it.

Prostitution as such isn't the problem, but often these areas aren't safe because they also attract pimps and junkies.

Drugs should be generally avoided for obvious reasons but also because a lot of the stuff going around is distributed by mafia-like organisations and is often stretched and thus dangerously impure.

Most U/S-Bahn platforms are equipped with electronic information and emergency devices labelled 'SOS/Notruf/Information' and illustrated with a large red bell. If you require emergency assistance, push the 'SOS' button. The Information button allows you to speak directly with one of the station masters. Fierce-looking private guards accompanied by even fiercer-looking muzzled dogs occasionally ride along in U-Bahn trains and are a convincing deterrent. If you're riding an S-Bahn train to the outer – especially eastern – districts late at night, stay in the compartment right behind the driver which is usually the safest.

Very annoying but not usually dangerous are the many panhandlers, often positioned at U-Bahn exits. The days when beggars sat passively on the pavement with a hat before them are a thing of the past. The new millennium bum can be quite aggressive and tends to unleash a tirade of dissatisfaction with life, wife and government on anyone who fails to hand over some cash. At night in restaurants you'll be swarmed by vendors of roses or kitschy plastic toys. They're a pain but harmless and will move away as soon as you indicate lack of interest.

Also irritating *in extremis* are the security staff at most Berlin museums, who follow you from room to room and watch your every move lest you breathe too close to a Picasso or touch the pharaoh's death mask (God forbid).

LEGAL MATTERS

The police in Berlin are well trained, fairly 'enlightened' and usually treat tourists with respect. Most members of the police force can speak some English. By German law, you must carry some form of picture ID like your passport, a national identity card or a driving licence. Reporting theft to the police is a simple, if occasionally time-consuming, matter. The first thing you will have to do, however, is show your passport or identity card.

Drivers should carry a driving licence and obey road rules carefully. Occasionally, you may find yourself caught in a 'mousetrap', temporary spot-check stations set up randomly by police. Pull over immediately if signalled to do so. You will be asked to show your driver's licence and registration papers and may be subjected to an alcohol test.

Penalties for drinking and driving are stiff. The highest permissible blood-alcohol level is 0.05% nationwide. If you are caught with higher alcohol blood levels, your licence will be confiscated immediately and a court then decides within three days whether or not you get it back. The same applies if you are involved in an accident with a blood-alcohol level exceeding 0.03%, regardless of whether or not the accident was your fault.

Drug possession is illegal in Germany, but in liberal Berlin laws are not always strictly enforced. Carrying small amounts (less than 10 grams) of hash or grass for personal consumption will not usually be prosecuted. The same cannot be said for harder drugs like heroin, cocaine or crack cocaine, possession of which results not just in considerable fines but may let you make the acquaintance of a Berlin jail as well.

German political demonstrations can quickly take on a violent character, especially when the *Autonomen*, a left-wing anarchist group, is involved. In Berlin, major demonstrations by this group have been known to escalate into violent riots. Most take place on the 1 May holiday and are usually centred in Kreuzberg and Prenzlauer Berg. Police will often seal off side streets and entire blocks and ask passers-by to prove their identity. It's a good idea to avoid such demonstrations.

Should you need legal representation, call your embassy or the 24-hour emergency lawyer hotline on ☎ 324 22 82 for a referral.

BUSINESS HOURS

Official shop trading hours in Germany were liberalised a few years ago and are now from 7 am to 8 pm on weekdays and to 4 pm on Saturday. Bakeries may sell fresh rolls for three hours on Sunday morning and cake for a couple of hours in the afternoon. Consumer interest in this development has been mixed. In central Berlin, it has been widely welcomed and most stores are open for the maximum hours. In the outer suburbs, however, retail stores have gone back to the old system of closing at 6 pm on weekdays and 1 or 2 pm on Saturday. Exceptions are supermarkets and department stores. In suburban areas and smaller towns in Brandenburg, you'll also find that many stores close for two or three hours at lunchtime.

Most larger train stations have a supermarket or general goods store that's open until at least 9 or 10 pm. Petrol stations are also convenient – if expensive – places to stock up on basic food and drink when everything else is closed.

Banking hours are generally from 8.30 am to 1 pm and from 2.30 to 4 pm Monday to Friday (many stay open to 6 pm on Thursday), though many banks in Berlin's centre stay open throughout the day. Travel agencies and other offices are usually open from 9 am to 6 pm weekdays and til noon on Saturday. Government offices, though, close for the weekend as early as 1 pm on Friday. Opening hours for museums vary greatly, though most are closed on Monday.

PUBLIC HOLIDAYS & SPECIAL EVENTS

National public holidays in Berlin include: New Year's Day *(Neujahrstag)*, Good Friday *(Karfreitag)*, Easter Sunday *(Ostersonntag)*, Easter Monday *(Ostermontag)*, Labour Day on 1 May *(Tag der Arbeit)*, Ascension Day *(Christi Himmelfahrt)*, Whit Sunday (Pentecost) and Whit Monday *(Pfingstsonntag and Pfingstmontag)*, Reunification Day on 3 October *(Tag der Wiedervereinigung)*, and Christmas and Boxing/St Stephen's Day *(erster und zweiter Weihnachtstag)*.

Shops, banks, public offices etc are closed on these holidays, though you may find some stores open at the larger train stations. Cinemas, theatres, nightclubs and other entertainment venues, though, are usually in session. Museums, sights and other attractions are most likely closed on 24, 25, 26 and 31 of December as well as on 1 January. Restaurants are open except on December 24 and 25.

Berlin's calendar is filled with an interesting collection of cultural events, festivals and fairs. For additional events relating to the gay and lesbian scene, see the Entertainment chapter.

January
Internationale Grüne Woche (International Green Week)
Officially a week-long consumer fair for food, agriculture and gardening, it's actually more like an excuse for hopping from booth to booth gorging on exotic morsels from around the world. It's held at the ICC trade fair centre; for information call ☎ 303 80.

Schauplatz Museum (Museum Showcase)
A month-long showcase of theatre performances, concerts, readings, films, lectures and discussions enlivening Berlin's museums. Includes the 'Lange Nacht der Museen' (Long Night of the Museums) when many exhibits stay open until well after midnight. For information call ☎ 28 39 74 44.

February
Internationale Filmfestspiele Berlin (International Film Festival Berlin)
Also known as Berlinale, this is Germany's answer to the Cannes and Venice film festivals and attracts its own stable of stars (few) and starlets (plenty), directors and critics from around the world. About 750 films are shown in a two-week span at various theatres around town. Check listings in newspapers or the entertainment magazines *Zitty* and *tip* for details. Many performances are quickly sold out, so check the schedule as soon as you can, then call the cinema for ticket availability. Tickets can be bought at the theatres and at ticket offices. For information call ☎ 25 48 90.

March
Internationale Tourismus Börse or ITB (International Travel Fair)
The largest travel show in the world takes over the ICC trade fair centre in early March with international exhibitors showing off their country's attractions. It's a good place to come for ideas for your next trip. For information call ☎ 303 80.

April
Festtage (Festival Days)
An annual series of gala concerts and operas under the auspices of the Staatsoper Unter den Linden which brings renowned conductors, soloists and orchestras to Berlin for 10 days.

euro currency converter DM1 = €.51

Concerts are held at the Philharmonie concert hall, operas are at held at the opera house. For information call ☎ 20 35 44 81.

May

Karnival der Kulturen
(Carnival of Cultures)
Berlin's answer to London's Notting Hill Carnival, this is a lively street festival with a parade of whacky costumed people dancing and playing music on floats. Information is available on ☎ 622 20 24.

Theatertreffen Berlin
(Theatre Meeting Berlin)
Three weeks of the latest productions from new and established German-language ensembles from Germany, Austria and Switzerland. It's held at various venues around town; for information call ☎ 25 48 90.

June

Christopher Street Day
The city's biggest annual gay party, in late June, is centred around a street parade from Savignyplatz in Charlottenburg to Unter den Linden in Mitte.

July

Classic Open Air
A series of classical concerts held al fresco on the Gendarmenmarkt in early July. Information at ☎ 843 73 50.

Love Parade
Berlin's top annual techno event, held in mid-July, attracted 1.5 million people in 1999. The parade is followed by nonstop partying in clubs and bars. Information is available on ☎ 390 66 60.

August

Lange Nacht der Museen
(Long Night of the Museums)
The summer version of the January event. Concerts, readings and plays provide additional entertainment. Information is on ☎ 20 24 00.

Lindenfest (Linden Tree Festival)
Another street festival held at Unter den Linden between Wilhelmstrasse and Schlossbrücke with concerts, cabaret and booths featuring traditional arts, crafts and food. Call ☎ 252 16 89 for information.

September

Berliner Festwochen
(Berlin Festival Weeks)
A month-long celebration featuring concerts, exhibits, plays and other cultural events with a particular focus (eg the Berlin Airlift in 1998,

Gustav Mahler in 1999). Information is available on ☎ 25 48 90.

October

Aaa
An international car exhibition held at the ICC trade fair centre.

Art forum Berlin
An international art fair hosted by Berlin's leading gallery owners. Information on ☎ 303 80.

November

JazzFest Berlin
Top-rated jazz festival with performances held at venues throughout the city. Information on ☎ 25 48 91 00.

December

Weihnachtsmärkte (Christmas markets)
Christmas markets are held from late November to around 21 December at several locations around Berlin, including Breitscheidplatz (Map 7, 10 am to 9 or 10 pm daily); Alexanderplatz (Map 8, 1 to 10 pm daily); and the Marktplatz in Spandau (9 am to 7 pm daily). The outlying district of Köpenick sets up stalls from mid-December around the town hall (from noon to 8 pm weekdays, from 10 am to 8 pm weekends).

DOING BUSINESS

With the world's third largest economy, Germany has long been Europe's most important address for doing business. And given that Berlin is once again the country's capital – and that enormous funds are pouring in to make the city a corporate showcase on a level with London and New York – the city's profile as a business centre is expected to skyrocket.

Of all German cities, Berlin has the highest concentration of English speakers, which makes getting around – and getting down to business – a great deal easier. Before you arrive, contact the trade or commercial office of the German embassy in your country, which can provide you with valuable assistance. The German Ministry of Economics publishes a thorough English-language reference manual entitled *Doing Business in Germany: A Contact List for U.S. Firms*. Although ostensibly geared towards US business, the trade and development agencies throughout Germany listed here should prove useful to anyone. Free copies may be obtained by writing to Bundesministerium für Wirtschaft, Scharnhorststrasse 36, 10115 Berlin (☎ 20 14 77 51, fax 20 14 70 36)

Berlin in Your Pocket (DM20) is an informal basic primer on how to survive and make the most of your time in the city. It's filled with such practicalities as tips on housing, hiring, taxes, networking, vital phone numbers and relocating in general. It's available at bookshops, including the British Bookshop (Map 8, ☎ 238 46 80) at Mauerstrasse 83-84 in Mitte.

Business Services

Regus Business Centers provide the full range of turn-key business operations (such as office rental, secretarial services, convention organisation and telecom needs, including video conferencing). They have a reputation for being price-conscious, reliable and service-oriented. Their most central office is near Zoo station at Kurfürstendamm 11 (☎ 88 44 11 00, fax 88 44 15 20); check the Yellow Pages for other branches.

Full-service copy shops are found around the city, but for some reason there's a cluster of them near U-Bahn station Eisenacher Strasse in Schöneberg. Copyhaus has two branches on Grunewaldstrasse at No 18 and 78 (Map 5, ☎ 235 53 80) and is open from 8 am to midnight Monday to Saturday and from 1 to 9 pm on Sunday. The staff tend to be on the snobbish side. Cheaper and friendlier for basic copy and print needs is Kopier Blitz nearby at Akazienstrasse 15 (Map 5, ☎/fax 782 49 11). Pro Business (Map 5, ☎ 499 78 50) at Maassenstrasse 7 is a full-service digital printing and copy store, open from 9 am to 10 pm weekdays, from 10 am to 4 pm Saturday and from 1 to 9 pm Sunday.

Most larger hotels offer the usual business services such as fax and Internet connections, though at inflated prices. Translation services include those of Scharpe & Ahrend (☎ 85 99 91 80), at Perelsplatz 18 in Friedenau. To rent audiovisual equipment such as projectors and sound systems you might try General Audio & Television Equipment (☎ 393 44 00) at Alt-Moabit 91d.

Exhibitions & Conferences

If you're planning a larger event in Berlin, your first contact should be Berlin Tourismus Marketing (BTM, ☎ 264 74 80, fax 26 47 48 99) at Am Karlsbad 11 in Tiergarten. Their 88-page publication *Meeting and Incentive in Berlin* (in English and German) provides a detailed overview of available facilities and services. The ICC Berlin (Internationales Congress Centrum Berlin) in western Charlottenburg is the city's major conference space (Map 5, ☎ 30 38 30 49, fax 30 38 30 32).

WORK

Given Germany's four million plus unemployed, chances of finding (legal) work in Berlin as a foreigner are slim to none. Nationals from EU countries don't need a work permit and basically enjoy the same rights as Germans. However, they do need an EU residency permit *(EU-Aufenthaltserlaubnis)* from the local authority, which is just a formality.

All others must apply for a work permit at the *Arbeitsamt* (Employment Office) and for a residency permit at the *Ausländerbehörde* (Foreigners' Office), a tedious process to say the least. Special conditions apply to citizens of so-called 'recognised third countries', including the USA, Canada, Australia, New Zealand, Japan, Israel and Switzerland. Citizens of these countries who have a firm job offer are usually granted the necessary permits, providing the job cannot be filled by a German or EU citizen.

You can begin your job search either before leaving home or on arrival in Germany. You must be well qualified and be able to back up your skills with an impressive array of certificates: Germans place great importance on formal qualifications. Once you receive a firm offer, the Arbeitsamt checks that the position cannot otherwise be filled, then issues a work permit specific to that position.

The Arbeitsamt also operates an electronic database of vacant positions and can help with finding part-time work. Temp agencies are another option, with ADIA (☎ 884 10 00), at Ku'damm 220, being one of the largest. The Saturday edition of the *Berliner Zeitung*, the *taz* and the Sunday edition of the *Berliner Morgenpost* are also good places to start looking.

Work as an au pair is relatively easy to find and there are numerous approved au pair agencies you can approach. *The Au Pair and Nanny's Guide to Working Abroad* (Vacation Work), by Susan Griffith & Sharon Legg, will help. *Work Your Way Around the World*, also by Susan Griffith and published by Vacation Work, is another suggestion.

In these days of record postwar unemployment, authorities are cracking down on illegal workers, especially on building sites, where raids are fairly common. You are also unlikely to make friends among your German colleagues, who will see you as a threat to their wage and work conditions. Busking is always an option, but be aware that Germans often equate it with begging.

Getting There & Away

If you live outside Europe, flying is the easiest way to get to Berlin. Even if you're already in Europe, a flight may still be the fastest and cheapest option, especially from faraway places like Greece, Spain or southern Italy. Otherwise, train travel is the most efficient and comfortable form of transport in Germany, though buses are a viable, and often cheaper, alternative from some capital cities. Keep in mind that, no matter which method of transport you choose, seats fill up quickly and prices often increase considerably during summer school holidays.

AIR

There are hardly any direct flights to Berlin from overseas and, depending on the airline you use, you're likely to fly first into another European city like Frankfurt, Amsterdam, Paris or London, then catch a connecting flight. If you can't get a connecting flight, or it is too expensive, you might consider taking the train instead. From Frankfurt, for instance, hourly Inter-City Express (ICE) trains make the direct journey to Berlin in just under five hours, with a 2nd-class one-way ticket costing DM180. If you're flying into Düsseldorf, there's at least one train an hour headed for Berlin. The trip takes 5¼ hours and costs DM162, unless you're using the ICE train in which case the journey takes four hours and costs DM181.

Buying Tickets

If you're flying to Berlin from outside Europe, the air fare will be the biggest expense in your budget. Before buying your ticket, it's worth putting aside a few hours to research the current state of the market.

Start early as some of the cheapest tickets must be bought months in advance, and popular flights sell out early. Ask other travellers for recommendations, look at the ads in newspapers and magazines (including those catering specifically for the German community in your country), consult reference books and watch for special offers. Then phone several agents for bargains. Find out the fare, the route, how long the ticket is valid and any restrictions that may apply.

Cheap tickets are available in two distinct categories: official and unofficial. Official ones have a variety of names including advance-purchase tickets, advance-purchase excursion (Apex) fares, super-Apex and simply budget fares.

Unofficial discount tickets are released by the airlines through selected travel agents, and it's worth shopping around to find them. If you call the airlines directly, they will almost never quote you the cheapest fares available. In most cases, a return ticket works out cheaper than two one-way tickets.

The cheapest rates to Berlin from the UK, the USA or South-East Asia may often be advertised by obscure agencies whose names haven't yet reached the telephone directory. Many such firms are honest and solvent, but there are a few rogues who will take your money and disappear, to reopen elsewhere a month or two later under a new name. If you feel suspicious, or they insist on full cash payment in advance, go somewhere else or be prepared to take a big risk. Once you have the ticket, ring the airline to confirm that you are actually booked onto the flight.

You may decide to pay more than the rock-bottom fare in favour of the safety of a better-known travel agent. Firms such as STA Travel and Council Travel (with offices worldwide), Travel CUTS in Canada and Flight Centres International in Australia are not going to disappear overnight.

Always make a photocopy of your ticket and keep it somewhere separate. This will simplify getting a replacement in case of loss or theft.

Round-the-world (RTW) tickets are often real bargains and can work out to be no more expensive – or even cheaper – than an ordinary return ticket. Official airline RTW tickets are usually offered by a combination of two or more airlines and permit you to

Air Travel Glossary

Cancellation Penalties If you have to cancel or change a discounted ticket, there are often heavy penalties involved; insurance can sometimes be taken out against these penalties. Some airlines impose penalties on regular tickets as well, particularly against 'no-show' passengers.

Courier Fares Businesses often need to send urgent documents or freight securely and quickly. Courier companies hire people to accompany the package through customs and, in return, offer a discount ticket which is sometimes a phenomenal bargain. However, you may have to surrender all your baggage allowance and take only carry-on luggage.

Full Fares Airlines traditionally offer 1st class (coded F), business class (coded J) and economy class (coded Y) tickets. These days there are so many promotional and discounted fares available that few passengers pay full economy fare.

Lost Tickets If you lose your airline ticket an airline will usually treat it like a travellers cheque and, after inquiries, issue you with another one. Legally, however, an airline is entitled to treat it like cash and if you lose it then it's gone forever. Take good care of your tickets.

Onward Tickets An entry requirement for many countries is that you have a ticket out of the country. If you're unsure of your next move, the easiest solution is to buy the cheapest onward ticket to a neighbouring country or a ticket from a reliable airline which can later be refunded if you do not use it.

Open-Jaw Tickets These are return tickets where you fly out to one place but return from another. If available, this can save you backtracking to your arrival point.

Overbooking Since every flight has some passengers who fail to show up, airlines often book more passengers than they have seats. Usually excess passengers make up for the no-shows, but occasionally somebody gets 'bumped' onto the next available flight. Guess who it is most likely to be? The passengers who check in late.

Promotional Fares These are officially discounted fares, available from travel agencies or direct from the airline.

Reconfirmation If you don't reconfirm your flight at least 72 hours prior to departure, the airline may delete your name from the passenger list. Ring to find out if your airline requires reconfirmation.

Restrictions Discounted tickets often have various restrictions on them – such as needing to be paid for in advance and incurring a penalty to be altered. Others are restrictions on the minimum and maximum period you must be away.

Round-the-World Tickets RTW tickets give you a limited period (usually a year) in which to circumnavigate the globe. You can go anywhere the carrying airlines go, as long as you don't backtrack. The number of stopovers or total number of separate flights is decided before you set off and they usually cost a bit more than a basic return flight.

Transferred Tickets Airline tickets cannot be transferred from one person to another. Travellers sometimes try to sell the return half of their ticket, but officials can ask you to prove that you are the person named on the ticket. On an international flight tickets are compared with passports.

Travel Periods Ticket prices vary with the time of year. There is a low (off-peak) season and a high (peak) season, and often a low-shoulder season and a high-shoulder season as well. Usually the fare depends on your outward flight – if you depart in the high season and return in the low season, you pay the high-season fare.

fly anywhere you want on their route systems so long as you do not backtrack. Other restrictions are that you usually must book the first sector in advance (cancellation penalties then apply). There may be restrictions on how many stops (or km/miles) you are permitted. Usually the tickets are valid for 90 days up to a year from the date of the first outbound flight.

Prices start at about UK£800/US$1300/ A$1700, depending on the season and length of validity. An alternative type of RTW ticket is one put together by a travel agent using a combination of discounted tickets. These can be much cheaper than the official ones but will normally carry more restrictions.

Travellers with Special Needs

If you have special needs of any sort – you're vegetarian or require a special diet, you're travelling in a wheelchair, taking the baby, terrified of flying, whatever – let the airline know early so that staff can make the necessary arrangements. Remind them when you reconfirm your booking (at least 72 hours before departure) and again when you check in at the airport. It may also be worth ringing several airlines before you make your booking to find out how each would handle your particular needs.

With advance warning, airports and airlines can be surprisingly helpful. Most international airports provide escorts from check-in desk to plane where needed, and there should be ramps, lifts, accessible toilets and reachable phones. Aircraft toilets, on the other hand, are likely to present a problem. Travellers should discuss this with the airline at an early stage and, if necessary, with their doctor.

Guide dogs for the blind will often have to travel in a specially pressurised baggage compartment with other animals away from their owner, though smaller guide dogs may be admitted to the cabin. Deaf travellers can ask for airport and in-flight announcements to be written down for them.

Children aged under two travel for 10% of the full fare (or free on some airlines) as long as they don't occupy a seat. They don't get a baggage allowance in this case. 'Skycots', baby food and nappies (diapers) should be provided by the airline if requested in advance. Prams and strollers can often be taken on as hand luggage.

Children aged between two and 12 can usually occupy a seat for half to two-thirds of the full fare. They do get a standard baggage allowance.

Departure Tax

Departure taxes and airport security fees are included in the price of any airline ticket purchased in Germany. You should not have to pay any more fees at the airport. There's no tax if you depart by sea or land.

Other Parts of Germany

Scheduled domestic flights connect Berlin to all major German airports and vice versa, usually via Tempelhof and Tegel airports. Predictably, Lufthansa (☎ 0180-380 38 03) is the main operator, though there's also services offered by Eurowings (☎ 68 51 28 33); Deutsche BA (☎ 01803-34 03 40 or ☎ 69 10 21), a subsidiary of British Airways; and LTU (☎ 0180-520 65).

The UK

London is the discount-flight capital of Europe and finding a cheap air fare to Berlin should not be a problem. The main airlines serving Berlin are British Airways and Lufthansa, with several flights daily. For the latest fares, check out the travel page ads of the Sunday newspapers, *Time Out*, *TNT* and *Exchange & Mart*. All are available at newsstands. Another good source of information on cheap fares is the magazine *Business Traveller*.

Bucket shops abound in London. They generally offer the cheapest tickets, though usually with restricted validity. However, many may not be registered with the ABTA (Association of British Travel Agents), which guarantees a refund or an alternative if you have paid for your flight and the agent goes out of business.

One of the more reliable, although not necessarily cheapest, agencies is STA (☎ 0171-361 6161 for European flights),

euro currency converter DM1 = €.51

which has several London branches, including at 86 Old Brompton Rd, London SW7 3LQ.

Trailfinders (☎ 0171-937 5400 for European bookings) is a similar operation whose London office is at 215 Kensington High St specialises in short-haul flights. Their head office at 194 Kensington High St has a travel library, bookshop, visa service and immunisation centre. Other Trailfinders branches are in Bristol, Birmingham, Glasgow and Manchester.

Another agency worth trying is Campus Travel with several London branches, including one at 52 Grosvenor Gardens, London SW1W OAG (☎ 0171-730 3402 for European flights).

Continental Europe

Discount flights to Berlin are available from many major cities in Continental Europe. Sometimes it may actually be cheaper – and faster – to catch a plane than to use ground transport, especially on longer journeys.

Smaller regional airlines, like Eurowings, are a good alternative to national carriers. They specialise in inexpensive short hops, often from regional airports that may be more convenient than the big hubs. Full-time students and those under 26 occasionally qualify for special discount rates.

The USA

Flights to Germany from major cities in the USA abound, though only Lufthansa and Delta have direct flights into Berlin. Lufthansa connects Frankfurt with Chicago, New York, Los Angeles and other major US cities. American carriers serving Frankfurt include American Airlines, Delta and United Airlines. There are also direct flights to other German cities, including LTU's flights to Düsseldorf from Los Angeles. Generally, though, flights to Frankfurt are the cheapest.

The *New York Times*, the *Los Angeles Times*, the *Chicago Tribune*, the *San Francisco Examiner* and many other major Sunday newspapers produce weekly travel sections in which you'll find lots of travel agents' advertisements.

Air fares rise and fall in a cyclical pattern. The lowest fares are available from early November to mid-December and then again from mid-January to Easter, gradually rising in the following months. Peak months are July and August, after which prices start dropping again.

Standard fares on commercial airlines are expensive and best avoided, especially since various types of discounts on scheduled flights are usually available.

In winter, round-trip tickets to Frankfurt may cost as little as US$300 from New York, US$350 from Chicago and US$400 from Los Angeles. In summer, tickets average US$700 from New York, US$850 from Chicago and US$950 from Los Angeles.

Council Travel (☎ 800-226 8624) and STA Travel (☎ 800-777 0112) are reliable budget travel agencies with offices throughout the USA. Call or check their Web sites for the branch nearest you. Council Travel's Web address is www.counciltravel.com while STA's is www.sta-travel.com.

If you're feeling particularly enterprising, try Priceline (☎ 800-774 2354 63), an auction-based booking system for flights. It works like this: you tell them how much you want to pay for a return flight and provide the dates and your credit card number. If an airline's offer matches or undercuts your bid, Priceline automatically books the flight and charges your account. The catch – and it's a big one – is that tickets are non-exchangeable and non-refundable and you may end up flying at odd times on odd airlines. For more details or to submit a bid see Priceline's Web site at www.priceline.com.

Stand-by Fares These tickets are often sold at 60% of the standard price for one-way tickets. You need to have a general idea of departure dates and destination and will usually be presented with a choice of flights a few days before departure. Flights available may not get you exactly to where you want to go, but the savings are so huge that you might opt for an onward train or bus.

New York-based Airhitch specialises in stand-by tickets between the USA and Europe. They're very cheap with one-way flights from the US east coast to Europe costing just US$159 (US$239 from the west coast). Service can be terrible, though, especially at their European partner offices, which you will need to work with in order to get back. Staff there are often poorly informed, unhelpful and sometimes don't speak intelligible English. Flight selection is greatest to/from the east coast, with connections to the west coast limited to just two airlines and three flights a week.

Airhitch has offices in New York (☎ 800-326 2009 or ☎ 212-864 2000), Los Angeles (☎ 800-397 1098 or ☎ 310-726 5000) and San Francisco (☎ 800-834 9192 or ☎ 415-834 9192). Its Web address is www.airhitch. org. Another outlet providing pretty much the same service is Air-Tech in New York (☎ 212-219 7000). Its Web site can be found at www.airtech.com.

Courier Flights Travelling as a courier means that you accompany freight to its destination. You don't have to handle any shipment personally, either at departure or arrival, and most likely will not even get to see it. All you need to do is carry an envelope containing the freight papers with you on board and hand it to someone at your destination. The freight takes the place of your check-in luggage, so you will be restricted to what you are allowed to carry on the plane. You may have to be a US resident and present yourself in person before the company will take you on. Also keep in mind that only a relatively small number of these tickets is available, so it's best to call two or three months in advance and be somewhat flexible with departure dates.

Major US gateways are Los Angeles, Chicago and New York and a New York-Frankfurt return ticket may cost as little as US$100 in the low season. Generally, you are required to return within a specified period (sometimes within one or two weeks, but often up to one month). The best source for courier flights is Worldwide Courier Association (☎ 800-780 4359 or ☎ 716-464 9020), at 757 W Main St, Rochester, NY 14611. Its comprehensive Web site is at www.wallstech.com.

Canada

Air Canada has direct flights into Berlin-Schönefeld. Travel CUTS (☎ 888-838 2877), which specialises in discount fares for students, has offices in all major cities. Also check the travel sections of the *Globe & Mail*, the *Toronto Star* and the *Vancouver Sun* for travel agents' ads. For courier flights contact FB On Board Courier Services (☎ 514-633 0740 in Toronto or ☎ 604-338 1366 in Vancouver).

Australia

STA Travel and Flight Centres International are major dealers in cheap air fares, though your local travel agent may also offer some heavily discounted fares. Check the Saturday travel sections of the *Sydney Morning Herald* and Melbourne's *Age*. But don't be surprised if they happen to be 'sold out' when you contact the agents (who then offer you a more expensive fare) or if they turn out to be low-season fares on obscure airlines with lots of conditions attached.

Discounted return air fares on major airlines through reputable agents can be surprisingly cheap, with low-season fares around A$1399 and high-season fares up to A$2300. The following are agencies selling tickets at good-value prices:

Flight Centres International
    Martin Place Flight Centre
    (☎ 02-9235 0166) Shop 5, State Bank Centre, 52 Martin Place, Sydney, NSW 2000
    Bourke Street Flight Centre
    (☎ 03-9650 2899) 19 Bourke St, Melbourne, Vic 3000
    City Flight Centre
    (☎ 09-325 9222) 25 Cinema City Arcade, Perth, WA 6000
STA Travel
    (☎ 02-9411 6888) Shop 17, 3-9 Spring St, Chatswood, Sydney, NSW 2067
    (☎ 03-9349 2411) 222 Faraday St, Carlton, Vic 3053
    (☎ 08-9380 2302) 1st Floor, New Guild Building, University of Western Australia, Crawley, Perth, WA 6009

New Zealand

STA Travel and Flight Centres International are popular travel agents in New Zealand as

GETTING THERE & AWAY

well. The cheapest fares to Europe are routed through the USA, and a RTW ticket may be cheaper than a simple return. Air New Zealand has flights from Auckland to Frankfurt, either with a stopover in Asia or in Los Angeles. Otherwise, you can fly to Melbourne or Sydney to pick up a connecting flight. Useful agencies include:

Campus Travel
 (☎ 07-838 42 42) Gate 1, Knighton Rd, Waikato University, Hamilton
Flight Centres International
 Auckland Flight Centre
 (☎ 09-309 6171) Shop 3A, National Bank Towers, 205-225 Queen St, Auckland
STA Travel
 (☎ 09-307 0555) 2nd Floor, Student Union Bldg, Princes St, Auckland University, Auckland

Airline Offices

Berlin's Lufthansa city centre office (Map 7, ☎ 88 75 38 00) is at Kurfürstendamm 220. The 24-hour central reservation number is ☎ 0180-380 38 03. The Lufthansa number at Tegel airport is ☎ 88 75 61 27. Contact numbers for other airlines serving Berlin airports include:

Aeroflot
 ☎ 226 98 10
Air Canada
 ☎ 882 58 79
Air France
 ☎ 01805-36 03 70
British Airways/Deutsche BA
 ☎ 41 01 26 47
Buzz Airlines
 ☎ 0695 007 01 33
Delta Airlines
 ☎ 0180-333 78 80
El Al
 ☎ 201 77 90
KLM
 ☎ 01805-21 42 01 or ☎ 41 01 38 44
LOT Polish Airlines
 ☎ 261 15 05
Malév Hungarian Airlines
 ☎ 264 95 45
Swissair
 ☎ 01805-25 85 75

TRAIN

With the completion date of the futuristic Lehrter Bahnhof pushed back well into this decade, the bulk of train travel will continue to be borne by Bahnhof Zoo in the western city centre and Ostbahnhof in the eastern centre. Many of the long-distance trains stop at both. Depending on your final destination, you may find that services arriving at one station link with services leaving from another. To connect, take the U-Bahn or S-Bahn (DM3.90), but allow ample time for transfer. If you have a train ticket to or from Berlin – or a rail pass – you may use it to travel on the S-Bahn network (but not the U-Bahn) for free.

For ticket and timetable information (available in English) by telephone you can ring ☎ 01805-99 66 33 from anywhere in Germany for DM0.24 per minute. The same information is available on the Internet at www.bahn.de (look for the link to 'International Guests').

Bahnhof Zoologischer Garten

Bahnhof Zoo (or Zoo station) is where most visitors to Berlin first arrive. It's also the station with the best infrastructure and the one you're most likely to use even if you're not travelling anywhere. Besides featuring shops and restaurants with extended hours, there are coin lockers for DM2 or DM4; the left-luggage office (open from 5 am to 11 pm) charges DM4 per item per day.

The large Deutsche Bahn Reisezentrum (ticket reservation and information office) is open from 5.15 am to 11 pm. Outside the main entrance on Hardenbergplatz is the BVG local transport information kiosk (Map 7), where you can get maps, information and tickets. In the back of the main hall, in the basement, is an establishment called McWash which has spic-and-span toilets (DM1.50) and shower facilities (DM10).

Next to McWash is the EurAide office, an excellent one-stop service station for English-speaking travellers. Staff can help with buying the right train ticket, making a seat reservation or finding a place to stay. Summer hours are from 8 am to noon and 1 and 6 pm daily (to 4.30 pm from 30 September through the winter months).

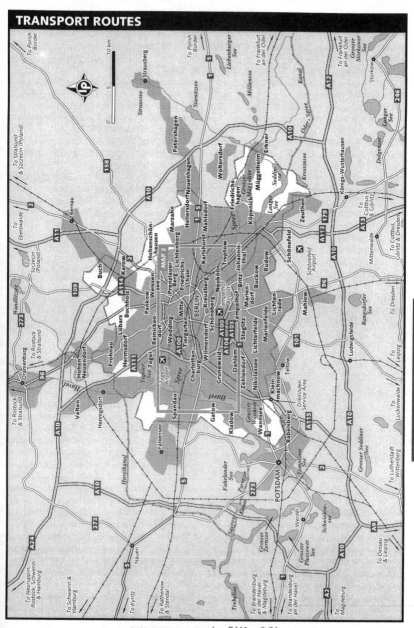

TRANSPORT ROUTES

Other Parts of Germany

The German train system is justifiably known as the most efficient in Europe. There are more than 41,000km of track serving over 7000 cities and towns throughout the country. All trains have 1st and 2nd class compartments.

Bahnhof Zoo is the main station for long-distance trains to cities west of Berlin, including Hanover, Frankfurt and Cologne. There are also frequent services to Hamburg and Munich and a direct train to Leipzig. Ostbahnhof handles regional services around Brandenburg, Saxony and, less so, Mecklenburg-Western Pomerania.

Berlin's other main station is Bahnhof Lichtenberg on Weitlingstrasse in the district of Lichtenberg. This is the hub for trains to Stralsund, Rostock and other cities in Mecklenburg-Western Pomerania, as well as services to Cottbus, Dresden, Erfurt, Halle and Magdeburg.

Train Types

The Deutsche Bahn (DB) operates several types of trains:

InterCity Express (ICE) – long-distance space-age bullet train, stops at major cities only

InterCity (IC) & EuroCity (EC) – long-distance trains almost as fast as the ICE, stop at major cities only

InterRegio (IR) – long-distance trains with more frequent stops than ICs

RegionalBahn (RB) – local trains in rural areas with frequent stops

Regional Express (RE) – regional trains serving primarily rural areas

StadtExpress (SE) – regional trains primarily connecting cities

Stadtbahn (S-Bahn) – local trains operating within a city and its urban area

Buying Tickets

The best places to buy your tickets are train stations or at authorised travel agencies (look for the DB logo). Conductors also sell tickets at a surcharge of DM5 (DM10 in ICE trains). Most regional and local trains now operate without a conductor, requiring passengers to buy a ticket *before* boarding or else risk paying a fine. We highly recommend that you make reservations (DM5)

for long-distance travel, especially on ICE and IC trains and during holiday periods and in summer.

Costs

The average price of 2nd-class train travel throughout Germany is currently DM0.27 per km; for 1st class it's DM0.41 per km. Travelling on IC or EC trains requires a supplement ticket of DM7.

Though train travel in Germany is efficient, it's not necessarily cheap. Children, students and seniors qualify for reduced prices but if you're neither, and don't have a rail pass, you can cut costs by taking advantage of several special tickets and offers. If you have some flexibility, the following two offer mind-boggling savings:

Guten-Abend-Ticket
This ticket is valid for unlimited train travel from 7 pm until 2 am (from 2 pm Saturday). It costs DM59 in 2nd class (DM69 in 2nd class on an ICE train) and a DM15 surcharge applies on weekends.

Schönes-Wochenende-Ticket
This ticket allows you and up to four other people to travel anywhere in Germany from midnight Friday/Saturday until 2 am Monday for just DM35 (yes, that's five people for DM35!) The catch is that you have to use local trains and *not* ICE, IC, EC or IR trains. That's not so bad, though. It might take a while, but you can still get clear across the country on the slower trains.

German Rail Passes A Deutsche Bahn rail pass is available to non-Germans only and available through your travel agent or at major train stations in Germany (bring your passport). Passes are available for unlimited travel for four/seven/10 days within a one-month period. Regular rates are US$174/240/306 in 2nd class. If you're aged between 12 and 25, you qualify for the German Rail Youth Pass which costs US$138/174/239. Two adults travelling together should check out the German Rail Twin Pass for US$261/360/459.

Europe

Berlin is well connected through direct rail links to several other European countries.

Trains to Paris, Amsterdam and Brussels depart from Zoo station, while those headed to destinations east – like Moscow, Prague, Budapest and Vienna – leave from Bahnhof Lichtenberg. If you are planning on travelling to Berlin by train, check with your local travel agent for the best connections and ticket prices.

BUS

The Zentraler Omnibus Bahnhof (ZOB, Central Bus Station, Map 5), at Masurenallee 4-6 in Charlottenburg opposite the spindly Funkturm radio tower (U2 to Kaiserdamm or S45 to Witzleben), is open from 5.30 am to 10 pm. The travel agency here, Reisebüro ZOB (☎ 301 80 28 for information, ☎ 302 52 94 for reservations), is open from 9 am to 6 pm weekdays, to noon Saturday and is closed Sunday. Tickets may also be bought from other travel agencies and some ride-share agencies (*Mitfahrzentralen*). ZOB's left-luggage office is open from 5.30 am to 9.30 pm daily.

Other Parts of Germany

Berlin-based BerlinLinienBus (within Berlin ☎ 86 09 60, outside toll-free 0800-666 69 99) is the main company offering services within Germany. Their SuperSpar fares are available to anyone aged 13 to 26, students of any age and to seniors over 60. Details about BerlinLinienBus routes and services are available on the Web at www.berlinlinienbus.de (in German). Destinations within Germany, their frequencies (in the peak summer months), trip durations and SuperSpar and full fares include:

destination	frequency (weekly)	duration (hrs)	fare (DM)
Bremen	4	6½	56/99
			86/99
Düsseldorf	2	8¾	72/132
			120/132
Frankfurt/Main via Magdeburg & Göttingen	7	9¼	76/143
			110/143
Hamburg	7	3¼	41/57
			41/67
Hanover	daily	4½	35/67
			59/67
Leipzig	7	1½	20/38
			34/44
Munich	7	8½	76/139
			129/149
Rügen Island (including Binz, Sellin, Baabe & Göhren)	2	4¾	37/69
			55/99

Europe

In addition to BerlinLinienBus, Gullivers (☎ 311 02 11) also offers bus services to destinations outside of Germany. Their discounted fares apply to students and anyone under 26 or over 60. Bikes may be taken on for DM50/80 one way/return. On some routes, sleeper seats (practically full beds) are available for an extra DM10 to DM40. If you are outside Germany and want to buy tickets, call toll-free 00800-48 55 48 37. Gullivers' Web site address is www.gullivers.de (in German).

Czech Republic BerlinLinienBus makes overnight trips to Prague (6½ hours, DM55/90 for full fare or DM50/81 for SuperSpar fare), either direct or via Dresden. In Prague, tickets may be bought at Bohemia Euroexpress International (☎ 227-18549), at Konevova 126.

France BerlinLinienBus travels to Paris via Brussels daily in 14 hours for DM139/209 (full fare) or DM109/179 (SuperSpar). In Paris, it is represented by Eurolines (☎ 01-49 72 51 51), Gare Routière International de Paris-Galliéni, at 28 Ave du Général de Gaulle. Gullivers fares are identical but its buses make the trip in one hour less.

Netherlands Both Gullivers and BerlinLinienBus make daily trips to/from Amsterdam. The journey takes about nine hours, discounted fares are DM79/139, and full fares cost DM99/169. In Amsterdam, the Eurolines office (☎ 560 87 87) at Julianaplein 5 sells BerlinLinienBus tickets.

Poland BerlinLinienBus goes to Warsaw twice weekly in 11¼ hours and charges

GETTING THERE & AWAY

DM70/115 (full fare) or DM56/104 (Super-Spar). Their Warsaw representative is Pekaes Bus (☎ 621 34 69), ul Zurawia 26.

The UK BerlinLinienBus offers services to Victoria Station in London via Amsterdam or Brussels daily except Wednesday. The trip takes 21 hours and costs DM169/279 (full fare) or DM139/229 (SuperSpar). In London, buy tickets from Eurolines (☎ 01582-404 511) at 52 Grosvenor Gardens, Victoria, London SW1 OAU. Gullivers buses, which go via Brussels, are a bit faster (16½ hours) and about DM10 cheaper.

CAR & MOTORCYCLE
The A10 ring road links Berlin with other German and foreign cities in every direction, including the A11 to Szczecin (Stettin) in Poland; the A12 to Frankfurt/Oder; the A13 to Dresden; the A9 to Leipzig, Nuremberg and Munich; the A2 to Hanover and the Ruhrgebiet cities; and the A24 to Hamburg.

HITCHING
Lonely Planet does not encourage hitchhiking for all the obvious reasons. In Germany, it has also gone somewhat out of fashion with fewer people trying and fewer willing to pick them up.

If you're headed for Leipzig, Nuremberg, Munich and beyond, go to the Dreilinden service area on the A115. Take either the U1 to Krumme Lanke, then bus No 211 to Quantzstrasse, and walk down to the rest area. Alternatively, take the S1 or S7 to Wannsee, then bus Nos 113 or 211 to the Isoldestrasse stop. Bring a sign showing your destination in German and consider waiting until you find a car going right to where you want to go.

Those headed to Hamburg or Rostock should go to the former border checkpoint Stolpe by catching the U6 to Alt-Tegel, then bus No 224 to Stolpe.

Ride-Share Agencies
Berlin has several ride-share agencies (*Mitfahrzentralen*). Fares comprise a commission to the agency and a per-kilometre charge to the driver. Rides to Leipzig cost DM20 usually, to Frankfurt/Main DM51, Munich DM56, Cologne DM50, Budapest DM95 and Paris DM89, all including commission. Check the Web site www.mitfahrzentrale carnet.com for additional fares.

Agencies include ADM Mitfahrzentrale (Map 7, ☎ 194 40) at Zoo station on the Vinetastrasse platform of the U2. There's also a second branch (Map 8, ☎ 241 58 20) in the U-Bahn station Alexanderplatz, as you cross from the U2 to U8.

CityNetz has offices in the Kurfürstendamm U-Bahn station (Map 7, ☎ 882 76 04) and at Bergmannstrasse 57 in Kreuzberg 61 (☎ 693 60 95). There's also a central number (☎ 194 44) which can be called from 8 am to 8 pm daily.

Other agencies include the Mitfahrzentrale Prenzlauer Berg (☎ 448 42 75) at Oderberger Strasse 45 and the Mitfahrzentrale (☎ 216 40 20) at Yorckstrasse 52, which caters primarily for gays and lesbians.

The people answering the phone in these offices usually speak English well. If you arrange a ride a few days in advance, be sure to call the driver the night before and again on departure morning to make sure the plans have not changed.

ORGANISED TOURS
There are many options for organised travel to Berlin. The German National Tourist Office in your country may be able to provide a list of tour operators (see Tourist Offices in the Facts for the Visitor chapter). It is always worth shopping around for value, but such tours rarely come cheap. While they can save you hassles, they also rob you of independence.

Within Europe especially, major airlines often offer short city break packages, which include air fares, accommodation, transfers and sometimes a guided city tour with additional time for independent explorations. Look for these deals in the travel sections of national newspapers or check with your travel agent.

TRAVEL AGENTS
Travel agencies offering cheap flights and tours advertise in the *Reisen* classified section

The elephant gate entrance to Berlin zoo.

Schiller monument, Gendarmenmarkt.

Bronze socialist relief, Neue Marstall building.

Berlin's mascots near Gendarmenmarkt.

Sarcophagus at the Soviet Memorial Treptow.

Brezhnev and Honecker kissing, one of the East Side Gallery's most famous images.

The 'cardboard car' bursts through to freedom.

Houseball sculpture by Claes Oldenburg.

(Kleinanzeigen) of the popular city magazines *Zitty* and *tip*. One of the better discount
operators is Alternativ Tours (Map 7, ☎ 881
20 89), at Wilmersdorfer Strasse 94 in
Wilmersdorf, which specialises in unpub-
lished, discounted fares to anywhere in the
world. It's open from 9 am to 8 pm weekdays
and from 10 am to 1 pm Saturday. Take the
U7 to Adenauerplatz.

Another good option is Rainbow Tours
(Map 7, ☎ 318 63 00), at Kantstrasse 116 in
Charlottenburg, which operates incredibly
cheap multiday bus trips to places like
Prague, London, Munich and Paris. Its Web
site at www.rainbowberlin.de has more details in German. The agencies listed below
are also reliable and reputable.

Atlas Reisewelt is a full-service chain of mainstream travel agencies with branches at
Alexanderplatz 5 (Map 8, ☎ 242 73 70) and
Münzstrasse 14 (Map 4, ☎ 247 76 48) in
Mitte, as well as at Schönefeld airport (☎ 60
91 56 50). These are good places to buy train
tickets or make bus, ferry and package-tour
reservations.
Flugbörse is a good place for discounted air tickets, including student and youth fares. There
are 11 branches throughout Berlin. Check the
Yellow Pages.
Frauen Unterwegs – Frauen Reisen (☎ 215 10
22), at Potsdamer Strasse 139, specialises in
travel for women only.
Kilroy Travel has especially good deals on air
tickets, bus travel and car hire. Central
branches are at Hardenbergstrasse 9 (Map 7) in
Charlottenburg and Georgenstrasse 3 (Map 8)
in Mitte. The central phone number is ☎ 310
00 40. Kilroy also sells GO25 and ISIC cards
(see Students & Youth Cards in the Facts for
the Visitor chapter).
STA Travel primarily caters for students and
young people, though anyone can buy tickets
here. There are branches at Goethestrasse 73 in
Charlottenburg (Map 7, ☎ 311 09 50) and at
Dorotheenstrasse 30 in Mitte (Map 8, ☎ 20 16
50 63). ISIC cards are issued here as well.
Over the Rainbow (☎ 69 51 26 52) is a gay and
lesbian travel agency in the main hall of Tempelhof airport (Map 6), open from 10 am to 9
pm weekdays.

Several agencies specialise in travel to Eastern Europe. Polnisches Reisebüro Darpol
(Darpol Polish Travel Agency, Map 3, ☎ 342
00 74) is at Kaiser-Friedrich-Strasse 19, corner of Zillestrasse, in Charlottenburg. If Russia is in your travel plans, check with Sputnik
Travel (☎ 20 30 22 46), at Friedrichstrasse
176 in Mitte. Information on travel to the
Czech Republic is available from Čedok
(Map 8, ☎ 204 46 44) at Leipziger Strasse
60. Ungarn Tours (Map 8, ☎ 247 82 96), at
Karl-Liebknecht-Strasse 9, sells bus and air
tours to Budapest and beyond.

WARNING

The information in this chapter is particularly vulnerable to change: Prices for international travel are volatile, routes are
introduced and cancelled, schedules change,
special deals come and go, and rules and
visa requirements are amended. Airlines and
governments seem to take a perverse pleasure in making price structures and regulations as complicated as possible. You should
check directly with the airline or a travel
agent to make sure you understand how a
fare (and ticket you may buy) works. In addition, the travel industry is highly competitive and there are many lurks and perks.

The upshot of this is that you should get
opinions, quotes and advice from as many
airlines and travel agents as possible before
you part with your hard-earned cash. The
details given in this chapter should be regarded as pointers and are not a substitute
for your own careful, up-to-date research.

Getting Around

Despite considerable progress, much of central Berlin is still one gigantic construction site, which continues to impede the flow of traffic. Gridlock, mysteriously rerouted roads and sudden dead ends that weren't there yesterday are among the obstacles you're likely to encounter while navigating the core districts.

A better choice is not to drive at all and to use Berlin's excellent public transport system – one billion passengers a year can't be wrong. A huge network of U-Bahn (underground) and S-Bahn (suburban-metropolitan) trains, buses, trams and ferries extends pretty much into every corner of Berlin and the surrounding areas, and tickets are quite economical.

THE AIRPORTS

Berlin has three airports. Tegel (TXL), about 8km north-west of Zoo train station, primarily serves destinations within Germany, Europe and North America. There's a left-luggage office (open from 5.30 am to 10 pm), a BTM tourist information counter, a post office and a bank in the main hall.

Schönefeld (SXF), about 22km southeast of Zoo station, handles mostly international flights within Europe, and to/from Asia, Africa and Central America. Facilities include a currency exchange desk and a post office. The baggage-storage office is in front of Terminal C and opens from 5.30 am to 10 pm daily.

The only airport in central Berlin is Berlin-Tempelhof (THF, Map 6), which functions as the main hub for domestic departures and flights to central Europe.

The central information number for all of Berlin's airports is ☎ 0180-500 01 86.

Annual flight passenger volume through Berlin is expected to double to 20 million by 2010, which is why plans have been devised to expand Schönefeld into Berlin's single mega-airport by 2007. Renamed the Berlin Brandenburg International (BBI), it will have the capacity to serve around 30 million passengers per year. As a result, Tegel will be closed down and services to/from Tempelhof will be limited.

TO/FROM THE AIRPORTS

Tegel

Tegel is connected by bus No 109 to Zoo station, a route that travels via Kurfürstendamm and Luisenplatz. Express bus X9 goes to Lützowplatz at Kurfürstenstrasse via Budapester Strasse and Zoo station. The trip between the airport and the western city centre takes about 30 minutes. If you want to connect to a U-Bahn, take either line to Jakob-Kaiser-Platz to switch to the U7, or bus No 128 to Kurt-Schumacher-Platz to connect to the U6.

The first-class express bus, TXL Bus, travels between Tegel and Potsdamer Platz/Unter den Linden in about 30 minutes. The fare is DM9.90 but this gets you air-conditioning, free newspapers and a display screen with flight departure information. A taxi between Tegel and Zoo station costs about DM35.

Schönefeld

Schönefeld airport is served by the Airport Express train from Zoo station every 30 minutes from 4.30 am to 11 pm. The slower alternative is the S9, which runs from Zoo station via Alexanderplatz every 20 minutes between 4 am and midnight. The less frequent S45 links the Schönefeld and Tempelhof airports. The S-Bahn station (which is also a main railway station) is about 300m from the terminal, and is connected by a free shuttle bus. Bus No 171 links the terminal directly with the U-Bahn station Rudow (U7), with connections to central Berlin. For a taxi between Schönefeld and Zoo station figure on spend between DM50 and DM70.

Tempelhof

Tempelhof airport (Map 6) is served by the U6 (exit Platz der Luftbrücke) and by bus

No 119 from Kurfürstendamm via Kreuzberg. A taxi to/from Zoo station will cost you about DM30.

PUBLIC TRANSPORT

Berlin's public transport system is composed of services provided by the Berliner Verkehrsbetriebe (BVG, ☎ 194 49), open from 6 am to 11 pm daily, which operates U-Bahn trains, buses, trams and ferries; and the Deutsche Bahn (DB, ☎ 01805-99 66 33) which is in charge of suburban and regional trains like the S-Bahn, Regionalbahn (RB) and Regionalexpress (RE).

Since the system is operated jointly, one type of ticket is valid on all forms of transport (with the few exceptions noted below). The system is fairly efficient overall but, given continuing extensive construction, delays and schedule changes may occur. The BVG number to call for 24-hour, up-to-date route information is ☎ 25 62 25 62. For DB information, dial ☎ 29 71 29 71.

The BVG information kiosk (Map 7) on Hardenbergplatz, outside Zoo station, has free route maps and general information on all means of transport around Berlin. The kiosk is open from 8 am to 10 pm daily and you can also buy tickets and passes there. For information on S-Bahn, RE and RB connections, visit the Reisezentrum office inside the station.

Tickets & Passes

Berlin's metropolitan area is divided into three tariff zones – A, B and C. Tickets are valid in at least two zones, AB or BC, or in all three zones, ABC. Unless you're venturing to Potsdam or the very outer suburbs, you'll only need the AB ticket. Dogs and one piece of luggage are free. The most common types of tickets are:

Ganzstrecke (Entire Route System)
This ticket covers unlimited travel for two hours in zones ABC, valid on all forms of transport (DM4.20).
Kurzstrecke (Short Trip)
This ticket covers three stops on the U-Bahn or S-Bahn, or six stops on buses or trams. One change is allowed, but only between trains - not bus to train or bus to bus (DM2.50).

Langstrecke (Long Trip)
This ticket covers unlimited travel for two hours within two of the three zones (AB or BC) in any direction on all forms of transport except RE and RB trains (DM3.90).
Tageskarte (Day Pass)
This ticket covers unlimited travel until 3 am the following day (DM7.80 for zones AB or BC, DM8.50 for zones ABC). The group day pass (Gruppentageskarte) is good for up to five people travelling together (DM20/22.50).
7-Tageskarte (7-Day Pass)
This ticket covers unlimited travel during any seven-day period after validation until midnight on the seventh day and is transferable (DM40 for zones AB, DM42 for zones BC, DM48 for zones ABC).
WelcomeCard
This is a tourist office sponsored card that buys 72 hours of unlimited travel in zones ABC for one adult and up to three children aged under 14, plus various other discounts (DM32). (See Tourist Offices in the Facts for the Visitor chapter for details.)

Buying & Using Tickets

Bus drivers sell single and day tickets, but tickets for U/S-Bahn trains and other multiple, weekly or monthly tickets must be purchased in advance. Most are available from the orange vending machines (which feature instructions in English) in U/S-Bahn stations, as well as from the ticket window at station entrances and the BVG information kiosk.

Tickets must be validated in one of the red machines (Entwerter) at the platform entrances to S-Bahn and U-Bahn stations before boarding. Buses have Entwerter machines on board. If you're using a timed ticket like the Langstrecke, validate it just as your train or bus arrives to ensure full value. If you're caught by an inspector without a ticket (or even an unvalidated one), there's a DM60 fine.

U-Bahn/S-Bahn

The most efficient way to travel around Berlin is by U-Bahn or S-Bahn. There are 10 U-Bahn and 13 S-Bahn lines which operate from 4 am until just after midnight. On weekends, the U9 and the U12 operate all night on a limited service (about two trains an hour). Most S-Bahn trains continue to operate hourly between midnight and 4 am

euro currency converter DM1 = €.51

GETTING AROUND

on Friday and Saturday. Rail pass holders can use the S-Bahn for free.

The next station (including an *Übergang*, or transfer point) is announced on most U-Bahn (but not S-Bahn) trains and is also displayed at the end of carriages on some newer trains. Be aware when the station you need is coming up. To help you do this, large route maps are plastered on the ceilings above the doors in most cars. Large versions of the same maps are on station platforms.

Regional Trains
The S-Bahn network is supplemented by the Regionalbahn (RB) and the Regional-express (RE) whose routes are also marked on the BVG network map. Only BVG Ganzstrecke and DB rail tickets (including rail passes) are valid on these routes.

Bus
These are rather slow, but being comfortably ensconced on the upper level of a double decker is a mighty fine – and inexpensive – way to do some relaxed sightseeing. One popular route is that of bus No 199 which goes from Grunewald to Platz der Luftbrücke via the Ku'damm and Kreuzberg. An even better option is bus No 100 (see the boxed text 'Seeing Berlin From Bus No 100').

Bus stops are marked with a large 'H' (for *Haltestelle*) and the name of the stop. Drivers sell tickets and can give change. The next stop is usually announced over a loudspeaker or displayed on a digital board. Push the button on the handrails to signal to the driver that you want to get off. After 8 pm, you can only board through the front door and, if you already have a ticket, you must present it upon entering.

Nightbus Some 70 bus lines take over from the U/S-Bahn between 1 and 4 am, running roughly at 30-minute intervals. Buses leave from the major nightlife areas like Zoo station, Hackescher Markt in Mitte

---

Seeing Berlin From Bus No 100

Perhaps the best – and certainly the cheapest – way to get to know Berlin quickly is a tour on the double-decker city bus No 100. Shuttling between Zoo station and Prenzlauer Berg, it passes by nearly every major city sight. And all you need is a DM3.90 bus ticket, which allows you to on and off as often as you want within the two hours of its validity.

Since there's no commentary, it's a good idea to pick up a map and information leaflet from the BVG information kiosk outside Zoo station, the route's western terminus. This is also the ideal place to board, especially if you want to garner one of those coveted front window seats from where the views are truly panoramic.

The first sight you see after the bus leaves Zoo station is the landmark Gedächtniskirche (Memorial Church) and the beginning of the Ku'damm before reaching the famous Zoological Garden. From here, the bus turns north into the Tiergarten where you'll pass the triumphant golden figure atop the Victory Column. Look quickly right as the bus crosses the Strasse des 17 Juni and you'll spot the Brandenburg Gate down the broad boulevard. Your next stop is Schloss Bellevue, the Berlin residence of Germany's president. The bus then follows streets paralleling the Spree river before passing the Reichstag. Soon after, it'll drive right through the Brandenburg Gate, a privilege given only to taxis and city buses.

Now you're in former East Berlin and heading down Unter den Linden, passing such sights as the Berlin Dom and Humboldt University. Next you'll reach Alexanderplatz with its monster TV tower, and a few minutes later you'll arrive at the eastern bus terminus near Europe's largest Jewish cemetery. If you don't interrupt your trip, the entire one-way journey takes about 45 minutes (more during heavy traffic), which should leave you loaded up with enough sightseeing ideas to last at least a week.

and Nollendorfplatz in Schöneberg, and cover the entire Berlin area, including the outer districts. Normal fares apply.

Changeovers at major transfer stations are timed in such a way that you should only have to wait a few minutes. A free network map is available at the BVG office (Map 7).

Tram

Trams used to be rickety throwbacks to the days before U/S-Bahns but nowadays most have been replaced by comfortable new models. They operate only in the eastern sections, having been abolished in the west in 1967.

About 30 lines crisscross the entire eastern half of Berlin and a network map is available at the BVG office (Map 7).

Ferry

The BVG operates several ferry services but the only one you're ever likely to need is the F10 which shuttles between Kladow and Wannsee. The trip in itself is quite scenic and, since regular BVG tickets apply, is an inexpensive excursion. Ferries operate hourly all year, weather permitting, usually from 9 am to sunset. For information about sightseeing cruises, see Organised Tours later in this chapter.

CAR & MOTORCYCLE

In principle, Berlin is easier to drive in than many other big European cities because it was more or less rebuilt from scratch after WWII with a modern city layout. However, until roadworks and construction – especially in the eastern parts – are finished (and god knows when that will be), you'll encounter some confusion. In spite of the massive building projects, traffic generally moves fairly smoothly. A real convenience is the A10 ring road which gets you easily around the urban perimeter.

Parking in garages is expensive (about DM2 to DM3 per hour), but it'll often be your only choice if you want to be near the main shopping areas or attractions. In the western city centre (Map 7), for instance, you'll find car parks on Augsburger Strasse, in the Europa-Center and immediately west

of the zoo on Budapester Strasse. The day rate is around DM20.

Free street parking, while impossible to find in these central areas, is usually available in residential streets, especially in the eastern districts. Watch for signs indicating parking restrictions or you risk a ticket or even being towed.

Parking meters are rare but the 'pay and display' system is quite widespread. This requires you to buy a ticket for the time you intend to park from a ticket-vending machine as soon as you've parked your car (it should be kerbside just a few metres away). Then display your receipt visibly on the dashboard inside the car. Hourly rates are usually DM2. Check the machine or signposts for enforcement hours.

If you're staying at a hotel, keep in mind that most don't have their own garages and you will either have to find parking on your own or have the hotel staff park it for you, which will add about DM25 per night to your bill.

Car Rental

You'll find all the major international car-rental chains represented in Berlin. Their lowest standard rates begin at around DM100 daily and between DM400 to DM500 weekly, including VAT and unlimited kilometres. The best deals are special weekend tariffs, in effect from Friday noon to Monday 9 am, from DM120. Some arrangements also include collision insurance which can save up to DM40 a day. You must be at least 21 to rent from most agencies.

Robben und Wientjes, a local agency with branches at Prinzenstrasse 90/91 in Kreuzberg (☎ 61 67 70) and at Prenzlauer Allee 96 (☎ 42 10 36), usually has the best deals in town with rates from DM28 per day.

International car rental agencies clustering on and around Budapester Strasse near the zoo are Hertz (Map 7, ☎ 261 10 53) at No 39, Avis (Map 7, ☎ 230 93 70) next door, SixtBudget (Map 7, ☎ 261 13 57) at No 18; and EuropCar (☎ 235 06 40) at nearby Kurfürstenstrasse 101-104. For other branches and agencies, check the Yellow Pages under *Autovermietung*.

GETTING AROUND

Better rates and excellent conditions are usually available through a US-based company called AutoEurope, which subcontracts with all the major agencies. Reservations can be made 24 hours a day via a tollfree number with an English-speaking operator. Cars are available in all sizes and categories, and there's no surcharge for one-way rentals or airport drop-offs.

There's also no charge for cancellations or changes, and the minimum rental age is 19. You can even travel into Poland and the Czech Republic if you tell the company at the time of booking, though there is an extra charge. There is also a three-day minimum rental (but no penalty for turning it in early).

If you need a car and you're already in Germany, dial ☎ 0130-82 21 98. From North America it's ☎ 800-223 5555; from Australia ☎ 1-800 12 64 09; from New Zealand ☎ 0800-44 07 22; from France ☎ 0800-90 17 70; and from Britain ☎ 0800-89 98 93.

A small economy car will cost you around US$70 for the three-day minimum and US$110 for a weekly rental, which includes unlimited kilometres, VAT and third-party insurance but not collision insurance, which may increase daily rates by up to US$15. Check with your credit card provider, as some do cover collision insurance. Even then, you may end up spending less than when renting directly with a local agency.

Car Purchase

Unless you're staying in Berlin or Germany for a while, buying a car here is an unwise decision due to the costs and paperwork involved. EU nationals must register the car with the Ordnungs-und Strassenverkehrsamt (Public Order & Traffic Office). You will need proof of ownership, proof of insurance and a passport or ID. You'll also be subject to a motor vehicle tax.

Non-EU nationals, while allowed to buy a car, may *not* register it since you have to be a German or EU resident to do so. You could have a local friend or relative register a car for you, though they may not feel comfortable about jeopardising their driving record and insurance rates in the event that you have an accident.

Having said that, Berlin is among the best places in Germany to shop around for used cars. A good place to look is the weekly newspaper *Zweite Hand*, which has a separate car edition with thousands of listings. Make sure that you don't buy a vehicle without a valid 'TÜV' certificate of roadworthiness.

Motorcycle Rental

American Bike Rent (☎ 03301-70 15 55) is at Magnus-Hirschfeld-Strasse 26, north of Berlin in Lehnitz. Daily 24-hour/weekend rates for Harley-Davidsons range from DM139/163 to DM168/176 and the first 90km are free. The seven-day rates, including the first 720km, are DM815 to DM985. There is a deposit of DM1500 on cash rentals. Opening hours are from 2 to 7 pm on weekdays from April to October. Take the S1 to Lehnitz.

Another possibility is G Passeckel (☎ 781 18 73), at Eisenacher Strasse 79 in Schöneberg, which has smaller bikes for DM60 to DM80/day (DM400 deposit) and bigger ones for DM100 and DM120/day (DM800 deposit). It is only open from 9 am to 6.30 pm on weekdays from March to October, and Saturday in fine weather. Take the U7 to Eisenacher Strasse.

Hitching

Hitching is never entirely safe in any country in the world, and we don't recommend it. Travellers who decide to hitch should understand that they are taking a small but potentially serious risk. People who do choose to hitch will be safer if they travel in pairs and let someone know where they are planning to go.

TAXI

Taxi stands with 'call columns' *(Rufsäulen)* are located beside all main train stations and throughout the city. Flag fall is DM4.20, then it's DM2.20 per km for the first 6km and DM2 per km thereafter. Night (11 pm to 6 am) and weekend charges are higher by DM0.20 per km. A fifth passenger costs DM2.50 on top of the fare. If you order a taxi by phone, flag fall goes up to DM6.

Sample fares: Nollendorfplatz to Schlesisches Tor is DM21.50; and Hermannplatz to Schlesisches Tor is DM11.50. Cab numbers include Würfelfunk (tollfree ☎ 0800-222 2255), Taxi Funk (☎ 690 22) and Funk Taxi (☎ 25 10 26).

If you need to travel quickly over a short distance you can use the DM5 flat rate which entitles you to ride for five minutes or 2km, whichever comes first. This deal only applies if you flag down an unoccupied moving taxi and ask for the DM5 rate before getting into the car.

If you have a problem with a cabbie (this is unlikely to happen), get a receipt showing the price, date, time and route, have them sign and stamp it, then complain to Innung des Berliner Taxigewerbes (☎ 344 40 59), Darwinstrasse 1.

If you've had one – or two or three – drinks too many and can't drive home anymore, call City Floh (☎ 441 73 44) from 7 pm to 5 am. Within minutes, someone will arrive on a collapsible moped, put it into your trunk and drive you home. The base fee is DM10, each kilometre costs DM2.50.

Fairly new to Berlin are Velotaxis (☎ 44 35 89 90), pedicabs that seat two people. The cost is DM2 per person per kilometre. The Japanese and elderly tourists love 'em.

BICYCLE

Berlin is fairly user-friendly for cyclists, although you need to keep your wits about you in heavy traffic, especially where there are no bike lanes. Helmets are not required by law.

Taking a bicycle in specially marked carriages of the S-Bahn or U-Bahn costs DM2.50. On the U-Bahn, bikes are allowed only between 9 am and 2 pm and from 5.30 pm until closing time on weekdays (any time at the weekend). If you want to take your bike on a DB train, it costs DM6 if the distance is under 100km, otherwise DM12. DB's bike hotline is on ☎ 0180-319 41 94.

Outlets renting bicycles in Berlin include:

Bike City (☎ 39 73 91 45) has bikes for DM10 (students DM5). There's no deposit but you must bring ID. In the warmer months, mobile rental stations (open 10 am to 6 pm daily) are usually on the Schlossplatz by the Staatsrat

building (Map 4)at U-Bahn station Hansaplatz (Lessingstrasse exit); and at Pohlstrasse 89, corner of Kluckstrasse (U15 to Kurfürstenstrasse). To confirm locations, call the office or the hotline at ☎ 0177-210 66 61.

Fahrradservice (☎ 447 66 66), at Reinhardtstrasse 6 in Mitte, has various types of bikes for around DM20 per 24-hour rental. Weekly rates are between DM50 and DM60. The weekend tariff of DM35 is good from Friday night to Monday morning. Deposit is DM100. Hours are from 10 am to 8 pm on weekdays and until at least 1 pm on Saturday.

Fahrradstation is the largest bike rental agency and has branches all over the city, including the main one in Hof VII off the Hackesche Höfe in Mitte (Map 8). Other branches are at Bergmannstrasse 9 in Kreuzberg and Auguststrasse 29. The central reservation number is ☎ 28 38 48 48. City cruisers cost DM15/39/59 per day/3-day weekend/week rental. Mountain bikes are DM20/49/69. There's a deposit of DM200.

WALKING

The historic centre of Berlin is surprisingly compact and best explored on foot. Walking lets you experience the city at ground level and generally gives you a better sense of the different flavours of the various neighbourhoods. It's safe to walk anywhere in the central city, including in the large parks like Tiergarten, though perhaps not at night time. Several great self-guided walking tours are outlined in the Things to See & Do chapter later in this book. If you don't want to walk by yourself, you can also join a guided English-language tour (see the Walking Tours section later in this chapter).

ORGANISED TOURS
Bus Tours

Most city sightseeing tours operate on the get on, get off as often as you wish principle, and there's very little difference between operators. Most take in 12 main sights – including Kurfürstendamm, Brandenburger Tor, Schloss Charlottenburg, Berliner Dom and Alexanderplatz – on loops that take about two hours without getting off.

Taped commentary comes in – count 'em – eight languages. Buses depart roughly every 30 minutes, with the first tour usually around 10 am from somewhere near the Gedächtniskirche, and the last tour departs sometime around 6 pm (earlier in winter). The cost is DM30.

Severin + Kühn buses (Map 7, ☎ 880 41 90) leave from Kurfürstendamm 216; BBS (Map 7, ☎ 35 19 52 70) depart from Kurfürstendamm, on the corner of Rankestrasse; and BVB (Map 7, ☎ 885 98 80) leave from Kurfürstendamm 229, which is opposite Café Kranzler.

All three operators also have a Super Berlin Tour, a more conventional, narrated non-stop 3½-hour tour which costs DM39 and is offered twice daily in the morning and afternoon. A 50% discount for children under 13 is offered for tours with any of these three companies.

Between Easter and October, there's also Top-Tour-Berlin (☎ 25 62 47 40) – operated by BVG – which has departures every 30 minutes from outside Café Kranzler at Kurfürstendamm 18. It makes 20 stops and costs DM35 for adults, DM29 for children aged six to 14. Tickets bought after 3 pm are valid until the end of the following day.

Walking Tours

Berlin has three companies that operate English-language tours, and all are excellent, informative and entertaining.

Certainly some of the best walking tours we've ever taken are those operated by The Original Berlin Walks (☎ 301 91 94). Its Discover Berlin tour covers the heart of the city and its enthusiastic guides provide eye and mind-opening historical and architectural insights. Tours leave at 10 am and 2.30 pm daily from late March to the end of October, and at 10 am only for the rest of the year.

The Infamous Third Reich Sites tour takes you past the former sites of Hitler's bunker, the Gestapo headquarters, Göring's Air Ministry and more. Also offered is the Jewish Life in Berlin tour which takes in the sights of the Spandauer Vorstadt, including the New Synagogue. Both tours run on a more limited schedule. Call for details or pick up a leaflet at EurAide in Zoo station or the tourist office.

All tours last between two and three hours (DM15/10, free for children under 14) and leave from outside the main entrance of Zoo station (Map 7) at the top of the taxi rank. Just show up armed with a BVG *Langstrecke* ticket (DM3.90; see the Public Transport section earlier in this chapter). Rail-pass holders don't need one for the Discover Berlin and Jewish Life tours as the S-Bahn is used.

Berlin Walks' main competitor, the Yellow Walking Tour Company (☎ 692 31 49), conducts the Insider Tour, which is also great fun. It's run by a team of young, hip Australians who pepper their commentary with anecdotes and interesting trivia.

Their tour covers all the main sights in both western and eastern Berlin – from Zoo station to Alexanderplatz – in three to four hours. It's all on foot, so be sure to wear comfortable shoes! Tours cost DM15 and leave at 10 am and 2.30 pm daily (10 am only from November to March) from outside McDonald's, also on Hardenbergplatz outside Zoo station. The price includes a nifty brochure packed with useful information about Berlin.

The last in the trio of English-language walking tour operators is Terry's Top Hat Tour, which enjoys a good reputation as well. It leaves twice daily from the New Synagogue and the Circus and Backpacker hostels in Mitte, costs DM10 and lasts about four hours. Call the hostels for details (see the Places to Stay chapter).

Boat Tours

In the warmer months, tourist boats cruise Berlin's waterways, calling at main historical sights in the centre as well as at picturesque parks and castles. Food and drink are sold on board, but they're quite expensive, so take along something to sip or nibble.

Stern und Kreis Schiffahrt (☎ 536 36 00) operates various cruises from April to December. A 3½-hour cruise from Jannowitzbrücke near the Märkisches Museum (Map 8) past the northern boundary of Tiergarten park to Schlossbrücke, near Schloss Charlottenburg (Map 3), costs DM15/25.50 one-way/return and is offered up to six times daily. A one-hour spin around Museumsinsel from the docks near Bodestrasse (Map 8) operates up to 16 times daily (DM14). Night tours, departing at 7.30 pm Friday and Saturday, cost DM21.50 (2½ hours).

Children under six travel for free, those under 14 receive a 50% discount. Students and seniors get 15% off, though not on weekends and holidays. A Kombi-Tageskarte, which entitles you to unlimited rides aboard regular Stern und Kreis Schiffahrt cruises as well as U/S-Bahn trains, buses and trams in Berlin and Potsdam, costs DM26.

Reederei Bruno Winkler (☎ 349 95 95) has sightseeing cruises on the Spree River and the Landwehr Canal from March to September. The main landing stage is at Schlossbrücke, just east of Schloss Charlottenburg. Three-hour tours leave at 10.20 am and 2.20 pm twice daily (DM22). You can also hop aboard at the Friedrichstrasse landing (Map 8) at Reichstagufer which cuts the return-trip cost to DM18. Seniors and students get a DM2 discount. There are also English-language audiotapes with commentary available.

Berliner Wassertaxi (Map 8, ☎ 65 88 02 03), based just north of the Schlossbrücke in Mitte, has one-hour spins (DM12/9) along the Spree between Spreekanal and Bahnhof Friedrichstrasse, leaving every half-hour between 10 am and 4.30 pm daily.

Things to See & Do

Berlin is such a vibrant city that it's unlikely you'll run out of things to do. And it's all changing at such lightning speed that you'll be able to make your own discoveries. Just pick a quarter to wander in, walk the streets, soak up the atmosphere and try to imagine where it will all be in a few years hence.

Places of interest, museums, sights and other diversions are described in this chapter by district. Each of Berlin's seven core districts – Mitte, Tiergarten, Charlottenburg, Schöneberg, Kreuzberg, Friedrichshain, Prenzlauer Berg – are covered in great detail. Some sections feature neighbourhood walking tours that take you to an area's lesser-known corners and attractions. Subsequent sections provide an overview of what there is to see and do in Berlin's outer districts. The chapter concludes with a listing of recreational activities. Berlin's wonderful public transport system is the best method of getting around the city, other than your own two feet.

Mitte

Mitte is the birthplace of Berlin and, certainly from a visitor's standpoint, the most attractive of the city's 23 districts, with its enormous density of sights, museums, entertainment and hotels. The heart of Berlin has been here since the double city of Berlin-Cölln was founded in the 13th century near today's Nikolaiviertel. Whether part of the Brandenburg-Prussia kingdom, the German Empire, the Weimar Republic, the Third Reich or the GDR, Mitte has always been the nexus of politics, culture and commerce. And it didn't take long after the Wende before it became the hub of united Berlin.

Your sightseeing choices here are immense. You'll find world-class museums in profusion. Some of the greatest architects – Schinkel, Nering, Langhans to name a few – have left their mark with neoclassical and

Berlin Highlights

Coming up with a list of best things to do in Berlin is no small task, thanks to the sheer number of sights, experiences and attractions the city has to offer. What follows is a list – in no particular order – of things we have enjoyed on our visits to Berlin and that we thought you might like as well. Some may seem obvious, others surprising, but all will make for special memories.

- Bar hopping till sunrise in Mitte, Friedrichshain or Prenzlauer Berg
- Close-ups of the Reichstag dome and views of the city from above
- Touring the city with Berlin Walks or Insider Tours
- Walking in the footsteps of history along Unter den Linden
- Daniel Libeskind's dramatic new Jewish Museum
- Clubbing at Maria im Ostbahnhof or any other of Berlin's in-spots in unusual sites
- Shopping and fine architecture at the Friedrichstadtpassagen
- Visiting the Pergamon Museum and Egyptian Museum
- KaDeWe and its opulent Food Halls
- Breakfast and scene watching at a Schöneberg cafe
- Seeing history in the making around Potzdamer Platz
- Feasting on some of the best doner kebabs this side of Istanbul
- Classical music at the Berliner Philharmonie
- Cruising Berlin's lakes, rivers or canals
- Strolling and picnicking in the fairytale setting of Pfaueninsel
- Seeing Berlin aboard Bus 100 for DM3.90
- Best views from above: TV Tower, French Cathedral, Siegessäule

baroque structures throughout the district. A stroll along Unter den Linden, Berlin's grand boulevard, will take you past a phalanx of sites that tell the city's story. For entertainment, you can hang out in a cool pub, watch the night turn into day in a throbbing nightclub, attend an acclaimed opera or see top-notch theatre.

Encircled by six other districts, Mitte covers roughly the same area taken up by the entire city at the beginning of the 19th century. WWII reduced nearly 80% of the historical buildings into bombed out and smouldering husks of their former grandeur. Since the area was part of the Soviet sector, it fell to the GDR to do the clean-up. East Berlin became that short-lived country's capital which, despite being a violation of the agreement made between the Allies, was probably a good thing since it made restoration a matter of pride.

Indeed, much of the restoration work from those decades is exemplary as can be seen, for instance, on Gendarmenmarkt or along Unter den Linden. At the same time, though, salvageable structures like the Hohenzollern dynasty's City Palace succumbed to the wrecking ball for ideological reasons only to be replaced by aesthetic violations like the Palace of the Republic. Quarters like the Spandauer Vorstadt and Friedrichstadt were left to languish through decades of neglect.

Mitte's many faces – its historical sights, monuments, architectural delights (and monstrosities), vibrant nightlife, imposing churches, hotels, cafes and museums – are a microcosm of Berlin's entire history. But, as a visit to the Reichstag area or to Potsdamer Platz will quickly show, it's also a place to observe the future in the making.

UNTER DEN LINDEN

Berlin's most splendid boulevard extends for about 1.5km from the Brandenburg Gate to Schlossplatz. If you have little time in Berlin, a stroll along here is an absolute must. Most major sights are strung out like

Berlin's Museums

Berlin has 170 museums but many of the major ones are being consolidated and reorganised, requiring their temporary closure.

Berlin's most internationally important museums are run by the Staatliche Museenzu Berlin - Preussischer Kulturbesitz (State Museums of Berlin - Prussian Cultural Collection, denoted in this book with 'SMPK'). Information about any of them is available via a hotline on ☎ 20 90 55 55. Admission to most is DM4/2 per entry, but some require that you purchase the **SMPK Day Pass** for DM8/4 which is then also valid at all other SMPK museums on that day. Day Passes are obligatory at the Pergamon Museum, Hamburger Bahnhof, New National Gallery, New Picture Gallery, Egyptian Museum and the Berggruen Collection. The Drei-Tages-Touristenkarte for DM15 gives unlimited access for three consecutive days to all SMPK museums. Admission to all SMPK museums is free on the first Sunday of the month.

At most museums, SMPK or otherwise, display captions are usually in German only. Some places have English-language pamphlets available at ticket counters or information desks which you may borrow for free or take with you. Increasingly popular are taped, self-guided audiotours in several languages (free to DM8).

Most of Berlin's museums are closed on Monday. Exceptions are: German Resistance Memorial, German Historical Museum at Kronprinzenpalais, Hanfmuseum, Deutsche Guggenheim, Käthe-Kollwitz-Museum, Centrum Judaicum, Plötzensee Memorial, Bauhaus Archiv/Museum of Design, Brücke Museum, Museum am Checkpoint Charlie, House of the Wannsee Conference, Puppentheater-Museum, Topographie des Terrors, German-Russian Museum Berlin-Karlshorst, and Infobox Potsdamer Platz. For more details about the museums themselves, see the individual entries in this chapter.

pearls on both sides of this broad esplanade and provide a thorough introduction to the city's fascinating past.

Before being developed into a show-piece road, Unter den Linden was merely a riding path connecting the city palace with the Tiergarten, once the royal hunting grounds. Under Elector Friedrich Wilhelm (ruled 1640-88), the eponymous linden trees were planted, but it took another century before most of the harmonious ensemble of baroque, neoclassical and rococo structures were completed. Wartime brought especially heavy destruction to the western end of Unter den Linden; most of what you see here today reflects postwar architectural tastes. The stretch east of Friedrichstrasse, though, has been beautifully restored.

Brandenburger Tor (Map 8)

The landmark Brandenburg Gate – Berlin's only surviving city gate – marks the transition of Unter den Linden into Strasse des 17 Juni. It was designed by Carl Gotthard Langhans in 1791 and modelled on the entrance to the Acropolis in Athens. Once the boundary between East and West Berlin, it is now the very symbol of reunification.

The gate is crowned by the **Quadriga**, a two-wheeled chariot drawn by four horses and driven by the winged goddess of victory. It was designed in 1793 by Johann Gottfried Schadow. What a well-travelled goddess 'Victory' became; spirited to Paris in 1806 by Napoleon after his occupation of Berlin, she triumphantly returned in 1814, freed from the French by a gallant Prussian general.

The gate's north wing contains the **Raum der Stille** (Room of Silence), where the weary can sit and contemplate peace. The south wing contains a tourist office branch (see the Facts for the Visitor chapter).

The Gate opens onto **Pariser Platz**, which is being restored to its prewar grandeur, when it was called the 'emperor's reception hall'. By the time it's finished, it will be framed by statuesque buildings on three sides. The **embassies** of the United States, Britain and France will be complemented by banks, offices and the Academy of Arts

headquarters. Meanwhile, the hawkers of GDR and Soviet military trinkets, Russian dolls and ever-smaller painted pieces of the Wall have moved to the west side of the Gate. Compare prices before buying, and bargain.

From its perch in the square's south-east corner, the **Hotel Adlon**, the grande dame of Berlin caravansaries, has held court over Pariser Platz since 1997. Its first incarnation (1907) was considered one of the world's most luxurious hotels, which counted Charlie Chaplin, Greta Garbo and Thomas Mann among its guests. These days once again a top address for presidents, musicians, diplomats, actors or the merely moneyed, it oozes sophistication from the moment the doors swing open onto a majestic lobby topped with a stunning stained-glass cupola.

Reichstag (Map 8)

Only a short detour north of the Brandenburg Gate, the Reichstag (1894) is another Berlin landmark. In May 1999, it once again became the seat of the Bundestag, the German parliament. British architect Sir Norman Foster has created a completely state-of-the-art parliamentary facility, preserving only the building's historical shell.

Its most striking feature is a giant glass dome hovering above the plenary hall. Visitors may take an elevator to a rooftop viewing terrace, then walk to the top of the glistening 'beehive' via a spiralling ramp. At the dome's centre is a mirror-clad funnel that reflects the light in myriad directions. Once at the top, you'll be at eye level with construction cranes and able to survey the sweeping government district mushrooming around here. There's a cafe and elevators operate until midnight. Last admission though is at 10 pm (free). Tours of the Reichstag itself are free but must be reserved by writing to Deutscher Bundestag, Besucherdienst, 11011 Berlin.

An imposing structure – measuring 137m by 97m – the Reichstag has been the focus of momentous events in German history. After WWI, Philipp Scheidemann proclaimed the German Republic from one of its windows. The Reichstag fire on the night of 27 February 1933 destroyed large sections, allowing Hitler to blame the communists and to cement his power. A dozen years later, bombs and the victorious Soviets nearly finished the job. The photograph of a Red Army soldier raising the red flag atop the burning building is world famous. Restoration – *sans* dome – wasn't finished until 1972.

At midnight on 2 October 1990 the reunification of Germany was enacted here. In the summer of 1995 the Reichstag again drew the world's attention when the artist Christo and his wife Jeanne-Claude wrapped it in fabric for two weeks. Sir Norman's reconstruction began shortly thereafter.

North and east of the Reichstag, office buildings for members of parliament and their staff are taking shape, while the **Federal Chancellery** (Map 3) is set to occupy a spot west of the Reichstag on the northern edge of Tiergarten.

Just south of the Reichstag, near the start of Scheidemannstrasse, is the **Wall Victims Memorial** dedicated to those who died trying to cross the Wall – one only nine months before it was dismantled.

Pariser Platz to Friedrichstrasse (Map 8)

Strolling east on Unter den Linden, you'll see the hulking **Russian Embassy** (1950), a white-marble Stalinist behemoth, at No 63-65. It is built in the so-called *Zuckerbäckerstil* (wedding-cake style) of architecture in vogue during the Stalin era. A tall wall allows only glimpses of the compound, but if you're interested in this type of monumental building, swing by Karl-Marx-Allee east of Alexanderplatz, which is lined with them (also see the Friedrichshain section later in this chapter).

On the north side of the next block, at No 40, is **Berlin Story** (☎ 20 16 61 39), a bilingual exhibit organised by the Berlin Historical Society, a strong supporter of proposals to reconstruct the city palace. On view are photos, pictures, scale models and the quaint Kaiserpanorama, a sort of primitive movie theatre. There is a huge selection of books on Berlin, including many in English.

The exhibit is open from 10 am to 8 pm daily (entry by donation).

Back on the south side of Unter den Linden is the box office of the **Komische Oper**, one of three of the city's state-sponsored opera houses (the main entrance is on Behrenstrasse 55-57). A theatre has stood in this spot since 1764, but the core of the current structure dates only to 1892. After WWII, the original interior – a plush, richly festooned baroque extravaganza – was largely restored, clashing with the decidedly functional 60s facade. (Also see the Entertainment chapter.)

Before WWII the intersection of Friedrichstrasse and Unter den Linden was one of the liveliest corners in Berlin, home to restaurants and cafes, including the original incarnation of that revered Berlin institution, the **Café Kranzler**. (For details about the current Café Kranzler see the Charlottenburg section later in this chapter.)

Deutsche Guggenheim (Map 8)

The Dresdner Bank building at the intersection with Charlottenstrasse (No 13-15) shares space with the Deutsche Guggenheim museum (☎ 202 09 30), which opened in November 1997. This is the fifth permanent exhibition space set up by the New York-based Guggenheim family, which incidentally is of German descent. The 510 sq metre gallery, with soaring ceilings and minimalist decor, hosts three to four high-calibre shows annually. Hours are from 11 am to 8 pm daily. Cost is DM8/5, except Mondays which are free. There's also a small shop and cafe.

Staatsbibliothek (Map 8)

Opposite the Deutsche Guggenheim at No 8 is the Staatsbibliothek (State Library, 1914) which, at 107m long and 170m wide, is one of the largest buildings in central Berlin. Founded by the Great Elector, Friedrich Wilhelm, in 1661, the library's collection contains nine million books and periodicals, including precious manuscripts (eg the poems of Hafiz, 1560), original musical sheets (eg by Bach, Mozart and Beethoven) and maps (eg Germany by

Nicolas von Kues, 1491). Books published after 1956 are housed at a second branch near Potsdamer Platz.

The ivy-covered building is accessed via an inner courtyard which leads to a huge entrance hall. A giant, sombre staircase lends it the gravity of a serious research facility and, indeed, its labyrinth of reading rooms is filled with studious types hunched over big tomes, furiously scribbling notes. (For hours and tour information, see the Libraries section in the Facts for the Visitor chapter.)

Humboldt Universität (Map 8)

Humboldt University (1753), the next building to the east, began life as a palace of Prince Heinrich, brother of King Friedrich II. In 1810 it became a university on the initiative of Wilhelm von Humboldt, then a minister of cultural affairs. Humboldt managed to assemble an illustrious faculty that included the philosophers Hegel and Fichte, and the university quickly rose to prominence throughout Europe. Marx and Engels both studied here, and notable professors included the Brothers Grimm, Albert Einstein, Max Planck and the nuclear scientist Otto Hahn. Numerous Nobel Prize winners came out of Humboldt. A touch terminal in the foyer provides more historical and practical information (in German only) and the student cafeteria is a good place for cheap meals (see the Places to Eat chapter).

The equestrian **statue of Friedrich II** (1851) by Christian Daniel Rauch, which normally stands in the middle of Unter den Linden outside the university's main entrance, is still under restoration.

Bebelplatz (Map 8)

Across from the university is Bebelplatz, previously known as Opernplatz and renamed in 1947 after the co-founder and leader of the Social Democratic Party (SPD). On 10 May 1933 the Nazis held their first official book burning here of authors they considered subversive, including Bertolt Brecht, Heinrich Mann and Jack London. It was a portentous event that signalled the death of the cultural greatness

Berlin had achieved over the previous two centuries. A poignant below-ground memorial of empty bookshelves by the Israeli artist Micha Ullmann marks the spot.

Bebelplatz is framed by several historical buildings. On the eastern side of the square is the renowned **Staatsoper Unter den Linden** (State Opera, 1743), one of Berlin's earliest neoclassical structures. A gabled portico is supported by six Corinthian columns and bears the inscription 'Fridericus Rex Apolloni et Musis', a reference to Friedrich II's intention to build a temple for Apollo and the Muses.

Opposite is the **Alte Königliche Bibliothek** (Old Royal Library, 1780), now part of the law faculty of the university and nicknamed *Kommode* (chest of drawers) for its bulky shape. On the square's south-eastern corner looms the giant copper dome of **St Hedwig Cathedral** (1773), which was partly modelled on the Pantheon in Rome. It was Berlin's only Catholic church until 1854. The adjacent building was once home to the Dresdner Bank and later housed the GDR's Central Bank.

Opernpalais & Kronprinzenpalais (Map 8)

The next two buildings to the east on the right-hand side are the Kronprinzessinenpalais (Crown Princesses' Palace) and Kronprinzenpalais (Crown Princes' Palace). The former has been renamed **Opernpalais** and houses a stuffy cafe famous for its cake selection, as well as a pub and cocktail bar. The best time to visit is summer when the lively beer garden is open.

The baroque, colonnaded Kronprinzenpalais (1664) indeed served as a royal residence until the end of WWI. After 1919 it housed a department of the National Gallery, which was closed by the Nazis in 1937. In GDR days it was used as a guesthouse for visiting dignitaries. Since 1999, part of the exhibit of the Deutsches Historisches Museum (see below) from across the street is on view here, while the museum is undergoing restoration and expansion. It's open from 10 am to 6 pm, closed Wednesday (free).

Schinkelmuseum (SMPK, Map 8)

Just south of the Crown Prince's palace – on Werderscher Markt, corner of Oberwallstrasse – is the Schinkel-designed **Friedrichswerdersche Kirche** (1830) with the Schinkelmuseum (☎ 20 90 55 55). Besides a collection of neoclassical sculpture, it contains an exhibit on the life and work of the multiskilled architect and sculptor himself in the upstairs gallery. Hours are from 10 am to 6 pm Tuesday to Sunday (DM4/2).

The chunky-looking building south of the church housed the German national bank under the Nazis. In GDR days it was the country's true seat of power as headquarters of the central committee of the SED party. It is now being prepared to house the Federal Ministry of Foreign Affairs.

Neue Wache (Map 8)

Back on Unter den Linden, opposite the Opernpalais, is the restored Neue Wache (New Guardhouse, 1818), built by Schinkel for King Friedrich Wilhelm III (ruled 1797-1840). (For details, see Tour I of the special Architecture section in the Facts about Berlin chapter.)

Deutsches Historisches Museum (Map 8)

The rose-coloured baroque building Zeughaus, just east of the Neue Wache, was designed in 1706 by Andreas Schlüter as the royal armoury. An inner courtyard features Schlüter's famous 22 masks of dying warriors. The structure normally contains the Museum of German History with artefacts, paintings, maps and photos tracing German history from 900 AD to the present, as well as excellent changing exhibits.

Closed until 2001, the museum is undergoing extensive restoration and expansion under the guidance of Chinese-American architect IM Pei. The original edifice will be topped by a dramatic glass roof, and just north of here a modern wing, which will be used for special exhibits, is being constructed. Meanwhile, portions of the permanent exhibit are on view at the Crown Prince's Palace (see the section on it earlier this chapter).

MUSEUMSINSEL (MAP 8)

East of the Museum of German History, the lovely **Schlossbrücke** (Palace Bridge), with its Schinkel-designed marble statues, leads to a little Spree island called Cölln, the site of Berlin's earliest medieval settlement. Its northern tip is better known as Museum Island for the cluster of world-class museums located here. Unfortunately, badly needed restoration has resulted in the closure of three of the five museums for an extended period of time. Until at least 2001, only the Altes Museum and the Pergamon Museum will be open.

The Museumsinsel museums are an outgrowth of a late 18th century trend among Europe's royal houses to share their private collections with the public. The British Museum in London, the Louvre in Paris, the

Berlin Nicknames

Berliners are known for having a way with words. They also have a fertile imagination, evidence of which you'll find in the numerous nicknames they've given to their landmarks. Here's a sample:

Kaiser Wilhelm Memorial Church	Hohler Zahn (Hollow Tooth)
Memorial Church & New Hall of Worship	Lipstick & Powdercase
House of World Culture	Schwangere Auster (Pregnant Oyster)
Reichstag Cupola	Eierwärmer (English Egg Cosy)
TV Tower	Telespargel (Tele-Asparagus)
Funkturm	Langer Lulatsch (Long Lulatsch)
ICC Congress Centre	Raumschiff (Space Ship)
Victory Column	Gold Else (Golden Else)
Air Lift Memorial	Hungerharke (Hunger Rake)
Wilhelminian pissoirs	Café Achteck (Café Octagon)

Prado in Madrid and the Glyptothek in Munich all date back to this time. Not to be outdone – and egged on by his advisers and supporters – Friedrich Wilhelm III commissioned Schinkel for the construction of the Altes Museum (1829). As a result of the royal collections growth, in 1841, Friedrich Wilhelm IV decided to turn the entire island into a museum complex. The **Neues Museum** was completed in 1855, followed by the **Alte Nationalgalerie** (1876), the **Bodemuseum** (1904) and finally the **Pergamon Museum** (1930).

Altes Museum & Neues Museum (SMPK)

Squatting on the northern edge of the Lustgarten, the Altes Museum (Old Museum, ☎ 20 90 55 55) at Am Lustgarten is an imposing neoclassical edifice (for details see the special Architecture section in the Facts about Berlin chapter).

On the upper floor are highlights from the collection of 18th and 19th century masterpieces from the Old National Gallery, which will be closed for renovation until at least 2001. Look here for sculpture by Christian Daniel Rauch and Johann Gottfried Schadow as well as paintings by Renoir, Monet, Manet, Cézanne and Constable. Also of note are the brooding images of Romanticists Arnold Böcklin and Anselm Feuerbach, the Prussian military scenes of Adolph Menzel and the strong works of Max Liebermann, Max Beckmann, Max Slevogt and Lovis Corinth. On the ground floor is a collection of antique sculpture. Museum hours are from 10 am to 6 pm, closed Monday (DM8/4, SMPK Day Pass).

Immediately behind the Altes Museum is the SMPK **Neues Museum** (New Museum) by Friedrich August Stüler, whose wartime ruins are only now being restored. Upon its scheduled completion in 2005 it will consolidate the Egyptian collections from the nearby Bodemuseum and the Egyptian Museum in Charlottenburg.

Alte Nationalgalerie (SMPK)

The Alte Nationalgalerie (Old National Gallery) at Bodestrasse 1-3 is just east of the Neues Museum and another Stüler design. It looks like a Corinthian temple perching on a raised platform and is reached via a sweeping double staircase. Scheduled to reopen in 2001, its permanent exhibit of 18th and 19th century masterpieces has been temporarily incorporated into that of the Gallery of the Romantics at Charlottenburg Palace.

Bodemuseum (SMPK)

Opened in 1904 during the reign of Emperor Wilhelm II, the neobaroque Bodemuseum at the island's northernmost tip is scheduled to reopen on its 100th anniversary. Designed by Ernst von Ihne, it was originally called Kaiser-Friedrich-Museum but renamed for its first director Wilhelm von Bode in 1956.

Pergamon Museum (SMPK)

If you only have time for one museum in Berlin, make it the Pergamon (☎ 20 90 55 55). A feast of classical Greek, Babylonian, Roman, Islamic and Middle Eastern art and architecture, it will amaze and enlighten you.

Under the roof of a monumental edifice that took nearly 20 years to build (completed in 1930) are three world-class collections: the Collection of Classical Antiquities (CCA); the Museum of Near Eastern Antiquities (MNEA); and the Museum of Islamic Art (MIA). Audioguides with four hours of taped commentary (in eight languages) are available for hire at DM8. Also look for plastic trays holding sheets in English, French and German that provide detailed background on the main exhibits. Each sheet costs 10 Pfennig. Payment is by an honour system; just place the money in the box as you exit.

The Pergamon is open from 10 am to 6 pm Tuesday to Sunday (DM8/4, SMPK Day Pass). You'll need at least two hours to do this place justice. If your time is limited, stick to the highlights detailed below.

Collection of Classical Antiquities The first major exhibit you'll see is also one of the most spectacular and what gives the museum its name: the **Pergamon Altar** (165 BC) from Asia Minor, a gargantuan raised

A familiar sight: Berlin's cobblestoned laneways.

Berlin's power station lights up the canal.

Brandenburg Gate.

The Quadriga chariot sits majestically above the Brandenburg Gate.

DAVID PEEVERS

A modern sculpture frames the Gedächtniskirche on Tauenzienstrasse.

Berlin Cathedral restored to its pre-WWII splendour.

marble shrine the height of a three storey building. It's mindboggling to think that what you see here was merely the entrance area of an entire complex. Check out the scale models to help put it all in perspective.

The 120m **frieze** framing the hall's wall shows the gods doing battle with the giants. Note the amazing anatomical precision, down to pectorals and facial expressions. Behind the altar, and reached by walking up its steps, is the **Telephos Frieze** which depicts the life story of the legendary founder of Pergamon.

The exhibit continues past the north (left) door with plenty of antique sculpture. If you're pressed for time, skip it or just check out the **Hellenistic architecture** of room 8, entered through the marble foyer of a 2nd century BC temple, where you'll find a stunning floor mosaic.

The other CCA highlight, though, awaits in Room 6 (Roman architecture), behind the south (right) door: the splendidly preserved **Gate of Miletus**, built under Emperor Hadrian in the early 2nd century AD. Merchants and customers once flooded through here onto the market square of Miletus, a Roman trading town in Asia Minor that functioned as a bridge between Asia and Europe. Note the gate's symmetry and intricate decorative detail. The **Orpheus Mosaic** in the same room is from a villa in Miletus.

Museum of Near Eastern Antiquities

Passing through the Gate of Miletus, you seamlessly enter another culture and century: Babylon during the reign of Nebuchadnezzar II (604-562 BC). This collection's *pièce de résistance* is the world famous **Ishtar Gate** fronted by a 30m-long 'Processional Way' (the original was 250m long). The walls of both the gate and way are covered in cobalt blue and ochre glazed bricks and feature reliefs of striding lions (a symbol of the goddess Ishtar), horses, dragons and unicorns. The walls of the gate itself are 15m high, which is presumed to be only half of their original height.

Room 5 is also worth a closer look for its unique **mosaic wall** from a temple in Uruk (3000 BC). The wall is put together from countless clay pegs in different colours arranged in a decorative pattern. This was not done so much for aesthetic reasons but rather to add a layer of reinforcement to the temple's brittle adobe walls.

Museum of Islamic Art The MIA is on the upper floor and reached via a staircase from the MNEA. It showcases art and objects from the 7th to the 19th centuries AD, including carpets, wood carvings, ceramics and books. The first highlight awaits in Rooms 9 and 10 in the form of the exterior wall of the fortress-like **Caliph's Palace in Mshatta**, probably built during the reign of Califh al-Walid II (743-744 AD). Mshatta itself, which means 'winter camp', was located near today's Jordanian capital Amman. The section on display here is part of a wall that once surrounded a complex measuring 144m by 144m and was guarded by 25 towers. The delicate-looking facade is smothered in decorative detail featuring vines and tendrils as well as whimsical animals and mythical figures.

Room 14 contains an impressive **Mihrab** (1226 AD), a prayer niche from Kaschan in Iran, ablaze with shiny golden, blue and turquoise tiles with Arabic inscriptions and adornments. Not to be missed either is the 17th century **Aleppo Room** (Room 17) from the house of a Christian merchant in today's Syria. Each square centimetre of wall space is overlaid with colourful wooden panelling painted with dizzying detail. If you look closely, you can make out *The Last Supper* and *Mary and Child* amid all the ornamentation (straight ahead, on the right of the door).

Berliner Dom

On its eastern end, Museumsinsel is anchored by the towering mass of the neobaroque Berlin Cathedral (1905), the former court church of the royal Hohenzollern dynasty. It's almost miraculous that this ostentatious symbol of monarchical power survived the GDR's fervour for erasing all traces of Berlin's imperial past, especially since it suffered grave damage during WWII. Rebuilt mostly with money pouring in from the western churches, its restoration was, in fact, not completed until 1993, three years after the Wende.

The colossal structure (114m long, 73m wide, 85m high) is crowned by a central copper dome topped with a golden cross and ringed by four smaller towers. To get a sense of its vastness, climb the 270 steps to the **viewing gallery** at the base of the dome. Besides giving you nice views over the central city, it also lets you admire the intricate church design from a bird's-eye perspective.

The main church itself is richly decorated. The niches in the northern and southern apses hold the ornate sarcophagi of members of the Hohenzollern family. More of these elaborate coffins, including those designed by Schlüter for King Friedrich I (1713) and his second wife Sophie Charlotte (1705), are on view in the **crypt**. Only a small selection is currently open to the public.

Cathedral visiting hours are from 9 am to 8 pm daily with hourly guided tours (in German) from 10.30 am to 3.30 pm. Admission is DM8/5 for the church, crypt and viewing gallery (DM5/3 for church and crypt only). English-German services are held at 6 pm Thursday. Organ recitals take place at 3 pm almost daily from May to September.

Lustgarten

The cathedral is fronted by the Lustgarten (Pleasure Garden) which began life in the late 16th century as a vegetable and herb garden for the adjacent palace kitchen. In 1650, Berlin's first potatoes were harvested here. The Soldier King, Friedrich Wilhelm I, had it converted into a parade ground, but in 1830 Schinkel turned it back into a small park to complement his then brand-new Altes Museum. The Nazis paved it over and now, after much debate, the garden is being restored to its Schinkel-era appearance.

SCHLOSSPLATZ AREA (MAP 8)

Nothing of today's sterile Schlossplatz, called Marx-Engels-Platz under the GDR, serves as a reminder of the magnificent edifice that stood here from 1451 to 1951, the Berliner Schloss (City Palace). Begun as a fortress-like structure during the reign of Elector Friedrich II, it was enlarged, then

reconfigured and renovated many times, finally taking up the entire area of today's square. A rectangular building with two inner courtyards, its most pleasing architectural features were a triumphal-arch portal and an octagonal chapel with a huge cupola.

WWII left its mark, but structurally the palace was not beyond repair and, in fact, served as a makeshift museum right after 1945. In 1950, though, the GDR's Walter Ulbricht arbitrarily declared that it was 'a ruin not worthy of reconstruction' and, arrogantly ignoring protests from east and west, had the 500-year-old building blown up to make room for mass demonstrations and military parades. It was a decision even East Berlin political honchos later regretted.

Palast der Republik

In place of the royal palace, the GDR eventually built their Palast der Republik (Palace of the Republic, 1976), a clumsy pile of concrete and steel with a glitzy facade of rust-coloured mirror glass. Until 1990 it was home of the GDR parliament, the Volkskammer (People's Chamber) and site of SED party conventions. The complex was also accessible to the common people during congresses, balls and concerts (Harry Belafonte once sang here) held in a hall that seated up to 5000. There was also a gallery, restaurants and bars.

In 1990 it was discovered that the 'palace' was contaminated with asbestos, forcing its immediate closure. For years demolition looked inevitable but, while discussion about its fate has continued, it's been left to crumble, an eyesore in a blossoming Berlin. In 1993-94, one step ahead of Christo and his wrapped Reichstag, a French artist clad the structure with plastic sheets designed to look like the old Berliner Schloss. This sparked interest in rebuilding the original structure and the formation of the Berlin Historical Association. (See the section on the Berlin Story exhibit earlier in this chapter).

Around Schlossplatz

Only the triumphal-arch portal from which Karl Liebknecht proclaimed a Socialist German Republic in 1918 was spared during demolition of the Berliner Schloss. It was later incorporated into the **Staatsratsgebäude** (State Council Building), a surprisingly pleasant construction from the early 1960s on the south side of Schlossplatz.

The kaleidoscopic windows in the foyer depict the 'historical evolution' of the GDR from the ill-fated revolutionary days of 1918-19 to the founding of the communist state in 1949. The portraits in the centre show Rosa Luxemburg and Karl Liebknecht, co-founders of the German Communist Party (KPD).

East of the State Council Building, across Breite Strasse, is the **Neue Marstall** (New Royal Stables), once home to horses and carriages and now containing the City Archives. Note the bronze reliefs on the wall facing the Palace of the Republic which depict socialist heroes and pivotal revolutionary events.

Immediately south at Breite Strasse 35-36 is the ornately gabled **Ribbeckhaus** (1624), Berlin's only remaining residential Renaissance building. Today it contains the Centre for Berlin Studies, with the City Library next door (for information about both, see the Libraries section in the Facts for the Visitor chapter).

FRIEDRICHSTRASSE (MAP 8)

The area around U/S-Bahn station Friedrichstrasse has been Berlin's premier theatre district since the late 19th century, although the station itself has an even more 'dramatic' history. Until 1990, Bahnhof Friedrichstrasse was the main gateway for western German visitors to East Berlin. Immediately to the north of the U-Bahn station exit stands the unassuming squat building that once housed the border checkpoint. Called **Tränenpalast** (Palace of Tears), this was where western visitors had to say goodbye to their eastern friends and family. Many tears of sorrow were shed within these walls, hence the name. Today it's a concert and cabaret venue as well as a nightclub (see the Entertainment chapter) with a colourful slab of the Wall outside its entrance.

Just across Weidendammbrücke is the **Berliner Ensemble** theatre at Bertolt-Brecht-

Platz 1, originally called Theater am Schiffbauerdamm (the name refers to the shipbuilders who once worked here on the banks of the Spree). It made headlines within days of its 1892 opening with the premiere of Gerhart Hauptmann's *The Weavers*, a play under imperial ban for being critical of social conditions. When the Kaiser heard of the performance, he immediately cancelled his subscription to the royal box.

In 1903, Max Reinhardt got his first crack at directing here, but the theatre did not reach its zenith until after WWII when it became the permanent venue of the Berliner Ensemble, the troupe founded by Bertolt Brecht and his wife Helene Weigel in 1949. A **statue** of the seated Brecht, hands folded in his lap and surrounded by three black marble pillars engraved with quotations from his works, is outside the theatre.

About 200m east of the theatre, still on Schiffbauerdamm, the **Ministry of the Environment** will be located right across the road from the **Federal Press Office** on the Reichstagufer.

Turning right on Albrechtstrasse will take you through a pleasant residential area to Schumannstrasse. At No 13a is the **Deutsches Theater** (1850) where classical operettas formed the standard repertoire until Otto Brahm – a dedicated supporter of Hauptmann and other naturalists – took over in 1894. The theatre experienced its heyday under Reinhardt, who succeeded Brahm and who directed it, with interruptions, from 1905 to 1932 (Also see the boxed text 'Max Reinhardt – Impresario Extraordinare').

Retrace your steps, then follow Reinhardtstrasse east back to Friedrichstrasse and the **Friedrichstadtpalast** with its gaudy facade. The structure you see today dates from just 1985 and replaced the one from 1869. Originally a market hall, it later housed a circus and was converted to a stage by Max Reinhardt in 1919. Lavish, commercial musical revues with showgirls and live orchestras take place here today.

For more on any of these theatres, see the Entertainment chapter.

Max Reinhardt – Impresario Extraordinaire

Max Reinhardt (1873-1943) was one of the seminal figures in the history of German theatre. Under his stewardship, Berlin became the country's leading stage in the first three decades of the 20th century. Born in Vienna of Jewish descent (his birth name was Max Goldmann), Reinhardt soon traded a traineeship in banking for a career in the theatre. When, in 1894, Otto Brahm hired him as an actor at the Deutsches Theater (DT), his mercurial career path was launched.

At the age of 27, while still acting at the DT, he co-founded Berlin's first literary cabaret – Schall und Rauch – on New Year's Eve 1900. In 1902 he became director of the Kleines Theater and simultaneously ran the Neues Theater from 1903 to 1906, making a name for himself with a production of Maxim Gorki's *Nachtasyl* (Night Asylum, 1903). In 1905 he inherited the mantle of the Deutsches Theater from Brahm and, on the side, also founded the Kammerspiele a year later.

MICK WELDON

Stylistically, Reinhardt completely turned his back on the Naturalism favoured by his mentor Brahm and broke new ground by using technological innovations to enhance the illusionary effects of the theatre. He integrated light effects, music, the new turning stage and other devices into his lavish productions, including his famous version of Shakespeare's *A Midsummer Night's Dream*. He demanded and extracted great performances from his actors.

During WWI, Reinhardt also directed the Neue Volksbühne, which he had founded in 1913. In 1919, he opened the Grosse Schauspielhaus (later the Friedrichstadtpalast) and co-founded the Salzburg Festival. In 1920, he suddenly handed the directorship of his Berlin theatres to Felix Hollaender and spent the next four years shuttling between theatres in Vienna, Salzburg and Berlin. Drawn back to the Berlin of the 'Golden Twenties' in 1924, he founded the Komödie am Kurfürstendamm and returned to running the DT until 1932. Reinhardt left Germany as soon as Hitler came to power, first going to Austria until 1938, then emigrating to the USA after the *Anschluss* (annexation). He died in New York on 30 October 1943.

ORANIENBURGER TOR AREA (MAP 4)
Brecht-Weigel Gedenkstätte

Bertolt Brecht and his wife, Helene Weigel, made their Berlin home at Chausseestrasse 125 from 1953 until their respective deaths in 1956 and 1971. It is a short walk northwest of Oranienburger Tor U-Bahn station (U6) and has been preserved as the Brecht-Weigel House (☎ 28 30 57 00). Inside, Brecht's spacious but rather modest living and working quarters on the 1st floor are functionally furnished with leather chairs from the 1930s and also some Biedermeier pieces. His large library contains everything from German classics to books on the FBI and detective stories. The tiny bedroom where he died (probably of a heart attack) remains as if he'd just left, with hat and woollen cap hanging on a door hook and Chinese artwork on the walls.

Weigel's living quarters on the ground floor are comparatively cluttered and have a surprisingly petit bourgeois character, reflected in her passion for collecting (jugs, porcelain, glass etc).

Guided tours (in German) leave on the hour and half hour between 10 and noon Tuesday to Friday, also from 5 to 7 pm Thursday, from 9.30 am to 2 pm Saturday and hourly between 11 am to 6 pm Sunday (DM6/3). Call for reservations since tours are limited to eight people. The entrance is upstairs to the right from the rear courtyard.

Museum für Naturkunde

A short walk north is the Humboldt University's surprisingly fascinating Museum für Naturkunde (Natural History Museum, ☎ 20 93 85 40) at Invalidenstrasse 43. Pride of place goes to the world-famous **Dinosaur Hall** with its star exhibit: a 23m long and 12m tall skeleton of a *Brachiosaurus brancai*, in fact the world's largest exhibited dinosaur skeleton. The other six dinosaur skeletons in the hall are smaller but no less interesting and neither is the fossilised archaeopteryx, the prehistoric species that forms the evolutionary link between reptiles and birds.

Evolution in general is the underlying theme of the exhibits in 16 vast rooms. Another show-stopper is 'Bobby', a preserved gorilla that was the first such animal raised in captivity from baby to adulthood. The museum is open from 9.30 am to 5 pm Tuesday to Sunday (DM5/2.50, U6 to Zinnowitzer Strasse).

The building just east of the museum is set to be the new home of the Transportation Ministry.

Hamburger Bahnhof (SMPK)

About a 10 minute walk west of the Museum für Naturkunde, the Hamburger Bahnhof (☎ 20 90 55 55), at Invalidenstrasse 50-51, is Berlin's premier contemporary art museum. It opened in November 1996 and picks up where the Neue Nationalgalerie at the Kulturforum leaves off. Big names, including Joseph Beuys, Andy Warhol, Robert Rauschenberg, Anselm Kiefer and Keith Haring, form the core collection, which spans the last four decades.

The exhibit space is centred on a vaulted central hall, which has the loftiness of a Gothic cathedral. With walls painted a gleaming white and supported by an exposed skeleton of steel beams, it is the perfect environment for megasized canvases and large scale installations. Smaller art is displayed in the 80m-long vaulted Ostgalerie and side wings.

At least as interesting as the art (and to some of us, perhaps even more so) is the architecture of the building. From the outside, the gleaming white, three-winged former train station exudes a palatial aura, though the clock in the right tower points to its more mundane origin. At night, the structure is bathed in a mystical blue and green, the result of an installation by Dan Flavin.

Museum hours are from 10 am to 6 pm Tuesday to Friday, from 11 am weekends (DM8/4, SMPK Day Pass).

GENDARMENMARKT AREA (MAP 8)

Once a thriving market, the quiet, graceful Gendarmenmarkt is Berlin's most beautiful square. Its name comes from the Gendarme regiment which had its headquarters and main stables here from 1736 to 1773. The twin churches of Deutscher Dom (German Cathedral) and Französischer Dom (French Cathedral) combine with Schinkel's **Konzerthaus** (see the special Architecture section in the Facts about Berlin chapter) to form a superbly harmonious architectural trio. Unifying elements include the columned porticoes and the domed towers of the two churches. Only the French cathedral is used as a place of worship.

A magnificent **statue of Friedrich Schiller**, one of Germany's greatest writers, stands in the centre of the square. Squirreled away by the Nazis, it ended up in the west, from where it returned to East Berlin in 1988 following an exchange of artworks between the two German states.

All Gendarmenmarkt buildings suffered severe structural damage during WWII, and restoration wasn't completed until 1984, just in time for the 35th anniversary of the founding of the GDR. The closest U-Bahn station is Französische Strasse (U6).

Deutscher Dom

The German Cathedral was completed in 1708 and consists of a pentagonal central structure surrounded by apses. It took another 80 years before it got its dazzling galleried dome, designed by Karl Gontard, which is supported by a ring of slender Corinthian columns. Renovated after the Wende, the Dom reopened in 1996 as a museum featuring **Fragen an die Deutsche**

Geschichte (☎ 22 73 21 41), an excellent exhibit on German history from 1800 to the present, previously housed at the Reichstag.

A slightly claustrophobic ground floor, which focuses on the beginnings of the democratic movement in Germany in the early 19th century, gives way to a four-storey high cylindrical central space with an interesting installation of mannequins dressed in historical, 'typical' German outfits. Displays are presented chronologically on three galleried tiers, with each floor dedicated to one particular period (pre-WWI, between the wars and post-WWII). There's a nice cafe on the 4th floor. The exhibit is open from 10 am to 6 pm Tuesday to Sunday (free).

Französischer Dom

The mirror image of the Deutscher Dom, the French Cathedral was once the main church of the French Huguenots who, persecuted in their own country, settled in Berlin in the late 17th century. Built between 1701 and 1705, the cathedral was modelled after the main Huguenot church in Charenton, which had been destroyed in 1688. Its floor plan reveals a rectangular structure with semicircular conches. By 1785 it too had acquired its landmark Gontard-designed, domed tower, matching that of the German Cathedral.

Inside is the **Hugenottenmuseum** (Huguenot Museum, ☎ 229 17 60) which chronicles the fate of these French Protestants in France and in Berlin-Brandenburg from the 17th to the 20th century. On display are books, art, manuscripts and documents. Descriptions are in French and German. Hours are from noon to 5 pm Tuesday to Saturday, from 11 am Sunday (DM3/2).

For a great view, climb the tower to an outdoor **viewing gallery**, which is open from 9 am to 7 pm daily (DM3/2). Concerts on the church's **carillon** take place periodically on weekends.

Friedrichstadtpassagen

The area around the Gendarmenmarkt was once known as Friedrichstadt, a residential community custom-planned by Friedrich I, with Friedrichstrasse as its main artery.

Over the centuries, this main thoroughfare evolved into Berlin's liveliest and most elegant boulevard – until WWII and division put an end to this nexus of urban vitality. After the Wende, Friedrichstrasse became the focus of an ambitious renewal project. Between Französische Strasse and Mohrenstrasse, an international team of architects created a trio of interconnected office and shopping complexes – the Friedrichstadtpassagen – in the hope of breathing new life into the languishing boulevard.

Called 'Quartiers,' these structures are like jewel boxes; their innocuous exteriors hiding sparkling treasures within. Quartier 207 is home to French department store Galeries Lafayette where Jean Nouvel has created a central translucent glass funnel that reflects light with the intensity of a hologram.

At Quartier 206 the usual clique of international designer boutiques has its hallowed halls. Take a look even if Donna Karan doesn't do it for you, the architecture is definitely worth it for the elegant composition in multihued marble, kaleidoscopically arranged in geometric patterns beneath a tent-like glass roof. Quartier 205 has ceilings of cathedral dimensions and a light court accentuated with a three-storey high installation by John Chamberlain.

POTSDAMER PLATZ AREA

Just east of the Kulturforum museum complex (see section later in this chapter), in an area once occupied by the Wall, a slow and difficult birth is taking place with Berlin's largest-scale new development. (See the Potsdam Platz map in this chapter.)

Since construction began in 1993, Potsdamer Platz has been ranked as one of Berlin's top tourist attractions, which is no surprise. The mammoth effort to rebuild the centre of an entire living, breathing city in one fell stroke is unprecedented. It's a challenge, and an opportunity, to reflect on the *Zeitgeist* at the dawn of a new millennium.

For an overview of the scope of the construction, visit the **Infobox** (☎ 226 62 40), a nail-polish red, three storey container on stilts above U-Bahn station Potsdamer Platz (U2). Inside is a free multimedia exhibit

The Reincarnation of Potsdamer Platz

The dawn of Potsdamer Platz came with the construction of the first railway line to Potsdam in 1838. From the late 19th century through the Weimar era, the square evolved into the heart of metropolitan life and entertainment in Berlin, mirroring New York's Times Square in vibrancy and intensity. Thousands of people came through here daily, stopping for coffee at Café Josty, a beer at Pschörr brewery or rendezvousing in the lobby of the elegant Hotel Esplanade. By the 1920s, Potsdamer Platz had become such an important traffic nexus that Europe's first – albeit hand-operated – traffic light was installed (1924) to control the flow of more than 100,000 people, 20,000 cars and 30 tram lines passing through each day.

War sucked all life out of Potsdamer Platz, which suffered 80% destruction, and it soon plunged into a coma before being bisected by the Wall in 1961. On the GDR side was the infamous 'death strip' while in the west sprawled an abandoned and desolate wasteland. Nearly all remaining historic buildings here were demolished at that time, except the ruined Hotel Esplanade, the erstwhile *belle* of Bellevuestrasse. (In fact, the cafe of this hotel was moved by Sony, with the help of some wizardly technology, when the hotel was torn down in 1996. It has been incorporated into the new Sony centre.)

With the fall of the Wall – and communism – capitalism, abhorring a vacuum, took over instantly. It didn't take long to realise the enormous commercial potential of this huge slice of prime real estate, which was soon gobbled up by powerful investors like Daimler-Benz (now DaimlerChrysler), Sony and A&T, a development company.

called 'See the City of Tomorrow Today' which explains all elements of the gigantic project with scale models, historical footage, interactive computers, posters and more. Some of the exhibits are in English. It will remain open from 9 am to 7 pm daily (to 9 pm Thursday) until at least December 2000. For a bird's-eye view of the new city within a city, head to the Infobox's rooftop terrace (DM2).

A work in progress for some time to come, the Potsdamer Platz area is slowly taking shape. By the time you're reading this, Helmut Jahn's glass and steel **Sony Center** should have opened, while the **DaimlerCity** complex was inaugurated in October 1998. More than DM4 billion has been invested in this 23,000 sq metre mixed-use area whose overall layout is based on a plan by Renzo Piano (best known as the mastermind behind Paris' Centre Pompidou) and Christoph Kohlbecker.

They were joined by an illustrious cast of architects including Arata Isozaki, creator of the waffle-patterned, coffee-coloured **Berliner Volksbank** building; Rafael Moneo

who conceived the sleek, minimalist **Grand Hyatt Hotel**; and Richard Rogers who planned office buildings and the **Potsdamer Platz Arkaden**, a stylish three storey shopping mall sheltered by a glass canopy.

Piano himself designed six of the 19 structures, including the entertainment ensemble of **Musical Theater, IMAX** and **Casino**, all orbiting a central plaza called Marlene-Dietrich-Platz. The adjacent **Debis Building** with its dramatic cathedral-like atrium that's well proportioned for Jean Tinguely's bizarre *Méta-Maxi* sculpture is also his work. More public art by international hot shots like Keith Haring, Jeff Koons and Robert Rauschenberg graces the outdoor spaces.

The result is pleasant but not the kind of daring new development with cutting-edge, 21st century architecture that many had hoped for and expected. Architects were hamstrung from the start when Berlin city planners required them to follow an approach called 'critical reconstruction'. The size and appearance of the new structures were tightly regulated, with an eye towards

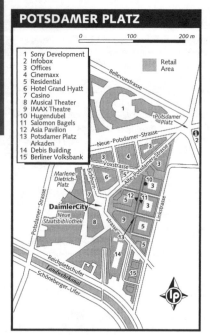

POTSDAMER PLATZ

1 Sony Development
2 Infobox
3 Offices
4 Cinemaxx
5 Residential
6 Hotel Grand Hyatt
7 Casino
8 Musical Theater
9 IMAX Theatre
10 Hugendubel
11 Salomon Bagels
12 Asia Pavilion
13 Potsdamer Platz Arkaden
14 Debis Building
15 Berliner Volksbank

avoiding anything too avant-garde, postmodern or 'monumental'. With facades made from natural materials like terracotta, sandstone or clinker, they've certainly succeeded at that goal. But where they've failed, at least to this point, is in creating a lively, appealing quarter bustling with people happy to be there.

THIRD REICH GOVERNMENT QUARTER (MAP 8)

Wilhelmstrasse, just east of Potsdamer Platz, was the traditional government centre from the late 18th century through the Third Reich era. The chancellery, presidential palace and the foreign ministry were all located along here. During the Third Reich the area became the nexus of power and perversion in Hitler's Nazi Germany.

Since only the Air Force Ministry has survived from that time, you will have to exercise your imagination to picture what the area must have looked like. All other

structures were either destroyed outright in the war or later demolished by the Russians and East Germans.

For an immersion into the quarter's history, take the 'Infamous Third Reich Sites' walking tour offered by The Original Berlin Walks (see Walking Tours in the Getting Around chapter).

Neue Reichskanzlei

Hitler's Neue Reichskanzlei (New Chancellery, 1938) ran nearly the entire length of Vosstrasse, west of the intersection with Wilhelmstrasse. Albert Speer worked some 4000 people through a mad 24-hour schedule, completing the massive structure in only 11 months, two days ahead of schedule. It must have been an impressive sight. More than 400m long and built of yellow stucco and grey stone, it featured a columned entrance leading to a large inner courtyard.

One of the hallways inside measured 146m, a few metres longer than the Hall of Mirrors in Versailles (where the humiliating WWI peace treaty was signed). Only the finest building materials were used, including various kinds of marble, bronze, glass and mosaics. The Führer allegedly asked Speer to make the floors particularly slippery, joking that diplomats should have no trouble making their way here as they were used to walking on slippery terrain.

After the war, the Russians stripped out all that marble and creatively recycled it in their memorials in Treptower Park and on Strasse des 17 Juni.

The unsightly apartment complex now occupying the site dates from the late 80s and contains flats that were much coveted in the GDR. Residents included champion figure skater Katharina Witt.

Hitler's Bunker

The legendary Führerbunker, where Hitler took cyanide and then, for good measure, shot himself through the head on 30 April 1945, stood about 200m west of the Neue Reichskanzlei Chancellery on Vosstrasse, in the garden of the Alte Reichskanzlei. Today, the spot is covered by a large grassy area with some fledgling trees.

The Holocaust Memorial – Anatomy of a Debate

Capping more than a decade of debate and indecision, Berlin is finally poised to have a memorial honouring the six million Jews killed during the Holocaust. In June 1999, the Bundestag approved a design by the New York architect Peter Eisenman and, if all goes according to schedule, construction will begin in early 2000. It will be located on Ebertstrasse (Map 8) just south of the future American Embassy, on an area once marred by the Berlin Wall. The cost, DM15 million, is to be shared equally by the state of Berlin, the federal government and a nonprofit organisation.

1988

The story begins pre-Wende with journalist Lea Rosh's call for a monument to the murdered Jews. The West German government shows interest but the issue gets buried amid reunification euphoria. When picked up again in 1993, Chancellor Kohl supports the idea of a monument and calls for a design contest.

1995

A committee decides on a design by Jackob Marcks consisting of a gigantic slanted concrete plane engraved with the names of ALL murdered Jews. Kohl boycotts the idea and demands a new discussion. Others want a new contest. Rosh likes Marcks' design. The Berlin Senate postpones a decision.

1996

The Bundestag debates the issue without results.

1997

A new contest begins.

1998

A monumental design by Peter Eisenman is favoured by Kohl and others. Cultural and political leaders, including Günter Grass, Elie Wiesel, Martin Walser and Berlin's mayor, want to scratch the memorial altogether. Eisenman creates a less grandiose version, but there are voices demanding a third contest. Others propose to set up a branch of Steven Spielberg's Shoa Foundation instead. Lea Rosh insists on a memorial.

1999

More confusion ensues when a group of politicians and clerics support a design by theologian Richard Schröder in the form of a column inscribed with the 6th Commandment 'Thou Shalt Not Kill' in German, Hebrew and other languages. The idea is rejected by the Bundestag (now led by Chancellor Gerhard Schröder).

June 1999

Eisenman's downscaled version finds enough supporters (314 vs 209) in the Bundestag. It takes the form of a huge accessible field comprised of 2700 concrete pillars of varying height which, from afar, looks like a cemetery. An information centre is planned as well.
  Stay tuned.

Hitler had the bunker built in 1943 when the bombing of Berlin became serious but only spent his last six weeks in it. It was entered through an earlier shelter from 1935, known as the Vorbunker, and was extremely deep. The ceiling plate was one metre below ground, and the roof alone was 30cm-thick concrete topped by 20cm of soil.

After the war, the Soviets tried to blow up the whole thing but the concrete proved impervious to explosives and so they burned and flooded it. The ceiling was reportedly blown up bit by bit until the whole thing caved in and it was filled in with rubble during construction of the adjacent apartment building in 1988. There are rumours, however, that sections of the bunker still exist.

Reichsluftfahrtsministerium

The massive building on the corner of Wilhelmstrasse and Leipziger Strasse started life as Hermann Göring's Reichsluftfahrtsministerium (Air Force Ministry, 1935-36). It matches the monumental building style its architect Sagebiel already used in his expansion of Tempelhof airport. Ironically, it survived Allied bombing largely unscathed and was first used as a temporary meeting facility by the East German government. Later it became the GDR's House of Ministries.

After the Wende, the Treuhand-Anstalt, the agency charged with selling off East German companies and property after reunification, moved into the complex, now renamed Detlev-Rohwedder-Haus (after the first Treuhand chief who was murdered by Red Army Faction terrorists in 1991). At the time of research, it was being set up as the new home of the Ministry of Finance.

Gestapo Headquarters

On Niederkirchner Strasse, just east of the Martin-Gropius-Bau, is the site of the former Gestapo headquarters for which Göring took over the School of Applied Arts building in 1933. Only partly destroyed, it soon fell into disrepair and was demolished in the 50s. As Gestapo headquarters, it was one of the most feared buildings in Berlin during the Third

Reich. People unfortunate enough to be brought here were interrogated and tortured; many were transferred to concentration camps and killed. Himmler later merged the Gestapo with the SS under his prime henchman Reinhard Heydrich, the mastermind behind the 'Final Solution to the Jewish Question' at the Wannsee Conference. (See the Zehlendorf section in the Western Districts section later in this chapter).

The exhibit **Topographie des Terrors** (Topography of Terror, ☎ 25 48 67 03), Niederkirchner Strasse 8, next to the Martin-Gropius-Bau, documents these and other Nazi crimes. It's open 10 am to 6 pm Tuesday to Sunday from October to April and 10 am to 8 pm from May to September (free).

The building across the street was originally the Prussian parliament building, then went through a brief stint under the Nazis as the notorious People's Court (1934-35), before being turned into an air force officers' club by Göring. Nowadays it is the **Abgeordnetenhaus**, the seat of Berlin's city parliament. A stretch of the **Berlin Wall** runs along Niederkirchner Strasse from the Martin-Gropius-Bau to Wilhelmstrasse. (See the boxed text 'The Berlin Wall' later in this chapter.)

Martin-Gropius-Bau

The Martin-Gropius-Bau (☎ 25 48 67 77) at Niederkirchner Strasse 7 started life in the 1870s as a Museum of Applied Arts, designed by the uncle of Bauhaus architect Walter Gropius. It's a beautiful cube centred around a richly ornamented light court. The facades too are decorated with mosaics and terracotta reliefs.

Ruined during the war, it was only restored as an exhibition venue in the late 1970s. After another renovation, it reopened in the summer of 1999 with a historical retrospective of the first 50 years of the Federal Republic of Germany. It will continue to be used for large-scale special exhibitions. Hours are from 10 am to 8 pm Tuesday to Sunday (admission varies).

The same building also houses the Museum der linge (Museum of things, ☎ 2548 6900), which documents daily life throughout the 20th century through art, objects and bric-a-brac (free, same hours).

ALEXANDERPLATZ AREA (MAP 8)

Former East Berlin's main hub, Alexanderplatz – known as 'Alex' for short – was named after Tsar Alexander I who visited Berlin in 1805. Until then it had been called Ochsenplatz (oxen square). Today it's a mere shadow of the low-life district Alfred Döblin called 'the quivering heart of a cosmopolitan city' in his novel *Berlin Alexanderplatz* (1929). Redesigned several times in the late 1920s and badly bombed in WWII, the square's current socialist look dates from the 1960s. On 4 November 1989, some 700,000 people gathered here to rally against the GDR regime. They were vociferous but peaceful, and they were heard; five days later, the Wall came down.

The first impression of Alexanderplatz is overwhelming. Nothing seems to be built on a human – or humane – scale. A cacophonous jumble of concrete and glass high-rises combines with a treeless asphalt desert to form one of the most hideous and disorienting squares this writer has ever seen. This is a good place for a quick overview of the soulless architectural styles in vogue in the GDR. It's hard to imagine that it actually looked even more drab before the Wende – at least the giant billboards atop rooflines and the neon advertisements have added, well, splashes of colour.

Alexanderplatz has forever been a major public-transport hub. Today, trains stop both below ground and on the elevated train tracks slicing right through the square.

Aware of Alex's status as an aesthetic eyesore, the city commissioned acclaimed architect Hans Kollhoff to come up with a new design fit for the 21st century. He produced a futuristic assemblage consisting largely of New York-style skyscrapers. It's a controversial concept and whether it will be realised at all remains, like so much in Berlin, the focus of a lively debate.

Alexanderplatz has few sights, a minor one being the **World Time Clock** (1969) by Erich John with its enamel and aluminium panelling (don't use the subterranean men's loo nearby unless you want to be stared down by 101 men on the prowl). The other attraction is the **TV Tower** (1969), a spiky 365m-tall monstrosity. Just below the antenna is a shiny steel sphere which, when hit by sunlight, produces the reflection of a huge cross – a source of embarrassment to the atheist GDR and of glee in the west where they dubbed this phenomenon 'the Pope's revenge'.

If it's a clear day and the queue isn't too long, it's worth paying the DM8/3 admission (adults/children) to go up the tower. It's open from 9 am to 1 am daily (10 am to midnight during November to March). At the 207m level is the **Telecafé**, which makes a complete revolution every half an hour.

Marienkirche

The Gothic Marienkirche, just west of Alex on Karl-Liebknecht-Strasse, is one of Berlin's few surviving medieval buildings. Inside, note the baroque pulpit designed by Andreas Schlüter (1703) with its lavish canopy topped by a gaggle of cherubs set against gilded rays of sunlight. Another major attraction is the 23m-long *Totentanz* (Dance of Death) fresco, created in the late 15th century, which is being restored. It portrays a shrouded figure of Death in 14 guises leading people from all walks of life to their graves. The church is open from 10 am to 4 pm Monday to Friday, from noon at weekends (free).

Nearby is the opulent **Neptunbrunnen** (Neptune Fountain, 1891) by Reinhold Begas which was moved here from Schlossplatz. The female figures symbolise the rivers Rhine, Elbe, Oder and Weichsel.

Rotes Rathaus

A block south on Rathausstrasse stands the palatial Rotes Rathaus (Red Town Hall, 1860), home of Berlin's governing mayor and the Berlin Senate. It gets its name from the colour of the brick used in its construction (not from the political leanings of its occupants). The building successfully blends Italian Renaissance elements with northern German architecture. Note the terracotta frieze on the facade (1879) which depicts the entire city history starting with the 13th century. The representative staircase, with its four allegorical statues symbolising various trades, as well as the ceremonial halls, may be visited for free from 9 am to 6 pm weekdays, except during official functions.

NIKOLAIVIERTEL (MAP 8)

The Nikolaiviertel (Nicholas Quarter) lies just south-west of the Rotes Rathaus and is bounded by the broad Mühlendamm to the south. Some of Berlin's oldest houses stood here until destroyed by bombs in 1944. What you see today is the not entirely unsuccessful attempt by socialist architects to re-create a medieval village. Purists will be shocked to learn that hardly any of these buildings have actual historical origins and that most are made with the same ubiquitous prefab concrete slabs used for most other GDR-era buildings. Some wags have even dubbed it 'Disneyvietrel'.

Nonetheless, the GDR tried hard to celebrate the 750th anniversary of the founding of Berlin in an appropriate fashion. The result is a maze of narrow alleys lined by diminutive houses, all lorded over by the spindly twin spires of the **Nikolaikirche** (Church of St Nicholas), a three-nave church that is Berlin's oldest (1230). One of the few buildings that was restored rather than newly built, it contains a moderately interesting exhibit on the city's history from its beginnings to 1648. The most prized piece in its small collection of religious sculpture is the **Spandauer Madonna**, which was carved from sandstone around 1290. The church museum (☎ 24 00 20) is open from 10 am to 6 pm Tuesday to Sunday (DM5/2.50).

The 18th century **Knoblauchhaus** (☎ 24 00 20) at Poststrasse 23 is the oldest original residential building in the Nikolaiviertel. It served as the home of the Knoblauch family for nearly 170 years until 1928. One of the family members, Eduard Knoblauch, was the architect of the original New Synagogue in Oranienburger Strasse. The 1st floor chronicles the history of the family, while the 2nd contains six period rooms

showcasing bourgeois living in the age of Biedermeier. It's open from 10 am to 6 pm Tuesday to Sunday (DM3/1). In the basement is the rustic yet elegant Historische Weinstuben restaurant.

The house **Zum Nussbaum** at Am Nussbaum 3 also contains a convivial restaurant-pub, the original of which once stood on the nearby Fischerinsel. It's said to have been the favourite watering hole of local legend, humorist and cartoonist Heinrich Zille in the 1920s. A copy of the **Gerichtslaube**, the courts of justice, also stands in Poststrasse and contains a couple of pricey restaurants. (For more on eating in the Nikolaiviertel, see the Places to Eat chapter.)

Ephraim-Palais

The Ephraim-Palais (☎ 24 00 20), on the corner of Mühlendamm and Poststrasse, was the home of Friedrich II's treasurer, Veitel Heine Ephraim. It is considered to be one of Berlin's prettiest buildings thanks largely to its curved rococo facade with delicate gilded ironwork balconies and sculptural ornamentation.

The original building, which stood some 20m from the current location, was destroyed during the construction of the Mühlendamm bridge in 1935. The precious facade, though, was dismantled and stored for decades in West Berlin. In 1984, it was given to East Berlin to be used in the construction of the Nikolaiviertel.

These days, the Ephraim-Palais hosts exhibitions of Berlin art from the time of Friedrich II to 1945. Hours are from 10 am to 6 pm Tuesday to Sunday (DM5/2.50).

Hanfmuseum

The Hanfmuseum (Hemp Museum, ☎ 242 48 27), at Mühlendamm 5, is Germany's only museum devoted to the subject of hemp. Here botany hobbyists can expand their knowledge of their favourite plant by studying its cultural, medicinal and religious significance. There's also a section on the discussion about the legalisation of hemp. Hours are from 10 am to 8 pm Tuesday to Friday, from noon weekends (DM5, free for children under 10).

MOLKENMARKT AREA (MAP 8)

The busy intersection of Mühlendamm, Stralauer Strasse and Spandauer Strasse, immediately south of the Nikolaiviertel, marks the Molkenmarkt area. The name refers to its medieval origin as a dairy market, though it requires a good imagination to recognise it as such amid the roaring traffic. On the south side stands the building complex of the GDR Ministry of Culture which incorporated the former **mint** (1935) and the baroque **Palais Schwerin**.

Looming above it all is the **Alte Stadthaus** with its 100m-high colonnaded and domed tower built in the early 20th century for the city administration after the Rotes Rathaus had become too small. Later, the GDR's *Ministerrat* (Council of Minister) moved into the structure.

Head north on Jüdenstrasse, then right on Parochialstrasse which leads to the baroque **Parochialkirche** (1703) at Klosterstrasse 67. Designed by Johann Arnold Nering (whose other works include the oldest section of Charlottenburg Palace), the church was completely burnt in WWII and has been left unrestored. Its layout shows four conches framing a central square tower. With its bare walls, open ceiling (you can actually see the roof timbering), draughty doors and stone floors, it has a much more powerful effect than Charlottenburg's Memorial Church. The Parochialkirche is now primarily used for exhibits and concerts.

Also on Klosterstrasse is the **Palais Podewil** at No 68-70, a lovely 18th century patrician manor turned cultural centre (see the Entertainment chapter). A few steps farther north is another church ruin, that of the **Franziskaner Klosterkirche** (Franciscan Abbey Church), formerly a three-nave, cross-vaulted basilica made from red bricks and dating to the latter half of the 13th century. Though a secured ruin, what's left of the church has a fragile quality and there are, in fact, warning signs urging you not to stand too close to the walls in case they collapse. In summer, this space too is used for exhibits and concerts.

The building behind the church ruins at Littenstrasse 13-17 is the **Justizpalast** (Courts of Justice), built at the turn of the century and worthwhile checking out for its handsome Art Nouveau staircases. The historic restaurant-pub **Zur letzten Instanz** is nearby at Waisenstrasse 14. (See the section on Berliner Kneipen in the Entertainment chapter.)

MÄRKISCHES UFER (MAP 8)

The area around Märkisches Museum U-Bahn station yields a couple of moderately interesting sights. Head east from the station, then north on Inselstrasse to get to the spot where the Spree canal rejoins the river. To the left loom the monotonous high-rises of the **Fischerinsel**, the name given to the southern tip of the Spree island of Cölln (Museum Island occupies the northern end). As the name suggests, this used to be a fishing settlement, a crammed maze of alleyways lined by simple two-storey houses with claustrophobic courtyards, all interspersed with raucous pubs and tiny stores. Not much fishing these days.

Turning left into Märkisches Ufer leads to the baroque **Otto-Nagel-Haus** at No 16-18 which is now home of the Prussian Picture Archives. At No 12 is an exact copy of a rococo house that once stood on the opposite bank. The highlight here is the **Ermeler-Haus** at No 10, one of Berlin's most handsome town villas, despite being another replica. Now part of the art'otel Ermelerhaus (see the Places to Stay chapter), its lovely rococo interior is best enjoyed during a meal in the upmarket restaurant.

Back track to Wallstrasse, and turn left towards the Märkisches Museum within the small **Köllnischer Park**. This area once formed a part of the city fortifications built under Soldier King Friedrich Wilhelm I. A reminder is the so-called **Wusterhausensche Bär** (literally 'Bear of Wusterhausen'), a guard tower which, despite the name, has nothing to do with the three brown bears housed in a pit in the park. They are the **official city mascots** and are named Schnute (born 1981), Maxi (1986) and Tilo (1990).

Märkisches Museum

The red-brick pile at Am Köllnischen Park 5 is the Märkisches Museum (Museum of the March Brandenburg, ☎ 30 86 60), which was the largest history museum in the GDR. The exterior is a hotchpotch of replicas of actual buildings in Brandenburg. The tower, for instance, is modelled after that of the bishop's palace in Wittstock, while St Catherine's church in the town of Brandenburg inspired the Gothic gables. A copy of the Roland statue from the same town guards the museum entrance.

The exhibits are as eclectic as the museum's exterior and are divided into several thematic sections, including general city history from 1648 to 1815; primeval and early history; arts and crafts; paintings, furniture and sculpture etc. A highlight is the nifty **automatophones**, 18th century mechanical musical instruments, which are wound up and made to go through their noisy paces at 3 pm every Wednesday and at 11 am on Sunday. The museum is open from 10 am to 6 pm Tuesday to Sunday (DM5/2.50, free on Wednesday).

SPANDAUER VORSTADT (MAPS 4 & 8)

The Spandauer Vorstadt (Spandau suburb) is one of Berlin's hippest areas and teems with nightclubs, bars and restaurants. Besides Oranienburger Strasse, the main artery, much of the action takes place in side streets like Auguststrasse and Tucholskystrasse.

The quarter, bordered by Friedrichstrasse in the west and Karl-Liebknecht-Strasse/Prenzlauer Allee in the east, gets its name from the time when the main road to Spandau – today's Oranienburger Strasse – ran right through here. These days, it's often mistakenly called 'Scheunenviertel' (Barn Quarter), which is actually only the small section of Spandauer Vorstadt around Rosa-Luxemburg-Platz (see Scheunenviertel later in this chapter).

For centuries, the area was the centre of Berlin's Jewish community and since the opening of the New Synagogue it is becoming so again today.

The S1 or S2 to Oranienburger Strasse, the U6 to Oranienburger Tor or any S-Bahn to Hackescher Markt will put you right in the thick of things.

Hackesche Höfe (Map 8)

The Hackesche Höfe (Hackesche Courtyards, 1907) are among eastern Berlin's greatest success stories. After a three-year restoration, the series of courtyards reopened to great fanfare in late 1996. A multi-use complex combining apartments with restaurants and cafes, theatres, galleries and boutiques, it's a tourist favourite. While this unfortunately taints it with an overly commercial feel, it's definitely worth a visit.

Fronted by a beautiful facade, the main entrance off Rosenthaler Strasse immediately puts you into the prettiest courtyard, Hof I (Endellscher Hof). Its facades are smothered in kaleidoscopic, intricately patterned tiles by Art Nouveau artist August Endell. Also here is the Chamäleon Varieté (see the Entertainment chapter), which uses a banquet hall of the former and fashionably famous wine-restaurant Neumann as a performance space. Hof II (Theaterhof) features the Café Aedes, the Hackesches Hof-Theater and several architects' studios. The other six courtyards contain more galleries, fashion boutiques, bookstores and a nightclub.

Sophienstrasse (Map 4)

The Hackesche Höfe spill out onto Sophienstrasse, which was lavished with attention by the GDR regime in preparation for the 750th city anniversary in 1987. At the time, many of the 19th century houses along here were placed under protection and restored.

Of historical interest is the **Handwerkervereinshaus** at No 18 with the former assembly halls of the craftsmen's association founded in 1844. This group later formed the germ cell of the workers' movement in Berlin, eventually leading to the founding of the Sozialdemokratische Partei (SPD) in 1869 by August Bebel and Wilhelm Liebknecht. Both spoke to the workers in several meeting halls here, the largest of which held 1400 people. Called **Sophiensaele**, the space is now used for concerts, theatre and, primarily, dance performances.

Just past the Handwerkervereinshaus look for the entrance to the quiet and dignified

Sophienhöfe whose trio of courtyards contains galleries and the popular Barcomi's cafe (see the Places to Eat chapter). The connecting walkways are lined with primary coloured neon lights.

Already in view is the hulking presence of the baroque **Sophienkirche** (1713) surrounded by a gated churchyard. The only church in Mitte that survived WWII, it's a single-nave, galleried confection with understated decor and a delicate stucco ceiling. The handsome tower, with its copper and gilded top, was added in 1730. Unfortunately, it's usually closed but can be seen on tours (in German; call ☎ 282 58 77 for details). If the gate off Sophienstrasse is locked, walk to the corner with Grosse Hamburger Strasse, turn left and the entrance will be via a gap between two apartment buildings.

Neue Synagoge (Map 4)

At Oranienburger Strasse 29 is the beautifully restored Neue Synagoge (New Synagogue) crowned by the gold and silver Schwedler Dome, once again a Berlin landmark. Built in the Moorish-Byzantine style, the synagogue opened in 1866 as the nation's largest synogogue (3200 seats) in the presence of Otto von Bismarck and other Prussian dignitaries.

During the Kristallnacht pogrom on 9/10 November 1938, SA thugs tried to set fire to it – as they had to almost all other 13 synagogues in Berlin – but were prevented by a district police chief. A plaque on the synagogue facade commemorates this act of courage. The synagogue was nonetheless desecrated by the Nazis, though it wasn't destroyed until hit by bombs in 1943.

In the GDR era the ruins were left to linger until the mid-80s. Reconstruction began before the Wende on the 50th anniversary of Kristallnacht with a ceremony attended by Erich Honecker. The synagogue reopened in May 1995, this time with then-Chancellor Helmut Kohl and President Roman Herzog present.

Today it is not just a house of worship but a research and community centre called **Centrum Judaicum** (☎ 28 40 12 50). Its permanent exhibit 'Open the Gates: The New Synagogue 1866-1995' provides an overview of Jewish life and culture in Berlin and Brandenburg. On display are photographs, original furnishings, documents and liturgical objects. Hushed 'sound fragments' of the synagogue's construction and destruction, as well as murmurings of prayer and everyday life in the quarter before the Holocaust, heighten the mood.

The Centrum Judaicum is open from 10 am to 5.30 pm Sunday to Thursday, from 10 am to 1.30 pm Friday (DM5/3). Guided tours (DM3/1.50) leave at 4 pm on Wednesday and at 2 and 4 pm on Sunday. Expect a lot of security checks.

Next door at No 31 is the **Jewish Gallery** (☎ 28 28 62), open daily except Saturday.

Tacheles (Map 4)

Since its dramatic rescue from the wrecking ball in 1990, the Tacheles at Oranienburger Strasse 54-56 has become one of Berlin's most unusual attractions. Shortly after the Wende, about 50 artists began occupying the partially ruined former department store (1909) with the intent of having it declared a protected building. The squatters accomplished this in 1992, paving the way for turning the Tacheles into an alternative art and culture centre spread out over 6000 sq metres.

Today, the dilapidated structure – with its graffiti-covered walls and brittle staircases – houses about two dozen artists' studios, several galleries, a theatre and a cinema, as well as a cafe and nightclub. The chaotic backyard is a constantly evolving 'sculpture garden' featuring upturned and painted vans and such. It's all run by a self-governed nonprofit organisation, largely made up of the artists themselves.

Over the years, the Tacheles has become one of the best-known entertainment complexes in Berlin, beloved by locals and visitors alike. Surprisingly, it has lost little of its edge, even though it's included in tourist office advertising material and is on the route of tour buses from Denmark and Bavaria.

Since its lease expired in 1997, the Tacheles has been under constant threat

Berlin's Jewish Renaissance

Berlin has the fastest growing Jewish community in the world, thanks largely to a steady and progressive influx of Russian Jewish immigrants. In December 1998, the city's official Jewish population numbered some 12,000 people, including 1000 members of the orthodox congregation of Adass Yisroel. These figures are likely to be even higher, in actuality, because many Jews choose not to be affiliated with a synagogue.

There are now seven synagogues, two mikve ritual baths, several schools and a handful of Kosher restaurants in Berlin. In May 1995, more than 4000 people attended the reopening of the New Synagogue on Oranienburger Strasse in the historic Jewish quarter. It has since become a centre of Jewish life in Berlin. Not primarily a house of worship, it houses the Centrum Judaicum, a community centre and exhibition space highlighting the contributions Jews have made to Berlin. Their story in this city, though – as just about everywhere else in Europe – is a tortured one of persecution, murder and injustice.

Records show that Jews settled here as early as 1295, but throughout the Middle Ages they had to contend with being blamed for any kind of societal or economic woe. When the plague struck in 1348-49, the rumour that it was they who had poisoned the wells led to the first major pogrom; a second one followed in 1446. In 1510, 38 Jews were publicly burnt after having been 'found guilty' of desecrating communion wafers and of killing Christian children. All other Jews were expelled.

Financial interests stood behind the edict passed by the Great Elector Friedrich Wilhelm in 1671, in which he invited the settlement in Berlin of 50 Jewish families who had been banished from Vienna. Later that year, he extended the offer to Jews in general and, as an enticement, allowed them to officially practise their faith. Berlin's oldest Jewish cemetery, on Grosse Hamburger Strasse in Mitte, dates from this time, while the first synagogue was built in 1714.

The year 1743 saw the arrival in Berlin of the philosopher Moses Mendelssohn, who paved the way for Jewish emancipation. About 50 years later, the first Jewish family was granted full civic rights, but it wasn't until 1812 that the Emancipation Edict made all Jews full citizens of

from developers seduced by the real estate's lucrative proximity to the government district. Yet Berliners have made the Tacheles their sacred cow, and ensuring its survival has become sort of a cause célèbre. As we go to press, it seems that it's been given a new lease on life, having been promised another decade on the site. Stay tuned.

Scheunenviertel (Map 4)

The Scheunenviertel (Barn Quarter) is framed by Münzstrasse, Alte Schönhauser Strasse, Torstrasse and Karl-Liebknecht-Strasse. U-Bahn station Weinmeisterstrasse puts you right in the middle of it.

Traditionally a poor area, it was regarded as a dumping ground for the city's down-and-out. Prostitution, petty and not-so-petty

crime and revolutionary rumblings flourished in its narrow lanes lined by dumpy houses. In the early 20th century, the Scheunenviertel absorbed huge numbers of new Jewish immigrants from Eastern Europe, and its streets and shops soon rang with the sound of Yiddish. Most newcomers were Hasidic Jews who, at least initially, didn't integrate very well with the existing and more liberal Jewish community living a few blocks west.

The Scheunenviertel got its name because in 1672, the Great Elector, Friedrich Wilhelm, decided to move the hay barns – a fire hazard – beyond city limits to the area of today's Rosa-Luxemburg-Platz. This square is now occupied by the **Volksbühne**, an interesting theatre founded by workers in

Berlin's Jewish Renaissance

Prussia with equal rights and duties. By the end of the 19th century, many of Berlin's Jews, numbering about 5% of the population, had become thoroughly German in speech and identity.

When a wave of Hasidic Jews escaping the pogroms of Eastern Europe arrived in the late 19th century, they found their way to today's trendy Scheunenviertel district – at that time an immigrant slum affording cheap housing. By 1933, the Jewish population in Berlin had grown to around 160,000, roughly one-third of the total Jewish population in Germany.

The well-documented horrors of WWII sent most into exile and left 55,000 dead. About 1000 to 2000 Jews are believed to have survived the war years. They called themselves 'U-Boats' for their ability to submerge in wartorn Berlin. Jews married to non-Jews were somewhat protected, though still subjected to harassment and pressure.

It wasn't until the collapse of the Soviet Union brought a new wave of immigrants that the population began to grow again. Today, Jewish Berlin is experiencing a significant renaissance. Interest in Jewish culture among Berliners is high. An appreciation of traditional Jewish foods, including the increasingly popular bagel, is a growing trend, and cultural events of all sorts are well attended by Jews and non-Jews alike. To find out more about the Jewish community in Berlin, go to the excellent English-language Web site at www.hagalil.com/brd/berlin/berlin.htm.

Synagogues in Berlin

Services are held on Friday night and Saturday morning. For details call ☎ 88 20 80. The orthodox congregation of Adass Yisroel meets at Tucholskystrasse 40 in Mitte; for information call ☎ 281 31 35. Other congregations are located at:

Joachimstaler Strasse 13 (Map 7), Charlottenburg (orthodox)
Pestalozzistrasse 14-15 (Map 7), Charlottenburg (liberal)
Fraenkelufer 10-16 (Map 6), Kreuzberg (conservative)
Herbartstrasse 26, Charlottenburg (conservative)
Rykestrasse 53 (Map 4), Prenzlauer Berg (conservative)
Oranienburger Strasse 29 (Map 4), Mitte (traditional egalitarian)

1913; its first director was none other than Max Reinhardt.

It has always had a reputation for avantgarde, radical productions, a tradition continued under its current director Frank Castorf. Nearby, at Kleine Alexanderstrasse 28, is the **Karl-Liebknecht-Haus**, which housed the central committee of the KPD, the communist party from 1926 to 1933. Appropriately, the PDS, the successor party of East Germany's SED, has its offices here today.

Charlottenburg

The tragic early death of a beloved queen gave birth to the hamlet of Charlottenburg. When Sophie Charlotte, wife of King

Friedrich I, died in 1705, the king gave town rights to the little settlement that had sprung up around the queen's summer palace and named the whole thing in her honour. Its fledgling population grew slowly. Even in 1870 the area still had a distinct rural character and a mere 17,000 inhabitants.

When Berlin became capital of the German Empire, the population exploded. By 1890, Charlottenburg had 77,000 people, by 1914, there were 320,000. These years also saw the opening of the Technical University (1884) and the College of Arts (1902). Charlottenburg's first heyday came after WWI when it became Berlin's cultural hub with theatres, cabarets, jazz clubs and literary cafes lining its main artery, the fashionable Kurfürstendamm, and its side streets.

Much of the creative spirit – and decadence – that characterised the 'Golden Twenties' had their roots here.

The area's widespread destruction during WWII is still poignantly portrayed in the ruined Memorial Church. Recovery, though, came fast. After division, Charlottenburg quickly emerged as the heart of West Berlin. Hotels, restaurants, shops and nightlife clustered here; to anyone travelling to Berlin before the Wende, this was the place to be. Since 1990, much of Charlottenburg's pinnacle position has been usurped by the Mitte and Prenzlauer Berg districts, but to this day it remains a vibrant and interesting part of the city.

WALKING TOUR (MAP 7)

Our tour begins at Zoo Station and ends at U-Bahn station Wittenbergplatz. It covers the core of the western city centre, West Berlin's main commercial area during the 'island years' of division.

Zoo Station to Fasanenstrasse

The gateway to Berlin, Zoo station opened in 1881 and gets its name from the wonderful **Zoologischer Garten** just east of it (for more on the zoo itself, see the Tiergarten section later in this chapter). Along with the Ostbahnhof in the eastern city centre Zoo station is the city's busiest station for long-distance travel. In the 70s and 80s, the area was a notorious drugs haunt, a sad reality graphically portrayed in *Wir Kinder vom Bahnhof Zoo* (Children from Bahnhof Zoo). It was the biography of the teenager Christiane F, who managed to escape the cycle of heroin addiction, prostitution and violence. The book was later made into a movie.

From the station, head north-west on Hardenbergstrasse where, immediately after passing the railway tracks overhead, you'll see the **Amerika Haus** on your left. The **British Council** has its facility next door. Both are popular cultural institutes with libraries and concerts, readings and other events.

Walk to the intersection with Fasanenstrasse. The modernistic structure on the south-east corner is the **Ludwig-Erhard-Haus**

with the Chamber of Commerce and the Berlin Stock Exchange. The squat structure on the north-west corner is the concert hall **Hochschule der Künste** (College of Arts), whose main building is right behind. Just north of it is the sprawling campus of the **Technische Universität**, one of Berlin's three main universities. It is bounded by the Landwehrkanal to the north-east, Hardenbergstrasse and its continuation Marchstrasse to the west, and Fasanenstrasse to the east.

Fasanenstrasse

Head south on Fasanenstrasse to the corner with Kantstrasse. Stop to take a look at the **Kantdreieck**, an office building topped with a strange 'sail', designed by Josef Paul Kleihues. Opposite looms the magnificent **Theater des Westens** (1896) whose architect, Bernhard Sehring, managed to squeeze a multitude of architectural styles – baroque, neoclassical, Art Nouveau – into a single building. Until the completion of the Deutsche Oper in 1961, this ornate theatre served a stint as the city opera house. Today it's primarily a venue for musicals.

A block south is the **Jüdisches Gemeindehaus** (Jewish Community House), Fasanenstrasse 79-80. It is built on the site of a former synagogue destroyed during the Kristallnacht pogroms on the night of 9 November 1938. Its lone surviving feature – the portal – is integrated into today's modern structure which also contains a memorial site to victims of the Nazi regime. Inside are meeting rooms, exhibition space, a library and Arche Noah, a kosher restaurant (see the Places to Eat chapter). As with most Jewish sites in Berlin, it's usually guarded by police.

South of Kurfürstendamm, Fasanenstrasse becomes decidedly fashionable. Elegant 19th century town houses, containing apartments with as many as 10 or 12 rooms, line the leafy boulevard. Take a peek inside behind some of the ornate entrances which often lead to lavish foyers with stucco ceilings, romantic murals or marble fireplaces. Occasionally you'll also see those frilly Art Nouveau lifts, made from wrought iron or brass, which look like giant bird cages.

At Fasanenstrasse 23, surrounded by a garden, is a lovely restored villa occupied by the **Literaturhaus**, where you can attend readings and book signings or check out the gallery. There's also a good bookstore and the sophisticated Café Wintergarten (see the Places to Eat chapter).

Käthe-Kollwitz-Museum

Adjacent to the Literaturhaus, in a restored and protected 1871 villa at Fasanenstrasse 24, is the private Käthe-Kollwitz-Museum (☎ 882 52 10), dedicated to one of Germany's greatest woman artists. There is an extensive collection of Kollwitz graphics, lithographs, woodcuts, sculptures and drawings which form the core of the exhibit. Amassed by the painter and gallery owner Hans Pels-Leusden, it shows her work in all its versatility and complexity.

Kollwitz was born in 1867 in Königsberg (today's Kaliningrad) and died in Moritzburg near Dresden in 1945, having lived in Berlin's poor Prenzlauer Berg district for nearly 50 years. She studied at art schools in Berlin and Munich and also spent time in Florence and Paris.

Through her art Kollwitz expressed deep commitment to and concern for the working class, the underdog, the suppressed and the poor in a timeless and accessible fashion. Among the museum highlights are the anti-hunger lithography *Brot* (Bread, 1924) and the woodcut series *Krieg* (War, 1922-23). Her favourite themes also included motherhood and – particularly haunting – death, which is often shown as a strangely nurturing figure, cradling its victims. The collection also includes several self-portraits completed between 1899 and 1938.

The skylit top floor is the ideal setting to showcase Kollwitz's sculptures. Exhibits include *Mutter mit Zwei Kindern* (Mother with two Children, 1924-37) and a copy of the monument by Gustav Seitz (1958) which stands on Kollwitzplatz (see the Prenzlauer Berg section later in this chapter) – showing her seated as an old woman. It's worth noting that the eagle-eyed guards, so prevalent at most of Berlin's museums, are refreshingly absent here, creating an intimate, almost meditative atmosphere.

Works of the permanent collection are rotated and supplemented annually by two to three special exhibitions of artists in some way connected to Kollwitz. The museum is open from 11 am to 6 pm Wednesday to Monday (DM8/4). A taped audio tour (in English, French or German) is available for an additional DM3.50.

Kurfürstendamm

Backtrack to Kurfürstendamm – known as Ku'damm – Berlin's main commercial thoroughfare. Speciality, chain and department stores elbow for space between the Memorial Church and Rathenauplatz, 3.5km further west. The greatest concentration of shops, though, is around its eastern end.

It was Bismarck who was responsible for making Ku'damm what it is today. A mere riding path until 1880, leading to the hunting grounds in the Grunewald forest, Bismarck had it turned into a 53m-wide paved boulevard flanked by grandiose residential buildings. The 1920s added the luxury hotels and shops, art galleries, restaurants and performance venues that still characterise the street today.

MICK WELDON

Käthe Kollwitz: one of Germany's greatest woman artists.

Head east on Ku'damm where, on the corner of Joachimstaler Strasse, is the reincarnated **Café Kranzler**, a Berlin institution and the successor to one of the city's most fashionable coffee houses. The original stood on the south-west corner of Unter den Linden and Friedrichstrasse in Mitte from 1825 until its destruction in WWII. The place is still popular today despite being an overpriced tourist trap. The outdoor terrace – perfect for people watching – is its one redeeming feature.

Erotik Museum

Turning left into Joachimstaler Strasse leads you right to Berlin's Erotik Museum (☎ 886 06 66), a surprisingly tasteful and artful exhibit at the intersection with Kantstrasse. It is the brainchild of Beate Uhse, a respected businesswoman and marketing queen of sex toys and pornography (she's even traded her company on the stock exchange). An elevator whisks you to the museum's top floor where well-lit and sophisticated displays tell the story of human sexuality through the ages. Included are meerschaum-smoking devices engraved with time-honoured themes, extremely funny scrolls from 19th century Japan, Balinese fertility demons, 'pillow books' and hilarious erotic films from the very early days of cinema. The selection of 17th century chastity belts elicits lots of giggles, especially from women who incidentally made up about half of all visitors on the day we went. The museum is open from 9 am to midnight daily (DM10/8). And yes, you must be over 18 to enter.

Kaiser-Wilhelm-Gedächtniskirche

From the museum, head east on Kantstrasse to arrive at one of Berlin's most famous landmarks, the neo-Romanesque Kaiser Wilhelm Memorial Church (1895). The Allied bombing of 22 November 1943 left only the husk of the church's west tower standing. Engulfed by roaring commercialism, it stands quiet and dignified on Breitscheidplatz. In 1961, a modern octagonal **hall of worship** with its bluer-than-blue stained-glass windows was built next to it (open from 9 am to 7.30 pm daily). The **Gedenkhalle** (Memorial Hall) below the ruined tower contains original ceiling mosaics, marble reliefs, liturgical objects and photos before and after the bombing (open from 10 am to 4 or 5 pm Monday to Saturday).

Breitscheidplatz

This lively square, ruled by pedestrians and skateboarders, is where everyone from tired tourists to street performers gather. An eye-catcher is the unusual **Weltbrunnen** (World Fountain, 1983). Made from reddish granite it shows a world split open with sculptures of humans and animals clustering in various scenes. Naturally Berliners have found a nickname for it – 'Wasserklops' (water meatball).

It's all lorded over by the **Europa-Center** (1965), a soaring shopping and restaurant complex topped by that symbol of capitalism, the Mercedes star. Inside is the tacky **Flow of Time Clock** by Bernard Gitton; it measures hours, minutes and seconds via a series of vials and spheres that fill up with vile, radioactive-looking green liquid. The main **BTM tourist office** is on the ground floor of the centre's Budapester Strasse (north) side.

At its southern edge, Breitscheidplatz is bordered by Tauentzienstrasse, the flashy continuation of Kurfürstendamm which culminates at Wittenbergplatz where the **KaDeWe** department store is the main attraction (see the Shopping chapter). Wittenbergplatz U-Bahn station has been beautifully restored and has a real old fashioned feel. The much photographed tubular sculpture (1987) nearby is a symbol of the divided city.

SCHLOSS CHARLOTTENBURG (MAP 3)

Schloss Charlottenburg is an exquisite baroque palace and one of the few remaining sites in Berlin that reflects the former splendour and grandeur of the royal Hohenzollern clan. In 1695 Elector Friedrich III (later King Friedrich I) commissioned Johann Arnold Nering to build a summer residence for his wife Sophie Charlotte (1688-1705). It was later enlarged by Johann Friedrich Eosander.

Over time, as the representational needs of the Hohenzollerns increased, other noted architects – like Schinkel, Knobelsdorff and Langhans – also took a whack at it. Nothing less than Versailles provided the inspiration for the three-wing structure which got its landmark central domed tower in 1812. It's topped by a gilded statue of the goddess Fortuna that moves with the wind, making it a sort of glamorous weather vane.

Bombed in 1943, the rebuilding of Schloss Charlottenburg became a priority after the East Germans dynamited the only other halfway surviving Hohenzollern palace, the Berliner Schloss on Unter den Linden, in 1951. When reconstruction was completed in 1966, the restored **equestrian statue of the Great Elector** (1699) by Andreas Schlüter was returned to the courtyard outside the main entrance.

Schloss Charlottenburg is on Spandauer Damm, 3km north-west of Zoo station. Along with several important buildings in the Schlossgarten (Palace Garden), there are seven fine museums in and around the palace (free). To get here, take the U2 to Sophie-Charlotte-Platz and then bus No 110 for three stops (or walk north from the station along Schlossstrasse for about 1km).

Each of the palace buildings charges separate admission (see below) but if you decide to see most of them, you should get the Day Card (DM15/10, family DM25). Note that this does not give you entry to the museums.

Nering-Eosander Building

Named after its two architects, the central – and oldest – section of the palace contains the former royal living quarters, which must be visited on a long-winded, 50 minute tour in German (ask for a pamphlet with detailed room-by-room descriptions in English at the ticket office).

The tour takes in 21 rooms, each of which are extravaganzas in stucco, brocade, gilt and overall opulence. Among the highlights are: the **Hall of Mirrors** (Room 118); the lovely **Oval Hall** (Room 116) with views of the French gardens and the Belvedere; the wind gauge in **Friedrich I's bedchamber,** which also contains the first-ever **bathroom**

in a baroque palace (Room 96); the fabulous **Porcelain Chamber** (Room 95), smothered in Chinese blueware and figures from floor to ceiling; and the **Eosander Chapel** (Room 94) with its trompe d'oeil arches. Finally, the **Great Oak Gallery** derives a dignified English feel from its rich wainscoting and large oil canvasses.

After the tour, you are free to explore the upper floor with more paintings and silverwork, vases, tapestries, weapons, Meissen porcelain and other items essential to a royal lifestyle. A lavish banquet table laid out with plates, cutlery, decorations etc – all made of silver – unashamedly displays the extreme luxury to which the royal family was accustomed.

Tours take place from 9 am to 5 pm Tuesday to Friday, from 10 am to 5 pm weekends (DM8/4). On some weekends and during summer holidays the demand for tickets may exceed capacity, so show up as early as possible.

Knobelsdorff Wing

The reign of Friedrich II saw the addition of the elongated eastern Knobelsdorff Wing (1746). Here you'll find some of the palace's most beautiful rooms, including the confection-like **White Hall**, the former dining hall with its elaborate concave ceiling; the **Golden Gallery**, a rococo fantasy of mirrors and gilding; and the **Concert Hall**. All rooms feature precious paintings by 18th century French masters like Watteau, Chardin, Boucher and Pesne.

To the right of the staircase are the comparatively austere **Winterkammern** (Winter Chambers) of Friedrich Wilhelm II. Noteworthy here are the four Gobelin tapestries in rooms 351 and 352. On the ground floor is the Schinkel-designed bedroom of Queen Luise. Hours are 10 am to 6 pm Tuesday to Friday, 11 am to 6 pm weekends (DM5/3).

Galerie der Romantik (SMPK) On the ground floor of the Knobelsdorff Wing is the spectacular Galerie der Romantik (Gallery of the Romantics, ☎ 20 90 55 55) with superb works of German Romantic and Biedermeier artists. A collection highlight are the two dozen paintings spanning the entire career of Caspar David Friedrich. Look out for some of his most famous pieces, including *Abbey in the Oak Wood*, with its mysterious and heavy mood, as well as the evocative *Monk by the Sea* (both 1810).

Also here are the Gothic fantasies of Karl Friedrich Schinkel and landscapes by the Berlin artist Carl Blechen, as well as works by members of the 19th century school of the Nazarenes who sought to revive the devout style of the Renaissance. Works from the Biedermeier period include those by Eduard Gaertner, who captured many scenes of historical Berlin in his paintings. The gallery is open from 10 am to 6 pm Tuesday to Friday, from 11 am weekends (DM4/2).

Schlossgarten

The Schlossgarten (Palace Garden) was originally laid out in French style following plans by Godeau, but this was changed when natural English gardens came into vogue at the turn of the 18th century. After WWII, a compromise was struck; the area adjacent to the palace is in the French style, the English park is behind.

Several ornate buildings are integrated into the garden landscape. The **Schinkel Pavilion** was built as the summer residence of King Friedrich Wilhelm III in 1824 and contains paintings, sculpture and crafts from the early 19th century, including works by Schinkel himself. It's open from 10 am to 5 pm Tuesday to Sunday, with shorter hours between late October and late March (DM3/2).

The rococo **Belvedere** folly (1788), which has the same hours and admission, was designed by Langhans and served as a teahouse for Friedrich Wilhelm II. Today it contains an impressive porcelain collection by the royal manufacturer KPM, covering the periods from rococo to Biedermeier.

The neoclassical **Mausoleum** accommodates the tombs of Queen Luise (1776-1810) and her husband Friedrich Wilhelm III (1770-1840), among others. It features sculpture by Christian Daniel Rauch and is open from 10 am to 5 pm Tuesday to Sunday, late March to October (DM2/1).

Museum für Vor- und Frühgeschichte (SMPK)

The Museum für Vor- und Frühgeschichte (Museum of Primeval & Early History, ☎ 20 90 55 55) occupies the west wing (or Langhans Building) of Schloss Charlottenburg and presents archaeological artefacts from Stone, Bronze and Iron Age cultures in Europe and the Middle East.

On the ground floor, a selection of **skulls** (some real, some partly reconstructed) from proto-humans to Homo Sapiens illustrates the evolution of human life. The 10,000-year-old **elk skeleton** is a crowd pleaser, as are the **dioramas** of prehistoric cave life and hunting scenes. There are remarkable collections of Bronze Age tools, weapons and ornaments and thorough explanations of how various human cultures became known – in archaeological circles – by the shape of the pottery they created or by their burial practices.

The most outstanding collection is that of Trojan antiquities on the 2nd floor in the **Schliemann Saal**, named after archaeologist Heinrich Schliemann (1822-90) who discovered the site of ancient Troy in Hissarlik in today's Turkey. After the fall of Berlin, many of the objects unearthed by Schliemann were looted by the Red Army and taken to museums in Moscow and Leningrad (now St Petersburg). What's left in Berlin is nonetheless an impressive array of bronzes, huge clay amphorae for storing wine and oil and other objects. Also here are replicas of gold jewellery and other objects from Schliemann's 'Priamos Treasure' whose originals are at the Pushkin Museum in Moscow.

Display panels throughout the museums are in several languages, including English. Museum hours are from 10 am to 6 pm Tuesday to Friday, from 11 am weekends (DM4/2).

SCHLOSS AREA MUSEUMS (MAP 3)

In addition to the splendour of the royal palace and its outbuildings, there are five mostly superb museums in the immediate vicinity. Unless otherwise noted, hours are from 10 am to 6 pm, closed Monday.

Ägyptisches Museum (SMPK)

The undisputed highlight of the Ägyptisches Museum (Egyptian Museum, ☎ 20 90 55 55), south of the palace in the East Stüler Building at Schlossstrasse 69b, is the **bust of Queen Nefertiti**, she of the long graceful neck and stunning looks (even after all these years – about 3300, give or take a century or two). The bust, dramatically spotlit in a darkened room, was never finished (the right eye, for example, is not inlaid) as this was just a model for other portraits of the queen, who was the wife of Pharaoh Ikhnaton (ruled 1379-62 BC). His bust is in one of the niches in the main exhibition room.

All the objects were found at Amarna, an ancient city on the Nile halfway between Thebes and the Mediterranean Sea. The site was excavated by the Deutsche Orient Gesellschaft (German Orient Society), led by Ludwig Borchardt, in 1912. Whatever they found they took with them, though at least one major item on view here was actually a gift from the Egyptian government – the **Kalabsha Gate**, a sandstone arch from the 20th century BC. Covered in reliefs and 7.35m high, it was given to Germany as thanks for help in saving archaeological treasures during construction of the Aswan Dam (1960-70).

Just beyond, the main room is divided into alcoves, each devoted to a particular person or subject, such as 'Ikhnaton's family', 'courtiers and soldiers', or 'women and music'. The circular room upstairs holds the museum's second-most cherished object, the **Berlin Green**, a small bust (500-400 BC) of a man carved from green stone that is almost expressionistic in style.

Museum hours are from 10 am to 6 pm Tuesday to Sunday (DM8/4, SMPK Day Pass). Pamphlets (some in English) with details about several of the exhibits are available for DM0.10 each near the Kalabsha Gate.

Sammlung Berggruen (SMPK)

In the West Stüler Building, just opposite the Egyptian Museum, is the Sammlung Berggruen (Berggruen Collection, ☎ 20 90 55 55) entitled 'Picasso and His Time'. It is on loan until at least 2006 from Dr Heinz Berggruen, art connoisseur and FOP (friend of Picasso). There are some 75 paintings, drawings and sculptures by Picasso himself and about as many works by Cézanne, Van Gogh, Gauguin and Braque. On the 2nd floor are 31 smaller pieces by Paul Klee from 1917 to 1940 as well as three Giacometti sculptures.

Nearly all of Picasso's creative periods are represented, starting with the Blue and Rose periods (eg *Seated Harlequin*, 1905), followed by early cubist paintings (eg the portrait of George Braque, 1910). These contrast greatly with the classicist *Seating Act, Drying her Feet* from 1921. Later paintings seem more familiar, such as *The Yellow Pullover* (1939) which shows a woman, Dora Maar, with lion claws for hands.

The museum is open from 10 am to 6 pm Tuesday to Friday, from 11 am weekends (DM8/4, SMPK Day Pass). An excellent 50 minute audio tour is available for hire though, unfortunately, it's in German only (DM6/4).

Bröhan Museum

The lovely Bröhan Museum (☎ 321 40 29), just south of the Berggruen Collection at Schlossstrasse 1a, focuses on decorative arts and design from 1889 to 1939 (Art Nouveau, Art Deco and Functionalism). It was donated to the city by Karl Bröhan in 1982. On the ground floor are the outstanding fully furnished and decorated **Art Nouveau and Art Deco rooms** (eg by Hector Guimard and Émile Ruhlmann). The collection of silverwork, glass, porcelain and enamelware seems endless but astonishes at every turn. There's furniture from France, porcelain from Scandinavia and Germany and paintings by members of the Berliner Sezession from the late 19th to early 20th century, including Jaeckel and Baluschek.

The top floor has changing exhibitions and a remarkable **Henry van de Velde** (1863-1957) room with furniture, tableware and other objects designed by this multitalented Belgian. Hours are from 10 am to 6 pm Tuesday to Sunday (DM6/3).

Abgusssammlung Antiker Plastik

Across the street at Schlossstrasse 69b is the Abgusssammlung Antiker Plastik (Antiquity Collection, ☎ 342 40 54) with copies of Greek and Roman sculpture from 600 BC to 400 AD. Hours are from 2 to 5 pm Thursday to Sunday (free). It's in the same building as the Heimatmuseum Charlottenburg (☎ 34 30 32 01), a local history museum where hours are from 10 am to 5 pm Tuesday to Friday, from 11 am weekends (free).

FUNKTURM AREA (MAP 5)

About 3km south-east of Charlottenburg Palace, near Theodor-Heuss-Platz, is Berlin's trade fair centre (Messe) and the ICC (International Congress Centre). By far the most visible structure in this area, though, is the **Funkturm** (radio tower) whose filigree outline bears similarities to Paris' Eiffel Tower. It dates from the 1920s and measures 138m in height. There's a restaurant at 55m and a viewing platform at 125m.

From the top there's a good view of the AVUS, Germany's first car-racing track at its opening in 1921 and now just a part of the city autobahn. AVUS stands for *Automobil-, Verkehrs- und Übungsstrecke* (car, traffic and practice track). The Nazis made it part of the autobahn system and it was altered after the war. Today, official races are rare, though it's usually filled with normal motorists trying to break land-speed records. In fact, until recently, the AVUS had no speed limit but, owing to pressure from environmentalists, the maximum is now 100km/h.

OLYMPIC STADIUM AREA

The **Olympic Stadium** (off Map 5), built by Hitler for the 1936 Olympic Games, lies about 4.5km west of Schloss Charlottenburg. It was here that the African-American runner Jesse Owens won four gold medals and put paid to the Nazi theory that Aryans were all-powerful *Übermenschen* (a super race). The 85,000-seat stadium, one of the best examples of Nazi-era monumentalism, is still very much in use for soccer, track and other sporting events.

Definitely not built to last 1000 years as the Nazis had planned, the structure is crumbling already. There was much talk about tearing it down to build a new stadium but now it seems that it's being scheduled for extensive renovation instead. Meanwhile, the stadium is open to visitors on non-event days from 9 am to sunset (DM1/0.50). To get there take the U2 to Olympia-Stadion Ost, then follow the signs for a 15 minute walk.

The **Maifeld**, a huge field west of the stadium, was used for Nazi mass rallies (it holds more than half a million people) and later became the drilling ground for occupying British forces which, until 1994, had their headquarters nearby. On its western edge is the 77m **Glockenturm** (Clock Tower), which offers superb views over the stadium, the city and the Havel. Check out the Nazi bell – it weighs 2.5 tonnes and was rung only twice; to signal the start and the finish of the Olympic Games. The tower is open from 10 am to 5.30 pm daily, May to October (DM3/1.50).

North-west of here, on the corner of Glockenturmstrasse and Passenheimer Strasse, is the **Waldbühne**, a Nazi-built outdoor amphitheatre for 20,000 that is now used in summer for concerts, film screenings and other cultural events.

Tiergarten

The central district of Tiergarten gets its name from the sprawling city park that straddles the central city from Zoo station to Brandenburg Gate. Like a trifle, Tiergarten consists of three distinct layers, each with a different flavour and consistency. In the north, there's Moabit, first settled by French Huguenots and later a workers' quarter. The southern section, which ends at Kurfürstenstrasse, wears the face of the 60s and harbours several luxury hotels, the former and future diplomatic quarter and the Kulturforum museum complex. Sandwiched between the two is Tiergarten park itself, Berlin's green heart.

Along with Mitte, Tiergarten is poised to undergo dramatic changes as a result of the government move. In Moabit, suits will soon replace workers' overalls as it morphs into a place of work and play for members of parliament and their staff, lobbyists, service industries and whoever else desires to be near Germany's government leaders.

The **Ministry of the Interior** (Map 3) has already moved into spanking new digs at the Spree-Bogen Complex on Alt Moabit, and the **Federal Chancellery** (Map 3) is taking shape on the park's north-eastern edge. Just north of here, the gaping holes and pivoting cranes next to the Lehrter Stadtbahnhof S-Bahn station point to the development of the **Lehrter Zentralbahnhof**, Berlin's futuristic central train station. (Completion dates have been pushed back and forth many times, so we won't even venture a guess here.) A costly extension of the U5 from Alexanderplatz to this station, a pet project of former Chancellor Kohl, has been rather controversial. Detractors argue that it's a waste of taxpayers' money because several S-Bahn lines currently connect the two. And of course they've already found a nickname for it: 'Kanzlerlinie' (Chancellor Line). Another mega-undertaking is the 3.3km-long **Tiergarten Tunnel** which will reroute traffic beneath the park away from the government buildings.

MOABIT (MAP 3)

The northernmost section of Tiergarten is also the oldest, settled after 1718 by French Huguenots fleeing religious persecution in their country. They called their colony *Terre des Moabites* (Land of the Moabits) because that was where, according to the Old Testament, Eli Melech and his family had found refuge. Over time, the name was shortened to simply Moabit. In the late 19th century, the area became part of the ring of working-class neighbourhoods that encircled the city centre to the north and east.

Moabit's face is changing but for now its few charms are easily assimilated on a stroll along Alt-Moabit from U-Bahn station Turmstrasse, the area's commercial heart. Before heading east, however, take a quick detour to the **Arminius Markthalle**, the nicest of the three surviving historical market halls and a good place to stock up on

fresh produce, dairy goods and meats (see the Shopping chapter). You reach it by walking a few steps west on Turmstrasse from the station and turning right into Jonasstrasse. The market hall is right there on the corner with Arminiusstrasse.

Back on Turmstrasse, head south one block to the road called Alt-Moabit and walk east. The Spree-Bogen Complex with the Ministry of the Interior will soon be on your right. Just past here is the **St Johannis Kirche** (1835), an early work by Karl Friedrich Schinkel with an arcaded Italianate portico and an extremely steep staircase leading up to the church door, which is usually locked.

Farther east lies the vast **Justizzentrum** (Centre of Justice) which incorporates the criminal courts, the municipal courts and a giant prison. It takes up the entire block from Wilsnacker Strasse to Rathenower Strasse in the east; Turmstrasse forms the northern boundary. The fortress-like jail has hosted numerous German heavyweight criminals, including several Red Army Faction (RAF) terrorists, Erich Honecker and Erich Mielke, the final Stasi director.

The adjacent criminal courts are entered via Portal IV on Turmstrasse, near the corner with Rathenower Strasse. The court building itself is an imposing, cathedral-like concoction from 1906 whose monumental foyer does not fail to intimidate. Security is tight, with turnstiles and a troupe of security staff. A list of court proceedings open to the public is posted in the lobby. However, only the name of the accused and the room of the hearing are listed, not the nature of the crime.

Either walk or take bus No 187 from outside the courts to get back to Turmstrasse station.

Gedenkstätte Plötzensee

About 3km north of the centre of Moabit (and technically in the district of Charlottenburg) is the Plötzensee Memorial (☎ 344 32 26), on Hüttigpfad, to the victims of the Nazi regime. From 1933 to 1945 about 2500 people, most of them political prisoners of all persuasions and nationalities, died between these walls. In a single night in

1943, following an air raid, 186 prisoners were hanged only so that they could not escape from the partly destroyed prison. A year later, many of the conspirators of the failed assassination attempt on Hitler on 20 July 1944 – and their (mostly uninvolved) relatives and friends, a total of 86 people – were also murdered here; a process the Führer had captured on film.

Housed in a plain red-brick shed at Plötzensee prison, the memorial is chillingly simple. Most haunting is the execution room, its emptiness pierced by an iron bar with five hooks on it. The other room documents the arbitrary practices of the Nazi judicial system.

An excellent free English brochure is available at the desk. The memorial is open daily from 8.30 am to 4.30 pm (in January and November), to 5.30 pm (February and October), to 6 pm (March to September) and to 4 pm (December). Admission is free. Bus No 123 (eg from U-Bahn station Hansaplatz, U9) travels to the Gedenkstätte Plötzensee stop.

TIERGARTEN PARK (MAPS 3, 5 & 7)

The 167-hectare Tiergarten park is one of the largest city parks in the world. A combination of groomed paths, woodsy groves, lakes and meadows, it is popular with joggers, strollers, picnickers and nature lovers year round. In spring, when the rhododendron bushes are in full bloom, the area around Rousseau Island becomes an oasis for the senses.

The Great Elector, Friedrich Wilhelm (ruled 1640-88), used the land as hunting grounds, though he made the job easy on himself by having the animals confined to a fenced-off area measuring 1km by 3km. It became a park in the 18th century and was landscaped by master gardener Peter Lenné (1789-1866) in 1830. During the frigid winter of 1946-7, Berliners chopped down virtually all the trees for firewood.

Strasse des 17 Juni (Map 3)

The broad boulevard known as Strasse des 17 Juni, which bisects Tiergarten, was built by King Friedrich I to connect the city palace with Schloss Charlottenburg. Hitler's showy entrance to Berlin, it was called East-West Axis during the Nazi era. Its present name commemorates the 1953 workers' uprising in East Berlin, which brought the GDR to the brink of collapse.

On the northern side, just west of the Brandenburg Gate, is the **Sowjetisches Ehrenmal** (Soviet Memorial), flanked by the first two Russian tanks (Nos 200 and 300) to enter Berlin in 1945. The reddish marble is said to have come from Hitler's Neue Reichskanzlei (New Chancellery) on Wilhelmstrasse. (More of this recycled marble was used in building the Soviet Memorial in Treptower Park.)

Like the arms of a starfish, five large roads merge into the roundabout called Grosser Stern, farther west along Strasse des 17 Juni. At its centre is the 69m-high **Siegessäule** (Victory Column, 1873) which rather cockily commemorates 19th century Prussian military exploits. The mosaic frieze behind the curtain of columns on the raised ground floor depicts the founding of the German Empire in 1870-71. The Nazis moved the column here in 1938 from Königsplatz (now Platz der Republik) in front of the Reichstag. Crowned by a gilded statue of Victory (called 'Gold-Else' by Berliners), it has a spiral staircase (285 steps) leading to the top for an eyeful of the park and surrounds. It is open 9 am to 6 pm daily, closed Monday morning (DM2/1, free if under 14).

Soviet Memorial commemorating Russian military occupation in 1945.

Schloss Bellevue (Map 3)

Just north-east of the Siegessäule (Victory Column) is Schloss Bellevue (1785), built for Prince Ferdinand, the youngest brother of Friedrich II, and now the German president's official residence. Until 2005, Johannes Rau and his family will reside in this neoclassical, U-shaped structure whose chalk-white facade is broken up by Corinthian columns and topped by a tympanum with sculptural decoration. Kaiser Wilhelm II disliked the building and used it as a school for his children. The Nazis turned it into a museum of German ethnology and later a guesthouse.

Akademie der Künste (Map 3)

The building at Hansatenweg 10 is the main exhibition space of the Akademie der Künste (Academy of Arts, ☎ 39 07 60), which has its roots in King Friedrich I's Prussian Academy of Arts (founded 1696). It hosts exceptionally fine revolving exhibits, often in conjunction with other museums. On Pariser Platz, the academy's new administrative headquarters are taking shape on the foundations of its Prussian predecessor. The Tiergarten space is open from 10 am to 7 pm daily, from 1 pm Monday (DM8/4, Wednesday free).

Haus der Kulturen der Welt (Map 3)

The Haus der Kulturen der Welt (House of World Cultures, 1957, ☎ 39 78 71 75) is in the oddly shaped structure – nicknamed 'pregnant oyster' – on John-Foster-Dulles-Allee on the northern edge of Tiergarten. Originally a congress hall, the structure with its dramatic cantilevered roof was the American contribution to the International Building Exhibition of 1957.

Unfortunately, it was fraught with disaster right from the start and nearly burned down during construction. In 1980, part of the roof collapsed but it was rebuilt and inaugurated as an exhibition space for non-European art and culture in 1988.

The changing photo and art exhibits inside – usually from Africa, Asia or Latin America – are worth a look. It's open from 10 am to 8 pm Tuesday to Sunday (admission charge varies). In the warmer months there are chime concerts at noon and 6 pm from the 68-bell, black marble and bronze **Carillon** – the largest in Europe – to the south-east.

Zoologischer Garten (Map 7)

After putting the finishing touches on Tiergarten, Peter Lenné turned his attention to the south-western corner of the park where King Friedrich Wilhelm IV had donated the grounds for a zoo. Germany's oldest zoo (☎ 25 40 10) opened in 1844, largely stocked with the king's pheasants and animals from the Pfaueninsel (see section later in this chapter), while the adjacent **aquarium** followed in 1869. During WWII most of the animals were killed in bombing raids, though the last elephant, Siam, is said to have been driven insane by the pandemonium and trumpeted nonstop in terror.

Currently some 14,000 animals representing 1400 species roam the extensive grounds, many of them in open – but moated – habitats. Enter via the impressive **Elephant Gate** (complete with chinoiserie roof) at Budapester Strasse 34, open from 9 am to dusk daily (to 6.30 pm at the latest), the aquarium until 6 pm. The zoo and the aquarium each charge admission of DM12/10/6 for adults/students/children; a combined ticket is DM19/16/9.50.

KULTURFORUM AREA (MAP 5)

In the 1950s, one of Germany's premier architects of the time, Hans Scharoun, was asked to create a design concept for what would become known as the Kulturforum. This cluster of top-notch museums and concert venues is located on the south-eastern edge of Tiergarten, just west of the Potsdamer Platz developments.

Scharoun started things off with the **Berliner Philharmonie** (1961), Herbert-von-Karajan-Strasse 1, a concert hall with otherworldly acoustics (also see the special Architecture section in the Facts about Berlin chapter). He also designed the adjacent smaller **Kammermusiksaal** (Chamber Music Hall, 1987), the Musical Instruments Museum (1985) and the New State Library (1978) across the street at Potsdamer

Strasse 33. Other museums were designed by Ludwig Mies van der Rohe (New National Gallery, 1968) and the team of Heinz Hillmer, Rolf Gutbrod and Christoph Sattler (Museum of Decorative Arts and Copperplate Etchings Gallery).

Most museums are accessible via a central plaza that opens up to Herbert-von-Karajan-Strasse. Unless noted, they are open from 10 am to 6 pm Tuesday to Friday and from 11 am weekends. For admission prices, see the individual entries. The nearest U/S-Bahn station is Mendelssohn-Bartholdy-Park, a 10 minute walk east. Bus Nos 129, 142 and 148 stop closer to the complex.

Musikinstrumenten-Museum

The Musical Instruments Museum (☎ 25 48 10) at Tiergartenstrasse 1 focuses on the evolution of musical instruments from the 16th to the 20th centuries. Harpsichords from the 17th century, medieval trumpets and shepherds' bagpipes may not start a stampede for tickets, but the museum displays them all in a unique and interesting way. Historical paintings and porcelain figurines portray people playing the instruments, and there are earphones sprinkled throughout the museum to hear what they sound(ed) like. Other nuggets include Steinway pianos and curiosities like a musical walking stick.

Pride of place goes to the **Gray Organ** (1820) from Bathwick, England, but our favourite is the **'mighty Wurlitzer' organ** (1929) with more buttons and keys than a troop of Beefeater guards. From a ramp above, you can peer through windows at the bizarre collection of percussion and other instruments connected to this musical behemoth, which give it control over an entire orchestra of sound effects.

Guided tours (DM3) at 11 am on Saturday culminate with a noon recital on this white and gold confection (you don't have to go on the tour to hear this). Chamber music concerts take place most Sundays at 11 am. Hours are from 9 am to 5 pm Tuesday to Friday, from 10 am weekends (DM4/2).

Kunstgewerbemuseum (SMPK)

The never-ending marble ramps inside the Kunstgewerbemuseum (Museum of Decorative Arts, ☎ 20 90 55 55) have an almost Escher-like quality. The museum shows arts and crafts ranging from 16th century chalices of gilded silver to Art Deco ceramics and 20th century appliances.

Highlights on the ground floor – which covers the Middle Ages up to the Renaissance – include gem-encrusted reliquaries; the **Welfenschatz** (Welf treasure), which includes a domed reliquary supposed to have contained the head of St George; Venetian glass; and the **Lüneburger Ratssilber**, which consists of 34 silver items from the late Gothic and early Renaissance periods.

Upstairs (Renaissance to Art Deco), don't miss Carlo Bugatti's crazy suite of furniture (1885) blending elements of Islamic, Japanese and Native American design. Also here are historical board games, amazing works in (unfortunately) ivory and Meissen porcelain. The Chinese Room from the Graneri Palace in Turin, Italy, is another highlight.

The basement (Modern and Contemporary Design) houses a huge collection of product design, international glassware, jewellery and furniture from today's top designers. Admission is DM4/2.

Kupferstichkabinett (SMPK)

The Copperplate Etchings Gallery (☎ 20 90 55 55) is a speciality museum of drawings and prints from the Middle Ages to the present. Fans of Albrecht Dürer, Pieter Brueghel the Elder, Rembrandt, Lucas Cranach the Elder, Picasso and Giacometti will be happy here. A highlight is the illustrations to Dante's *Divine Comedy* by Botticelli. Illuminated manuscripts round out the displays.

What you see is in fact only a fraction of the entire collection, as exhibits are rotated to prevent deterioration of the fragile paper. This is also the reason for the protective glass casings and muted lighting. All explanatory panels are in German only, so it's better if you already know how to appreciate this type of art. Admission is DM4/2.

Neue Gemäldegalerie (SMPK)

If you only have time for one Kulturforum museum, make it the Neue Gemäldegalerie (New Picture Gallery, ☎ 20 90 55 55), which reopened in June 1998 in a gloriously designed building. Focused on European painting from the 13th to the 18th centuries, it merges collections from the Bodemuseum (in the former East) with the one from the Gemäldegalerie in Dahlem (in the former West). Galleries are accessed from the amazing football field-sized, pillared Great Hall, lit via circular skylights.

More than 1100 major paintings vie for your attention in this vast museum, and it's easy to become overwhelmed. Grab a map in the huge foyer and prepare to spend at least two hours just to gain an overview. Admission is DM8/4 (SMPK Day Pass) and includes free audioguides (German or English) with commentary on selected paintings. If you want to concentrate on particular masters, here are some of the highlights:

Dürer (room 4)
Cranach the Elder (room 5)
Holbein the Younger (room 6)
Rubens (rooms VII and VIII)
Rembrandt (room 16)
Gainsborough and Reynolds (room 20)
Canaletto and Tiepolo (room XII)
Caravaggio (room XIV)
Titian and Tintoretto (room XVI)
Botticelli (room XVIII)

Neue Nationalgalerie (SMPK)

The Neue Nationalgalerie (New National Gallery, ☎ 20 90 55 55) lies a short walk south of the main Kulturforum complex at Potsdamer Strasse 50. Displaying 19th and 20th century paintings and sculptures, it roughly picks up where the New Picture Gallery leaves off. Expect to see works by Klee, Munch, Miró, Max Ernst, Juan Gris and Henry Moore. The main emphasis, however, is on German expressionism, and you shouldn't miss the works of Otto Dix (eg *Old Couple*, 1923), Max Beckmann's triptychs and the wonderful 'egghead' figures of George Grosz.

The exhibitions echo the fearful symmetry of the building; paintings on the walls just zoom away from you like railroad tracks into the distance. You'll definitely be treated to predatory stalking by the ever-attentive staff, but there's a hopping cafe in the basement where you can escape them. And the sculpture garden in the back is a great place to put up your feet and catch a few rays if the sun is shining. For more on the building, see the special Architecture section in the Facts about Berlin chapter. Admission is DM8/4 (SMPK Day Pass).

St Matthäus Kirche

Standing a bit forlorn within the modern museum complex, red-brick St Matthäus Kirche was originally built to provide a place of worship to the legions of diplomats from the adjacent diplomatic quarter. Today it is still one of the few churches with **English-language services**, held at 12.30 pm on Sundays in winter and at 9 am in summer. It's also used as an art gallery (free). A well-kept secret is the birds-eye view from atop the bell tower. Part with DM1, brave the 129 spiralling steps and you'll be rewarded with a 360-degree view over Tiergarten, Potsdamer Platz, the Kulturforum complex and the city at large. The church is open from noon to 6 pm Wednesday to Sunday.

Neue Staatsbibliothek

The rambling building on the east side of Potsdamer Strasse houses Scharoun's Neue Staatsbibliothek (New State Library, ☎ 26 61). Open since 1978, it is an academic lending and research library with huge reading rooms. Library hours are from 9 am to 9 pm weekdays and to 3 pm Saturday. Tours take place at 10.30 am every third Saturday of the month.

Gedenkstätte Deutscher Widerstand

The Gedenkstätte Deutscher Widerstand (German Resistance Memorial Museum, ☎ 26 54 22 02), at Stauffenbergstrasse 13-14, is housed in the Bender Block just west of the Kulturforum. Home to Hitler's army command centre during the Third Reich, it was here that Claus Schenk Graf von Stauffenberg and three co-conspirators were shot to death the night of the failed assassination attempt on the Führer. A plaque and statue commemorate the event. Despite the building's grim history, no one seems to find it inappropriate that the Ministry of Defence will soon move into part of the complex.

The exhibit itself addresses an important – and little known – facet of the Third Reich. An extensive hodgepodge of photographs, documents and explanatory panels shows how such diverse groups as workers, students, Jews, soldiers, prisoners, exiles and others risked life and livelihood to thwart Hitler's mob.

Unfortunately it's all presented in a rather encyclopaedic (read: boring) way and, with the total absence of English explanations, non-German speakers are reduced to looking at the pictures which, in this case, don't always say a thousand words.

The skimpy English-language pamphlet, available for DM5, does not do justice to this complicated chapter of history. It's rather sad that an exhibit of such great importance was not designed with a broader audience in mind.

Hours are from 9 am to 6 pm weekdays, to 1 pm weekends. Guided tours take place at 11 am on Sunday (admission is free).

Bauhaus Archiv/Museum für Gestaltung

About 1km to the west along the Landwehr Canal at Klingelhöferstrasse 14 is the Bauhaus Archive/Museum of Design (☎ 254 00 20), devoted to the artists of the Bauhaus School who laid the basis for much of contemporary design and architecture (see boxed text 'The Bauhaus'). The collection includes works by Klee, Wassily Kandinsky, Oskar Schlemmer and other Bauhaus followers. Furniture, blueprints, models and graphic prints are presented in an appealing and easily assimilated fashion. (For more on the building itself, see the special Architecture section in the Facts about Berlin chapter.) The museum is open from 10 am to 5 pm Wednesday to Monday (DM5/2.50).

The Bauhaus

Founded in Weimar in 1919 by Berlin architect Walter Gropius, the Bauhaus School aimed to unite art with everyday functionality, from doorknobs and radiators to the layout of entire districts and apartment blocks. The movement attracted some of the era's most talented artists and architects, including Paul Klee, Wassily Kandinsky, Piet Mondrian, Lionel Feininger and Oskar Schlemmer.

Gropius' radical ideas raised too many eyebrows in Weimar and in 1925 the Bauhaus relocated to Dessau, where it enjoyed its most fruitful phase. Disciples peppered the city with Bauhaus structures and mass-marketed their successes – simple but elegant lamps, chairs and wallpaper, to name a few items.

In 1932 the Bauhaus moved to Berlin to escape oppression by the Nazis, who claimed that it undermined traditional values. ('How can a flat roof be German?' they asked). The school was dissolved by Hitler in 1933 and its leading lights fled the country. After WWII, the Bauhaus was hailed as the cutting edge of modern architecture but its chief followers remained in exile.

– Jeremy Gray

Schöneberg (Map 5)

South of Tiergarten, Schöneberg is a comfortable hybrid between the sedateness of its western neighbour, Wilmersdorf, and the wackiness of Kreuzberg to the east. Nicely restored 19th century apartment buildings line residential streets, many of them packed with pubs, cafes and global-village restaurants.

It's hard to imagine that as recently as the 1980s Schöneberg – especially the area around Winterfeldtplatz – was a squatter's stronghold. An ambitious gentrification program finally pushed them out, making room for upwardly mobile Generation Xers, including many young families. Schöneberg is trendy and chic, its people having the necessary money and education to appreciate the finer things in life.

Schöneberg has also been an active centre of the gay scene since the 1920s, a period vividly chronicled by one-time area resident Christopher Isherwood in *Goodbye to Berlin*. To this day, the city's main gay haunts still cluster around Nollendorfplatz and along Motzstrasse and Fuggerstrasse with all scenes catered for.

Schöneberg's most famous daughter is Marlene Dietrich who grew up on Leberstrasse and is buried in Friedhof Friedenau (see boxed text 'Cemetery Hopping'). Another internationally famous name associated with this district is John F Kennedy. It was at Schöneberg's town hall where he uttered the famous words: 'Ich bin ein Berliner'.

NOLLENDORFPLATZ AREA

Nollendorfplatz marks the beginning of the gay district. Christopher Isherwood lived at Nollendorfstrasse 17, a block south of the square. The treatment of homosexuals under the Third Reich is commemorated by a triangular red granite **memorial plaque** set into the wall of the south-western exit of Nollendorfplatz U-Bahn station. Homosexuals suffered tremendously from persecution under the Nazis although their treatment has been generally ignored. Those who didn't conceal their orientation had to wear pink triangles and were, at best, socially ostracised. Many ended up being deported to concentration camps and killed.

The imposing neobaroque building right on Nollendorfplatz is the former **Metropol Theater** (not to be confused with the Metropol Theater in Mitte), now a mediocre nightclub (see the Entertainment chapter). Note the tastefully erotic frieze gracing its facade.

From the square, Maassenstrasse leads south to the **Winterfeldtplatz**, site of a wonderful produce market on Wednesday and Saturday mornings (see the Shopping chapter). The Saturday market especially is perfect for observing the trendy Schöneberg scene at play. Young families with small children gather on the square's east side for

a chat and a coffee, while fashionable 'dinks' (double income, no kids) dig into lavish breakfasts at the many cafes. The church looming above the square is the **St-Matthias-Kirche**.

KLEISTPARK AREA

A number of interesting sites cluster around U-Bahn station Kleistpark. The park itself is a few steps north on Potsdamer Strasse and is entered via the graceful sandstone **Königskolonnaden** (Royal Colonnades), designed in 1780 by Karl von Gontard (who was responsible for the domes atop the German and French cathedrals on Gendarmenmarkt). Sculptural ornamentation, including figures of angels and gods, decorate the arcades. The colonnades originally stood at the end of Königsstrasse (today's Rathausstrasse) in Mitte but were moved here in 1910 because of road construction. Kleistpark itself used to be a botanical garden.

At the western edge of the park stands the imposing **Kammergericht** (chamber courts of justice) which was where the notorious Nazi Volksgericht (People's Court), led by the fanatical judge Roland Freisler, held some of its show trials. About 2500 political prisoners received death sentences here, many of them going on to be executed at Plötzensee Prison (see Gedenkstätte Plötzensee under Tiergarten earlier this chapter). From 1945 to 1990, the Allied Control Council had its seat here. These days, the Berlin Constitutional Court uses a part of the building.

North of here, on the corner of Goebenstrasse and Potsdamer Strasse, stood the **Sportpalast**, a huge hall with room for up to 9000 which, besides hosting bicycle races and concerts, was also where, on 18 February 1943, Goebbels, standing before thousands of war-chastened but still fanatical Berliners, exclaimed: *'Wollt ihr den totalen Krieg?'* (Do you want total war?) The answer was yes, and the rest is history. In 1973, the Sportpalast was torn down.

Potsdamer Strasse is a fairly grotty, rundown street that has actually seen *worse* days when it was a haven for drug addicts and prostitutes. Some of that still goes on today, but mostly this is a completely normal business street with second-hand boutiques, Woolworth's, photo stores, fruit and vegie shops etc. South of Kleistpark station, it turns into Hauptstrasse where, at No 152, David Bowie and Iggy Pop once lived.

RATHAUS SCHÖNEBERG

Schöneberg's town hall on John-F-Kennedy-Platz is most famous for being the place where JFK committed his famous 'I am a doughnut' faux pas in 1963 (see the boxed text 'I Am a Doughnut – John F Kennedy, 1962'). From 1948 to 1990, the Rathaus was the seat of the West Berlin Senate and the governing mayor (now back at the Red Town Hall in Mitte). Its clock tower used to rise 81m but was shortened by about 10m in 1950 to accommodate the **Liberty Bell**.

Seven million Americans had donated money towards this replica of the original Philadelphia Bell which was given to Berliners as a gesture of support. It was presented to the city by General Lucius D Clay, commander of the US army in Germany.

Kreuzberg

For 30 years, Kreuzberg was the ugly duckling of Berlin districts. With its border location in the west, but south of Mitte and west of Friedrichshain, it became a catch basin for the socially disadvantaged – the poor and immigrants – and for students, squatters, punks and supporters of an alternative lifestyle. Subcultures flourished in this climate and so did some radical – and occasionally violent – spin-offs (see the boxed text 'Kreuzberg in Flames'). All were attracted by cheap rent and accepted the often substandard living conditions.

With the collapse of the Wall, Kreuzberg suddenly found itself not at the edge but in the heart of the New Berlin, making it desirable turf for developers and the upwardly mobile. Gentrification is quickly taking place and in some areas commercial rent has quintupled since 1990. Housing rents shot up as well, pushing out students who've moved on to cheaper pastures like Prenzlauer Berg and Friedrichshain.

'I am a Doughnut' – John F Kennedy, 1962

West Berlin had pulled off the PR coup of the Cold War. It was August 1963, exactly two years since the Wall separating East and West Berlin had been put up by the GDR, and the Leader of the Free World and everybody's favourite blue-eyed boy, John Fitzgerald Kennedy, 35th president of the United States, had agreed to speak.

From the steps of Rathaus Schöneberg, the silver-tongued orator flayed the forces of darkness to the east and applauded the powers of light in the west, concluding with the now famous words: 'All men free, wherever they live, are citizens of Berlin, and therefore, as a free man, I take pride in the words, *Ich bin ein Berliner*.' Looking at old film footage of that momentous event, it's difficult to know whether the crowd of 500,000 was cheering in support of JFK's sentiments or howling with laughter. The President of the United States had just told them: 'I am a doughnut.'

Unlike English, German does not use the indefinite article ('a' or 'an') before professions, nationalities etc. Thus *Ich bin Student* is 'I am *a* student' in English, while 'I am a Berliner' is rendered *Ich bin Berliner* in German. *Ein Berliner* in German is short for *ein Berliner Pfannkuchen*, a round jam-filled bun sprinkled with powdered sugar and – as was JFK – very popular in the capital.

There's no record of what happened to JFK's chief of protocol or his linguistic advisers after the speech. Everyone probably had a good laugh and forgot about the 'doughnut debacle'. But sometimes you still see, at souvenir shops around town, little plastic Berliners emblazoned with the words 'Ich bin ein Berliner'.

Kreuzberg in Flames

In the 1980s, the area of Kreuzberg 36 (SO 36) gained notoriety for its ferocious street fights pitting the police against militant left-wing anarchists, the so-called Autonomen. The traditional day of rioting was the 1 May holiday (Labour Day) which brought out a huge contingent of cops armed to the teeth and equipped with water cannons and tear gas. Violence raged through the streets, but in 1987 things got badly out of hand.

No longer content with merely throwing rocks and bottles, the frenzied mob barricaded themselves and declared SO 36 a 'lawless zone'. They then broke into a supermarket on Wiener Strasse, looted the shelves (alcohol being particularly popular) and finished the job by setting the entire store on fire. The police stood by helplessly as the radicals cheered on the flames.

After the Wende, when Kreuzberg began its gentrification process, the Autonomen quickly moved on to Prenzlauer Berg, staging their May riots there. Now that that district has gone mainstream too, they may soon again have to find a new frontier.

Kreuzberg is divided into two distinct sections. The western half (referred to as Kreuzberg 61 after the old postal code) is more upmarket, with dignified 19th century apartment houses with ornate facades. The eastern half, Kreuzberg 36, was once the home of the alternative political scene and is still famous for its raging nightlife (though things have quietened down considerably since the Wende). Traditionally a working-class quarter, it is crisscrossed by corridors of Mietskasernen (tenements built around successive courtyards) in various states of disrepair. As recently as 1994 around 20% of all apartments here did not have a private bath and 4% still had the toilet in the hallway.

In terms of area, Kreuzberg is the second-smallest district (after Friedrichshain) but with roughly 150,000 residents is also

among the most densely populated. Fully one-third of the population is of foreign descent, most of them Turkish. In fact, Turks so dominate the area around Kottbusser Tor and Görlitzer Bahnhof that the U1, which runs to this area, is sometimes referred to as the 'Istanbul Express'.

NORTH-WEST KREUZBERG (MAPS 6 & 8)

This part of Kreuzberg may not be a big draw in terms of aesthetics, but it does offer a number of interesting sights, including the famous Checkpoint Charlie. The area described in this section roughly encompasses the triangle formed by U-Bahn stations Kochstrasse to the north, Yorckstrasse to the south-west and Mehringdamm to the south.

Checkpoint Charlie (Map 8)

Almost nothing remains of Checkpoint Charlie, but if you want to stand on the spot of the famous border crossing, go to the intersection of Friedrichstrasse and Zimmerstrasse (U6 to Kochstrasse). The main gateway for foreigners between the two Berlins during the Cold War, this was the third Allied checkpoint and thus named 'Charlie' with reference to the third letter in the phonetic alphabet (alpha, bravo, charlie, dora ...)

Since the Wende, sleek modern office buildings, including one designed by Philip Johnson, have replaced the barbed wire and barriers. The modest trailer that served as the duty office of western military police is now on view at the Allied Museum in Zehlendorf (see the Western Districts section later in this chapter). An old watchtower and the famous sign 'You are leaving the American Sector' are the only tangible reminders of that spooky chapter in German history.

Haus am Checkpoint Charlie (Map 8)

The history of the Berlin Wall is commemorated in the Haus am Checkpoint Charlie (☎ 253 72 50) at Friedrichstrasse 44. You have to wade through a haphazard maze of tattered exhibits and posters to find some fascinating nuggets about the heroic efforts of former GDR citizens to escape their keepers. Interesting displays include a handcrafted one-man submarine and photographs of people fleeing in concealed compartments in cars and luggage. One family actually made its tortured way to freedom in a homemade hot-air balloon. A continually playing video explains the very real and frightful history played out here.

While the museum must be commended for its multilingual displays (in German, English, French and Russian), it's also dated, grimy, poorly organised and badly in need of revamping. It's quite sad, especially since this is one of Berlin's most popular museums. A cluster of Formica tables by the exit serves as a cafe. Also here is yet another gift shop selling chips of the Wall and other Cold War memorabilia.

The museum is open from 9 am to 10 pm daily (DM8/5). If you think that's not enough, there's the opportunity to throw some extra money into a 'donation box'.

Anhalter Bahnhof Area (Map 6)

As you emerge from the Anhalter Bahnhof U-Bahn station, you'll spot some elegant arches which are all that remain of the neo-Renaissance **Anhalter Bahnhof**, until WWII the finest and busiest railway station in Berlin. Badly bombed, it languished and was finally demolished in the early 60s by the East Germans. For some reason, they kept a small piece of the facade which now stands forlornly on the giant empty lot. The **Tempodrom**, a popular entertainment venue, is scheduled to get its permanent home here.

A short walk west gets you to the **Gruselkabinett** (Cabinet of Horrors, ☎ 26 55 55 46), at Schöneberger Strasse 23a, the only publicly accessible above-ground air-raid shelter in Berlin (enter via the gap in the long red-brick building on Schöneberger Strasse). In 1997 it was converted into a somewhat confusing exhibit that is a combination war museum, medieval house of horrors and country-fair spook show. In the 'historical section', you'll find a smattering of actual belongings left behind by those who holed up here to escape bombing raids.

A broken-through section of the outer wall reveals its 2.13m thickness. The ground floor is given over to the gory subject of medieval surgery techniques, graphically (and laughably) demonstrated by groaning dummies. And then there's the top level where you'll be accosted by giant gorillas leaping out of the dark. If all this sounds like it might be fun for children, well, be warned that it's pretty intense. Hours are from 10 am to 7 pm Sunday, Monday, Tuesday and Thursday, to 8 pm Friday, from noon to 8 pm Saturday (DM12/10/9 for adults/students/children).

Deutsches Technikmuseum (Map 6)

The gigantic Deutsches Technikmuseum (German Museum of Technology, ☎ 25 48 40) at Trebbiner Strasse 9 is one of the most exciting, involving and stimulating museums in Berlin and one of the largest of its kind in the world (take the U15 to Möckernbrücke or Gleisdreieck). Housed in a cluster of structures of the former Anhalter Bahnhof freight depot, the museum explains technical principles in an entertaining, practical and hands-on way. It's easy to spend an entire day here, especially if you bring the kids.

The museum has several sections, each focused on a particular field of technology. In the printing department, you can make your own business cards on historical machines. In the automation section, there's a copy of the world's first computer – the Z1 by Konrad Zuse – plus demonstrations of computer music and games.

Production technology comes alive in historical workshops where each step, for instance in the making of jewellery, is shown (the finished products are available for a donation). Train lovers won't want to miss the 40 historical locomotives dating back as far as 1800. There's also a six-hectare **Museumspark,** with two reconstructed, working windmills, while another facet of energy technology is explained at the solar-energy station.

Especially popular with kids is the interactive **Spectrum**, where they can carry out about 250 experiments explaining the scientific underpinnings of technology. Learn what makes the sky blue or how a battery works. Spectrum is housed in an annex on Möckernstrasse, about 300m east of the main museum building. The year 2000 will see the opening of yet another structure which will house the department of shipping and air travel.

Museum hours are from 9 am to 5.30 pm Tuesday to Friday, from 10 am to 6 pm weekends (DM5/2).

Around Mehringplatz (Map 6)

An aerial photograph reveals the impressive circular shape of Mehringplatz, the plaza just north of the Hallesches Tor U-Bahn station. In the 19th and early 20th centuries, this was a rather fashionable neighbourhood favoured by politicians, diplomats and aristocrats. Sadly, it was completely destroyed in the war and overall has not been imaginatively rebuilt.

South of Mehringplatz, at Blücherplatz, is the **Amerika-Gedenkbibliothek**, or AGB (American Memorial Library, ☎ 69 08 40), built to commemorate the Berlin Airlift of 1948-49 and the largest circulating library in Germany (also see the Libraries section in the Facts for the Visitor chapter). The small **cemeteries** right behind the AGB hold the graves of composer Felix Mendelssohn-Bartholdy, writer ETA Hoffmann and poet Adalbert von Chamisso.

West of Mehringplatz, at the intersection of Stresemannstrasse and Wilhelmstrasse, stands the **Willy-Brandt-Haus**, a glass, steel and concrete flat-iron building that houses the Berlin headquarters of the Social Democratic Party (SPD). Designed by Helge Bofinger, it opened in 1996 and was named after the one-time Berlin mayor and later German chancellor (1969 to 1974). A sculpture by artist Rainer Fetting – showing Brandt in cool pose, one hand in pocket, the other outstretched – stands in the light-flooded triangular atrium. The atrium is also used for art exhibits, discussions and concerts. Opening hours are from 10 am to 8 pm Monday to Saturday, from 11 am to 6 pm Sunday (free).

Jüdisches Museum

The most prominent and provocative addition to Berlin's museum scene is the Jüdisches Museum (Jewish Museum, ☎ 25 99 33) by Daniel Libeskind. It's at Lindenstrasse 9-14, a short walk east of Kochstrasse U-Bahn station.

The daring structure by the Polish-born architect is a rare example of crisp modernism in the landscape of the New Berlin. Zinc-clad walls rise skyward in a sharply angled zigzag ground plan that's an abstract interpretation of a star. The general outline is echoed in the windows: triangular, trapezoidal and irregular gashes in the building's gleaming skin.

The interior too is not merely exhibit space but a metaphor for the history of the Jewish people. The museum is entered through an underground walkway from the adjacent Berlin Museum. It leads to a small interior plaza from which three 'roads' radiate. The first road is a cul-de-sac, leading to the **Holocaust Tower**, one of a series of 'voids' – enclosed hollow spaces – that symbolise the loss of humanity, culture and people. The second street culminates in the **ETA Hoffmann Garden**, a field of concrete columns which represents Jewish emigration and exile. The main walkway leads to a flight of stairs providing access to three exhibition floors.

Actual exhibits won't be on view until at least October 2000. On display will be ceremonial objects, portraits of Jewish personalities, books, a historical archive and more. At the time of writing, fascinating architectural tours of the museum were conducted in German and English several times weekly (DM8/5). Phone ☎ 28 39 74 44 for reservations (mandatory).

KREUZBERG WALKING TOUR (MAP 6)

Though devoid of major conventional sights, this tour will introduce you to the many faces of this fascinating district, from Kreuzberg 61, the charming, middle-class neighbourhood around the Kreuzberg hill, to Kreuzberg 36, the epicentre of Turkish Berlin and still home to a fringe underground scene. It starts at U-Bahn station Mehringdamm in Kreuzberg 61, travels via Südstern station and ends at Schlesisches Tor station.

West of Mehringdamm

From U-Bahn station Mehringdamm (U6 and U7) head south, cross Gneisenaustrasse and walk a few more steps to the **Schwules Museum** (Gay Museum, ☎ 693 11 72) at Mehringdamm 61, second courtyard. Its exhibits are hit or miss – some are excellent, but others can be rather offensive, like the one on flagellation or about that master fraud, the late William Burroughs. The museum, which also has a library and an archive, is open from 2 to 6 pm Wednesday to Sunday with a guided tour at 5 pm on Saturday (DM7/4).

Retrace your steps back north to the intersection, then turn west into Yorckstrasse where you'll walk past the spiky twin towers of the **Bonifatiuskirche**, a neo-Gothic concoction wedged in between a row of regular apartment buildings. As you turn left into Grossbeerenstrasse, note the building with the two giants buttressing a 2nd floor balcony. This is one feature of the attractive **Riehmers Hofgarten**, a large complex with open green spaces built for the well-to-do in the early 20th century (also see the Places to Stay chapter). It covers the entire block along Grossbeerenstrasse until Hagelbergerstrasse. A few more steps get you to Kreuzbergstrasse and to the foot of the Kreuzberg hill for which the district is named.

Kreuzberg & Viktoriapark

Note the rather decrepit **Café Achteck**, the nickname given to the green, octagonal *pissoirs* (public latrines) from the Wilhelminian era. This one is no longer functioning and is fenced off to be quietly consumed by rust (there's a better one on nearby Chamissoplatz seen later on this tour). Also here is a suggestive **statue of Neptune** showing the god and an ocean nymphet obviously enjoying each other's company. The pond behind it is the catchment of an artificial **waterfall** which comes rushing down a narrow, rock-lined canal – quite a lovely sight, though enjoyed in summer only.

Most of the Kreuzberg hill, which rises 66m, is covered by the rather unruly, rambling **Viktoriapark** which can be 'climbed' via some steep, short trails. It was designed by Gustav Meyer, a student of the famous garden architect Peter Lenné.

Punctuating the peak is the Schinkel-designed **Kreuzberg memorial** to the Wars of Liberation which pitted Napoleon against Prussian troops in 1813. The 19m-high, cathedral-like spire, perched on a massive pedestal, is reached via a double staircase. Decorated with dramatic detail, the memorial is laid out in the shape of a cross and is also topped by one. *Kreuz* is the German word for 'cross' and so this is actually what gave the hill, which was previously known as Tempelhofer Berg, its name. Unfortunately, the statue memorial is usually defaced with bad graffiti and seems to be under perpetual restoration.

The views from up here are, yes, fabulous, especially in winter when it's easy to peer over the leafless treetops. On New Year's Eve, this is one of the most coveted spots to be. The entire hill becomes party central with thousands of youngsters drinking and gawking at the fireworks. There's also a rather nice cafe/beer garden/disco called Golgatha on the park's western side (see the Entertainment chapter). The buildings at the bottom of the southern slope belong to a large brewery.

Luftbrückendenkmal & Tempelhof Airport

Tempelhof airport (technically in the district of Tempelhof) was one of the main landing sites for Allied planes during the Berlin Airlift of 1948-49. (For more information see the boxed text 'The Berlin Airlift' in the Facts about Berlin chapter). To get there, descend the Kreuzberg on its eastern side to Methfesselstrasse, head south, then east back to Mehringdamm. Right in front of you is the Platz der Luftbrücke, easily recognised by the **Luftbrückendenkmal** (Airlift Memorial, 1951), colourfully called *Hungerharke* (hunger rake).

The trio of spikes represents the three Allied air corridors that ensured Berlin's survival during the Soviet blockade of roads and railways. But the monument itself really is a symbol of when the Allies became protectors instead of occupiers. The names of the 79 airmen and other personnel who died during this amazing effort are engraved in the plinth.

Tempelhof airport itself looks like textbook Nazi architecture, composed as it is of bulky, chunky structures that appear to stretch on endlessly. In fact, it pre-dates the Third Reich by some 10 years, though the Nazis did enlarge it considerably. The fierce-looking eagles clinging to some of the facades are actually from the Weimar Republic era, which explains why they survived postwar de-Nazification. These days, Tempelhof handles mostly domestic departures and smaller planes.

East of Mehringdamm

Walk north on Mehringdamm, then turn right on Fidicinstrasse past the home of the English-language theatre Friends of Italian Opera (see the boxed text 'Thespian Delights' in the Entertainment chapter) and the graceful **Wasserturm** (water tower, 1888). Made from red brick, it looks very much like Rapunzel's tower, its lower sections being practically windowless with only the top ringed by arched openings.

Turn left into Kopischstrasse, then follow it to **Chamissoplatz**, a gorgeous square centred around a peaceful little park and framed by stately 19th century buildings with wrought-iron balconies. One of the few Berlin neighbourhoods largely untouched by WWII, it timewarps you back to the late 19th century and has an almost unreal, movie-set quality. Indeed, directors often use these streets as backdrops for films about 'Old Berlin'. A still functioning Café Achteck pissoir on Chamissoplatz further adds authenticity to the scene.

One block north of the square is Bergmannstrasse, the lively main artery of Kreuzberg 61. It's a fun road teeming with funky second-hand and book shops, restaurants and cafes. Take in the atmosphere while strolling along here, eventually making your way east to Marheinekeplatz. The

highlight of this large square is the **Marheineke Markthalle**, one of Berlin's three surviving historic market halls. Browse through the aisles where produce, cheeses and sausages are piled high. Avoid the ones with cheap clothing, stationery, and junky toys. The impressive red-brick church situated at the square's north-eastern corner is the **Passionskirche**, the occasional site of classical concerts.

Continue east on Bergmannstrasse past a cluster of **cemeteries**. Lots of notables lie buried here, Weimar Republic chancellor Gustav Stresemann being one of the better known. Also here are the architect Martin Gropius (died 1880), the sculptor Adolf Menzel (1905) and Schiller's girlfriend, Charlotte von Kalb (1843). Just beyond is U-Bahn station Südstern.

Südstern to Kottbusser Tor

Südstern marks the unofficial end to the 'better' half of Kreuzberg. Beyond here lies south-east Kreuzberg – named SO36, after the old postal code – much of which has the atmosphere of a bustling bazaar thanks to its predominantly Turkish population. An excellent introduction to the scene is provided by the so-called **Türkenmarkt** (Turkish Market), held every Tuesday and Friday afternoon along the Maybachufer (also see the Shopping chapter). To get there from Südstern, walk north-east on Körtestrasse, then right on Urbanstrasse and left into Graefestrasse which runs into Kottbusser Damm.

Right here is the Maybachufer (Maybach Bank) – and the Paul-Lincke-Ufer opposite – the most scenic section of the Landwehrkanal in this otherwise fairly run-down quarter. Both banks are lined by handsomely renovated pre-WWI apartment buildings and, in good weather, throngs of happy folk gather inside and outside the numerous pubs and restaurants that have sprung up.

Less appealing is the architecture around Kottbusser Tor U-Bahn station, a few steps north along Kottbusser Damm, where the sins of the 70s are all too apparent. Take a look at the hideous **Neue Kreuzberger Zentrum** for a perfect example of misdirected modernisation.

Kottbusser Tor is the hub of Turkish Kreuzberg. Grocers, bakeries, supermarkets, shops, department stores and cafes have a distinctive oriental flavour. Turkish women bustle about, their hair hidden beneath colourful kerchiefs and their bodies concealed beneath shapeless frocks. The younger ones often spice up the traditional garb with pink lipstick, their coats just short enough to reveal ankles in black nylons. More often than not, though, they have emancipated themselves from ancient conventions and prefer the same contemporary fashions as their German peers.

Oranienstrasse to Schlesisches Tor

From the Kottbusser Tor station, head north on Adalbertstrasse where the **Kreuzberg Museum** (☎ 25 88 62 33) is in a converted factory at No 95a. This is a useful place for learning more about the history of the district. The museum is open Wednesday to Sunday afternoons (free).

Adalbertstrasse intersects with **Oranienstrasse**, still one of Berlin's main nightlife drags. Though considerably tamer today, its cafes, bars, clubs and restaurants retain the radical underground feel that helped SO36 make headlines in the wild 80s. For details about the scene, see the Entertainment chapter.

Turn right on Oranienstrasse, then left into Mariannenstrasse which culminates in Mariannenplatz, in summer a popular site for street parties with outdoor picnics and barbecues. At Mariannenplatz 2 is the **Künstlerhaus Bethanien** (☎ 616 90 30), an art centre with studios rented cheaply to young artists. The building began life in 1847 as a hospital and Theodor Fontane, before he become a writer, spent a brief stint here as a pharmacist. The house, which organises frequent exhibits, is open to the public from 2 to 7 pm Wednesday to Sunday (admission varies, but it's often free).

Walk to the north end of the square, then turn right into Wrangelstrasse, which vividly illustrates the cramped living conditions still endured by many Kreuzberg residents. Note the rear courtyards of these buildings, only some of which have been renovated. Wrangelstrasse travels past the **Eisenbahn Markthalle**, another one in the trio of surviving late 19th century market halls with lots of cheap food and junk stalls.

Wrangelstrasse eventually intersects with Skalitzer Strasse, a main shopping thoroughfare leading to Schlesisches Tor U-Bahn station. Before the Wende, this was the terminus of the U1. Immediately beyond, the Spree River served as a natural border between West and East Berlin.

Our tour ends here but in case you're wondering about that amazing red-brick bridge just east of here, it is the **Oberbaumbrücke** (1896). With its jaunty turrets and pinnacles, crenellated walls and arched walkways it looks very much like a medieval drawbridge leading up to a fortified castle. It once again links Kreuzberg with the district of Friedrichshain. Just beyond the bridge is the East Side Gallery, the longest stretch of surviving Wall (see the next section).

Friedrichshain

Like neighbouring Prenzlauer Berg and Kreuzberg, Friedrichshain – formerly in East Berlin – has traditionally been a workers' quarter. Good transportation infrastructure (the river Spree and the railway) helped entice industry to settle in this district in the late 19th century. Many of the factories were kept alive by the GDR but since the Wende most have closed due to lack of profitability, eliminating 20,000 jobs.

Friedrichshain's appearance reflects its humble origins. Much of it is still crisscrossed by block after block of dilapidated Mietskasernen. In recent years, though, the district has experienced an influx of students and squatters, drawn by low rent and the earthy, proletarian atmosphere. At the same time, older residents who can afford to live elsewhere, have moved out.

This demographic restructuring has resulted in an emerging nightlife and entertainment scene centred around Boxhagener

Platz and along Simon-Dach-Strasse. Underground culture flourishes on Rigaer Strasse, north of the Frankfurter Allee, where countless squatters have opened makeshift bars and clubs in their occupied buildings.

Friedrichshain's grey monotony is softened by the Volkspark, one of the largest in the eastern districts. Aficionados of architecture have the monumental Stalinist Karl-Marx-Allee to look forward to.

EAST SIDE GALLERY (MAP 6)

The longest and most famous remaining section of the notorious 'border security system' – aka the Wall – runs for 1.3km along Mühlenstrasse from Warschauer Strasse in the south-east almost up to Hauptbahnhof train station in the northwest. The stretch is covered in 111 large-scale paintings by 52 German and 59 foreign artists whose works reflect the euphoric spirit of 1989, the year the Wall came down. Some have political messages, others show surreal imagery, yet others are purely decorative. Here you'll find the famous images of the Trabant bursting through the Wall, and Erich Honecker and Leonid Brezhnev French-kissing.

Unfortunately, graffiti 'artists' have added their two cents over the years, and the wind and weather have taken their toll as well. Protected as a monument since 1992, there's talk of covering the gallery with glass in order to prolong its life for at least a few more years. Until that happens, it will just be left to crumble. This is not a gallery where you have to pay admission; just walk along it. The better place to start is from the Warschauer Strasse end (U/S-Bahn to Warschauer Strasse, then a five minute walk downhill). The medieval-looking red-brick bridge you'll see is the recently restored Oberbaumbrücke (see the Kreuzberg section earlier in this chapter).

KARL-MARX-ALLEE (MAP 4)

Karl-Marx-Allee, leading south-east off Alexanderplatz, was East Germany's 'first socialist road' and the backdrop for GDR military parades. It is an architectural oddity and a perfect metaphor for the inflated sense of importance and grandeur of the former GDR regime. First called Stalinallee after WWII, it was renamed in 1961 following Stalin's death.

Built in two segments between 1952 and 1965, the older section, which runs from Strausberger Platz to Frankfurter Tor, is a good example of the bombastic Zuckerbäckerstil (wedding cake style) in vogue during Stalinist Russia. Both sides of the 90m-wide boulevard are flanked by 'people's palaces' – in fact concrete behemoths with small flats for workers – that are between 100m and 300m long and seven to nine storeys high. They are replicas of those on Lenin Allee in Moscow. (In an ironic twist, it was the very construction of the people's palaces that led to the workers' uprising on 17 June 1953, which brought the GDR to the brink of collapse – see the History section in the Facts about Berlin chapter for details.)

At the time of construction, these apartment buildings were considered state-of-the-art. They all had private sanitary facilities, central heating and lifts. But construction materials were poor and it didn't take long before they started to crumble. On some of them, you can still see the partly eroded facades, allowing a peek at how they were made. Placed atop the concrete shell is a steel grid upon which are glued huge rectangular tiles, now shattered and grimy with age. In 1993, a large bank bought most of these buildings and began restoring them.

Between 1959 and 1965, the second segment of Karl-Marx-Allee was constructed from Alexanderplatz to Strausberger Platz. Five to 10-storey apartment blocks, in the finest GDR prefab, line this section, which is 125m wide. But, just to show that the GDR regime wanted their people to have *some* fun as well, the boulevard also boasts two large cinemas which, after renovation, are again operational. They are the **Kosmos** (1962) at No 131 and the **International** (1963) at No 33.

Since no buses run along Karl-Marx-Allee, its monumentalism must be appreciated on foot or by car.

The Berlin Wall

In 1999 Berlin celebrated its first decade without 'die Mauer', the ugly scar and symbol of in-humanity and oppression that bisected the city for 28 years. The East German government erected this so-called 'Anti-Fascist Protection Barrier' in 1961 to curb the exodus of its own residents to the west. Extended several times, it snaked through the countryside for some 160kms, 44 of them within Berlin. Its ugly prefab concrete slabs – that you could reach out and touch or paint on the western side – were protected by a no-man's land of barbed wire, land mines, attack dogs and watch towers in the east.

More than 5000 people tried to scale the Wall; 3200 were captured, 160 were killed. The first victim, who tried to jump into the west from the window of his house, died only a few days after the Wall went up. The full extent of the cruelty of the system became blatantly apparent on 17 August 1962 when 18-year-old Peter Fechtner was shot during his attempt to flee and then left to bleed to death while the East German police looked on.

Today, little more than 1.5km of the Wall is left, much of it having been hammered away by memento seekers. Entire sections were shipped to museums worldwide but most was sim-ply recycled for use in road construction. Crosses commemorating those who died at this bar-baric border are scattered throughout Berlin.

Some stretches, however, still stand, silent symbols not just of an era of division but also of the triumph of freedom and individuality over an oppressive and unjust political system.

East Side Gallery

This is a 1300m-long section along Mühlenstrasse (Map 6) painted by more than 100 inter-national artists during post-reunification euphoria. Take the U/S-Bahn to Warschauer Strasse. (Also see the Friedrichshain section in the Things to See & Do chapter.)

Niederkirchnerstrasse

This 160m section runs along Niederkirchnerstrasse from Martin-Gropius-Bau to Wilhelm-strasse (Map 8). Take the U/S-Bahn to Potsdamer Platz.

Invalidenfriedhof

This cemetery, just north of the Hamburger Bahnhof Museum of Contemporary Art (Map 4) has two sections measuring about 150m in total. Take the U6 to Zinnowitzer Strasse.

Berlin Wall Memorial

The new Gedenkstätte Berliner Mauer (Map 4) composed of a lengthy section of the Wall, plus reconstructed border installations, is on the corner of Bernauer Strasse and Ackerstrasse. Take the S-Bahn to Nordbahnhof.

VOLKSPARK FRIEDRICHSHAIN (MAP 4)

Berlin's first public park dates back to 1840 in celebration of the centenary of Friedrich II's ascension to the throne. Peter Lenné provided the original plans and in 1875 his student, Gustav Meyer, designed an expan-sion. During WWII, the park sported two flak towers which doubled as repositories for treasures from Berlin museums. Most of these fell victim to a devastating fire in 1945. Blown up after the war, the towers' remains were topped with rubble from bombed buildings to form the two artificial mounds called **Bunkerberge** at the park's centre and on its north-eastern edge.

One of the park's nicest features is the **Märchenbrunnen** (Fairytale Fountain, 1913) on the corner of Am Friedrichshain and Friedenstrasse, though it would benefit from some restoration. Flanked by a romantic, halfmoon-shaped superstructure, it consists of multiple, tiered basins studded with sculptures representing fairytales of the Brothers Grimm (eg Cinderella, the Frog Prince). In the warmer months, the fountain is a popular cruising spot for gay men. You can reach the park on bus No 100.

The park also has a couple of GDR-era monuments. A short walk south-east of the fountain, along Friedenstrasse, stands **Gedenkstätte für die Deutschen Interbrigadisten**, a grandiose memorial dedicated to the German soldiers who fought against fascism as part of the International Brigades in the Spanish Civil War (1936-39). Just look for the sculpture of a sword-swinging, raised-fisted soldier. The bronze relief on the left depicts the battle of Madrid.

In the park's north-eastern corner is another monument (1972) commemorating the joint fight of Polish soldiers and the German resistance during WWII. On the southern edge is the cemetery for nearly 200 demonstrators who died during the revolutionary riots in March 1848.

Prenzlauer Berg

Framed by Mitte and Friedrichshain to the south and middle-class Pankow and Weissensee to the north, Prenzlauer Berg has, in recent years, evolved from a working-class backwater to one of the prettiest and most happening of Berlin's neighbourhoods. Many facades still bore the scars of war at the time of the Wende, but restoration has since been proceeding at a furious pace. At the same time, a wonderfully diverse cafe and pub scene has sprouted. Eager, young entrepreneurs open up shops, studios, galleries and offices, bringing with them energy, ideas, and optimism needed to inject new life and colour into this district.

Even during GDR days, Prenz'lberg – as Berliners refer to it – was a special district.

In many ways it was the mirror image of Kreuzberg. Both were frontier districts, wedged against the Wall, neglected and brimming with old, claustrophobic living spaces. Both attracted people in search of an alternative lifestyle: avant-garde artists, writers, homosexuals and political activists. Even squatting was prevalent here.

The Prenzlauer Berg tradition of going against the majority goes a long way back. In this century, a comparatively low 23% voted for the Nazis in 1932, and during GDR elections in 1986 some 5% protested silently against the regime by refusing to participate in the voting – sham that it was, with only the SED party on the ballot. If 5% seems small, remember that the simple act of not voting meant extending an invitation to the Stasi.

Today, Prenz'lberg is very much Berlin's Latin Quarter. Thousands of students, attracted by the cheap rent and vibrant nightlife, have moved here.

WALKING TOUR (MAP 4)
This walk takes in the southern section of Prenzlauer Berg between U-Bahn stations Senefelderplatz and Eberswalder Strasse. As you exit the first, note the functioning **Café Achteck** pissoir, one of the last remaining ones in Berlin. Cross the little park to Kollwitzstrasse and head north. Immediately on your left is a rather unusual **adventure playground** which engages children in creative play. There's a workshop where kids actually build with hammers and nails, a bike-repair shed, a smithy, various climbing structures and much more. The playground, open to kids aged six to 14, is supervised by a social worker and is free. This progressive project was the first such playground in eastern Berlin when it opened in 1990.

Continuing on Kollwitzstrasse soon gets you to the triangular Kollwitzplatz at whose centre is an expressive bronze sculpture of the aged Kathe Köllwitz by Gustav Seitz (1958). She looks tired, possibly from a lifetime of concern with the destitute around her. Children often clamber around this larger-than-life sculpture or sit in her maternal lap. Kollwitz, who produced an entire series of mother and child drawings, would probably have liked this. Between 1891 and 1943, Kollwitz and her physician husband Karl lived on the corner of Kollwitzstrasse and Knaackstrasse. The house was destroyed in 1943.

Continue south-east on Knaackstrasse and you'll soon arrive at a Prenzlauer Berg landmark, the statuesque **Wasserturm** (water tower, 1875). Resting atop a slight mound, it replaced its predecessor, built in 1853 on nearby Windmühlenberg, as it proved too narrow and short to supply sufficient water. This newer one was in use until 1915. During the Third Reich, its basement was used as a torture chamber. Today, this rather unique structure contains flats.

Just north of the tower at Rykestrasse 53 is a **synagogue**, the only one in Berlin to survive both Kristallnacht (apparently because Nazi party officials resided nearby) and Allied bombing. It's actually in the back of a courtyard and usually inaccessible, though you can see it from the pavement through a gate.

Turning left on Wörtherstrasse will take you back to Kollwitzplatz. From here, head north on Husemannstrasse. This entire street received a serious sprucing up from the East German government in the context of Berlin's 750th anniversary celebrations in 1987. Yet Husemannstrasse has the same artificial patina as the Nikolaiviertel in Mitte, created at the same time. Lots of cutesy, supposedly turn-of-the-century shops opened here. Today they contain antiques and junk, along with a fairly meagre selection of furniture, books and GDR paraphernalia.

Turn left into Sredzkistrasse, where the giant complex of the former **Schultheiss brewery** will soon come into view. Parts of this yellow-brick Art Nouveau structure from the late 19th century have a cathedral-like appearance. The entire place survived time and wars relatively unscathed. At the time of research the culture centre **Kulturbrauerei** (Cultural Brewery), which already occupied several buildings in its north-eastern corner, was being expanded into a mega-complex taking up the entire former

brewery. (Enter from Knaackstrasse 97, also see the Entertainment chapter). Integrated within the centre will be an expanded and modernised version of the **Sammlung Industrielle Gestaltung** (Collection of Industrial Design), a collection of objects that typified daily life in the GDR. Swing by or check with the tourist office about updated hours and admission prices.

From Knaackstrasse, turn left, then left again into Danziger Strasse, which takes you right to Eberswalder Strasse U-Bahn station. Before boarding the train, make a quick detour south to Kastanienallee 7-9 where you'll find the historic **Berliner Prater**. Originally a beer hall, it became an assembly place for the Berlin workers' movement late last century. August Bebel and Rosa Luxemburg were among those who gave speeches here. Today, the Prater is a secondary stage of the Volksbühne theatre, with provocative, off-beat productions. The vast beer garden just behind it attracts an intergenerational crowd in summer. In winter, the adjacent restaurant is a traditional favourite with the grey-haired crowd.

NORTHERN PRENZLAUER BERG (MAP 4)

Northern Prenzlauer Berg is quite different from the Kollwitzplatz area and is actually more genuinely GDR (Paul-Robeson-Strasse, for instance, is quite a typical street scene). Just south of the Schönhauser Allee U-Bahn stop, on the corner of Greifenhagener Strasse and Stargarder Strasse, is the **Gethsemane Kirche**, which was one of the centres of the dissident movement that led to the collapse of the East German government.

At the eastern end of Stargarder Strasse, where it meets Prenzlauer Allee, looms the dome of the **Carl-Zeiss-Planetarium** (☎ 421 84 50). It has Berlin's most modern telescope, which explores the universe as part of multimedia shows with music and laser. It's popular with school kids, so pick the evening show if you want quiet. Shows take place at 10.30 am weekdays, on Wednesday, Saturday and Sunday afternoons, and at 8 pm on Friday and Saturday (DM8/6, S8 or S10 to Prenzlauer Allee).

South-east of the planetarium is **Ernst-Thälmann-Park**, not just the name of the park but also of the modern, model high-rise housing complex built for the GDR elite in the mid-80s. South of the planetarium at Prenzlauer Allee 75 is the **Local History Museum** (Map 4, ☎ 42 40 10 97), open from 10 am to noon and from 1 to 5 pm Tuesday and Wednesday, to 7 pm on Thursday, and from 1 to 5 pm on Sunday (free).

North-east of the planetarium, between Sültstrasse and Sodtkestrasse, is an interesting housing development from 1930 called **Flamensiedlung** (Flemish Colony), so named because it was inspired by the architecture of the low countries. Architects Bruno Taut and Franz Hillinger tried to break up the monotony of the dark and dim Mietskasernen by creating green open spaces and adding balconies.

Northern Districts

PANKOW

Pankow, Berlin's northernmost district, was once the centre of the East German government elite. It has preserved a pleasant, small-town atmosphere but is modest in terms of visitor attractions. Part of its appeal lies in the forests and parks that blanket more than one-third of the land. Its main artery, Breite Strasse, is reached after a 500m walk north from S-Bahn station Pankow (S8 and S10) along Berliner Strasse. Where the two streets meet stands the medieval **Dorfkirche**, a diminutive Gothic red-brick church with octagonal towers (open only for Sunday service). Another 500m or so west is Pankow's imposing neobaroque **Rathaus**, site of the Soviet show trial of the commander of the Sachsenhausen concentration camp. Still farther west is the popular **Bürgerpark** (people's park); it merges into the Schönholzer Heide with a Soviet cemetery for soldiers fallen in the Battle of Berlin.

Schloss Niederschönhausen

Pankow's main sight is Schloss Niederschönhausen (1664) which, after the founding of the GDR in 1949, became that country's 'White House' for Staatspräsident (State President) Wilhelm Pieck who lived here until 1960. His successor, Walter Ulbricht, used the palace for four more years until the completion of the Staatsratsgebäude (State Council Building) in Mitte (see that section earlier in this chapter). It then became a government guesthouse hosting, among many others, Mikhail Gorbachev. Until 1991, the entire compound was completely inaccessible to the general public.

The rather unremarkable two storey palace is set within a walled garden (closed from December to Easter) that is surrounded by the public, Peter Lenné-designed Schlosspark (always open). The little Panke, the river that gives Pankow its name, flows through here. Access to the Schloss area is via formerly guarded iron gates. Coming from Breite Strasse, walk north on Ossietzkystrasse where, after about 750m, you'll reach the southern gate. You can also take tram No 52 or 53 from S-Bahn station Pankow to the Tschaikowskystrasse stop and walk east on Tschaikowskystrasse for about 400m, which will lead you to the western gate.

The entire quarter around the palace, especially along Majakowskiring, was a closed community where the party brass made its home. Access passes were needed to get inside, thus ensuring that the general public couldn't see the lavish villas and overall luxury in which their rulers wallowed – while denying almost everyone else basic amenities like a car or telephone.

WEISSENSEE

Thinly populated Weissensee is north of Prenzlauer Berg and east of Pankow. It is one of the more pleasant of the former East Berlin districts, having preserved a provincial flair and a fair amount of green space. Weissensee escaped large scale destruction during WWII and much of its 19th century architecture survived.

Weissensee gets its name from the **Weisser See**, an almost circular lake on Berliner Allee (U2, S8 or S10 to Schönhauser Allee, then tram No 23 or 24 to Berliner Allee/Indira-Gandhi-Strasse stop).

THINGS TO SEE & DO

On a nice day, the place is crawling with families and young couples, and fleets of rowing and pedal boats dot the placid waters. On its eastern shore is an old-fashioned lakeside pool.

East of here, at Berliner Allee 185, is the **Brecht Haus** where Bertolt Brecht and Helene Weigel first lived after returning from exile in 1949. The villa, in classicist style, is now a gallery (☎ 926 80 44) and also used for readings. North of the lake, in a little park, is an open-air theatre, the Freilichtbühne, where concerts and film screenings take place in the warmer months.

Weissensee is also home to Europe's largest Jewish Cemetery (see the boxed text 'Cemetery Hopping').

Hundemuseum

A delicacy for canine lovers is the quirky Hundemuseum (Dog Museum, ☎ 474 20 31) in the Blankenburg section of Weissensee at Alt-Blankenburg 33. The museum's seven rooms are crammed with a mind-blowing collection of items, including stuffed and porcelain dogs, medals, posters, candlesticks, glassware and more. In total there's 20,000 dog-related items. Not surprisingly, the Hundesmuseum is listed in the *Guinness Book of Records*.

Opening hours for this unusual museum are 3 to 6 pm Tuesday, Thursday and Saturday, 11 am to 5 pm Sunday, and admission costs DM2/1. To get there, take the S8 or S10 to Blankenburg, from where it's a 10 minute walk east.

Cemetery Hopping

Dead legends continue to exert a morbid fascination over the living, and Berlin's cemeteries are certainly stacked with them. Here's our little guide to the city's star-studded resting places:

Dorotheenstädtischer Friedhof – Mitte

This one wins, hands down, the top award for greatest density of celebrity corpses. A veritable pantheon of German greats lie buried here, including the architects Schinkel and Schadow, composers Paul Dessau and Hanns Eisler, Heinrich Mann, Bertolt Brecht and his wife, Helene Weigel. Brecht, in fact, lived in the house bordering the cemetery, allegedly to be close to his idols, the philosophers Hegel and Fichte, who are also buried here. In 1985, German playwright and Berliner Ensemble director Heiner Müller joined their ranks.

Look for a chart of grave locations at the end of the walkway leading to the gated graveyard. It's open roughly from 8 am to sunset, though it's best to check the sign by the entrance for details or else you'll be in for a fence climbing adventure if the gates are locked. (Map 4, U6 to Zinnowitzer Strasse.)

Friedhof Friedenau – Schöneberg

To pay homage to the city's most fabled daughter, Marlene Dietrich, you have to travel to this tiny cemetery. Here, in the far right corner, the 'Blue Angel' makes her final home in a decidedly unglamorous plot. Her tombstone bears her first name only, as well as the inscription: 'Here I stand on the marker of my days'. It's on Fehlerstrasse. (Map 5, U9 to Friedrich-Wilhelm-Platz, then about a 400m walk north-west via Görresstrasse.)

Matthäus-Kirchhof – Schöneberg

This pretty little churchyard holds the famous bones of the Brothers Grimm, who taught at the Humboldt University, as well as the physician and politician Rudolf Virchow. There's also a memorial tombstone to Claus Schenk Graf von Stauffenberg and his fellow conspirators executed by the Nazis after their failed attempt to assassinate Hitler in 1944. A pamphlet with

Eastern Districts

LICHTENBERG

Nondescript Lichtenberg lies east of Friedrichshain and west of Hohenschön-hausen and Marzahn. In 1995, it was the first district to elect a mayor from the Partei Demokratischen Sozialisten (PDS) party, successor to the GDR's SED. Nostalgia for the communist era is surprising given that Lichtenberg was home to the headquarters of the feared Ministry for State Security or 'Stasi'. From its offices on Normannen-strasse, the invasive surveillance system extended less to foreign enemies than to the GDR's own citizens (see the boxed text 'The Stasi – Fear and Loathing in the GDR'). Lichtenberg also has a zoo, a Schloss and another important memorial exhibit, the Museum Karlshorst.

Schloss Friedrichsfelde & Tierpark

Schloss Friedrichsfelde (1695, ☎ 513 81 41), at Am Tierpark 125, is a late-baroque palace that was completely renovated between 1973 and 1981. It is now a classical concert venue and contains a small museum of fine and applied arts from the 17th and 18th centuries, with the usual collection of paintings, tapestries, furniture, porcelain, silver and glassware (open from 10 am to 6 pm Tuesday to Sunday).

To compensate its citizens for the loss of access to the famous Zoologischer Garten in West Berlin, the government of East Berlin

Cemetery Hopping

additional names and grave locations is available for DM1 from the cemetery office. (Map 5, S1/U7 to Yorckstrasse or U7 to Kleistpark.)

Jüdischer Friedhof – Mitte

Berlin's oldest Jewish cemetery (1672), destroyed by the Nazis in 1938, is on Grosse Hamburger Strasse. It contained the graves of more than 10,000 people, including the philosopher Moses Mendelssohn who inspired the title role in Gotthold Ephraim Lessing's *Nathan the Wise*. (Map 4, S-Bahn station Hackescher Markt.)

Jüdischer Friedhof – Prenzlauer Berg

On Schönhauser Allee is the second of Berlin's Jewish cemeteries. It opened in 1827 after the oldest one on Grosse Hamburger Strasse in Mitte ran out of space. Among the famous people buried here are the impressionist painter Max Liebermann (1935), the composer Giacomo Meyerbeer (1864) and the publisher Leopold Ullstein (1899). It's closed on weekends and Friday afternoon. Men must cover their head upon entering. (Map 4, U2 to Senefelder Platz.)

Jüdischer Friedhof – Weissensee

This is Berlin's – and Europe's – largest Jewish cemetery (1880) with more than 100,000 graves. Even before the Wende, West Berlin Jews buried their dead here, although it was behind the Iron Curtain. Just beyond an imposing yellow-brick gate lies a circular area with a memorial to concentration camp victims. Beyond sprawls a veritable forest of tombstones and mausoleums, sheltered by a thick canopy of ancient trees. A chart by the entrance reveals the locations of the plots of some of the better known residents, including painter Lesser Ury and publisher Samuel Fischer. The cemetery is closed on Saturday and Jewish holidays. Men must cover their heads upon entering.

(Take bus No 100 to the eastern terminus, cross Michelangelostrasse and walk through the housing estate to Puccinistrasse. After about 100m, turn right into Herbert-Baum-Strasse.)

decided to convert the former Schlosspark into a zoo. **Tierpark Friedrichsfelde** (☎ 51 53 10) opened in 1954 and at last count (end of 1998) had over 8000 animals representing nearly 1000 species. The Tierpark is open from 9 am to dusk daily (7 pm at the latest).

Since the Tierpark and the Schloss are on the same grounds, only combined tickets are available, costing DM12/10/6 for adults/students/children. The U5 drops you off right near the Tierpark entrance.

Museum Berlin-Karlshorst

This fascinating memorial exhibit (☎ 509 86 09) focuses on the relationship between Germany and the Soviet Union from 1917 to the Wende. Documents, objects, uniforms and photographs explore every stage in the relations, with a particular focus on WWII. Themes such as German-Soviet relations before Hitler's rise to power, the daily grind of life as a soldier, and the fate of Soviet civilians during the war are all dealt with in an informative and objective manner.

The villa which houses the exhibit has a turbulent history. It was here, on the night of 8 to 9 May 1945, where the unconditional surrender of the German army was signed, thus officially ending the fighting of WWII in Europe.

The Stasi – Fear and Loathing in the GDR

The walls had ears. Modelled after the Soviet KGB, the East German Ministerium für Staatssicherheit (Ministry for State Security, 'Stasi' for short) was founded in 1950. It was secret police, central intelligence agency and bureau of criminal investigation, all rolled into one. Called the 'shield and sword' of the paranoid SED leadership – which used it as an instrument of fear and oppression to secure its power base – the Stasi grew steadily in power and size over the four decades of its existence. By the end, the ministry had about 91,000 official full-time employees. Its secret weapons, though, were the 173,000 IMs (inoffizielle Mitarbeiter, unofficial employees) recruited from among the general public to spy on their co-workers, friends, family and neighbours. Even the tiniest piece of information was documented. By the time the system collapsed, there were files on six million people.

The Stasi's all-pervasiveness is unimaginable, as is the extent of the invasion of privacy it perpetrated on its own citizens. Its methods knew no limits with wire-tapping, video-taping observation, and opening of private mail being the more conventional techniques. Perhaps the most bizarre form of Stasi terror was the conservation of a suspected 'enemy's' body odour. Samples taken during interrogations – usually by wiping the unfortunate victim's crotch with a cotton cloth – were stored in hermetic glass jars. If a person needed to be identified, specially trained groin-sniffing dogs – euphemistically known as 'smell differentiation dogs' – sprang into action.

This twisted world is documented in a fascinating exhibit called Stasi – Die Ausstellung (Map 8, ☎ 22 41 74 70) on view at Mauerstrasse 34-38 in Mitte. It helps if you read German, though you can get much of the general context from the pictures and charts. It is open from 10 am to 6 pm Monday to Saturday (free).

In order to see the original office of Erich Mielke, the last Stasi director, as well as cunning surveillance devices, communist paraphernalia and blood-chilling documents about GDR internment camps, travel to the former Stasi headquarters in the eastern district of Lichtenberg. Here, at Ruschestrasse 103 (House 1), is the Forschungs- und Gedenkstätte Normannenstrasse (☎ 553 68 54), a research and memorial exhibit about this spooky organisation. It's open from 11 am to 6 pm Tuesday to Friday, from 2 pm weekends. Admission is DM5/3. Take the U5 to Magdalenenstrasse.

During the war, the building served as a casino for Wehrmacht officers; later it became the headquarters of the Soviet Military Administration in Germany (SMAD). The **office of Marshal Zhukov**, the Soviet supreme commander, can still be seen, as can the **Great Hall** in which the terms of surrender were signed. Taped speeches by top Nazi officials are played via earphones, and various TV screens continuously show war footage. Outside is a battery of **Soviet military weapons**, including a Howitzer canon and the *Katjuscha* multiple rocket-launcher (called 'Stalin organ').

The museum is at Zwieseler Strasse 4, corner of Rheinsteinstrasse, in the Lichtenberg suburb of Karlshorst (S3 to Karlshorst, north on Treskowallee, then right on Rheinsteinstrasse for a 10 minute walk). Hours are from 10 am to 6 pm Tuesday to Sunday. Admission here, as at all war-related memorial exhibits, is free. Display panels are in German and Russian only, but an English-language pamphlet (free) and also a well-written booklet (DM4) are available at the counter in the basement.

MARZAHN

If you're curious about what was considered 'state-of-the-art' housing in the GDR as late as the 1980s, just take the S7/75 to Springpfuhl, followed by tram Nos 8 or 18, and you'll find yourself in the heart of Marzahn. After being 'assaulted' by the hideous aesthetics, get ready for a serious mind-warp: **Alt-Marzahn**, a minuscule patch of medieval history reconstructed amid the soulless concrete canyons. It's all here; a lovely church with step-gabled tower, cobblestone lanes, a wooden windmill, even a small farm. Sort of Disneyland – GDR-style – built on the grounds of the actual settlement from the 1300s.

You can learn more about that at the **Heimatmuseum Marzahn** (☎ 542 40 53), which also contains the much more interesting **Friseurmuseum** (Hairdressing Museum), teaching you all you never wanted to know about the mysteries of washing, cutting, curling and dying hair. It even offers a glimpse into the intricate world of wigmaking. A

highlight is furniture designed by Henry van de Velde for a Berlin hair salon. It's all open from 10 am to 6 pm Tuesday and Thursday, from 1 to 5 pm Sunday (DM2/1).

HELLERSDORF

Hellersdorf is a mirror image of Marzahn with Plattenbauten ghettos galore containing 40,000 flats. Whatever charm there is can be found amid the 19th century villas in the suburb of Mahlsdorf. This is also where you'll find the **Gründerzeit Museum** (☎ 567 83 29) which sheds light on how people lived during the early years of the German Empire (roughly 1870 to 1890). The museum has a curious history. It was started by the GDR's most famous transvestite, Charlotte von Mahlsdorf, born Lothar Bergfelde. Alas, like Britain's Quentin Crisp *(The Naked Civil Servant)*, who saw greener pastures in New York, Die Charlotte flew the coop to Sweden in 1995.

Some of the famous pack rat's collection went with her, but lots was left behind and bought by the Hellersdorf district administration. When they failed to settle the entire bill, Charlotte sued, got her day in court and won. The future of the museum, however, remains uncertain. Call before you venture out. It's at Hultschiner Damm 333 (S5 to Mahlsdorf, then tram No 62 for two stops).

HOHENSCHÖNHAUSEN

More green space, a couple of lakes (Orankesee and Obersee) and a villa colony make Hohenschönhausen slightly more appealing than its immediate neighbours. As far as sights, there's really just one and a pretty chilling one it is.

The **Gedenkstätte Hohenschönhausen** (☎ 962 42 19), Genslerstrasse 66, is a memorial site in a former prison that went through three notorious incarnations. From May 1945 to October 1946, it served as the Soviet-run 'Speziallager Nr 3' (Special Camp No 3), a processing centre for as many as 20,000 German prisoners condemned to the Gulag. The Soviets then turned it into a regular prison, mostly dreaded for its 'U-Boats' – windowless, subterranean cells used to administer water

'Luxury Living' – Made in the GDR

Marzahn, Hohenschönhausen and Hellersdorf are faceless satellite cities founded as recently as 1979, 1985 and 1986 respectively. Their most distinctive feature is row upon row of gigantic, nondescript, prefab housing developments – the so-called *Plattenbauten* – rushing skyward like concrete stalagmites. In Marzahn alone, more than 62,000 flats for 160,000 people were built between 1976 and 1979, giving it the dubious distinction of being Germany's largest new-building complex. Most of these warrens of tiny apartments rise up to 17 storeys high. Entrance doors are painted with colours, symbols or animals to make it easier – especially for kids – to find one's way home.

MICK WELDON

Horrifyingly sterile by most people's standards, the flats were in great demand in the GDR because, unlike many buildings in the central districts like Prenzlauer Berg or Friedrichshain, they had private sanitary facilities, lifts and central heating. Other amenities, like playgrounds and parking, were considered desirable bonuses.

Not surprisingly, nowadays, these places are largely inhabited by people from the lower end of the social spectrum. An exodus of the better-off back into the city or the countryside is offset by an influx of working-class families with gaggles of kids, asylum seekers and welfare recipients who are assigned apartments here by the city. Tension between the various groups does nothing to enhance living conditions. Neither do high unemployment levels and rampant vandalism.

Yearning for the 'good old days' of the GDR seems to be high. All three districts are governed by district mayors belonging to the PDS, the successor of the communist SED.

torture. In 1951 the place was turned over to the GDR government which converted it into its central Stasi prison. Suspected enemies of the regime were detained, interrogated and tortured here until as late as 1989.

Free guided tours operate at 1 pm Tuesday, Wednesday and Thursday and at 11 am Friday and Saturday. Call ahead for a reservation. Take the S7 to Marzahn, then head back south on tram No 6, 7, or 17 to Genslerstrasse.

Southern Districts

NEUKÖLLN (MAP 6)

Neukölln, Berlin's most populous district (315,000 people), is a study in contrasts. The north, bordering Kreuzberg, has traditionally been a stronghold of the proletariat and continues to be dominated by poorer segments of the population, including many immigrants. The main drag, Karl-Marx-Strasse, is a busy high street where pale and downtrodden people – knocked about by life's misfortunes – hang around street corners or spend their measly earnings in cheap import stores and low-end chains.

The southern suburbs of Britz, Buckow and Rudow, on the other hand, have preserved a tranquil small-town character, with tree-lined avenues, single-family homes and a largely middle-class population. An exception is Gropiusstadt, a massive high-rise housing development that is a good example of the kind of architectural sins committed in the 1970s.

Volkspark Hasenheide

This wonderfully rambling park links Neukölln with Kreuzberg and has its origins as the royal family's rabbit preserve (hence

Rebuilding the city's centre at Potsdamer Platz.

JONATHAN SMITH

The Blue Angel's grave in Schöneberg.

RICK GERHARTER

One way to cross Berlin's many waterways.

DAVID PEEVERS

Berlin Cathedral.

French Cathedral.

Odd couple: the Gedächtniskirche and a modern hall of worship.

Schloss Bellevue, currently the German president's official residence.

the name which translates as 'rabbit heath'). Landscape architect Peter Lenné also worked his magic in the Hasenheide in 1838. After WWII it was turned into a public park, with walking paths, playgrounds, an outdoor natural theatre and an animal sanctuary. Today it is still a popular hangout for neighbourhood folks who meet up for a game of *boules*, a chat or a stroll. The 70m-high **Rixdorfer Höhe** is another one of Berlin's Trümmerberge (rubble mountains).

Britz

Architecture fans will be fascinated by the **Hufeisensiedlung** (Horseshoe Colony), a planned housing development from the late 1920s in the suburb of Britz. It is the brainchild of Bruno Taut and Martin Wagner, who set out to create generous and humane living spaces as appealing alternatives to the cramped and lightless tenements of the inner city.

The structure on Lowise-Reuter-Ring perfectly illustrates the principles at work. Around an existing pond, they created a park-like area and surrounded it with a rounded three storey structure in the form of a horseshoe. What looks like a huge single building actually consists of individual sections each set at a slightly different angle to achieve the rounded effect. All the flats have balconies facing the park and each section has its own small garden. It all looks clean, neat and quite handsome.

While here, also check out the street called **Hüsung** just west of Lowise-Reuter-Ring. Here you'll find uninterrupted rows of narrow, two-storey, single-family homes that follow the diamond-shaped outline of the street. Their tiny front lawns are separated from the pavement with hedges of identical height; trees are evenly spaced, about 10m apart. The amazing symmetry and homogeneousness of this development is both a tad oppressive and visually interesting.

The 'Horseshoe' and the 'Diamond' are easily reached by taking the U7 to Parchimer Allee and walking north for about 250m.

Another attraction in Britz is **Schloss Britz** (☎ 606 60 51) at Alt-Britz 73, reached by walking about 500m west from U-Bahn station Parchimer Allee. It's the former estate of the family Britz, who founded the village in the 12th century and owned the castle and village until the 17th century.

There are concerts on most Fridays. Tours of the Schloss' historical rooms take place from 2 to 6 pm Wednesday, though it's probably not worth the effort (DM4/2). The Schloss park is open from 9 am to dusk.

Gropiusstadt

South-east of Britz is Gropiusstadt, West Berlin's answer to Marzahn and other barren colonies of the former East Berlin. Built from 1964 to 1975, it's a glass and concrete desert with flats for some 50,000 people. Although based on designs by Bauhaus founder Walter Gropius, the end result probably made him spin in his grave. His vision of a pedestrian-friendly community with lots of green, open spaces and up to four-storey tall buildings was turned into a forest of high-rises, some with as many as 31 floors, that stand close enough together to see the neighbours brush their teeth. There are no real attractions here for visitors, but if you just want to get a feel for the place, get off at any of the four U-Bahn stations south of, and including, Johannisthaler Chaussee (U7). There's a shopping centre at the Wutzkyallee stop.

TREPTOW

Treptow in former East Berlin gets its character from the Spree River and the large recreational area formed by the Plänterwald forest and Treptow Park. Once a manufacturing stronghold, Treptow is staking its survival on a high-tech future. The former GDR television production site in Adlershof is being turned into a media city. A science and business park, with institutes for the Humboldt Universität, is also being developed. Prime attractions for visitors are the monumental Soviet War Memorial in Treptow Park and, for kids primarily, the Spree-Park.

Treptower Park

Treptower Park, along with the Plänterwald, forms a recreational area of 230 hectares stretching west from the Spree. Stern und Kreis Schiffahrt operates cruises from May to October, and rowing and pedal boats are available for rent as well. The little island to the south is the **Insel der Jugend**, reached via an arched bridge. In the daytime a cafe popular with families, it turns into a hard-core nightclub on weekend nights (see the Entertainment chapter). From here you can also see the tiny island called **Liebesinsel** (Love Island), a good place to take your loved one on a pedal boat.

The statuesque building set a bit away from the shore is **Haus Zenner/Eierschale** (☎ 272 72 11), at Alt-Treptow 14-17, a popular restaurant with a tradition dating back to 1606. It was recently desecrated when a Burger King moved in on the ground floor, though the restaurant upstairs is only marginally better. Ignore both and quaff a cold one in the riverside beer garden instead.

Sowjetisches Ehrenmal Right at the heart of the park is the city's largest Soviet memorial (1949), a gargantuan complex attesting both to the immensity of the losses of WWII and to the overblown self-importance of the Soviet state under Stalin. The monument is always open. From the S-Bahn station Treptower Park, head south for about 750m on Puschkinallee, then enter the park through the bombastic stone gate.

As you approach the complex, you'll first pass a statue of Mother Russia, grieving for her dead children. The actual entrance to the memorial is flanked by two mighty walls made from red marble retrieved from Hitler's New Chancellery and fronted by kneeling soldiers.

From here a wide plaza, lined on either side by eight sarcophagi representing the then 16 Soviet republics, opens up. Each of the blocks is covered with reliefs portraying scenes from the war and quotes from Stalin (in Russian and German). The large field in the centre is the burial site of the 5000 soldiers that fell in the Battle of Berlin. It culminates in a mound topped with a 13m-high statue of a Russian soldier clutching a child, his great sword resting on a shattered swastika. In the plinth is a socialist-realism mosaic of grateful Soviet citizens, including workers, peasants and some Central Asian minorities.

Archenhold Sternwarte A short walk south of the monument is Germany's first public observatory (☎ 534 80 80), opened in 1909 at the initiative of astronomer Friedrich Simon Archenhold. In 1915, Albert Einstein gave a talk here on his theory of relativity. After thorough renovation the observatory now contains changing exhibits on space-related themes. It is open from 2 to 5.30 pm Monday to Thursday, to 7.30 pm Friday to Sunday (DM4/3). It is best reached by walking north into the park from S-Bahn station Plänterwald.

Spree-Park

Unless you're travelling with children, you can probably skip the Spree-Park (☎ 53 33 52 60), a small-scale amusement park with a tame array of attractions, including (not so) wild water rides, a Ferris Wheel, a roller coaster and the 'cowboy town' Colorado City. A number of casual eateries and snack bars are on the grounds as well. The park is at Kiehnwerderallee 1-3 and usually open from 9 am to 6 pm weekdays, from 10 am to 7 pm weekends during March to late October. Admission, including rides, is a hefty DM29/27. The closest S-Bahn station is Plänterwald, from where it's a 15 to 20 minute walk north-east. Or you can take U1 or U15 to Schlesisches Tor, then bus No 265 to the Rathaus Treptow stop. The entrance is on Neue Krugallee.

Museum der Verbotenen Kunst (Map 6)

Behind the ugly grey facade of a former GDR border watchtower, still standing in what used to be the former 'Death Strip, is the petite Museum der Verbotenen Kunst (Museum of Forbidden Art, ☎ 204 20 49). It features changing exhibitions dealing with Germany's 40 years of division and is open noon to 6 pm on weekends. From U-Bahn station Schlesisches Tor (U1/15) walk southeast for about 10 minutes or take bus No 265. From S-Bahn station Treptower Park, it's about the same distance north-west.

Anna Seghers Gedenkstätte

Fans of the writer Anna Seghers (1900-83) might want to make a pilgrimage to her former flat at Anna-Seghers-Strasse 81 (☎ 677 47 25), which contains a library and small exhibit documenting her life and work. A devout communist, Seghers (whose real name was Netty Radvanyi, nee Reiling) spent WWII in Mexico and chose East Berlin as her domicile upon her return from exile. Her most famous work is *The Seventh Cross* (1941), a chilling account of the terrors of the Nazi regime. Hours are 9 am to noon and 2 to 7 pm Tuesday, and 9 am to noon and 2 to 5 pm Wednesday and Thursday (DM4/2). The nearest S-Bahn station is Adlershof.

KÖPENICK

Köpenick, at the far south-eastern tip of Berlin, has the largest area and fewest people (109,000) of all city districts. It is also by far the greenest, with forests and lakes covering about two-thirds of the land. Berlin's largest lake (Müggelsee), largest forest (Köpenicker Stadtforst) and highest natural elevation (Müggelberge, 115m) are all here. There's lots of boating, swimming, sailing, windsurfing, rowing and hiking.

Köpenick, the area's third medieval settlement after Spandau and Berlin, was granted town rights in 1232, 30 years before Berlin, from which it remained independent until 1920. Culture and architecture fans have a protected Altstadt, baroque palace and the former fishing village Kietz to look forward to.

Despite its obvious natural assets, the GDR located lots of industry in Köpenick. At one point, there were about 100 factories with 35,000 jobs. Most have since closed, though smaller companies and 'cleaner' industries – like electronics and cosmetics companies – remain.

Easily reached on the S3 from all major central Berlin S-Bahn stations, Köpenick makes an excellent half-day or day break from the big-city bustle of Berlin. The district's tourist office (☎ 655 75 50) is at Alt-Köpenick 34 and open 9 am to 7 pm weekdays, 10 am to 2 pm weekends.

Gedenkstätte Köpenicker Blutwoche

In the early 20th century, Köpenick was a stronghold of the KPD (communist) and SPD (Social Democrat) parties. After WWI, Köpenick workers did their part in staving off the attempted putsch of right-wing radical Wolfgang Kapp on 13 March 1920 (see the History section in the Facts about Berlin chapter). Under the leadership of Alexander Futran, they stalled army troops loyal to Kapp as they marched on Berlin. Futran was captured and executed, but Köpenick remained red. Thirteen years later, when Hitler rose to power, the communist flag was defiantly raised over Köpenick.

The Nazis naturally didn't let such provocation pass unpunished. In June 1933, the SA captured and tortured hundreds of Nazi opponents, killing 91. Most of the atrocities took place in the courthouse prison of the **Amtsgericht Köpenick**. The events of the so-called *Köpenicker Blutwoche* (Köpenick's Bloody Week) are commemorated in a small **memorial exhibit** (☎ 657 14 67) at the prison, at Puchanstrasse 12, which also contains a reconstructed cell. It's open from 10 am to 6 pm Thursday, from 2pm Saturday (free). A **monument** (1969), showing a raised clenched fist, honours the victims of the Blutwoche; it's on Platz des 23 April just south of here.

Altstadt

Much of Köpenick's Altstadt, including buildings and roads, has recently been restored. Unlike most of Spandau's old town, Köpenick's Altstadt is not pedestrianised and many of its ancient cobblestone streets still follow their medieval layout. The oldest street is Böttcherstrasse but for a parade of historic houses go to Strasse Alt-Köpenick. The oldest is the one at No 36 (built in 1616). House No 14 dates to 1800, Nos 6 and 10 to 1830.

Easily recognised is the **Rathaus** (1904), a red-brick, neo-Gothic jumble with frilly turrets and a jutting 54m tower. Also note the step-gabled mock facade typical of northern German architecture.

Der Hauptmann von Köpenick

Outside the Rathaus stands the bronze statue of the Hauptmann von Köpenick (the Captain of Köpenick), a legendary character famous for making a laughing stock of Prussian authority. Born Wilhelm Voigt, he was a ne'er do well who had spent much of his life in prison for petty offences. Upon his final release in 1906, the unemployed cobbler decided to turn honest and start over in another country. All he needed was a passport. There was only one problem; as an ex-con without job or money, chances of being granted one were pathetically slim.

On 16 October 1906, with Voigt's frustration having reached a boiling point, he hatched an ingenious plan. He went to a costume shop, bought a captain's uniform, stepped outside and promptly took command of the first group of soldiers who happened to pass by, ordering them to march on the Rathaus of Köpenick. There, he and his men occupied the town hall, arrested the mayor and confiscated the city treasury. No one ever bothered to ask who he was or whether he had the authority to do so. His uniform was all the identification they needed. With everyone standing stiffly at attention, Voigt disappeared with the money.

As soon as the press got wind of the ruse, the entire world was laughing at the absurdity of Prussian militarist authority and Voigt became an instant media celebrity. Voigt, however, didn't get away with his trickery. Ten days later, he was caught and sentenced to four years in prison. But even the Kaiser was so amused by the incident that he ordered the cobbler released after only two years. For the next few years, Voigt travelled to all corners of the world – Vienna to London, Budapest to New York City – giving interviews and signing film, book and music contracts.

But with the outbreak of WWI, Voigt's fame fizzled; no one was laughing at Prussian militarism any longer. Dejected, he settled in Luxembourg and died in 1922, as poor and downtrodden as he had been most of his life.

The Rathaus Köpenick has dedicated a small, free exhibit in his – ahem! – honour.

Schloss Köpenick

The simple but graceful Köpenick Palace stands on the Schlossinsel, an island in the Dahme, and was built in Dutch baroque style between 1677 and 1681. It served as a residence for Prince Friedrich until he became Elector Friedrich III (and later King Friedrich I). Subsequently it went through periods as a prison and a teaching seminary before the GDR moved its Decorative Arts Museum here in 1963. It's been under renovation since 1997 and isn't expected to reopen until 2003.

In late October 1730, a military court met in the Schloss' Wappensaal, a lavish and ornate hall on the 2nd floor, to determine the fate of Captain Friedrich and Captain Hans, the former accused of attempted desertion, the other of being an accessory. The verdict? Hans went to the guillotine, and Friedrich, who happened to be the son of King Friedrich Wilhelm I, went on to become King Friedrich II.

Opposite the Schloss is the baroque **Schlosskapelle** (1885), built according to plans by Charlottenburg palace architect Johann Arnold Nering. It's all surrounded by the lovely **Schlosspark**.

Kietz

South-east of the Altstadt, the Kietz is Köpenick's medieval fishing village and is still lined by nicely restored single and two-storey buildings where the fisherfolk lived as far back as the 18th century. The Kietz is home to the unique **Wäscherei-Museum** (Laundry Museum, ☎ 651 64 24), at Luisenstrasse 23, which keeps alive the time in the 19th century when Köpenick was a centre of the laundry business. Bizarre displays include steam-powered washing machines, gas-fuelled irons and ancient mangles.

Guided tours (in German) are delivered with lots of humour but unfortunately are run from 3 to 6 pm only on the first Friday of the month (DM3/1).

To get to the Kietz, take tram No 62 to the Müggelheimer Strasse/Wendenschlossstrasse stop.

Grosser Müggelsee

The Müggelsee is called 'Grosser' for good reason. Measuring 4km in length and 2.5km in width, it's the largest lake in the Berlin area. The north-western shore is bordered by the suburb of **Friedrichshagen**, best reached on tram No 61 from S-Bahn station Friedrichshagen. In 1753, Friedrich II settled this area with 100 Bohemian families whose job it was to grow mulberry trees to feed the silkworms that supplied silk for weaving. At the end of the 19th century, a circle of poets and writers that included Gerhart Hauptmann formed here as well.

Where the Spree merges with the lake are the Stern und Kreis Schiffahrt cruise company's landing docks. Several boats daily make the half-hour trip to the forested southern shore (with good hiking – this is where you'll find the Müggelberge) and back between May and October. One-way costs DM4 or DM6 depending on where you get off, return is DM9. West of the lake, the **Köpenicker Stadtforst** stretches southward for miles, eventually leading to the Müggelberge.

Also on the shore are two lakeside pools; **Seebad Friedrichshagen** just east of the north shore landing docks, and **Strandbad Müggelsee** on the eastern shore in the medieval fishing village of Rahnsdorf (take tram No 61).

Grünau

Grünau is a handsome colony founded in 1749 on the western bank of the Dahme River, south of the Köpenick Altstadt. This section of the river, called **Langer See**, was the site of the Olympic regattas in 1936. Here you'll find the **Wassersportmuseum** (Water Sports Museum, ☎ 674 40 02), at Regattastrasse 141, with an exhibit on the history of water sports in Berlin-Brandenburg.

On display are flags, medals, clothing, newspaper articles, photos, boats and boat accessories. Hours are from 9 am to noon and from 2 to 4.30 pm Tuesday and Wednesday and also on Saturday afternoon (free). To get there, take the S8 to Grünau, followed either by a five minute walk north or a short ride on tram No 68 to the Wassersportallee stop. Alternatively, you could take tram No 62 to the Müggelbergallee stop and cross the Dahme on a little ferry on the same ticket.

Western Districts

SPANDAU (Map 9)

Spandau (population 220,000), about 10km north-west of Zoo station, is Berlin's second-largest district and makes a lovely excursion and respite from the city. Having been spared from heavy bombing, it is one of the few places in Berlin that still has a historic centre – the Altstadt – complete with narrow cobblestone lanes, a market square and a medieval church. Its most striking attraction, though, is the almost entirely intact 16th century citadel.

Spandau's other main asset is its forests (especially the **Spandauer Forst** in the north), which take up about one-quarter of the district and are great for walking. You might encounter deer, rabbits and, though rarely, wild boar.

Spandau is not like Berlin, as the locals will quickly tell you. In 1920, during the formation of Greater Berlin, the people of Spandau heavily resented their loss of independence. To this day, they talk about 'going to Berlin' when travelling outside their district.

In recent history, Spandau has been associated with the Nazi war criminal Rudolf Hess, who was imprisoned in the Allierte Kriegsverbrechergefängnis (Allied War Criminal Prison) on Wilhelmstrasse in the western Spandau suburb of Staaken. Nothing but a guard's block is left of the prison today. It was torn down as soon as Hess, who was the only prisoner in the end, died in 1987.

THINGS TO SEE & DO

Spandau Zitadelle

The extremely well-preserved Spandau Zitadelle (1560-94) is one of the most impressive structures in Berlin. Built on a little island in the Havel River, the citadel is protected by a moat on three sides, the fourth side opening up to the river. Its basic layout is that of a square with each corner protected by a bastion – essentially a stony section shaped like an arrowhead. Its dramatic outline is best appreciated in winter when you can see it through the leafless trees of the surrounding park.

As you enter via the bridge off Strasse Am Juliusturm, you will pass the gate featuring the restored coat of arms of the Hohenzollern dynasty with its characteristic two black eagles. Wandering around the central courtyard is free but besides a few sculptures and statues there isn't that much to look at.

More interesting is a climb up the 36m-high **Juliusturm**, the crenellated tower in the south-west corner, from where you can better appreciate the citadel's layout and also enjoy a view over the Havel and Spree rivers and to the Altstadt. From 1873 to 1919, Bismarck had the *Reichskriegsschatz* (literally meaning 'imperial war treasure') stored here. This was an amount in gold equivalent to 120 million Reichsmark, which was a portion of the reparation payments collected from the French after the war of 1870-71.

Also of interest is the **Stadtgeschichtliches Museum Spandau**, the local history museum in the former Zeughaus (armoury). Another exhibit on the history of the citadel is inside the **Kommandantenhaus** (commander's house). Also here is the ticket office where tickets, good for both museums and the tower (weather permitting), cost DM4/2. Hours are from 9 am to 5 pm Tuesday to Friday, from 10 am weekends. The citadel is about 200m west of the U-Bahn station Zitadelle (U7).

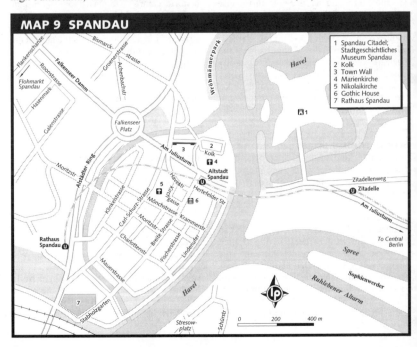

MAP 9 SPANDAU

1 Spandau Citadel;
  Stadtgeschichtliches
  Museum Spandau
2 Kolk
3 Town Wall
4 Marienkirche
5 Nikolaikirche
6 Gothic House
7 Rathaus Spandau

Altstadt

The Altstadt lies a short walk west of the citadel and consists of two sections separated by Strasse Am Juliusturm. The older part, called **Kolk**, lies immediately on your right (north) after you've crossed the Havel. Compared with the vastness of the citadel, this area seems toy-sized. Wander the quiet, narrow lanes lined by tiny houses, including a few half-timbered ones. The **Garnisonskirche** (Garrison Church), also known as Marienkirche, dates from 1848 but was destroyed in WWII and rebuilt in 1964. West of here stands a 78m-long remnant of the medieval 6m-high **town wall**.

Most of the pedestrianised Altstadt lies south of the Strasse am Juliusturm. This is Spandau's commercial heart, and shops line both its main streets, Carl-Schurz-Strasse and Breite Strasse. The graceful church on the corner of Carl-Schurz-Strasse and Mönchstrasse is the **Nikolaikirche**, which played a pivotal role during the Reformation. Outside is a statue of Elector Joachim II, the first Brandenburg ruler to convert to Protestantism in 1539. On 1 November of that year, the first public Protestant service was held in this church. A Protestant minister delivered the sermon while a Catholic priest ministered the holy communion. A few years later, Protestantism became the dominant religion in the entire March of Brandenburg.

The Nikolaikirche was first mentioned in a record of 1240 but the structure you see today dates from the 15th century. The walls of the west tower, which doubled as fortress and watchtower, are up to 3m thick. The church itself is a three-nave Gothic hall design, its whitewashed walls decorated with oil paintings. Of interest is the bronze baptismal font (1398) and the baroque pulpit (1714). Pride of place, though, goes to the late-Renaissance altar (1582) whose centre panel depicts the Last Supper.

During WWII, a wall was erected around the altar to protect it, which is how it survived the fire storm of 1944. The Nikolaikirche is only open from 11 am to 3 pm on Saturday and from 2 to 4 pm Sunday. On the south side of the church you can peer through a glass window at the foundations of what is purported to be a Dominican monastery excavated in the 1980s.

At Breite Strasse 32 stands the **Gothisches Haus** (Gothic House, ☎ 333 93 88), a brick town house from the second half of the 15th century. There's a small museum on Spandau history on the 1st floor, including a Biedermeier room and a 19th century kitchen. The ground floor boasts a net-vaulted ceiling. Hours are 9 am to 5 pm weekdays and 10 am to 1 pm weekends (free).

WILMERSDORF

The sprawling district of Wilmersdorf runs from Kurfürstendamm in the north to Zehlendorf in the south, with about half of its area taken up by the Grunewald forest. Like its neighbours to the north and east – Charlottenburg and Schöneberg, respectively – it's largely middle-class residential. Although short on sights and attractions, many visitors become familiar with Wilmersdorf because of its density of hotels. Restaurants and bars abound as well, though the quarter is hardly considered trendy, except perhaps for the area around Ludwigkirchplatz and along Pariser Strasse.

Grunewald Forest (Map 2)

The Grunewald forest, covering a total area of 32 sq km, is bordered by the Havel River in the west, Heerstrasse in the north, Clayallee in the east and the Schlachtensee lake in the south. Until 1903 it was used as the hunting grounds for the royal family. During WWII and the Berlin Blockade, more than 70% of its trees were felled for heating purposes, so what you see today is mostly newgrowth forest. The Grunewald is at the top of the list of favourite outings among Berliners and provides just as much entertainment, respite and distraction for visitors.

Teufelsberg The forest's northern section is dominated by the Teufelsberg, at 115m the highest Trümmerberg in Berlin, made from 25 million cubic metres of war debris. Since 1950, it has been a popular recreational spot, especially on rare snowy days when the sledding and ski slopes (!) and the small ski jump have kids howling with glee.

There's also a climbing rock and trails for mountain bikes, and in autumn the sky is filled with colourful kites. The little lake at the bottom of the hill is the **Teufelssee** (not suitable for swimming). Just north of the lake is the high moor, Teufelsfenn.

Havelchaussee A lovely footpath runs along the entire right bank of the Havel River. For drivers there's the Havelchaussee which cuts through the forest from Scholzplatz/Am Postfenn (south off Heerstrasse and the only place from where the drive can be started) in the north to the Zehlendorf suburb of Nikolassee in the south. If you can, avoid driving here on sunny spring Sundays, when it's bumper to bumper traffic for the entire 6km.

About 2.5km into the drive or the walk is the **Grunewaldturm**, a 56m-high tower formerly known as Kaiser-Wilhelm-Turm after Wilhelm I, whose marble statue stands in the tower hall. From the viewing gallery, reached after climbing 204 steps, a marvellous view extends over the river, the suburbs of Gatow and Kladow and all the way to the Pfaueninsel (see the following Zehlendorf section), sometimes even to Potsdam. The tower is open from 10 am to dusk daily, in summer often through until midnight. The climb costs DM1.50/0.80. By public transport, it is reached by taking the S1 or S7 to Wannsee and then bus No 218 to Grunewaldturm.

Grunewaldsee & Jagdschloss Grunewald

The Grunewald lakes are very popular with Berliners and their dogs. The largest lake, Grunewaldsee, even has a dog beach. Unfortunately, the concept of 'pooper-scoopers' hasn't yet caught on here which means you have to keep an eye on the trail. It also renders the place basically unsuitable for small children.

Jagdschloss Grunewald (☎ 813 35 97), south of the lake, is a Renaissance palace built by Elector Joachim II in 1542. He called the place Haus am Grünen Walde (House in the Green Woods) which is how the forest and the area got its name. Inside

is a surprisingly good gallery with German and Dutch paintings from the 15th to the 19th centuries. Exquisite works include oils by Lucas Cranach the Elder, an early 15th century altar and *Venus and Armor* by the Dutchman Jan Lievens (1630-73). Another exhibit, the **Jagdzeugmagazin** (Hunting Collection) with hunting-related items, antlers and paintings depicting hunting scenes, can easily be skipped.

The palace is at Am Grunewaldsee 29. It's open from 10 am to 5 pm Tuesday to Sunday, from mid-May to mid-October, otherwise hours are from 10 am to 4 pm weekends only (DM4/2). Take the U1 to Dahlem-Dorf, then bus No 183 to the Königin-Luise-Strasse/Clayallee stop, followed by a 15 minute walk west through the forest.

ZEHLENDORF

Zehlendorf is one of Berlin's greenest districts (only Köpenick is greener), with about half of its land covered by forest, rivers and lakes. The elegant suburbs of Dahlem and Wannsee with their villas and estates contribute greatly to Zehlendorf's small-town character. To visitors and locals, the district has much to offer. The southern half of Grunewald forest and Wannsee lake are great areas for outdoor activities, while several museums provide intellectual stimulation. A couple of palaces, important historical sites, a university and lovely gardens further add to its appeal.

Dahlem Museums

The biggest draw in leafy Zehlendorf used to be the Dahlem Museum complex, a cluster of seven world-class museums. We say 'used to be' because it has been affected like no other by the sweeping reorganisation of Berlin's collections.

The entire Gemäldegalerie (Picture Gallery), for instance, has moved into its new home at the Kulturforum (see the Tiergarten section earlier in this chapter). The collection of the **Museum of Islamic Art** has been merged with that at the Pergamon Museum. The **Museum of Indian Art** and the **Museum of East Asian Art** closed in May 1998 and won't re-open until at least 2001 while the collections are being reorganised. For the time being, only the following two museums remain open.

Museum für Völkerkunde (SMPK) The Museum of Ethnology (☎ 20 90 55 55), at Lansstrasse 8, takes you on a journey back in time and around the world to the early Americas, Australasia, Africa and South and East Asia. Its collections on Europe, the Islamic Orient and Native Americas are only shown during special exhibits.

Highlights of the **pre-Columbian collection** are the stone sculptures from Guatemala, and figurines, sculptures and weapons from the Mayan culture. The gold jewellery and helmets are sparkling examples of this rich civilisation. Cult objects from New Guinea, Tonga, Melanesia and other islands, some of which used to belong to Captain James Cook, form part of the South Seas section. The enormous outriggers in the boat hall are serious crowd-pleasers, while upstairs such treats as a royal Hawaiian feather coat await. Also here, in the **East Asian section**, is a 19th century carved teak wall from a house in central Java. In the basement are the two touchy-feely rooms containing the **Junior Museum** for children and the **Blinden Museum** for the blind.

Museum hours are from 10 am to 6 pm Tuesday to Friday, from 11 am weekends (DM4/2).

Museum Europäische Kulturen

This museum was previously known as the Museum für Volkskunde (Folklore Museum, ☎ 20 90 55 55) and is located at Im Winkel 6-8, a short walk east of Dahlem-Dorf station along Königin-Luise-Strasse. It was still being converted at the time of research and will eventually be reopened with a permanent exhibit called 'Cultural Contacts in Europe: the Fascination of the Image'. Hours are from 10 am to 6 pm Tuesday to Friday, from 11 am weekends (DM4/2).

Museumsdorf Düppel

The Museumsdorf Düppel (Düppel Museum Village, ☎ 802 66 71), at Clauertstrasse 11, is a re-creation of a medieval village on the grounds of an actual settlement that stood here from 1170 to 1220. Over a dozen reed-thatched buildings have been reconstructed and are surrounded by fields and woods. Demonstrations of various old-time crafts, such as blacksmithing and pottery, take place on Sunday and are popular with children. Hours are 3 to 7 pm Thursday and 10 am to 5 pm Sunday, from April to October (DM3/1.50). Take the S1 to Zehlendorf station, followed by a 20 minute walk south-west or a ride on bus No 115, 211 or 629.

Botanischer Garten

Berlin's stunning botanical garden (☎ 83 00 60, or recorded message at ☎ 83 00 61 27) is a symphony of perfume and colour at Königin-Luise-Strasse 6-8, about a 15 minute walk east of U-Bahn station Dahlem-Dorf. Little over 100 years old, it boasts more than 20,000 plant species beautifully arranged on 43 hectares. It's open from 9 am to dusk daily, though never later than 9 pm. Also on the grounds is the **Botanisches Museum**, open from 10 am to 5 pm Tuesday to Sunday (DM6/3 for both gardens and museum).

Domäne Dahlem

Just north of U-Bahn station Dahlem-Dorf, at Königin-Luise-Strasse 49, is the Domäne Dahlem (☎ 832 50 00), an open-air museum that illustrates the daily workings of a large Berlin farm, with equipment from the past 300 years. It is centred around a farmhouse from 1680 that's filled with glass, household items, tableware, paintings and more. Other buildings include barns, workers' sheds, the horseshoe smithy and the woodwork shed. In the yard are historical tractors and farming equipment. Various craft shops, including pottery and carpenter's shops where the occasional demonstrations take place, are here as well. The museum is open from 10 am to 6 pm Wednesday to Monday (DM3/1.50). There are guided tours at 4 pm on Saturday.

Freie Universität

Scattered about Dahlem are the buildings of the Freie Universität (Free University, FU), founded in 1948 in reaction to

Berlin's traditional Humboldt University in Mitte coming increasingly under the influence of Marxist-Leninist doctrine. Its democratic-minded students and professors risked harassment, dismissal and even arrest. Initially, lectures at the *free* university took place in empty villas but in 1955, the Henry-Ford-Bau opened as the first permanent structure, financed with a grant from the Henry Ford Foundation.

Creating an entirely new university was also an opportunity to do away with elements of Germany's antiquated university system. FU students were given a voice through a student council, and quaint organisations like (saber) duelling fraternities were prohibited. In the 60s, students at the FU provided the spark for the nationwide student movement which, among other things, demanded further reforms in the political and university systems.

Allierten-Museum

The Allierten-Museum (Allied Museum, ☎ 818 19 90), at Clayallee 135, is an excellent multimedia exhibit that documents the history and challenges faced by the western Allies in post-WWII Berlin. The complex is easily recognised by the many large scale objects displayed in its yard, including the historic guard trailer from Checkpoint Charlie, a colourful piece of the Wall, a GDR border guard tower, a US military plane and a French military train.

The exhibit itself is divided into two periods. The first, from 1945 to 1950, is housed in the former Outpost cinema for US soldiers and covers subjects like the Allied victory, the relationship between the occupiers and the vanquished and the tough times of the Berlin Airlift. It all continues next door, culminating with the fall of the Wall, reunification and the withdrawal of occupying forces in 1994.

One especially fascinating exhibit is the partial re-creation of the Berlin Spy Tunnel, built by the CIA in order to tap into the central telephone system of the Soviets. Two metres wide and 450m long, it recorded half a million calls from May 1955 to 1956 until a double agent blabbed to the Soviets.

Unfortunately, this fascinating museum is sadly undervisited, probably because it's perceived to be hard to get to. This is not really the case; the trip from, say, Wittenbergplatz station on the U1 takes about 20 minutes, followed by a five to 10 minute walk north on Clayallee. It's worth the effort. Hours are from 10 am to 6 pm Tuesday to Sunday and admission is free. All explanatory panelling is in German, English and French.

Brücke Museum

This small museum (☎ 831 20 29) is dedicated to the expressionist painters of Die Brücke (The Bridge), a group founded in Dresden in 1910 by Karl Schmidt-Rottluff, Erich Heckel and Ernst Ludwig Kirchner. It's at Bussardsteig 9, about 2km north-west of Dahlem-Dorf (bus No 115). Emil Nolde, Max Pechstein and Otto Müller later joined the circle, which soon moved to Berlin and dissolved in 1913. The group's style is characterised by simplified shapes and figures that nonetheless do not quite cross into the abstract. Bright, strong colours heighten the expressiveness. The Nazis called this work subversive and had much of it destroyed.

Paintings by all six artists are displayed in four rooms, with skylights that seem to intensify the colours even more. Two rooms deal with work produced after the group's dissolution. Hours are from 11 am to 5 pm Wednesday to Monday (DM7/3).

Wannsee

Villa-studded Wannsee, a Zehlendorf suburb, is one of the best parts of town. The area gets its name from the **Grosse Wannsee** lake which spills over into the **Kleiner Wannsee**. On the shores of the latter, the Romantic poet Heinrich Kleist and his lover Henriette Vogel committed suicide in 1811. Kleist's grave is located on the south-eastern side of Wannsee bridge (enter at Bismarckstrasse 3).

The lake environment is a paradise for sailors, windsurfers and rowers, and the **Strandbad Wannsee**, a popular lakeside pool built in 1907, provides welcome respite from the heat on summer days (see the Swimming section later in this chapter).

In the north-east, the Grunewald forest hugs the lake's shore, while the **Berliner Düppel Forest** sprawls out to the west.

Cruises Stern und Kreis Schiffahrt (☎ 536 36 00 or ☎ 803 87 50) cruises the Wannsee and adjacent waters between April and October. The *Grosse Havelrundfahrt* (Big Havel Tour) runs from Wannsee to Kladow and Pfaueninsel to Potsdam and back. The journey is offered at least twice and up to six times daily, takes about one hour each way and costs DM11.50, return DM15.50.

The *7-Seen-Rundfahrt* (Seven Lakes Tour) operates six or seven times daily and takes you through various Havel lakes (including the Kleiner Wannsee and Lake Glienicke. The trip lasts two hours and costs DM14. These and other tours leave from the docks near S-Bahn station Wannsee (S1 and S7).

Students and seniors get a 15% discount Monday to Friday. Any day, children under six go free, those to age 14 get 50% off and those between 14 and 18 qualify for a 20% discount.

If you just want a little spin on the water, take Ferry No 10 which operates hourly year round (weather permitting) between Wannsee and Kladow for the price of a regular BVG ticket (DM3.90).

Pfaueninsel

The dreamy environment of the Pfaueninsel in the Havel River was the romantic fantasy of King Friedrich Wilhelm II. Here he built a frilly little palace perfect for frolicking around with his mistress away from the curious eyes of the court. Today it contains a small **museum** (☎ 805 30 42) which can only be seen on guided tours with prior reservation from May to October (DM4/2).

The prolific Peter Lenné designed the gardens where the peacocks that gave the island its name still strut their stuff proudly. Since the entire place is a protected reserve, the *verboten* list is rather long and includes smoking, cycling, swimming, animals and radios. Picnicking, though, remains legal and this is a nice place to do it.

Ferries leave from the docks at the end of Nikolsloer Weg. If you're driving, you must take Nikolsloer Weg to get here (your map may show other routes but they're off limits to public traffic). Those using public transport should take the hourly bus No 216 from S-Bahn station Wannsee. The little ferry shuttles from 8 am to 8 pm between May and August, to 6 pm in April and September, from 9 am to 5 pm in March and October and from 10 am to 4 pm between November and February. The return ride costs DM2/1 and includes admission to the island.

Haus der Wannsee Konferenz

In January 1942, a group of elite Nazi officials led by Reinhard Heydrich, chief of the Reich Security Main Office met at this historic villa right on the lakeshore at Am Grossen Wannsee 56-58. The purpose of their gathering was to decide on the fate of the Jewish people. Debate was swift and deadly. The 'Final Solution', they agreed, would be to deport and exterminate ALL Jews in a systematic and organised fashion, starting at once.

These days, the same walls house the Wannsee Conference memorial exhibit (☎ 805 00 10). You can stand in the room where discussions took place and study the minutes of the conference, taken by Adolf Eichmann. Also here are the portraits and career synopses of the main perpetrators, many of whom were allowed to live to ripe old age. The rest of the exhibit chronicles, in a thorough and graphic way, the horrors leading up to and perpetrated during the Holocaust. Photographs and documents portray the ever-increasing acts of cruelty inflicted upon the Jews.

Exhibit hours are from 10 am to 6 pm weekdays, from 2 pm weekends (free). You must ring the bell to enter and you can borrow an English-language pamphlet from the desk. There's also an excellent booklet in English on sale for DM5. Bus No 114 makes the trip here from S-Bahn station Wannsee every 20 minutes.

Schloss Glienicke & Around

Schloss Glienicke, on Königsstrasse at the very south-western tip of Berlin, is surrounded by a romantic Lenné-landscaped park. The palace itself, a rambling cluster of buildings, got its current look from the prolific Karl Friedrich Schinkel who, after 1824, expanded the earlier structure at the behest of Prince Carl of Prussia (third son of King Friedrich Wilhelm III). Inside is an exhibit on the intricacies of landscape gardening and a few furnished period rooms, which are seriously skippable (DM3/2).

Schinkel also created the gazebo-like structure called **Grosse Neugierde** (Great Curiosity), inspired by the monument to Lysicrates in Athens. You'll find it in the park's south-western corner from where it overlooks the Havel and the outskirts of Potsdam. Schinkel also converted a former billiard house into the **Kasino**, an Italian villa with a double pergola, west of the palace. The **Klosterhof** nearby consists of reassembled pieces of a Carthusian monastery in Italy.

Prince Carl himself was an avid collector of antiquities and much of what you see he personally brought to Berlin (some might say, stole) from places like Pompeii and Carthage.

The palace on the southern side of Königsstrasse is the **Jagdschloss Glienicke** (Glienicke Hunting Palace), purchased by Prince Carl in 1859 and later expanded in neobaroque style by Ferdinand von Arnim.

As spy novel aficionados will know, the **Glienicker Brücke** just west of the palaces was the dramatic setting of spy exchanges during the Cold War. The green steel construction spans the Havel over a length of 125m and connects Berlin with Potsdam.

Palace and bridge are easily reached from S-Bahn station Wannsee via bus No 116, which runs at 20 minute intervals.

Activities

Berlin's many parks and forests are tailor-made for walking and jogging, both activities that can easily be enjoyed by visitors as well. Another easy way to keep fit is swimming – there are dozens of pools to choose from. Soccer, volleyball, handball and other team sports are popular too but you usually have to join a club to participate.

In the outer suburbs especially, you'll find large sports centres that combine a pool, squash and tennis courts, fitness studio, sauna etc, all under one roof. One of the more central is the Sport-und Erholungszentrum (SEZ, Map 4) in the district of Friedrichshain (see Indoor Pools later in this section), which even incorporates an ice rink.

For details about tickets to sports events (soccer, basketball, ice hockey, horse racing and more), see the Spectator Sports section in the Entertainment chapter.

FITNESS CENTRES

Many gyms are clubs where you have to sign a minimum one-year contract, shell out a registration fee and pay monthly dues. The following are among the ones that sell day passes for what seems to be the going rate of DM45.

The granddaddy of gyms, Gold's Gym (Map 4, ☎ 442 82 94), at Immanuelkirchstrasse 3-4 in Prenzlauer Berg, has a weights room, aerobics classes and sauna. It's open to 11 pm, to 6 pm weekends (take tram No 1, eg from U-Bahn station Rosa-Luxemburg-Platz to Knaackstrasse).

Ars Vitalis (Map 5, ☎ 788 35 63), Hauptstrasse 19 in Schöneberg is a modern gym with aerobics, weights and cardio training, plus sauna and pool. It's open 10 am to 11.30 pm, 11 am to 9 pm weekends.

For the discerning fitness freak, there's the state-of-the-art Healthland (Map 8, ☎ 20 63 53 00), Behrenstrasse 48 in Mitte, which offers spinning classes on top of the usual range of fitness offerings. It's open from 6 am to 11 pm, from 10 am to 10 pm weekends; day passes here are DM50.

Jopp Frauen-Fitness (Map 7, ☎ 21 01 11), as its name suggests, is a women-only facility with five branches around town, the most central being at Tauentzienstrasse 13, opposite the Memorial Church. Normal hours are from 7 am to 11 pm, from 10 am to 8 pm weekends.

SWIMMING

Berlin has plenty of outdoor and indoor pools with several in each district. In 1996, their operation was taken over by the

What's Free

It's easy to spend a fortune in Berlin and most museums and activities will cost some money. What follows is a list of places you can go and things you can do while keeping your wallet closed. Everything is described in greater detail in this book.

Museums & Memorial Exhibits (Always Free)
- Allied Museum
- Infobox
- German Historical Museum at Kronprinzenpalais
- German History Exhibit at Deutscher Dom
- German Resistance Memorial Exhibit
- Stasi – Die Ausstellung
- Research & Memorial Exhibit Normannenstrasse
- Plötzensee Memorial Exhibit
- Topography of Terror
- Hohenschönhausen Prison
- Museum Berlin-Karlshorst
- House of the Wannsee Conference
- Local History Museums of Kreuzberg, Prenzlauer Berg and Charlottenburg
- Collection of Antiquities
- Willy-Brandt-Haus
- Hohenschönhausen Prison Memorial
- Köpenick Blood Week Memorial
- Water Sports Museum in Grünau
- Gothic House in Spandau

Museums (Occasionally Free)
- Deutsche Guggenheim – Monday
- Märkisches Museum – Wednesday
- Academy of Arts – Wednesday
- All SMPK Museums – First Sunday of the month (these include the Old Museum, Schinkelmuseum, Pergamon Museum, Hamburger Bahnhof, New Picture Gallery, Copperplate Etchings Gallery, Museum of Decorative Arts, New National Gallery, Egyptian Museum, Berggruen Collection, Gallery of the Romantics, Museum of Primaeval and Early History, Museum of Ethnology, Museum of European Cultures).

Entertainment & Activities
- Nightclubs – some have no cover charge on certain weeknights
- Stroll along Unter den Linden and admire the architecture
- Window-shop amid the bright lights of Kurfürstendamm
- Tuesday or Wednesday at the A-Trane or Quasimodo jazz clubs
- A spring afternoon in the gardens of Schloss Charlottenburg
- Smells and sights of the Turkish Market in Kreuzberg
- Picnicking in Berlin's many city parks and forests
- Carillon (glockenspiel) recitals at the House of World Cultures, French Cathedral
- Organ recitals at the Berliner Dom or other churches
- Tomb hunting at the Dorotheenstadt or any other of Berlin's cemeteries

Berliner Bäder-Betriebe (BBB), which resulted in price hikes but also in the gradual renovation of some rather antiquated (in some cases outright historic) facilities.

Some pools are closed in the mornings when school groups take over. Others are reserved to specific groups – women, men, nudists, seniors – at certain times of the week. Outdoor and lakeside pools are usually open from 8 am to 8 pm daily, from May to September. During that time, some of the indoor pools may be closed. In general, opening hours vary by day, pool and season. For specifics, either call the pool directly or the BBB Hotline on ☎ 01803-10 20 20, check the German-language Web site at www.bbb.berlin.de, or pick up a pamphlet at any pool. Unless otherwise noted, tickets are DM6, discount DM4. Sets of 10 tickets are DM50/30.

Indoor Pools

Berlin has indoor pools, of varying standards, in just about every district. Try the following.

Bad am Spreewaldplatz (Map 6, ☎ 612 70 57), Wiener Strasse 59 in Kreuzberg 36 – has a wave pool, water cascades, a slide and sauna in addition to a 25m lap pool (U1 or U15 to Görlitzer Bahnhof).

Blub (off Map 6, ☎ 606 60 60), Buschkrugallee 64 in Neukölln – 'fun' pool popular with kids. Attractions include a wave pool, a waterfall, a 120m slide, a sea-water pool, hot whirlpools, sauna and restaurants. Four-hour admission is DM21/18 for the pool only or DM26/23 with sauna. Hours are from 10 am to 11 pm daily (U7 to Grenzallee).

Sport- und Erholungszentrum (SEZ, Map 4, ☎ 42 18 23 20), Landsberger Allee 77 in Friedrichshain – a mega sports facility encompassing seven pools (including a wave pool), a slide and saunas. The complex also houses an ice-skating rink and a fitness studio. Pool admission is DM10/5 for 2½ hours or DM6/3 for 1½ hours. Between 7 and 10 pm, it's DM8/4 (S8 or S10 to Landsberger Allee).

Stadtbad Charlottenburg (Map 3, Alte Halle – ☎ 34 38 38 60, Neue Halle – ☎ 34 38 38 65), Krumme Strasse 9-10 – this facility has two pools; its Alte Halle (Old Hall) is one of the world's few pools that's also a protected monument. With its Art Nouveau ceiling and colourful tiles dating back to 1898, it definitely has museum character, a 25m pool and a sauna.

(During nude bathing on Tuesday, Wednesday and Friday nights, the place is crawling with gay men.) The Neue Halle (New Hall) is more suited for serious swimmers and has a 50m lap pool (U2 or U7 to Bismarckstrasse).

Stadtbad Mitte (Map 4, ☎ 30 88 09 10), Gartenstrasse 5 – this is renovated Bauhaus structure (1928) with a 50m lap pool (S1 or S2 to Nordbahnhof).

Stadtbad Neukölln (Map 6, ☎ 68 24 98 11), Ganghoferstrasse 5 – called the most beautiful pool in Europe at its opening in 1914, it's certainly one of Berlin's most impressive swimming temples with mosaics and frescoes, wooden panelling, marble and brass. There are 25m and 20m pools. Admission to the sauna area with dry sauna, Roman bath and steamroom costs DM25/20 (U7 to Rathaus Neukölln).

Outdoor & Lakeside Pools

One of the great summer delights in landlocked Berlin is its many lakes, but if you prefer some amenities try one of the following lakeside pools.

Freibad Halensee (Map 5, ☎ 891 17 03), Königsallee 5a in Wilmersdorf – nicely situated in a forest and popular with those who prefer to do their swimming *au naturel*. Occasionally closed for poor water quality. Take bus No 115 to Herbertstrasse. Coming from Kurfürstendamm, walk down Bornstedter Strasse, then via a pedestrian bridge across the autobahn.

Freibad am Olympia-Stadion, Osttor (eastern gate) (☎ 30 06 34 73), Olympischer Platz, Charlottenburg – swim in the 50m pool where Olympic athletes have swum. In this Nazi-designed facility, you can do your laps watched by oversized sculptures of athletes and four gigantic clocks (U2 to Olympia-Stadion Ost).

Sommerbad Kreuzberg (Map 6, ☎ 616 18 80), Prinzenstrasse 113-119, Kreuzberg 36 – better known as Prinzenbad (Princes' Pool), this is the most central, multicultural and popular facility, often crawling with love-struck teenagers. There are two 50m pools, a slide and a nudist section (U1 or U15 to Prinzenstrasse).

Strandbad Müggelsee (☎ 648 77 77), Fürstenwalder Damm 838 in Köpenick – idyllically located on the Müggelsee's eastern shore and especially suitable for children because of its sandy beach and flat water with reasonable quality (S3 to Friedrichshagen, then tram No 61 to the Strandbad Müggelsee stop).

Strandbad Wannsee (☎ 803 54 50 or ☎ 803 56 12), Wannseebadweg 25 in Zehlendorf – claims to be the largest lakeside pool in Europe and has been in business since 1926. Often referred to as Berlin's 'Lido', its 1000m of sandy beach are about as crowded as the real thing in Italy. Besides swimming, you can rent boats, take an exercise class, eat and drink at several restaurants or relax in a giant wicker chair typically found at German coastal resorts. The water quality is decent (S1, S3 or S7 to Nikolassee, then bus No 513 to Strandbad Wannsee).

SAUNAS

Germans are far from prudish and saunas are usually mixed and nude, so check your modesty at the reception desk. There are, however, hours set aside for women only, so if it matters to you, call ahead to find out those times. The cheapest saunas are those at public pools, where three-hour admission costs DM15/11. These include Schwimmhalle Thomas-Mann-Strasse (Map 4, ☎ 423 07 55) at Hans-Eisler-Strasse 1 in Prenzlauer Berg, Stadtbad Wilmersdorf (Map 5, ☎ 821 02 60) at Mecklenburgische Strasse 80 in Wilmersdorf, Schwimmhalle Weinstrasse (Map 4, ☎ 241 29 75) at Weinstrasse 9 in Friedrichshain, and Stadtbad Charlottenburg, Stadtbad Neukölln and Bad am Spreewaldplatz already listed in the Indoor Pools section above.

Privately operated facilities usually have more amenities and can be downright luxurious. The Thermen am Europa-Center (Map 7, ☎ 261 60 31) is a stylish facility at Nürnberger Strasse 7 next to the Memorial Church. It incorporates nine saunas, indoor and outdoor pools, fitness rooms, restaurants and a terrace for tanning. It's open from 10 am to midnight daily (to 9 pm Sunday). Day admission is DM35, three hours cost DM30 and if you come for the final three hours of the day, it's DM27.

Hamam (Map 6, ☎ 615 14 64), downstairs from the lesbian Schoko Café at Mariannenstrasse 6 in Kreuzberg, is a women-only Turkish bathhouse. There's no pool but a steam room and a variety of beauty services. It's open daily from noon to 10 pm (Monday from 3 pm) and charges DM12 for one hour and DM18 for 2½ hours.

ICE SKATING

Berlin has a number of well-maintained municipal indoor ice rinks that are open from October to early March. The cost is DM6/3, plus DM5 to DM7 to rent skates. Skating periods vary with each facility but usually last three hours. Call for schedules. The rink at the SEZ (see the Indoor Pools section earlier in this section) is open from 9 am to 10 pm daily between November and March (to 8 pm Sunday). Day admission is DM5, plus DM5 for skate rental.

Municipal rinks include the following:

Eisstadion Berlin-Wilmersdorf (Map 5, ☎ 824 10 12), Fritz-Wildung-Strasse 9, Wilmersdorf (U1 to Heidelberger Platz).
Erika-Hess-Eisstadion (Map 4, ☎ 45 75 55 55), Müllerstrasse 185, Wedding (U6 to Reinickendorfer Strasse).
Sportpark Neukölln (Off Map 6, ☎ 68 09 35 34), Oderstrasse 182, Neukölln (U8 to Hermannstrasse).

CYCLING

The Berlin office of the cycling association called Allgemeiner Deutscher Fahrradclub (ADFC) has put out a *Radwegekarte* map that shows all bike routes in Berlin. The map costs DM15 and is available at bookstores and at the ADFC office (☎ 448 47 24) at Brunnenstrasse 28 in Mitte. To get there, take the U8 to Bernauer Strasse. Opening hours are from noon to 8 pm weekdays and from 10 am to 4 pm Saturday.

The countryside surrounding Berlin's urban core offers lots of lovely cycling routes. Check at major bookshops (see the Shopping chapter) for guides with detailed route descriptions. *Mit dem Rad durch Berlin* by Peter Becker is one option, another is *Auf Tour – Ohne Auto Mobil,* published by the BVG public transport agency.

Taking a bicycle in specially marked carriages of the S-Bahn or U-Bahn trains normally costs you DM2.50 but it's free if you hold a monthly ticket. On U-Bahn trains there are time restrictions on taking bicycles, they are allowed only between 9 am and 2 pm and from 5.30 pm to closing time on weekdays (any time on weekends).

RUNNING

Berlin is a great place for running and jogging because of its many parks. By far the most popular – because of its size and central location – is the Tiergarten, though the Volkspark Hasenheide in Neukölln, the Tegeler Forst in Tegel and the Grunewald in Wilmersdorf/Zehlendorf are also popular. The trip around the scenic Schlachtensee here is 5km. If you prefer to run in historic surroundings, try the gardens of Schloss Charlottenburg, though it won't prove too challenging for seasoned joggers because of its size.

TENNIS & SQUASH

Most of the larger racquet-sports centres are in the suburbs and are generally inconvenient to reach by public transport. One of the more central ones is Tennis & Squash City (Map 7, ☎ 873 90 97) at Brandenburgische Strasse 53 in Wilmersdorf (U7 to Konstanzer Strasse). It has five tennis courts, 11 squash courts and eight badminton courts. Prices vary according to court, time of day and day of the week but range from DM22 to DM59 for one hour of tennis and from DM10 to DM32 for 45 minutes of squash. There's also a solarium and a sauna, open from 7 am to 1 am daily.

Tennis, Squash und Fitnesscenter (☎ 333 40 83), with branches at Galenstrasse 33-35 in Spandau (U7 to Rathaus Spandau) and Richard-Tauber-Damm 36 in Marienfelde (☎ 742 10 91), has indoor tennis and squash courts, plus sauna, solarium and a fitness studio (S2 to Buckower Chaussee, then a 20 minute walk).

For squash fans only, a good central option is Fit Fun (Map 7, ☎ 312 50 82), Uhlandstrasse 194, open from 9 am to midnight daily. Its 13 courts are often busy with students from the nearby TU. Rates start at DM20, for students from DM12.

CASINO

The Spielbank Berlin (☎ 85 59 90) has recently moved into glamorous new digs on Marlene-Dietrich-Platz in the Potsdamer Platz area (see the Potsdamer Platz map earlier in this chapter). It claims to be Germany's largest casino with tables and slot machines spread over three floors and divided into the Casino Leger (no dress code) and Casino Royal (dress-up). Admission to the slot machine section is DM2, to the tables DM5. It's open from 10.30 to 3 am daily. You must be over 21 to enter.

COURSES
Language

Some of the best German-language courses are offered by the Goethe Institute (Map 4, ☎ 25 90 63, fax 25 90 64 00), a nonprofit cultural and language organisation, at Neue Schönhauser Strasse 20. Courses cater to all age groups and stages of proficiency – from absolute beginner to professional level. The program is divided into three general levels: *Grundstufe* (basic), *Mittelstufe* (intermediate) and *Oberstufe* (advanced); each is further divided into sublevels.

Intensive courses cost DM2940 to DM3140 (eight weeks), DM1690 (four weeks) and DM1360 (two weeks), excluding accommodation and meals. Courses are offered throughout the year, but it's best to contact the Goethe Institute directly to find out the specific dates. The staff in the Berlin office are knowledgeable, helpful to a fault and speak excellent English. You can also find detailed information on the Internet at www.goethe.de.

A highly rated private school teaching German to foreigners is the Europa Sprachenschule (Europa Language School, Map 6, ☎ 618 88 63, fax 618 95 57) at Taborstrasse 17 in Kreuzberg 36. It offers 20-unit weekly intensive courses at beginner and advanced levels for DM66 (groups of up to 15) to DM180 (groups of five). The monthly 80-unit course fee is DM264/720. Other options are available too. Courses start monthly but it is possible to join ongoing courses.

Places to Stay

Berlin attracts tourists all year round, with the peak months being from May to September. If you'll be travelling during that time, make reservations at least several weeks ahead of arrival. From November to March, on the other hand, visitor numbers plunge significantly and special deals abound (except around the Christmas and New Year holidays).

Berlin offers the gamut of lodging options, from camping and small private pensions to international business chains and historic, palatial establishments. Just as the city itself is undergoing a facelift, so are many of its older hotels. While some places close for a month or so, others undergo gradual renovation while remaining in business. Since this may mean noise and dust during your stay, ask ahead if you're sensitive to this kind of thing.

Many small hotels and pensions take up one or several floors of historic apartment buildings. Usually you have to ring the street-level bell to get in. Since many of these family-run places are not staffed around the clock, make a quick call to ensure that someone will be there when you arrive. Upon checking in, you should be given a set of keys (sometimes a deposit is charged), so you can let yourself in at any time.

Germany's reputation for cleanliness extends to accommodation; even budget places are usually spotlessly clean. Television and direct-dial phones (or even in-room phones) are not standard amenities in older hotels, so check if this is important to you. Lifts, on the other hand, are not as rare as you might think and are often of the quaint 'bird-cage' variety.

Occasionally you'll find hotels and pensions tucked away in a rear building of a sprawling 19th-century tenement complex. There's usually a bell but no intercom, so you either have to navigate using the layout sketches by the main gate or, better yet, call ahead and ask the proprietor to meet you downstairs.

If you're driving, note that most central hotels don't have a parking lot. Street parking may be elusive, requiring you to leave your car in an expensive public garage (about DM25 per night) that may even be located quite a distance from the hotel. Top-end hotels may have their own lots or valet parking, though in either case this will still add DM25 per day to your hotel bill.

Note that this chapter is particularly vulnerable to changes which may occur spontaneously as rooms get renovated, managers switch and independent hotels are bought out by chains. All rates quoted below, therefore, serve merely as guidelines.

CAMPING

Camping facilities in Berlin are neither plentiful nor particularly good. All are far from the city centre and complicated to reach unless you're motorised. They fill up quickly, with a lot of space taken up by RVs (recreational vehicles). Call ahead to enquire about vacancy. Office hours at all camping grounds are from 7 am to 1 pm and from 3 to 9 pm daily. Charges are DM9.70 per person plus DM7.20 for the smallest tent to DM12.70 for a large tent with car space; showers are DM1. For specifics, contact the Deutscher Campingclub (☎ 218 60 71) at Geisbergstrasse 11 in Schöneberg.

Camping grounds convenient to public transport include *Campingplatz Kohlhasenbrück (☎/fax 805 17 37, Neue Kreisstrasse 36)* which is open early March through late October. It's in a peaceful location overlooking the Griebnitzsee in the suburb of Zehlendorf, about 15km south-west of the centre. Take the S7 to Griebnitzsee station from where it's a 10 minute walk. Alternatively, get off at the previous stop, Wannsee, and take bus No 118, which runs directly to the camping ground.

If Kohlhasenbrück is full, 2km east along the Teltow Canal is *Campingplatz Dreilinden (☎ 805 12 01, Albrechts-Teerofen)* which is open early March to late October.

It's 30 minutes on foot from the Grieb-nitzsee S-Bahn station; bus No 118 from Wannsee station also stops there.

Getting to Berlin's other camping grounds requires at least two changes on public transport. *Campingplatz Kladow* (☎ *365 27 97, fax 365 12 45, Krampnitzer Weg 111-117)* is 18km west of the city centre in Spandau and open all year. To get here, take the U7 to Rathaus Spandau, then bus No 134 to the Alt-Kladow stop, where you change for bus No 234. *Campingplatz Gatow* (☎ *365 43 40, fax 36 80 84 92, Klad-ower Damm 213-217)* is a nearby alternative and also served by bus No 134.

Campingplatz Am Krossinsee (☎ *675 86 87, fax 675 91 50, Wernsdorfer Strasse 45)* is in Köpenick, 35km to the south-east, and open all year. You'd have to take the S8 to Grünau, then tram No 68 to Schmückwitz and from there bus No 755 to Königs Wusterhausen.

HOSTELS
DJH Hostels
Berlin has three DJH hostels, which fill up fast on weekends and in summer; in spring and fall, they are often booked out by noisy school groups. All require DJH or HI membership cards; see Hostel Cards in the Facts for the Visitor chapter if you don't already have one. None have cooking facilities, but rates include breakfast, and lunch and dinner are available. The hostels stay open all day year round but all have curfews.

To secure yourself a bunk, you should write several weeks in advance to Deutsches Jugendherbergswerk, Zentralreservierung, Kluckstrasse 3, 10785 Berlin. State precisely which nights you'll be in Berlin and enclose an international postal reply coupon so they can send back confirmation. You can also send a fax to 262 95 29. They do not take phone reservations, but if you just want to inquire about availability, call ☎ 262 30 24 from 8 am to 3 pm weekdays (Friday to 2 pm). Their Web site is at www.djh.de.

The most central DJH hostel is the impersonal *Jugendgästehaus Berlin (Map 5, ☎ 261 10 97, fax 262 95 29, email jh-berlin@jugendherberge.de, Kluckstrasse 3)* in Schöneberg near the Landwehr Canal with 364 beds (U15 to Kurfürstenstrasse). Bunks in multibed rooms are DM34/42 for juniors/seniors. Curfew is at midnight.

Jugendgästehaus am Wannsee (☎ *803 20 34, fax 262 95 29, email jh-wannsee@ jugendherberge.de, Badeweg 1)* has 264 beds and a lovely lakeside location on the Grosser Wannsee south-west of the city. Take the S1 or S7 to Nikolassee, walk west over the footbridge, turn left at Kron-prinzessinnenweg, and the hostel will be in sight on the right. This should take no more than 10 minutes. They too charge DM34/42 for juniors/seniors in four-bed rooms, and the key deposit is DM20. Curfew is at 1 am.

Jugendherberge Ernst Reuter (☎ *404 16 10, fax 404 59 72, email jh-ernst-reuter@ jugendherberge.de, Hermsdorfer Damm 48-50)* is in the far north-west of Berlin. Take the U6 to Alt-Tegel, then bus No 125 right to the door. An overnight stay at this 110-bed facility costs DM28/35 for juniors/seniors. Curfew is at 1 am.

Independent Hostels & Guesthouses
DJH cards are not needed for any of the hostels below. None have curfews and several are run by ex-backpackers who have travelled extensively, know what people want and need, and are extremely savvy and well informed about Berlin.

Charlottenburg *Jugendhotel Berlin (Map 5, ☎ 322 10 11, fax 322 10 12, Kaiserdamm 3)* asks DM55/49/46 per person in singles/doubles/triples, which includes breakfast but not the DM7 sheet fee for stays under three nights. This facility caters primarily to those aged 27 and under, but they will accept older people on a space-available basis, at discouragingly high rates (DM183/143/92). All rooms have bath and WC. To get there, take the U2 to Sophie-Charlotte-Platz.

Friedrichshain This up-and-coming area has sprouted a couple of convivial hostels with staff that can make you feel 'plugged into' Berlin within a day or two.

Odyssee Globetrotter Hostel (Map 6, ☎ 29 00 00 81, Grünberger Strasse 23, 2nd backyard, 1st floor) is run by a quartet of young guys who grew up in pre-Wende East Berlin (and are happy to tell a tale or two about those days). It offers 82 beds in new, clean dorms with lockers, as well as private rooms. Check-out is at a civilised 1 pm and the all-you-can-eat breakfast buffet costs just DM5. The reception area doubles as a happening bar/lounge (both open 24 hours) with pool table and cheap beers (yes, the parties are legendary). Dorm bunks are DM24 to DM32, singles/doubles DM50/72, sheets included. We've only heard good things about this place from readers and other travellers. From Ostbahnhof, take bus Nos 240 or 147; from U/S-Bahn Warschauer Strasse it's a five minute walk north.

Another winner is *Frederik's Hostel (Map 4, ☎ 29 66 94 50, fax 29 66 94 52, email hostel@frederiks.de, Strasse der Pariser Kommune 35)*. Thirty large and quiet rooms are spread out in what was once a Jewish girls' school. There's a large garden, 24-hour reception, Internet access, bike rental and an overall congenial atmosphere. Beds in spacious dorms cost DM22 to DM25, singles/doubles/triples are DM49/32/29 per person and sheets are DM4. Take the U5 to Weberwiese.

Kreuzberg *Hotel Transit (Map 6, ☎ 789 04 70, fax 78 90 47 77, Hagelberger Strasse 53-54)*, in a pleasant corner of Kreuzberg, has multibed rooms with shower for DM33 per person, big breakfast included. Singles/doubles go for DM90/105. Popular with backpackers, the Transit also often fills up with school groups in spring and fall.

Die Fabrik (Map 6, ☎ 611 71 16, fax 618 29 74, Schlesische Strasse 18) is in a converted factory and has beds in a huge dorm for DM30 per person. Singles/doubles/triples/quads are spread out over five floors (no lift) and available for DM66/94/120/144; breakfast is an extra DM10 and served at the downstairs *Café Eisenwaren.* Take the U15 to Schlesisches Tor.

The *Gästehaus (Map 6, ☎ 618 20 08, mobile ☎ 0177-618 20 08, fax 618 20 06,*

Wiener Strasse 14), operated by Wohnagentur Freiraum, is in a renovated historic building near cafes and nightlife in Kreuzberg 36. Singles/doubles/triples/quads are DM40/70/100/110. Take the U1/12/15 to Görlitzer Bahnhof.

The *Jugendgästehaus Schreberjugend (Map 6, ☎ 615 10 07, fax 61 40 11 50, Franz-Künstler-Strasse 4-10)* has 124 rooms and charges DM38.50 per night per person in two or three-bed rooms. Singles are DM77. Prices include breakfast; sheet sleeping bags cost DM6 for stays under three nights. Take the U6 or U15 to Hallesches Tor.

The friendly *Pension Kreuzberg (Map 6, ☎ 251 13 62, Grossbeerenstrasse 64)* caters primarily for backpackers, which is reflected in the prices. A night in a multibed room costs DM42 per person, while plain singles/doubles go for DM70/90. Shower and WC are shared.

Mitte Beg, borrow and/or steal to secure a bed at *Circus – The Hostel (Map 4, ☎ 28 39 14 33, fax 28 39 14 84, email circus@mind.de, Rosa-Luxemburg-Strasse 39-41)*. The staff here are particularly friendly and helpful. We watched the front-desk crew comfort and assist hot, tired and sometimes short-tempered backpackers again and again and would give them a '10' every time. Comfortable, clean singles/doubles/triples cost DM45/70/90. Beds in four to six-bed rooms are DM25 to DM27. Breakfast is not included and there's a one-off DM3 sheet fee. Highly recommended. Take the U2 to Rosa-Luxemburg-Platz.

The friendly *Backpacker (Map 4, ☎ 262 51 40, 28 39 09 65, fax 28 39 09 35, email backpacker@snafu.de, Chausseestrasse 102)* is a short walk from nightlife areas and offers simple digs for DM25 to DM28 in four to six-person dorms, DM30 in triples and DM38 in doubles, all per person. Sheets are DM5. There are cooking facilities, and services include bike rental. Take the U6 to Zinnowitzer Strasse – north exit.

At the time of research, a new hostel was about to open above the Kalkscheune cultural centre (see Entertainment). Called

PLACES TO STAY

Clubhouse Hostel *(Map 8, ☎ 28 09 79 79, Johannisstrasse 2)*, is central to all nightlife yet in a quiet sidestreet (though there may be noise from Kalkscheune events). Per person rates were set at DM50/40/35 in singles/doubles/triples and DM25 in five to seven-bed dorms.

Prenzlauer Berg *Lette 'm Sleep (Map 4, ☎ 44 73 36 23, fax 44 73 36 25, email info@ backpackers.de, Lettestrasse 7)* is a welcome addition to the hostel scene and right in the heart of some of Berlin's hottest nightlife. It's received ringing endorsements from readers who've called it 'spotlessly clean' and 'the most friendly'. Per person charges are DM45 in doubles (with kitchenette) or DM25 to DM35 in three to six-bed dorms. It's a five minute walk from U-Bahn Eberswalder Strasse. Get there on the U2.

Schöneberg The central *Studentenhotel (Map 5, ☎ 784 67 20, fax 788 15 23, Meininger Strasse 10)* offers bed and breakfast for DM60 in a single, DM44 per person in a double room and DM40 in a quad; facilities are communal. Take the U4 to Rathaus Schöneberg.

The *CVJM (Map 5, ☎ 264 91 00, fax 261 43 08, Einemstrasse 10)*, the German YMCA, charges DM39 to DM42 for B&B in doubles or multibed rooms with shared showers. Take the U2 or U15 to Nollendorfplatz.

The *Gästehaus Luftbrücke (Map 5, ☎ 78 70 21 30, fax 781 13 47, Kolonnenstrasse No 10-11)* has 23 rooms (some nonsmoking) with shared facilities for DM45. Take the U7 to Kleistpark. You must ring to enter here as well as at the nearby *Jugendgästehaus Feurigstrasse (Map 5, ☎ 781 52 11, fax 788 30 51, Feurigstrasse 63)*, a quieter option where bed and breakfast range from DM28 to DM39, depending on the time of year. There's a one-time charge of DM5 for sheets.

Tegel About 12kms north-west of Berlin's city centre is the area of Tegel. If you're on a really tight budget and don't mind 'roughing it', head for the big tent at the *Internationales Jugendcamp Fliesstal (☎ 433 86 40, fax 434 50 63, Ziekowstrasse 161)*, open

in July and August only. There's room for 260 people with spaces in communal tents costing DM10 per person (including blankets, foam mattresses and showers).

Proper beds in small tents are also available for DM15. Check-in is after 5 pm; no reservations are taken. Officially this place is only for those aged 14 to 27, but usually no one gets turned away. The official maximum stay is three nights. Wake-up is at 8 am and the place is closed until 5 pm. Inexpensive food and self-catering are available.

The tents are right behind the *Jugendgästehaus Tegel (☎ 433 30 46, fax 434 50 63)*, a stately, red-brick building with 220 beds. A night in three to eight-bed dorms goes for DM37.50 per person, including sheets and breakfast buffet. There's no curfew, but the cut-off age of 27 is more rigorously enforced here. To get to either hostel or camp is quite a haul: take the U6 to Alt-Tegel, then bus No 222 to Titusweg.

Wedding The *Jugendgästehaus Nordufer (Map 3, ☎ 45 19 91 12, fax 452 41 00, Norduffer 28)* is operated by the same nonprofit Berliner Jugendclub (Berlin Youth Club) that also runs the Jugendgästehaus Tegel. Norduffer has 130 beds in 38 rooms and also charges DM37.50. It's also more central: take the U9 to Westhafen, then walk left across the bridge and left again into Norduffer. Here you also need to be under 27.

The *Bund Deutscher Pfadfinderinnen (Association of German Girl Scouts, off Map 4, ☎ 493 10 70, fax 494 10 63, Osloer Strasse 12)* charges DM30 per night with sheets costing an extra DM8. There's a self-catering kitchen, but they also serve breakfast for DM4 or DM6. Hot and cold dinners are available. You must phone ahead for reservations; take the U9 to Osloer Strasse.

Wilmersdorf The sprawling, 450-bed *Jugendgästehaus Central (Map 7, ☎ 873 01 88, fax 861 34 85, Nikolsburger Strasse 2-4)* offers B&B for DM38 per person in double and multibed rooms; the one-time DM7 sheet charge applies to stays under three nights. Take the U1 to Hohenzollernplatz or U9 to Güntzelstrasse.

The *Studentenhotel Hubertusallee (Map 5, ☎ 891 97 18, fax 892 86 98, Delbrückstrasse 24)*, near the Hubertussee lake, charges DM80/110/126 per night for singles/doubles/triples with shower and WC. Students with a recognised card pay only DM45/70/90. Prices include breakfast. This place is open from March to October only. From Ku'damm, catch bus No 119 (going west) to the Hasensprung stop or bus No 129 to the Delbrückstrasse stop.

In the same area is the newly opened *Jugendgästehaus St-Michaels-Heim (Map 5, ☎ 89 68 80, fax 89 68 81 85, email St.-Michaels-Heim@t-online.de, Bismarckallee 23)* which has 35 modern and friendly rooms with shared showers for DM30 to DM33 per person without breakfast. At the attached hotel, singles/doubles start at DM70/150, also with shared facilities.

Jugendhotel Vier Jahreszeiten (Map 5, ☎ 873 20 14/17, fax 873 82 23, Bundesallee 31a) costs DM39 for B&B in one to five-bed rooms. From November to February, rates drop by up to DM8 (U9 to Güntzelstrasse).

Other Districts Still fairly central is *Haus Wichern (Map 3, ☎ 395 40 72, fax 396 50 92)* at Waldenser Strasse 31 in Tiergarten-Moabit. Contemporary and clean, it charges DM42 per person in doubles or quads. There's a one-time fee of DM5 for sheets for stays of under three nights. It's in a neat building with muralled facades depicting various crafts and trades. Take the U9 to Turmstrasse.

Karl-Renner-Haus (Off Map 5, ☎ 833 50 29/30, fax 833 91 57, Ringstrasse 76) is in Steglitz and has beds in two to six-bed rooms for DM35 (breakfast included) or DM38 in rooms with shower. There's a DM5.50 charge for sheets the first night only. Take the S1 to Lichterfelde West.

Also in Steglitz is *Jugendgästehaus Lichterfelde (☎ 71 39 17 34, fax 71 39 17 51, Osdorfer Strasse 121)*, which caters exclusively to guests between the ages of 16 and 26 and charges DM40/55 for singles/doubles. Breakfast is included. Take the S25 to Osdorfer Strasse.

Jugendhotel am Flussbad (☎ 65 88 00 94, fax 65 88 00 93, Gartenstrasse 50) is a long way out in Köpenick. It has seven dorms with communal showers and WC and charges DM25 to DM35 per person, plus DM5 for linen. Take the S3 to Köpenick, then the S10 to Spindlerfeld.

PRIVATE ROOMS

The BTM no longer books private rooms, but several private agencies specialise in this kind of thing. One option is *Bed & Breakfast in Berlin (☎ 44 05 05 82, fax 44 05 05 83, email bedbreakfa@aol.com, Tietjenstrasse 36)* in Tempelhof. They represent 750 beds with singles costing DM55 to DM62, doubles for DM86 to DM98 and triples DM130 to DM140, including commission but not the 16% VAT.

Other agencies worth trying include *Agentur Wohnwitz (☎ 861 82 22, fax 861 82 72, Holsteinische Strasse 55)* in Wilmersdorf and *Berliner Zimmer (☎ 312 50 03, fax 312 50 13, Goethestrasse 58)* in Charlottenburg.

HOTELS
Bookings

Berlin Tourismus Marketing, the tourist office, handles room reservations for its partner hotels only. Reservations can be made in person at the tourist office branches in Budapester Strasse and at the Brandenburg Gate (see the Tourist Offices section in the Facts for the Visitor chapter for addresses). Phone reservations must be made via an expensive new hotline (☎ 0190-75 40 40) that can only be accessed from within Germany. Calls to this number cost DM2.42 per minute. Free bookings may be made via the Internet at www.btm.de.

Private booking services include Berlin-Direkt-Touristik (toll-free ☎ 0130-21 30 or ☎ 787 77 70) at Feurigstrasse 27 in Schöneberg, which can make free reservations at its 250 member hotels (covering all price categories). A third option is Reservierungs-Dienst (☎ 313 88 58) at Blissestrasse 62 in Wilmersdorf.

You can, of course, also contact a hotel or pension directly and we have provided phone and fax numbers and, where available, email addresses. If you call, you may often be quoted the most expensive available room first. Just make it a habit to ask if a cheaper room or rate is available – there usually is.

Most of the smaller, independent hotels and pensions don't accept credit-card reservations and may require a down payment by money order or bank draft. There's usually no funny business involved with this kind of thing, but always ask for a written confirmation of your booking and prepayment.

If you're asked to specify your arrival time, be sure to stick to it (or call if you're delayed). Otherwise, if you haven't prepaid anything, you may find that your room has been given to someone else.

Prices

Berlin is certainly no budget town when it comes to accommodation. Even simple pensions may charge DM130 or so for a double room without great comfort or style. In the off-season (especially in winter), be sure to ask for special rates. Proprietors of small, independent facilities are often inclined to drop prices if business is slow. Many also lower rates for stays of three nights or more. At larger hotels and international business chains, rates often plunge at weekends and during lulls in trade-show activity. Naturally the opposite is true if the city is full.

A wonderful feature of German hotels and pensions is that room rates almost always include breakfast, usually in the form of a lavish buffet with cheeses and cold cuts, jams and honey, various breads and rolls, a choice of cereals and unlimited coffee or tea. Since these are all-you-can-eat, they can easily keep you fed until mid-afternoon. Unless noted, all room rates quoted below include breakfast.

Hotels – Budget

Rooms in this category (doubles for DM100 or less) are truly low or no-frills and you will have to share a shower and WC, though most rooms have at least a sink. Many places listed here also have larger, more expensive rooms with full private facilities and more amenities.

Charlottenburg There are a few reasonably priced places near Zoo station and north of the Ku'damm. The artist-owned *Pension München (Map 5, ☎ 85 79 120, fax 85 79 12 22, Güntzelstrasse 62, 3rd floor)* has lots of character and comes highly recommended. Its eight, cheerfully decorated rooms with modern amenities cost DM66/90 (with shared facilities) or DM110/130 (with private shower and WC). Breakfast, served in a pleasant, tiled room, costs an extra DM9.

Pension Fischer (Map 7, ☎ 218 68 08, fax 213 42 25, Nürnberger Strasse 24a, 2nd floor) has 10 rooms with decor that may give you 50s flashbacks but who's to complain with rates of DM50/70 (or DM70/130 with facilities). Breakfast costs DM8 to DM10. For a more contemporary flair, try *Hotel-Pension Majesty (Map 7, ☎ 323 20 61, fax 323 20 63, Mommsenstrasse 55)* which has 11 tastefully appointed rooms that cost DM80/100 (in-room sink only) or DM110/165 (with shower).

An excellent bet is *Pension Peters (Map 7, ☎ 312 22 78, fax 312 35 19, email penspeters@aol.com, Kantstrasse 146)*, which is pleasantly furnished with a modern, homey look. There are just eight rooms costing DM75/95 or DM110/130 (with private shower). Just up the road is *Hotel Crystal (Map 7, ☎ 312 90 47, fax 312 64 65, Kantstrasse 144)*, which is much larger, with 33 rooms, but also reasonably priced from DM120/150 with facilities to DM70/90 without.

Mitte Word has gotten out that *artist Hotelpension Die Loge (Map 4, ☎ /fax 280 75 13, email die-loge@t-online.de, Friedrichstrasse 115)* offers one of the best deals in town, which is why its seven rooms are often booked far in advance. With rates of DM90/130 for singles/doubles (which drop to DM60/100 for stays of three nights and more), this should come as no surprise. Rooms have all modern amenities and the affable young couple who run the place even serve up a romantic candlelit breakfast for DM10 per person, but only after 11 am. Wait for it!

Gay & Lesbian Hotels

By law, no hotel may turn away gay couples, though some may pretend to be full, or frown upon homosexual guests. A few, all in Schöneberg, cater exclusively for gays and lesbians.

Toms Haus (Map 5, ☎ 218 55 44, fax 213 44 64, Eisenacher Strasse 10) is a winner with the leather crowd. There's no check-in between 3 and 6 pm. Singles/doubles with shared shower and WC cost DM110/140. Men only.

Above the Connection nightclub is **ArtHotel Connection** (Map 7, ☎ 217 70 28/29, fax 217 70 30, Fuggerstrasse 33). Stylishly furnished rooms feature all amenities and full private bathrooms. Guests are allowed. Singles range from DM99 to DM150, doubles are DM120 to DM210. Rates include breakfast and drop 20% from Monday to Thursday. For gays and lesbians.

enjoy bed & breakfast (☎ 215 16 66, fax 21 75 22 19) is a private room referral service operated by Mann-O-Meter (Map 5, Motzstrasse 5). Rates start at DM35 per person, breakfast included. For gays and lesbians.

In the same vein is **Hotel Künstlerheim Luise** (Map 8, ☎ 280 69 41, fax 280 69 42, email luise@compuserve.com, Luisenstrasse 19). The place was recently expanded and given a full make-over with an international league of artists designing each of 33 rooms. Basic rooms start at DM50/70, those with facilities top out at DM120/200.

Schöneberg Budget options, both of them in the heart of the area's gay quarter, include the large but dumpy **Hotel Sachsenhof** (Map 5, ☎ 216 20 74, fax 215 82 20, Motzstrasse 7), which has depressing rooms but a good breakfast buffet (costing DM10 extra). Rooms start at an affordable DM57/99 (rising to DM120/186 for larger ones with facilities). The friendly **Hotel Gunia** (Map 5, ☎ 218 59 40, fax 218 59 44, email HotelGunia@t-online.de, Eisenacher Strasse 10) charges DM80/110 for rooms with shared bathrooms and DM100/150 for those with private facilities.

Tiergarten The family-run **Hotel Les Nations** (Map 3, ☎ 392 20 26/27, fax 392 50 10, email Les-Nations-Berlin@t-online.de, Zinzendorfstrasse 6) is popular among younger travellers from around the world. Comfortable basic rooms cost DM60/100, though those with shower and WC go for DM135/195. Some are nonsmoking and there's parking on the premises. A special bonus for night-owls: breakfast is served around the clock.

Wilmersdorf Hotel Steiner (Map 7, ☎ 891 90 16, fax 892 87 21, Albrecht-Achilles-Strasse 58) offers quirky charm and is an excellent budget option. Rooms (the pink one is a scream) are largish, functionally furnished and popular with an artsy crowd. Rooms with shared facilities are DM75/100; with shower and WC costs DM95/140.

Hotel-Pension Margrit (Map 7, ☎ 883 77 17, fax 882 32 28, Brandenburgische Strasse 24, 2nd floor) is in a lovely restored building (with lift) and has clean but low-frills rooms at very acceptable prices. The singles/doubles with shower cost DM60/115. If you want full private facilities, rates increase to DM95/150.

Hotels – Lower Mid-Range

Hotels in this category (doubles from DM100 to DM175) are still affordable and generally good value. Don't expect the full range of amenities, though some rooms may have telephone and TV.

Charlottenburg There are a few well-priced places near Zoo station and north of the Ku'damm. The excellent **Pension Knesebeck** (Map 7, ☎ 312 72 55, fax 313 95 07, Knesebeckstrasse 86) has five rooms with showers for DM90/140 and nine rooms without for DM60/110. Furnishings are eclectic but comfortable and the proprietor is very friendly.

euro currency converter DM1 = €.51

Another option on this street is **City-Hotel Westerland** (Map 7, ☎ 312 10 04, fax 313 64 89, Knesebeckstrasse 10) whose unremarkable facade conceals a rather pleasant and comfortable environment. Some of the older rooms go for a very reasonable DM90/110, though rates are higher for newly renovated ones. All have private shower and WC. There's also a bike rental service.

Pension Gudrun (Map 7, ☎ 881 64 62, fax 883 74 76, Bleibtreustrasse 17) is housed in a wonderful old building with a facade of folk reliefs that suit the old-fashioned but agreeable interior. It's got a great location and friendly owners. Singles/doubles with shower are DM90/120, those with shower and WC go for DM98/130.

The attractive **Pension Alexandra** (Map 7, ☎ 885 77 80, fax 88 57 78 18, Wielandstrasse 32) has simple singles/doubles for DM110/135, or DM155/185 with full facilities. It's just a few steps north of Kurfürstendamm so it's handy for shopping.

For 1920s nostalgia, head to the pint-sized **Hotel-Pension Nürnberger Eck** (Map 7, ☎ 235 17 80, fax 23 51 78 99, Nürnberger Strasse 24a), which has been a hotel since that roaring era of jazz and cabaret. Each of the eight rooms features period furniture and modern facilities. Original art, some left by former guests, decorates the public areas. Rates are a relative bargain: singles cost DM80 to DM100, doubles go for DM130 to DM160.

Near fashionable Savignyplatz is the snug **Pension Viola Nova** (Map 7, ☎ 313 14 57, fax 312 33 14, Kantstrasse 146), which attracts a varied clientele from backpackers to tourists to business folks because of its price range and its accommodating owners. Simple rooms without private bathrooms are DM80/110, while those with shower cost DM110/150. If you want shower and WC, you pay DM130/160. Breakfast is an additional DM9.50.

Hotel Augusta (Map 7, ☎ 883 50 28, fax 882 47 79, Fasanenstrasse 22) is a charming, frilly establishment that offers good-value singles/doubles without shower for DM110/150. For rooms with shower and WC, rates go up to DM145/195.

Hotel Carmer 16 (Map 7, ☎ 31 10 05 00, fax 31 10 05 10, Carmerstrasse 16) was recently spiffed up and given some modern and friendly touches. Rooms have stucco ceilings and cost DM130/160 with shower and WC. The cheaper ones, costing DM80/120, have shared facilities but are perfectly adequate.

On the same street, **Hotel Alpenland Berlin** (Map 7, ☎ 312 39 70, 313 84 44, Carmerstrasse 8) has renovated rooms spread over four floors (no lift) and ranging in price from DM75 to DM140 for singles and DM110 to DM190 for doubles. Some rooms on the 4th floor have shared facilities and are cheaper.

Friedrichshain *Juncker's Hotel Garni* (Map 6, ☎ 293 35 50, fax 29 33 55 55, email junckers-hotel@t-online.de, Grünberger Strasse 21) offers good value for money and is within walking distance of this district's evolving nightlife scene. Their 30 rooms are decked out with contemporary furniture and range from DM90/110 to DM140/170, depending on location and size. All rooms have private shower and WC. Breakfast is an extra DM10 per person.

Kreuzberg Not far from Potsdamer Platz, *Hotel am Anhalter Bahnhof* (Map 6, ☎ 251 03 42, fax 251 48 97, email Hotel-AAB@ t-online.de, Stresemannstrasse 36) is a good bet if you want just simple, reasonably priced digs. Rooms are divided over three floors. Those facing away from the street have showers and WCs and cost from DM140/180. Singles without facilities start at DM80, doubles at DM110, triples at DM150 and quads at DM160.

Schnitzel fumes may waft through your window if you're staying at *Gasthaus Dietrich Herz* (Map 6, ☎ 691 70 43/44, fax 693 11 73, Marheinekeplatz 15), a hotel-restaurant right in the fun district of Kreuzberg 61. Some of the 16 homey rooms have a balcony. The cost is DM80 to DM120 for singles and DM120 to DM140 for doubles. Staying here gives you a real flavour of old-fashioned Berlin.

Mitte & Prenzlauer Berg The family-operated *Pension Merkur* (Map 4, ☎ 282 82 97, fax 282 77 65, Torstrasse 156), within walking distance of Mitte's most happening nightlife, is in a ratty-looking building but rooms are quite adequate. Rates range from DM65/95 for a simple single/double to DM150/168 for those with private shower and WC.

Hotel Kastanienhof (Map 4, ☎ 44 30 50, fax 44 30 51 11, Kastanienallee 65), between Prenzlauer Berg and Mitte, has singles with private shower and WC for DM130 and doubles for DM160. Bigger, quieter rooms are also available at DM190/265. There's a nonsmoking breakfast room and the staff are quite savvy.

Schöneberg & Tiergarten *Hotel-Garni Arco* (Map 7, ☎ 235 14 80, fax 211 33 87, email arco-hotel@t-online.de, Geisbergstrasse 30) is a welcoming, gay-friendly place with warm furnishings. There are 20 comfortable rooms, all with private facilities, from DM100/140 to DM140/180.

The modern *Hotel Delta Berlin* (Map 5, ☎ 26 00 20, fax 26 00 21 11, email Delta.Hotel.Berlin@t-online.de, Pohlstrasse 58) sports a charming, creative design and nice sun terrace. Each room looks different; some have circular windows, one even has a circular bathroom. Nonsmoking rooms are available and there's also a bar and room service. Some rooms, all with private bathrooms, are a steal at DM107/119, others though can cost as much as DM252/304. Gay and lesbians are welcomed. This hotel is also child and dog friendly.

Wilmersdorf Those in search of a truly unique and quirky Berlin abode should try getting a room at the *Propeller Island Lodge* (Map 7, ☎ 893 25 33, fax 891 87 20, Paulsborner Strasse 10). There are only five but each sports a design from the warped imagination of artist-owner Lars Stroschen. The Symbol Room, for instance, is smothered – floor to ceiling – in black and white symbols. In the Orange Room, even the bed sheets are sunset-coloured. And the Dwarf Room? Well, it's only 1.42m

high! There are two shared bathrooms and kitchen access. Room prices are DM140 (except for the Dwarf Room which is DM50) and do not include breakfast. Add DM50 for one-night stays. You must call ahead for reservations.

Hotel Bogota (Map 7, ☎ 881 50 01, fax 883 58 87, email hotelbogota@t-online.de, Schlüterstrasse 45) gets top marks, and has been praised in several readers' letters. Housed inside an early 20th-century building, it's inexpensive and quiet, yet close to the Ku'damm action. Furnishings in the 125 rooms are old-fashioned but classy. Rooms cost DM78/125 with shared facilities, DM100/145 with private shower and DM130/170 with full facilities. A bike rental service operates in summer.

The small and friendly *Pension Curtis* (Map 7, ☎ 883 49 31, fax 885 04 38, Pariser Strasse 39-40, 2nd floor) has cosy singles for DM70 to DM90 and doubles for DM90 to DM140, with shower. Discounts for longer stays are available. If they're fully booked, there are three other pensions offering similar rates in the same building – Austriana, Rügen and Marco Polo.

It may not win awards for stylishness, yet *Hotel Agon* (Map 7, ☎ 885 99 30, fax 885 99 31 23, email hotel-agon-berlin@t-online.de, Xantener Strasse 4) scores points for its winsome and personable atmosphere. Rooms are large and comfortable, offer all amenities and start at DM117/147.

Hotel Savigny (Map 7, ☎ 881 30 01, fax 882 55 19, Brandenburgische Strasse 21) is a good, well-priced establishment in an historic Berlin building with high ceilings and a lift. The large and traditional rooms have all amenities. Singles range from DM90 to DM130, doubles cost between DM150 and DM190.

The modern yet quirky *Hotel Albatros* (Map 5, ☎ 89 78 30, fax 89 78 31 00, email Albatros-Hotel@t-online.de, Rudolstädter Strasse 42) is a big place with 139 rooms and eight apartments. The decor is fresh, welcoming and colourful and rooms are quite reasonable, costing DM99/120 without and DM120/190 with private shower and WC.

Men are out of luck at the *Frauenhotel Artemisia (Map 7, ☎ 873 89 05, fax 861 86 53, Brandenburgische Strasse 18, email Frauenhotel-Berlin@t-online.de)*, a stylish and quiet women-only haven. Soothing salmon, charcoal and mint dominate the colour scheme of the bright and individually decorated rooms which cost from DM100/170. The rooftop terrace, a great spot for sunbathing or having breakfast in summer, gets rave reports. Unfortunately, there are only eight rooms, so be sure to book ahead.

Hotels – Upper Mid-Range

Hotels in this category (doubles between DM175 and DM250) are comfortable without being formal and usually small enough to offer personal attention. Most rooms in these places meet modern standards, though some may occasionally have a few less expensive ones with shared facilities.

Charlottenburg *Hotel California (Map 7, ☎ 88 01 20, fax 88 01 21 11, email info@hotel-california.de, Kurfürstendamm 35)* puts you near the city's best shopping and restaurants. Rooms, some nonsmoking, are large and decked out in a fresh and appealing colour scheme, and there's a sauna on the premises. Singles range from DM155 to DM225, doubles from DM195 to DM295.

For a place with style and comfort, try *Hotel Askanischer Hof (Map 7, ☎ 881 80 33, fax 881 72 06, Kurfürstendamm 53)*, which has counted David Bowie and Wim Wenders among its guests. Rooms are large, decked out in frilly Art Nouveau style and have the usual amenities. Nonsmoking rooms and room service are available. Rates are DM175 to DM210 for singles and DM230 to DM280 for doubles.

Just off Ku'damm in a ritzy side street, you'll find *Hotel-Garni Atlanta (Map 7, ☎ 881 80 49, fax 881 98 72, Fasanenstrasse 74)* which has 30 rooms, all outfitted with private bathrooms, from DM155/185. Some of the larger rooms cost DM20 more.

Hotel Consul (Map 7, ☎ 30 31 10 60, fax 303 12 20 60, email info@hotel-consul. com, Knesebeckstrasse 8-9) is a quiet and friendly place which combines efficiency with charm and thus appeals to business types and tourists alike. There are 70 rooms, including several for non-smokers, costing DM169/269 with full bathroom facilities; some with shower only go for DM119/170. Also ask about special weekend rates.

Friedrichshain & Kreuzberg The location of the *East Side Hotel (Map 6, ☎ 29 38 33, fax 29 38 35 55, Mühlenstrasse 6)* is a bit noisy, but the view of the East Side Gallery, one of the last remaining stretches of the Wall, may be sufficient compensation. Rooms with full facilities in this pleasantly renovated 19th-century hotel are friendly and well lit and cost DM140 to DM188 for singles and DM166 to DM235 for doubles.

Hotel Riehmers Hofgarten (Map 6, ☎ 78 10 11, fax 786 60 59, Yorckstrasse 83), in a lovely part of Kreuzberg near Viktoriapark, is an intimate 25-room, upmarket hotel that deserves special notice. It's housed in an elegant 1892 edifice that orbits a courtyard that is sure to delight romantics. Singles/doubles cost DM170/200 or DM210/240, depending on size and location.

Schöneberg & Tiergarten *Hotel Auberge (Map 7, ☎ 235 00 20, fax 23 50 02 99, Bayreuther Strasse 10)*, in an interesting old building, has 29 spacious singles/doubles with private bathroom ranging from DM160/210 to an exorbitant DM300/380.

The modern *Scandotel Castor Berlin (Map 5, ☎ 21 30 30, fax 21 30 31 60, email castor@t-online.de, Fuggerstrasse 8)* is a behemoth of a building with 78 singles/doubles in a bright colour scheme, all with shower and WC, from DM170/185 to DM228/265. There's a bar, a nonsmoking floor and parking in the yard (DM10). Children to age 12 stay free in their parents' room (a portable bed is provided).

Hotel Imperial (Map 7, ☎ 88 00 50, fax 882 45 79, email Imperial.Hotel.Berlin@ t-online.de, Lietzenburger Strasse 79-81) is a full-service affair with parking garage, sauna, restaurant, bar and meeting facilities. Rooms feature all the usual high-end amenities and go for DM175/225; some of the larger ones are DM195/265. Gay and lesbians welcome. The Imperial is also child and dog friendly.

Near the government quarter, *Hotel Park Consul (Map 3, ☎ 39 07 80, fax 39 07 89 00, Alt-Moabit 86a)* is a modern establishment catering largely to a business clientele. Amenities include hotel parking and non-smoking rooms. Rates start at DM165/195. *Hotel Tiergarten (Map 3, ☎ 39 98 96 , fax 393 86 92, Alt-Moabit 89)* is nearby and roughly in the same vein but with a bit more character. Rates start at DM150/180 for a single/double with shower and WC. If you want quiet, ask for a room at the back. Non-smoking rooms are available.

Wilmersdorf The *Olivaer Apart Hotel (Map 7, ☎ 88 58 60, fax 88 58 62 22, Konstanzer Strasse 1)* is a contemporary place that should make business types feel right at home. It's also near Kurfürstendamm and has stylishly minimalist rooms with all the facilities for DM140/180. Nonsmoking rooms and parking on the premises are available.

Lots of chrome and a sparse, yet surprisingly warm decor characterise *Hotel Alexander (Map 7, ☎ 881 60 91, fax 881 60 94, Pariser Strasse 37)*. This hotel counts film makers and other artists, as well as business people, among its loyal clientele. Singles/doubles with shower and WC start at a fairly reasonable DM120/180 but crest at DM160/210; triples are DM180. Special weekend rates may be available.

If you bring the kids to stay at the *Hotel-Pension Wittelsbach (Map 7, ☎ 873 63 45, fax 862 15 32, Wittelsbacher-strasse 22)*, they may never want to leave. The family floor is a veritable fairytale setting, with Sleeping Beauty, a medieval castle and toys galore. Some of it is a bit hokey but kids love it. Quieter accommodation is found on the other floors. Rates are DM130/180 to DM180/250.

Hotels – Top End
The hotels in this category (doubles over DM250) supply all the frills and amenities the international jet-setter would expect – pools, fitness centres, cable TV, mini bar,

restaurants, business desks etc. Breakfast, often optional and usually lavish, may add DM30 on to your nightly bill.

Charlottenburg If there was such a thing as an 'ecologically correct' hotel, the stylish *Hotel Bleibtreu (Map 7, ☎ 88 47 40, fax 88 47 44 44, email info@bleibtreu-hotel.com, Bleibtreustrasse 31)* would be it. The aesthetic decor is a meditation in understatement boasting specially designed furniture of untreated oak, 100% virgin wool carpets and walls bathed in organic paint. Tucked behind a flower shop, cafe and deli, the Bleibtreu also operates a first-rate restaurant and bar that are popular with locals. Rooms start at DM249/289, cresting at DM349/389; breakfast buffet is DM26.

Family-run with panache and aplomb is *Hecker's Hotel (Map 7, ☎ 889 00, fax 889 02 60, email info@heckers-hotel.com, Grolmanstrasse 35)*, which offers cutting-edge cool in its spacious, streamlined public areas, including a glass-front lobby. Popular with celebrities in search of privacy, its 72 over-sized rooms are decked out with soothing earth-tone furnishings. Some have walk-in closets, king-size beds and marble bathrooms. Rates start at DM200/250; breakfast buffet is DM23.

You can't get more central than the business-style, 302-room *Hotel Palace Berlin (Map 7, ☎ 250 20, fax 262 65 77, email Hotel@palace.de)*, which is inside the Europa-Center and has views of the Memorial Church. The rooms, recently subjected to a rigorous facelift, are the very definition of luxury (minibar, air-con, TV, etc), though it's all done in a rather functional manner. Sauna, solarium and pool round out the full-service offerings. Rates start at a whopping DM360/410, breakfast included.

Another splurge option is the nearby *Hotel Steigenberger Berlin (Map 7, ☎ 212 70, fax 212 71 17, Los-Angeles-Platz 1)*. This pleasant, 397-room hotel, which is popular with the business crowd, offers all the mod cons and is seconds away from the Ku'damm and the Memorial Church. Rates start at DM310/360, rising to DM490/540; breakfast adds another DM31.

euro currency converter DM1 = €.51

PLACES TO STAY

Hotel Mondial (Map 7, ☎ 88 41 10, fax 88 41 11 50, email hotel-mondial@t-online.de, Kurfürstendamm 47) offers the same full range of amenities and facilities – including a pool, sauna and solarium – but on a more intimate scale. There are just 97 rooms, some with extra wide doors enabling wheelchair access. Rates start at DM220/280 and peak at DM380/480.

Mitte The odds of bumping into a celebrity actor or powerful politician are pretty good at Berlin's premier abode, the *Hotel Adlon Kempinski* (Map 8, ☎ 226 10, fax 22 61 22 22, email adlon@kempinski.com, Unter den Linden 77). With front-row vistas of the Brandenburg Gate and offering a sumptuous 'restored-historical' ambience, this full-service hotel leaves no desire unfulfilled. Staff are multilingual, the pool-sauna area makes for some heavenly relaxation, and shopping, nightlife and sights are just a stroll away. Rooms start at DM390/460 and are commensurately lavish; the breakfast buffet is an extra DM39.

The art of living is celebrated at the *art'o-tel Ermelerhaus* (Map 8, ☎ 24 06 20, fax 24 06 22 22, email reservation@artotel.de, Wallstrasse 70-73), a boutique hotel that fuses a modernist wing with an 18th-century patrician townhouse via a dramatic atrium. Staying here feels a bit like camping out at a museum as public areas and rooms abound with original works by leading contemporary German painter, Georg Baselitz. Rates start at DM235/275, breakfast included, but it's almost worth the splurge.

As far as chain hotels go, the huge 354-room *Berlin Hilton* (Map 8, ☎ 202 30, fax 20 23 42 69, Mohrenstrasse 30) offers something beyond the usual range of amenities: it's housed in a striking glass palace within walking distance of Gendarmenmarkt, shopping at the Friedrichstadtpassagen, the opera and other major Mitte sights. Singles cost DM270 to DM350, doubles range from DM295 to DM390, breakfast included.

Tiergarten The classy *Sorat Hotel Spree-Bogen* (Map 3, ☎ 39 92 00, fax 39 92 09 99, email spree-bogen@SORAT-Hotels.com, Alt Moabit 99), which occupies a converted dairy, offers a fusion of contemporary chic and early 20th century industrial architecture. It's a state-of-the-art affair that sits right on an idyllic stretch of the Spree river, with the government quarter just around the next bend. Minimalist rooms feature designer furniture, and the public areas are friendly and imbued with a creative spirit. Rates start at DM230/300, including the sumptuous breakfast buffet.

On the opposite – southern – edge of the Tiergarten district is the postmodern *Grand Hotel Esplanade* (Map 5, ☎ 25 47 80, fax 265 11 71, email info@esplanade.de, Lützowufer 15); just look for the mirrored-glass behemoth squatting beside a picturesque stretch of canal. Celebrities, top executives and the merely monied relax here with a massage, are chauffeured around in the hotel-owned Rolls Royce or sip a cocktail at the oh-so-fashionable Harry's New York Bar (see Entertainment). You too can join in for DM358/441, breakfast included.

LONG-TERM RENTALS

If you're planning to stay in Berlin for a month or longer, you might consider renting a room or an apartment through a *Mitwohnzentrale* (flat-sharing agency) which matches people willing to let their digs temporarily with those in need of a temporary home. Accommodation can be anything from rooms in shared student flats to furnished apartments. Rates vary according to the agency and the type of accommodation but are always less than what you'd pay in hotels. In general, the longer you rent, the less expensive it gets. Even if you're not staying for an entire month, it may still work out cheaper to pay the monthly rent and leave earlier.

Added to the rate will be the agency's commission which comes to around 25% of the rent, plus 16% VAT. In other words, if the month-long flat rental is DM800, your total will be DM1128 (DM200 commission, DM128 VAT).

In order to find a place, you first must fill out an application with a Mitwohnzentrale, specifying the desired rental period, the maximum rent you want to pay, the type of accommodation you prefer etc. Next, the agency gives you a list of places that meet your needs. You then need to phone the landlords (you may be able to find someone nice at the agency to do this for you if your German isn't up to it), visit the rooms/apartments that interest you, and pick your favourite. In the case of a successful rental agreement, the entire sum, including commission, is payable to the agency in advance (unless you're staying for several months, in which case you may be able to arrange for monthly payments).

Agencies to try include:

Erste Mitwohnzentrale (☎ 324 30 31) at Sybelstrasse 53, Charlottenburg.

Mitwohnagentur Kreuzberg (☎ 786 20 03) at Mehringdamm 72, Kreuzberg.

HomeCompany (☎ 194 45) at Joachimsthaler Strasse 14, Charlottenburg.

Casa Nostra (☎ 235 51 20) at Winterfeldtstrasse 36, Schöneberg.

PLACES TO STAY

Places to Eat

Berlin is a cosmopolitan city, and thanks to its large immigrant population you'll find quite a United Nations of cuisines represented here. Ethnic dishes have sometimes been adapted to local tastes and available ingredients, but this in itself can make for interesting culinary experiences. Berlin has not traditionally had a reputation for great food or sophisticated restaurants, but a new generation of chefs – many of them trained overseas – ensure that the overall quality has undeniably improved.

FOOD
Local Etiquette
Dining out is usually a casual affair and there are few restaurants where patrons would feel compelled to dress up. Dinner time is usually around 8 pm, so if you're heading for a popular eatery – especially on a Friday or Saturday night – make a reservation. Only in the most formal establishments (and American chains like the Hard Rock Café or TGI Friday's), or if you've made a reservation, will someone seat you at an assigned table; normally you'll just seat yourself. In student cafes and other casual eateries you may occasionally be asked to share your table with another party. You are expected to consent but you need not socialise with your table mates or even introduce yourself.

Most restaurants figure on only one or two seatings per night, so don't feel that you need to leave quickly after you've finished your meal. You may stay on for another hour or so just nursing a drink, chatting and enjoying the atmosphere. The bill will only be presented to you when you request it.

Service, unfortunately, remains a sore point; you can safely presume it will be bad. Long waits, lukewarm food, inattentiveness and plain rudeness are rampant. In recognition of this fact, the Berlin Hotel & Restaurant Guild has called upon service personnel to help improve the city's image by adopting a better attitude and being less

stingy with smiles. As far as we can tell, they've still got a long way to go.

Smoking continues to be practised relentlessly – even in vegetarian restaurants – and nonsmoking sections are rare or ineffective (see the boxed text 'Smoke Gets in Your Eyes').

Smoke Gets in Your Eyes

Berliners are some of the heaviest tobacco smokers in the world. Entering a pub, club or restaurant can be a lung-searing, eye-watering experience that will leave your clothes reeking and your hair in need of an instant wash. Some places do have seating sections for nonsmokers but that makes almost no difference when you're sharing a small room with 50 puffers.

But there are a couple of things you can do to minimise health, hygiene and laundry hazards. Always try to sit on the ground floor of any place you enter, as smoke rises. Sitting by a door or window is also a good idea; any draft you have to put up with will be worth it.

When you know you're going to be spending some hours in a packed club or cafe, don't put on the only remaining clean shirt in your suitcase or backpack. Instead, wear what we've come to call a designated 'cafe shirt', you know, the one that's only worn in nicotine-dense environments.

If you have long hair, wear it up or pile it up under a hat or a scarf.

Pick restaurants with high ceilings, or modern establishments with efficient ventilation. If you don't mind having an entire restaurant to yourself, have your meal in the afternoon; most kitchens are open all day.

A final point on smoking etiquette. You're in Berlin and the people here smoke. You'll only get incredulous stares if you ask people not to light up. Just pretend you're in an old Bette Davis movie.

Cost

If you don't insist on lavish, sit-down meals, you need not spend a lot of money on food. German *Imbiss* (snack) stalls are a wonderful way to fill up inexpensively, as are the ubiquitous Turkish takeaway places. At the latter you can get a Turkish *lahmacun* (pizza) for about DM3 or a doner kebab (thin meat slices – usually chicken or lamb – served with salad vegetables and a garlicky yogurt sauce in a toasted pitta bread) for around DM4.

Cafes are great places to eat cheaply since they offer not only cakes but also small bistro-type dishes like quiche lorraine, baguette sandwiches, soups etc, usually for under DM10. Most are cosy, congenial places where you can also relax over a newspaper or write those postcards.

If you want a more substantial hot meal, lunch is almost always cheaper than dinner. Chinese and Indian restaurants in particular often offer special three-course bargain lunches for around DM10. Old-style German restaurants sometimes have a *Stammgericht*, which is a daily changing main dish served at lunchtime only and also costing around DM10.

Going out for dinner can also be affordable – even at fancier restaurants – as long as you stick to one main course and a single beverage. If you want alcohol, have beer. If you want wine, order a glass of the house wine and avoid ordering a bottle. Pizzerias have among the cheapest and most reliable meals. Besides pizza, you can also get a wide array of pasta dishes and salads. You should easily be able to get away with spending DM20 or less per person, including a drink.

A service charge is always included in the bill and German restaurant staff tend to be paid fairly well anyway. Nevertheless, unless the service was truly abhorrent, most people leave a small tip, usually just rounding up the amount of the bill. So if, say, your bill comes to DM37, you might make that DM40.

DRINKS
Nonalcoholic

Berlin tap water is fine to drink but asking for a glass at a restaurant will raise brows at best and may be refused altogether because they want to sell you an expensive bottle of mineral water (*Mineralwasser*). This almost always has bubbles. Truly still wáter, like Evian, is rare and more expensive. Soft drinks are widely available, but for some reason the diet versions are not. If they taste slightly different from what you're used to, it's because they've been reformulated to meet German tastes. A refreshing summer drink is *Apfelschorle*, which is apple juice mixed with sparkling mineral water.

Coffee is king both in Berlin and Germany in general, and is usually fresh and strong. It comes in cups (*Tasse*) or pots (*Kännchen*) and you should specify what you want when ordering. Condensed milk and sugar will usually be served alongside. In trendy cafes you'll often see people nursing a huge cup of coffee, called *Milchkaffee* (milk coffee) and contains a large amount of hot milk.

One warning: the bottomless cup is *not* a concept here, and a single cup can cost as much as DM5. If you just want a quick cuppa, grab it at the stand-up counters of the Eduscho or Tschibo coffee stores where it'll cost around DM2.50.

If you're ordering tea, and don't want a pot, ask for *ein Glass Tee* (a glass of tea). It'll usually be served in the form of a teabag with sugar and maybe a slice of lemon. If you want milk, ask for *Tee mit Milch*.

Alcoholic

Beer The most common alcoholic beverage is – no surprise – beer, of which the Germans have made a science. All brews adhere to the *Reinheitsgebot* (Purity Law) passed in 1516 in Bavaria. There's a confusing number of choices, the most popular being the fairly bitter-tasting *Pils* and the sweeter, foamy *Weizenbier*. *Schwarzbier*, like Köstrizer, is as black as Guinness but not as creamy and heavy tasting, and is widely available too. Other terms to know are *helles Bier* and *dunkles Bier* which are light and dark beers, respectively. *Berliner Weisse*, or 'Berlin White', is a foaming, low-alcohol wheat beer usually mixed with red (raspberry) or green (woodruff) syrup. *Alsterwasser* is a mix of Pils and lemonade and a popular summer drink.

Wine You'll find wines from around the world in Berlin's restaurants and bars. Those from California and Australia are particularly trendy at the moment and, accordingly, expensive. Chilean wines, on the other hand, offer excellent value. Wines from other European countries, like Spain, Italy and France, are common as well.

Despite what you may have heard – or tasted – back home, German wines are actually very good. Their reputation as being sweet and headache-inducing is largely undeserved. Germany just doesn't produce a great amount of wine and the Germans drink all the good stuff. It's only the swill that ends up being exported. In supermarkets, the cheaper wines are almost as cheap as bottled water or soft drinks, and even those are quite good indeed. A delicious bottle of crisp, dry *(trocken)* white wine can easily be found for DM4.

Riesling, Müller-Thurgau and Silvaner are the three most celebrated German varietals. Unless you order a bottle, wine is usually served in glasses holding 20cL. A *Weinschorle* is white wine mixed with sparkling mineral water. Wine is drunk as an aperitif or with meals.

See the Language chapter later in this book for a glossary of food and drink terms that might come in useful.

RESTAURANTS

Berliners love going out for dinner and have literally thousands of restaurants and cafes to choose from. Wherever you are in the city, there's no need to travel far since every neighbourhood has its own cluster of eateries running the gamut of cuisines and price categories.

Unless noted otherwise, restaurants mentioned here are open daily for lunch (usually from 11 am or noon) and dinner. Those that do dinner only usually open around 5 or 6 pm. In keeping with Berliners' propensity to go out late and stay out until the early hours of the morning, many restaurants keep their doors open way past dinner time, often until 2 am or even 4 am on weekends, though food service usually stops around midnight.

American

For more than the stereotypical burger and rib variety, head to *Juleps (Map 7, ☎ 881 88 23, Giesebrechtstrasse 3)*, a warmly lit cocktail bar and restaurant in Charlottenburg. The menu reflects the various influences of the multi-ethnic cauldron that is the US, though slightly deeper pockets are required to enjoy it all.

A time-worn Trabant adds the local touch to Berlin's *Hard Rock Café (Map 7, ☎ 88 46 20, Meinekestrasse 21)*, surely the mother of all theme restaurants. It's renowned for its 'pig sandwich' (with smoked pork, DM19.50), though the usual assortment of burgers and salads is, of course, available.

TGI Friday's (Map 8, ☎ 23 82 79 60, Karl-Liebknecht-Strasse 5) in Mitte is the Berlin branch of this successful US chain. The menu includes lots of 'fun food' like buffalo wings, ribs and pizza to keep the kids happy. Thumbs down for the prices (burgers DM18!), though the friendly service makes for a welcome break from Berlin's usual surly restaurant/bar staff.

Jimmy's Diner (Map 7, ☎ 882 31 41, Pariser Strasse 41) in Wilmersdorf is the oldest American diner in Berlin and a great place to soak up that *American Graffiti* vibe. Squeeze into one of the crimson faux-leather booths, then sink your teeth into one them thar juicy burgers (from DM11).

If they're full, try the nearby *Fabulous Route 66 50's Diner (Map 7, ☎ 883 16 02, Pariser Strasse 44)* instead. More pricey and perhaps a tad overdesigned, it's good fun nonetheless and the food convinces too. Best thing: booths with miniature jukeboxes (DM1 buys two songs).

Australian

Woolloomooloo (Map 3, ☎ 34 70 27 77, Röntgenstrasse 7) in Charlottenburg is Berlin's oldest Australian restaurant. Craving a bit of 'roo? Kangaroo dinners go for around DM30, though the marinated crocodile steak scores points as well. Wash it all down with pints of foamy Foster's. In summer there's a nice beer garden with a view of the Spree. Dinner only.

A gilded griffon stands guard at Schloss Glienicke.

'Golden Else' crowns the Victory Column.

The New Synagogue.

A sun motif at Sanssouci Park in Potsdam.

The new glass dome of the Reichstag, now home to the German parliament.

Old hiding the new: entrance to the Reichstag.

An abstract star emblazons the Jewish Museum.

Caribbean

Carib (Map 5, ☎ *213 53 81, Motzstrasse 30)* in Schöneberg will transport you – sort of – to the West Indies on a dark and chilly Berlin night. The decor borders on tacky, but the food is mouth watering nonetheless. Jerk chicken is DM21, the vegetarian sampler DM24. Dinner only.

Chinese

For authentic Cantonese head to the bustling *Good Friend (Map 7,* ☎ *313 26 59, Kantstrasse 30)*, low on ambience but big on delicious food. It's all enjoyed by a hungry clientele that includes lots of Chinese. In case the original dishes prove too challenging, there are others adapted to western palates. Most meals cost around DM20.

In Mitte is *Bambussprosse (Map 8,* ☎ *282 18 04, Reinhardtstrasse 12)*, a small, largely kitsch-free restaurant where most meals cost under DM10 and lunch specials (served until 3 pm) go for DM6 to DM7.50. All dishes are available as takeaway as well. It's open daily from noon to midnight.

Ostwind (Map 4, ☎ *441 59 51, Husemannstrasse 13)* is a stylish, pastel maze of a restaurant where you can sit at regular tables or in lotus position on pillows in raised booths. The food is creative and above average, with most dishes priced under DM20. There's a cross-cultural breakfast buffet on Sunday (DM16). Open daily for dinner and for lunch also on weekends.

Ethiopian

Café Arada (Map 4, ☎ *44 05 68 88, Lychener Strasse 4)* is a tiny Ethiopian eatery, also in Prenzlauer Berg. The few tables are almost always crowded with diners chowing down on exotic meat and vegetarian fare served with ginger and garlic. Utensils are banished and it's all scooped up with bread called *injera*. A la carte dishes are DM11.50 to DM14, speciality plates for four persons are DM38 to DM72. Closed Monday.

French

Cour Careé (Map 7, ☎ *312 52 38, Savignyplatz 5)* is a nice brasserie that's especially popular in summer, when you can watch the goings-on in the square from the lovely garden. It's good for snacks like *Flammekuche* (DM9) but also well-priced bistro-style mains like lamb cutlet (DM18).

Paris Bar (Map 7, ☎ *313 80 52, Kantstrasse 152)* is *the* place to come for some serious celebrity watching. When in town, David Bowie and Jack Nicholson have been known to drop by, and film directors like Wim Wenders and Volker Schlöndorff are regulars. Nobody seems to mind that the staff are snobbish and the menu (mains DM25 to DM50) often overstretches the chef's skill.

borchardt (Map 8, ☎ *20 39 71 17, Französische Strasse 47)*, near Gendarmenmarkt and Galeries Lafayette, is an elegant eatery that seeks to recapture the lost grandeur of pre-WWI Berlin. Dine amidst marble columns and beneath lofty stucco ceilings while waiters with crisp long aprons whisk from kitchen to tables carrying plates of ambitious French food with Germanic touches. Deep pockets are de rigeur. Make reservations.

In Mitte is *Reinhard's (Map 8,* ☎ *242 52 95, Poststrasse 28)*, an offshoot of the original on Kurfürstendamm and an island of sophistication in the touristy Nikolaiviertel. This chic brasserie serves Franco-German food, with plats du jour priced around DM18. It's open from 9 am to 1 am.

Wine and cheese is the favourite combination at *Nö (Map 8,* ☎ *201 08 71, Glinkastrasse 24)*, a cluttered assortment of dining rooms located in Mitte. The menu focuses on hearty Alsatian fare, reasonably priced between DM10 and DM20. For DM22.50, you can taste up to five wines, served alongside cheese and a baguette. It's open weekdays for lunch and dinner, on Saturday for dinner only.

In Prenzlauer Berg, you'll find *Gugelhof (Map 4,* ☎ *442 92 29, Knaackstrasse 37)* which blends Swiss, Alsatian and Baden cooking. Reliable standards include cheese fondue and *raclette* (two person minimum) and *choucroute* (a sauerkraut-based dish). Prices hover around the DM20 mark. Open from 10 am, breakfast is served until 4 pm.

German

Charlottenburg *Aschinger (Map 7, ☎ 882 55 58, Kurfürstendamm 26)* is a great place, especially for the budget-strapped. A cosy cellar, it offers 15 filling dishes at DM9.80, an all-you-can-eat salad bar for DM4.80 and breakfasts for DM5 (coffee is extra). You must order at the self-service counter. A delicious dark beer is brewed right on the premises (DM2.80 for 20cL). If you're done drinking, cover your glass or else you'll keep getting served another.

Luisenbräu (Map 3, ☎ 341 93 88, Luisenplatz 1), is another microbrewery and a good place to relax over a beer and a pretzel after a day of museum-hopping around Schloss Charlottenburg. Filling fare is served to mop up the delicious brews, including a daily dish for DM9.80.

Kreuzberg If you think a schnitzel is a schnitzel is a schnitzel, go to the time-tested *Gasthaus Dietrich Herz (Map 6, ☎ 691 70 43/44, Marheinekeplatz)*, at the eastern end of the market hall, to find out it ain't necessarily so. A dozen varieties, often bigger than the plates they're served on, start at DM12.95, though for the health-conscious there are salads for under DM10. Open from 8 am daily, from 9 am Sunday. (Also see the Places to Stay chapter for its accomodation prices.)

For a quintessential Berlin experience, head to the rustic *Grossbeerenkeller (Map 6, ☎ 251 30 64, Grossbeerenstrasse 90)*. Here you'll be served German soul food at its finest, including such delicious arterycloggers as fried potatoes, roast pork and matjes in cream sauce (these dishes are all under DM20). It's open from 4 pm daily, from 6 pm Saturday.

For a more upmarket experience and a wider selection in food, try the venerable *Weltrestaurant Markthalle (Map 6, ☎ 617 55 02, Pücklerstrasse 34)*. The chef digs deep into his repertory of German dishes from all regions, ranging from DM15 to DM25. The *Königsberger Klopse* (meat dumplings in caper sauce) are a speciality. Open from 9 am, from 7 pm Sunday. Also good for breakfast.

Mitte *Keyzer Soze (Map 4, ☎ 28 59 94 89, Tucholskystrasse 33)* is a hip, uncluttered restaurant that takes you on a culinary journey around Germany. *Maultaschen* (ravioli-like noodles) from Swabia, spiced fingersized sausages from Nuremberg and, of course, the *Berliner Boulette* (hamburger patty) all have their place on the menu. Prices are decidedly civilised (nothing over DM18), which is why this place is usually packed. Service is accordingly slow.

The menu at *Stäv (Map 8, ☎ 282 39 65, Schiffbauerdamm 8)* reflects a distinct Bonn-Berlin connection. Originally based in Bonn, the owner decided to open a second branch in Berlin so as not to deprive homesick politicians, journalists and bureaucrats of the Rhenish cuisine they'd come to love. (By the way, the name is short for *Ständige Vertretung*, the euphemism used for the West German embassy in the former GDR.)

The time-honoured *Zum Nussbaum (Map 8, ☎ 242 30 95, Am Nussbaum 3)* in the Nikolaiviertel has the distinction of being the oldest restaurant in Berlin. Its wood-panelled walls have hosted the hungry and thirsty since 1571. Originally located on Fischerstrasse in Cölln, it was bombed to bits in WWII and painstakingly resurrected in its current location. Despite regular tourist invasions, the place has remained friendly and affordable (mains DM12 to DM20).

Nearby, the *Zur Gerichtslaube (Map 8, ☎ 24 31 32 45, Poststrasse 28)* is another historic – if rebuilt – restaurant with character. Seated beneath a Gothic-style vaulted ceiling, you'll dine on such stick-to-the-ribs fare as pig's knuckles with pea puree. Some dishes cost under DM20.

Inside the Nikolaiviertel's Knoblauchhaus is the *Historische Weinstuben (Map 8, ☎ 242 41 07, Poststrasse 23)* which has an outstanding selection of German wines from all regions, including the eastern German growing areas of Saale-Unstrut and Saxony. The wines are pricey (costing DM12 and up for a glass) but go surprisingly well with the hearty Berlin fare served alongside.

At the **Kellerrestaurant** (Map 4, ☎ 282 38 43, Chausseestrasse 125), in the vault-like basement of the Brecht-Weigel House, you can indulge in rustic dishes from the cookbook of Helene Weigel, Brecht's wife. Concoctions like Barbary duck with green cabbage and potatoes (DM24) are typical, though there are cheaper specials. Lunch and dinner weekdays, dinner only on weekends.

Prenzlauer Berg Offenbachstuben (Map 4, ☎ 445 85 02, Stubbenkammerstrasse 8) is a GDR relic that has weathered the Wende with panache. It's stuffy but classy and especially suited for carnivores who can choose from a menu that seems to feature the entire animal world, including venison, pheasant and rabbit. Mains cost DM17 to DM30. It's dinner only and come early as things start to quieten down around 10 pm.

Spandau At **Zitadellenschänke** (☎ 334 21 06, Am Juliusturm), right in the Spandau citadel, tables groan under lavish medieval banquets beneath vaulted ceilings and accompanied by minstrel song. Seven courses cost DM76.50, five courses are DM52.50, and à la carte is available too. Reservations are recommended since it's the kind of place that draws large office and birthday parties. Dinner only on weekends, lunch and dinner on weekdays. (See the Spandau map in the Things to See & Do chapter.)

Tiergarten Alte Meierei (Map 3, ☎ 39 07 97 21, Alt-Moabit 99) is a stylish gem tucked away in the stable section of a former dairy. It serves updated versions of classic Berlin dishes to a moneyed clientele. Dinner mains start at DM28. If you're a gourmet on a budget, go at lunch time.

Greek

Istoria (Map 4, ☎ 44 05 02 10, Kollwitzstrasse 64) is a lively Greek cafe on Kollwitzplatz in Prenzlauer Berg. Besides classics like gyros, souvlaki and bifteki (all well under DM20), look for creative delicacies like tiger shrimp in a tomato-based, garlic-Cointreau sauce. There's also a choice of half a dozen breakfasts from DM5 to DM13. Nearby is **Abbot & Costello** (Map 4, ☎ 442 07 24, Husemannstrasse 10), which has simple country decor, a longish bar and serves updated versions of classic Greek food for around DM20. Open daily for dinner.

Competition among Greek restaurants is especially fierce in Schöneberg. **Ypsilon** (Map 5, ☎ 782 45 39, Hauptstrasse 163) doubles as a neighbourhood hang-out for the local Greek population and a happening dinner spot for trendoids. The huge room often fills with the clatter of communicative patrons, but the food is good and well-priced (fish dishes around DM25 are a speciality). Dinner only, live music on weekends. A few doors down, you'll find the similar **Nemesis** (Map 5, ☎ 781 15 90, Hauptstrasse 154), which is also dinner only.

A personal favourite is **Ousies** (Map 5, ☎ 216 79 57, Grunewaldstrasse 16), a lively Greek taverna with an exhaustive menu of hot and cold appetisers (the appetiser sampler for DM14 is excellent and enough to fill you up), plus succulent spiced

---

Berlin Cuisine

Though few locals seem to favour it, there is still such a thing as traditional Berlin cuisine, though it's hard to distinguish from general German cooking. Overall, it tends to be calorific, hearty and heavy on artery-clogging meat dishes. Pork, prepared in umpteen ways, is a staple. Dishes frequently found on menus include Kasseler Rippen (smoked pork chops) and Eisbein (pork knuckles). Both usually share the plate with sauerkraut and either mashed or boiled potatoes.

A definite Berlin classic is Currywurst, a spicy sausage served with a tangy curried sauce. There's much debate about which Imbiss serves the best such concoction.

Ground meat often comes in the form of a Boulette, a cross between a meatball and a hamburger and eaten with a dry roll. Other regulars on Berlin menus are roast chicken, schnitzel, sauerbraten (marinated beef) and matjes (pickled herring).

meat dishes like bifteki for around DM15 to DM20. Dinner only. Reservations advised.

Indian

Charlottenburg *Ashoka (Map 7, ☎ 313 20 66, Grolmanstrasse 51)* is a tiny hole-in-the-wall where curries and meat-based dishes cost a mere DM6.50 to DM9.50 and just fly over the counter from the steamy open kitchen. The same excellent food (though vegetarian only) is served at *Satyam (Map 7, ☎ 312 90 79)* at Goethestrasse 5.

A seductive melange of ginger, coriander and cumin also wafts out from *Kalkutta (Map 7, ☎ 883 62 93, Bleibtreustrasse 17)*. It's said to serve some of the best Indian food in town (especially the tandoori dishes), with main courses starting at DM12.

Kreuzberg *Chandra Kumari (Map 6, ☎ 694 12 03, Gneisenaustrasse 4)* is a small, kitschfree restaurant with dishes that blend Sri Lankan and Indian flavours. The menu starts at DM7.50 for a vegetarian lentil dish. The piece de resistance, though, is the Hochzeitsmenu (wedding menu – but you can skip the tux and veil), a veritable banquet costing DM95 for two. The chef uses only hormone-free meat.

With its heavy pine tables and boldly pigmented canvases, *Amrit (Map 6, ☎ 612 55 50, Oranienstrasse 203)* may be furnished like a Swedish living room, but the food is Indian at its finest. Portions are ample, fragrant and steamy and cost from DM10 to DM20. There's even Indian wine.

Prenzlauer Berg At the excellent *Himalaya (Map 4, ☎ 441 25 01, Lychener Strasse)* specialities include lamb dishes priced around DM12.50 and more than 20 vegetarian meals priced from DM6.50 to DM10.50. It's open daily from noon to midnight. Nearby is the equally convincing *Bahu (Map 4, ☎ 44 05 54 91, Rykestrasse 15)* which does pan-Indian fare from mild to so wickedly hot you feel like you're auditioning as a fire eater.

Schöneberg There's a cluster of Indian restaurants on Goltzstrasse, but for years

Rani (Map 5, ☎ 215 26 73) at No 32 has been the only one that packs them in day after day. Less than DM10 buys a big plate of rice smothered with meat or vegetable-based curry which, in fine weather, is best consumed al fresco at the street-side tables. Open 9 am to 2 am daily.

Specialities from throughout India are served at *Maharani (Map 7, ☎ 213 40 22, Fuggerstrasse 28)* where lunch specials cost a mere DM10, most à la carte mains are DM10 to DM13.50 and multicourse dinners weigh in at DM18.50. The decor, though, is traditional Raj kitsch.

International

Charlottenburg *Lubitsch (Map 7, ☎ 882 37 56, Bleibtreustrasse 47)* is a sleek bistro popular with sophisticates chatting and chomping amidst stucco, wood and turquoise tinted walls. The menu changes daily with prices ranging from DM12 to DM40. Open from 9.30 am, from 6 pm Sunday.

Marché (Map 7, ☎ 882 75 78, Kurfürstendamm 14-15), a casual self-service establishment, has excellent salads from DM4.50 and pastas from DM9.50. Meaty main courses are also available, and there's a cafe (coffee from DM2.50) with tables inside and on the terrace. Lots of vegetarian choices.

Kreuzberg The menu of *Bergmann 103 (Map 6, ☎ 694 83 23, Bergmannstrasse 103)* suits international culinary tastes. Best bet, perhaps, is the Alsatian Flammekuche, though we hear the Turkish-style dishes are worth trying too. Sadly service is breathtakingly slow and perfunctory. Expect to pay from DM10 to DM20 for main courses, served from 9.30 am to 1 am daily.

In a yellow corner building, *Deininger (Map 6, ☎ 694 19 93, Friesenstrasse 23)* has an eclectic menu and different all-you-can-eat dishes (DM12) every Monday and Tuesday night. Sunday brunch (from 10 am to 3 pm) is also DM12 (children eat for free). It's dinner only on weekdays, opening from 10 am on weekends. Reservations are advised.

Advena (Map 6, ☎ 618 81 09, Wiener Strasse 11), in Kreuzberg 36, is a quiet oasis on this busy street. Open daily after 10 am, this restaurant has excellent vegetarian specials (DM8.50 to DM12), salads (DM6) and soups (DM5.50) served in a candle-lit, relaxing atmosphere. On Sunday the breakfast buffet is available until 4 pm.

Mitte The *Hackescher Hof (Map 8, ☎ 283 52 93, Rosenthaler Strasse 40-41)* has sacrificed its cultured atmosphere to become just another tourist trap. It's almost always full, which keeps staff simmering at potentially explosive stress levels. One good thing about this cafeteria-sized place is its sky-high ceiling which helps the smoke dissipate more quickly. Hours are from 7 am to 2 am daily.

Beautifully located in a restored courtyard with a large terrace, *Maxwell (Map 4, ☎ 280 71 21, Bergstrasse 22)* is one of Berlin's exceptional restaurants, though primarily frequented by a suit-and-tie crowd. Using only locally grown products, the chef puts substance before culinary pyrotechnics which results in main courses costing from DM35 to DM50.

Ganymed (Map 8, ☎ 28 59 90 46, Schiffbauerdamm 5), a renovated GDR leftover next to the Berliner Ensemble, has a stucco ceiling, a beautiful antique bar buffet and glasses arranged in dazzling symmetry. The food is sophisticated German with prices to match (DM30 for most mains), though there's also a business lunch for DM15.

It took chef Kolja Kleeberg of *Vau (Map 8, ☎ 202 97 30, Jägerstrasse 54/55)* just one year to garner a coveted Michelin star for his ambitious culinary concoctions. The decor is minimalist with seating on slim leather banquettes and wicker chairs, but it all gets an elite touch from high-quality canvases. Three-course lunches are around DM50, dinner costs about double that. A la carte mains start at DM20 for lunch, DM50 for dinner. Closed Sunday.

Schöneberg *Toronto (Map 5, ☎ 781 92 30, Crellestrasse 17)* is as contemporary and unpretentious as the city after which it's named. Open from 9 am daily (from 10 am Sunday), it offers a menu that fearlessly blends ethnic cuisines into interesting concoctions. The

three-course meal is good value at DM30, but daily specials and à la carte dishes from DM15 are also available.

Storch (Map 5, ☎ 784 20 59, Wartburgstrasse 54) is an upmarket yet comfy place where guests are often greeted by owner Volker Hauptvogel himself. Tuxedo-clad waiters serve delicious dishes with Alsatian touches to a yuppie crowd. Figure on about DM30 for main courses, though the Flammekuche go for DM14 to DM17. Open for dinner only.

Tiergarten A hot tip for gourmets on a puny budget is the friendly *Kiezküche (Map 3, ☎ 39 73 91 37, Waldenser Strasse 2-4)* (enter the large yard and it's on the 1st floor behind the steel door in the first building on your left). The place is run by a non-profit organisation that trains disadvantaged youth as certified chefs and restaurant managers in a 3½-year program. And they get to practise on you! Refined recipes such as poached salmon in sauce chantilly for a miraculous DM7 are typical. It's open from 11.30 am to 2 pm weekdays. Seating is cafeteria-style.

Wilmersdorf *Hamlet (Map 7, ☎ 882 13 61, Uhlandstrasse 47)* is a beautiful and stylish brasserie whose chef performs small miracles with French cuisine complemented by North African inflections (eg couscous with tiger shrimp and lamb sausages) for around DM30. It's open from 7.30 am to 3 am daily.

A few steps away is *Manzini (Map 7, ☎ 885 78 20, Ludwigkirchstrasse 11)*, a timelessly trendy tunnel-shaped restaurant where chandeliers dangle above diners settled into snug green leather banquettes. Patrons have palates cultured enough to enjoy such creative mergers as pheasant with champagnekraut and baby potatoes (DM28), though the risottos convince too. Open from 8 am to 2 am daily.

Italian
Charlottenburg *Biscotti (Map 7, ☎ 312 39 37, Pestalozzistrasse 88)* is an upmarket trattoria with wicker, white linen, leafy

plants and a refined menu of exquisite meat and fish dishes, priced from DM25 to DM35 and pasta goes for around DM20. It's dinner only, closed Sunday.

Il Pulcino (Map 7, ☎ 313 91 28, *Leibnizstrasse 74)* is a busy neighbourhood Italian spot with good pizza and pasta. It's mainstream, rustic and mid-priced, with pasta from DM13 to DM18 and chicken dishes around DM20.

Bleibtreustrasse boasts three good Italian restaurants that couldn't be more different. The swank *XII Apostoli* (Map 7, ☎ 312 14 33, *Bleibtreustrasse 49)*, inside the Savignypassage alley, is one of Berlin's rare 24-hour restaurants, though we hear the most pleasant time to come is actually for breakfast (DM6.50 to DM19.50). Otherwise it brims with people with money to burn on pricey pizzas named after the apostles, and mains of DM30 and up. Part of the appeal is the hilariously over-the-top, church-like decor with lots of Rubenesque cherubs, kitschy frescoes and gaudy chandeliers.

Equally popular is *Ali Baba* (Map 7, ☎ 881 13 50) at No 45. The pizza here is always fresh and the place fills quickly. With prices cresting at DM13 you don't need to be princely rich to eat here (mini pizzas are just DM2). A few doors down at No 55 is *Toto* (Map 7, ☎ 312 54 49), a classic trattoria with chequered tablecloths and honest-to-goodness Italian food. It's not cheap but this ain't Kansas either, and on a crowded night the atmosphere gets quite lively.

Pizzeria Piccola Taormina (Map 7, ☎ 881 47 10, *Uhlandstrasse 29)* is a noisy, blue-walled labyrinth, and with fast, good-value pizzas (from the DM2 mini variety up to a quite filling DM15) and pastas (DM5.50 to DM11) it's possible to escape for DM10 including coffee. Locals like the style, and the aromas wafting along the street can be irresistible.

Kreuzberg *Sale e Tabacchi* (Map 8, ☎ 252 11 55, *Kochstrasse 18)* is an island of good taste not far from the former Checkpoint Charlie. Integrated into the *taz* newspaper headquarters, its tables are often crowded with reporters and editors. The chef likes to

spin culinary creations around exquisite ingredients like lobster tails, artichoke hearts and veal cutlets, which is why it costs between DM20 and DM40 for a main course here. It's open from 9 am to 2 am weekdays, from 10 am weekends.

Mitte Some restaurants manage to transcend trends and offer consistently reliable food. One of them is *Cantamaggio* (Map 4, ☎ 283 18 95, *Alte Schönhauser Strasse 4)*, which doled out delicious pasta and more substantial mains (DM17 to DM30) long before tour operators 'discovered' the Scheunenviertel. Tables here are always crowded – sometimes with actors and directors from the nearby Volksbühne – so phone ahead for reservations.

One of the hippest trattorias in town is *Lappeggi* (Map 4, ☎ 442 63 47, *Kollwitzstrasse 56)* in Prenzlauer Berg, frequented by a mixed clientele of artists, actors, media types and managers. What they all have in common is fat wallets and appreciation for the exquisite concoctions coming out of the kitchen. There's a nice terrace with a view of the Kollwitzplatz scene.

Fressco (Map 4, ☎ 282 96 47, *Oranienburger Strasse 48-49)*, a nonsmoker deli clad in beautiful Mediterranean tiles, offers freshly prepared quiches, baguette sandwiches, casseroles, salads and the like at merciful prices (mostly under DM10). Hours are from 9.30 am to 2 am daily. A second branch *(Map 6, ☎ 25 29 93 09, Stresemannstrasse 34)* in Kreuzberg is much quieter, except during lunch-time rush hour.

Zucca (Map 8, ☎ 24 72 12 12, *Am Zwirngraben, S-Bahn arches 11 and 12)* is an elegant bar and dining hall with such design accents as mirrors, chandeliers and antique-style murals. The food is Italian and changes often; check the blackboard for daily specials priced from DM15 to DM23. Ciabatta sandwiches can be had for around DM10, and the cappuccino is delicious.

Die Zwölf Apostel (Map 8, ☎ 201 02 22, *Georgenstrasse 177-180)* is the less sophisticated clone of the XII Apostoli in Charlottenburg. Tourists unwind here over huge pizzas baked in the woodfire oven and sold at half price until 5 pm. You'll be dining beneath the vaulted S-Bahn arches covered with colourful biblical scenes. Open daily from 9 am to 1 am.

Schöneberg & Kreuzberg

Petite Europe (Map 5, ☎ 781 29 64, Langenscheidtstrasse 1) has a local neighbourhood feel and serves good-value, no-nonsense Italian food in a rustic setting. It's very popular, so show up early if you want a table or, better yet, call for a reservation. Dinner only.

Another excellent bet is *Lucky Pizzeria (Map 5, ☎ 781 12 93, Willmanndamm 15)* where the pizza comes in three sizes. It's cosy, cheap and congenial and has been around for 30 years – which is saying something in ever-changing Berlin. Dinner only.

Flavour-packed fare is what you'll find at *Trattoria á Muntagnola (Map 7, ☎ 211 66 42, Fuggerstrasse 27)*. Garlic strings and heavy chandeliers dangle from the beamed ceiling above red-and-white chequered tablecloths. Fresh pasta dishes are priced around DM20, though meaty fare is more.

Japanese

Sachiko Sushi (Map 7, ☎ 313 22 82, S-Bahn Arch 584) in Charlottenburg is a floating sushi bar. Sushi servings, sitting on plates coloured to correspond with the price, float by you in a little 'river' built into the oval bar. Your final tab is calculated by adding up the plates (DM7 to DM10 each). Best buy is the lunch special which gets you three plates plus all the green tea you can drink for DM17.

At *Sushi-Bar (Map 4, ☎ 281 51 88, Friedrichstrasse 115)* in Mitte, artistic sushi plates cost DM15 to DM20. *Nigiri* (bars of rice topped with fish slices) cost DM4 to DM6 per two-piece serving and *maki-sushi* (rice roll with various fillings wrapped in seaweed) tops out at DM15. The food is always fresh and excellent and the Sushi-Bar is open from noon (from 2 pm weekends) until 10 pm.

You wouldn't expect to find one of Berlin's best – and most reasonably priced – sushi bars in working-class Neukölln, but that's just where *Tabibito (Map 6,*

☎ 624 13 45, Karl-Marx-Strasse 56) makes its home. Authentic and intimate, what's on the menu depends on the season and on what chef Mitsuru himself picks up during his daily trips to the Hamburg port. Sushi platters (eight nigiri and six maki pieces) cost DM34. Teriyaki, tempura and yakitori all go for under DM20. This place is a real find. Dinner only, closed Tuesday.

Many sushi places are more like takeaways than proper restaurants. In Schöneberg, *Kiraku Sushi (Map 5, ☎ 216 52 02, Motzstrasse 9)* is clean and reasonably priced with nigiri portions for DM7 to DM10. Open daily, closed until 4 pm Sunday. Also recommended in this district is *Flying Fish Sushi (Map 5, ☎ 782 06 63, Eisenacher Strasse 67)*.

The plainly named *Sushi (Map 7, ☎ 881 27 90, Pariser Strasse 44)* in Wilmersdorf has a 'six-pack' of rolled salmon-avocado pieces for DM5.50 and nigiri from DM5. Open daily, closed until 4 pm Sunday. There's a second branch (Map 5) in Schöneberg at Goltzstrasse 24.

Jewish

Several Berlin restaurants now serve certified Kosher food, reflecting the city's growing Jewish community. The oldest – and a bit old-fashioned – is *Arche Noah (Map 7, ☎ 882 61 38, Fasanenstrasse 79)* inside the Jewish Community House in Charlottenburg. Besides the quite expansive à la carte menu, multicourse dinners are served daily for DM21, DM24 and DM26. The Tuesday night hot and cold buffet with 30 items for DM35 starts at 6.30 pm. Restaurant hours are from 11.30 am to 3.30 pm and from 6.30 to 11 pm Sunday to Friday. Lunch only on Saturday.

Beth Café (Map 4, ☎ 281 31 35, Tucholskystrasse 10) in Mitte is a good-value cafe-bistro with a pretty inner courtyard. Come here for lox on toast, salads, gefilte fish and other staples of Jewish cuisine. It's affiliated with the congregation of Adass Jisroel and open from 11 am to 10 pm daily except Saturday (to 8 pm Monday).

To stock up on matzo balls, Manischevitz and gefilte fish, try *Plätzl (Map 7, ☎ 217 75 06, Passauer Strasse 4)*, a Kosher grocery

PLACES TO EAT

store and deli opposite the KaDeWe department store. In the same vein are **Kolbo** *(Map 4, ☎ 281 31 35, Auguststrasse 77-78)* in Mitte and **Schalom** *(Map 7, ☎ 312 11 31, Wielandstrasse 43)* in Charlottenburg.

A few other restaurants also serve Jewish and Israeli food, but they don't have the Kashrut certificate. Best know among them is the stylish **Café Oren** *(Map 4, ☎ 282 82 28, Oranienburger Strasse 28)* in Mitte where the food has a heavy Middle Eastern influence. The Orient-Express (DM19), a platter loaded with a good variety of mezze (appetisers) is a favourite. The menu is in Hebrew, English and German, and you can read foreign language newspapers. Open from 10 am to 1 am daily. Reservations are advised.

A newish entry up the street is **Rimón** *(Map 4, ☎ 28 38 40 32, Oranienburger Strasse 26)* which has some eastern European specialities like latkes and blintzes in addition to Middle Eastern foods like felafel, hummus and couscous. Prices range from DM15 to DM20 for mains. (Also see Rimón Imbiss in the Snacks & Fast Food section later in this chapter.)

Right by the Rykestrasse synagogue in Prenzlauer Berg is **Am Wasserturm** *(Map 4, ☎ 442 8807), Knaackstrasse 22)*. Its extensive menu goes far beyond the usual Jewish food with interesting concoctions, including some vegie choices, for all budgets. In fine weather, the sunny outdoor terrace is the place to be.

Mexican
Tres Kilos *(Map 6, ☎ 693 60 44, Marheinekeplatz 3)*, a chic Mexican cantina and restaurant, has been a mainstay of Kreuzberg sophisticates for years. Sipping a spine-tingling margarita while surveying the scene from the terrace is definitely a summer ritual. Inside, the brightly pigmented decor goes well with the jalapeño-packed fare, which is good but on the overpriced side (burritos DM20 and up). Dinner nightly.

Next door at No 4 is the equally popular but much more low-key **Locus** *(Map 6, ☎ 691 56 37)* which is also cheaper. Yet another contender, more rustic and cheaper

still, is the **Lone Star Taqueria** *(Map 6, ☎ 692 71 82, Bergmannstrasse 11)*. Mains here are priced from DM7.50 to DM20 and there's a happy hour from 5 to 8 pm.

Las Cucarachas *(Map 4, ☎ 282 20 44, Oranienburger Strasse 38)* in Mitte has rather mediocre food but is always buzzing with Berliners and tourists alike. Mains start at DM10, though you're more likely to spend twice that.

A winner in Prenzlauer Berg is **Frida Kahlo** *(Map 4, ☎ 445 70 16, Lychener Strasse 37)*, a lively restaurant-bar decked out in colourful canvasses. The scene is as lively as the decor most nights. In summer, the action spills out onto the pavement with views of Helmholtz square. Open from 10 am daily.

Mixed in among the American diners along Pariser Strasse in Wilmersdorf is **Poco Loco** *(Map 7, ☎ 881 18 68, Pariser Strasse 18)* which looks kitschy yet fun, with poster-covered walls and colourful dolls and figurines dangling from the ceiling. The food's good and filling, and served from 3 pm to the early morning.

Middle Eastern & Russian
If you'd like to be transported to Egypt, venture to the magical world of **Der Ägypter** *(Map 7, ☎ 313 92 30, Kantstrasse 26)* in Charlottenburg, filled with the tantalising scents of exotic dishes. Most include a sampler of bread and appetisers centred around felafel, fuul (spicy beans), eggplant or lamb. Prices range from DM14 to DM30. Dinner only.

Pasternak *(Map 4, ☎ 441 33 99, Knaackstrasse 22-24)* was one of the first restaurants in Prenzlauer Berg. Housed in an attractive renovated building, it revives Russian nostalgia with updated versions of traditional favourites (borscht, pelmeni, beef stroganoff) costing around DM20. Dining takes place at heavy wooden tables surrounded by equally sturdy leather chairs. Hours are from 10 am to 2 am daily and reservations are advised.

South-East Asian
Goa *(Map 4, ☎ 28 59 84 51, Oranienburger Strasse 50)* in Mitte is the kind of place

where grown-up hippies, postmodern trendoids and tourists from Dubuque feel equally at home. The menu takes you on a journey around Asia, featuring safe versions of curries, stir-fries, dumplings and the like, including many meatless options (mains from DM15 to DM25). Open from 10 am to the wee hours daily.

Stepping into *Tuk-Tuk (Map 5, ☎ 781 15 88, Grossgörschenstrasse 2)* in Schöneberg, feels like walking into an intimate bamboo den in Jakarta. Here you can dine on meat-based (from DM20) or vegetarian (from DM18) Indonesian dishes while listening to soothing gamelan music. Dinner only.

The *Angkor Wat (Map 3, ☎ 393 39 22, Paulstrasse 22)* in Tiergarten, is an exotic, cavernous place that serves Cambodian fondue, which involves cooking your own meat and vegies in a cauldron right at your table (DM60 for two). Other, usually coconut milk-based, dishes go for around DM20. Dinner only weekdays, lunch and dinner weekends.

Spanish & Latin American

Barbar Bar (Map 7, ☎ 313 38 08, Krumme Strasse 41), located in Charlottenburg is a romantically candle-lit place with picture windows and a small menu of Spanish-themed chicken and vegetarian dishes all under DM15.

El Borriquito (Map 7, ☎ 312 99 29, Wielandstrasse 6) nearby offers a rustic Spanish country-inn atmosphere and a menu that runs the gamut of pork, beef, lamb and fish dishes. The paella for DM18.50 is excellent, but vegetarians should go elsewhere. Mains range from DM15 to DM25. Dinner only.

Don Quijote (Map 7, ☎ 881 32 08, Bleibtreustrasse 41) has excellent tapas and fish. It's open for dinner on weekdays as well as for Sunday lunch.

In Mitte, *Brazil (Map 4, ☎ 208 63 13, Gormannstrasse 22)* is a cavernous, trendy place that tries to re-create the lost grandeur of the colonial era. Specialities include *frango estufado* (chicken braised in wine) for DM18, though many guests are partial to the appetiser platters for DM15.

The salads from DM10 are fresh and excellent too. Dinner only.

Bar-Celona (Map 4, ☎ 282 91 53, Hannoversche Strasse 2) is a friendly restaurant-bar near the Brecht-Weigel House. It serves delicious paella for DM20 to DM26 (two person minimum) and tapas around DM6.

A fashionable crowd, munching on tapas, tortillas and bocadillas starting at DM3, enjoys the lively atmosphere at *Pasodoble (Map 5, ☎ 784 52 44, Crellestrasse 39)* in Schöneberg. Full dishes cost around DM20. Dinner only, closed Sunday.

Thai

Thai-Vietnamese cooking in its infinite variety is on the menu at *Sticks (Map 7, ☎ 312 90 42, Knesebeckstrasse 15)*, making it likely that you'll find your favourite among the fragrant rice dishes and duck and seafood specialities. Mains range from DM16.50 to DM22.50, the lunch menu (served from noon to 6 pm) is DM15, and there's even a separate vegetarian menu. On Sunday it's dinner only.

Another Thai option is *Kamala (Map 4, ☎ 283 27 97, Oranienburger Strasse 69)* in Mitte, an immensely popular petite basement eatery that's usually packed to the gills. The plain decor contrasts with the colourful dishes, including lip-smacking curries and noodles, with meat and vegetarian varieties (main courses DM15.50 to DM20).

At *Mao Thai (Map 4, ☎ 441 92 61, Wörther Strasse 30)* in Prenzlauer Berg, the menu is as intriguing as the carved statuettes and original Asian art. The celeb-heavy crowd comes for the sublime Thai cuisine which has complex flavouring and can be quite spicy. Prices are up there but for budget gourmets there's a lunch menu for DM14.50 (served until 4 pm weekdays). Make reservations.

Turkish

Despite the huge number of Turks that call Berlin home, there are relatively few Turkish restaurants, though there are countless doner kebab takeaway places.

A hit with both meat lovers and vegetarians alike is *Hitit (Map 5, ☎ 322 45 57,*

PLACES TO EAT

Knobelsdorffstrasse 35) in Charlottenburg, a cool and elegant eatery with wall reliefs and a marble fountain. The appetiser platter is a winner, though main courses (DM15 to DM30) of grilled meat, as well as the vegetarian casseroles, convince as well. Service is good too.

Although named after the Iraqi capital, *Bagdad (Map 6, ☎ 612 69 62, Schlesische Strasse 1)* in Kreuzberg 36 has mostly Turkish mains (DM11 to DM20) and salads from DM4, served at dinner time only (closed Monday).

Merhaba (Map 6, ☎ 692 17 13, Hasenheide 39) is Berlin's only gourmet Turkish restaurant, and it's also in Kreuzberg. The decor is contemporary and the outdoor garden is pleasant, but there's much debate about whether the quality of the primarily meat-based mains justifies their prices (DM20 to DM30).

In Mitte is *Malete (Map 4, ☎ 280 77 59, Chausseestrasse 131)*, a friendly, low-key cafe-restaurant. Interesting salads cost around DM10, vegetarian dishes cost from DM10 to DM19.50 and flavourful meaty fare starts at DM20. Open from 9 am to 1 am weekdays, from 10 am to 2 am weekends.

Derya (Map 4, ☎ 281 75 36, Chausseestrasse 116), a few steps away, is similar but has the added asset of a sprawling beer garden anchored by a sprightly fountain. There's an emphasis on vegetarian dishes. Open from 8 am daily.

Prenzlauer Berg has *Miro (Map 4, ☎ 44 73 30 13, Raumerstrasse 29)*, where you'll dine in an exotic environment designed by owner/artist Adnan Kalkanci. Seating is at tables or on traditional pillows. Vegetarians won't feel left out here. Open from 10 am to midnight daily.

Vegetarian

In meat-heavy Germany, vegetarians usually have a tough time, but in cosmopolitan Berlin there are more choices than elsewhere. Most restaurants and cafes now offer at least one vegetarian dish as well as a range of fresh salads. Best bets are ethnic eateries, especially Indian, Thai and Vietnamese places, some of which are completely vegetarian. Places

listed below specifically cater for herbivores, though for more options also check the other restaurant listings where we've usually noted if vegetarian meals are available.

Samadhi (Map 7, ☎ 313 10 67, Goethestrasse 6) in Charlottenburg is ideal for vegetarians hankering after an Asian fix. A wide selection of fragrant dishes covers the bases from Vietnamese to Indian to Chinese to Thai, but it's all prepared authentically and as spicy as you can stand. Appetisers/main courses start at DM8/16. The weekday lunch menu is DM11.50. Saturday dinners are nonsmoking.

For simple vegetarian fare, try *Einhorn (Map 7, ☎ 881 42 41, Mommsenstrasse 2)* near Bleibtreustrasse in Charlottenburg. It has a buffet with salads from DM2.60 per 100g and main dishes from DM6. Hours are from 9 am to 6.30 pm on weekdays and from 10 am to 4 pm on Saturday.

The vegetarian gourmet won't want to miss *Abendmahl (Map 6, ☎ 612 51 70, Muskauer Strasse 9)* in Kreuzberg 36, whose inventive menu also includes fish dishes. Starters cost from DM8, main courses from DM25. The restaurant name means 'The Last Supper', which may explain the Catholic kitsch decor. Dinner only.

Another good place is *Naturkost Vegetarisches Buffet (Map 6, ☎ 694 29 82, Mehringdamm 48)* in Kreuzberg 61, which has takeaway or sit-down choices. Blackboard specials are under DM10. It's open from 9 am to 6.30 pm weekdays, from noon to 2 pm Saturday.

For a journey into the vegetable kingdom, head to the *Little Shop of Foods (Map 4, ☎ 44 05 64 44, Kollwitzstrasse 90)*, more of a restaurant than a shop, despite the name. It's a no-nonsense environment enlivened with beautiful floral tiles and wainscotting. The chef makes use of whatever is fresh and in season which results in delicious, sometimes eccentric, dishes from DM6 to DM13.

CAFES

Cafes are an inspired German institution and the number and variety of them in Berlin is astonishing. They're wonderful places to relax over a cup of coffee while reading a newspaper or magazine or chatting away with friends. The afternoon *Kaffee und Kuchen* (coffee and cake) is a German cafe tradition, though these days it's mostly practised by the older generations.

Most cafes are casual eateries attracting people of all ages and walks of life. Most have expanded their culinary repertoire to include hot and cold snacks and some even serve more substantial meals.

Cafes usually change identity in a chameleon-like way over the course of a day, starting out as a breakfast place, then offering a small lunch menu and cakes in the afternoon before turning into a restaurant-bar or just a bar at night. In fact, many places listed here would fit just as well into the earlier Restaurant section or the Pubs & Bars section of the Entertainment chapter.

Charlottenburg

Café Kranzler (Map 7, ☎ 882 69 11, Kurfürstendamm 18-19), near Zoo station, is one of Berlin's oldest coffee houses and a traditional *Konditorei* (cake shop). Since it largely caters to tourists now, it has expanded its menu to everything from pasta to schnitzel to spare ribs. The terrace is good for people-watching, though when it's crowded (and it usually is), the service can be quite lame. It's open from 8 am to midnight daily. Another Ku'damm institution with yummy cakes and a less commercial flair is *Café Möhring (Map 7, ☎ 881 20 75)* at No 213.

Those with a sweet tooth should not miss *Leysieffer (Map 7, ☎ 882 79 61, Kurfürstendamm 218)*. The shop on the ground floor sells a mouthwatering bonanza of chocolates and truffles, while the courtly cafe-bistro upstairs serves refined pastries and savoury morsels beneath tall stuccoed ceilings and mirrored walls. It's open from 9 am to 8 pm Monday to Saturday, from 10 am to 6 pm Sunday.

A well-known classic inside the Literaturhaus is *Café Wintergarten (Map 7, ☎ 882 54 14, Fasanenstrasse 23)*, a cosy oasis for deep conversation over a simple coffee or delicious international fare (around DM20). In summer the garden tables are the most coveted. It's open from 9.30 am to 1 am daily.

The Joy of Breakfast

One of life's little luxuries is a leisurely breakfast, and Berliners have just about perfected the art. Any day of the week, a motley bunch of the city's hungover, idle rich, students and late risers gather at the countless breakfast cafes to tuck into big plates of eggs, meats, cheeses, breads, butter, jam and a plethora of other foods.

On Sunday, many places set up fantastic brunch buffets that may include various salads, lox and cream cheese, quiches, pasta, hot meats and whatever else takes the chef's fancy that day. It's easy to pig out at these all-you-can-eat banquets.

Pricewise, breakfasts can cost as little as DM5 for coffee, a croissant and jam, or as much as DM20 for a lavish spread. Most cafes serve breakfast until 4 or 5 pm. Try the following breakfast spots which do more than scramble a few eggs and serve coffee. They are all explained in greater detail in this chapter or in the Entertainment chapter.

Charlottenburg
Aschinger, XII Apostoli, Café Aedes, Café Hardenberg, Café Kranzler, Café Wintergarten, Lubitsch, Schwarzes Café

Kreuzberg
Atlantic, Café Adler, Advena, Barcomi's, Hannibal, Kichererbse, Café Morena, Weltrestaurant Markthalle

Mitte
Aedes East, Barcomi's, Café Einstein Unter den Linden, Gugelhof, Hackescher Hof, Café Orange

Prenzlauer Berg
Houdini, Istoria, November, Schall und Rauch, Anita Wronski

Schöneberg
Café Berio, Café Einstein, Café Lux, Café M, Café Mirell, Montevideo, Café Sidney, TTT

PLACES TO EAT

Café Aedes (Map 7, ☎ 31 50 95 35, S-Bahn Arch 599), right outside Savignyplatz S-Bahn station, has become the 'in' haunt of Berlin architects whose work is often shown in the adjacent gallery. The interior is as cool as its customers, though you may have to raise your voice occasionally when the trains rumble overhead. Hours are from 8 am to midnight daily.

Comfy as an old shoe, *Schwarzes Café (Map 7, ☎ 313 80 38, Kantstrasse 148)* has made a career out of being a favourite lair of students, travellers and post-60s hippies. Best seating is in the tiny enclosed courtyard. Breakfast is served around the clock (from DM8.50) in this 24-hour cafe. It's also famous for its – ahem – creatively designed toilets.

Students from the art school and technical university across the street treat *Café Hardenberg (Map 7, ☎ 312 26 44, Hardenbergstrasse 10)* as an extension of the student cafeteria. Open from 9 am to 1 am, it's usually full, which can have a deleterious effect on the service, so pack some patience.

Friedrichshain

Of the many new places that have sprung up in this district, a few stand out for their congenial atmosphere and cheap prices. *Conmux (Map 6, ☎ 29138 63, Simon-Dach-Strasse 35)* in the heart of the main drag, has industrial decor and builds a menu around vegies, meat and fish prepared in a home-style way. Filling mains range from DM8 to DM15. Open 10 am to 2 am daily.

Nearby is *Truxa (Off Map 6, ☎ 29 00 30 85, Wühlischstrasse 30)*, a friendly establishment which does everything from ciabatta sandwiches to pasta, nachos to fish, all at budget prices (DM8 to DM18). Tapas are DM3 to DM6. Open from around 3 pm daily.

Kreuzberg

Café Adler (Map 8, ☎ 251 89 65, Friedrichstrasse 206), across from where Checkpoint Charlie once stood and facing the famous 'You Are Now Leaving the American Sector' sign, is a friendly place, even if most of its customers are tourists. It's open from 9 am to midnight daily.

Hannibal (Map 6, ☎ 611 23 88, Wiener Strasse 69), situated in Kreuzberg 36, is a happening contempo cafe with seats from old S-Bahns and lamps that look like upturned hubcaps. It's open from 8 am to 3 am daily (from 9 am Sunday), and there are lots of dishes around DM10, including burgers and salads.

Always busy, *Café Morena (Map 6, ☎ 611 47 16, Wiener Strasse 60)* is a Kreuzberg 36 classic with a Spanish twist. Best thing: their pancakes, piled high with fruit and drizzled with maple syrup, served until 5 pm. Bagels, burgers, omelettes and other goodies have also carved out their niches on the menu. Open from 9 am to 4 am daily.

Right on Bergmannstrasse, the main drag in Kreuzberg 61, is *Atlantic (Map 6, ☎ 691 92 92, Bergmannstrasse 100)*, a communicative corner cafe that's usually packed with hipsters and young families. It's a great place to absorb the local scene. Open daily from 9 am to 2 am.

Barcomi's (Map 6, ☎ 694 81 38, Bergmannstrasse 21), is a hole-in-the-wall coffee shop that's as busy as Grand Central Station during rush hour. Main attractions are the freshly roasted coffees which go well with the equally fresh muffins and bagels. Open 9 am to midnight daily, from 10 am Sunday.

For a change in taste, you could try one of the Arabic breakfasts at the popular *Kichererbse (Map 6, ☎ 694 98 69, Bergmannstrasse 96)*, which is open from 10 am to 1 am. Choose from eight combinations, including the *Khan-El Khalili* which gets you Egyptian beans, fetta, felafel, salad and fruit for DM10. If you're not having breakfast, sample the couscous dishes or vegetable casseroles, which are all reasonably priced.

A jewel in downtrodden Neukölln is *Café Rix (Map 6, ☎ 686 90 20, Karl-Marx-Strasse 141)* with a lovely Art Deco ambience combined with gold-leaf stucco ceilings. The cross cultural menu ranges from felafels to tagliatelle to tortilla chips, all of them cheap (under DM15). If the smoke gets too heavy, you can always sit in the nice, quiet courtyard.

Mitte

If not invaded by bus-tripping tourists, *Café Orange (Map 4, ☎ 282 00 28, Oranienburger Strasse 32)*, next to the New Synagogue, is a smart hangout with lofty stucco ceilings and a pleasant atmosphere. Pizza, pasta and salads are surprisingly affordable (under DM10), though more substantial meat and fish dishes cost around DM20. Or you can just come for people-watching and a huge (though pricey) cup of coffee. It's open from 9 am to 1 am daily.

In S-Bahn arch No 192 on Georgenstrasse near Museumsinsel is *Cafe Odéon* (Map 8), which has coffee and cake as well as small snacks like quiche lorraine and sausages for DM7 to DM9. The walls are plastered with old-fashioned, enamelled advertising signs. It's open from 10 am to 7 pm Sunday to Thursday, to midnight on Friday and Saturday.

Unlike it's Kreuzberg cousin, Mitte's *Barcomi's (Map 4, ☎ 28 59 83 63, Sophienstrasse 21)* is more of a deli than a cafe, though you can still get bagels, muffins and coffee. Other options include marinated cheeses and delicious but expensive build-your-own sandwiches. It's located in the central courtyard of the Sophienhöfe. Hours are from 9 am to 10 pm (from 10 am Sunday).

Inside the nearby Hackescher Höfe is a clone of Charlottenburg's Café Aedes, called *Aedes East (Map 8, ☎ 282 21 03)*. Thankfully, the atmosphere here is more relaxed and the bistro menu – featuring ratatouille, tortelloni and the like for around DM15 – is quite acceptable. It's open from 10 am daily.

Prenzlauer Berg

Houdini (Map 4, ☎ 441 25 60, Lychener Strasse 35) has popular breakfasts served until 5 pm and candle-lit dinners of soups, pasta and potato dishes, mostly under DM10. At the split-level *Anita Wronski (Map 4, ☎ 442 84 83, Knaackstrasse 26-28)*, one of the original Prenzlauer Berg cafes, you can observe locals and tourists at play, though the view of the historic water tower through the picture windows is also

enjoyable. It's a popular breakfast place on weekends (served until 3 pm) and is open from 10 am to 3 am.

Sparse, uncluttered decor characterises *November (Map 4, ☎ 442 84 25, Husemannstrasse 15)*, a friendly corner cafe whose huge picture windows give you that fishbowl feeling. It's perfect for a quiet chat over a strong cuppa (or beer, if you prefer). Breakfast is served until afternoon. Open from 10 am to 2 am daily.

Schöneberg

Cafes belong to Schöneberg like froth belongs on cappuccino. The two-level *Café Berio (Map 5, ☎ 216 19 46, Maassenstrasse 7)* offers classical music and cakes that are as sweet as the gooiest love letter. It's pretty trendy and especially busy during Saturday's Winterfeldtplatz market. At night it's swarmed by the gay crowd. Hours are from 9 am to 1.30 am daily.

Café Sidney (Map 5, ☎ 216 52 53, Winterfeldtstrasse 40) has a loosely inspired Australian theme that incorporates chrome, wicker and palm trees. It's open from 9 am to 3 am Friday and Saturday (to 2 pm on other days), but it's best on Saturday morning when the picture windows provide front-row seats of the market.

For a perfectly prepared cup of tea, try *TTT (Map 5, ☎ 21 75 22 40, Goltzstrasse 2)*, a serene place decorated with East Asian aesthetic restraint. The afternoon tea (DM16, served from 4 to 6 pm) is a rich spread including a pot of your choice, sandwiches, scones and cookies. All teas – some 150 varieties – are also available for purchase. Hours are from 8.30 am to midnight daily (from 10 am Sunday).

Cult status goes to *Café M (Map 5, ☎ 216 70 92, Goltzstrasse 33)* despite decor that's as grungy as a train station waiting room. (Actually, this is rather fitting given the place's original name 'Mitropa', after a train catering service company. Ordered to drop the name, the owners simply shortened it to M.) It's overpriced and overrated but the cool and trendy keep coming, and so it's still a good place to take in the scene. Open from 8 am to the wee hours.

euro currency converter DM1 = €.51

PLACES TO EAT

Next door, at No 35, is the much more low-key and multicultural **Café Lux** (Map 5, ☎ 215 96 74) which features kaleidoscopic canvases and killer cakes. Open from 9 am to 3 am.

Big breakfasts under potted palm trees is what you get at **Café Mirell** (Map 5, ☎ 782 04 57, Crellestrasse 46), open from 8 am daily (from 9 am Sunday). In the evening the kitchen switches to inexpensive Italian and Oriental dishes, and there's a budget-priced appetiser menu as well.

Montevideo (Map 7, ☎ 213 10 20, Viktoria-Luise-Platz 6) has mirrored walls, the cool charm of an American diner and breakfasts from around the world (Japanese, American, Canadian, Dutch, Italian, Finnish etc) from DM9.50 to DM19. Opening hours are from 8 am to 2 am daily (from 10 am Sunday).

Tiergarten

Berlin's most elegant cafe is **Café Einstein** (Map 5, ☎ 261 50 96, Kurfürstenstrasse 58), a Viennese-style coffee house ensconced in a rambling historic villa. In summer, you can enjoy your bean – perhaps in tandem with a slice of delicious apple strudel – in the orchard out back. If you're seriously hungry, you can dig into rich Austrian food with main courses priced around DM30. The staff, alas, tend to be a bit precious. Open daily 10 am to 2 am. A second branch is at Unter den Linden 42 (Map 8), where some tables are literally beneath the linden trees in the median strip of this boulevard.

Balmy summer nights are the best time to be at the **Café am Neuen See** (Map 7, ☎ 254 49 30, Lichtensteinallee 1), a lakeside oasis in the Tiergarten park. Beer garden service can be pretty slow but that just gives you more time for people-watching and looking out over the lake. Hours are from 8 am to midnight, February to October. The rest of the year, it's open from 10 am to 10 pm only at weekends.

SNACKS & FAST FOOD

Berlin is a paradise for snackers who are on the go, with Turkish, Greek, Italian, Middle Eastern, Chinese – you name it – specialities available at Imbiss stands and stalls throughout the city.

Soup Kultur (Map 7, ☎ 74 30 82 95, Kurfürstendamm 224) near Zoo station in Charlottenburg is a pint-sized stand-up place operated by a young team that serves delicious soups from around the world, from hearty potato to refreshing gazpacho to exotic South African sousboontje. Prices range from DM4.90 to DM8.50.

Nearby, **Gosch** (Map 7, ☎ 88 68 28 00, Kurfürstendamm 212) is a branch of the legendary fish bistro on Sylt island in the North Sea. It's a wonderful place for superbly fresh fish, from takeaway sandwiches for DM3 to more substantial fare like salmon and tuna steaks.

Bagels are making inroads into German food consciousness, partly thanks to a new chain called **Salomon Bagels** where the lowly bagel is treated with spiritual reverence. (The back of the menu features a lengthy dissertation entitled 'The history of the bagel as seen from a Solomonic standpoint'.) Be that as it may, this is a friendly establishment that serves tasty sandwiches for around DM6; bagels alone are DM1.50 each. Branches are at Joachimstaler Strasse 13 (Map 7, ☎ 881 81 96) in Charlottenburg and at the Potsdamer Platz Arkaden mall (☎ 25 29 76 26); see the Potsdamer Platz map in the Things to See and Do chapter.

Another one to try is **Bagels & Bialys** (Map 8, Rosenthaler Strasse 46-47), a trailblazer of the bagel trend. Located near the Hackesche Höfe in Mitte, it is a popular place for tourists to sustain their stamina and – with hours to 3 am – the night-time crowd's as well. Also on the menu: submarine sandwiches and shwarma.

For sumptuous Spanish-style toasted sandwiches, packed with ingredients like mozzarella or gorgonzola, tomato and salami (DM3 to DM5), head to the **Sandwich Kiosk** on Heinrichplatz (Oranienstrasse) in Kreuzberg (to 7 pm daily).

Nearby is the newest branch of **Habibi** (Map 6, Oranienstrasse 30), a granddaddy of Berlin's felafel and shwarma circuit whose original establishment at Winterfeldtplatz 24 in Schöneberg (Map 5) is as busy as a beehive all day long. With opening hours until 3 am (until 5 am weekends), it's a favourite place to indulge midnight snack attacks of the night-time crowds frequenting area bars. A third branch is also in Schöneberg at Akazienstrasse 9 (Map 5).

Some people give **Rimón Imbiss** *(Map 4, ☎ 28 38 40 32, Oranienburger Strasse 26)* even higher marks for its mouthwatering felafel sandwiches. These literally spill over with fresh vegetables and a trio of fluffy chick-pea balls all smothered in a tangy, garlicky sauce. At DM4.80 each, they're a dream come true for the cash-strapped. This is the takeaway of the restaurant by the same name (details in the Jewish section earlier this chapter).

Want the best doner kebab this side of Istanbul? Drop by the **Rosenthaler Imbiss** *(Map 4)*, a short distance away on Rosenthaler Platz in Mitte, right outside the north-western U-Bahn exit. Do not confuse this one with the other Imbiss immediately to the left. For around DM4.50, the portions are huge, the meat is light (not greasy) and is shaved into thin slivers, the bread is toasted to perfection, the salads are fresh and the yoghurt sauce has just the right amount of garlic.

Taco Rico *(Map 5, ☎ 23 62 13 43, Martin-Luther-Strasse 21)* in Schöneberg is a good place for those hankering for decent Mexican food but who are unwilling to pay the inflated prices of regular restaurants. Here you can fill up on enchiladas and burritos for well under DM10.

Dogs go haute at the memorably named **Hot Dog** *(Map 5, ☎ 215 69 32, Goltzstrasse 15)*. Purists' will find their tastes satisfied, while more adventurous types might want to order the dog buried beneath a heap of aromatic chilli. Vegetarian varieties are available too.

On the same street is **Fish & Vegetables** *(Map 5, ☎ 821 68 16, Goltzstrasse 32)*, an Imbiss and takeaway with stellar budget-priced Thai dishes (the Pad Thai noodles are a killer) which you watch being made to order in the steamy open kitchen. The stand-up tables are always full (sharing is OK) and there's nothing over DM10 on the menu.

Across the street is **Shayan** *(Map 5, ☎ 215 15 47, Goltzstrasse 23)* with Persian delicacies. Sandwiches are DM5, rice dishes DM7 to DM9 and kebabs DM5 to DM18.

Queue up with the rest of them at **Asia Pavillion** inside the Potsdamer Platz Arkaden mall. At DM4.50, huge plates of steaming hot fried noodles just fly over the counter, and most everything else is less than DM10.

Another place for a quick, cheap meal is the **Nordsee** chain, with outlets throughout town, including one at Karl-Liebknecht-Strasse 6 *(Map 8, ☎ 213 98 33)* near Alexanderplatz. It specialises in fish and seafood and has excellent sandwiches to go from DM2.80. The food is clean, fresh and tasty and available from 10 am to 9 pm daily (from 11 am Sunday).

FOOD COURTS

The food hall on the 6th floor of the **KaDeWe** *(Map 7, Tauentzienstrasse 21)* is legendary. Pick from a dozen varieties of caviar, a scrumptious selection of antipasti and a mind-boggling assortment of cheese and sausages (1800 varieties of each, we are told). It's all beautifully presented and interspersed with small bars and food counters where the moneyed cap off successful shopping sprees with a glass of Moet & Chandon (DM16.50). Putting together a picnic here will cost you a bundle, though, and you may fill your stomach more cheaply – and just as well – in the cafe on the 7th floor.

Wertheim bei Hertie *(Map 7, Ku'damm 231)* also has a nice, less precious and pricey selection, and a good cafe as well.

Galeries Lafayette *(Map 8, Friedrich-stadtpassagen)*, which is situated outside Französische Strasse U-Bahn station, has a basement food court where gourmets with deep pockets perch at polished counters, sliding oysters down their gullets or digging into plates of calamari rings served on a bed of arugula.

For much more reasonable prices and delicious down-to-earth food, simply wander a couple of buildings south to the small cluster of self-service counters in the basement of **Quartier 205** (Map 8). The bistro on the right has appetising rice and noodle dishes straight from the pan for around DM12, while NK Insel on the left serves filling pasta dishes for DM7 to DM9. For dessert you can pick up a scrumptious pastry from the bakery in the centre.

The new Potsdamer Platz Arkaden mall (see the Potsdamer Platz map in Things to See & Do) also has a few eating choices in the basement, plus a couple of excellent eateries outlined under Snacks & Fast Food earlier in this chapter.

STUDENT CAFETERIAS

These are called *Mensa* at German universities, which comes from the Latin for 'table' and has nothing to do with the elite intellectual society. Indeed, you don't have to be a genius to realise that these places are some of the best dining deals in Berlin. Anyone, student or not, may eat at the **Technische Universität Mensa** *(Map 7, Hardenbergstrasse 34)* on the 1st floor (the entrance is across from Steinplatz). Non-students pay slightly more, but you can still fill your tray with a three-course lunch for under DM10. It's open from 11.15 am to 2.30 pm weekdays. The *cafe* on the ground floor is open from 8 am to 7.45 pm and has drinks, snacks and basic mains for DM4 or DM5. On the 2nd floor is a smaller restaurant which is slightly more expensive (three courses for about DM12).

The **Humboldt Universität Mensa** *(Map 8, Unter den Linden 6)* has the same hours (enter the main portal, take the first door on your left, turn right at the end of the corridor and follow your nose). You must either show student ID (from any university) or pay non-student prices. The **Freie Universität** at Kiebitzweg 6 in Zehlendorf (take the U1 to Thielplatz) has a Mensa as well (same hours).

KANTINEN

On weekdays, you can enjoy a hot subsidised meal (DM5 to DM10) in a government cafeteria where you clear your own table. Each of Berlin's 23 districts has a town hall and all of them have Kantinen open to the public. All serve lunch only.

Central ones include: **Rathaus Charlottenburg** *(Map 3, Otto-Suhr-Allee 100)* near Schloss Charlottenburg (in the basement) and **Rathaus Kreuzberg** *(Map 6, Yorckstrasse 4-11)* on the 10th floor with great views.

Arbeitsämter (employment offices) also have cheap Kantinen. A good one is in **Arbeitsamt IV** *(Map 8, Charlottenstrasse 90)* in northern Kreuzberg on the 5th floor (take the U6 to Kochstrasse).

SELF-CATERING

To prepare your own food, start your shopping at the discount Aldi, Lidl, Plus or Penny Markt supermarket chains, which have outlets throughout Berlin, as well as the less common Tip. You may have to wait in long checkout queues but you will pay considerably less for basic food items. These are also the cheapest places to buy beer and table wines. More upmarket chains include Kaiser's, Reichelt, Spar and Bolle.

Aldi is on Joachimstaler Strasse (Map 7), on the 1st floor opposite Zoo station, at Uhlandstrasse 42 (Map 7) and at Leibnizstrasse 72 (Map 7) near Kantstrasse in Charlottenburg. Tip and Penny Markt are side by side near the corner of Hohenstaufenstrasse and Martin-Luther-Strasse in Schöneberg. Kaiser's locations include outlets on Nollendorfplatz in Schöneberg (Map 5), Wittenbergplatz in Tiergarten (Map 7) and at Bleibtreustrasse 19 in Charlottenburg (Map 7). There's a Plus at Grolmanstrasse 48 (Map 7) nearby. Spar outlets are everywhere as well.

A few tips on German supermarket etiquette: at the checkout, you must pack away your purchases yourself. And you'd better be quick, as you don't want to hold up the queue and draw withering stares from stressed-out hausfraus! Start packing the items away as soon as they've been passed over the scanner or punched into the register. Most Germans bring along re-usable plastic or canvas bags in which to carry their groceries. If you don't have your own, plastic bags are sold for 30 or 50 Pfennig.

The best places to buy fresh produce is at a farmers' market (see the Shopping chapter).

Entertainment

Berliners take their culture, and fun, very seriously. All in all, there are 36 theatres, 49 off-theatres, 22 children's theatres, 14 cabarets, 95 cinemas, 170 museums and 300 galleries.

Berlin's nightlife is spread over seven main areas. For upmarket, mainstream venues, go to Savignyplatz and side streets like Bleibtreustrasse and northern Grolmannstrasse in Charlottenburg. The western theatre district is centred on and around Ku'damm. The area around Gneisenaustrasse, Bergmannstrasse and Marheinekeplatz in Kreuzberg 61 is alternative but with trendy touches, while on Oranienstrasse and Wiener Strasse in Kreuzberg 36 a subcultural, grungy vibe continues to flourish.

Around Winterfeldtplatz in Schöneberg, you'll find fewer tourists and lots of thirty-somethings tip-toeing between their alternative lifestyles and the demands of their careers and parenthood. The area around Nollendorfplatz and along Fuggerstrasse and Motzstrasse is ground zero of Berlin's gay bar and club scene.

Since the Wende, most of the more exciting nightlife has shifted to the eastern districts which are more gritty, experimental and interesting. The energy here is electric with new bars, clubs and restaurants opening in profusion and previously dull streets erupting into life, seemingly overnight.

The newest frontier is Friedrichshain where lots of hip, inexpensive bars and restaurants have sprung up along Simon-Dach-Strasse and around Boxhagener Platz. Rigaer Strasse, north of Frankfurter Allee, is squatter's land and underground cafes and clubs pop up all the time in the occupied buildings. Since these are illegal, they are usually short-lived, forced to close as soon as the cops catch on. You'll have to rely on the kindness of strangers to fill you in on what's hot. (The guys who run the Odyssey hostel – see the Places to Stay chapter – are the most plugged-in people we've found.)

Friedrichshain is now what Prenzlauer Berg was until a couple of years ago. But as the area has been 'discovered' it has lost some of its vibrancy, which is not to say that it isn't fun any more. New and colourful places will be there to discover for some time to come, with the 'old' scene centred around Käthe-Kollwitz-Platz and its side streets, and the bolder places springing up around Helmholtzplatz north of Danziger Strasse.

The spotlight, though, is definitely on Mitte with its great density of bars, clubs and cafes – especially along Oranienburger Strasse, Auguststrasse, Hackescher Markt and adjacent streets. This is the revitalised old Jewish quarter which has evolved into a wonderfully pulsating district, despite an inevitable increase in tourism and commercialism. The eastern theatre district is nearby along Friedrichstrasse.

Listings

The best sources for comprehensive what's-on listings are *Zitty* (DM4) and *tip* (DM4.50). Both are published biweekly and are chock-full with insider tips and in-depth articles that capture the constantly evolving Berlin *Zeitgeist*. *Tip* tends to be more mainstream and for a slightly older crowd, while *Zitty* is a tad edgier. The monthly *Prinz* (DM4.50) and *Berlin Programm* (DM3) are not nearly as up-to-date and happening. Another source is *Ticket*, distributed on Thursday as a free supplement to subscribers of the daily newspaper *Tagesspiegel*, which is also for sale at newsstands for DM1.

For essential news about the perpetually evolving club scene in Berlin, pick up the free bi-weekly *Flyer*, which is available at clubs and bars around town. *030* is a similar publication, though geared more to a teenage audience. All magazines are in German only, but you should be able to make sense of the listings even with a minimal command of the language.

Tickets

Outlets selling tickets to cultural and sports events are scattered all over the city. A commission charge of 15% of the ticket price is customary. Most agencies accept phone reservations with credit cards. If time permits, tickets will be mailed to you; if not, they'll be waiting for you at the box office.

Ticket offices abound in the area around the Ku'damm, including Theaterkasse Centrum (Map 7, ☎ 882 76 11) at Meineckestrasse 25 and Concert & Theaterkasse City (Map 7, tollfree ☎ 0130-71 92 71 or ☎ 313 88 58) at Knesebeckstrasse 10. In Schöneberg, you'll find Box Office Theaterkasse (Map 5, ☎ 215 54 63) at Nollendorfplatz 7. A Showtime Ticket counter (Map 7, ☎ 217 77 54) is in the KaDeWe department store at Tauentzienstrasse 21. See the Theatre section for details on Hekticket which offers 50% off last-minute theatre tickets.

CINEMAS

Films are quite expensive in Berlin and Saturday night tickets to a luxurious multiplex can cost as much as DM17. Seeing a show on *Kinotag* (film day, usually Tuesday or Wednesday) or before 5 pm saves about DM5. Independent neighbourhood theatres are also cheaper, with evening prices ranging from DM10 to DM14. Discounts for students are sometimes available as well.

Foreign films are usually dubbed into German. Look for the acronym 'OF' (Originalfassung) for films screened in the original language (no subtitles); films shown in the original language with subtitles are denoted 'OmU' (Original mit Untertiteln). German cinemas often lag a few months behind a film's first release, especially for US productions.

Most of the large movie houses on Kurfürstendamm show dubbed Hollywood fare. Among the grandest are the historic *Zoo-Palast (Map 7, ☎ 25 41 47 77, Hardenbergstrasse 29a)*, formerly the main venue of the Berlin International Film Festival, and the *Delphi Film Palast (Map 7, ☎ 312 10 26, Kantstrasse 12a)*, adjacent to the Theater des Westens. A new addition to Berlin's movie scene is the *IMAX (Map 8, ☎ 44 31 61 31 for*

reservations, Marlene-Dietrich-Platz 4) in the new Potsdamer Platz development. (See the Potsdamer Platz map in the Things to See and Do chapter). Admission is DM11.50/20 for one/two shows. Also here is *Cinemaxx (Map 8, ☎ 44 31 63 16 for reservations)*, a multiplex with Hollywood blockbusters. Thursday before 5 pm is 'happy hour' with all tickets costing just DM6.

Cinemas with frequent OmU or OF showings include:

Arsenal (Map 7, ☎ 218 68 48, Welserstrasse 25) in Schöneberg screens mostly English-language films, including Hollywood classics and underground productions. Take the U4 to Victoria-Luise-Platz.

Babylon (Map 6, ☎ 61 60 96 93, Dresdner Strasse 126) in Kreuzberg 36 shows mostly recent-release OmU mainstream fare. Take the U1, U8, or U15 to Kottbusser Tor.

Eiszeit (Map 6, ☎ 611 60 16, Zeughofstrasse 20) in Kreuzberg 36 has a daily changing program of more obscure, alternative film fare. Take the U1 to Görlitzer Bahnhof.

Kurbel (Map 7, ☎ 883 53 25, Giesebrechtstrasse 4) in Charlottenburg has three theatres with mostly OF screenings of first-release Hollywood blockbusters. Take the U7 to Adenauerplatz.

Odeon (Map 5, ☎ 78 70 40 19, Hauptstrasse 116) in Schöneberg screens English-language recent releases. Take the U4 to Innsbrucker Platz or S1, S45 or S46 to Schöneberg.

Olympia (Map 7, ☎ 881 19 78, Kantstrasse 162) near Zoo station has mainstream and independent productions from the USA and the UK. Take the U9 to Kurfürstendamm or U2/9/12 to Bahnhof Zoo.

Urania Filmbühne (Map 5, ☎ 218 90 91, An der Urania 17) in Schöneberg is a revival house with the odd English-language movie. Take the U1, U2, or U15 to Wittenbergplatz.

PUBS & BARS

No matter where you are in Berlin, you're never far from a bar or a pub. A few words on etiquette: it's usual not to pay for your drinks upon ordering or when they are served. A tab is kept and you pay when leaving.

Charlottenburg

Hegel (Map 7, ☎ 312 19 48, Savignyplatz 2) is the preferred watering hole of academics and the more cultured of Berlin's expat

Russians. Drinks have names like *Zarenblut* (Tsar's blood) and *Hegel's Todestrunk* (Hegel's death drink), and things in this tiny place get downright nostalgic when someone takes a turn on the piano.

Friedrichshain

For a dose of real Berlin grit, visit Rigaer Strasse, most of which is in the hands of squatters who have opened some pretty earthy pubs and cafes in these illegal haunts. Most of these have no fixed opening hours and many are rather short-lived as they get busted by the police and are forced to close. At the time of writing, a couple of semi-established hardcore hold-outs included *Fischladen* at No 83 and *Schizzo Tempel* (Map 4) at No 77.

There are also a couple of licensed establishments. *Filmriss (Map 4, ☎ 2 21 96 27, Rigaer Strasse 103)* is a former squat house gone respectable. Now a dark and dank cafe-pub, it also shows old and new cult flicks twice a week – for free! Get there early, it's small and very popular. *X-Beliebig (Map 4, no phone)*, at the corner of Liebigstrasse, is a bar with occasional live bands and meals for DM3.

Supamolly (Off Map 6, Jessner Strasse 41) survived a period as a squatter haunt and is now a pub and live venue. Usually it's music, though theatre and film screenings pad the program. Cover is cheap, often under DM5.

Kreuzberg

Café Anfall (Map 6, ☎ 693 68 98, Gneisenaustrasse 64) is a counterculture pub-cafe and legendary punk temple in Kreuzberg 61. Anfall opens at 5 pm (from 9 pm on Monday) and has wild decor which changes every month or so, as well as good, but loud, music. (Take the U7 to Südstern.)

Zyankali Bar (Map 6, ☎ 251 63 33, Grossbeerenstrasse 64) has an unusual glass bar with odd trinkets and curios on display. Besides cocktails with bizarre names, one of the more unusual drinks is hemp beer.

Oranienstrasse is Kreuzberg 36's main entertainment mile. *Flammende Herzen (Map 6, ☎ 615 71 02)* at No 170 and *Bierhimmel (Map 6, ☎ 615 31 22)* at No 181 are long time favourites. Both are good places to hang over a paper or for a chat, and are also popular with gays and lesbians. *Franken (Map 6, ☎ 614 10 81, Oranienstrasse 19)* is often packed with SO 36 club-goers and otherwise offers a smoke-filled living room ambience. Open from 8 pm daily; cocktails from DM5.

The *Junction Bar (Map 6, ☎ 772 76 77, Gneisenaustrasse 18)* is a long-standing basement venue with a musical menu that includes funk, soul, rock and jazz. Open from 8 pm daily.

Würgeengel (Map 6, ☎ 615 55 60, Dresdner Strasse 122) – German for 'angel of death' – pays homage to the 1962 Luis Buñuel movie by that name. The dramatic blood-red velvet walls, matching big plump sofas and unique tile and stucco ceiling, however, are more reminiscent of a Belle Epoque brothel. The cocktails are killers, but the place feels like a straightjacket when crowds from the shows at the adjacent Babylon cinema get out.

Mitte

Broker's Bier Börse (Map 8, ☎ 282 39 65, Schiffbauerdamm 8) is a unique and fun beer hall where demand determines the price of drinks (after 5 pm). Just as in a mini stock exchange, current prices are posted on a digital board above the bar. If drink orders are up, prices go down – and vice versa. Every once in a while a heavy brass bell is rung and all hell breaks loose because that's when prices go cut-rate. Sure, it's a touristy thing but fun nonetheless. Small meals are available too. It opens at 8 am.

Highlights on the Oranienburger Strasse drag include *Café Silberstein (Map 4, ☎ 281 28 01)* at No 27, a gallery-bar with oversized metal chairs and avant-garde sculptures. Packed to the gills on weekend nights, the music is kept at talking level and there's a small sushi bar for those craving a protein burst. The Silberstein is not to be confused with *Meilenstein (Map 8, ☎ 282 89 95)* at No 7, a pub where prostitutes working Oranienburger Strasse go for a warm-up drink between, ahem, jobs.

Obst und Gemüse (Map 4, ☎ 282 96 47), on the same street at No 48/49, gets its

ENTERTAINMENT

name from the fruit and vegetable shop that used to occupy the spot. Its popularity may make it hard to get even a foot in the door to get a drink from the self-service bar.

Nearby is the funky *Onyx (Map 8, ☎ 283 22 49, Grosse Präsidentenstrasse 10)*. Divided into two sections, it has retro decor, oddly pleasant whorehouse lighting and furniture placed on raised aluminium platforms.

The Irish pub **Oscar Wilde** *(Map 4, ☎ 282 81 66, Friedrichstrasse 112a)* is a patriotic, hard-core drinking establishment at Friedrichstrasse 112a with occasional live music. Guinness, Kilkenny and Murphy's are on tap and there's a fine selection of pub grub like Irish breakfast for DM12, Irish stew for DM11.50 and, yep, Irish steak for DM25.

For a whiff of *Ostalgie* (new word fusion of Ost and Nostalgie, meaning nostalgia for the GDR), have a drink at *VEB Ostzone (Map 4, no phone, Auguststrasse 92)*, creatively furnished with GDR memorabilia and paraphernalia (framed pictures of Honecker and Marx, Trabbi parts etc).

Nearby *Zosch (Map 4, ☎ 280 76 64, Tucholskystrasse 30)* is a scene fixture popular with student-age patrons that has friendly service, vaulted brick ceilings and occasional bands in the basement (often free).

Prenzlauer Berg

Plenty of popular cafe-pubs with outdoor tables in warm weather are clustered around Käthe-Kollwitz-Platz. (Take the U2 to Senefelderplatz.) Old-timers include *Weitzmann (Map 4, ☎ 442 71 25, Husemannstrasse 2)* and, opposite at No 1, the historic *Restauration 1900 (Map 4, ☎ 449 40 52, Husemannstrasse 1)*, which specialises in fine German cuisine.

A short walk away, time hasn't worn the edge off *Kommandatur (Map 4, ☎ 442 77 25, Knaackstrasse 20)*, which is still trashy, smoky, noisy and packed as tight as a pickle jar. And they just keep coming back. For something not quite so Germanically dark, try the Australian-themed *Uluru Resort (Map 4, ☎ 44 04 95 22, Rykestrasse 17)*, which often has live music and a boisterous and friendly atmosphere.

While the pubs and bars around Kollwitz-platz get all the attention, the really humming places are a few blocks away, north of Danziger Strasse. (Take the U2 to Eberswalder Strasse.) Lychener Strasse, for instance, is a happening street where, at No 6, you'll find **La Bodeguita del Medio** *(Map 4, ☎ 441 74 12)*, a clamorous Cuban watering hole with a multicultural crowd and an assortment of rum and tequila, plus tapas from DM6. It takes its name from what was allegedly Ernest Hemingway's favourite Cuban drinking place.

For a more 'civilised' atmosphere, head across the street to **Weinstein** *(Map 4, ☎ 441 18 42)* at No 33, a snug wine bar where you can sample fermented grape juice from most German growing regions from DM4.50 per 20cL glass. Walls are lined by wooden casks, decoratively arranged bottles and other vinicultural paraphernalia.

The name of **Wohnzimmer** *(Map 4, ☎ 445 54 58, Lettestrasse 6)*, right by the Lette 'm Sleep hostel, translates as 'living room' which aptly describes the comfy and laid-back atmosphere that reigns in this tiny communicative pub cum cafe cum cocktail bar. It's a 'second home' for some of Prenzlberg's youth and usually jammed.

Schöneberg

You'll find lots of bars and cafes along Goltzstrasse, the main drag in this neighbourhood. Also see the Cafe section in the Places to Eat chapter and the Cocktail Bars section later in this chapter.

Slumberland *(Map 5, ☎ 216 53 49, Goltzstrasse 24)* is pretty much a district legend drawing in the trendies with its pseudotropical ambience (plastic palm trees and sand floor). Open nightly from 9.30 pm.

A happening drag away from the tourist beat is Crellestrasse which has a cluster of fun pubs and cafes, including **Café Mirell** *(Map 5, ☎ 782 04 57)* at No 46 (also see the Places to Eat chapter) and the timeless **Leuchtturm** *(Lighthouse, Map 5, ☎ 781 85 01)* at No 17, which woos customers with its retro ambience, walls plastered in kitschy oil paintings and blues blaring out from the speakers.

Cocktail Bars

Berlin is rediscovering glamour, or at least that's what the recent mushrooming of sophisticated cocktail bars seems to suggest. And it's not just the deep-pocketed suit-and-tie and little-black-dress crowd that's sipping manhattans or martinis, lifted pinkie finger and all. Scensters with pierced belly buttons, hip mothers in baggy clothing, retro-types in zoot suits and pocket chains, media types with dark glasses, college kids in vintage gear – they are all found sidling up to endless bars or settling into designer sofas. No one seems to mind the steep prices (DM12 to DM25) but thankfully for the budget-conscious, happy hour has come to Berlin. Sip away!

Charlottenburg has **Gainsbourg** *(Map 7, ☎ 313 74 64, Savignyplatz 5)*, an American bar that speaks to a thirty-something arty crowd. The best thing is the warmly lit, clubby atmosphere and the award-winning cocktails mixed by master-shaker Frido Keiling. **La Casa del Habano** *(Map 7, ☎ 31 10 30, Fasanenstrasse 9)*, inside the Hotel Savoy near Zoo station, is a clubby, wood-panelled cigar lounge. Enjoy your stogy and whiskey in surroundings that once hosted Henry Miller and friends.

In Mitte, **Pip's** *(Map 4, ☎ 283 29 04, Auguststrasse 84)* timewarps you back to the 70s with eccentric decor that includes washing machine drums. It's friendly, comfortable and not overly pretentious. Cocktails start at DM11 (or DM8 before 9 pm Sunday to Thursday). Open at 8 pm. **Jubinal** *(Map 4, ☎ 28 38 73 77)* is a similarly happening spot with a nicely calibrated look. Music ranges from Klezmer to jazz, and cocktails start at DM13.

Flourishing Friedrichshain has its own home-grown brand of cocktail bars. **Mana Mana** *(Map 4, no phone, Niederbarnimstrasse 23)* is a low-key hang-out popular with punks (only 'friendly' ones, we're assured). The decor looks wild and creative, and so are the bands that occasionally perform here. Cocktails are 'dirt-cheap' as far as cocktails go (DM6 to DM10).

Prices are a bit higher (DM10 to DM14) at **Euphoria** *(Map 6, ☎ 29 00 46 83)*, on the corner of Grünberger Strasse and Simon-Dach-Strasse, but you can always stick with the 'daily special' for just DM7. Happy hour is from 5 to 7 pm. There's also a restaurant with fish, meat and pasta dishes under DM20, though food is more of an afterthought here. Nearby is the **Dachkammer** *(Map 6, ☎ 296 16 73, Simon-Dach-Strasse 39)*, whose subdued cocktail bar upstairs is great for a chat or relaxing. A more pubby atmosphere reigns on the ground floor.

Prenzlauer Berg has the **X-Bar** *(Map 4, ☎ 443 49 04, Raumerstrasse 17)* where you'd need wads of money and lots of stamina to drink yourself through the epic cocktail menu. Maybe that's why there are two happy hours (from 6 to 8 pm and from midnight to 1 am). There's a sushi bar in the back. Open from 6 pm daily.

Places in the western districts are considerably more grown-up with prices to match. In Schöneberg, **Mister Hu** *(Map 5, ☎ 217 21 11, Goltzstrasse 39)* is dark and grotto-like and has a daily happy hour from 5 to 8 pm when all cocktails are DM9.95. The **Zoulou Bar** *(Map 5, ☎ 784 68 94, Hauptstrasse 4)* is a tiny, trendy establishment that seeks to evoke 1930s America and sometimes gets more crowded than a Stones concert. **N.N. Bar** *(Map 5, ☎ 787 50 33, Hauptstrasse 159)* is a chic, tube-shaped lounge with a bar as long as the cocktail menu. Nearby is **N.N. Train** *(Map 5, ☎ 78 71 06 17, Hauptstrasse 162)* in a converted S-Bahn carriage.

Tiergarten has a couple of favourites for the expense-account crowd. **Bar am Lützowplatz** *(Map 5, ☎ 262 68 09, Lützowplatz 7)* was once named 'Best Bar in Germany'. Pouting beauties and paunchy gents sip perfect cocktails at the endless bar or drape themselves into comfortable armchairs. Happy hour from 5 to 9 pm, open until 4 am.

Not to be outdone in the accolade department, **Harry's New York Bar** *(Map 5, ☎ 254 78 21, Lützowufer 15)*, inside the Grand Hotel Esplanade, was voted 'Bar of 1996' by *Playboy* magazine. With its refined atmosphere – enhanced by a black piano and blood-red leather couches – it usually crawls with people who are either way too rich or too thin.

Berliner Kneipen

Old-fashioned Berlin pubs have their own tradition of hospitality – beer, schnapps, hearty food and a bizarre brand of Berlin humour all served up in rustic, smoke-filled surroundings. Occasionally, you'll come across a *Kneipe* (pub) that natives from the neighbourhood – usually balding working-class stiffs with paunches – have staked out as their private turf. Gruff demeanour and hostile stares greet you as you enter their smoky lair through a heavy wooden door. You, a stranger, have dared to invade their territory (let it be known that there's equal treatment for *all* strangers, German or foreign). Sure, it's local colour, but you'll probably have a better time somewhere else. We've picked out a few places where you can comfortably soak up some atmosphere along with that good German beer.

In Charlottenburg, *Dicke Wirtin (Map 7, ☎ 312 49 52, Carmerstrasse 9)*, off chic Savignyplatz, is an earthy Kneipe populated with students from the nearby Technische Universität. The menu features four daily stews for under DM6 and has six varieties of beer on tap from DM4.50.

Stories abound about the historic *Zur letzten Instanz ('The Final Authority', Map 8, ☎ 242 55 28, Waisenstrasse 14)* in Mitte. The pub, which claims a tradition dating back to the 1600s, sits next to a chunk of medieval town wall. It got its present name 150 years ago, we are told, when a couple came in from the nearby courthouse to celebrate their just finalised divorced. By the time they were well oiled and ready to leave, they'd decided to remarry – at which point one of those present exclaimed, 'This pub is the court of final authority!' It's open from noon to 1 am Monday to Saturday, to 11 pm on Sunday.

Another historic place is *Zum Nussbaum (Map 8, ☎ 242 30 95, Am Nussbaum 3)*, once the drinking hole of early 20th century caricaturist Heinrich Zille and the humorist Otto Nagel. It has been re-established as part of the Nikolaiviertel. (Also see the Places to Eat chapter).

E&M Leydicke (Map 5, ☎ 216 29 73, Mansteinstrasse 4), located in Schöneberg, is another of Berlin's oldest surviving pubs (founded in 1877). Flavoured schnapps and fruit wines are bottled on the premises. It's open from 4 pm. (Take the U1, U2 or U7 to Yorckstrasse.)

Beer Gardens

As soon as the last winter storms have blown away, pallid Berliners re-acquaint themselves with the sun. Restaurants, bars and cafes start cramming their pavements, gardens or courtyards with tables and chairs to ring in beer garden season. It's convivial and fun, especially in the peak summer months when there's daylight until about 11 pm. For sustenance, snacks – sometimes even barbecued ribs, steaks, corn on the cob and the like – are usually available.

A cult place in Kreuzberg is the open-air *Golgatha (Map 6, ☎ 785 24 53, Dudenstrasse 48-64)* in Viktoriapark. It's been around for as long as we can remember and is still a comfortable, low-key place. You can dance in your Birkenstocks here, ya rascal.

Whether *Prater (Map 4, ☎ 448 56 88, Kastanienallee 7-9)* in Prenzlauer Berg is really Berlin's oldest beer garden doesn't really matter. Fact is, it's definitely one of the prettiest and a great place to quaff away beneath a canopy of mature chestnuts. It's part of a complex that includes a small stage operated by the Volksbühne and a restaurant serving hearty German fare from DM9 to DM18.

In the south-western district of Zehlendorf is *Loretta am Wannsee (☎ 803 51 56, Kronprinzessinenweg 260)*, a huge garden with over 1000 chairs that's a favourite for capping off a summer Sunday on the lake. (Take the S1, S3 or S7 to Wannsee.) Also in Zehlendorf is *Luise (☎ 832 84 87, Königin-Luise-Strasse 40-44)*, a legendary student haunt with space for 700. (Take the U1 to Dahlem-Dorf.)

Places with wonderful beer gardens that are covered elsewhere in this book include: *Pfefferberg* in Prenzlauer Berg and *Podewil* in Mitte. (See the Cultural Centres section later in this chapter); *Café am Neuen See* in Tiergarten and *Ypsilon* in Schöneberg (see the Places to Eat chapter).

CLUBS

Berlin has a reputation for unbridled and very late nightlife – nothing happens until midnight. As in every major city, it's hard to keep up with the ever-changing club scene. Before stepping out, call ahead to make sure the club's still there or, better yet, consult any of the what's-on rags (see the Listings section earlier in this chapter).

Cover charges (when they apply) range from DM5 to DM20 and sometimes include a drink. In the 90s, Berlin became the epicentre of techno (see the boxed text 'Techno Town') and it's still big, as evidenced by the annual Love Parade which is drawing bigger crowds each year. But as techno has gone mega-commercial, the scene has diversified and now anything goes – salsa, hip hop, house, heavy metal, goa, German *Schlager* (silly pop songs), swing, reggae, 80s New Wave, 70s rock 'n roll, even tango and foxtrot.

If you put a pin for every club on a map of Berlin, the biggest cluster would be in the eastern districts of Mitte, Friedrichshain and Prenzlauer Berg, which illustrates how much the scene has shifted since the Wende.

Charlottenburg

Abraxas (Map 7, ☎ 312 94 93, *Kantstrasse 134*) in Charlottenburg is unpretentious and timeless and does jazz and Latin rhythms nightly except Monday. The cover charge is DM5 to DM10.

Salsa (Map 7, ☎ 324 16 42, *Wielandstrasse 13*) is a local institution, in business since 1981. Enjoy an evening to the beat of salsa and merengue, with live bands on weekends and beautiful couples holding forth on the dance floor. It opens at 5 pm and cover is DM6, with live band DM10.

Friedrichshain

Maria am Ostbahnhof (Map 6, ☎ 29 00 61 98, *Strasse der Pariser Kommune 8-10*) is one of Berlin's hippest new techno and drum 'n bass temples, housed in the hallway of an abandoned postal distribution centre. A large lobby with bar leads to a vast dance floor, while the upstairs lounge has great city views. The cover charge is DM5

Techno Town

Lay down a bass track that sounds like direct thermonuclear hits on an oil drum, toss in some eerie electronic wailing and gasping snatches of melody, run it through some Star Wars technology and deliver it all through speakers the size of God's summer home. Then add an oddly mellow crowd of twenty-something 'ravers' with pierced anatomy, plastic miniskirts, tight t-shirts and – more often than not – loaded up on Ecstasy.

Somewhere high above the dance floor post a DJ who manipulates the sound and the crowd like a postmodern fakir charming his snake. Pour it all into a venue with decor from the sexual dream of a robot, with bodies writhing rhythmically from midnight until way past dawn. And there you have it: Techno 101. A sound, a mantra and a way of life that Berlin has somehow made its own.

Rave. Gabber. Jungle. Trance. The variations seem endless, but it all started with the machine-music first spun by the Düsseldorf band Kraftwerk – influenced by Detroit-grown House – in the 1970s. Twenty years later, techno moved mainstream: you can now hear it in supermarkets, elevators and TV commercials.

With Berlin's annual Love Parade (1999 attendance: 1.5 million), techno has even gained recognition as a legitimate 'political movement', though it's difficult to spot the activism behind the unofficial motto: 'Friede, Freude, Eierkuchen' (Peace, Happiness, Pancakes). Even so, since the organisers regularly register the mega-event as a political demonstration, the Berlin Senate has to cough up buckets of Deutschmark to pay for the huge post-party clean-up. They don't seem to mind and, after all, the parade's public relations potential is enormous. Not to mention the shot in the arm for the city's economy, courtesy of the hundreds of thousands of visitors descending on Berlin from around Germany, Europe and, indeed, the world.

to DM15, drinks are DM5 for beer to DM15 for cocktails. Open from 10 pm Wednesday to Saturday.

The chic *Matrix (Map 6, ☎ 29 49 10 47, Warschauer Platz 18)* has a gritty industrial charm and is ensconced below the Warschauer Strasse U-Bahn arches. Top DJs like Marusha and Hazel B occasionally pop in to spice up house and techno parties. The scene, mostly those in their early 20s, spreads across several dance floors. The cover charge is DM10 to DM20. Open from 11 pm Friday and Saturday.

To wallow in GDR nostalgia, head to *Tagung/Cube Club (Map 6, ☎ 292 87 56, Wühlischstrasse 29)*. Upstairs is a cafe-bar (open daily), and the intimate basement club opens after 11 pm Thursday to Saturday. The cover charge is from zero to DM5.

Kreuzberg

Anything goes in Berlin, and those who don't believe it should visit the *KitKat Club (Map 6, ☎ 611 38 33, Glogauer Strasse 2)* during Sex Trance Bizarre parties on Friday and Saturday nights. Wear your 'sexual fantasy outfit' (meaning fetish – or basically no – clothes) and leave all inhibitions at home. What goes down on and beyond the dance floor usually belongs in a porno flick or at least the bedroom. Watching only is discouraged, as are aggressive approaches. Hey, it's just all good, clean fun, right? The KitKat is open after 11 pm Wednesday to Saturday (Thursday is 'Bottoms Up' gay night). Take the U1 to Görlitzer Bahnhof.

On a tamer scale, *Schnabelbar (Map 6, ☎ 615 85 34, Oranienstrasse 31)* has great music and atmosphere and a minuscule dance floor in the back. The musical menu covers the spectrum from jazz to house to black. Best of all, there's usually no cover charge. Open after 10 pm daily. Take the U15 to Görlitzer Bahnhof.

SO 36 (Map 6, ☎ 61 40 13 06, Oranienstrasse 190) belongs to Kreuzberg like cream on strawberries. Once the main haunt of the alternative punk scene, it now has a diversified schedule of live concerts and theme nights – hip hop to house, ballroom (!) to techno. On Wednesday the place belongs to gays and lesbians. Open nightly, the cover charge is DM6 to DM28. Take the U15 to Görlitzer Bahnhof.

The outer appearance of *Insel (Off Map 6, ☎ 53 60 80 20, Alt-Treptow 6)* – a mock medieval castle on Spree island reached via a romantic bridge – belies the hard-core sounds that charge through here most weekends. Expect Gothic, industrial, metal and jungle after 10 pm on Friday, Saturday and Sunday. The cover charge is DM5 to DM15. Take the S-Bahn to Plänterwald.

Mitte

In the basement of a popular bar is *Bergwerk (Map 4, ☎ 280 88 76, Bergstrasse 68)* which does open-mike nights on Wednesdays and mostly mainstream sounds otherwise. With its easy-going atmosphere, it draws a mixed clientele. Open from 11 pm nightly (from 10 pm Sunday); the cover charge is DM7 to DM10.

Boudoir (Map 4, ☎ 613 44 97, Brunnenstrasse 192, 2nd courtyard), is an intimate disco-bar in a series of small rooms painted a violent red, with 60s GDR furniture. Open after 10 pm on Friday and Saturday (occasionally also on Thursday and Sunday), it's always full and fun (DM5 to DM15). To get there take the U8 to Rosenthaler Platz.

Discount (Map 4, ☎ 28 59 80 10, Gartenstrasse 103) is an intimate venue with a kitschy, spaced-out look that gets its name from the supermarket that once occupied its premises. Come here for house, techno and electronic sounds after 11.30 pm every Friday and Saturday. The cover charge is DM10, beer is DM5, and cocktails cost from DM8.

The Volksbühne theatre may shock with its provocative productions, but in its *Grüner Salon (Green Salon, Map 4, ☎ 28 59 89 36, Rosa-Luxemburg-Platz)* an atmosphere of sophistication and nostalgia reigns. This is the place to come for tango, salsa and swing nights, taking place on various days of the week. Dance lessons are held as well. Open after 6 pm, closed Tuesday. Similar things go on at the theatre's *Roter Salon (Red Salon, Map 4, ☎ 24 06 58 06)* where readings and live music supplement the dance schedule. Open from 9 pm daily.

Kurvenstar (Map 8, ☎ 28 59 97 10, Kleine Präsidentenstrasse 4) is a recent entry with whacky 70s-syle decor and a motley melange of music, dancing and global food. Open after 9 pm daily.

Lizard Lounge (Map 4, ☎ 44 35 94 99, Veteranenstrasse 21) is downstairs from the Acud, a multifunctional venue (gallery, cafe and cinema). The music is mixed and changes often, from ska to reggae to jungle and Asian underground. The cover charge is DM5 to DM10 and it's open Wednesday and Friday (upstairs daily).

Oxymoron (Map 8, ☎ 28 39 18 86, Rosenthaler Strasse 40/41), inside the Hackesche Höfe, is a cafe by day, a lounge and restaurant by night and, after 11 pm, morphs into a chic bar-dance club where jazz and rock seamlessly blend with drum 'n bass and soft hip hop. The best thing may well be the pompous baroque decor accented with plump velvet sofas, sensuously curved gold-leaf mirrors, chandeliers and luxurious drapes. Admission is DM5 on weekdays, DM10 on weekends, and concerts cost DM15.

Sage Club (Map 8, ☎ 278 50 52, Köpenicker Strasse 76), inside the Heine-Heine-Strasse U-Bahn station (U8), is a hit with sophisticated twenty-somethings. There are two dance floors, three bars (75 cocktails), plus a lounge and garden. Funk, soul, rock, house and trance music is on the turntables, a 'fire'-spewing dragon looms above the dance floor and Gothic pillars form part of the fantasy decor. The cover charge is DM10. Open from 9 pm Thursday, from 11 pm Friday and Saturday and from 8 pm Sunday.

Sophienklub (Map 4, ☎ 282 45 52, Sophienstrasse 6), a left-over from GDR days, changes the music style nightly – jazz, brasil, house, soul, funk, reggae, but definitely *no* techno. It has a nice, fairly low-key atmosphere, is open Sunday, Tuesday, Friday and Saturday and costs DM10 on weekends, less during the week. There's also a billiard room and – from May to September only – a cafe. Take the U8 to Weinmeisterstrasse.

The *Tränenpalast (Palace of Tears, Map 8, ☎ 20 61 00 11, Reichstagsufer 17)*, in a retired border-crossing facility, is best known as a cabaret and concert venue, though on Saturday nights it usually turns into a disco with great parties.

Techno fiends won't want to leave Berlin without a pilgrimage to *Tresor (Map 8, ☎ 609 37 02, Leipziger Strasse 128a)*, the city's oldest techno temple inside the actual money vault of a former department store. Upstairs in a former bank building is the affiliated *Globus*, which plays more hip hop, funk and soul. Both are open Wednesday (DM5), Friday (DM15) and Saturday (DM20).

Another classic is *WMF (Map 4, ☎ 262 79 01, Johannisstrasse 19)* housed in the former guesthouse of a GDR *apparatschik* (a high official in the Communist party). Come here for drum 'n bass and house on Friday and Saturday; Sunday is the 'GayMF'. Admission is DM15.

Prenzlauer Berg

The trendy *Akba Lounge (Map 4, ☎ 441 14 63, Sredzkistrasse 64)* combines a quiet, tunnel-shaped ground floor cafe with an intimate club upstairs. It plays some of the loudest music in Berlin – from latin house to acid jazz. Take the U2 to Eberswalder Strasse. *Bibo Bar (Map 4, ☎ 443 97 98, Lychener Strasse 12)* is a cocktail bar cum dance club that draws a wild, whacky and communicative crowd to a nightly changing beat. Admission is often free.

Duncker (Map 4, ☎ 445 95 09, Dunckerstrasse 64) plays old stuff – mostly rock. Spend a couple of hours here (open from 10 pm daily) and then move on to something more lively. Take the S8 or S10 to Prenzlauer Allee or U2 to Eberswalder Strasse.

The *Subground (Map 4, ☎ 44 38 31 16, Schönhauser Allee 176)* thrives at the Pfefferberg cultural centre (see the Cultural Centres section following), reflecting the centre's multicultural orientation with world music from Senegal to Sweden. Opening hours vary, but usually there's something on from Wednesday to Sunday. The cover charge is DM10 to DM15.

Schöneberg & Tiergarten

Metropol/Loft (Map 5, ☎ 21 73 36 80, Nollendorfplatz 5) has seen better days, despite

ENTERTAINMENT

the new Egyptian theme following a recent revamping. A live concert venue from Sunday to Thursday, it morphs into a disco (70s/80s nights, rock, indie pop etc) after 10 pm on Friday and Saturday. The Loft is a more intimate concert venue. Sunday afternoon is usually reserved for gay parties.

90 Grad (Map 5, ☎ 262 89 84, Dennewitzstrasse 37) in Tiergarten is still chic and trendy after many years in the party business and is now especially popular among gay clubbers. Recently renovated, DJs spin a mixed program of funk, soul, progressive house and mainstream. Note: no techno here. There's a cool chill out and chat bar in the back. It's open from 11 pm Thursday to Saturday, from 9 pm Sunday and admission is DM10.

For fiery salsa nights, head to *El Barrio* (Map 5, ☎ 262 18 53, Potsdamer Strasse 84), a sultry cellar where couples are caught up by Latin rhythms. There's occasional live music, and dance classes in salsa and merengue are offered regularly. Call for a schedule. It's open from 10 pm daily, is free during the week, and costs DM8 on weekends.

CULTURAL CENTRES

Cultural centres are an important part of Berlin's entertainment scene. These multi-use venues are usually housed in converted warehouses, department stores, breweries and other large buildings. The space is divided into several rooms dedicated to various forms of entertainment, including all or a mix of the following: cinema, dance and concert halls, theatre, bars, cafes, restaurants, gallery space, circus and studios. Depending on the centre, events are mainstream to cutting edge, usually with a good dose of multiculturalism thrown in. The price of admission depends on the event.

Arena (Map 6, ☎ 533 73 33, Eichenstrasse 4), in an old bus depot in Treptow, is a big party place with frequent concerts by headliners like Alanis Morissette. Take the U15 to Schlesisches Tor or the S-Bahn to Treptower Park.

In Mitte the *Kalkscheune* (Map 8, ☎ 28 39 00 65, Johannisstrasse 2) holds forth with a sophisticated eclectic program that may include tango nights, jazz sessions and chanson evenings.

The hot spot in Prenzlauer Berg is the *Kulturbrauerei* (Map 4, ☎ 441 92 69, Knaackstrasse 97), which was closed for renovation at the time of writing, but promises to become one happening mega-complex.

Nearby is the more alternative *Pfefferberg* (Map 4, ☎ 449 65 34) at Schönhauser Allee 176. It's particularly strong in promoting cross-cultural projects, with all types of events featuring black music, ska and reggae. Take the U2 to Senefelderplatz.

Podewil (Map 8, ☎ 24 74 96, Klosterstrasse 68-70) in Mitte, offers a mixed bag of film, dance, theatre and live music (much of it contemporary classic) as well as a cafe, all in a historic building dating from 1704. The beer garden is open to 9.30 pm in summer. Take the U2 to Klosterstrasse.

An adventure playground for adults is *Tacheles* (Map 4, ☎ 282 61 85, Oranienburger Strasse 54-56), housed in a dilapidated, graffiti-covered building. Its post-atomic look belies its active cultural program that includes dance, jazz concerts, the *Café Camera*, cabaret, readings, workshops, bizarre art galleries and studios, a cinema, theatre space and more. The *Gartenhaus* beer garden is great in summer, and there's also the *Zapata* nightclub (mostly techno). (For more on the Tacheles, see the Mitte section in the Things to See & Do chapter).

The beloved *Tempodrom* (Map 6, ☎ 61 28 42 35) has moved to (temporary) new digs in the courtyard of the same former postal centre that's already home to Maria am Ostbahnhof (see the Clubs section earlier in this chapter). Formerly in a big circus tent in the Tiergarten park, this multicultural venue was forced to move for being located too close to the new government quarter. A permanent facility at Anhalter Bahnhof is supposed to open in 2001.

Another multimedia culture club is the *UFA-Fabrik* (Off Map 6, ☎ 75 50 30, Viktoriastrasse 10-18), in the former UFA film studios in Tempelhof. There's music, theatre, dance, cabaret and circus shows all year round. Between June and September performances take place on an open-air stage. Workshops, seminars and production studios round out the program. Take the U6 to Ullsteinstrasse.

LIVE MUSIC
Classical

Music lovers should try to hear a concert at the **Berliner Philharmonie** *(Map 5, ☎ 25 48 81 32, Herbert-von-Karajan-Strasse 1)*, famous for its supreme acoustics. Inside the 1960s building, designed by Hans Scharoun, the audience sits in several galleries wrapped around a central area reserved for the orchestra. The adjacent **Kammermusiksaal**, a smaller chamber-music venue, was built between 1984 and 1987, also according to plans by Scharoun. The box office opens from 3.30 to 6 pm weekdays, from 11 am to 2 pm weekends and holidays. Tickets cost from DM24 to DM78 and all seats are excellent, so just take the cheapest. Take the U15 to Kurfürstenstrasse, then bus No 148.

Another treat is a concert at the lavish **Konzerthaus** *(Map 8, ☎ 203 09 21 01/02, Gendarmenmarkt 2)* in Mitte, formerly the Schauspielhaus and home to the renowned Berlin Symphony Orchestra. The box office, below the main staircase, opens from noon to 8 pm Monday to Saturday, to 4 pm Sunday. Tickets range from DM10 (standing tickets) to DM75. Discounts are available to students and seniors with ID.

The concert hall at the **Hochschule der Künste** *(College of Arts, Map 7, ☎ 31 85 23 74, Hardenbergstrasse 33)* is also busy in season. The box office is open from 3 to 6.30 pm Tuesday to Friday, from 11 am to 2 pm Saturday.

Organ and other concerts are held in many of the city's churches, museums and other venues, including the **Marienkirche** *(Map 8, Rathausstrasse)* in Mitte; *St* **Matthäus Kirche** *(Map 5, Matthäikirchplatz)* in Tiergarten; the **Berliner Dom** *(Map 8)* on Museumsinsel; the **Französischer Dom** *(Map 8)* on Gendarmenmarkt; the **Kaiser Wilhelm Memorial Church** *(Map 7)* in Charlottenburg; and the **Eosander Chapel** of Charlottenburg Palace *(Map 3)*.

A special summer treat is a concert at the **Waldbühne** *(Map 2, ☎ 23 08 82 30, Am Glockenturm)* in Charlottenburg, a natural amphitheatre for 20,000 à la Los Angeles' classic Hollywood Bowl. Originally a theatre and celebration venue built by the Nazis, it now hosts rock, pop and jazz concerts in addition to classical fare. Popular too are the movie nights with films projected onto a giant screen. Take U2 to Olympia-Stadion Ost, then walk or take the free shuttle; or take bus No 18 from Olympia-Stadion Ost station right to the Waldbühne stop.

Jazz

The **A-Trane** *(Map 7, ☎ 313 25 50, Bleibtreustrasse 1)* in Charlottenburg, is still *the* place in Berlin for jazz. Local, national and international artists appear here nightly. Styles run the gamut from modern jazz and bebop to avant-garde, mainstream and vocal jazz. Benches and coffee house-type tables and chairs wrap around the small stage so there's not a bad seat in the house. The cover charge is DM10 to DM20 but some nights, usually Tuesday and Wednesday, are free.

Quasimodo *(Map 7, ☎ 312 80 86, Kantstrasse 12a)*, in the basement next to the cafe by the same name, has nightly live jazz, blues or rock acts. Shows start around 10 pm and the cover charge is DM15 to DM35, though Tuesday and Wednesday are free here as well. The stylish cafe – with walls featuring lurid canvases of jazz scenes and performers – opens at 5 pm and is the place for a preshow drink.

The occasional jazz concert attracts people of all ages and walks of life to **b-flat** *(Map 4, ☎ 280 62 49, Rosenthaler Strasse 13)* which at other times is a modern cafe-bar. **Flöz** *(Map 5, ☎ 861 10 00, Nassauische Strasse 37)*, located in Wilmersdorf, has mostly modern jazz and boogie, and a slightly more mature clientele. The cover price varies, ranging from DM10 to DM18. The pub section which has a pool table opens at 8 pm, and the concert space in the basement opens at 9 pm. Take the U7 or U9 to Berliner Strasse.

ENTERTAINMENT

OPERA & MUSICALS

The *Staatsoper Unter den Linden (Map 8, ☎ 208 28 61 for schedule, ☎ 20 35 40 for box office, ☎ 208 28 61 for ticket availability, Unter den Linden 5-7)* in Mitte hosts lavish productions with international talent in an exquisite building from 1743. The opera house was founded by Frederick the Great, and Felix Mendelssohn-Bartholdy once served as music director. After the Wende, the artistic leadership fell to Daniel Barenboim who has placed much emphasis on Wagner and pre-Mozart operas. All operas are performed in the original language. The box office is open from 10 am to 6 pm weekdays, and from 2 pm weekends. Tickets cost between DM12 and DM145. Take the U6 to Französische Strasse.

Pre-Wende, the *Deutsche Oper Berlin (Map 7, ☎ 343 84 01, Bismarckstrasse 35)* was West Berlin's answer to the Staatsoper. A 1961 glass and steel behemoth, it lacks in visual appeal but not in quality. Classical works of mostly Italian and French composers – Verdi, Puccini, Bizet, Massenet, to name a few – feature prominently in program schedules, as do contemporary composers. All operas are performed in the original language.

The box office is open from 11 am to 7 pm Monday to Saturday, and from 10 am to 2 pm Sunday. Tickets range from DM17 to DM142 for opera and from DM17 to DM70 for ballet. Students and seniors are entitled to 50% off tickets purchased in person at least one week before the performance. The same discount is available to anyone for remaining tickets on the day of the performance. Weekday performances are rarely sold out.

Back in Mitte is the *Komische Oper (Map 8, ☎ 47 99 74 00, Behrenstrasse 55-57)*, with musical theatre, light opera and operetta and dance theatre performances. Founded in 1947, it makes opera accessible to anyone through its lively productions of light-hearted works performed in a very theatrical way. All productions are sung in German. The box office at Unter den Linden 41 is open from 11 am to 7 pm Monday to Saturday, from 1 pm until 90 minutes before curtain on Sunday. Tickets cost from DM15

to DM108. There's a 50% discount on tickets after 11 am on the day of performance.

Despite its name, the *Neuköllner Oper (Map 6, ☎ 68 89 07 77, Karl-Marx-Strasse 131-133)* is more an alternative opera than the real thing. The repertory has included rare operas by Mozart and Schubert, but also children's and experimental shows. It's all staged with little money and much creativity in a prewar ballroom. Younger people and residents of this traditionally working-class neighbourhood love the accessibility and gritty charm. Tickets range in price from DM14 to DM39. Take the U7 to Karl-Marx-Strasse.

The newly built *Musical Theater Berlin (☎ 47 02 46 00, Marlene-Dietrich-Platz 1)*, in the Potsdamer Platz development, opened in June 1999 with the world premiere of *Der Glöckner von Notre Dame* (The Hunchback of Notre Dame), based on the novel by Victor Hugo. Daily performances (except Monday) are in German, with tickets costing DM80 to DM195. (See the Potsdamer Platz map in the Things to See & Do chapter.)

The *Theater des Westens (Map 7, ☎ 882 28 88, Kantstrasse 12)* near Zoo station, is Berlin's traditional venue for musicals, both touring and home-grown productions. These are usually performed in German and quality varies widely. Seats cost DM18 to DM65, and the box office is open from 11 am to 7 pm Tuesday to Saturday, from 2 to 5 pm Sunday. Note that it's hard to see much from the cheapest seats.

CABARET

A number of venues are trying to revive the lively and lavish variety shows first in vogue during the Golden Twenties. Programs include dancers, singers, jugglers, acrobats and other entertainers who each perform a short number.

In Mitte, the *Friedrichstadtpalast (Map 8, ☎ 23 26 23 26, Friedrichstrasse 107)* was entertainment central in the GDR and still offers ritzy Las Vegas-style musical revues today. There's an 80-head ballet and excellent in-house orchestra and singers. Shows are often sold out and packed with coach tourists. The

Cabaret in Berlin: Let the Good Times Roll – Again!

For all intents and purposes, Berlin *is* cabaret. No other form of entertainment is so intensely linked with the German capital – and not just since Bob Fosse and Liza Minelli gave us their classic movie. Cabaret reached its heyday in the freewheeling Golden Twenties. Night after night, more than 150 theatres drew in the crowds for a varied program of singers, showgirls, jugglers, magicians and other artists, many of whom had broken away from the circus.

Cabaret's spirit was nurtured by the political and societal circumstances of the 1920s. The collapse of the monarchy had brought an end to centuries of censorship, and artists were quick to capitalise on their new-found freedom. Political satire flourished, with inherently corrupt Weimar Republic politicians providing plenty of fodder for biting routines. At the same time, the crippling hyperinflation of 1923 imbued people with a sense of fatalism, driving them to party as though there was no tomorrow. The arrival of new music – especially jazz (or *Yatz*, as it was called here) – further loosened libidos. Berlin became Europe's party town – the capital of cocaine and decadence. It was a world of lurid delights and amoral dalliances so cleverly chronicled by Christopher Isherwood in *Goodbye to Berlin*.

Hitler's rise to power put an instant cork into this brief period of unbridled laissez-fare; war and division followed. Since the Wende, though, cabaret has undergone a renaissance, albeit in a much tamer form. In many venues, you're more likely to encounter the *Pirates of Penzance* than an opium-besotted androgyne. Even drag queens have become respectable. In places such as the Wintergarten you'll find carefully choreographed, top-Deutschmark spectacles for the tourist market, so we recommend you stick to smaller venues like the Bar jeder Vernunft and Scheinbar for a glimpse of the wild days of the Golden Twenties.

MICK WELDON

---

box office is open from 1 to 6 pm Monday, to 7 pm Tuesday to Friday and from 2 to 7 pm Saturday and Sunday. Tickets are priced between DM19 and DM99.

Chamäleon Varieté (Map 8, ☎ 282 71 18, Rosenthaler Strasse 40/41), a much more intimate venue in the Hackesche Höfe, has the usual slapstick, juggling acts and singing but it's all put together in an unconventional, entertaining way. On Friday and Saturday there's a midnight show in addition to the one at 8.30 pm (closed Mondays). The box office is open from noon to 9 pm Monday to Thursday, to midnight Friday and Saturday and from 4 to 9 pm Sunday. Admission is DM27 to DM39, the midnight show is a flat DM27.

Another 20s-style variety show is staged at the petite *Scheinbar (Map 5, ☎ 784 55 39,* *Monumentenstrasse 9)* in Schöneberg where pantomimes, jugglers and clowns are part of the act. Shows are at 8.30 pm Wednesday to Sunday. Tickets, available before the show, range from DM12 to DM25. Take the U7 to Kleistpark.

Tickets are hot at the cool *Wintergarten-Das Variété (Map 5, ☎ 23 08 82 30, Potsdamer Strasse 96)* in Tiergarten, which features top magicians, clowns and artistes from around the world. The programs, which change every few months, vary in quality, but it's worth checking out. Unfortunately, a night at the Wintergarten will set you back a bundle. Tickets range from DM48 to DM98, but drinks and the mediocre food will stretch your budget even more. The box office is open from 10 am to 8 pm daily. The original Wintergarten

ENTERTAINMENT

(1887-1944) was in the Hotel Central on Friedrichstrasse.

One of the best cabaret-varietés in town is the exquisite *Bar jeder Vernunft (Map 7, ☎ 884 20 884, Schaperstrasse 24)* in an Art Nouveau-style tent decked out with dazzling mirrors and booths bathed in red velvet. Programs often have an experimental and/or bizarre character. After the show, the place turns into a happening piano bar. The box office is open from noon to 7 pm daily. Tickets cost from DM33 to DM66.

Cabaret, by the way, is not to be confused with 'Kabarett', which is political and satirical revues featuring a team of *Kabarettisten* in a series of monologues or skits. They can be hilarious, though you should have at least passable German language skills in order to truly appreciate them. The main troupes are:

BKA-Berliner Kabarett Anstalt (Map 6, ☎ 251 01 12, Mehringdamm 32-34) in Kreuzberg has daily shows for DM20 to DM35. Disco after 11 pm on Saturday.

Die Distel (The Thistle, Map 8, ☎ 204 47 04, Friedrichstrasse 101) in Mitte is closed Sunday and Monday. Tickets cost DM12 to DM39.

Die Radieschen (The Radishes, Map 8, ☎ 30 86 28 10, Am Köllnischen Park 6-7), corner of Rungestrasse in Mitte, has daily shows for DM20 to DM25.

Die Stachelschweine (The Porcupines, Map 7, Europa-Center, ☎ 261 47 95) in Charlottenburg has shows Tuesday to Saturday. Tickets cost DM20 to DM40.

Die Wühlmäuse (The Voles, Map 7, ☎ 213 70 47, Nürnberger Strasse 33) in Wilmersdorf, shows daily except Monday for DM20 to DM40.

THEATRE

Berlin has more than 100 theatres, so there should be something for everybody. In the eastern city centre, they cluster around Friedrichstrasse; in the western part of the city they concentrate along Ku'damm. Many theatres are closed on Monday and from mid-July to late August.

Good seats are usually available on the evening of a performance, as unclaimed tickets are sold an hour before curtain time, sometimes at steep discounts. Most theatres offer discounts (up to 50%) to students and seniors.

Thespian Delights

If your German is fluent enough to follow the plot of *Faust* or *Woyzeck* on a Berlin stage, our hats are off to you. Thankfully, cosmopolitan Berlin has plenty to offer to visiting theatre lovers who slept through their German lessons. The following venues stage English-language production all or some of the time:

Despite its name, Friends of Italian Opera (Map 6, ☎ 691 12 11, Fidicinstrasse 40) has nothing to do with fat ladies in frills (in fact its name is code for Mafia in Some Like it Hot). It is, in fact, Berlin's oldest English-language theatre. Both resident Berlin troupes and visiting ensembles perform almost nightly at the 60-seat Kreuzberg 61-based facility.

STÜKKE (Map 6, ☎ 692 32 39, Hasenheide 54), in Kreuzberg 36, is a small fringe theatre that often opens its stage to non-German Berlin-based actors for experimental fare and solo performances. Not always in English.

The Baracke (Map 8, ☎ 28 44 12 21, Schumannstrasse 10), a spin-off of the Deutsches Theater, has experienced a stratospheric rise in popularity since its founding in 1996. The 99-seat minimalist venue has become Berlin's premier venue for off-beat and avant-garde theatre. Plays like Mark Ravenhill's *Shopping & Fucking* are typical. Most performances are in German, but check the listings for visiting English ensembles.

Another theatre which doesn't require German language skills is the Hackesches Hof-Theater (Map 8, ☎ 283 25 87, Rosenthaler Strasse 40/41) in Hof II of the Hackesche Höfe. Its program is an unlikely mix of pantomime, theatre and Yiddish music concerts, but it all seems to work very well.

Half-price theatre tickets are also available from Hektichet on the day of the performance. Branches are on the ground floor in the Zoo-Palast cinema at Hardenbergstrasse 29a (Map 7) and at Liebknechtstrasse 12

(Map 8), near Alexanderplatz (both ☎ 24 31 24 31 or ☎ 230 99 30). Choices are obviously limited to what's left unsold that day. Sales commence at 2 pm daily and tickets must be bought and paid for in person at the office but will actually be waiting for you at the venue.

Listed below is a cross section of mainstream and fringe theatres. Also check the listings in city magazines and newspapers for additional (mostly smaller, experimental) theatres. Berlin's not stuffy, so you can attend theatre and cultural events dressed as you please.

The **Deutsches Theater** (DT, Map 8, ☎ 28 44 12 25, Schumannstrasse 13a) in Mitte has a rich tradition and counts Max Reinhardt among its former directors (1905-33). Over the years, it has gone from strength to strength with its solid productions of mostly German dramas, both classic (from Sophocles to Ibsen) and modern (Klaus Chatten, Werner Schwab). The box office is open from 11 am to 5.30 pm Monday to Saturday, from 3 pm Sunday. Tickets are DM12 to DM52. There's a second, smaller stage next door at the **Kammerspiele** (literally 'chamber theatre').

The **Berliner Ensemble** (Map 8, ☎ 28 40 81 55, Bertolt-Brecht-Platz 1) is the name of the troupe founded by Brecht on his return from exile after WWII. It plays at the former Theater am Schiffbauerdamm where *The Threepenny Opera* launched Brecht's career in 1928. Rudderless since the death of its last director, Heiner Müller, in 1996, it has been under the stewardship of Claus Peymann since 1999. The box office opens from noon to 6 pm Monday to Friday, from 3 pm weekends; tickets cost from DM13 to DM56. (For more on Brecht, see the boxed text 'Bertolt Brecht' in the Facts about Berlin chapter.)

Sex, blood, screams and pain; the graphic performances at the **Volksbühne** (Map 4, ☎ 24 06 5, Am Rosa-Luxemburg-Platz) in Mitte are not for tender souls. Nonconformist and radical, cutting-edge and provocative are the maxims of its eccentric director Frank Castorf. Performances also take place on a smaller stage at the Berliner Prater, Kastanienallee 7-9, in Prenzlauer Berg (Map 4).

The box office is open from noon to 6 pm daily and admission is either DM20 or DM30, depending on the production.

The **Maxim Gorki Theater** (Map 8, ☎ 20 22 11 15, Am Festungsgraben 2), near Humboldt University in Mitte, offers a usually high-calibre array of 20th century classics with an emphasis on Russian and Eastern European playwrights. Standard works by Tennessee Williams and Harold Pinter often round out the schedule. The box office is open from 1 to 6.30 pm Monday to Saturday and from 3 pm Sunday. Tickets range from DM22 to DM45.

Noteworthy theatres outside of Mitte include the **Renaissance-Theater Berlin** (Map 7, ☎ 312 42 02, Hardenbergstrasse 6) in Charlottenburg whose productions are a little more on the lightweight, entertaining side. Tickets (DM22 to DM48) are available until 8 pm daily.

The Wilmersdorfer **Schaubühne am Lehniner Platz** (Map 7, ☎ 89 00 23, Kurfürstendamm 153), in a converted 1920s cinema, is one of Germany's leading stages and features mostly modern and classic plays by German authors. The box office is open from 11 am to 6.30 pm Monday to Saturday and from 3 pm Sunday. Tickets range from DM16 to DM56.

Children's & Youth Theatre

Berlin has several youth-oriented theatres, all of which perform in German. The best, and best-known, is the **Grips Theater** (Map 3, ☎ 391 40 04, Altonaer Strasse 22) in Tiergarten, which does high-quality, topical and critical plays for children and teenagers. Take the U9 to Hansaplatz. The **Berliner Kammerspiele** (Map 3, ☎ 391 55 43, Alt-Moabit 98), also in Tiergarten, stages fairly demanding productions for mature teenagers.

People of any age and language background can enjoy puppet theatre. Excellent troupes include the **Berliner Figuren Theater** (Map 6, ☎ 786 98 15, Yorckstrasse 59) in Kreuzberg, **Puppentheater Firlefanz** (Map 4, ☎ 283 35 60, Sophienstrasse 10) in Mitte and **Schaubude Puppentheater Berlin** (Map 4, ☎ 423 43 14, Greifswalder Strasse

81-84) in Prenzlauer Berg. *Cabuwazi (Map 6, ☎ 611 92 75, Wienerstrasse 59h)* in Kreuzberg is a popular children's circus.

DANCE

Berlin's dance scene has announced that it wants to be taken seriously and several venues and companies are doing their best to ensure that the city will become a centre of dance in Europe. The following places are all venues for high-calibre modern and experimental dance performances. Check the listings magazines for the current schedule.

Hebbel Theater (Map 6, ☎ 25 90 04 27, Stresemannstrasse 29) in Kreuzberg
Tanzfabrik Berlin (Map 6, ☎ 786 58 61, Möckernstrasse 68) in Kreuzberg
Tanzwerkstatt Berlin im Kunsthaus Podewil (Map 8, ☎ 24 74 96, Klosterstrasse 68-70) in Mitte
Sophiensaele (Map 4, ☎ 283 52 66, Sophienstrasse 18) in Mitte

The Staatsoper Unter den Linden, Deutsche Oper and Komische Oper currently all have their own ballet companies (see the Opera section earlier in this chapter), but plans are under way to merge the trio into a single company, the BerlinBallet. Scantily-clad dancing showgirls are on view at the Friedrichstadtpalast (see the Cabaret section earlier in this chapter).

GAY & LESBIAN BERLIN

If you're reading this, you probably don't need to be told that Berlin is about the 'gayest' city in Europe. To Christopher Isherwood, Berlin meant boys and to some of us, it still does (but nowadays it's spelled 'boyz'). It's estimated that up to 500,000 gays and lesbians call Berlin home; their number was augmented mostly by Ossies (slang for people from the former East Berlin) after the Wende, since East Berlin was the only place in the GDR where you could have any semblance of a lifestyle.

Anything goes in the gay Berlin of the 1990s – and we mean *anything* – so please take the usual precautions. Discos and clubs are everywhere but don't really get going until about midnight. Before clubbing you can eat at a gay-owned and/or operated restaurant and nurse a drink at one of the dozens of gay cafes and bars. Darkrooms are very common and basically *de rigeur* for new pubs or bars.

For listings check the gay and lesbian freebie *Siegessäule* or the strictly gay *Sergej Szene Berlin. Zitty* and *O30* also have listings. If you require even more information and listings than we or they are able to provide, get a copy of the bilingual *Berlin von Hinten* (Berlin from Behind, Bruno Gmünder Versand, DM19.80). For referrals, advice and tips on hot new venues, pay a visit to the friendly folks at the Mann-O-Meter (Map 5, ☎ 216 80 08) info office at Motzstrasse 5 in Schöneberg.

There are three main gay areas in Berlin: around Nollendorfplatz in Schöneberg; Oranienstrasse in Kreuzberg 36 (take the U15 to Görlitzer Bahnhof); and Prenzlauer Berg, particularly around Gleimstrasse (take the U2 to Schönhauser Allee).

Cinemas

With its dangling Bohemian glass chandeliers, wainscoting, glitter curtain and parquet floor, the *Kino International (Map 4, ☎ 247 56 00, Karl-Marx-Allee 33)* in Mitte is a show in itself. On Monday nights, it goes 'MonGay' with homo-themed classics, imports and previews of upcoming features. The glam lobby bar is open before and after the show. It opens at 9 pm and screenings start at 10.30 pm.

A theatre with predominantly gay-lesbian flicks is *Xenon (Map 5, ☎ 782 88 50, Kolonnenstrasse 5-6)* in Schöneberg, incidentally Berlin's second-oldest movie theatre. It has lots of imports and watch out for Dykescreen, its occasional lesbian film series.

Cafes & Bars

The friendly *Anderes Ufer (Map 5, ☎ 787 00 38 00, Hauptstrasse 157)* in Schöneberg has been around for over 20 years. Also popular with heteros, it has an intellectual flair complemented by changing gallery exhibits. *Da Neben (Map 5, ☎ 21 75 38 27, Motzstrasse 5)*, is a pleasant cafe good for a chat and a beer, and has breakfast all day.

Maxim Gorki Theatre shows 20th century classics.

The old Metropol Theatre.

Hot, but not bothered, clubbers at the Metropol disco.

Germany's gay capital celebrates with the annual Christopher Street Day Parade.

Galeries Lafayette: don't just shop, admire the architecture.

Stunning symmetry: Quartier 206 of the Friedrichstadtpassagen complex.

It's operated by the crew of Mann-O-Meter. The volunteer-run *Café PositHIV (Map 5, ☎ 216 86 54, Alvenslebenstrasse 26)* provides a nonthreatening environment for those infected with HIV, their friends and anyone else for that matter.

Interesting places in Kreuzberg 36 include *Roses (Map 6, ☎ 615 65 70, Oranienstrasse 187)*, with over-the-top baroque, queeny decor. *Café Anal (Map 6, ☎ 618 17 64, Muskauer Strasse 15)*, a gay and lesbian Berlin fixture, is an arty-farty cafe and very low-key. It allegedly was a favourite hangout of cult-film director Rosa von Praunheim. In Kreuzberg 61, *Melitta Sundström (Map 6, ☎ 692 44 14, Mehringdamm 61)* is a relaxed cafe with walls decked out in colourful, friendly art.

Schall und Rauch (Map 4, ☎ 448 07 70, Gleimstrasse 23), in Prenzlauer Berg, is a chic cocktail bar with an award-winning design and designer prices willingly paid by a young and buff crowd. It's open to 3 am daily.

Clubs Right by the East Side Gallery in Friedrichshain is *Die Busche (Map 6, ☎ 589 15 85, Mühlenstrasse 11-12)*, the biggest gay-lesbian place in eastern Berlin. On Wednesday night, the *SO36* (Map 6) in Kreuzberg hosts the legendary Hungrige Herzen (Hungry Hearts) party. Other venues with occasional gay-lesbian events include: *Tränenpalast, Tresor, Sage Club, Oxymoron, Kalkscheune* and *90 Grad*. For addresses, check under the Clubs section earlier in this chapter.

Special Events

For specific information on gay events, contact Mann-O-Meter (Map 5) on ☎ 216 80 08. February sees the award ceremony of the Teddy, the Gay & Lesbian film prize as part of the Berlin International Film Festival. Around Easter, there's a gay leather meet. In May, the Gay & Lesbian Run and Totally Twisted, a gay and lesbian theatre festival, take place. June wouldn't be complete without the Christopher Street Parade. The Lesbian Film Festival is held in October, followed in November by the International Gay & Lesbian Film Festival.

Men Only

Bars Schöneberg has the greatest concentration of bars. *Hafen (Map 5, ☎ 214 11 18, Motzstrasse 19)* is full of gay yuppies fortifying themselves before they move on to (some say sneak into) *Tom's Bar (Map 5, ☎ 213 45 70)* next door, with its cavernous and very dark and active cellar. Originally popular with the leather crowd, Tom's now attracts mostly a younger bunch and also a fair share of tourists. Hafen opens at 8 pm, Tom's at 10 pm, but if you're OFB (out for business) don't arrive at the latter before midnight.

Next to Connection (see the Clubs section following) is the up-and-coming (no pun intended) *Prinzknecht (Map 7, ☎ 218 14 31, Fuggerstrasse 33)*, a chic American-style bar with bare brick walls, chrome lamps and Georgia O'Keefe floral canvases.

Knast (Map 7, ☎ 218 10 26, Fuggerstrasse 34), on the corner of Welserstrasse, was Berlin's first leather bar in the 1980s. These days, it's particularly popular with forty-something gays and a good place to start the evening. The same is true of *Andreas Kneipe (Map 7, ☎ 218 32 57, Ansbacher Strasse 29)*, a convivial pub with lots of locals and lots of cruising.

New Action (Map 5, ☎ 211 82 56, Kleiststrasse 35), corner of Eisenacher Strasse, is an eccentric bar for the rubber, leather and military crowd. *Lenz (Map 5, ☎ 217 78 20, Eisenacher Strasse 3)*, is a beautiful cocktail bar (150 different drinks) for beautiful boyz.

Café Amsterdam (Map 4, ☎ 448 07 92, Gleimstrasse 24) in Prenzlauer Berg is down-to-earth and open to 6 am at the weekend. The ever-changing DJs here play great music. *Pick Ab (Map 4, ☎ 445 85 23, Greifenhagener Strasse 16)* is a low-key neighbourhood pub with a darkroom. Agewise, it's a mixed bag.

Clubs *Connection (Map 7, ☎ 218 14 32, Fuggerstrasse 33)* in Schöneberg is arguably the best gay disco in town (DM10, first drink free) and has a huge darkroom. *Jaxx (Map 5, ☎ 213 81 03, Motzstrasse 19)* is a sort of combination sex 'shop'/cinema with a labyrinth of small video cabins. Thursday is

ENTERTAINMENT

'Bottoms Up' gay night at the *KitKat Club*, while the *WMF* turns GayMF on Sunday with its gay tea dance complete with go-go boys and steeled bods. (For addresses, see the Clubs section earlier in this chapter.)

Saunas Berlin has several gay saunas but one of the biggest, cleanest and most active is the *Gate Sauna (Map 8, ☎ 229 94 30, Wilhelmstrasse 61)*, south-east of the Brandenburg Gate in Mitte. Apart from two floors of modern and clean saunas and steam rooms, it has a bar and TV and video room. Hours are from 11 am to 7 am and nonstop over weekends.

Also popular is the *Apollo Sauna (Map 7, ☎ 213 24 24, Kurfürstenstrasse 101)* in Charlottenburg, a traditional gay sauna with steam rooms, cruising hallways and cabins. It's famous for its Slivovitz sauna infusions. Open from 1 pm to 7 am daily, weekends nonstop.

One of the nicest saunas in town is *Treibhaus Sauna (Map 4, ☎ 448 45 03, Schönhauser Allee 132)* in Prenzlauer Berg, open from 3 pm to 7 am, weekends nonstop.

Lockers at any of these saunas cost from DM19 to DM27 (cabins are an extra DM8 to DM10). Weekday specials and student discounts are sometimes available.

Cruising Check with Mann-O-Meter for the latest on the cruising scene. In the meantime, the following are some 'classic' haunts: Löwenbrücke bridge in the Tiergarten near the Siegessäule; the Märchenbrunnen in Volkspark Friedrichshain (Map 4), and Grunewald Park (especially for the leather scene). Nude swimming days (Tuesday, Wednesday and Friday) at the Alte Halle in the Stadtbad Charlottenburg (Map 3) are also popular.

Women Only

As usual, the lesbian scene is smaller and more subdued than the gay scene, but what venues it lacks in number is made up for in substance. A pleasant cafe is the smoke and alcohol-free *Café Seidenfaden (Map 8, ☎ 283 27 83, Dircksenstrasse 47)* in Mitte, open to 10.30 pm (closed Monday). The

oldest lesbian bar-club (1973) in the city is the timelessly plush *Pour Elle (Map 5, ☎ 218 75 33, Kalckreuthstrasse 10)* in Schöneberg. Open to 5 am daily, it's frequented by well-off lesbians over 35.

The *Sonntagsclub (Map 4, ☎ 449 75 90, Greifenhagener Strasse 28)* in Prenzlauer Berg, has lesbians-only nights. *Begine (Map 5, ☎ 215 43 25, Potsdamer Strasse 139)* in Schöneberg is a warm cafe and cultural centre for women with occasional lesbian evenings. The program includes concerts, readings, films and singing.

The *Schoko-Café (Map 6, ☎ 615 15 61, Mariannenstrasse 6)* in Kreuzberg (above the Turkish hammam) is a convivial meeting point with a good cake selection. *SO 36* has a Jane Bond evening for lesbians and drag queens on the third Friday of the month (see the Clubs section earlier in this chapter).

The *MS Sanssouci (Map 6, ☎ 611 12 55)* is back in business. Bopping lazily in the Spree at Gröbernstrasse, just north of the Oberbaumbrücke, it regularly hosts its MS Titanica parties for women of all preferences (lesbians, drag, straight). Call ☎ 78 70 30 94 for details.

SPECTATOR SPORTS
Athletics

The ISTAF, an international track and field meet, is held in early September at the Olympic Stadium. Tickets may be ordered on ☎ 30 38 44 44. Later the same month, you have the opportunity to watch or participate in the Berlin Marathon. The route starts at Charlottenburger Tor on Strasse des 17 Juni and finishes at the Memorial Church (for information call ☎ 302 53 70).

Basketball

Berlin's European-class basketball team, ALBA, won the German championship in the 1996-97 season. Home games usually take place at 3 pm on Saturday in the Max-Schmeling-Halle (Map 4) which seats about 8000. Tickets, which start at DM11.25 for national league games (DM21.25 for European league), are available at the stadium or may be booked on ☎ 53 43 80 00.

Horse Racing

Berlin has three racecourses. Galopprennbahn Hoppegarten (☎ 03342-389 30) is at Goetheallee 1 in Dahlwitz-Hoppegarten, north-east of the city. Built in 1867, it is one of the fanciest European racetracks and is 2350m long. Races take place on Sunday at 1 pm from April to October. Standing room costs DM7, seats are from DM10 to DM20. To get there take the S5 to Hoppegarten.

Trabrennbahn Karlshorst (☎ 50 01 70) in the eastern district of Lichtenberg dates back to 1862 but was completely destroyed in WWII. Rebuilt after the war, it was the only trotting course in the GDR. Meetings are at 2 pm on Saturday (admission DM2/1) and sometimes at 6 pm on Tuesday (free entry). To get there, take the S3 to Karlshorst or tram No 21, 26, 27 or 28 to Treskowallee/Ehrlichstrasse.

In Tempelhof, at Mariendorfer Damm 222, is Trabrennbahn Mariendorf (☎ 740 11 21), founded in 1913. It's the trotting course of choice for hobnobbing city politicos and businessfolk. Races take place year round at 6 pm on Wednesday (free) and at 1.30 pm on Sunday (admission DM5/3). Take the U6 to Alt-Mariendorf or Bus No 176 or 179 to Trabrennbahn.

Ice Hockey

Ice hockey has become a very popular spectator sport in Berlin, which has two teams in the national league. The Berliner Capitals (☎ 885 60 00) play at the Eissporthalle on Jaffestrasse in Charlottenburg. You can get tickets for the games from the hall itself, at the head office at Kurfürstendamm 214 or at other ticket offices. Standing tickets will set you back DM20, while seats cost between DM30 and DM60.

The other team, EHC Eisbären, plays on Weissenseer Strasse at the Sportforum Hohenschönhausen in the eastern district by that name. Tickets (standing DM25, seats from DM40 to DM50) are available at the hall, from the club hotline (☎ 53 43 50 00) or from ticket offices. Take the U5, S8 or S10 to Frankfurter Allee, then tram No 23 to Sportforum.

Soccer

Berlin's club Hertha BSC has had its ups and downs but has managed to stay in Germany's first division, the Bundesliga, for the past few years. The team's home games are played at the Olympic Stadium usually at 3.30 pm on Saturday. The playing season lasts from early September to May/June with a winter break over December and January.

Seats under cover cost between DM34 and DM56, those in the open are DM12. If a famous team like Bayern München or Borussia Dortmund is visiting, the stadium gets packed and prices shoot up by DM10. On most other days, you should be able to get tickets on game day at the stadium box office which opens two hours before kick-off. Advance tickets are available from the Hertha BSC head office (☎ 300 92 80) at Hanns-Braun-Strasse, Friesenhaus 2 in Charlottenburg (take the U2 to Olympia-Stadion Ost) or at ticket offices (eg at the KaDeWe department store).

Two national championship finals take place every year in Berlin. In January there is the annual indoor soccer championship, hosted by the DFB (the German National Soccer Association) and played in the Max-Schmeling-Halle (Map 4, information on ☎ 44 30 44 30). Hugely popular is the DFB Pokalendspiel, the German National Soccer Association cup final. It's played at the Olympia-Stadion but tickets are hard to come by and should be ordered months in advance by writing to Berliner Fussball-bund, Humboldtstrasse 8a, 14193 Berlin, call ☎ 896 99 40.

Tennis

The German Open women's tournament takes place every May at the Rot-Weiss tennis club in the Grunewald forest near the Hundekehlesee lake. It usually attracts high-ranking players and was won by the recently retired Steffi Graf umpteen times. The Open is a very popular event and tickets, especially for the later rounds, are hard to come by. Costing from DM46 to DM115, they can be booked on ☎ 89 57 55 20 and ☎ 89 57 55 21 or through the tourist office hotline ☎ 25 00 25.

ENTERTAINMENT

Shopping

Berlin's decentralised character is reflected in the fact that it doesn't have a single major shopping artery like London's Oxford Street or New York's Fifth Avenue. Rather, you'll find numerous shopping areas in the various neighbourhoods, many of which have a very localised feel. For mainstream and haute couture, for instance, you'd head for Charlottenburg, while multi-ethnic Kreuzberg is known for its eclectic second-hand and junk stores, and Mitte for its art galleries.

The closest Berlin gets to having an international shopping strip is along Kurfürstendamm (Ku'damm) and its extension, Tauentzienstrasse, though Friedrichstrasse in Mitte is up and coming as well. This is not to say that shopping in Berlin isn't fun. You can unearth many unique things, especially clothing, art and high-end porcelain – all of which can be quite pricey. If you don't have a trust fund, give the flea markets a try. It's worth taking a couple of hours to rake through the muck if you dig up some treasure you could only have found in Berlin.

A good source of hip and unusual stores is *The Art of Shopping*, an annual booklet available in bookshops and some stores.

WHAT TO BUY
Antiques & Collectibles
The greatest concentrations of antique stores are around Nollendorfplatz in Schöneberg (furniture, household goods, lamps etc); around Savignyplatz in Charlottenburg (up-market classic furniture, Berlin collectibles, and jewellery); on Bergmannstrasse in Kreuzberg 61 (funky clothing, accessories, and decorative arts); and along Husemannstrasse in Prenzlauer Berg (GDR memorabilia, furniture, and books).

Near the Museumsinsel museums is the Berliner Antikmarkt, not really a market but a series of shops housed in S-Bahn arches Nos 190-203 along Georgenstrasse (between Planckstrasse and Geschwister-Scholl-Strasse). Shops specialise in periods like Art Nouveau or the 1950s, or in collectibles such

as lamps, military regalia or porcelain. Cheap it ain't, though with some luck you might still find some bargains.

Galleries
Berlin has about 300 private galleries holding forth in courtyards, stately patrician villas, old warehouses or factories and in spacious, elegant collections of rooms on major boulevards. They used to be concentrated along Ku'damm and Fasanenstrasse, but the more cutting-edge studios and galleries are now in Mitte, especially along Auguststrasse and in and around the Hackesche Höfe and Sophienhöfe.

Since we can only list a few here, consult the listings magazines for additional addresses and current shows. The best up-to-date source is the German-English *Berlin Artery – Der Kunstführer* (DM3.50) available at newsstands, bookstores and some museums.

Aedes East Galerie (Map 8, ☎ 282 70 15), at Rosenthaler Strasse 40-41, Hackesche Höfe specialises in international architectural exhibits, often with neat models. It's open from 11 am to 6.30 pm Tuesday to Friday, from 11 am to 3 pm Saturday and from noon to 5 pm Sunday.

Galerie am Chamissoplatz (Map 6, ☎ 69 40 12 45), at Chamissoplatz 6 in Kreuzberg 61 has contemporary paintings, sculpture and drawings, many of them satirical. It's open from 1 to 6 pm Tuesday to Friday, from 3 pm Saturday.

Galerie Anselm Dreher (Map 7, ☎ 883 52 49), at Pfalzburgerstrasse 80 in Wilmersdorf, has contemporary and concept art by many foreign, mostly American, artists. It's open from 2 to 6.30 pm Tuesday to Friday, from 11 am to 2 pm Saturday.

Galerie Arndt & Partner (Map 8, ☎ 280 81 23), at Auguststrasse 35 shows video installations and experimental art. It's open from noon to 6 pm Tuesday to Saturday.

Galerie Brusberg (Map 7, ☎ 882 76 82), at Kurfürstendamm 213 displays classical modern and contemporary art, much of it figurative, by established artists. It's open from 10 am to 6.30 pm Tuesday to Friday, to 2 pm Saturday.

Galerie Eigen + Art (Map 4, ☎ 280 66 05), at Auguststrasse 26 in Mitte, displays new expressive art, much of it from eastern German artists. It's open from 2 to 7 pm Tuesday to Friday, from 11 am to 5 pm Saturday.

Galerie Gunar Barthel (Map 7, ☎ 88 68 33 06), on the 1st floor at Fasanenstrasse 15 in Charlottenburg, shows contemporary German art, with an emphasis on artists from the eastern states. It's open from 11 am to 7 pm Tuesday to Friday, to 2 pm Saturday.

Galerie Pels-Leusden (Map 7, ☎ 885 91 50), in Villa Grisebach, at Fasanenstrasse 25 is one of Berlin's leading galleries with an emphasis on classical modern art as well as German and other contemporary artists. It also holds art auctions. It's open from 10 am to 6.30 pm weekdays, to 2 pm Saturday.

Galerie Springer & Winckler (Map 7, ☎ 315 72 20), at Fasanenstrasse 13, focuses on international contemporary art. It's open from 10 am to 7 pm Tuesday to Friday (closed lunchtime), from 11 am to 3 pm Saturday.

Galerie Wohnmaschine (Map 4, ☎ 30 87 20 15), at Tucholskystrasse 35 in Mitte, has frequently changing art, some avant-garde, from Berlin and international artists. Open from 2 to 7 pm Tuesday to Friday, from noon to 5 pm Saturday.

Zellermayer Galerie (Map 7, ☎ 883 41 44), at Ludwigkirchstrasse 6 in Wilmersdorf, displays contemporary art and sculpture, plus photography and concept art. Open from 1 to 6 pm Tuesday to Friday, from 11 am to 2 pm Saturday.

Books

General Interest Hugendubel (Map 7, ☎ 21 40 60) at Tauentzienstrasse 13, is one of Berlin's best bookstores and seems to have just about every German title in print, plus a decent selection of English novels. Browsing is encouraged and comfortable sofas invite reading. You may even bring books to the in-store cafe. A smaller branch is in the Potsdamer Platz Arkaden mall (see the Potsdamer Platz map in the Things to See & Do chapter).

Similar in selection, though quite old-fashioned in its layout, is Kiepert bookstore, which has branches at Hardenbergstrasse 4-5 in Charlottenburg (Map 7, ☎ 311 00 90) and at Friedrichstrasse 63 (Map 8, ☎ 208 25 11) in Mitte.

Also in Mitte is Berliner Universitäts-buchhandlung (Berlin University Bookshop,

Map 8, ☎ 240 94 31), at Spandauer Strasse 2, which has lots of glossy art books, German travel guidebooks and maps, plus cultural and historical material about Berlin.

The bookshop inside the Literaturhaus (Map 7, ☎ 882 65 52) at Fasanenstrasse 23 is an island of calm off the busy Ku'damm and has just what its name promises: great literature (and competent staff).

For international papers and magazines in most languages, try the BHG Presse Zentrum in the main hall of Zoo station (Map 7) or the Europa Presse Center on the ground level of the Europa-Center (Map 7) on Budapester Strasse.

English Cosmopolitan Berlin has a number of bookstores which specialise in English-language materials. The friendly British Bookshop (Map 8, ☎ 238 46 80), at Mauerstrasse 83-84 in Mitte, has books on the history of Berlin and of Germany in general, an excellent selection of the latest British and US novels, and general reference books on subjects like German cuisine, the arts and travel, including Lonely Planet books. Staff are multilingual and very knowledgeable.

Books in Berlin (Map 7, ☎ 313 12 33) at Goethestrasse 69 in Charlottenburg has new and used English-language books. For used books there's also Fair Exchange (Map 6, ☎ 694 46 75) at Dieffenbacherstrasse 58 in Kreuzberg 61. Try the well-established Marga Schoeller Bücherstube (Map 7, ☎ 881 11 12), at Knesebeckstrasse 33-34 in Charlottenburg for its sophisticated assortment of literature and nonfiction.

Travel Most bookshops have a travel section, but some stores specialise in guidebooks and maps. Outdoor (Map 6, ☎ 693 40 80), at Bergmannstrasse 108 in Kreuzberg 61, has many books and maps at discounted prices and caters especially for budget travellers. A new entry is Reisebuch (Map 4, ☎ 283 86 107), at Auguststrasse 89 in Mitte, run by a couple of enterprising young women. Schropp (☎ 859 49 11 or ☎ 859 45 38), at Lauterstrasse 14-15, right at Rathaus Friedenau (take the U9 to Friedrich-Wilhelm-Platz), has a wide selection, as does

Globetrotter Ausrüstungen (see the Camping & Outdoor Gear section later in this chapter).

Speciality The Richard Schikowski (Map 5, ☎ 218 54 95) store at Motzstrasse 30 in Schöneberg has a unique collection of books on the occult. At Friesenstrasse 27 in Kreuzberg 61 is Hammet (Map 6, ☎ 691 58 34), named after Dashiell Hammet, which has nothing but detective and crime stories, including many in English. Biographische Literaturhandlung (☎ 881 45 04) at Düsseldorfer Strasse 4 in Wilmersdorf stocks books by and about women, including many biographies. Bücherbogen, with branches inside S-Bahn arch No 585 (Map 7, ☎ 313 25 15) at Savignyplatz and at Kochstrasse 19 (☎ 251 13 45), specialises in books on architecture and art, many of them English titles.

Gay & Lesbian One of the best shops for gay literature is Prinz Eisenherz (Map 7, ☎ 313 99 36), at Bleibtreustrasse 52 in Charlottenburg. In Prenzlauer Berg, at Gleimstrasse 23, there's Adam (Map 4, ☎ 448 07 67), which has books and magazines but also condoms and dildos for men and women. Bruno's (☎ 21 47 32 93), at Nürnberger Strasse 53 in Schöneberg, has the usual assortment plus videos (for men only). Lesbians should check out Chronika Buchhandlung (☎ 693 42 69), at Bergmannstrasse 26 in Kreuzberg 61 (take the U7 to Gneisenaustrasse). Most mainstream bookstores usually have a gay and lesbian section as well.

Camping & Outdoors

For outdoor, expedition and camping gear, have a look at the range of Der Aussteiger (Map 4, ☎ 441 04 14), at Schliemannstrasse 46 in Prenzlauer Berg, and compare it with Bannat (Map 7, ☎ 882 76 01) at Lietzenburger 65 (corner of Fasanenstrasse) in Wilmersdorf. Also in Prenzlauer Berg is Mont Klamott (Map 4, ☎ 448 25 90), Kastanienallee 83, which has a large assortment for hikers, canyoners, climbers and others. The young team also has an arsenal of tips to offer.

Step by Step (Map 5, ☎ 784 84 60), at Kaiser-Wilhelm-Platz 4 in Schöneberg, has an excellent selection of hiking boots and other outdoor equipment. One of the best-known and largest stores is Globetrotter Ausrüstungen (off Map 5, ☎ 850 89 20) at Bundesallee 88 in Friedenau (take the U9 to Walter-Schreiber-Strasse).

For general sports equipment, try the Berlin branch of Niketown (Map 7, ☎ 250 70) at Tauentzienstrasse 7b near the KaDeWe. Also worth a browse is Karstadt Sport (Map 7, ☎ 88 02 40), Joachimstaler Strasse 5-6, right by Zoo station.

In general, high-quality outdoor items are quite expensive in Germany and you may find that you can get better prices at home.

Fashion

Mainstream Good streets for 'regular' clothing are Wilmersdorfer Strasse, the Ku'damm and Tauentzienstrasse. Gap (Map 7, ☎ 219 00 90), at Tauentzienstrasse 13, is a branch of the American chain selling well-made, classic casual wear for men and women. West of here at Ku'damm 16 (corner of Joachimstaler Strasse) is the Diesel Jeans Store (Map 7, ☎ 883 58 81), where you can get the entire collection of this fashionably overpriced designer label.

Solid, quality clothing for men and women at decent prices is sold at Peek & Cloppenburg (Map 7, ☎ 24 90 51), a large department store at Tauentzienstrasse 19, just west of the KaDeWe. Young fashions are available at the ubiquitous H&M with branches around town, including the one at Tauentzienstrasse 13a (☎ 213 90 92) and another on the corner of Friedrichstrasse and Französische Strasse in Mitte (Map 8). There's even a kids' store at Ku'damm 234.

Those preferring to go natural should pay a visit to Vivaverde (Map 5, ☎ 213 33 61), at Motzstrasse 28, where cotton, silk, linen and other materials are turned into comfortable, sometimes even stylish, shapes.

Schuhtick has some of the coolest trotters in town – office to nightclub – but usually with stratospheric price tags. Relief is in sight at Schuhtick Last Minute (Map 5,

☎ 214 09 80), at Maasenstrasse 5, where many styles ring in for well under DM100.

Designer Most upmarket designer stores hold court on Ku'damm and side streets, though Friedrichstrasse in Mitte is quickly catching up. The German fashion designer Jil Sander, whose clothes are known for their straight lines and understated look, has a store at Kurfürstendamm 185 (Map 7, ☎ 885 41 45), in the same building as the Gianni Versace boutique (☎ 885 74 60) with its colourful, eccentric clothing. At No 50 are the understated fashions by Claudia Skoda (☎ 885 10 09), sold from her cucumber-cool aluminium-clad store.

You'll find Gucci (☎ 885 63 00), with its classic leather and other types of accessories, at No 73 on Fasanenstrasse, and Chanel at No 30. Bleibgrün (☎ 885 00 80), at Bleibtreustrasse 29, sports one-of-a-kind fashions and shoes. Escada (☎ 238 64 04), at Friedrichstrasse 176, has through the roof prices for stylish frocks favoured by the well-heeled.

'Sexy wear for sexy women' is the slogan of Jutta Teschner's lingerie shop Fishbelly (Map 5, ☎ 788 30 15), at Grunewaldsrasse 71a in Schöneberg. From brief to bustier to babydoll – you'll find big names and her own designs. For the finest in bodywear, head to Les Dessous (Map 7, ☎ 883 36 32), at Fasanenstrasse 42 in Wilmersdorf, where the money you part with outweighs that silken negligee you get in return.

Eccentric & Clubwear Schwarze Mode (Map 5, ☎ 694 54 75), at Grunewaldstrasse 91 in Schöneberg does fetish fashions of the weirdest variety. Come here for vinyl, leather and rubber, then browse the erotic bookstore next door. Hautnah (Map 7, ☎ 882 34 34), at Uhlandstrasse 170 in Charlottenburg, has three floors of much the same but is a little less kinky.

Groopie de Luxe (Map 5, ☎ 217 20 38), at Goltzstrasse 39 in Schöneberg, has one-of-a-kind outfits and accessories of superior quality that will make you look good at anything from a trance party to a 30s Swing night. Mid-priced and hip.

Planet (Map 7, ☎ 885 27 17), at Schlüterstrasse 35, has party and clubwear for well-heeled techno fiends. The much smaller Planet 2nd Hand around the corner at Mommsenstrasse 65 is more affordable.

Kaufhaus Schrill (Map 7, ☎ 882 40 48), at Bleibtreustrasse 46 in Charlottenburg, has crazy outfits and accessories. Come and browse and get your inspiration for that next techno party. Market (☎ 883 62 55), at Uhlandstrasse 29, has designer club wear and day wear, but it's quite pricey.

Second-Hand Several stores with funky pre-worn attire have set up shop along Maassenstrasse and Goltzstrasse in Schöneberg, including Razzo (☎ 252 23 95) at Goltzstrasse 32 and Megadress Berlin (Map 5) at No 13. Garage (Map 5, ☎ 211 27 60), a few blocks north at Ahornstrasse 2, is for the dedicated treasure hunter. Here you buy by weight (1kg costs DM25) but much of it is tattered or soiled. More upmarket, and still in Schöneberg, is Made in Berlin (Map 5, ☎ 262 24 31) at Potsdamer Strasse 106.

In Kreuzberg 61 are the crammed Checkpoint (Map 6, ☎ 694 43 44) at Mehringdamm 57 and the big Colours (Map 6, ☎ 694 33 48) in the backyard of Bergmannstrasse 102 (on the 1st floor).

Humana is a chain of thrift shops with branches throughout town, including big ones on the corner of Kantstrasse and Joachimstaler Strasse (Map 7) and at Frankfurter Tor (Map 4, ☎ 422 20 18) on Karl-Marx-Allee. Check the phone book for additional branches.

For superb gowns and cocktail dresses from the 50s to the 80s, visit Sterling Gold with branches at Paul-Lincke-Ufer 44 in Kreuzberg (☎ 611 32 17) and inside the Heckmann Höfe (Map 4, ☎ 28 09 65 00), off Oranienburger Strasse 32, in Mitte. It's not cheap, but it has classy, well-preserved stuff.

Home Furnishings

You'll find plenty of imaginative household wares and decorative knick-knacks at Eins, Zwei, Drei, inside the stylish Quartier 205

(Map 8) in the Friedrichstadtpassagen (see the Where to Shop section later in this chapter). There's another branch in the Europa-Center (Map 7, ☎ 265 26 51). Filiale (Map 5) at Winterfeldtstrasse 42 in Schöneberg has a similar selection of fun items. Glasklar (Map 7, ☎ 313 10 37), at Knesebeckstrasse 13 in Charlottenburg, has gorgeous glassware in all shapes and sizes.

In the S-Bahn arches at Savignyplatz is Arno Lamps (Map 7, ☎ 315 94 90), a large store with an inspired collection ranging from lavish chandeliers to functional office lamps from more than 200 manufacturers. Gunther Lambert (☎ 881 30 36), at Uhlandstrasse 181, sells country-style tableware, furniture, glass and more. At Kiran (Map 7, ☎ 313 46 25), at Bleibtreustrasse 5a, you can stock up on old and new handwoven carpets from Turkey and Persia sold in an exotic ambience. Wohnkultur (☎ 313 29 77), at Grolmannstrasse 53-54, has inviting table settings and cutlery from France and Italy as well as tablecloths from Austria.

Jewellery
Simple Pleasures (Map 5), at Winterfeldtstrasse 37 in Schöneberg, sells handmade rings, necklaces and earrings, much of it in a cool matte silver and incorporating semiprecious stones. The prices here are surprisingly reasonable.

In a higher price bracket is Treykorn (Map 7), in the Savignypassage off Bleibtreustrasse (S-Bahn to Savignyplatz). This gallery-like store features unique artistic creations (the workshop is inside) which most of us can only afford to look at. The material to make your own jewellery can be found at Tukadu (Map 8), an eccentric bead boutique at Rosenthaler Strasse 46-47, where a cheeky cherub rotates beneath the ceiling. Agata (Map 8), at Friedrichstrasse 153, has a huge selection of stylish jewellery, mostly silver but also pearls and some gold, at affordable prices.

Famous international jewellers including Bulgari and Cartier have sparkling shops on ritzy Fasanenstrasse, at No 70 and No 28 respectively.

Music
ProMarkt (Map 7, ☎ 886 88), inside the Ku'damm Karree mall at Kurfürstendamm 206, has a bevy of mainstream CDs at good prices, including lots of special offers. There are even listening stations so you can try before you buy, still a rarity in Germany. Also in Charlottenburg, Zweitausendeins (Map 7, ☎ 312 50 17), at Kantstrasse 41, stocks lots of world music, classical and pop, much of it at steep discounts.

Specialist music stores include Canzone (Map 7, ☎ 312 40 27), in S-Bahn arch No 583 (S-Bahn to Savignyplatz) for world music, and Gelbe Musik (Map 7, ☎ 211 39 62) at Schaperstrasse 11 in Wilmersdorf for avant-garde and minimalist sounds.

Musikhaus Riedl (☎ 204 11 36) on Gendarmenmarkt specialises in classical music. There's a second branch at Uhlandstrasse 38 (Map 7, ☎ 883 73 95). Musikmarkt Schallplatten (☎ 229 14 75), at Friedrichstrasse 165, still has lots of GDR tunes on the shelves.

For the latest club sounds – drum 'n bass, trance, goa, classic techno and more – go to Flashpoint (Map 4, ☎ 44 65 09 59) at Bornholmer Strasse 88 in Prenzlauer Berg. In a similar vein is Mr Dead & Mrs Free (Map 5, ☎ 215 14 49), at Bülowstrasse 5 in Schöneberg, which specialises in imports and independent labels, including vinyl.

Unter den Gleisen (☎ 285 91 44), at Friedrichstrasse 128 in Mitte, still has lots of vinyl and new and used CDs as well as GDR relics.

The store of the Berlin label and producer Piranha (Map 7, ☎ 31 86 14 21) is at Carmerstrasse 11 in Charlottenburg. Here you'll find rarities, collectibles and mainstream music from around the globe.

Porcelain & Gifts
Meissener Porzellan (Map 8, ☎ 204 35 81), at Unter den Linden 39, sells the famous porcelain manufactured in that Saxon city. It's lovely to look at but, with prices starting at DM100 for an unpainted piece, it's a gaspingly expensive purchase. Even just a painted ashtray measuring 7cm by 10cm will set you back DM275.

In the same price bracket is KPM (Map 7, ☎ 881 18 02), which stands for Königliche Porzellan Manufaktur (royal porcelain manufacture) and is located at Kurfürstendamm 26a. Also on the Ku'damm, at No 216, is Rosenthal Studio (☎ 881 70 51), a branch of the nationwide chain of selling tableware, vases and cutlery.

O-Ton Keramik (Map 6), at Oranienstrasse 165a in Kreuzberg 36, has expensive but very idiosyncratic handmade vases, bowls, pots, cups etc. You can watch it all being made at the potter's wheel in the back of the shop.

Specialities

The Hanf-Haus (Map 5, ☎ 782 31 69), at Eisenacher Strasse 71 in Schöneberg, sells anything made of hemp such as clothing, creams, shoes and paper. There's another branch (Map 6, ☎ 614 81 02) at Oranienstrasse 192 in Kreuzberg 36.

The Greenpeace Shop (Map 7, ☎ 313 20 85), at Kantstrasse 5, inside S-Bahn arch No 549, has natural textiles and ecological products.

Douglas is a large chain of perfume and cosmetic stores with about two dozen branches in Berlin, including two on the Ku'damm at No 33 (☎ 883 50 65) and No 216 (☎ 881 25 34).

If you're into painting or any other kind of art, you should visit the Hobby-Shop (Map 5, ☎ 216 55 87), a wonderfully crammed arts and crafts supply shop at the corner of Goltzstrasse and Frankenstrasse in Schöneberg. Pärschke (Map 5), at Potsdamer Strasse 96, specialises in stationery and office supplies. It has good prices and a fair amount of discounts.

Wine

For a good selection of Spanish wines – and competent counselling on what to buy – go to Der Rioja Spezialist (Map 5, ☎ 782 25 78) at Akazienstrasse 13 in Schöneberg. Viniculture (☎ 883 81 74), at Grolmannstrasse 44 in Charlottenburg, also has a good wine selection. At the corner of Barbarossastrasse and Goltzstrasse is Barbarossa (Map 5, ☎ 216 34 12), which doubles as an Italian deli.

WHERE TO SHOP
Kurfürstendamm/ Tauentzienstrasse

The Ku'damm, Berlin's premier shopping mile, stretches west of the Kaiser Wilhelm Memorial Church for about 3km, while Tauentzienstrasse wends its way south-east of the church to Wittenbergplatz. Here you'll find the usual chain boutiques selling inexpensive young fashions rubbing shoulders with elegant haute couture houses and porcelain shops. Thrown into the mix are electronics stores, pharmacies, shops selling perfume, stationery supplies and home furnishings, and department stores. The price levels here are average, except for the more exclusive boutiques in side streets like Fasanenstrasse and Bleibtreustrasse.

The stretch also features a number of indoor malls. Just west of Uhlandstrasse U-Bahn station, the Ku'damm Karree (Map 7) from the late 60s is dominated by the four-storey electronics store ProMarkt (see the Specialities section earlier in this chapter). The Europa-Center (Map 7), opposite the Memorial Church on Breitscheidplatz, stays open late and has a large supermarket, newsstands, boutiques and restaurants. Surprisingly for a tourist centre, the choice of goods and the prices here are quite good.

The eastern end of Tauentzienstrasse is dominated by the huge KaDeWe department store (see the Department Stores section later in this chapter).

Wilmersdorfer Strasse

Along this partly pedestrianised street (between Stuttgarter Platz and Schillerstrasse), you'll find many chain department and large clothing stores like C&A, Hertie and Karstadt. This is the place where locals buy affordable mainstream wares for daily use. The Wilmersdorfer Strasse stop of the U7 will put you in the thick of it.

Friedrichstadtpassagen

This chic new indoor shopping complex is right outside the Französische Strasse U-Bahn stop (U6) and is anchored by the Galeries Lafayette (Map 8), a branch of the famous Parisian department store (see the following section on Department Stores). It is connected by an underground tunnel to Quartier 205 and Quartier 206 (Map 8), smallish malls taken over by international designer boutiques like DKNY, Gucci and Strenesse. (Also see the Mitte section in the Things to See & Do chapter.)

Alexanderplatz
The shopping here is centred around the large Kaufhof department store, with a good assortment of mainstream items. Saturn is a megastore for electronics with good prices but poor service. Smaller boutiques and a Blockbuster Video store round out the offerings. Any U/S-Bahn train that stops at Alexanderplatz will get you there.

Pariser Strasse/Olivaer Platz
Many mid-range to upmarket boutiques selling fashionable and sometimes one-of-a-kind clothing and accessories are gathered along Pariser Strasse. It gets more exclusive the closer you get to Olivaer Platz, where expensive designer boutiques cluster. On Ku'damm, take bus No 109, 119, 129 or 219 west and get off at the Olivaer Platz stop.

Forum Köpenick
In the eastern suburb of Köpenick, you'll find this state-of-the-art American-style mall with three floors of mostly mainstream stores. There are boutiques for teens and twenty-somethings, perfume and shoe shops, cosmetics stores, a large grocery store in the basement and a food court to boost energy levels for the next round of 'mall crawling'. The Forum has been a huge success since its opening in 1997, in no small part because of its location right outside the Köpenick S-Bahn station on Bahnhofstrasse which, by the way, is lined by even more shops.

Karl-Marx-Strasse
For a dose of multiculturalism visit this street in Neukölln between Hermannplatz and the Neukölln U-Bahn station. The district has a large ethnic population, and the many Turkish, Greek, Croatian and other proprietors add their unique touches to the colourful and bustling ambience. You may not find much

worth buying here but it can be fun to watch and browse. Most of the large department stores (eg Karstadt) cluster around the Karl-Marx-Strasse U-Bahn stop (U7).

Altstadt Spandau
The old town of Spandau has been entirely pedestrianised which makes it a pleasure to shop in. There's nothing trendy about it, but if you just want to browse for conventional clothes, toiletries, household goods, stationery and such, you should be able to find what you need along Breite Strasse and Carl-Schurz-Strasse. Take the U7 and get off either at Altstadt Spandau or Rathaus Spandau.

DEPARTMENT STORES
KaDeWe
Short for Kaufhaus des Westens (Department Store of the West), this consumer temple and very symbol of capitalism, is located at Tauentzienstrasse 21 (Map 7, ☎ 212 10). This is truly one of Europe's grand stores, with about 30 million shopping fetishists leaving the registers ringing with about half a billion Deutschmarks each year. The assortment is so huge that, as the store says, 'if we don't have it, it probably doesn't exist'. In general, prices are competitive, if not low. The food hall on the 6th floor is legendary (see the Places to Eat chapter).

Wertheim bei Hertie
Berlin's second-largest department store, located at Kurfürstendamm 231 (Map 7, ☎ 88 00 30), is a nice complement to the KaDeWe with which it's affiliated. This one's less upmarket, slightly cheaper and has almost as good a selection.

Galeries Lafayette
Part of the Friedrichstadtpassagen in Mitte, this transplant of the French department store (Map 8) is more interesting for its architecture than its exclusive designer stores. Built like a circular atrium, its centrepiece is a funnel-shaped translucent glass core where the light bounces around in an impressive display. Offerings include French designer clothing, accessories and

cosmetics. It's expensive but presented tastefully. There's a food court in the basement (see the Places to Eat chapter).

Potsdamer Platz Arkaden

Embedded in the new DaimlerCity development on Potsdamer Platz, this stylish three-floor shopping mall (☎ 25 29 62 00) is an excellent place to shop. (See the Potsdamer Platz map in the Things to See and Do chapter.) There's an interesting range of shops – boutiques and many speciality stores – selling everything from funky eyewear to cigars to books to tuxedos. In the basement are a couple of supermarkets and fast food restaurants. The ice cream parlour on the upper floor is always packed. (Also see the Places to Eat chapter.)

Dussmann – Das Kulturkaufhaus

Not a department store in the conventional sense, Dussmann (Map 8, ☎ 20 25 24 40) at Friedrichstrasse 90 is a hip place to stock up on books (three floors), CDs (two floors) and GDR-era books and memorabilia. Unique services include free reading glasses if you left yours at home, gift wrapping, and portable chairs to rest weary legs. It's all rounded out by a cultural program that includes cabaret nights, live TV talkshows and readings. Best of all, it's open from 10 am to 10 pm.

MARKETS
Flea & Antique Markets

Berlin's many flea markets are treasure troves of unique memorabilia, typical Berlin curiosities, bric-a-brac, antiques, eccentric clothing and simply cheap used stuff. Bargaining is definitely encouraged and, depending on your skills, you should be able to get vendors to knock 10% to 50% off the asking price. As a general rule, offer half, then settle somewhere in between. Following is a list of regular markets.

Berliner Kunst- und Nostalgiemarkt (Berlin Art & Nostalgia Market, Map 8) is at Am Kupfergraben just beyond the north-western tip of Museumsinsel. Collectibles, books, ethnic crafts and GDR memorabilia (not always authentic) are for sale here from 8 am to 5 pm

weekends. Take bus No 100 to Lustgarten, then walk north for a few minutes, or get off at U/S-Bahn station Friedrichstrasse, then walk east along Georgenstrasse for 10 minutes (it leads into Kumpfergrabben).

Flohmarkt am Arkonaplatz (Map 4), in Mitte on Arkonaplatz (take the U8 to Bernauer Strasse), has 50s collectibles and more. Open Sunday from 10 am to 4 pm.

Flohmarkt Spandau, on Askanierring between Flankenschanze and Falkenseer Chaussee, has lots of private vendors, meaning prices are fairly low. It's open from 8 am to 4 pm weekends (take the U7 to Rathaus Spandau).

Grosser Berliner Trödel- und Kunstmarkt (Big Berlin Junk & Art Market, Map 5) on Strasse des 17 Juni, is just west of the S-Bahn stop Tiergarten. It's popular with tourists and expensive, since most vendors are professionals, but is undeniably fun to browse. Open from 8 am to 5 pm weekends.

Grosser Trödelmarkt on John-F-Kennedy-Platz in Schöneberg operates from 8 am to 4 pm weekends (take the U4 to Rathaus Schöneberg).

Farmers' Markets

Heaps of regular and exotic fruit and vegetables, mountains of delicious bread loaves, buckets spilling over with olives, delicious arrays of fetta cheeses – this mouthwatering culinary bonanza is what you'll find at the bazaar-like **Türkenmarkt** (Turkish market, Map 6) in Kreuzberg 36. It's a slice of Istanbul located on the Maybachufer, just off Kottbusser Damm. Prices are as low as you'll find anywhere and the people are friendly and helpful. Good picnic items include spiced fetta spread, best eaten with a freshly baked *Simit*, a ring-shaped sesame loaf. Official market hours are from noon to 6.30 pm Tuesday and Friday. Take U1, U8 or U15 to Kottbusser Tor, then walk south on Kottbusser Damm for about 300m.

Every Saturday morning, Winterfeldtplatz in Schönepark turns into a scene during the Winterfeldtmarkt (Map 5). Considered the best of Berlin's neighbourhood produce markets, its fruit and vegetables are among the freshest and the selection is good too, though prices tend to be quite high. Stalls selling dairy products, meats and sausages are here as well. Market hours are from 8 am to 2 pm.

It's also held on Wednesday, but to get a sense of the Schöneberg scene, you should come on Saturday. After browsing, treat yourself to breakfast at one of the area's many cafes. Take the U1, U2, U4 or U15 to Nollendorfplatz, then walk five minutes south on Maassenstrasse.

Market Halls

Berlin has some of the few surviving market halls in Germany and they are wonderful places for chowing down on some earthy snacks while stocking up on cheeses, breads, hams and produce. The halls were erected by the city late last century in order to move the street markets indoors. The first such hall opened in 1886 and by 1900 there were 14 of them. Some didn't survive the wars, others were closed for lack of profitability. The three remaining ones are high-ceilinged, fairly ornate structures that will time-warp you back to a different age. All are open from 8 am to 6 pm on weekdays and to 1 pm on Saturday.

In Tiergarten-Moabit, you'll find the Arminius Markthalle (Map 3, U9 to Turmstrasse) which has been in its red and yellow brick building at Arminiusstrasse 2 since 1891. A few years ago, the Lange's Imbiss (immediately on your left as you enter from Arminiusstrasse) gained fame as the main set for a well-known German TV series. You can admire the black and white photographs featuring the stars posing with the staff proudly displayed in the stand-up eating section across the aisle.

In Kreuzberg 61, on Marheinekeplatz, is the Marheineke Markthalle (Map 6, U7 to Gneisenaustrasse) which unfortunately has more stalls selling cheap toys and clothes than produce, dairy goods or meats – though there is some of that as well. Finally, in Kreuzberg 36 is the Eisenbahn Markthalle (Map 6, U1 or U15 to Görlitzer Bahnhof), at Eisenbahnstrasse 43-44, with the cool Weltrestaurant inside (see the Places to Eat chapter).

Excursions

Almost everything worth seeing around Berlin is in the surrounding state of Brandenburg, including Potsdam, Brandenburg (the town), the former Sachsenhausen concentration camp at Oranienburg, the Spreewald, Cottbus, Buckow, Rheinsberg, Chorin and Niederfinow. All these destinations are adequately served by train from Berlin.

Efficient rail links also mean that cities farther afield, such as Lutherstadt-Wittenberg in the state of Saxony-Anhalt and the Saxon cities of Dresden and Leipzig, are within quick reach and make for good excursions from the German capital.

Brandenburg

Brandenburg was originally settled by the Wends – the ancestors of the Sorbs – but they were overpowered in 1157 by Albrecht der Bär (Albert the Bear), who became the *Markgraf* (margrave) of Brandenburg. Friedrich I of the Hohenzollern dynasty arrived in the early 15th century, and by 1618 the electors of Brandenburg had acquired the eastern Baltic duchy of Prussia, eventually merging the two states into a powerful union called the Kingdom of Prussia. By 1871, this kingdom brought all the German states under its control, leading to the establishment of the German Empire.

Many Berliners will warn you about the 'Wild East' (a reference to Brandenburg's former status as a communist state), advising you not to stray too far afield in what they consider to be a backward and sometimes violent region. But Brandenburgers, ever *korrekt* in the Prussian style, sniff and ask what you can expect from a bunch of loud-mouthed and brash upstarts like the Berliners. Perhaps illustrating this enmity, in May 1996 Brandenburg held a referendum on whether to merge with Berlin; the result was an overwhelming *Nein*.

Organised Tours

Severin + Kühn (☎ 880 41 90), BVB (☎ 885 98 80) and BBS (☎ 35 19 52 70), who provide guided bus tours of Berlin, also offer four-hour tours to Potsdam and Sanssouci (with commentary in English and German) for DM59. Reservations are necessary. From May to early October, they also run a seven-hour tour of the Spreewald (DM57), which includes a punt ride on the canals. (See the Organised Tours section in the Getting Around chapter.)

POTSDAM
☎ 0331 • pop 142,000

Potsdam, on the Havel River some 24km from the centre of Berlin, is the capital of Brandenburg and the most popular day trip from Berlin. The city rose to prominence in the mid-17th century when Elector Friedrich Wilhelm (ruled 1640-88) made it his second residence after Berlin. Later, with the creation of the Prussian kingdom, Potsdam became a royal seat and garrison town, and in the mid-18th century Friedrich II (the Great, ruled 1740-86) built many of the marvellous palaces in Sanssouci Park to which visitors flock today.

In April 1945, RAF bombers devastated the historic centre of Potsdam, including the City Palace on Alter Markt, but fortunately most of the palaces in the park escaped undamaged. The Allies chose Schloss Cecilienhof for the Potsdam Conference of August 1945, which finalised the division of Berlin and Germany into occupation zones.

Potsdam-Information (☎ 27 55 80, fax 275 58 99, email ptm@potsdam.de) is at Friedrich-Ebert-Strasse 5, which is beside the Alter Markt. Opening hours are from 9 am to 8 pm on weekdays, till 6 pm Saturday and 4 pm Sunday, from April to October. Hours are 10 am to 6 pm weekdays and till 2 pm weekends from November to March. A smaller branch (same telephone number) at Brandenburger Strasse 18 has similar hours but mainly sells tickets.

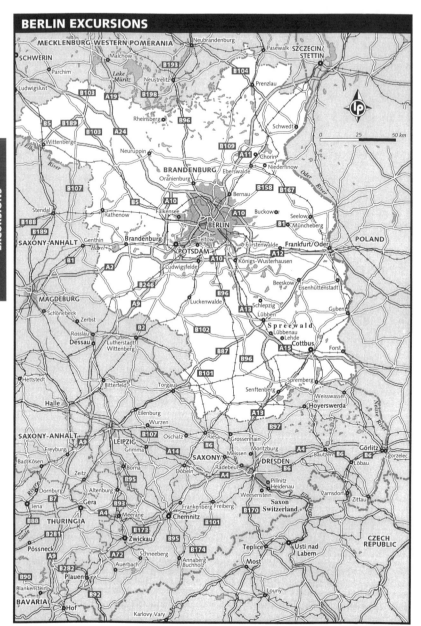

Both places sell the joint Berlin Wel-comeCard (see Tourist Offices in the Facts for the Visitor chapter), which entitles you to unlimited transport and free or dis-counted admission to many attractions in both cities for 72 hours (DM29).

Sanssouci-Information (☎ 969 42 00), near the historical windmill opposite Schloss Sanssouci, has details on the palaces in the park. It's open 8.30 am to 5 pm daily from April to October, and 9 am to 4 pm the rest of the year.

Potsdam will host the *Bundesgarten-schau* (National Garden Show) in the sum-mer of 2001, to be held at parks and gardens in and around town.

Sanssouci Park

Sprawling Sanssouci Park, located west of the city centre, is open from dawn to dusk (free entry). The palaces and outbuildings, which are on UNESCO's World Heritage List, all have different hours and admission prices. A day ticket allowing entry to all palaces and other sights in the park ('ac-cording to capacity', we are warned) costs DM20/15 for adults/children; a family card is DM25. But you have to work pretty fast to make it pay off.

Sanssouci Park is one of the most poorly signposted sights in Germany; pick up a free map at the tourist office for better ori-entation. Since the palaces are spaced fairly far apart (eg it's about 2km between the Neues Palais and Schloss Sanssouci and at least 10km to complete the entire circuit), a bicycle is the most efficient way to see as many of the sights as possible in a day. You can ride on the tracks in the park but not along the footpaths.

City Rad (☎ 61 90 52) rents bikes from Bahnhofsplatz on the north side of Potsdam Stadt train station. In winter, ring ☎ 280 05 95. Rental fees (plus up to DM150 deposit) are DM15/20 per day for touring/trekking bikes (students get a 30% discount).

Schloss Sanssouci

The highlight of Sanssouci Park is the Kno-belsdorff-designed Schloss Sanssouci (1747), a celebrated rococo palace with glorious in-teriors. You have to take the guided tour, so arrive early and avoid weekends and holi-days, or you may not get a ticket (DM10) at all. A maximum of 2000 visitors a day are al-lowed entry (UNESCO's rule) so tickets are usually sold out by 2.30 pm – even in the shoulder seasons. Entry is guaranteed if you're in Potsdam on an escorted tour (see Organised Tours earlier this chapter) or if you take the park and palace tour operated by Potsdam-Information which, at DM49, is pretty pricey.

Inside the palace, our favourite rooms in-clude the frilly rococo **Konzertsaal** (Concert Hall) and the bed chambers of the **Damen-flügel** (Ladies' Wing), including a 'Voltaire slept here' one. From the palace's northern terrace you can see **Ruinenberg** (1754), a group of classical 'ruins' – a folly built by Friedrich II.

Schloss Sanssouci is open 9 am to 5 pm Tuesday to Sunday from April to mid-Oc-tober (to 4 pm from November to April) with a half-hour break at 12.30 pm.

Around Schloss Sanssouci

Just opposite the palace is the **Historische Mühle** (historical windmill) designed to give the palace grounds a rustic air. The palace is flanked by Neue Kammern (New Chambers) and the Bildergalerie (Picture Gallery).

Highlights of the **Neue Kammern**, which was used both as a guesthouse and an or-angery, include the large Ovidsaal, with its gilded reliefs and green and white marble floor, and the Meissen porcelain figurines that occupy the last room to the west. It's open all year round from 10 am to 5 pm, closed Friday (DM4/2).

The **Picture Gallery** (1764) was Ger-many's first purpose-built art museum. It contains a rich collection of 17th century paintings by Rubens, Van Dyck, Caravag-gio and others. It's open 10 am to 5 pm with a half-hour break at 12.30 pm, from mid-May to mid-October; closed Monday (DM4/2). Just west of the Neue Kammern is the **Sizilianischer Garten** (Sicilian Gar-den) of subtropical plants laid out in the mid-19th century.

EXCURSIONS

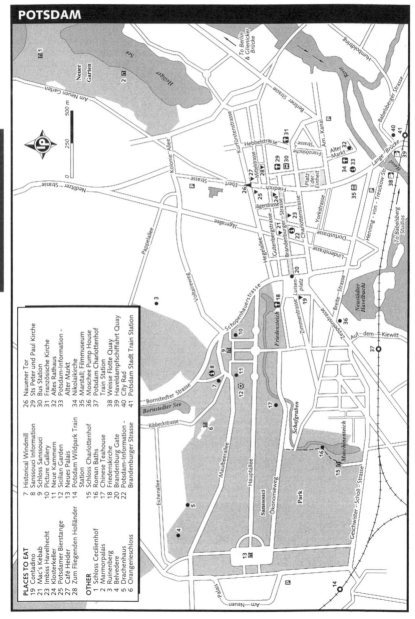

POTSDAM

PLACES TO EAT
19 Contadino
21 Mac's Kebab
23 Imbiss Havelhecht
24 Klosterkeller
25 Potsdamer Bierstange
27 Café Heider
28 Zum Fliegenden Holländer

OTHER
1   Schloss Cecilienhof
2   Marmorpalais
3   Ruinenberg
4   Belvedere
5   Drachenhaus
6   Orangenieschloss
7   Historical Windmill
8   Sanssouci Information
9   Schloss Sanssouci
10 Picture Gallery
11 Neue Kammern
12 Sicilian Garden
13 Neues Palais
14 Potsdam Wildpark Train
    Station
15 Schloss Charlottenhof
16 Roman Baths
17 Chinese Teahouse
18 Friedenskirche
20 Brandenburg Gate
22 Potsdam-Information -
    Brandenburger Strasse
26 Nauener Tor
29 Sts Peter und Paul Kirche
30 Bus Station
31 Französische Kirche
32 Altes Rathaus
33 Potsdam-Information -
    Alter Markt
34 Nikolaikirche
35 Marstall; Filmmuseum
36 Moschee Pump House
37 Potsdam Charlottenhof
    Train Station
38 Weisse Flotte Quay
39 Haveldampfschiffahrt Quay
40 City Rad
41 Potsdam Stadt Train Station

Orangerieschloss

The Renaissance-style Orangerieschloss (Orangery Palace) was built in 1864 as a guesthouse for foreign royalty. It contains six sumptuous rooms, including the **Raphaelsaal** with copies of the Italian Renaissance painter's work done by 19th century German artists. The **tower** on the west side can be climbed (DM2) for great views over the Neues Palais and the park. Part of the Orangerieschloss' west wing is still used to keep some of the more sensitive plants alive in the cold German winter. Hours are 10 am to 5 pm, with a half-hour break at 12.30 pm, closed Monday (DM5/3).

Two interesting buildings west of the Orangerieschloss and within easy walking distance are the pagoda-like **Drachenhaus** (Dragon House, 1770), housing a cafe-restaurant, and the rococo **Belvedere**, the only building in the park to suffer serious damage during WWII but which is now fully restored.

Neues Palais

The late-baroque Neues Palais (1769), once the summer residence of the royal family, is one of the biggest, most imposing buildings in the park and the one to see if your time is limited. The tour (DM6/4) takes in about a dozen of the palace's 200 rooms, including the **Grottensaal** (Grotto Hall), a rococophile's delight of shells, fossils and baubles set into the walls and ceilings; the **Marmorsaal**, a large banquet hall of white Carrara marble with a wonderful ceiling fresco; the **Jagdkammer** (Hunting Chamber) with lots of dead furry things and fine gold tracery on the walls; and several chambers fitted out from floor to ceiling in rich red damask (a sample is provided so you don't have to resist the temptation to touch it). Note the *Fahrstuhl* (1899), an electric 'stair lift' that transported aging royals from the ground to the 1st floor.

The **Schlosstheater** in the south wing has classical music concerts on weekends. The palais is open from 10 am to 5 pm, closed Monday, from mid-May to mid-October; and is open 10 am to 5 pm on weekends and holidays only from April to mid-May.

Schloss Charlottenhof & Around

Karl Friedrich Schinkel's main contribution to the park, the Schloss Charlottenhof (1826), must be visited on a 30-minute German-language tour (DM6/3), but don't wait around too long if the queues are long. In truth, the exterior (modelled after a Roman villa) is more interesting than the interior, especially the Doric portico and the bronze fountain to the east. Charlottenhof is open from 10 am to noon and 12.30 to 5 pm, closed Monday, April through October only.

A short distance to the north-east, on the edge of the little Maschinenteich (Machine Pond), are the **Römische Bäder** (Roman Baths), built in 1836 by a pupil of Schinkel and never used. The floor mosaics and caryatids inspired by the baths at Herculaneum are impressive, but we also liked the flounder spitting into a clamshell near the entrance. The Roman Baths are open 10 am to 5 pm with a half-hour break at noon from mid-May to mid-October, closed Monday (DM3/2).

If you follow the path crossing the Schafgraben (the narrow canal feeding the pond) to the north and then east, you'll come to what many consider to be the pearl of the park: the stunning **Chinesisches Teehaus** (Chinese Teahouse, 1757), a circular pavilion of gilded columns, palm trees and figures of Chinese musicians and animals. It keeps the same hours as the Roman Baths (DM2).

Altstadt

The baroque **Brandenburger Tor** (Brandenburg Gate), on Luisenplatz at the western end of the old town, pales in comparison to its namesake in Berlin but is actually older (1770). From this square, pedestrianised Brandenburger Strasse runs east to the **Sts Peter und Paul Kirche** (Church of Saints Peter & Paul, 1868). The **Französische Kirche** (French Church), to the south-east on Charlottenstrasse and once the seat of the town's Huguenots, was built in 1753.

North-west of here, on Friedrich-Ebert-Strasse, is the **Nauener Tor** (Nauen Gate, 1755), another monumental arch. It's on the edge of the **Holländisches Viertel** (Dutch Quarter), bounded by Friedrich-Ebert-Strasse, Hebbelstrasse, Kurfürstenstrasse and Gutenbergstrasse, which has 134 gabled red-brick houses built for Dutch workers who came to Potsdam in the 1730s at the invitation of Friedrich Wilhelm I.

South of here, past the monumental Platz der Einheit, looms the great neoclassical dome of Schinkel's **Nikolaikirche** (1850). It stands on Alter Markt whose eastern side is anchored by the **Altes Rathaus** (1753) which contains several art galleries, and is closed Monday (free).

West of the Alter Markt on Breite Strasse is the **Marstall**, the former royal stables designed by Knobelsdorff in 1746. Inside is the smallish **Filmmuseum**, a real delicacy for film buffs, which documents the early days of film making in Germany. Besides a bioscope, the prototype projector invented by Max Skladanowsky in 1895 (see Film in the Facts about Berlin chapter), there are dressing rooms of UFA's leading ladies, including Marlene Dietrich. You can also watch excerpts from classics like *Metropolis* and *The Blue Angel* and learn all about Hans Albers, one of Germany's main movie stars. Hours are 10 am to 6 pm Tuesday through Sunday, closed Monday (DM5/3).

East of here, along Breite Strasse, is the quirky **Moschee** (mosque), a Moorish-style structure built in 1842 as the palace's pump house. It's open from 10 am to 12.30 pm and 1 to 5 pm (DM4/2) on weekends only from May to October.

North-west of here, on the edge of Sanssouci Park, is the **Friedenskirche** (Church of Peace), a neo-Romanesque pile completed in 1854 and containing the mausoleum of Friedrich Wilhelm IV (ruled 1840-61).

Neuer Garten

This winding lakeside park, on the west bank of the Heiliger See and north-east of the city centre, is a fine place to relax after all the baroque-rococo and high art of Sanssouci Park. The **Marmorpalais** (Marble Palace, 1792) which is right on the lake and was designed by Carl Gotthard Langhans, has just been restored. Note the gilded angels dancing around the cupola. Opening hours are 10 am to noon and 12.30 to 5 pm

(till 4 pm otherwise), closed Monday. It's open from April to October only (DM4/3).

Farther north is **Schloss Cecilienhof**, an English-style country manor best known as the site of the 1945 Potsdam Conference. Large photos of the participants – Stalin, Truman and Churchill – are displayed inside. The conference room can be visited on a guided tour daily except Monday year round from 9 am to noon and 12.30 to 5 pm (4 pm in winter). Admission costs DM8/4.

Filmpark Babelsberg

Filmpark Babelsberg (☎ 721 27 55), Germany's one-time response to Hollywood, is located east of the city centre on August-Bebel-Strasse (enter from Grossbeerenstrasse). Filming has resumed (see the 'Hollywood on the Havel' boxed text), though people come here mostly for the heavily touted **Studio Tour**. It's a mini Universal Studios-type theme park, with a haunted house, live shows with audience participation, and a few hokey rides. The science fiction exhibit in the warped **Caligari Hall** with its expressionistic facade is a highlight.

Also good fun is the **VULKAN stunt show** in which actors jump from 30m heights, set themselves on fire and beat each other up, all in a carefully choreographed scenario taking place inside a giant fake volcano. There's also a **guided tram ride** (in German) around the backlot for a peek at the sound stages and production studios, as well as the props and costumes room.

The Filmpark is open from 10 am to 6 pm from March through October. Tickets are DM28/25. To reach Babelsberg directly from Berlin, take the S7 to Babelsberg station (one stop before Potsdam Stadt) and then bus No 692 to the Ahornstrasse stop.

Cruises

From April to early October, Weisse Flotte (☎ 275 92 10) operates boats on the Havel and the lakes around Potsdam, leaving from the dock below the Hotel Mercure near Lange Brücke. There are frequent boats to Wannsee (DM15.50 return), and Werder (DM16.50) and Spandau (DM22) are popular too. Haveldampfschiffahrt (☎ 270 62 29)

Hollywood on the Havel

Before there was Paramount (1914) and Warner Brothers (1918), the reels were already spinning in the Babelsberg dream factory, half a world away from Los Angeles. Production on the first movie, *Der Totentanz* (Dance of Death), starring Asta Nielsen, began in 1912. By the 20s, the talent of celebrated directors like Fritz Lang, FW Murnau, Ernst Lubitsch and Josef von Sternberg fuelled the Babelsberg myth.

Under the UFA banner, the studio churned out movie after movie, many of them now cherished classics, like Lang's *Metropolis*. One of the world's first mega-productions, it required the building of a gigantic production stage (still the largest in Europe) and 36,000 extras. By 1945, some 1300 films had come out of Babelsberg, including the first German talkie *The Blue Angel*, starring Marlene Dietrich, and countless Nazi propaganda flicks.

After WWII, from the ashes of UFA rose DEFA, the top production company in the GDR which made primarily antifascist and internationally successful children's fare. After the Wende, a French consortium bought DEFA and put film director Volker Schlöndorff *(Tin Drum)* at the helm of the Filmpark Babelsberg. Several TV and radio production companies, post-production facilities and computer animation firms also set up shop here. Filming (which stopped in 1989/90) has resumed but overall progress has been slow and it will be years, if ever, before Babelsberg reclaims its role on the world stage of movie making.

has steamboat tours (DM18/10) of the same areas leaving from the southern end of Lange Brücke (opposite the Weisse Flotte quay) daily except Monday and Friday from mid-April to late September.

Places to Eat

The rustic **Klosterkeller** *(☎ 29 12 18, Friedrich-Ebert-Strasse 94)* serves traditional regional dishes from about DM20 and

also has a wine bar, beer garden and cocktail bar. Close by, the two-floor **Potsdamer Bierstange** *(☎ 231 70, Friedrich-Ebert-Strasse 88)*, in the swanky Hotel Voltaire, has a lovely garden terrace, a 1920s feel inside and light dishes from DM10 to DM15.

Across the road is **Café Heider** *(☎ 275 42 11, Friedrich-Ebert-Strasse 29)*, right by the Nauen Gate, which was a prime meeting spot for GDR intellectuals and has daily specials for DM10 to DM13. **Zum Fliegenden Holländer** *(☎ 27 50 30, Benkerstrasse 5)* is an airy pub-restaurant on three levels, newly done up with lots of copper. Two-course lunch specials cost DM16.

Contadino *(☎ 951 09 23, Luisenplatz 8)* is a quality Italian place with soups for DM5.50, pizzas from DM8.50 and creative mains under DM20.

On pedestrianised Brandenburger Strasse are **Imbiss Havelhecht** at No 25 and, one block away, **Mac's Kebab**, both good for a quick bite.

Getting There & Away

Getting to Potsdam is easy and convenient. The S7 links central Berlin (eg Zoo station) with Potsdam Stadt train station, south-east of the town centre, about every 10 minutes. Potsdam Charlottenhof and Potsdam Wildpark stations are closer to Sanssouci Park and the palaces but getting there requires a change to a Regionalbahn (RB) train at Potsdam Stadt.

Potsdam's bus station, on Bassinplatz, is accessible from Rathaus Spandau on bus No 638 (hourly from 5 am to 9 pm). If you're headed for Schloss Cecilienhof, take bus No 116 from Wannsee to Glienicker Brücke in Potsdam and walk from there.

Berlin transport passes must cover zones A, B and C to be valid for the trip to Potsdam which means buying either the *Ganzstrecke* (entire route system ticket) for DM4.20 or the day pass for DM8.50. See the Getting Around chapter of this book for more information on public transport.

Getting Around

Potsdam has its own local trams and buses that are integrated with Berlin's public

EXCURSIONS

transport network; these converge on Lange Brücke near Potsdam Stadt train station. To reach Schloss Charlottenhof and the Neues Palais from Lange Brücke, take bus No 606; tram No 96 is also good for the former. Bus No 695 goes to Schloss Sanssouci, the Orangerieschloss and the Neues Palais. Tram No 92 heads north for the city centre and places beyond.

From the bus station on Bassinplatz, bus No 610 will get you almost as far as the Neues Palais.

BRANDENBURG AN DER HAVEL
☎ 03381 • pop 82,600

Brandenburg, about 60km south-west of Berlin, is virtually never referred to by its full name. It is the oldest town in the March of Brandenburg, with a history going back to at least the 6th century when Slavs settled near today's cathedral.

Although badly damaged in WWII, the town, with its baroque churches and many half-timbered houses, is being restored and makes an obvious day trip from Berlin.

The Havel River, the Beetzsee and their canals split Brandenburg into three sections: the Neustadt on an island in the centre, Dominsel to the north, and the Altstadt to the west. There are worthwhile sights in all three areas, which are connected by six bridges. The train station is 1.5km south of the central Neustädtischer Markt.

The tourist office (☎ 03381-194 33, fax 22 37 43) at Hauptstrasse 51 is open from 10 am to 6 pm weekdays and to 2 pm on Saturday.

Walking Tour

Begin a stroll through Brandenburg at the Romanesque **Dom**, on the northern edge of Dominsel. Begun in 1165 by Premonstratensian monks and completed in 1240, it contains the wonderfully decorated Bunte Kapelle (Coloured Chapel), with its vaulted and painted ceiling; the carved 14th-century Böhmischer Altar (Bohemian Altar) in the south transept (which may still be under renovation); a fantastic baroque organ (1723) in the choir loft which was restored in 1999; and the **Dommuseum** of liturgical treasures upstairs.

Much of the cathedral is being rebuilt, so some items may have moved around – or disappeared altogether! The Dom and museum are open from 10 am to 4 pm Monday to Saturday (to noon on Wednesday), and from 11 am on Sunday (museum from noon). Museum admission is DM3/2.

From the cathedral walk south on St Petri to Mühlendamm. Just before you cross the Havel to the Neustadt, look left at the **Hauptpegel** which measures the river's water level. On the other side is the **Mühlentorturm** (Mill Gate Tower) that once marked the border between the separate towns of Dominsel and Neustadt.

Molkenmarkt, which is the continuation of Mühlendamm and runs parallel to Neustädtischer Markt, leads to the **Pfarrkirche St Katharinen** (Parish Church of St Catherine), a Gothic hall church dating back to the early 1400s and currently undergoing renovation. South-west of the church, at the end of Steinstrasse, is the **Steintorturm**, the second of the four remaining city towers.

To reach the Altstadt, walk back up Steinstrasse to pedestrianised Hauptstrasse and then west over the Havel to the **Museum im Freyhaus**, Ritterstrasse 96, a local history museum with much emphasis on local pottery and mechanical toys produced by the EP Lehmann factory. It's open 9 am to 5 pm Tuesday to Friday, from 10 am weekends, closed Monday (DM4/2).

A short distance north-east is the redbrick Gothic **Altstädtisches Rathaus**, with a **statue of Roland** (1474) in front symbolising the town's judicial independence.

Places to Eat

Kartoffelkäfer (☎ 03381-22 41 18, Steinstrasse 56) has umpteen varieties of potato dishes with soups from DM5.25 and main courses from DM7.60 to DM25.

Blaudruck Café (☎ 0177-243 27 40, Steinstrasse 21) is a wild-looking restaurant-pub with game dishes and a great wine list. Daily specials start at DM8, and at night it opens its snazzy wine cellar. *Dom Café (☎ 03381-52 43 27, Burghof 11)*, just west of the cathedral, has salads from DM5.50

and mains from DM15. The cafe is only open between 11 am and 6 pm from April to September.

Steinstrasse is the place to go for snacks, with *Pizzeria No 31* at, surprise, No 31; *Orient Grill* at No 43 (doner kebabs from DM4); and *Asia-Snack* at No 65.

Getting There & Around

Frequent regional trains link Brandenburg with Zoo station (DM16.20, 35 minutes) and Potsdam (DM9.80, 20 minutes).

Tram Nos 6 and 9 run from Brandenburg Hauptbahnhof to Hauptstrasse via Steinstrasse and Neustädtischer Markt. A single ride is DM1.90, four tickets cost DM7.60. There's a Fahrradstation (☎ 03381-28 93 98) at the Hauptbahnhof with bicycles for DM13 a day.

SPREEWALD

The Spreewald, the watery 'Spree Forest' (287 sq km) of rivers, canals and streams 80km south-east of Berlin, is the closest thing the capital has to a playground. Day trippers and weekend warriors come here in droves to punt on more than 400km of waterways, hike the countless nature trails and fish in this region declared a 'Biosphere Reserve' by UNESCO in 1990. The focal points of most of this activity are the twin towns of Lübben and Lübbenau. The Spreewald is also home to most of Germany's Sorbian minority (see boxed text 'The Sorbs') who call the region the Blota. Its unofficial capital is Cottbus, 30km farther to the south-east.

Lübben & Lübbenau

There's an ongoing debate among Berliners over Lübben (Lubin in Sorbian, population 15,000) and Lübbenau (Lubnjow, population 23,800), which lie 13km apart. Which is the more historical/touristy/picturesque 'Spreewald capital'?

Lübben, a tidy and attractive town and the centre of the drier Unterspreewald

---

The Sorbs

The ancestors of the Sorbs, Germany's only indigenous minority (population 60,000), were the Slavic Wends, who settled between the Elbe and Oder rivers in the 5th century in an area called Lusatia (Luzia in Sorbian, from *luz* or 'meadow').

Lusatia was conquered by the Germans in the 10th century, subjected to brutal assimilation throughout the Middle Ages and partitioned in 1815. Lower Sorbia, centred around the Spreewald and Cottbus (Chosébuz), went to Prussia while Upper Sorbia around Bautzen (Budessin), 53km north-east of Dresden, went to Saxony. Upper Sorbian, closely related to the Czech language, enjoyed certain prestige in Saxony while the Kingdom of Prussia tried to suppress Lower Sorbian, which is similar to Polish. The Nazis tried to eradicate both.

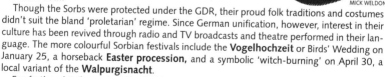

MICK WELDON

Though the Sorbs were protected under the GDR, their proud folk traditions and costumes didn't suit the bland 'proletarian' regime. Since German unification, however, interest in their culture has been revived through radio and TV broadcasts and theatre performed in their language. The more colourful Sorbian festivals include the **Vogelhochzeit** or Birds' Wedding on January 25, a horseback **Easter procession,** and a symbolic 'witch-burning' on April 30, a local variant of the **Walpurgisnacht**.

For further details, contact the Sorbian Institute (☎ 03591-497 20), at Bahnhofstrasse 6, 02625 Bautzen or the Institute of Sorbian Studies (☎ 0341-973 76 50), at Augustusplatz 9, 04109 Leipzig.

– Jeremy Gray

EXCURSIONS

(Lower Spreewald), has a history predating that of Lübbenau by at least two centuries. It boasts more interesting architecture and feels like a 'real' town.

Lübbenau, in the Oberspreewald (Upper Spreewald), is equally picturesque but positively crammed year round with tourists trying to get out onto the canals on *Kähne* (punt boats) – once the only way to get around in these parts. A visit to both towns has its merits.

Lübben Hauptbahnhof is on Bahnhofstrasse, south-west of the central Markt. To reach the centre of town walk north-east along Friedensstrasse and then through the Hain, a large park. The tourist office (☎ 03546-30 90, fax 25 43) is in Schloss Lübben at Ernst-von-Houwald-Damm 14 and opens from 10 am to 6 pm weekdays, to 4 pm Saturday and to 3 pm Sunday (shorter hours in winter).

Lübbenau's train and bus stations are on Poststrasse, about 600m south of the tourist office (☎ 03542-36 68, fax 467 70) at Ehm-Welk-Strasse 15. It is open from 9 am to 6 pm weekdays, to 4 pm on weekends from March to October. During the rest of the year it's open from 9 am to 4 pm weekdays only. If you want to learn more about the Spreewald Biosphere Reserve, go to Haus für Mensch und Natur (☎ 03542-89 21 11, fax 89 21 40) at Schulstrasse 9, open from 10 am to 5 pm weekdays and, between April and October, also on weekends.

Hiking The Spreewald has hiking and walking trails to suit everyone. The tourist offices sell the 1:25,000 *Oberspreewald* (No 4) and *Unterspreewald* (No 1) maps (DM9.80 each) which are a must if you're serious about hiking.

From Lübben an easy trail follows the Spree south to Lübbenau (13.2km) and north to Schlepzig (12.3km). From Lübbenau you can follow a nature trail (30 minutes) west to Lehde, the 'Venice of the Spreewald', which has the wonderful **Freilandmuseum** (DM6/4) of traditional Sorbian thatched houses and farm buildings. The Leipscher Weg, which starts near the Grosser Hafen on Dammstrasse in

Lübbenau, is part of the E10 European Walking Trail from the Baltic to the Adriatic and leads south-west to Leipe, accessible only by boat as recently as 1936. Another popular walk is from the Topfmarkt in Lübbenau north-east to the Wotschofska restaurant (3km), crossing 14 small bridges.

Boating The Kahnfährhafen in Lübben, the little harbour where you can board punts (DM5 to DM6 per person per hour), is along the Spree south-west of the tourist office. Bootsverleih Gebauer (☎ 03546-71 94) has one/two-person kayaks for DM7/8 for the first hour and DM4/5 for each additional hour. Day rates are DM30/35 during the week and DM35/42 at the weekend. Canoes cost DM10/7 for the first hour/subsequent hour and DM49/56 per day during the week/weekend.

In Lübbenau there's the Kleiner Hafen on Spreestrasse, about 100m north-east of the tourist office, and the Grosser Hafen, 300m south-east on Dammstrasse. From the former you can go on a two-hour tour of the canals for DM10 or paddle as far as Lehde (DM15, three hours) or Leipe (DM35, seven hours). The large Grosser Hafen has any number of punt and boat companies vying for business throughout the year.

Places to Eat – Lübben *Goldener Löwe* (☎ 03546-73 09, Hauptstrasse 15) is a somewhat touristy but decent place, with a lovely beer garden and freshwater fish dishes for DM12 to DM20. The *Café Ambiente* (☎ 03546-18 33 07), corner of Renatestrasse and Gerichtsstrasse, does breakfast and has light meals under DM10 (open 8 am to 6 pm). There are several cheap Imbiss (snack) stands just opposite the NKD Citykauf department store at the start of Hauptstrasse.

Places to Eat – Lübbenau The cosy *Lübbenauer Hof* (☎ 03542-831 62, Ehm-Welk-Strasse 20) is one of the nicest places for a meal, with main courses from DM17. The *Pension Spreewald-Idyll* (☎ 03542-22 51, Spreestrasse 13) has a good restaurant, with salads from DM5.50 and main courses from DM14. If you want to try eel, pike or perch (*Aal, Hecht, Zander*) pulled straight from the Spree, try **Strubel's** (☎ *03542-27 98, Dammstrasse 3)*, where mains are about DM20.

Cottbus

Cottbus (Chosebuz in Sorbian, population 115,000), about 115km south-east of Berlin, is a pretty town with some wonderful architecture and a decent number of cultural offerings. The tourist office (☎ 0355-242 54, fax 79 19 31) is at Berliner Strasse 1. The Sorbische Kulturinformation Lodka (☎ 0355-79 11 10), in the Wendisch Haus at August-Bebel-Strasse 82, provides information about the Sorbs – and serves authentic Sorbian specialities at its cafe.

Those who are interested in Sorbian culture should check out the **Wendisches Museum/Serbski muzej** at Mühlenstrasse 12. This museum thoroughly examines the Slavic people's history, language and culture. It's open from 8.30 am to 5 pm weekdays and from 2 to 6 pm weekends. Admission costs DM4/2. Other places in Cottbus worth inspecting include the 15th century **Oberkirche** on Oberkirchplatz, west of the central Altmarkt; the Art Nouveau **Staatstheater** on Schillerplatz to the south-west; and **Branitzer Park** to the south-east with its lovely 18th century baroque Schloss and the Seepyramide, a curious grass-covered pyramid 'floating' in a little lake nearby.

Getting There & Around

InterRegio (IR), Regionalexpress (RE) and Regionalbahn (RB) trains serve Lübben (50 minutes, DM22.20) and Lübbenau (one hour, DM24.40) several times hourly from Berlin-Lichtenberg. Hourly trains to Cottbus (1½ hours, DM33) departing from Ostbahnhof also stop at both towns.

The tourist office in Lübben rents bicycles for DM10 a day, as does K-Heinz Oswald (☎ 03546-40 63) at An der Spreewaldbahn 6, north-west of the centre. In Lübbenau, try Kretschmann (☎ 03542-433) at Poststrasse 16.

BUCKOW

☎ 033433 • pop 1800

The lovely town of Buckow is the 'pearl of the Märkische Schweiz', a 205-sq-km nature park of clear streams, lakes and beautiful, low-lying hills. About 55km east of Berlin, it has long been touted as the capital's 'lung', and not just since 1854 when Friedrich Wilhelm IV's physician advised His Majesty to visit this village where 'the lungs walk as on velvet'. Writer Theodor Fontane praised its 'friendly landscape' in *Das Oderland* (1863), the second book in his four-volume travelogue. In the early 1950s, Bertolt Brecht and Helene Weigel spent their summers here, away from hot and humid Berlin.

Buckow is surrounded by five lakes, the largest of which is Schermützelsee. Wriezener Strasse, the main street where you'll find the tourist office (☎ 659 82, fax 659 20) at No 1a, runs parallel to the lake before becoming Hauptstrasse. It's open from 9 am to noon and 1 to 5 pm weekdays, from 10 am to 5 pm weekends during April to October. Otherwise, Saturday hours are 10 am to 2 pm, and it's shut on Sunday.

Brecht-Weigel House

The house where the GDR's first couple of the arts spent their summers from 1952 to 1955 is at Bertolt-Brecht-Strasse 29. You can either walk due west on Werderstrasse or take the scenic route along Ringstrasse and Bertolt-Brecht-Strasse, admiring the posh villas and mansions that once housed the elite of the GDR.

Brecht's house (☎ 467) is a relatively simple affair with an overhanging roof, geometric patterns outside and a relief of Europa riding a bull over the front door. Among the photos, documents and original furnishings inside is the covered wagon from a production of *Mother Courage*; outside in the fine gardens are copper tablets engraved with Brecht's words. Opening hours are from 1 to 5 pm Wednesday to Friday, to 6 pm weekends, from April to October. During the rest of the year it's open from 10 am to noon and 1 to 4 pm Wednesday to Friday, from 11 am to 4 pm Sunday (DM3/1.50).

euro currency converter DM1 = €.51

EXCURSIONS

Activities

Buckow is paradise for hikers and walkers. You can follow the Panoramaweg from north of Buckow clear around the Schermützelsee (7.5km), the Drachenkehle north to Krugberg (5km), the Poetensteig to the north-east above the Kleiner Tornowsee, the Grosser Tornowsee to Pritzhagener Mühle (9km), or the Alter Schulsteig to Dreieichen (10km). The tourist office sells two useful maps with marked walks: *Märkische Schweiz Reisegebiet Karte* (DM6.50) and the 1:25,000 *Märkische Schweiz Topographische Karte* (DM9.75).

There's a *Strandbad* (lakeside pool) with a beach and diving board on the north-east tip of the Schermützelsee (entry costs DM3). At the dock just south you can rent rowing boats or go on a cruise with Seetours (☎ 232). In season, the large MS *Scherri* sails hourly between 10 am and 5 pm from Tuesday to Sunday while the little MS *Seeadler* sails from 10.30 am to 5.30 pm on weekends only. A trip to the Pension Buchenfried and Fischerkehle restaurant at the south-western end of the lake and back will cost you DM7/3.50, or for a one way trip DM5/2.50. Taking a bike along costs an extra DM2.

Places to Eat

The *Stobbermühle* (☎ 668 33) has food worthy of a hotel in a world-class city, with imaginative starters/main courses from DM7/18. Try the fabulous duck dishes (from DM20) or the lobster (DM36).

The *Fischerkehle* (☎ 374, Am Fischerberg 7) is a popular, 85-year-old place on the south-west shore of the lake.

For ethnic food, try the *Minh Hoa* (☎ 574 72, Königstrasse 33) which offers Vietnamese fare or the stylish *Chao'sche* (☎ 560 02, Bertolt-Brecht-Strasse 9) for Chinese.

The *Café Am Markt* (☎ 566 95, Markt 4) has pizza from DM6 and attracts a boisterous crowd (closed Monday).

The *Mini Grill* on Wriezener Strasse, almost opposite the tourist office, sells kebabs, pork steaks, sausages and other snacks from 11 am to 8 pm.

Getting There & Away

Buckow is not easily reached by public transport. The best way is to take the RB train to Müncheberg leaving Berlin-Lichtenberg every two hours, then change onto the bus to Buckow. Connections are good, and the journey takes just 1½ hours (DM25 each way).

SACHSENHAUSEN MEMORIAL & MUSEUM

In 1936 the Nazis opened a 'model' *Konzentrationslager* (concentration camp) for men in a disused brewery in Sachsenhausen, near the town of Oranienburg (population 26,000), about 35km north-west of Berlin.

Inmates (political undesirables, gays, Jews, Gypsies – the usual Nazi targets) were forced to make bricks, hand grenades and weapons, counterfeit dollar and pound banknotes (to flood Allied countries and wreak economic havoc) and even to test out boot leather for days on end on a special track. By 1945 about 220,000 men from 22 countries had passed through the gates of Sachsenhausen KZ. About 100,000 were murdered.

After the war, the Soviets and GDR leaders set up *Speziallager No 7* (Special Camp No 7) for political prisoners, rightists, ex-Nazis, monarchists or whoever didn't happen to fit into *their* mould. An estimated 60,000 people were interned at the camp between 1945 and 1950, and up to 12,000 are believed to have died here. There's a mass grave of victims at the camp and another one 1.5km to the north.

The triangular, walled camp (31 hectares in size) is about 2km north-east of Oranienburg train station. It's an easy, signposted 20-minute walk or you can catch bus No 804 or 805 as far as the corner of Bernauer Strasse and Strasse der Einheit.

The camp is open April to September from 8.30 am to 6 pm (to 4.30 pm the rest of the year), closed Monday (free admission). Maps, brochures and books are for sale at the camp information office.

Getting There & Away

The best and cheapest way to travel to Oranienburg is by taking an RB train from

Berlin-Lichtenberg, which makes the trip in 30 minutes for the price of a *Ganzstrecke* ticket (DM4.20 one way) or the DM8.50 *Tageskarte* (day pass). The S1 also goes to Oranienburg for the same price, but it's much slower.

See the Getting Around chapter for more information on tickets.

RHEINSBERG
☎ 033931 • pop 5500

Rheinsberg, some 90km north of Berlin, has much to offer visitors: a charming Renaissance palace, walks in the lovely Schlosspark, boating on the lake and Rhin River and some top-notch restaurants.

The town hugs the south-eastern shore of Grienericksee, a large lake. The central Markt lies about 1km north-west of the train station, with the friendly tourist office (☎/fax 20 59) in the Kavalierhaus. It's open from 9.30 am to 5 pm Monday to Saturday, from 10 am to 2 pm Sunday. Buses stop on Mühlenstrasse just south of Schlossstrasse.

Schloss Rheinsberg

A moated castle stood on Grienericksee from the early Middle Ages to protect the March of Brandenburg's northern border from the marauders of Mecklenburg. But Schloss Rheinsberg as we see it today only began to take shape in 1566, when its owner, Achim von Bredow, had it rebuilt in the Renaissance style. Friedrich Wilhelm I bought and expanded it in 1734 for his 22-year-old son, Crown Prince Friedrich (the future Friedrich II). He also cleaned up the town – paving roads, plastering house facades and tiling roofs.

Friedrich, who spent four years here studying and preparing for the throne (1734-40), later said this period was the happiest of his life. He oversaw much of the remodelling of the palace by Johann Gottfried Kemmeter and Knobelsdorff; some say this was his 'test', on a minor scale, of the much grander Schloss Sanssouci (1747) in Potsdam.

During WWII art treasures from Potsdam were stored at Schloss Rheinsberg. Alas, the palace was looted in 1945 and

used as a sanatorium by the communists from 1953. Today, it is a mere shadow of its former self, but it is being renovated at a furious pace.

A tour of the palace takes in about two dozen, mostly empty, rooms on the 1st floor, including the oldest ones: the **Hall of Mirrors**, where young Friedrich held flute contests; the **Tower Chamber**, where the future king studied and which he recreated in the Berliner Schloss in 1745; and the **Bacchus Room** with a ceiling fresco of a worn looking Ganymede. Among our favourites, though, are the **Lacquer Room**, with its chinoiserie; **Prince Heinrich's bedchamber**, with an exquisite trompe l'oeil ceiling; and the rococo **Shell Room**.

The ground floor of the north wing contains the **Kurt Tucholsky Gedenkstätte**, a small memorial museum dedicated to the life and work of the writer (1890-1935). He wrote a popular novel called *Rheinsberg – ein Tagebuch für Verliebte* (Rheinsberg – A Lovers' Diary) in which the young swain Wolfgang traipses through the Schloss with his beloved Claire in tow, putting the palace and the town of Rheinsberg firmly on the literary map.

The palace and museum are open from 9.30 am to 5 pm with a half-hour break at 12.30 pm from April to October, closed Monday. During the rest of the year, it opens at 10 am and closes at 4 or 5 pm. Admission to the palace is DM6/4, to the museum DM2/1.

Places to Eat

Among the excellent new restaurants in Rheinsberg is *Seehof* (☎ 383 03, *Seestrasse 19c*), a 1st-class restaurant with a lovely back courtyard. The *Schloss Rheinsberg* (☎ 27 77), inside the Deutsches Haus Atrium Hotel, is the town's silver-service restaurant – with prices to match.

More reasonable is *Zum Alten Fritz* (☎ 20 86, *Schlossstrasse 11*), an excellent place for regional specialities like Schlesischer Krustenbraten (ham with beans and parsley potatoes), costing DM18, or Märkische Rinderrouladen (beef olives à la March), costing DM19.

euro currency converter DM1 = €.51

Al Castello (☎ 380 84, Rhin Passage) on Rhinstrasse, has pizzas/pastas from DM7/8.50. The *Garden (☎ 378 11, Rhin Passage)* is a Chinese restaurant with starters/main courses from DM4.50/15 and weekday lunches from DM13.

Getting There & Away

RB trains from Berlin-Lichtenberg to Rheinsberg leave every two hours (1½ hours, DM24.40). The train station in Rheinsberg is 1km south-east of the Markt on Berliner Strasse.

CHORIN

Kloster Chorin (Chorin Monastery), in the little town by the same name some 60km north-east of Berlin, is considered to be one of the finest red-brick Gothic structures in northern Germany. Every summer it hosts the Choriner Musiksommer, a world-class music festival.

There is no tourist office, but the reception desk at the Hotel Haus Chorin (☎ 033 366-447) acts as a sort of de facto information centre.

Kloster Chorin was founded by Cistercian monks in 1273, and 500 of them laboured over six decades to erect their monastery and church of red brick on a granite base. The monastery was secularised in 1542 following Elector Joachim II's conversion to Protestantism and, after the Thirty Years' War, it fell into disrepair. Renovation of the structure, which was instigated by Schinkel, has gone on in a somewhat haphazard fashion since the early 19th century.

The entrance to the monastery, with its bright red and ornate facade, leads to the central cloister and ambulatory, where the music festival is held. To the north is the early-Gothic **Klosterkirche** with its wonderful carved portals and long lancet windows in the apse. Have a look along the walls at floor level to see the layer of granite supporting the porous handmade bricks. The monastery is open between 9 am and 6 pm daily from April to October and to 4 pm the rest of the year. Admission is DM4/2, parking costs DM5.

The celebrated **Choriner Musiksommer** takes place at 3 pm on most Saturdays and Sundays from June to August – expect to hear some top talent. For more information contact the organisers on ☎ 03334-65 73 10, Schickelstrasse 5, in Eberswalde Finow. Tickets are also available from ticket agencies in Berlin. Chamber music concerts are also held in the church, said to have near-perfect acoustics, at 4 pm on certain Sundays from late May to August.

Getting There & Away

Chorin is directly served every two hours from Ostbahnhof (50 minutes, DM16.20) by RE trains. The train station in Chorin is about 3km north-west of the monastery, but you can reach it via a marked trail in less than half an hour.

NIEDERFINOW

The Schiffshebewerk (ship's lift) at Niederfinow (population 700), about 10km southeast of Chorin and 55km from Berlin, is one of the most remarkable feats of engineering from the early 20th century. It's also fun, especially for kids.

A mechanical hoist (1934) allows barges to clear the difference of 36m in height between the Oder River and the Oder-Havel Canal. This being Germany, technical data about the structure is posted everywhere ('60m high, 27m wide, 94m long' etc), but it's still an amazing sight watching 1200-tonne Polish barges laden with coal being hoisted in a watery cradle up from the Oder and deposited in the canal. The lift can be viewed from Hebewerkstrasse for free, but it's much more fun to pay the DM2/1 and climb the steps to the upper platform to view the 10-minute operation from above. It's open between 9 am and 6 pm daily from May to September, to 4 pm the rest of the year.

Getting There & Away

Niederfinow is served at least hourly from Ostbahnhof with an easy change of trains in Eberswalde (one hour, DM16.20). The Schiffshebewerk is about 2km to the north of the train station, and the way is clearly signposted.

Beyond Brandenburg

LUTHERSTADT-WITTENBERG
☎ 03491 • pop 53,000

Lutherstadt-Wittenberg is about 100km south-west of Berlin in the state of Saxony-Anhalt. It is best known as the place where Protestant reformer Martin Luther launched the Reformation in 1517, an act of the greatest cultural importance to all of Europe and indeed the world. Wittenberg was also famous for its university where Luther was a full theology professor, and for being the seat of the elector of Saxony until 1547. Renaissance painter Lucas Cranach the Elder also lived here at that time.

From Wittenberg's main train station, the city centre is a 15-minute walk away. Go between the two train lines and then under the tracks and into Collegienstrasse, which is the city's main street. Collegienstrasse runs along an east-west axis through the Markt, turning into Schlossstrasse at its western end.

Wittenberg-Information (☎ 49 86 10, fax 48 86 11) is at Schlossplatz 2, opposite the Schlosskirche. It's open from 9 am to 6 pm weekdays, from 10 am to 2 pm Saturday, and from 11 am to 3 pm Sunday. *The Historic Mile* (DM4.80) is an excellent English-language guide to the city.

Lutherhaus
The Lutherhaus (☎ 40 26 71) is a museum devoted to the Reformation housed inside a former Augustinian monastery at Collegienstrasse 54. Luther stayed here in 1508 when he first came to teach at Wittenberg University and made the building his home for the rest of his life after returning in 1511. Inside is an original room furnished by Luther in 1535 and a copy of the papal bull threatening his excommunication.

It's open from 9 am to 6 pm Tuesday to Sunday during April to September; otherwise hours are 10 am to 5 pm (DM7/3).

The **Luthereiche**, the site where Luther burned (yet another) copy of the document,

Martin Luther was the central figure of the Reformation

is on the corner of Lutherstrasse and Am Bahnhof.

Melanchthon House
The humanist Philipp Melanchthon (1497-1560) became a close friend of Martin Luther, and eventually a reformer as well. He came to town in 1518 as a university lecturer and stayed until his death. Melanchthon's idea of reform went far beyond religious matters – his primary goal was the reform of the German education system, which at that time taught entirely in Latin.

Melanchthon helped Luther translate the Bible into German from Greek and Hebrew. Later, he was heavily sought by other universities but stayed in Wittenberg, especially after the elector gave him a house at Collegienstrasse 60 in 1536. Today it functions as a museum (☎ 40 26 71) open concurrently with the Lutherhaus (DM5/3).

Stadtkirche St Marien
The large altarpiece in this church was designed jointly by Lucas Cranach the Elder and his son and completed in 1547. It shows Luther, Melanchthon and other Reformation figures, as well as Cranach the Elder himself, in Biblical contexts. In 1525

euro currency converter DM1 = €.51

Luther married the ex-nun Katherina von Bora in this church, where he also preached. Note the octagonal bronze baptismal font and the many fine paintings, especially Cranach the Younger's *The Lord's Vineyard* behind the altar.

Markt

On the northern side of the Markt is the **Rathaus** (1540), a banner example of an affluent central-German Renaissance town hall. In front of the Rathaus are two large statues of Luther (1821) and Melanchthon (1865). On one corner of the Markt, at No 4, is the **House of Lucas Cranach the Elder**, with a picturesque courtyard. On the walls of the courtyard are photographs showing the shocking condition the house had fallen into under the GDR. Inside, the superb **Galerie im Cranach Haus** (☎ 420 19 15) has temporary art exhibitions.

Schloss Wittenberg

At the western end of town is Wittenberg Palace (1499) with its huge, rebuilt **Schlosskirche** (free entry; tour (in German) is DM2). A replica of the door, onto which Luther is said to have nailed his 95 Theses on 31 October 1517, is here. The original door was destroyed by fire in 1760 and has been replaced by a bronze memorial (1858) inscribed with the theses in Latin. Luther's tombstone lies below the pulpit, and Melanchthon's is opposite.

Places to Eat

Much of the town's food scene is along Collegienstrasse. Try Speckkuchen, a pizza-like base topped with bacon and eggs scrambled with cream and onions. Lutherbrot is a scrumptious gingerbread-like concoction with chocolate and sugar icing.

The *Stadtkantine* (☎ 41 13 89, Coswigerstrasse 19) is the best bet for a quick, cheap hot meal – try the stuffed pork olives for DM6.50. There's pub food like Irish stew and meat pies for under DM8 at the *Irish Harp Pub* (☎ 41 01 50, Collegienstrasse 71).

Zum Schwarzen Baer (☎ 41 12 00, Schlossstrasse 2) is a great place for snacks like Bratkartoffeln (DM4.50 to DM7), salads

(DM7.50 to DM12) or pizzas (the Kartoffel Pizza is DM14.50); there's a cool pub in the back. *Zur Schlossfreiheit* (☎ 40 29 80, Coswigerstrasse 24), goes in for historical theme dishes, such as Lutherschmaus (duck in a peppery sultana sauce) for DM16.50.

Getting There & Away

Wittenberg is directly served by fast IC trains every two hours from Ostbahnhof (1¼ hours, DM39).

DRESDEN

☎ 0351 • pop 485,000

About 200km south of Berlin, Dresden, capital of the state of Saxony, was famous throughout Europe as 'the Florence of the north' in the 18th century. During the reigns of August der Starke (August the Strong, ruled 1694-1733) and his son August III (ruled 1733-63), Italian artists, musicians, actors and master craftsmen, particularly from Venice, flocked to the court at Dresden.

The Italian painter Canaletto depicted the rich architecture of the time in many paintings that now hang in Dresden's Alte Meister Gallery in the Zwinger; also here are countless masterpieces purchased for August III with income from Saxon silver mines.

In February 1945 much of Dresden was devastated during Anglo-American firebombing raids. At least 35,000 people died in this atrocity, which happened at a time when the city was jammed with refugees and the war was almost over. It is generally recognised that the bombing of Dresden was inspired more by vengeance than strategic necessity.

Quite a number of Dresden's great baroque buildings were restored, but the city's former architectural masterpiece, the Frauenkirche, is still in the early stages of a laborious reconstruction.

The Elbe River cuts a ribbon between the low, rolling hills, and despite its ugly outlying districts, this sprawling city invariably wins the affection of visitors.

Most of Dresden's priceless art treasures are south of the Elbe in two large buildings, the Albertinum and the Zwinger, which are at opposite sides of the Altstadt. From Dresden

Hauptbahnhof, pedestrianised Prager Strasse leads north into this old centre. In Neustadt, Albertplatz, connected to Augustusbrücke via the charming pedestrianised Hauptstrasse, is one of the main attractions.

Dresden-Information (☎ 49 19 20, fax 49 19 21 16) is at Prager Strasse 21 and open from 9 am to 7 pm weekdays and to 4 pm Saturday. If you want to spend the night in Dresden, staff here can help you find hotel or private room accommodation from around DM35 per person (plus a fee of DM5 per person). A second branch is in the Schinkelwache, Theaterplatz 2, open from 10 am to 6 pm weekdays and to 4 pm weekends. Both offices sell the 48-hour Dresden-Card (DM27) which is good for unlimited public transport, admission to 11 museums and discounts on city and boat tours.

The Hamburger Hummelbahn (☎ 498 95 19) runs double-decker buses, 'choo-choo' trains and other touristy vehicles around the city, stopping at all the major sights (at clearly marked 'Hummelbahn' stops). Tours (also in English) leave from Postplatz from April to October several times daily, take 1½ hours and cost DM20/16.

Altstadt

A 10-minute walk north along Prager Strasse from the Hauptbahnhof brings you into the Altmarkt area, the historic hub of Dresden. On the right you'll see the rebuilt **Kreuzkirche** (1792), famous for its 400-strong boys' choir which performs every Saturday at 6 pm (free). Behind the church is the 1910 **Neues Rathaus**, topped by a shining golden statue of Hercules. Cross the wide Wilsdruffer Strasse to the **City Historical Museum** (*Stadtmuseum*) which chronicles the city's history until 1989. Housed in a building erected in 1775, the museum is closed Monday (DM3).

Neumarkt

North-west up Landhausstrasse is Neumarkt with the **Frauenkirche** wrapped in scaffolding at its eastern end. Until 1945 it was Germany's greatest Protestant church, its enormous dome known as the 'stone bell'. The church was destroyed in the bombing raids of 13 February 1945 and the rubble left as a war memorial.

After reunification, the movement to rebuild the church gained momentum and a huge archaeological dig and reconstruction project began. Today you can see most of the building's 10,000 pieces in open shelters on Neumarkt; reassembly of this huge puzzle is expected to take at least until 2006 (Dresden's 800th anniversary). To view the progress, take a one-hour guided tour (several daily, free, German only).

Leading north-west from Neumarkt is Augustusstrasse with the 102m-long *Procession of Princes* mural – made of 24,000 Meissen tiles – covering the outer wall of the old royal stables. Here you'll also find the interesting **Museum of Transport** (Verkehrsmuseum, ☎ 495 30 02) with very cool late 19th century vehicles including a railway car, huge-wheeled bicycles, dirigibles and carriages. It's open from 10 am to 5 pm Tuesday to Sunday (DM4/2).

Schlossplatz

Augustusstrasse leads directly to Schlossplatz and the baroque Catholic **Hofkirche** (1755), whose crypt contains the heart of August der Starke (August the Strong). Just south of the church is the neo-Renaissance **Residenzschloss** (Royal Palace), which is being reconstructed as a museum. Its completion is still far off, although the **Hausmannsturm** (tower) and an exhibit on the reconstruction are now open to the public (closed Monday, DM3/1.50).

Theaterplatz

On the western side of the Hofkirche is the Theaterplatz with Dresden's glorious neo-Renaissance **Semperoper**. The first opera house on the site opened in 1841 but burned down in 1869. Rebuilt in 1878, it was again destroyed in 1945 and only reopened in 1985 after the communists invested millions in its restoration. The Dresden opera has a tradition going back 350 years, and many works by Richard Strauss, Carl Maria von Weber and Richard Wagner premiered here.

The baroque **Zwinger** (1728) occupies the southern side of Theaterplatz and

euro currency converter DM1 = €.51

EXCURSIONS

EXCURSIONS

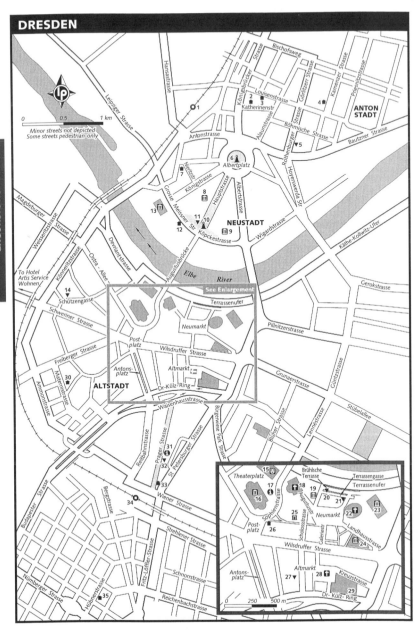

DRESDEN

Minor streets not depicted
Some streets pedestrian-only

0   0.5   1 km

ANTON STADT

NEUSTADT

ALTSTADT

Elbe River

See Enlargement

Neumarkt

Post-platz

Wilsdruffer Strasse

Antons-platz

Altmarkt

Dr-Külz-Ring

To Hotel Artis Service Wohnen

DRESDEN

PLACES TO STAY
2 Hostel Mondpalast
3 Jugendhotel Die Boofe
4 Hotel Stadt Rendsburg
7 Hotel Martha Hospiz
12 Westin Bellevue
26 Hotel Kempinski
    Taschenberg Palais
30 Jugendgästehaus
    Dresden
33 Mercure Newa Dresden
35 Rudi Arndt Hostel

PLACES TO EAT
5 Marrakech
11 Andrea Doria
14 brennNessel

20 Crêpes Galerie
21 Dampf Schiff;
    Klepper Eck
27 Zum Goldenen Ring
32 Schlemmerland

OTHER
1 Dresden Neustadt Train
   Station
6 Schiller Monument
8 Museum of Early Romanticism; Kügelhaus
9 Museum of Saxon Folk Art
10 Goldener Reiter Statue
13 Japanese Palace;
    Ethnological Museum
15 Semperoper

16 Zwinger; Zwinger
    Museums
17 Dresden-Information –
    Schinkelwache
18 Hofkirche
19 Museum of Transport
22 Frauenkirche
23 Albertinum
24 City Historical Museum
25 Residenzschloss;
    Hausmannsturm
28 Kreuzkirche
29 Neues Rathaus
31 Dresden-Information –
    Prager Strasse
34 Dresden Main Train
    Station

houses five museums. The most important are the **Old Masters Gallery**, which is open 10 am to 6 pm (DM7/4), closed Monday, and features masterpieces including Raphael's *Sistine Madonna*; and the **Historical Museum**, opening the same hours (DM3/1.50), with its superb collection of ceremonial weapons.

Other museums include the **Mathematics & Physics Salon**, open 9.30 am to 5 pm, closed Thursday (DM3/2) with old instruments, globes and timepieces; the **Zoological Museum**, open 9 am to 4 pm, closed Tuesday (DM2/1) with natural history exhibits; and the dazzling **Porcelain Collection**, open from 10 am to 6 pm, closed Thursday (DM3/2). They are all housed in opposite corners of the complex with separate entrances.

Brühlsche Terrasse

From Theaterplatz, head a few steps north towards the Elbe River to Terrassenufer and turn right. Soon you'll come upon the Brühlsche Terrasse, one of Europe's most spectacular promenades. Known as the 'Balcony of Europe', it is an elevated footpath above the southern embankment of the Elbe. In summer it's a must for strolling, with expansive views of the river, the paddle-steamers and, across the Elbe, the Goldener Reiter statue and Neustadt.

Beneath the promenade is the Renaissance brick bastion commonly known as the

Kasematten. The museum inside is open daily (DM6/4; audioguides in English and other languages are an additional DM2).

Albertinum

The Albertinum (☎ 491 47 30), just off the eastern end of the promenade, is home to many of Dresden's glorious art treasures. Here you'll find the **New Masters Gallery**, with renowned 19th and 20th century paintings, including many impressionists. The **Grünes Gewölbe** (Green Vault) harbours one of the world's finest collections of jewel-studded precious objects. Both are open from 10 am to 6 pm, closed Thursday (DM7/4 joint admission). Eventually the Grünes Gewölbe will be relocated to its original site in the Royal Palace.

Neustadt

Despite the name, Neustadt is an old part of Dresden largely untouched by the wartime bombings. After reunification it became the centre of the city's alternative scene, but with encroaching gentrification it's gradually losing its hard-core bohemian edge. Königsstrasse, which runs parallel and to the west of Hauptstrasse, is developing into a swish shopping district.

The **Goldener Reiter** statue (1736) of August der Starke stands at the northern end of the Augustusbrücke, which leads to Hauptstrasse, a pleasant pedestrian mall with the

euro currency converter DM1 = €.51

Museum zur Dresdner Frühromantik (Museum of Early Romanticism, ☎ 0351-804 47 60) at No 13. It's open from 10 am to 6 pm Wednesday to Sunday (DM3/1.50). On Albertplatz, at the northern end of Hauptstrasse, is an evocative marble **Schiller Monument**.

Other museums in the vicinity include the **Museum für Sächsische Volkskunst** (Museum of Saxon Folk Art, ☎ 491 46 19) at Köpckestrasse 1, open 10 am to 6 pm, closed Monday (DM3/2); and the **Japanisches Palais** (1737) on Palaisplatz, with Dresden's famous **Landesmuseum für Vorgeschichte** (Ethnological Museum, ☎ 814 48 51), open from 10 am to 5 pm, closed Friday (DM3/1.50).

Places to Stay

Accommodation in Dresden can be expensive, with average room rates among the highest in Germany. Fortunately, there are now a few budget places near the centre.

Jugendgästehaus Dresden (☎ 49 26 20, fax 492 62 99, Maternistrasse 22), is a fantastic place in an old communist party training centre. Beds cost DM33/38 for juniors/seniors in basic twin or triple rooms (add DM5 for private shower and WC). Singles cost an extra DM15.

Hostel Mondpalast (☎/fax 804 60 61, Katharinenstrasse 11-13) is a leading Neustadt budget option and has theme-decorated bedrooms. The simple singles/doubles cost DM37/62 while bunks in dorms are DM25.

Nearby *Jugendhotel Die Boofe* (☎ 801 33 61, fax 801 33 62, Louisenstrasse 20) offers near-hotel standards at DM49.50/79 singles/doubles, though it can get a bit noisy. The non-DJH *Rudi Arndt Hostel* (☎ 471 06 67, fax 472 89 59, Hübnerstrasse 11) is a 10-minute walk south of the Hauptbahnhof and offers dorm beds for seniors/juniors at DM29/24.

North of the Elbe, *Hotel Stadt Rendsburg* (☎ 804 15 51, fax 802 25 86, Kamenzer Strasse 1), built in 1884, offers basic rooms with shared bath for DM65/95, including breakfast. *Artis Service Wohnen* (☎/fax 864 50, Berliner Strasse 25), 1km west of the centre, has the same rates but without breakfast.

Hotel Martha Hospiz (☎ 817 60, fax 817 62 22, Nieritzstrasse 11) offers a few cheerful, simple single rooms for DM95, but most have private facilities and cost DM140/190 for singles/doubles.

Want a view? Head for the *Westin Bellevue* (☎ 80 50, fax 805 16 09, Grosse Meissner Strasse 15) for front-row seats to the Brühlsche Terrasse, the ferry terminal, Neues Rathaus and the Kreuzkirche. Rooms cost from DM160/180.

The *Mercure Newa Dresden* (☎ 481 41 09, fax 495 51 37, St Petersburger Strasse 34), is perfectly located right at the southern end of Prager Strasse, a minute's walk from the Hauptbahnhof. Rooms with all amenities start at DM158/168.

Hotel Kempinski Taschenberg Palais (☎ 491 20, fax 491 28 12, Taschenberg 3), in a restored 18th-century mansion just opposite the Zwinger, drips luxury. Rooms are DM390/450, though 'specials' may sometimes be available.

Places to Eat

Beneath the Brühlsche Terrasse, Terrassengasse is a great place for sitting and watching the world go by. Several cafes and inexpensive eateries also cluster here.

Crêpes Galerie (☎ 864 29 46), on Terrassengasse, has crêpes from DM8 to DM12 and drinks from DM3. *Dampf Schiff* (☎ 864 28 26) and *Klepper Eck* (☎ 864 24 39), both on the corner of Münzgasse, are casual places with street-side seating, good beer and decent food.

The *Zum Goldenen Ring* (☎ 495 23 20, Seestrasse 6), opposite the Kreuzkirche, has main courses for around DM13. The *brennNessel* (☎ 494 33 19, Schützengasse 18) is a good vegetarian restaurant.

In the Neustadt, *Andrea Doria* (☎ 803 29 49, Hauptstrasse 1a) has super service and nice street-side dining. Lunch main courses range from DM14 to DM20 and it's open to 2 am. *Kügelgenhaus* (☎ 527 91, Hauptstrasse 13), below the Museum of Early Romanticism, has a good range of local dishes, and there's a beer cellar as well. For something exotic at dinnertime, try *Marrakech* (☎ 804 55 66, Rothenburger Strasse*

The Zwinger building at Dresden houses five museums.

Kloster Chorin monastery.

Filmpark Babelsberg.

Lutherstadt Wittenberg marketplace.

Dresden's Procession of Princes mural is made up of 24,000 Meissen tiles.

Steaming along the Elbe river.

JOHANN
SEBASTIAN
BACH

Bach: maestro of music and empty pockets.

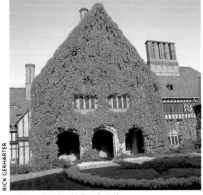

Schloss Cecilienhof in Potsdam.

16) which, despite its name, does mainly Uzbeki and Russian dishes, from DM8.

Schlemmerland, in Prager Strasse, is a collection of fast-food joints selling doner kebabs, pizzas, fish, pastries and Asian dishes – much of it for DM6 or less.

Getting There & Away
Despite the distance from Berlin, Dresden is only a two hour IC train ride away (DM59) with departures every two hours from Ostbahnhof. If you're driving, take the A113 to the A13 south. While you could, in theory, see the main sites of Dresden in a day, you'll probably be able to appreciate its museums and fine baroque palaces better if you stay overnight. Most trains also stop at Dresden's Neustadt train station but the Hauptbahnhof is more convenient.

Getting Around
Dresden's transport network charges DM2.70 for a one-zone single ticket and DM10 for four-ride strip tickets. Day passes are DM8 (single) or DM12 (family).

LEIPZIG
☎ 0341 • 480,000
Since the discovery of rich silver mines in the nearby Erzgebirge (Ore Mountains) in the 16th century, Leipzig has enjoyed almost continual prosperity. Today it is a major business and transport centre and the second-largest city in eastern Germany. It has a strong cultural tradition and still offers much for book and music lovers – Johann Sebastian Bach's time here is celebrated by a museum and an active choir.

Leipzig is also known for the annual trade fairs it has hosted since medieval times, and during the communist era these provided an important exchange window between east and west. After reunification, the city spent a huge sum of money on a new ultra-modern fairground in order to re-establish its position as one of Europe's great 'fair cities'. Never as heavily bombed as nearby Dresden, in recent years central Leipzig has undergone a restoration and construction boom that has brought new life to its many fine old buildings.

Leipzigers were among the first participants in the democratic revolution of 1989 when they took to the streets by the hundreds of thousands, placing candles on the front steps of the Stasi headquarters, and attending peace services at the Nikolaikirche. On 16 October 1989, 120,000 demonstrated for democracy – a mere four weeks later the Wall collapsed.

Leipzig's city centre lies within a ring road that follows the outline of the medieval fortifications. From the Hauptbahnhof, take the underpass below Willy-Brandt-Platz and continue south along Nikolaistrasse for five minutes; the central Markt is just a couple of blocks south-west. Leipzig's dazzling fairgrounds (or Neue Messe) are 5km north of the station (take tram No 16).

The excellent Leipzig Tourist Service (☎ 710 42 60/65, fax 710 42 71), at Richard-Wagner-Strasse 1 near the Hauptbahnhof, is open from 9 am to 7 pm weekdays, until 4 pm Saturday and until 2 pm Sunday. The Leipzig Card (DM9.90) is available here for free or discounted admission to museums and the zoo, plus unlimited public transport. Its free room-finding service is on ☎ 710 42 55.

Guided walking tours depart from this tourist office at 4 pm daily except Sunday (DM10). There are also daily bus tours at 10.30 am and 1.30 pm from April to December, lasting two and 2½ hours, and costing DM20/16 and DM28/20.

City Centre Walking Tour
Aside from the organised tours, a good way to see the city is by taking your own walking tour. You can start at the Markt, Leipzig's central square, whose eastern side is flanked by the Altes Rathaus (Old Town Hall, 1556). This stately Renaissance structure is also home to the Stadtgeschichtliches Museum (City History Museum), which is open from 2 to 8 pm Tuesday, and from 10 am to 6 pm Wednesday to Sunday (DM5/2.50).

Walk to the south end of the Markt, then turn right into Thomasgasse and left on Burgstrasse to get to the **Thomaskirche** (1212), with the tomb of composer Johann Sebastian Bach in front of the altar. The

EXCURSIONS

EXCURSIONS

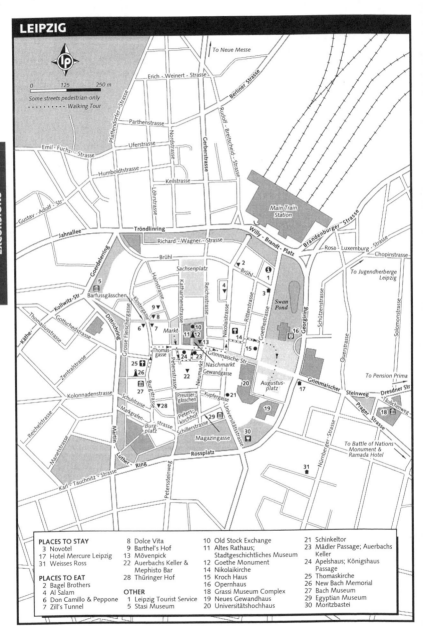

LEIPZIG

0   125   250 m

Some streets pedestrian-only
·········· Walking Tour

PLACES TO STAY	8 Dolce Vita	10 Old Stock Exchange	21 Schinkeltor
3 Novotel	9 Barthel's Hof	11 Altes Rathaus;	23 Mädler Passage; Auerbachs
17 Hotel Mercure Leipzig	13 Mövenpick	Stadtgeschichtliches Museum	Keller
31 Weisses Ross	22 Auerbachs Keller &	12 Goethe Monument	24 Apelshaus; Königshaus
	Mephisto Bar	14 Nikolaikirche	Passage
PLACES TO EAT	28 Thüringer Hof	15 Kroch Haus	25 Thomaskirche
2 Bagel Brothers		16 Opernhaus	26 New Bach Memorial
4 Al Salam	OTHER	18 Grassi Museum Complex	27 Bach Museum
6 Don Camillo & Peppone	1 Leipzig Tourist Service	19 Neues Gewandhaus	29 Egyptian Museum
7 Zill's Tunnel	5 Stasi Museum	20 Universitätshochhaus	30 Moritzbastei

church was extended and converted to the Gothic style in 1496 and was the site of the baptisms of Richard Wagner, Karl Liebknecht and all of Bach's children. Bach worked here as a cantor from 1723 until his death in 1750. Outside the church is the **New Bach Memorial** (1908) showing the composer standing against an organ, with his left-hand jacket pocket turned inside-out (he always claimed to be broke, and with 20 children from two marriages it's not surprising). Concerts by the famous *Thomanerchor*, the boys choir once led by Bach, are held regularly.

Retrace your steps north along Burgstrasse, then turn right on Thomasgasse to get to the sunset-coloured baroque **Apelshaus** (1607), with its lovely bay windows. Now a shopping mall known as the Königshaus Passage, in its heyday it hosted an impressive guest list including Peter der Grosse (Peter the Great) and Napoleon.

The Königshaus Passage leads directly into the **Mädler Passage** which is perhaps the most beautiful shopping arcade in the world. A mix of neo-Renaissance and Art Nouveau, it opened as a trade hall in 1914. Today it's home to chi-chi shops, restaurants, cafes and Auerbachs Keller (see Places to Eat).

The north exit of the Mädler Passage leads to Naschmarkt, dominated by the Old Stock Exchange (1687) and a **Goethe Monument** (1903), dedicated to the poet and dramatist who studied law at Leipzig University. Today the stock exchange is a cultural centre, with year-round concerts, plays and readings.

From the Naschmarkt, walk east along Grimmaische Strasse, then turn left into Nikolaistrasse for a peek inside **Nikolaikirche** (1165). This unusual edifice blends Romanesque and late-Gothic architecture with an amazing neoclassical interior. It was the central gathering point for peaceful demonstrators in May 1989. The church's pamphlet tells, in many languages, the story of how 600 loyal party members sent into the church to break up the services ended up listening to the sermon and joining the protesters.

Carry on east, through the Theaterpassage, to Augustusplatz, Leipzig's cultural nerve centre. The square is strewn with glass structures that are illuminated at night, lending the concrete slabs some much-needed warmth.

On its northside looms the functional **Opernhaus** (1960), while on the square's opposite end is the unforgiveably boxy **Neues Gewandhaus** (1981), home to the *Gewandhausorchester*, one of the oldest and best orchestras in the world. Looming on the western flank is the GDR-era **Universitätshochhaus** (1970), a skyscraper vaguely shaped like an open book.

Moving south past the Gewandhaus fountain you'll arrive at the **Moritzbastei**, once part of the city fortifications and now a sprawling student club. Half-hidden on the western side of the university building, up Universitätsstrasse, is the **Schinkeltor**, a mid-19th century gate that was one of the few bits of the original university to survive WWII and the GDR.

Museums

Opposite the Thomaskirche is the **Bach Museum**, open from 10 am to 5 pm daily (DM4/2.50), which has portraits, manuscripts and other memorabilia focusing on the composer's life in Leipzig. Bach wrote some of his greatest works – including *Johannes Passion, Matthäus Passion, Weinachtsoratorium and h-Moll Messe* – in this city.

In the Runde Ecke (Round Corner) building at Dittrichring 24 is the former local headquarters of the GDR Ministry for State Security (Stasi), now the **Stasi Museum** (☎ 961 24 43). It contains exhibits on propaganda, preposterous disguises, surveillance photographs and mounds and mounds of the papier-mâché the Stasi created when they shredded and then soaked secret documents before the fall of the GDR – take a chunk home, it's free and plentiful. Museum hours are from 2 to 6 pm Wednesday to Sunday (free admission).

The **Egyptian Museum** (☎ 973 70 10) at Leipzig University, Schillerstrasse 6, has a 9000-piece collection of Egyptian antiquities and ranks among the most important of

EXCURSIONS

such collections in Europe. Displays include stone vessels from the 3rd millennium BC, Nubian decorative arts, and sarcophagi. It's open from 1 to 5 pm Tuesday to Saturday and from 10 am to 1 pm Sunday (DM3/1.50).

The **Grassi Museum Complex** at Leipzig University, Täubchenweg 2 and 2c, contains three museums, all charging separate admissions and closed Monday. These include: the **Völkerkunde** (Ethnological Museum, ☎ 214 20), an enormous collection of cultural exhibits from around the world, open 10 am to 5.30 pm Tuesday to Friday (DM5/2); the Musikinstrumenten-Museum (Musical Instrument Museum, ☎ 214 21 20), with some 1000 instruments, open from 10 am to 5 pm Tuesday to Saturday, until 1 pm on Sunday (DM5/2); and the **Museum für Kunsthandwerk** (Arts & Crafts Museum, ☎ 214 21 75), displaying local items, open from 10 am to 6 pm Tuesday to Sunday, until 8 pm on Wednesday (DM4/2).

Battle of Nations Monument

South-east of the city centre is Leipzig's monolithic Völkerschlachtdenkmal (Battle of Nations Monument), a 91m-high monument built in 1913 commemorating the decisive victory by the combined Prussian, Austrian and Russian forces over Napoleon's army 100 years earlier. You can climb the tower for a good view of the city and surrounding area. It's open from 10 am to 5 pm during May to October (DM5/2.50).

Places to Stay

Keep in mind that Leipzig's hotels raise their prices and fill up quickly during large trade shows, so check ahead if you plan to spend the night.

Jugendherberge Leipzig (☎ 245 70 11, fax 245 70 12, Volksgartenstrasse 24), north-east of the city centre, charges DM24/29 for juniors/seniors. Take tram No 17, 27, 37 or 57 to the Löbauer Strasse stop.

Pension Prima (☎ 688 34 81, Dresdner Strasse 82), east of the city centre, has a great deal on simple single/double rooms for DM55/80, including breakfast. It's 2km east of the old town. Another budget option

is the renovated *Weisses Ross* (☎ 960 59 51, Rossstrasse 20) where rooms with shower cost DM70/110, those without DM60/95.

Hotel Mercure Leipzig (☎ 214 60, fax 960 49 16, Augustusplatz 5-6) offers probably the best deal in the city centre, with rooms with private bath for DM99/139. *Ramada Hotel Leipzig* (☎ 129 30, fax 129 34 44, Gutenbergplatz 1-5), 500m east of the city ring, has most creature comforts for the price of DM135 per room. *Novotel* (☎ 995 80, fax 995 82 00, Goethestrasse 11), opposite the train station, has air-conditioned singles/doubles for DM165.

Places to Eat

The *Thüringer Hof* (☎ 994 49 99, Burgstrasse 19), said to have been Martin Luther's favourite pub, has been entirely restored and now offers great veggie dishes from DM13 to DM17, and fish and meat mains from DM17 to DM26. For a lunchtime buffet, the historic *Barthel's Hof* (☎ 141 31 13, Hainstrasse 1) is hard to beat (DM14.40), while at dinnertime the buffet at *Mövenpick* (☎ 211 77 22, Am Naschmarkt 1-3) steals the show (DM19.50).

Barfussgässchen, one block west of the Markt, is chock-a-block with outdoor tables in fine weather. Along here you'll find two excellent pizzerias, *Dolce Vita* (☎ 479 15 27) and the upmarket *Don Camillo & Peppone* (☎ 960 39 10), for Saxon specialities head to *Zill's Tunnel* (☎ 960 20 78, Barfussgässchen 9).

The *Bagel Brothers* (☎ 980 33 30), corner of Brühl and Nikolaistrasse, serves generously filled bagels with a drink from just DM4.90. For tasty Middle Eastern food, head to *Al Salam* (☎ 980 28 77, Nikolaistrasse 33), where enormous felafels and doner kebabs go for DM4 and the vegetarian platter is DM7.50.

Founded in 1525, *Auerbachs Keller* (☎ 21 61 00), in Mädler Passage, is one of Germany's classic restaurants. Goethe's *Faust – Part I* includes a scene at Auerbachs Keller, in which Mephistopheles and Faust carouse with students before they ride off on a barrel. Ask to join a tour of the historic section of the restaurant, including the

Goethe room (where the writer constantly drank – excuse us, gleaned inspiration), the Weinfass and, beneath that, the genuinely spooky Hexenküche. Note the carved tree-trunk hanging in the Weinfass, featuring witches, Faust astride the barrel and a hooved Mephisto in hot pursuit. The tour includes a Verjüngungstrunk (rejuvenation drink), buffet or fixed-menu dinner and costs DM100 per person.

Getting There & Away
Located about 160km south of Berlin, Leipzig is quickly reached in less than two hours by IC trains leaving every other hour from Ostbahnhof (DM58). Although it is possible to get a good overview of Leipzig's main sights on a long day trip, you might consider spending the night.

Getting Around
Trams are the main form of public transport in Leipzig, with the most important lines running via Willy-Brandt-Platz in front of the Hauptbahnhof. Fares are zone *and* time-based, with DM1.70 (15-minute) and DM3.40 (60-minute) adult tickets available. Strip-tickets which are valid for five journeys cost DM8 for 15-minute rides, or DM16 for 60-minute journeys. There's also the off-peak '10-o'clock' ticket, valid from 10 am to 4 pm, costing DM6.

EXCURSIONS

Language

High German is the official and proper form of German throughout the country, though most people also speak a local or regional dialect. The same is true of Berlin, though only a small number of native Berliners speak pure Berlinisch.

The good news is that both High and Low German are distant relatives of English and many words survive in the current vocabulary, which makes things easier for English speakers.

The bad news is that, unlike English, German has retained clear formal distinctions in gender and case. Though not as difficult as Russian, which has more cases, German does have its tricky moments. Fortunately Germans are used to hearing foreigners make a hash of their grammar, and any attempt to speak the language is well received.

All German school children learn a foreign language – usually English – which means most can speak it to a certain degree. You might have problems finding English speakers in eastern Germany, however, where Russian was the main foreign language taught in schools before the *Wende* (change) in 1989.

Berlin is Germany's most multicultural city (with people from 184 nations), so it's not surprising that a multitude of languages are spoken here. In 1997, one in three immigrants was of Turkish descent and people from the former states of Yugoslavia accounted for 16.5% of the city's population. Other large groups are Poles (6.4%) and immigrants from the former Soviet republics (5.4%). There are also about 13,000 Italians and 11,000 Greeks.

The words and phrases in this language guide should help you through the most common travel situations. Those with the desire to delve further into the language should get a copy of Lonely Planet's *German phrasebook*, which contains a useful two-way dictionary.

Pronunciation

English speakers sometimes hold onto their vowels too long when speaking German, which causes comprehension problems. Nevertheless, there are long vowels, like *pope*, and short ones, like *pop*. Another common mistake is a tendency to pronounce all vowels as if they have umlauts (ä, ö and ü). It's worth practising the difference, as they often change the tense and meaning of a word. In most other respects German pronunciation is fairly straightforward. There are no silent letters, and many foreign words (eg *Band*, for 'rock band') are pronounced roughly the same as in English.

Vowels

a	short, as the 'u' in 'cut', or long, as in 'father'
au	as the 'ow' in 'vow'
ä	short, as in 'hat', or long, as in 'hare'
äu	as the 'oy' in 'boy'
e	short, as in 'bet', or long, as in 'obey'
ei	as the 'ai' in 'aisle'
eu	as the 'oy' in 'boy'
i	short, as in 'inn', or long, as in 'marine'
ie	as in 'siege'
o	short, as in 'pot', or long, as in 'note'
ö	as the 'er' in 'fern'
u	as in 'pull'
ü	similar to the 'u' in 'pull' but with stretched lips

Consonants

Most consonants and their combinations are roughly similar to English ones, with a few exceptions. At the end of a word, consonants **b**, **d** and **g** sound a little more like 'p', 't' and 'k' respectively. There are no silent consonants.

ch	throaty, as in Scottish *loch*
j	as the 'y' in 'yet'
ng	always one sound, as in 'strong'
qu	as 'kv'
r	trilled or guttural

s	as in 'see' or as the 'z' in 'zoo'
sch	as the 'sh' in 'shore'
st	usually pronounced 'sht'
sp	usually pronounced 'shp'
v	more like an English 'f'
w	as an English 'v'
z	as the 'ts' in 'tsar'

Grammar

German grammar can be a nightmare for English speakers. Nouns come in three genders: masculine, feminine and neutral – the corresponding forms of the definite article ('the' in English) are *der*, *die* and *das*, with the basic plural form, *die*. Nouns and articles will alter according to the case (nominative, accusative, dative and genitive). Note that German nouns always begin with a capital.

You should be aware that German uses polite and informal forms for 'you' (*Sie* and *Du* respectively). When addressing people you don't know well you should always use the polite form (though younger people will be less inclined to expect it). In this language guide we use the polite form unless indicated by 'inf' (for 'informal') in brackets.

Greetings & Civilities

Hello.	*Hallo.*
Good morning.	*Guten Morgen.*
Good day.	*Guten Tag.*
Good evening.	*Guten Abend.*
Goodbye.	*Auf Wiedersehen.*
Bye.	*Tschüss.*
Yes.	*Ja.*
No.	*Nein.*
Where?	*Wo?*
Why?	*Warum?*
How?	*Wie?*
Maybe.	*Vielleicht.*
Please.	*Bitte.*
Thank you (very much).	*Danke (schön).*
You're welcome.	*Bitte or Bitte sehr.*
Excuse me.	*Entschuldigung.*
I'm sorry/Forgive me.	*Entschuldigen Sie, bitte.*
I'm sorry. (to express sympathy)	*Das tut mir leid.*

Language Difficulties

I understand.	*Ich verstehe.*
I don't understand.	*Ich verstehe nicht.*
Do you speak English?	*Sprechen Sie Englisch?/Sprichst du Englisch?* (inf)
Does anyone here speak English?	*Spricht hier jemand Englisch?*
What does ... mean?	*Was bedeutet ...?*
Please write it down.	*Bitte schreiben Sie es auf.*

Paperwork

first name	*Vorname*
surname	*Familienname*
nationality	*Staatsangehörigkeit*
date of birth	*Geburtsdatum*
place of birth	*Geburtsort*
sex (gender)	*Geschlecht*
passport	*Reisepass*
identification	*Ausweis*
visa	*Visum*

Small Talk

What's your name?	*Wie heissen Sie?/Wie heisst du?* (inf)
My name is ...	*Ich heisse ...*
How are you?	*Wie geht es Ihnen?/Wie geht's dir?* (inf)
I'm fine, thanks.	*Es geht mir gut, danke.*
Where are you from?	*Woher kommen Sie/ kommst du?* (inf)
I'm from ...	*Ich komme aus ...*

Getting Around

What time does the ... leave/arrive?	*Um wieviel Uhr fährt ... ab/kommt ... an?*
boat	*das Boot*
bus	*der Bus*
train	*der Zug*
tram	*die Strassenbahn*
Where is the ...?	*Wo ist ...?*
bus stop	*die Bushaltestelle*
metro station	*die U-Bahnstation*
train station	*der Bahnhof*
main train station	*der Hauptbahnhof*
airport	*der Flughafen*
tram stop	*die Strassenbahn-haltestelle*
I want to go to ...	*Ich möchte nach ... fahren.*

the next	der/die/das nächste
the last	der/die/das letzte
ticket office	Fahrkartenschalter
one-way ticket	einfache Fahrkarte
return ticket	Rückfahrkarte
1st/2nd class	erste/zweite Klasse
timetable	Fahrplan
platform number	Gleisnummer
luggage locker	Gepäckschliessfach

I'd like to hire ...	Ich möchte ... mieten.
a bicycle	ein Fahrrad
a motorcycle	ein Motorrad
a car	ein Auto

Directions

Where is ...?	Wo ist ...?
How do I get to ...?	Wie erreicht man ...?
Is it far from here?	Ist es weit von hier?
Can you show me (on the map)?	Könnten Sie mir (auf der Karte) zeigen?

street	die Strasse
suburb	der Vorort
town	die Stadt
behind	hinter
in front of	vor
opposite	gegenüber
straight ahead	geradeaus
(to the) left	(nach) links
(to the) right	(nach) rechts
at the traffic lights	an der Ampel
at the next corner	an der nächsten Ecke
north	Nord
south	Süd
east	Ost
west	West

Around Town

I'm looking for ...	Ich suche ...
a bank	eine Bank/ Sparkasse
the church	die Kirche
the city centre	das Stadtzentrum
the ... embassy	die ... Botschaft
my hotel	mein Hotel
the market	den Markt
the museum	das Museum
the post office	das Postamt
a public toilet	eine öffentliche Toilette
a hospital	ein Krankenhaus

Signs

Eingang/Einfahrt	Entrance
Ausgang/Ausfahrt	Exit
Auf/Offen/ Geöffnet	Open
Zu/Geschlossen	Closed
Rauchen Verboten	No Smoking
Polizei	Police
WC/Toiletten	Toilets
Damen	Women
Herren	Men
Bahnhof	Train Station
Hauptbahnhof	Main Train Station
Notausgang	Emergency Exit

| the police | die Polizei |
| the tourist office | das Fremden- verkehrsbüro |

I want to change some money/ travellers cheques.	Ich möchte Geld/ Reisechecks wechseln.
What time does ... open/close?	Um wieviel Uhr macht ... auf/zu?
I'd like to make a phone call.	Ich möchte telefonieren.

beach	der Strand
bridge	die Brücke
castle/palace	die Burg/das Schloss
cathedral	der Dom
forest	der Wald
island	die Insel
lake	der See
market	der Markt
monastry/convent	das Kloster
mountain	der Berg
river	der Fluss
sea	das Meer/die See
tower	der Turm

Accommodation

I'm looking for ...	Ich suche...
a hotel	ein Hotel
a guesthouse	eine Pension
a youth hostel	eine Jugendherberge
a campground	einen Campingplatz

| Where is a cheap hotel? | Wo findet man ein preiswertes Hotel? |

LANGUAGE

Please write the address?	*Könnten Sie bitte die Adresse aufschreiben?*
Do you have a room available?	*Haben Sie ein Zimmer frei?*
How much is it per night/person?	*Wieviel kostet es pro Nacht/Person?*
May I see it?	*Darf ich es sehen?*
Where is the bathroom?	*Wo ist das Badezimmer?*
It's very noisy/ dirty/expensive.	*Es ist sehr laut/ dreckig/teuer.*

I'd like to book a ...	*Ich möchte ... reservieren.*
bed	*ein Bett*
cheap room	*ein preiswertes Zimmer*
single room	*ein Einzelzimmer*
double room	*ein Doppelzimmer*
room with two beds	*ein Zimmer mit zwei Betten*
room with shower and toilet	*ein Zimmer mit Dusche und WC*
dormitory bed	*ein Bett im Schlafsaal*

for one night	*für eine Nacht*
for two nights	*für zwei Nächte*

I'm/We're leaving now.	*Ich reise/Wir reisen jetzt ab.*

Shopping

I'd like to buy ...	*Ich möchte ... kaufen*
How much is that?	*Wieviel kostet das?*
Do you accept credit cards?	*Nehmen Sie Kreditkarten?*
bookshop	*Buchladen*
chemist/pharmacy	*Apotheke* (medicine) *Drogerie* (toiletries)
department store	*Kaufhaus*
laundry	*Wäscherei*

more/less	*mehr/weniger*
bigger/smaller	*grösser/kleiner*

Health

I need a doctor.	*Ich brauche einen Arzt.*
Where is a hospital?	*Wo ist ein Krankenhaus?*
I'm ill.	*Ich bin krank.*

It hurts here.	*Es tut hier weh.*
I'm pregnant.	*Ich bin schwanger.*

I'm ...	*Ich bin ...*
diabetic	*Diabetiker*
epileptic	*Epileptiker*
asthmatic	*Asthmatiker*

I'm allergic to antibiotics/ penicillin.	*Ich bin allergisch auf Antibiotika/ Penizillin.*

antiseptic	*Antiseptikum*
aspirin	*Aspirin*
condoms	*Kondome*
diarrhoea	*Durchfall*
medicine	*Medikament*
the pill	*die Pille*
sunblock cream	*Sonnencreme*
tampons	*Tampons*

Times & Dates

What time is it?	*Wie spät ist es?*
It's (10) o'clock.	*Es ist (zehn) Uhr.*
It's half past nine.	*Es ist halb zehn.*
in the morning	*morgens/vormittags*
in the afternoon	*nachmittags*
in the evening	*abends*
When?	*wann?*
today	*heute*
yesterday	*gestern*

Monday	*Montag*
Tuesday	*Dienstag*
Wednesday	*Mittwoch*
Thursday	*Donnerstag*
Friday	*Freitag*
Saturday	*Samstag/Sonnabend*
Sunday	*Sonntag*

January	*Januar*
February	*Februar*
March	*März*
April	*April*
May	*Mai*
June	*Juni*
July	*Juli*
August	*August*
September	*September*
October	*Oktober*
November	*November*
December	*Dezember*

Emergencies

Help!	*Hilfe!*
Call a doctor!	*Rufen Sie einen Arzt!*
Call the police!	*Rufen Sie die Polizei!*
Leave me in peace!	*Lassen Sie mich in Ruhe!*
Get lost!	*Hau ab!* (inf)
I'm lost.	*Ich habe mich verirrt.*
I've been raped/ robbed!	*Ich bin verge-waltigt/be-stohlen worden!*

Numbers

1	*eins*
2	*zwei /zwo*
3	*drei*
4	*vier*
5	*fünf*
6	*sechs*
7	*sieben*
8	*acht*
9	*neun*
10	*zehn*
11	*elf*
12	*zwölf*
13	*dreizehn*
14	*vierzehn*
15	*fünfzehn*
16	*sechzehn*
17	*siebzehn*
18	*achtzehn*
19	*neunzehn*
20	*zwanzig*
21	*einundzwanzig*
22	*zweiundzwanzig*
30	*dreissig*
40	*vierzig*
50	*fünfzig*
60	*sechzig*
70	*siebzig*
80	*achtzig*
90	*neunzig*
100	*einhundert*
1000	*eintausend*
10,000	*zehntausend*
one million	*eine Million*

FOOD & DRINK

breakfast	*Frühstück*
lunch	*Mittagessen*
dinner	*Abendessen*
menu	*Speisekarte*
restaurant	*Gaststätte/Restaurant*
pub/bar	*Kneipe*
supermarket	*Supermarkt*
snack bar	*Imbiss*

I'm a vegetarian.	*Ich bin Vegetarier(in).*
I'd like something to drink, please.	*Ich möchte etwas zu trinken, bitte.*
It was very tasty.	*Es hat mir sehr geschmeckt.*
The bill, please?	*Die Rechnung, bitte.*
Please keep the change.	*Das stimmt so.* (lit: 'that's OK as is')

Menu Decoder

Eating at a restaurant in a foreign country can easily be bewildering. Fortunately, throughout Germany, you'll usually find menus posted outside the entrance, giving you all the time you need to decide whether something speaks to your tastes. We've put together a short list of useful vocabulary terms to help you steer what you hunger for onto your plate.

Soups (*Suppen*)
Brühe – bouillon
Erbsensuppe – pea soup
Frühlingssuppe or *Gemüsesuppe* – vegetable soup
Hühnersuppe – chicken soup
Linsensuppe – lentil soup
Tomatensuppe – tomato soup

Meat (*Fleisch*)
Boulette – a cross between a meatball and a hamburger, eaten with a dry roll
Brathuhn – roast chicken
Bratwurst – fried pork sausage
Currywurst – a spicy sausage served with a tangy curried sauce
Eisbein – pickled pork knuckles
Ente – duck
Fasan – pheasant
Frikadelle – flat meatball

Hackbraten – meatloaf
Hackfleisch – chopped or minced meat
Hirsch – male deer
Huhn or Hähnchen – chicken
Kalbfleisch – veal
Kaninchen or Hase – rabbit
Kasseler Rippen – smoked pork chops
Lammfleisch – lamb
Putenbrust – turkey breast
Reh – venison
Rindfleisch – beef
Rippenspeer – spare ribs
Sauerbraten – marinated and roasted beef
Schinken – ham
Schnitzel – pounded meat, usually pork, breaded and fried
Schweinefleisch – pork
Truthahn – turkey
Wild – game
Wildschwein – wild boar

Seafood *(Meeresfrüchte)*

Aal – eel
Austern – oysters
Barsch – perch
Dorsch – cod
Fisch – fish
Forelle – trout
Hummer – lobster
Karpfen – carp
Krabben – shrimp
Lachs – salmon
Matjes – pickled herring
Miesmuscheln or Muscheln – mussels
Scholle – plaice
Seezunge – sole
Thunfish – tuna

Vegetables *(Gemüse)*

Blumenkohl – cauliflower
Bohnen – beans
Brokkoli – broccoli
Erbsen – peas
Gurke – cucumber
Kartoffel – potato
Kohl – cabbage; can be *rot* (red), *weiss* (white) or *grün* (green)
Möhre – carrot
Paprika – bell/sweet pepper
Pilze – mushrooms
Rosenkohl – brussels sprouts

Spargel – asparagus
Tomate – tomato
Zwiebel – onion

Fruit *(Obst)*

Ananas – pineapple
Apfel – apple
Apfelsine or Orange – orange
Aprikose – apricot
Banane – banana
Birne – pear
Erdbeere – strawberry
Kirschen – cherries
Pampelmuse – grapefruit
Pfirsich – peach
Pflaume – plum
Weintrauben – grapes
Zitrone – lemon

Some Common Dishes

Auflauf – casserole
Eier, Rühreier – eggs, scrambled eggs
Eintopf – stew
Königsberger Klopse – meatballs in caper sauce
Kohlroulade – cabbage leaves stuffed with minced meat
Rollmops – pickled herring
Salat – salad

Cooking Methods

Frittiert – deep-fried
Gebacken – baked
Gebraten – pan-fried
Gefüllt – stuffed
Gegrillt – grilled
Gekocht – boiled
Geräuchert – smoked
Geschmort – braised
Paniert – breaded

Drinks *(Getränke)*

Bier – bier
Kaffee – coffee
Milch – milk
Mineralwasser – fizzy bottled mineral water
Saft – juice
Tee – tea
Wein – wine

Glossary

You may encounter the following terms and abbreviations while in Berlin. For other terms, see the Language chapter.

(pl) indicates plural

Abfahrt – departure (trains & buses)
ADAC – Allgemeiner Deutscher Automobil Club (German Automobile Association)
Allee – avenue
Altstadt – old town
Ankunft – arrival (trains & buses)
Apotheke – pharmacy
Arbeitsamt – employment office
Arbeitserlaubnis – work permit
Ärztlicher Notdienst – emergency medical service
Aufenthaltserlaubnis – residency permit
Auflauf, Aufläufe (pl) – casserole
Ausgang, Ausfahrt – exit
Ausländerbehörde – Foreigners' Office
Autobahn – motorway
Autonom – left-wing anarchist
AvD – Automobilclub von Deutschland (Automobile Club of Germany)

Bahnhof – train station
Bahnpolizei – train station police
Bahnsteig – train station platform
Bau – building
Bedienung – service, service charge
Behinderte – (pl) disabled persons
Berg – mountain
Bezirk – district
Bibliothek – library
Bierkeller – cellar pub
Bratkartoffeln – fried or roasted potatoes
BRD – Bundesrepublik Deutschland or, in English, FRG (Federal Republic of Germany). The name for Germany today, it originally applied to the former West Germany.
Brücke – bridge
Brunnen – fountain or well
Bundesland – federal state
Bundesrat – upper house of German Parliament

Bundestag – lower house of German Parliament
Busbahnhof – large bus station

DB – Deutsche Bahn (German national railway)
DDR – Deutsche Demokratische Republik or, in English, GDR (German Democratic Republic). The name for the former East Germany. *See also* BRD.
Denkmal – memorial
Deutsche Reich – German Empire. Refers to the period 1871-1918.
DJH – Deutsches Jugendherbergswerk (German youth hostel association)
Dom – cathedral
DZT – Deutsche Zentrale für Tourismus (German National Tourist Office)

Eingang – entrance
Eintritt – admission
EU-Aufenthaltserlaubnis – EU residency permit

Fahrplan – timetable
Fahrrad – bicycle
Fest – festival
Feuerwehr – fire brigade
Flohmarkt – flea market
Flughafen – airport
Franks – Germanic people influential in Europe between the 3rd and 8th centuries
Freikorps – WWI volunteers
Fremdenverkehrsamt – tourist office
Fremdenzimmer – tourist room
FRG – Federal Republic of Germany; *see also* BRD
Frühstück – breakfast

Garten – garden
Gasse – lane or alley
Gastarbeiter – literally 'guest worker'; labourer arriving from Turkey, Yugoslavia, Italy or Greece in the 1960s to help rebuild Germany
Gästehaus, Gasthaus – guesthouse
Gaststätte – informal restaurant

GDR – German Democratic Republic (the former East Germany); *see also* BRD, DDR
Gedenkstätte – memorial site
Gepäckaufbewahrung – left-luggage office
Gespräch – reverse charge telephone call
Gestapo – Nazi secret police
Glockenspiel – literally 'bell play'; carillon sounded by mechanised figures often in the form of religious or historical characters
Gründerzeit – literally 'foundation time'; the period of industrial expansion in Germany following the founding of the German Empire in 1871

Hafen – harbour, port
halbtrocken – semi-dry (wine)
Hauptbahnhof – main train station
Hauptpostlagernd – poste restante
Heilige Römische Reich – the Holy Roman Empire, which lasted from the 8th century to 1806. The German lands comprised the bulk of the Empire's territory.
Herzog – duke
Hitlerjugend – Hitler Youth, organisation for boys
Hochdeutsch – literally 'High German'; standard spoken and written German developed from a regional Saxon dialect
Hof, Höfe (pl) – courtyard
Hotel Garni – a hotel without a restaurant where you are only served breakfast

Imbiss – snack bar, takeaway stand; *see* Schnellimbiss
Insel – island

Jugendgästehaus – youth guesthouse, usually of a higher standard than a youth hostel
Jugendherberge – youth hostel
Jugendstil – Art Nouveau

Kabarett – cabaret
Kaffee und Kuchen – literally 'coffee and cake'; traditional afternoon coffee break
Kaiser – emperor; derived from 'Caesar'
Kanal – canal
Kantine, pl Kantinen – government subsidised cafeterias in public buildings like town halls

Kapelle – chapel
Karte – ticket
Kartenvorverkauf – ticket booking office
Kino – cinema
Kirche – church
Kloster – monastery, convent
Kneipe – bar or pub
Kommunales Kino – alternative or studio cinema
Konditorei – cake shop
König – king
Konsulat – consulate
Konzentrationslager (KZ) – concentration camp
korrekt – correct, proper
Kristallnacht – literally 'night of broken glass'; the attack on Jewish synagogues, cemeteries and businesses by Nazis and their supporters on the night of 9 November 1938 that marked the beginning of full-scale persecution of Jews in Germany. Also known as Reichspogromnacht.
Kunst – art
Kurfürst – prince elector

Land, Länder (pl) – state
Landtag – state parliament
Lesbe, Lesben (pl) – lesbian
lesbisch – lesbian (adj)
lieblich – sweet (wine)
Lied – song

Markgraf – margrave; German nobleman ranking above a count
Markt – market
Marktplatz (often abbreviated to Markt) – marketplace or central square
Mehrwertsteuer (MWST) – value-added tax
Mensa – university cafeteria
Mietskaserne, (pl) Mietkasernen – tenement built around courtyards
Milchcafé – milk coffee, *café au lait*
Mitfahrzentrale – ride-sharing service
Mitwohnzentrale – an accommodation-finding service (usually long-term)
Münzwäscherei – coin-operated laundrette

Nord – north
Notdienst – emergency service

Ossis – nickname for East Germans
Ost – east
Ostalgie – word fusion of Ost and Nostalgie, meaning nostalgia for GDR days
Ostpolitik – former West German chancellor Willy Brandt's foreign policy of 'peaceful coexistence' with the GDR

Palast – palace
Pannenhilfe – roadside breakdown assistance
Parkhaus – car park
Parkschein – parking voucher
Parkscheinautomat – vending machine selling parking vouchers
Passage – shopping arcade
Pfand – deposit for bottles and glasses
Pfund – pound (500 grams)
Plattenbauten – prefab housing developments
Platz – square
Post or Postamt – post office

Rathaus – town hall
Reich – empire
Reichspogromnacht – *see* Kristallnacht
Reisezentrum – travel centre in train or bus stations
Rezept – prescription
Rezeptfrei – over-the-counter medications

Saal, Säle (pl) – hall, large room
Sammlung – collection
Säule – column, pillar
Schatzkammer – treasury
Schiff – ship
Schiffahrt – literally 'boat way'; shipping, navigation
Schloss – palace, castle
Schnaps – schnapps
Schnellimbiss – stand-up food stall
Schwul, Schwule (pl) – gay
See – lake
Sekt – sparkling wine
Selbstbedienung (SB) – self-service (restaurants, laundrettes etc)
Sozialistische Einheitspartei Deutschland – Socialist Unity Party of Germany (SED)
SS – Schutzstaffel; organisation within the Nazi party that supplied Hitler's bodyguards, as well as concentration-camp guards and the Waffen-SS troops in WWII
Stadt – city or town
Stadtbad, Stadtbäder (pl) – public bath
Stadtwald – city or town forest
Stasi – GDR secret police (from Ministerium für Staatssicherheit, or Ministry of State Security)
Stau – traffic jam
Stehcafé – stand-up café
Strasse (often abbreviated to Str) – street
Süd – south
Szene – scene (ie where the action is)

Tageskarte – daily menu or day ticket on public transport
Tal – valley
Teich – pond
Thirty Years' War – pivotal war in Central Europe (1618-48) that began as a German conflict between Catholics and Protestants
Tor – gate
Trampen – hitchhiking
Treuhandanstalt – trust established to sell off GDR assets after the Wende
trocken – dry (wine)
Trödel – junk, bric-a-brac
Trümmerberg – artificial hill built from wartime rubble
Trümmerfrau – 'rubble women', ie women who cleaned up bricks and rebuilt houses after WWII
Turm – tower

Übergang – transit point
Ufer – bank

verboten – forbidden
Verkehr – traffic
Viertel – quarter, district

Wald – forest
Waldfrüchte – wild berries
Wäscherei – dry cleaner, laundrette
Wechselstube – currency exchange office
Weg – way, path
Weihnachtsmarkt – Christmas market
Wende – 'change' or 'turning point' of 1989, ie the fall of communism that led to the collapse of the GDR and ultimately to German reunification

Wessis – literally 'Westies'; nickname for West Germans
West – west
Wurst – sausage

Zahnarzt – dentist
Zeitung – newspaper
Zeitgeist – the spirit or outlook of a specific time or period

Zimmer Frei – room available (accomodation)
Zimmervermittlung – room-finding service; *see also* Mitwohnzentrale
ZOB – Zentraler Omnibusbahnhof (central bus station)
Zuckerbäckerstil – the wedding-cake style of architecture which was typical of the Stalin era

Notes

LONELY PLANET

ON THE ROAD

Travel Guides explore cities, regions and countries, and supply information on transport, restaurants and accommodation, covering all budgets. They come with reliable, easy-to-use maps, practical advice, cultural and historical facts and a rundown on attractions both on and off the beaten track. There are over 200 titles in this classic series, covering nearly every country in the world.

 Lonely Planet Upgrades extend the shelf life of existing travel guides by detailing any changes that may affect travel in a region since a book has been published. Upgrades can be downloaded for free from **www.lonelyplanet.com/upgrades**

For travellers with more time than money, **Shoestring** guides offer dependable, first-hand information with hundreds of detailed maps, plus insider tips for stretching money as far as possible. Covering entire continents in most cases, the six-volume shoestring guides are known around the world as 'backpackers bibles'.

For the discerning short-term visitor, **Condensed** guides highlight the best a destination has to offer in a full-colour, pocket-sized format designed for quick access. They include everything from top sights and walking tours to opinionated reviews of where to eat, stay, shop and have fun.

CitySync lets travellers use their Palm™ or Visor™ hand-held computers to guide them through a city with handy tips on transport, history, cultural life, major sights, and shopping and entertainment options. It can also quickly search and sort hundreds of reviews of hotels, restaurants and attractions, and pinpoint their location on scrollable street maps. CitySync can be downloaded from **www.citysync.com**

MAPS & ATLASES

Lonely Planet's **City Maps** feature downtown and metropolitan maps, as well as transit routes and walking tours. The maps come complete with an index of streets, a listing of sights and a plastic coat for extra durability.

Road Atlases are an essential navigation tool for serious travellers. Cross-referenced with the guidebooks, they also feature distance and climate charts and a complete site index.

ESSENTIALS

Read This First books help new travellers to hit the road with confidence. These invaluable predeparture guides give step-by-step advice on preparing for a trip, budgeting, arranging a visa, planning an itinerary and staying safe while still getting off the beaten track.

Healthy Travel pocket guides offer a regional rundown on disease hot spots and practical advice on predeparture health measures, staying well on the road and what to do in emergencies. The guides come with a user-friendly design and helpful diagrams and tables.

Lonely Planet's **Phrasebooks** cover the essential words and phrases travellers need when they're strangers in a strange land. They come in a pocket-sized format with colour tabs for quick reference, extensive vocabulary lists, easy-to-follow pronunciation keys and two-way dictionaries.

Miffed by blurry photos of the Taj Mahal? Tired of the classic 'top of the head cut off' shot? **Travel Photography: A Guide to Taking Better Pictures** will help you turn ordinary holiday snaps into striking images and give you the know-how to capture every scene, from frenetic festivals to peaceful beach sunrises.

Lonely Planet's **Travel Journal** is a lightweight but sturdy travel diary for jotting down all those on-the-road observations and significant travel moments. It comes with a handy time-zone wheel, a world map and useful travel information.

Lonely Planet's eKno is an all-in-one communication service developed especially for travellers. It offers low-cost international calls and free email and voicemail so that you can keep in touch while on the road. Check it out on **www.ekno.lonelyplanet.com**

FOOD & RESTAURANT GUIDES

Lonely Planet's **Out to Eat** guides recommend the brightest and best places to eat and drink in top international cities. These gourmet companions are arranged by neighbourhood, packed with dependable maps, garnished with scene-setting photos and served with quirky features.

For people who live to eat, drink and travel, **World Food** guides explore the culinary culture of each country. Entertaining and adventurous, each guide is packed with detail on staples and specialities, regional cuisine and local markets, as well as sumptuous recipes, comprehensive culinary dictionaries and lavish photos good enough to eat.

OUTDOOR GUIDES

For those who believe the best way to see the world is on foot, Lonely Planet's **Walking Guides** detail everything from family strolls to difficult treks, with 'when to go and how to do it' advice supplemented by reliable maps and essential travel information.

Cycling Guides map a destination's best bike tours, long and short, in day-by-day detail. They contain all the information a cyclist needs, including advice on bike maintenance, places to eat and stay, innovative maps with detailed cues to the rides, and elevation charts.

The **Watching Wildlife** series is perfect for travellers who want authoritative information but don't want to tote a heavy field guide. Packed with advice on where, when and how to view a region's wildlife, each title features photos of over 300 species and contains engaging comments on the local flora and fauna.

With underwater colour photos throughout, **Pisces Books** explore the world's best diving and snorkelling areas. Each book contains listings of diving services and dive resorts, detailed information on depth, visibility and difficulty of dives, and a roundup of the marine life you're likely to see through your mask.

LONELY PLANET

OFF THE ROAD

Journeys, the travel literature series written by renowned travel authors, capture the spirit of a place or illuminate a culture with a journalist's attention to detail and a novelist's flair for words. These are tales to soak up while you're actually on the road or dip into as an at-home armchair indulgence.

The range of lavishly illustrated **Pictorial** books is just the ticket for both travellers and dreamers. Off-beat tales and vivid photographs bring the adventure of travel to your doorstep long before the journey begins and long after it is over.

Lonely Planet **Videos** encourage the same independent, tough-minded approach as the guidebooks. Currently airing throughout the world, this award-winning series features innovative footage and an original soundtrack.

Yes, we know, work is tough, so do a little bit of deskside dreaming with the spiral-bound Lonely Planet **Diary** or a Lonely Planet **Wall Calendar**, filled with great photos from around the world.

TRAVELLERS NETWORK

Lonely Planet Online. Lonely Planet's award-winning Web site has insider information on hundreds of destinations, from Amsterdam to Zimbabwe, complete with interactive maps and relevant links. The site also offers the latest travel news, recent reports from travellers on the road, guidebook upgrades, a travel links site, an online book-buying option and a lively travellers bulletin board. It can be viewed at **www.lonelyplanet.com** or AOL keyword: lp.

Planet Talk is a quarterly print newsletter, full of gossip, advice, anecdotes and author articles. It provides an antidote to the being-at-home blues and lets you plan and dream for the next trip. Contact the nearest Lonely Planet office for your free copy.

Comet, the free Lonely Planet newsletter, comes via email once a month. It's loaded with travel news, advice, dispatches from authors, travel competitions and letters from readers. To subscribe, click on the Comet subscription link on the front page of the Web site.

Lonely Planet Guides by Region

Lonely Planet is known worldwide for publishing practical, reliable and no-nonsense travel information in our guides and on our Web site. The Lonely Planet list covers just about every accessible part of the world. Currently there are 16 series: Travel guides, Shoestring guides, Condensed guides, Phrasebooks, Read This First, Healthy Travel, Walking guides, Cycling guides, Watching Wildlife guides, Pisces Diving & Snorkeling guides, City Maps, Road Atlases, Out to Eat, World Food, Journeys travel literature and Pictorials.

AFRICA Africa on a shoestring • Botswana • Cairo • Cairo City Map • Cape Town • Cape Town City Map • East Africa • Egypt • Egyptian Arabic phrasebook • Ethiopia, Eritrea & Djibouti • Ethiopian Amharic phrasebook • The Gambia & Senegal • Healthy Travel Africa • Kenya • Malawi • Morocco • Moroccan Arabic phrasebook • Mozambique • Namibia • Read This First: Africa • South Africa, Lesotho & Swaziland • Southern Africa • Southern Africa Road Atlas • Swahili phrasebook • Tanzania, Zanzibar & Pemba • Trekking in East Africa • Tunisia • Watching Wildlife East Africa • Watching Wildlife Southern Africa • West Africa • World Food Morocco • Zambia • Zimbabwe, Botswana & Namibia
Travel Literature: Mali Blues: Traveling to an African Beat • The Rainbird: A Central African Journey • Songs to an African Sunset: A Zimbabwean Story

AUSTRALIA & THE PACIFIC Aboriginal Australia & the Torres Strait Islands •Auckland • Australia • Australian phrasebook • Australia Road Atlas • Cycling Australia • Fiji • Fijian phrasebook • Healthy Travel Australia, NZ & the Pacific • Islands of Australia's Great Barrier Reef • Melbourne • Melbourne City Map • Micronesia • New Caledonia • New South Wales • New Zealand • Northern Territory • Outback Australia • Out to Eat – Melbourne • Out to Eat – Sydney • Papua New Guinea • Pidgin phrasebook • Queensland • Rarotonga & the Cook Islands • Samoa • Solomon Islands • South Australia • South Pacific • South Pacific phrasebook • Sydney • Sydney City Map • Sydney Condensed • Tahiti & French Polynesia • Tasmania • Tonga • Tramping in New Zealand • Vanuatu • Victoria • Walking in Australia • Watching Wildlife Australia • Western Australia
Travel Literature: Islands in the Clouds: Travels in the Highlands of New Guinea • Kiwi Tracks: A New Zealand Journey • Sean & David's Long Drive

CENTRAL AMERICA & THE CARIBBEAN Bahamas, Turks & Caicos • Baja California • Belize, Guatemala & Yucatán • Bermuda • Central America on a shoestring • Costa Rica • Costa Rica Spanish phrasebook • Cuba • Cycling Cuba • Dominican Republic & Haiti • Eastern Caribbean • Guatemala • Havana • Healthy Travel Central & South America • Jamaica • Mexico • Mexico City • Panama • Puerto Rico • Read This First: Central & South America • Virgin Islands • World Food Caribbean • World Food Mexico • Yucatán
Travel Literature: Green Dreams: Travels in Central America

EUROPE Amsterdam • Amsterdam City Map • Amsterdam Condensed • Andalucía • Athens • Austria • Baltic States phrasebook • Barcelona • Barcelona City Map • Belgium & Luxembourg • Berlin • Berlin City Map • Britain • British phrasebook • Brussels, Bruges & Antwerp • Brussels City Map • Budapest • Budapest City Map • Canary Islands • Catalunya & the Costa Brava • Central Europe • Central Europe phrasebook • Copenhagen • Corfu & the Ionians • Corsica • Crete • Crete Condensed • Croatia • Cycling Britain • Cycling France • Cyprus • Czech & Slovak Republics • Czech phrasebook • Denmark • Dublin • Dublin City Map • Dublin Condensed • Eastern Europe • Eastern Europe phrasebook • Edinburgh • Edinburgh City Map • England • Estonia, Latvia & Lithuania • Europe on a shoestring • Europe phrasebook • Finland • Florence • Florence City Map • France • Frankfurt City Map • Frankfurt Condensed • French phrasebook • Georgia, Armenia & Azerbaijan • Germany • German phrasebook • Greece • Greek Islands • Greek phrasebook • Hungary • Iceland, Greenland & the Faroe Islands • Ireland • Italian phrasebook • Italy • Kraków • Lisbon • The Loire • London • London City Map • London Condensed • Madrid • Madrid City Map • Malta • Mediterranean Europe • Milan, Turin & Genoa • Moscow • Munich • Netherlands • Normandy • Norway • Out to Eat – London • Out to Eat – Paris • Paris • Paris City Map • Paris Condensed • Poland • Polish phrasebook • Portugal • Portuguese phrasebook • Prague • Prague City Map • Provence & the Côte d'Azur • Read This First: Europe • Rhodes & the Dodecanese • Romania & Moldova • Rome • Rome City Map • Rome Condensed • Russia, Ukraine & Belarus • Russian phrasebook • Scandinavian & Baltic Europe • Scandinavian Europe phrasebook • Scotland • Sicily • Slovenia • South-West France • Spain • Spanish phrasebook • Stockholm • St Petersburg • St Petersburg City Map • Sweden • Switzerland • Tuscany • Ukrainian phrasebook • Venice • Vienna • Wales • Walking in Britain • Walking in France • Walking in Ireland • Walking in Italy • Walking in Scotland • Walking in Spain • Walking in Switzerland • Western Europe • World Food France • World Food Greece • World Food Ireland • World Food Italy • World Food Spain **Travel Literature:** After Yugoslavia • Love and War in the Apennines • The Olive Grove: Travels in Greece • On the Shores of the Mediterranean • Round Ireland in Low Gear • A Small Place in Italy

Lonely Planet Mail Order

Lonely Planet products are distributed worldwide. They are also available by mail order from Lonely Planet, so if you have difficulty finding a title please write to us. North and South American residents should write to 150 Linden St, Oakland, CA 94607, USA; European and African residents should write to 10a Spring Place, London NW5 3BH, UK; and residents of other countries to Locked Bag 1, Footscray, Victoria 3011, Australia.

INDIAN SUBCONTINENT & THE INDIAN OCEAN Bangladesh • Bengali phrasebook • Bhutan • Delhi • Goa • Healthy Travel Asia & India • Hindi & Urdu phrasebook • India • India & Bangladesh City Map • Indian Himalaya • Karakoram Highway • Kathmandu City Map • Kerala • Madagascar • Maldives • Mauritius, Réunion & Seychelles • Mumbai (Bombay) • Nepal • Nepali phrasebook • North India • Pakistan • Rajasthan • Read This First: Asia & India • South India • Sri Lanka • Sri Lanka phrasebook • Tibet • Tibetan phrasebook • Trekking in the Indian Himalaya • Trekking in the Karakoram & Hindukush • Trekking in the Nepal Himalaya • World Food India **Travel Literature:** The Age of Kali: Indian Travels and Encounters • Hello Goodnight: A Life of Goa • In Rajasthan • Maverick in Madagascar • A Season in Heaven: True Tales from the Road to Kathmandu • Shopping for Buddhas • A Short Walk in the Hindu Kush • Slowly Down the Ganges

MIDDLE EAST & CENTRAL ASIA Bahrain, Kuwait & Qatar • Central Asia • Central Asia phrasebook • Dubai • Farsi (Persian) phrasebook • Hebrew phrasebook • Iran • Israel & the Palestinian Territories • Istanbul • Istanbul City Map • Istanbul to Cairo • Istanbul to Kathmandu • Jerusalem • Jerusalem City Map • Jordan • Lebanon • Middle East • Oman & the United Arab Emirates • Syria • Turkey • Turkish phrasebook • World Food Turkey • Yemen **Travel Literature:** Black on Black: Iran Revisited • Breaking Ranks: Turbulent Travels in the Promised Land • The Gates of Damascus • Kingdom of the Film Stars: Journey into Jordan

NORTH AMERICA Alaska • Boston • Boston City Map • Boston Condensed • British Columbia • California & Nevada • California Condensed • Canada • Chicago • Chicago City Map • Chicago Condensed • Florida • Georgia & the Carolinas • Great Lakes • Hawaii • Hiking in Alaska • Hiking in the USA • Honolulu & Oahu City Map • Las Vegas • Los Angeles • Los Angeles City Map • Louisiana & the Deep South • Miami • Miami City Map • Montreal • New England • New Orleans • New Orleans City Map • New York City • New York City Map • New York City Condensed • New York, New Jersey & Pennsylvania • Oahu • Out to Eat – San Francisco • Pacific Northwest • Rocky Mountains • San Diego & Tijuana • San Francisco • San Francisco City Map • Seattle • Seattle City Map • Southwest • Texas • Toronto • USA • USA phrasebook • Vancouver • Vancouver City Map • Virginia & the Capital Region • Washington, DC • Washington, DC City Map • World Food New Orleans **Travel Literature**: Caught Inside: A Surfer's Year on the California Coast • Drive Thru America

NORTH-EAST ASIA Beijing • Beijing City Map • Cantonese phrasebook • China • Hiking in Japan • Hong Kong & Macau • Hong Kong City Map • Hong Kong Condensed • Japan • Japanese phrasebook • Korea • Korean phrasebook • Kyoto • Mandarin phrasebook • Mongolia • Mongolian phrasebook • Seoul • Shanghai • South-West China • Taiwan • Tokyo • Tokyo Condensed • World Food Hong Kong • World Food Japan **Travel Literature:** In Xanadu: A Quest • Lost Japan

SOUTH AMERICA Argentina, Uruguay & Paraguay • Bolivia • Brazil • Brazilian phrasebook • Buenos Aires • Buenos Aires City Map • Chile & Easter Island • Colombia • Ecuador & the Galapagos Islands • Healthy Travel Central & South America • Latin American Spanish phrasebook • Peru • Quechua phrasebook • Read This First: Central & South America • Rio de Janeiro • Rio de Janeiro City Map • Santiago de Chile • South America on a shoestring • Trekking in the Patagonian Andes • Venezuela **Travel Literature**: Full Circle: A South American Journey

SOUTH-EAST ASIA Bali & Lombok • Bangkok • Bangkok City Map • Burmese phrasebook • Cambodia • Cycling Vietnam, Laos & Cambodia • East Timor phrasebook • Hanoi • Healthy Travel Asia & India • Hill Tribes phrasebook • Ho Chi Minh City (Saigon) • Indonesia • Indonesian phrasebook • Indonesia's Eastern Islands • Java • Lao phrasebook • Laos • Malay phrasebook • Malaysia, Singapore & Brunei • Myanmar (Burma) • Philippines • Pilipino (Tagalog) phrasebook • Read This First: Asia & India • Singapore • Singapore City Map • South-East Asia on a shoestring • South-East Asia phrasebook • Thailand • Thailand's Islands & Beaches • Thailand, Vietnam, Laos & Cambodia Road Atlas • Thai phrasebook • Vietnam • Vietnamese phrasebook • World Food Indonesia • World Food Thailand • World Food Vietnam

ALSO AVAILABLE: Antarctica • The Arctic • The Blue Man: Tales of Travel, Love and Coffee • Brief Encounters: Stories of Love, Sex & Travel • Buddhist Stupas in Asia: The Shape of Perfection • Chasing Rickshaws • The Last Grain Race • Lonely Planet ... On the Edge: Adventurous Escapades from Around the World • Lonely Planet Unpacked • Lonely Planet Unpacked Again • Not the Only Planet: Science Fiction Travel Stories • Ports of Call: A Journey by Sea • Sacred India • Travel Photography: A Guide to Taking Better Pictures • Travel with Children • Tuvalu: Portrait of an Island Nation

Index

Text

A

Abgusssammlung Antiker
    Plastik 136
accommodation 177-89
    private agencies 181
Ägyptisches Museum 135
Air Force Ministry 55
air travel 87-92, **93**
    airline offices 92
    airports 98
    buying tickets 87-9
    departure tax 89
    fare changes 97
    glossary 88
    to/from Australia 91
    to/from Canada 91
    to/from Continental Europe
        90
    to/from New Zealand
        91-2
    to/from the UK 89-90
    to/from the USA 90-1
    travellers, special needs 89
Airlift Memorial 148
Akademie der Künste 139
Albertinum 255
Alexanderplatz 234
Alexanderplatz area 123-4
Allierten-Museum 170
Alte Nationalgalerie 112
Alte Stadthaus 125
Altes Museum 50, 112
Altes Rathaus 242
Altstadt Spandau 234
Amerika-Gedenkbibliothek
    147
Amtsgericht Köpenick 163
Anhalter Bahnhof 146
antiques 228
Antiquity Collection 136
architecture 44-55
    styles 47-9
    tours 49-55
arts 28-40
athletics 226
ATMs see money
Autonomen 82, 145

B

Babelsberg 243
Bach, Johann Sebastian 257
    museum 259
    New Bach Memorial 259
    tomb 257
Balcony of Europe 255
bargaining see money
bars see pubs
Basic Treaty 21
basketball 226
Battle of Berlin 19
Bauhaus Archiv/Museum of
    Design 52, 142
Bauhaus school 142
Bebelplatz 110
beer gardens 214
Begas, Reinhold 29
Behrens, Peter 46
Belvedere 241
Belvedere folly 134
Berggruen Collection 135
Berlin Airlift 20
Berlin Blockade 20
Berlin Spy Tunnel 170
Berlin Wall 21, 151-2
Berliner Sezession 30
Berliner Volksbank 54
bicycle travel 103
Bismarck 14
Blinden Museum 169
boat cruises 58, 104-5, 170,
    242-3, 246
boating 246, 248
Bodemuseum 112
book burning 110
books 70-1
bookshops 229-30
Botanischer Garten 169
Botanisches Museum 169
Brandenburg 237-50
Brandenburg an der Havel 244
    walking tour 244
Brandenburger Gate 108
Brandenburger Tor 241
Brecht, Bertolt 35, 36, 39, 116,
    156, 247
Brecht Haus 156
Brecht-Weigel House 247
Breitscheidplatz 132
Britz 161

Bröhan Museum 135
Brücke Museum 170
BTM tourist office 132
Buckow 247-8
Bunkerberge 152
bus travel
    to/from Berlin 95-6, **93**
    tours 103-4
    within Berlin 100
business hours 82-3
business services 84-5

C

cabaret 220-3
camping 177-8
    outdoor equipment 230
car travel
    to/from Berlin 96
    within Berlin 101-2
Carl-Zeiss-Planetarium 154
casino 176
castles & palaces
    Ephraim Palais 124
    Jagdschloss Grunewald 168
    Kronprinzenpalais 110
    Marmorpalais 242
    Neues Palais 241
    Opernpalais 110
    Orangerieschloss 241
    Palace of Tears 115
    Palais Podewil 125
    Palais Schwerin 125
    Palast der Republik 114
    Schloss Bellevue 139
    Schloss Cecilienhof 242
    Schloss Charlottenburg 132-3
    Schloss Charlottenhof 241
    Schloss Friedrichsfelde 157
    Schloss Glienicke 171
    Schloss Köpenick 164
    Schloss Niederschönhausen
        155
    Schloss Rheinsberg 249
    Schloss Sanssouci 239
    Schloss Wittenberg 252
CDU 25-6
cemeteries 147, 149, 156
Chamissoplatz 149
Charlottenburg 129-36
Checkpoint Charlie 145, 170

Bold indicates maps.

children, travelling with 79-80
    Deutsches Technikmuseum
      146-7
    Junior Museum 169
    Spree-Park 162
    youth theatre 223-4
Chorin 250
Choriner Musiksommer 250
churches & cathedrals
    Berliner Dom 113-14
    Deutscher Dom 117-18
    Franziskaner Klosterkirche
      125
    Französische Kirche 241
    Garnisonskirche 167
    Gethsemane Kirche 154
    Kaiser-Wilhelm-
      Gedächtniskirche 132
    Marienkirche 123
    Nikolaikirche 124, 167
    Parochialkirche 125
    Passionskirche 149
    Pfarrkirche St Katharinen 244
    St Johannis Kirche 137
    St Matthäus Kirche 141
    Sts Peter und Paul Kirche 241
    Sophienkirche 127
    Stadtkirche St Marien 251
    Thomaskirche 257
cinema 151, 210
climate 24
clubs 215-18
cocktail bars 213
Cold War 20-4
Communist Party (KPD)163
concentration camps 18
    Speziallager No 7 248
consulates 61-2
Cottbus 247
counselling services
    children 79
    gay & lesbian 78
    women 77
credit cards see money
cultural centre 218-19
cultural institutes 80-1
currency see money
customs 62
cycling 175

D
dadaism 30
Dahlem Museums 168

DaimlerCity 53-5, see also
    Potsdamer Platz
dance 37, 224
Debis building 54
department stores 234-5
Deutsche Guggenheim 109
Deutscher Dom 117-18
Deutsches Historisches
    Museum 111
Deutsches Technikmuseum
    146-7
Dietrich, Marlene 32, 33, 143
disabled travellers 78
districts 56, **57**
documents 59-61
Domäne Dahlem 169
Drachenhaus 241
Dresden 252-7, **254**
    Grünes Gewölbe 255
    Neumarkt 253-5
drinks 191-2
driving licence 60, 82
drugs 82
Dussmann – Das
    Kulturkaufhaus 235

E
East Side Gallery 151
ecology 24-5
economy 26
education 27
Egyptian Museum 259
Einstein, Albert 28
Elbe river 252
electricity 74
email 69
embassies 61-2
emergency 81
    lawyer hotline 82
entertainment 209-27
environment 24-5
Ephraim Palais 124
Erotik Museum 132
ETA Hoffmann Garden 147
etiquette 40-1
Eurocheques see money

F
Fasanenstrasse 130
fauna 25
fax services 68
Federal Republic of Germany
    (FRG) 20
ferry travel 101
festivals 83-4
film 31-5

Filmpark Babelsberg 242
Final Solution 18, 171
Fischerinsel 125
fitness centres 172
flora 25
Fontane, Theodor 247
food 190-208
    American 192
    Australian 192
    breakfast 203
    cafes 202-6
    Caribbean 193
    Chinese 193
    costs 191
    Ethiopian 193
    fast food 206-7
    food courts 207-8
    French 193
    German 194-5
    Greek 195
    Indian 196
    international 196-7
    Italian 197-9
    Japanese 199
    Jewish 199-200
    kantinen 208
    local etiquette 190
    Mexican 200
    Middle Eastern & Russian
      200
    self-catering 208
    South-East Asian 200
    Spanish/Latin American 201
    student cafeterias 208
    Thai 201
    traditional Berlin cuisine 195
    Turkish 201-2
    vegetarian 202
Forum Köpenick 234
Franziskaner Klosterkirche 125
Französische Kirche 241
Frauenkirche 253
Freie Universität 169
Freilandmuseum 246
Friedrichshain 150-3
Friedrichstadtpalast 115
Friedrichstadtpassagen 118-20,
    233-4
Friedrichstrasse 115
Friedrichswerdersche Kirche 49
Funkturm 136

G
Galerie der Romantik 133-4
Galerie im Cranach Haus 252
Galeries Lafayette 234
Garnisonskirche 167

Bold indicates maps.

gay travellers 77-8
  bookshops 230
  entertainment 224-6
  hotels 183
  memorial plaque 143
  Schöneberg 143
Gay Museum 148
Gedenkstätte Deutscher
  Widerstand 141-2
Gedenkstätte Hohenschön-
  hausen 159
Gedenkstätte Plötzensee 137-8
Gendarmenmarkt 117-18
geography 24
German Communist Party
  (KPD)163
German Democratic Republic
  (GDR) 21, 151-4, 157-8, 160
  collapse of 22-3
Gestapo Headquarters 122
Gethsemane Kirche 154
Goebbels, Joseph 17
Goldener Reiter 255
Gontard, Karl von 143
Göring, Hermann 17
Gothisches Haus 167
government 25-6
Grass, Günter 40
Grassi Museum Complex 260
Gropius, Walter 142, 161
Gropiusstadt 161
Grosser Müggelsee 165
Grünau 165
Gründerzeit Museum 159
Grünes Gewölbe 255
Grunewald Forest 167-8
Grunewaldturm 168
Gruselkabinett 146
gymnasiums 172

H
Hamburger Bahnhof 117
Handwerkervereinshaus 126
Hanfmuseum 124
Hansaviertel 51
Haus am Checkpoint Charlie
  145
Haus der Kulturen der Welt 139
Haus der Wannsee Konferenz
  171
Havel river 171, 237, 242, 244
health 75-6
Hegel, Georg Wilhelm Friedrich
  27
Hellersdorf 159
Hess, Rudolf 165

highlights 106
hiking 246, 248
history 11-24
  books 70-1
hitching
  to/from Berlin 96
  within Berlin 102
Hitler, Adolf 16-19
Hitler's Bunker 120-2
Hohenschönhausen 159-60
Holländisches Viertel 241
Holocaust Memorial 121
Honecker, Erich 22, 23
horse racing 227
Horseshoe Colony 161
hospitals 75
hostels 178-81
  cards 60
Hotel Grand Hyatt 54
Humboldt University 110
Hundemuseum 156

I
ice hockey 227
ice skating 175
indoor swimming pools 174
International Film Festival 83
international phonecards 68
International Travel Fair 83
Internet resources 69
Isherwood, Christopher 143, 221
Ishtar Gate 113

J
Jagdschloss Grunewald 168
Jews 17, 18, 41, 121, 128-9,
  147, 154, 171
jogging 176
Jüdisches Museum 147
Justizzentrum 137

K
KaDeWe 132, 234
Kaiser-Wilhelm-
  Gedächtniskirche 132
Kammergericht 143
Kant, Immanuel 27
Karl-Marx-Allee 151
Karl-Marx-Strasse 160, 234
Kasematten 255
Käthe-Kollwitz-Museum 131
Kennedy, John F 143, 144
Kietz 164-5
Kleist, Heinrich 170
Kleistpark 143

Kloster Chorin 250
Klosterkirche 250
kneipen 214
Knobelsdorff Wing 133
Knobelsdorff, Georg
  Wenzeslaus von 45
Kohl, Helmut 24
Kollwitz, Käthe 30, 131, 153
Komische Oper 109
Königskolonnaden 143
Köpenick 163-7
Köpenick, Hauptmann von 164
Kreuzberg 144-50
Kreuzberg memorial 148
Kreuzberg Museum 150
Kreuzkirche 253
Kronprinzenpalais 110
Kronprinzessinenpalais 110
Krüger, Franz 29
Kulturbrauerei 154
Kulturforum 139-43
Kunstgewerbemuseum 140
Künstlerhaus Bethanien 150
Kupferstichkabinett 140
Kurfürstendamm 131-2
Kurfürstendamm/
  Tauentzienstrasse 233

L
lakeside swimming pools 174
Lang, Fritz 32
Langhans, Carl Gotthard 45
language 41
  courses 176
laundry 74
legal matters 82
Lehrter Zentralbahnhof 137
Leipzig 257-61, **258**
  Apelshaus 259
  Goethe monument 259
  Nikolaikirche 259
  Völkerschlachtdenkmal 260
Lenné, Peter 148, 161, 171
lesbian travellers 77-8
  bookshops 230
  entertainment 224-6
  hotels 183
  memorial plaque 143
  Schöneberg 143
Lessing, Gotthold Ephraim 39
libraries 80
Lichtenberg 157-9
Liebermann, Max 30
Liebknecht, Karl 15
literature 38-41
Love Parade 84

Lübben 245-7
Lübbenau 245-7
Lucas Cranach the Elder 251-2
    House of Cranach 252
Luftbrückendenkmal 148
Luther, Martin 41, 251
    Luthereiche 251
    Schlosskirche 252
    tombstone 252
Lutherhaus 251
Lutherstadt-Wittenberg 251-2

M

magazines 71-2
Mahlsdorf, Charlotte von 159
maps 58
Marheineke Markthalle 149
Marienkirche 123
markets 235-6
    Türkenmarkt 149
Märkisches museum 125-6
Märkisches Ufer 125-6
Marmorpalais 242
Martin-Gropius-Bau 122-3
Marx, Karl 28
Marzahn 159
medical services 75-6
medieval village 169
Mehringplatz 147
Melanchthon, Philipp 251
    Melanchthon House 251
    tombstone 252
Metropol Theater 143
Meyer, Gustav 148, 152
Ministry for State Security 21, 157-8
Mitte 106-29
Moabit 137-8
Molkenmarkt area 125
money 62-7
motorcycle travel
    to/from Berlin 96
    within Berlin 101-2
Müller, Heiner 40
Museum Berlin-Karlshorst 158-9
Museum der Verbotenen Kunst 162
Museum Europäische Kulturen 169
Museum für Naturkunde 117
Museum für Völkerkunde 169
Museum für Vor- und Frühgeschichte 134

Museum of Transport 253
museums & art galleries 107
    Ägyptisches Museum 135
    Albertinum 255
    Allierten-Museum 170
    Alte Nationalgalerie 112
    Altes Museum 112
    Antiquity Collection 136
    Bach Museum 259
    Bauhaus Archiv/Museum of Design 52, 142
    Berggruen Collection 135
    Berlin Story 109
    Blinden Museum 169
    Bodemuseum 112
    Botanisches Museum 169
    Bröhan Museum 135
    Brücke Museum 170
    Deutsche Guggenheim 109
    Deutsches Historisches 111
    Deutsches Technikmuseum 146-7
    Domäne Dahlem 169
    Egyptian Museum 259
    Erotik Museum 132
    Friseurmuseum 159
    Galerie der Romantik 133-4
    Galerie im Cranach Haus 252
    Gay Museum 148
    Gedenkstätte Deutscher Widerstand 141-2
    Grassi Museum Complex 260
    Gründerzeit Museum 159
    Hamburger Bahnhof 117
    Hanfmuseum 124
    Haus am Checkpoint Charlie 145
    Haus der Kulturen der Welt 139
    Heimatmuseum Marzahn 159
    Huguenot Museum 118
    Hundemuseum 156
    Jüdisches Museum 147
    Kasematten 255
    Käthe-Kollwitz-Museum 30, 131
    Kreuzberg Museum 150
    Kunstgewerbemuseum 140
    Kupferstichkabinett 140
    Local History Museum 155
    Lutherhaus 251
    Märkisches Museum 125-6
    Martin-Gropius-Bau 122
    Museum Berlin-Karlshorst 158-9
    Museum der Verbotenen Kunst 162

    Museum Europäische Kulturen 169
    Museum für Naturkunde 117
    Museum für Völkerkunde 169
    Museum für Vor- und Frühgeschichte 134
    Museum of Transport 253
    Museum zur Dresdner Frühromantik 256
    Museumsdorf Düppel 169
    Museumsinsel 111-14
    Musikinstrumenten-Museum 140
    Neue Gemäldegalerie 141
    Neue Nationalgalerie 141
    Neues Museum 112
    New Masters Gallery 255
    Pergamon Museum 112-13
    Pfaueninsel 171
    private galleries 228-9
    Schinkelmuseum 111
    Schloss area museums 134
    Schloss Friedrichsfelde 157
    Sophienhöfe 127
    Stasi Museum 259
    Wäscherei-Museum 164-5
    Wassersportmuseum 165
Museumsdorf Düppel 169
Museumsinsel 111-14
music 37-8, 219,
    Love Parade 38, 215
    music shops 232
    opera & musicals 220
    techno 215
Musikinstrumenten-Museum 140

N

Napoleon 12-13
Nauener Tor 241
Nazi years 16-19
Nering-Eosander Building 133
Neue Gemäldegalerie 141
Neue Kammern 239
Neue Nationalgalerie 52, 141
Neue Reichskanzlei 120
Neue Staatsbibliothek 141
Neue Synagoge 127
Neue Wache 49, 111
Neuer Garten 242
Neues Museum 112
Neues Palais 241
Neues Rathaus 253
Neukölln 160-1
New Masters Gallery 255

Bold indicates maps.

newspapers 71-2
Niederfinow 250
Nietzsche, Friedrich 28
Nikolaikirche 124, 167, 242
Nikolaiviertel 124
Nollendorfplatz area 143
Nuremberg Laws 17

O

Olympic Stadium 55, 136
opera & musicals 220
Orangerieschloss 241
Oranienburger Tor 116-17
Oranienstrasse 150
organised tours 58, 80
  boat 104-5, 170-1, 242-3,
    246, 248
  Brandenburg 237
  bus 103-4
  to/from Berlin 96
  walking 104
orientation 56-8
Otto-Nagel-Haus 125

P

painting 28-31
palaces see castles & palaces
Palais Podewil 125
Palais Schwerin 125
Pankow 155
Pariser Platz 109
Pariser Strasse/Olivaer Platz
  234
parks
  Tiergarten park 138-9
  Treptower Park 161
  Volkspark Hasenheide 160-1
Parochialkirche 125
Partei Demokratischer
  Sozialisten (PDS) 26, 157
Pass Agreement 21
Passionskirche 149
Pergamon Museum 112-13
Pfarrkirche St Katharinen 244
Pfaueninsel 171
pharmacies 75
Philharmonie 52
philosophy 27-8
photography 73-4
Piano, Renzo 118-20
Picture Gallery (Bildergalerie)
  239
Planck, Max 28
Plattenbauten 44, 159-60
Plötzensee Memorial 137-8
politics 25-6

population 26-7
postal services 67-9
Potsdam 237-44, **240**
Potsdamer Platz 118-20, **120**
  Infobox 119
Potsdamer Platz Arkaden 54,
  235
Prenzlauer Berg 153-5
Procession of Princes mural
  253
Prussia, Kingdom of 237
public holidays 83-4
public transport 99-101
pubs 210-14

Q

Quadriga 29, 108

R

racial attacks 81
radio 72
Rathaus Schöneberg 144
Rauch, Christian Daniel 29
Red Army Faction (RAF) 22
Reformation 251-2
Reichsluftfahrtministerium
  122
Reichstag 108-9
Reinhardt, Max 35, 115, 116
religion 41
rental properties 188-9
reunification 23
Rheinsberg 249-50
Riefenstahl, Leni 34
Rixdorfer Höhe 161
Rotes Rathaus 123-4
Ruinenberg 239

S

Sachsenhausen memorial &
  museum 248-9
safety 81-2
Sts Peter und Paul Kirche 241
Sammlung Berggruen
  (Berggruen Collection) 135
Sanssouci Park 239
saunas 175
S-Bahn 99
Schadow, Johann Gottfried 29,
  108
Scharoun, Hans 46, 139
Schauspielhaus 49
Scheidemann, Philipp 15
Scheunenviertel 128-9
Schiller Monument 256

Schinkel, Karl Friedrich 29, 45,
  148, 172, 241
  Schinkel tour 49-50
Schinkelmuseum 111
Schloss Bellevue 139
Schloss Britz 161
Schloss Cecilienhof 242
Schloss Charlottenburg 132-3
Schloss Charlottenhof 241
Schloss Friedrichsfelde 157
Schloss Glienicke 171
Schloss Köpenick 164
Schloss Niederschönhausen 155
Schloss Rheinsberg 249
Schloss Sanssouci 239
Schloss Wittenberg 252
Schlossgarten 134
Schlosskirche 252
schlossplatz 114-15
Schlüter, Andreas 28
Schöneberg 142-4
Schröder, Gerhard 24
Schultheiss brewery 154
science 27-8
sculpture 28-31
Seghers, Anna 163
Seitz, Gustav 153
Semperoper 253
senior travellers 78
shopping 228-36
  antiques 228
  books 229
  camping gear 230
  fashion 230-1
  galleries 228-9
  household wares 231-2
  jewellery 232
  music 232
  porcelain 232-3
  wine 233
Siegessäule (Victory Column) 138
smoking 190
soccer 227
Social Democratic Party (SPD)
  147, 163
Socialist Unity Party of
  Germany (SED) 19, 21, 26
society & conduct 40-1
Sophiensaele 126
Sophienstrasse 126-7
Sorbs 41, 237, 245
  Freilandmuseum 246
  Wendisches Museum/
    Serbski muzej 247
Sowjetisches Ehrenmal (Soviet
  Memorial) 138, 162
Spandau 165-72, **166**

Spandau Zitadelle 166
Spandauer Vorstadt 126-9
   Hackesche Höfe 126
Spartacus League 15
SPD see Social Democratic Party
special events 83-4
spectator sports 226-7
Spielbank Berlin 176
Sportpalast 143
Spree-Park 162
Spreewald (Spree Forest) 245
squash 176
St Johannis Kirche 137
St Matthäus Kirche 141
Staatsbibliothek 109-10
Stadtkirche St Marien 251
Stasi see Ministry for State
   Security
Stasi Museum 259
Strasse des 17 Juni 138
Student Identity Card 60
swimming 172-5
synagogues 128-9, 154

T
Tacheles 127
Taut, Bruno 46, 161
taxes & refunds see money
taxi travel 102-3
telephone 67-8
television 72-3
Tempelhof airport 55, 148
tennis 176, 227
Theater des Westens 130
theatre 35-7, 222-3
   Berliner Ensemble 115
   children's 223-4
   Deutsches Theater 115
   English-language
      productions 222
   Sophiensaele 126
   Theater des Westens 130
   Theaterplatz 253
   Waldbühne 136

Thomaskirche 257
Tiergarten 51-2, 136-42
Tiergarten park 138-9
Tierpark 157-8
time 74
tipping see money
toilets 74-5
tourist offices 58-9
   abroad 59
   local 58
train travel
   regional 100
   to/from Berlin 92-5, **93**
tram travel 101
travel agents 96-7
travel insurance 59-60
travellers cheques see money
Treptow 161-3
Trümmerberge (rubble
   hill) 161, 167
TV Tower 123

U
U-Bahn 99
Ulbricht, Walter 19, 21, 34
unemployment 26
universities 80
   Humboldt Universität 110
Universum Film AG (UFA) 31
Unter den Linden 107-11

V
video 73-4
video systems 73
Viktoriapark 148
visas 59
Volkspark Friedrichshain 152-3
Volkspark Hasenheide 160-1

W
Wagner, Martin 161
walking tours 130-2
   Brandenburg 244
   Kreuzberg 147-50

Leipzig 257
Prenzlauer Berg 153-5
Spreewald 246
within Berlin 104
Wall Victims Memorial
   109
Wannsee 170-1
Wäscherei-Museum
   164-5
Wassersportmuseum 165
Wasserturm
   Mehringdamm 149
   Prenzlauer Berg 154
weights & measures 74
Weimar Republic 15-16
Weinhaus Huth 55
Weissensee 155-7
WelcomeCard 58, 239
Wende 158
Wertheim bei Hertie 234
Wilhelm II, Kaiser 14, 15
Willy-Brandt-Haus 147
Wilmersdorf 167-8
Wilmersdorfer Strasse
   233
Wolf, Christa 40
women travellers 76-7
work 85-6
World Time Clock 123
WWI 14-15
WWII 17-19, 158, 162
   aftermath 19

Y
Yalta Conference 19

Z
Zehlendorf 168-72
Zoo station 92, 130
Zoologischer Garten
   139
   Elephant Gate 139
Zuckerbäckerstil 151
Zwinger 253

Boxed Text

Bauhaus, The 142
Berlin Airlift, The 20
Berlin Cuisine 195
Berlin Highlights 106
Berlin Nicknames 111
Berlin Wall, The 152
Berlin's Jewish Renaissance 128-9
Berlin's Museums 107
Bertolt Brecht 36
Cabaret in Berlin: Let the Good Times Roll – Again! 221
Cemetery Hopping 156-7
Der Hauptmann von Köpenick 164
Gay & Lesbian Hotels 183

Hollywood on the Havel 243
Holocaust Memorial – Anatomy of a Debate, The 121
'I am a Doughnut' – John F Kennedy, 1962 144
Introducing the Euro 64-5
Joy of Breakfast, The 203
Kreuzberg in Flames 145
'Luxury Living' – Made in the GDR 160
Making an Art of Discounts 66
Marlene Dietrich 33
Max Reinhardt – Impresario Extraordinaire 116
Mystery of Hitler's Body, The 18

Reincarnation of Potsdamer Platz, The 119
Rise & Fall of Erich Honecker, The 23
Seeing Berlin From Bus No 100 100
Smoke Gets in Your Eyes 190
Sorbs, The 245
Stasi – Fear and Loathing in the GDR, The 158
Techno Town 215
Thespian Delights 222
What To Do In An Emergency 81
What's Free 173

S-Bahn Berlin GmbH
Deutsche Bahn Gruppe

Beetz-Sommerfeld RB35
Rheinsberg (Mark) RB12 Prenzlau
Stralsund RE3

Vehlefanz RB55
Bärenklau
Velten (Mark)
Oranienburg S1
Lehnitz
Borgsdorf
Birk...
Hennigsdorf (b.Bln) RB21
Hohen Neuendorf West
Hohen Neuendorf (b Bln)
Heiligensee
Schulzendorf (b.Tegel)
Frohnau
Hermsdorf
Waidmannslust
Alt-Tegel
Borsigwerke
Tegel
Rathaus Reinicke...
Eichborndamm
Karl-Bonhoeffer-Nervenklinik
Holzhauser Str
Lindauer Allee
Seidelstr.
Paracelsus-Bad
Scharnweberstr.
Residenzstr.
Kurt-Schumacher-Platz
Franz-Neumann-Platz
Am Schäfersee
Afrikanische Str.
Flughafen Berlin-Tegel Otto Lilienthal
X9, 109, 128
Rehberge
Nauener Platz
Leopoldplatz
Wedding
Westhafen

Wittenberge RE4
Nauen RB21
Brieselang
Finkenkrug
Falkensee
Seegefeld-Helitzwerke
Albrechtshof
Altstadt Spandau
Haselhorst
Paulsternstr.
Rohrdamm
Siemensdamm
Halemweg
Jakob-Kaiser-Platz

Rathenow RB13
Wustermark
Dallgow-Döberitz
Staaken
Eistal
Rathaus Spandau U7
Stresow
Spandau U7

Jungfernheide S41 S42
Beusselstr.
Birkenstr.
Reinickendorfer Str.
Turmstr.
Schwartzkopffstr.
Zinnowitzer Str
Oranienburger Tor
Oranien burger S...
Nord...

Ruhleben U2
Olympia-Stadion (Ost)
Westend S41 S42
Neu-Westend
Sophie-Charlotte-Pl.
Richard-Wagner-Platz
Mierendorffplatz
Deutsche Oper
Ernst-Reuter-Pl.
Hansaplatz
Tiergarten
Bellevue
Lehrter Stadtbahnhof
Friedrichstr.

Pichelsberg
Olympiastadion
Theodor-Heuss-Platz
Witzleben
Bismarckstr.
Zoologischer Garten
Unter den Linden
Potsdamer Platz
Französisch...

Heerstr.
Savignyplatz
Wilmersdorfer Str
Charlottenburg
Nollendorf platz U4
Mendelssohn-Bartholdy-Park
Anhalter
Mohr...
Kurfürstendamm
Wittenbergplatz
Kurfürstenstr
Uhlandstr.
Augsburger Str.
Bülowstr
Gleisdreieck
Möc...
Priort
Spichernstr.
Viktoria-Luise-Platz
Yorckstr.
Großgörschenstr.
Yorckstr.
Adenauerplatz
Hohenzollernplatz
Fehrbelliner Pl
Güntzelstr.
Bayerischer Platz
Mehri...
Marquardt
Konstanzer Str
Westkreuz S3 S5
Blissestr.
Berliner Str.
Eisenacher Str.
Kleistpark
Lu...
Halensee
Rathaus Schöneberg
P...
Hohenzollern damm
Heidelberger Platz
Bundesplatz
Schöneberg
Papestr.
Grunewald
Rüdesheimer Platz
Friedrich-Wilhelm-Platz
Innsbrucker Platz U4
Friedenau
Breitenbachplatz
Walther-Schreiber-Platz
Feuerbachstr.
Priesterweg
Podbielskiallee
Schloßstr.
Attilastr.
Golm
Dahlem-Dorf
Rathaus Steglitz
Südende
Thielplatz
Botanischer Garten
Lankwitz
Mari...
Griebnitzsee
Nikolassee
Oskar-Helene-Heim
Lichterfelde West
Lankwitz
Brandenburg RB10
Brandenburg RB20
Magdeburg RE1
Werder (Havel)
Wildpark
Charlottenhof
Babelsberg RB21
Onkel Toms Hütte
Lichterfelde Ost
Osdorfer Str.
Potsdam Stadt RB13 RB22 DB
Krumme Lanke U3
Lichterfelde Süd S25
Drewitz
Wannsee RB33 DB
Sundgauer Str.
Teltow
Rehbrücke
Schlachtensee
Mexicoplatz
Zehlendorf
Großbeeren
Pirschheide
Genshagener Heide
Blankenfelde
Caputh-Geltow
Wilhelmshorst
Saarmund
Schwielowsee
Michendorf
Ferch-Lienewitz
Seddin
Ludwigsfelde
Birkengrund
Thyrow

Dessau RB3
Belzig RB10
Jüterbog RE3
Bad Liebenwarda RE4

RE1 Magdeburg ↔ Cottbus
RE2 Brandenburg ↔ Cottbus
RE3 Stralsund ↔ Dessau
RE4 Wittenberge ↔ Bad Liebenwerda
RE5 Stralsund ↔ Hoyerswerda/Dresden
RE7 Schwedt (Oder) ↔ Berlin-Lichtenberg

RB10 Charlottenburg ↔ Belzig
RB12 Prenzlau/Rheinsberg (Mark) ↔ Frankfurt (Oder)
RB13 Rathenow ↔ Charlottenburg
RB14 Schöneweide ↔ Senftenberg
RB20 Brandenburg ↔ Charlottenburg
RB21 Hennigsdorf/ Nauen ↔ Griebnitzsee
RB22 Potsdam Stadt ↔ Eberswalde

RB24 Schönefeld-Flughafen ↔ Wünsdorf-Waldstadt
RB25 Lichtenberg ↔ Tiefensee
RB26 Schöneweide ↔ Strausberg Nord/Kostrzyn
RB27 Groß Schönebeck/Wensickendorf ↔ Karow
RB31 Lichterfelde Ost (SEV) ↔ Ludwigsfelde (SEV)
RB33 Wannsee ↔ Jüterbog
RB35 Beetz-Sommerfeld ↔ Birkenwerder

S1 Wannsee ↔ Oranien...
S2 Blankenfelde ↔ Nor...
S25 Lichterfelde Süd ↔ ...
S3 Erkner ↔ Ostbahnho...
S41 Jungfernheide ↔ Be...
S45 Schönefeld - Flughaf...
S46 Königs Wusterhause...
S5 Strausberg Nord ↔ ...

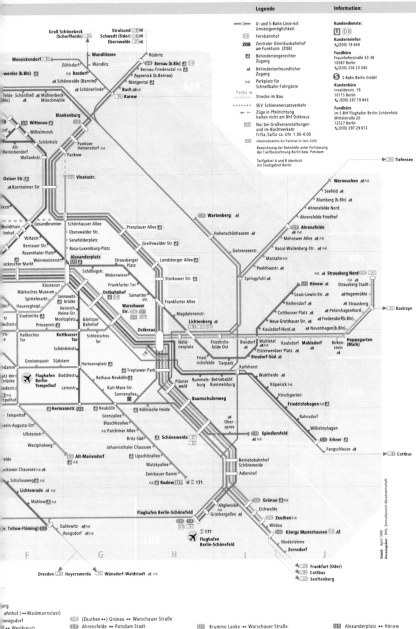

MAP 2 BERLIN

MAP 3

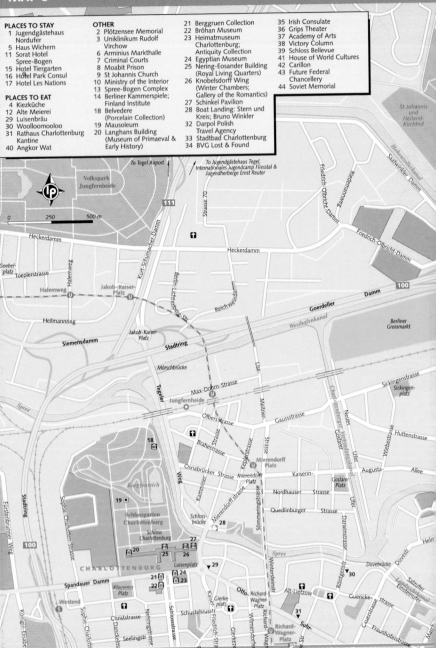

PLACES TO STAY
1 Jugendgästehaus Nordufer
5 Haus Wichern
11 Sorat Hotel Spree-Bogen
15 Hotel Tiergarten
16 Hôtel Park Consul
17 Hotel Les Nations

PLACES TO EAT
4 Kiezküche
12 Alte Meierei
29 Luisenbräu
30 Woolloomooloo
31 Rathaus Charlottenburg Kantine
40 Angkor Wat

OTHER
2 Plötzensee Memorial
3 Uniklinikum Rudolf Virchow
6 Arminius Markthalle
7 Criminal Courts
8 Moabit Prison
9 St Johannis Church
10 Ministry of the Interior
13 Spree-Bogen Complex
14 Berliner Kammerspiele; Finland Institute
18 Belvedere (Porcelain Collection)
19 Mausoleum
20 Langhans Building (Museum of Primaeval & Early History)

21 Berggruen Collection
22 Bröhan Museum
23 Heimatmuseum Charlottenburg; Antiquity Collection
24 Egyptian Museum
25 Nering-Eosander Building (Royal Living Quarters)
26 Knobelsdorff Wing (Winter Chambers; Gallery of the Romantics)
27 Schinkel Pavilion
28 Boat Landing: Stern und Kreis; Bruno Winkler
32 Darpol Polish Travel Agency
33 Stadtbad Charlottenburg
34 BVG Lost & Found

35 Irish Consulate
36 Grips Theater
37 Academy of Arts
38 Victory Column
39 Schloss Bellevue
41 House of World Cultures
42 Carillon
43 Future Federal Chancellery
44 Soviet Memorial

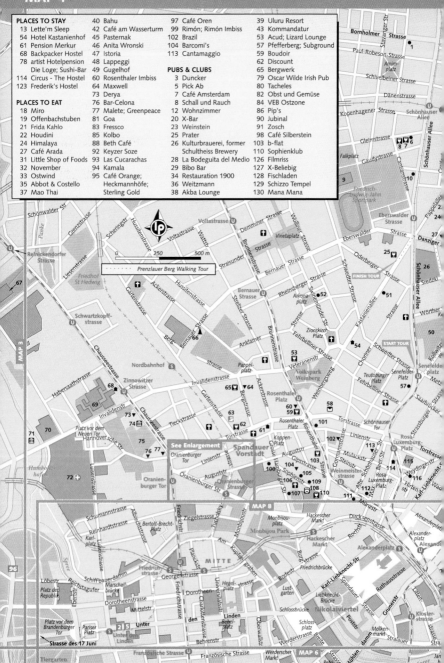

MAP 4

PLACES TO STAY
13 Lette'm Sleep
54 Hotel Kastanienhof
61 Pension Merkur
68 Backpacker Hostel
78 artist Hotelpension
   Die Loge; Sushi-Bar
114 Circus - The Hostel
123 Frederik's Hostel

PLACES TO EAT
18 Miro
20 Offenbachstuben
21 Frida Kahlo
22 Houdini
24 Himalaya
27 Café Arada
31 Little Shop of Foods
32 November
33 Ostwind
35 Abbot & Costello
37 Mao Thai
40 Bahu
42 Café am Wasserturm
45 Pasternak
46 Anita Wronski
47 Istoria
48 Lappeggi
49 Gugelhof
60 Rosenthaler Imbiss
64 Maxwell
73 Derya
76 Bar-Celona
77 Malete; Greenpeace
81 Goa
83 Fressco
85 Kolbo
88 Beth Café
92 Keyzer Soze
94 Las Cucarachas
95 Kamala
95 Café Orange;
   Heckmannhöfe;
   Sterling Gold
97 Café Oren
99 Rimón; Rimón Imbiss
102 Brazil
104 Barcomi's
113 Cantamaggio

PUBS & CLUBS
3 Duncker
5 Pick Ab
7 Café Amsterdam
8 Schall und Rauch
12 Wohnzimmer
20 X-Bar
23 Weinstein
25 Prater
26 Kulturbrauerei, former
   Schultheiss Brewery
28 La Bodeguita del Medio
29 Bibo Bar
34 Restauration 1900
36 Weitzmann
38 Akba Lounge
39 Uluru Resort
43 Kommandatur
53 Acud; Lizard Lounge
57 Pfefferberg; Subground
59 Boudoir
63 Discount
65 Bergwerk
79 Oscar Wilde Irish Pub
80 Tacheles
82 Obst und Gemüse
84 VEB Ostzone
86 Pip's
90 Jubinal
91 Zosch
98 Café Silberstein
103 b-flat
110 Sophienklub
126 Filmriss
127 X-Beliebig
128 Fischladen
129 Schizzo Tempel
130 Mana Mana

Prenzlauer Berg Walking Tour

See Enlargement

MAP 8

MAP 6

MAP 4

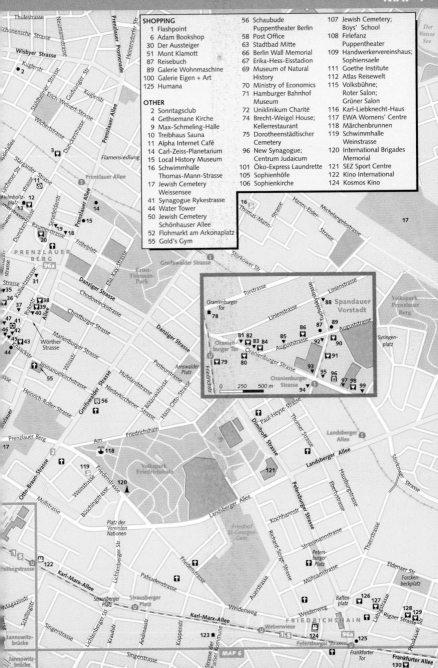

SHOPPING
1 Flashpoint
6 Adam Bookshop
30 Der Aussteiger
51 Mont Klamott
87 Reisebuch
89 Galerie Wohnmaschine
100 Galerie Eigen + Art
125 Humana

OTHER
2 Sonntagsclub
4 Gethsemane Kirche
9 Max-Schmeling-Halle
10 Treibhaus Sauna
11 Alpha Internet Café
14 Carl-Zeiss-Planetarium
15 Local History Museum
16 Schwimmhalle
   Thomas-Mann-Strasse
17 Jewish Cemetery
   Weissensee
41 Synagogue Rykestrasse
44 Water Tower
50 Jewish Cemetery
   Schönhauser Allee
52 Flohmarkt am Arkonaplatz
55 Gold's Gym

56 Schaubude
   Puppentheater Berlin
58 Post Office
63 Stadtbad Mitte
66 Berlin Wall Memorial
67 Erika-Hess-Eisstadion
69 Museum of Natural
   History
70 Ministry of Economics
71 Hamburger Bahnhof
   Museum
72 Uniklinikum Charité
74 Brecht-Weigel House;
   Kellerrestaurant
75 Dorotheenstädtischer
   Cemetery
96 New Synagogue;
   Centrum Judaicum
101 Öko-Express Laundrette
105 Sophienhöfe
106 Sophienkirche

107 Jewish Cemetery;
   Boys' School
108 Firlefanz
   Puppentheater
109 Handwerkervereinshaus;
   Sophiensaele
111 Goethe Institute
112 Atlas Reisewelt
115 Volksbühne;
   Roter Salon;
   Grüner Salon
116 Karl-Liebknecht-Haus
117 EWA Womens' Centre
118 Märchenbrunnen
119 Schwimmhalle
   Weinstrasse
120 International Brigades
   Memorial
121 SEZ Sport Centre
122 Kino International
124 Kosmos Kino

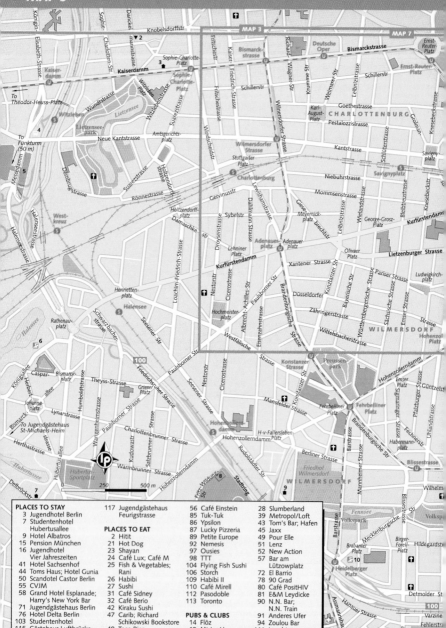

MAP 5

MAP 3
MAP 7

PLACES TO STAY
3 Jugendhotel Berlin
7 Studentenhotel Hubertusallee
9 Hotel Albatros
15 Pension München
16 Jugendhotel Vier Jahreszeiten
41 Hotel Sachsenhof
44 Toms Haus; Hotel Gunia
50 Scandotel Castor Berlin
55 CVJM
58 Grand Hotel Esplanade; Harry's New York Bar
71 Jugendgästehaus Berlin
76 Hotel Delta Berlin
103 Studentenhotel
115 Gästehaus Luftbrücke

117 Jugendgästehaus Feurigstrasse

PLACES TO EAT
2 Hitit
21 Hot Dog
23 Shayan
24 Café Lux; Café M
25 Fish & Vegetables; Rani
26 Habibi
27 Sushi
31 Café Sidney
32 Café Berio
42 Kiraku Sushi
47 Carib; Richard Schikowski Bookstore
48 Taco Rico

56 Café Einstein
85 Tuk-Tuk
86 Ypsilon
87 Lucky Pizzeria
91 Petite Europe
92 Nemesis
97 Ousies
99 TTT
104 Flying Fish Sushi
106 Storch
109 Habibi II
110 Café Mirell
112 Pasodoble
113 Toronto

PUBS & CLUBS
14 Flöz
19 Mister Hu

28 Slumberland
39 Metropol/Loft
43 Tom's Bar; Hafen
45 Jaxx
49 Pour Elle
51 Lenz
52 New Action
57 Bar am Lützowplatz
72 El Barrio
90 90 Grad
80 Café PositHIV
81 E&M Leydicke
90 N.N. Bar; N.N. Train
91 Anderes Ufer
94 Zoulou Bar
111 Leuchtturm

MAP 5

SHOPPING
1 Big Berlin Junk &
   Art Market
17 Hobby-Shop
18 Groopie de Luxe
20 Barbarossa
22 Megadress Berlin
29 Winterfeldtmarkt
30 Simple Pleasures
34 Mr Dead & Mrs Free
35 Kaiser's Supermarket
36 Schuhtick Last Minute
37 Filiale
46 Vivaverde
54 Garage
73 Pärschke
81 Made in Berlin
95 Schwarze Mode

100 Fishbelly
102 Grosser Trödelmarkt
105 Hanf-Haus
108 Der Rioja Spezialist
118 Step by Step

OTHER
4 Central Bus Station
5 ICC
6 Freibad Halensee
8 Eisstadion
   Berlin-Wilmersdorf
10 Stadtbad Wilmersdorf
11 Zahnklinik Medeco
12 Friedenau Cemetery
13 Internet Café Hai Täck
33 Pro Business
38 Box Office Theaterkasse

40 Mann-O-Meter;
   Da Neben Café
53 Urania Filmbühne
59 Bauhaus Archive/
   Museum of Design
60 Future Ministry of Defense
61 Italian Consulate
62 German Resistance
   Museum
63 New Picture Gallery
64 Copperplate Etchings
   Gallery
65 Museum of
   Decorative Arts
66 Musical Instruments
   Museum
67 Berliner Philharmonie;
   Kammermusiksaal

68 St Matthäus Kirche
69 New State Library
70 New National Gallery
74 Jacobs & Schulz
75 Wintergarten-Das Varieté
79 Begine
82 Lesbian Advice Centre
84 Kammergericht
86 Matthäus-Kirchhof
93 Ars Vitalis
94 Copyhaus II
99 Copyhaus I
101 Rathaus Schöneberg
107 Kopier Blitz
114 Scheinbar
116 Xenon Cinema
119 Odeon Cinema

MAP 6

PLACES TO STAY
1 Odyssee
  Globetrotter Hostel;
  Juncker's Hotel-Garni
9 East Side Hotel
36 Gästehaus
40 Die Fabrik Hostel;
  Café Eisenwaren
49 Jugendgästehaus
  Schreberjugend
56 Hotel am Anhalter
  Bahnhof
62 Pension Kreuzberg;
  Zyankali Bar

68 Hotel Riehmers
  Hofgarten
69 Hotel Transit
82 Gasthaus Dietrich Herz

PLACES TO EAT
4 Conmux
5 Abendmahl
18 Habibi
31 Sandwich Kiosk
32 Amrit
34 Advena
35 Hannibal
37 Café Morena

39 Bagdad
55 Fressco
58 Grossbeerenkeller
63 Rathaus Kreuzberg
  Kantine
70 Chandra Kumari
72 Naturkost
  Vegetarisches Buffet
76 Bergmann 103
78 Atlantic
79 Kichererbse
83 Locus
84 Tres Kilos
88 Merhaba

89 Deininger
91 Barcomi's
92 Lone Star Taqueria
103 Tabibito
107 Café Rix

PUBS & CLUBS
2 Euphoria
3 Dachkammer
5 Tagung/Cube Club
6 Maria am Ostbahnhof;
  Tempodrom (temporary)
7 Die Busche
10 Matrix

12 MS Sanssouci
16 Café Anal
19 Schnabelbar
21 Würgeengel
24 Flammende Herzen
25 Bierhimmel
26 Franken
27 Roses Bar
28 SO 36
42 Arena
44 KitKat Club
80 Junction Bar
86 Café Anfall
95 Golgatha

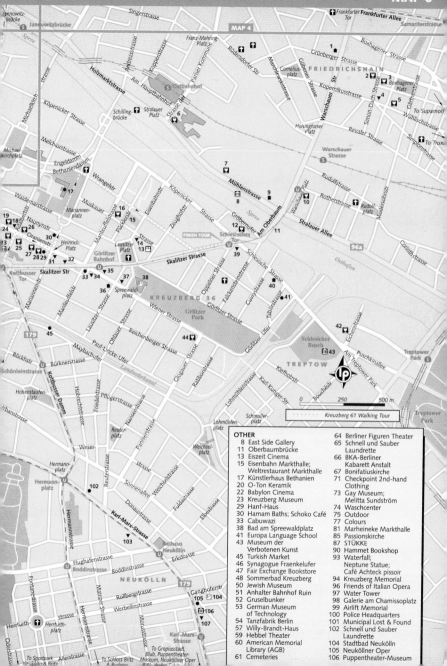

MAP 6

OTHER
- 8 East Side Gallery
- 11 Oberbaumbrücke
- 13 Eiszeit Cinema
- 15 Eisenbahn Markthalle; Weltrestaurant Markthalle
- 17 Künstlerhaus Bethanien
- 20 O-Ton Keramik
- 22 Babylon Cinema
- 23 Kreuzberg Museum
- 29 Hanf-Haus
- 30 Hamam Baths; Schoko Café
- 33 Cabuwazi
- 38 Bad am Spreewaldplatz
- 41 Europa Language School
- 43 Museum der Verbotenen Kunst
- 45 Turkish Market
- 46 Synagogue Fraenkelufer
- 47 Fair Exchange Bookstore
- 48 Sommerbad Kreuzberg
- 50 Jewish Museum
- 51 Anhalter Bahnhof Ruin
- 52 Gruselbunker
- 53 German Museum of Technology
- 54 Tanzfabrik Berlin
- 57 Willy-Brandt-Haus
- 59 Hebbel Theater
- 60 American Memorial Library (AGB)
- 61 Cemeteries
- 64 Berliner Figuren Theater
- 65 Schnell und Sauber Laundrette
- 66 BKA-Berliner Kabarett Anstalt
- 67 Bonifatiuskirche
- 71 Checkpoint 2nd-hand Clothing
- 73 Gay Museum; Melitta Sundström; Waschcenter
- 74 Outdoor
- 75 Colours
- 81 Marheineke Markthalle
- 85 Passionskirche
- 87 STÜKKE
- 90 Hammet Bookshop
- 93 Waterfall; Neptune Statue; Café Achteck pissoir
- 94 Kreuzberg Memorial
- 96 Friends of Italian Opera
- 97 Water Tower
- 98 Galerie am Chamissoplatz
- 99 Airlift Memorial
- 100 Police Headquarters
- 101 Municipal Lost & Found
- 102 Schnell und Sauber Laundrette
- 104 Stadtbad Neukölln
- 105 Neuköllner Oper
- 106 Puppentheater-Museum

MAP 7 - CHARLOTTENBURG

Charlottenburg Walking Tour

500 m
250

Neuer See

Landwehrkanal

Tiergarten

Zoologischer Garten

Charlottenburger Brücke

Strasse des 17 Juni

Technische Universität

Zoologischer Garten

Ernst-Reuter-Platz

Steinplatz

CHARLOTTENBURG

Deutsche Oper

Karl-August-Platz

Weimarer Strasse

Bismarckstrasse

Schillerstrasse

Goethestrasse

Pestalozzistrasse

Leibnizstrasse

Kantstrasse

Krumme Strasse

Wilmersdorfer Strasse

Bismarck-strasse

Kaiser-Friedrich-Strasse

Fritschestrasse

Stuttgarter Platz

Sybelstrasse

Charlottenburg

Leibnizstrasse

Savignyplatz

Grolmanstr

Kantstrasse

Uhlandstr

Kurfürstendamm

Knesebeckstr

Schlüterstrasse

Niebuhrstrasse

Mommsenstrasse

Pestalozzistrasse

Kantstrasse

Wielandstrasse

Giesebrechtstr

Meyerinck-platz

Adenauer-platz

Lewishamstrasse

Dahlmann Strasse

Droysenstrasse

Wilmersdorfer Strasse

Budapester Strasse

Olof-Palme-Platz

Kurfürstenstrasse

Wittenberg-platz

Bayreuther Strasse

Tauentzienstr

Nürnberger Strasse

Passauer Str

Ansbacher Strasse

Hohenstaufenstrasse

Viktoria-Luise-Platz

Welserstrasse

Geisbergstrasse

Kurfürstendamm

Rankestrasse

Augsburger Strasse

Los-Angeles-Platz

Lietzenburger Strasse

Nürnberger Platz

Spichernstrasse

Bundesallee

Joachimstaler

Joachim-staler-platz

Breitscheid-platz

Hardenbergplatz

Hardenbergstrasse

Budapister Str

Kantstrasse

Meinekestr

Fasanenstrasse

Uhland-strasse

Grolmanstr

Knesebeckstr

Bleibtreustr

George-Grosz-Platz

Lietzenburger Strasse

Pariser Strasse

Düsseldorfer Strasse

WILMERSDORF

Sächsische Strasse

Emser Strasse

Ludwigkirch-strasse

Ludwig-kirch-platz

Pfalzburger Strasse

Uhlandstrasse

Kaiser Strasse

Fasanenstrasse

Hohenzollerndamm

Spichernstrasse

Württembergische Strasse

Bayerische Strasse

Olivaer Platz

Konstanzer Strasse

Zähringer-strasse

Wittelsbacherstrasse

Pommersche Strasse

Xantener Strasse

Brandenburgische Strasse

Sächsische Strasse

Albrecht-Achilles-Str

Cicerostrasse

Nestor

Westfälische Strasse

Hochmeister-platz

Lehniner Platz

Kurfürstendamm

MAP 7 - CHARLOTTENBURG

PLACES TO STAY
4 Hotel Consul
5 City-Hotel Westerland
19 Hecker's Hotel
22 Pension Knesebeck
23 Hotel Alpenland
24 Hotel Carmer 16
55 Hotel Crystal
56 Pension Peters
57 Pension Viola Nova
82 Hotel Palace Berlin
105 Pension Gudrun; Kalkutta Indian Restaurant
113 Hotel-Pension Majesty
117 Hotel Askanischer Hof
118 Pension Alexandra
120 Hotel Mondial
121 Hotel California
131 Hotel Steigenberger Berlin
132 Pension Fischer; Hotel-Pension Nürnberger Eck
140 Hotel Auberge
147 Hotel-Garni Atlanta
148 Hotel Augusta
155 Hotel Imperial
156 Hotel Bleibtreu
157 Hotel Bogota
160 Hotel Agon
161 Olivaer Apart Hotel
175 ArtHotel Connection; Connection Disco
177 Hotel-Garni Arco
187 Pension Curtis
188 Hotel Alexander
189 Hotel Steiner
190 Propeller Island Lodge
191 Hotel-Pension Margrit
192 Hotel Savigny
193 Hotel-Pension Wittelsbach
194 Frauenhotel Artemisia
196 Jugendgästehaus Central

PLACES TO EAT
8 Café Hardenberg
9 Technical University Mensa
11 Café am Neuen See
14 Satyam
15 Samadhi
21 Sticks
30 Cour Careé
31 Ashoka
33 Toto
35 Der Ägypter
36 Good Friend
37 Schalom
38 Il Pulcino
42 Biscotti
43 Barbar Bar
48 XII Apost oli
49 Café Aedes
58 Schwarzes Café
59 Sachiko Sushi
60 Paris Bar
90 Marché
95 Café Kranzler; Top-Tour-Berlin Bus Tours
97 Aschinger
101 Lubitsch
104 Ali Baba
106 Einhorn
107 Don Quijote
111 El Borriquito

115 Julep's
123 Gosch
124 Café Möhring; Galerie Brusberg
126 Leysieffer
128 Soup Kultur
130 Salomon Bagels
134 Plätzl
143 Hard Rock Café
149 Café Wintergarten; Literaturhaus
153 Pizzeria Piccola Taormina
162 Poco Loco
172 Maharani
173 Trattoria á Muntagnola
178 Montevideo
181 Manzini
183 Hamlet
184 Fabulous Route 66 50's Diner
185 Sushi
186 Jimmy's Diner

PUBS & CLUBS
27 La Casa del Habano
28 Dicke Wirtin
29 Gainsbourg
34 A-Trane Jazz Club
45 Abraxas
54 Hegel
110 Salsa
141 Andreas Kneipe
171 Knast
174 Prinzknecht

SHOPPING
2 Kiepert Bookshop
16 Books in Berlin
20 Glasklar
25 Piranha
32 Prinz Eisenherz Bookshop
39 Aldi Supermarket
41 Zweitausendeins
46 Kiran
47 Treykorn Jewellery
51 Bücherbogen
52 Arno Lamps
53 Plus Supermarket
61 Galerie Springer & Winckler
63 Greenpeace Shop
72 Aldi Supermarket; AGW Exchange
74 Humana
86 Hugendubel; Gap; Jopp Frauen-Fitness Studio
88 Wertheim bei Hertie
91 Diesel
94 Karstadt Sport; Cyberb@r
96 KPM
99 Galerie Gunar Barthel
102 Kaufhaus Schrill
103 Marga Schoeller Bücherstube
108 Planet
109 Planet 2nd Hand
119 Kaiser's Supermarket
133 Peek & Cloppenburg
135 KaDeWe; Showtime Tickets; Tourist Office Info Point
136 Niketown
137 Kaiser's Supermarket
151 Galerie Pels-Leusden
152 Hautnah
154 Ku'damm Karree; ProMarkt
158 Jil Sander; Gianni Versace
163 Musikhaus Riedl
164 Galerie Anselm Dreher

165 Aldi Supermarket
166 Zellermayer Galerie
167 Bannat
169 Gelbe Musik
180 Les Dessous

OTHER
1 Deutsche Oper Berlin
3 Concert & Theaterkasse City
6 Renaissance-Theater Berlin
7 Kilroy Travel
10 Hochschule der Künste Concert Hall
12 Zoo Station; ADM Mitfahrzentrale; EurAide; McWash
13 Post Office
17 Synagogue Pestalozzistrasse
18 STA Travel
26 Fit Fun
40 Schnell und Sauber Laundrette
44 Rainbow Tours
50 Savignypassage
62 Kantdreieck
64 Theater des Westens
65 Delphi Film Palast; Quasimodo
66 Ludwig-Erhard-Haus
67 British Council
68 Amerika Haus
69 Reisebank
70 BVG Information Kiosk
71 Zoo-Palast Cinema; Hekticket
73 Erotik-Museum
75 Main Post Office
76 Zoo Main Entrance
77 Aquarium
78 Hertz; Avis
79 SixtBudget
80 Apollo Sauna
81 Thermen am Europa-Center
83 BTM Main Tourist Office
84 Europa-Center; Kabarett Die Stachelschweine
85 Euro-Change
87 BBS Bus Tours
89 Kaiser-Wilhelm-Gedächtniskirche
92 Olympia Cinema
93 Café Website
98 Jewish Community House; Arche Noah
100 Australian Embassy
112 Gay Counseling Centre
114 Kurbel Cinema
116 Alternativ Tours
122 Institut Français; French Consulate
125 Severin + Kühn Bus Tours
127 Lufthansa City Centre
129 BVB Bus Tours
138 American Express
139 Japanese Consulate
142 Theaterkasse Centrum
144 CityNetz Mitfahrzentrale
145 City-Wache Police Station
146 Synagogue Joachimstaler Strasse
150 Käthe-Kollwitz-Museum
159 Schaubühne am Lehniner Platz
168 Berliner AIDS-Hilfe
170 Die Wühlmäuse Kabarett
176 Arsenal Cinema
179 Bar jeder Vernunft
182 Schnell und Sauber Laundrette
195 Tennis & Squash City

MAP 8 - MITTE

Michael-
kirchstrasse
Heinrich-Heine-Strasse

Schillingsbrücke
Jannowitzbrücke
Michael-
kirchplatz

Schillingstrasse
Alexanderstrasse
Dircksenstrasse

Wadzeckstr

23
22

24
Alexander-
platz
25

Kopenicker Strasse
124
123
Brückenstr
Heinrich-Heine-Strasse

90
Jannowitz-
brücke
Jannowitz-
brücke Ufar

122

Schultze-
Delitzsch-
Platz

Annen-

86
88
87
Litten-
strasse
Waisenstr
91

Klosterstrasse
Jüdenstr

Stralauer

25
126
127
Markisches
Museum
Insektr
Wallstrasse
Neue Rossstr

46
45
44

500 m

Alexanderplatz
strasse
85

93
92

Grunerstrasse
Molken-
markt
Mühlendamm

43
47
48

98
99
94
96 97
95
Postr

102 101
103

104 105

Breite Strasse
Petri-
Platz

Spittel-
markt
Seydlitzstrasse

250

42
49
50
51

Spreeufer
100

Spandauer

Zum
Nussbaum

Liebknecht

84
Schloss-
platz

Fischerinsel
Gertraudenstr

Spittel-
markt

KREUZBERG
Axel-Springer-Str
Oranienstrasse
Waldeck-
park

Kommandantenstrasse

Alte Jakobstrasse

19
18
17
16
15

Rosenthaler
Markt
S
21
20

Rochstr
Friedrichsbrücke
52
41
39
40

Niederlagstr
83

Werderscher
Markt

Hausvogteiplatz
Niederwall-
strasse
Hausvogtei-
platz

128

Ritterstrasse

Oranienburger
Strasse

Burgstr
Hackescher
Markt
Monbijou-
platz
Monbijou Park

26
27

Lust-
garten

Am Zeughaus
54
53

81
Oberwallstrasse
55
80
106
79
Bebel-
platz

105
121

120
119
118
130 129

Jerusalemer
Strasse
Markgrafen

Strasse

Kochstrasse

28
29
38
37
36
Am Kupfer-
graben
Bahnhofstr
Dorotheenstr
56
57
78
77
Hegel-
platz
Universitätsstr
Linden

Charlottenstrasse

58
59
60
Planckstr
Georgenstrasse
den
Friedrichstrasse

76

117
116
115
114
108 107

113
131

Gendarmen-
markt

132
Stadtmitte
Mohrenstr
Taubenstrasse

142

144
146
147
148
Charlottenstrasse

145
143

Leipziger Strasse

Krausenstrasse
Schützenstrasse
Zimmerstrasse
Kochstrasse

Weidendamm-
brücke
Am Weiden-
damm

30
31
32

Mittelstr
63
62
61
64

74
75

Französische
Strasse
Französische
Strasse
Glinkastrasse
Jäger

Mauerstrasse
133

Wilhelmstrasse

141
139
138
140

13
14
12

Johannisstrasse

Ziegelstrasse

Bertolt-Brecht-
Platz
8
6 7
5
10 11
9

33

Reinhardt-
Karl-
platz
4
3
2
1
Albrechtstrasse
Schumannstrasse

35

Marschall-
brücke
damm
Wilhelm-

72
73
71 70

109
110

112

Behrenstrasse

134
136

Wallmann-
platz
Mohrenstr

Kronenstrasse

137
Potsdamer
Platz

Stresemannstrasse
Köthener Strasse
Niederkirchner Strasse

MITTE

Luisenstrasse
Reichstagufer
Spree

Neustädtische Kirchstr
Unter

Dorotheenstrasse
Unter den Linden
strasse

65
68 69
67
66

Pariser
Platz
111

135

Vosstrasse

Platz vor dem
Brandenburger Tor
Ebertstrasse
Ebertstrasse

34
Schiffbauer

Tiergarten

Leipziger
Platz

Potsdamer Platz Map p120

MAP 8 - MITTE

PLACES TO STAY
3   Künstlerheim Luise
71   Hotel Adlon Kempinski
126   art'otel Ermelerhaus
129   Berlin Hilton

PLACES TO EAT
5   Stäv
7   Ganymed
10   Bambussprosse
18   Zucca
20   Bagels & Bialys;
      Tukadu Bead Shop
36   Café Odeon
38   Die Zwölf Apostel
50   Nordsee
51   TGI Friday's
63   Café Einstein Unter den Linden
95   Reinhard's
96   Zur Gerichtslaube
97   Zum Nussbaum
107   borchardt
113   Nö
120   Vau
145   Café Adler
147   Sale e Tabacchi
148   Arbeitsamt IV Kantine

PUBS & CLUBS
6   Broker's Bier Börse
13   WMF
14   Kalkscheune; Clubhouse Hostel
15   Meilenstein
16   Onyx
17   Kurvenstar
31   Tränenpalast
89   Zur letzten Instanz
124   Sage Club
136   Tresor/Globus

SHOPPING
29   Berlin Art & Nostalgia Market
42   Berlin University Bookshop
59   Dussmann – Das
      Kulturkaufhaus
60   Agata Jewellery
75   Meissener Porzellan
115   Quartier 206
116   Galeries Lafayette
131   Quartier 205
132   Kiepert Bookshop
143   British Bookshop

THEATRE & MUSIC
1   Deutsches Theater;
      Kammerspiele
2   Baracke
9   Berliner Ensemble
12   Friedrichstadtpalast
30   Die Distel
53   Maxim Gorki Theater
74   Komische Oper

79   Staatsoper Unter den Linden
118   Konzerthaus
123   Die Radieschen Kabarett

OTHER
4   STA Travel
8   Brecht Statue
11   Fahrradservice
19   Hackesche Höfe: Aedes East
      cafe; Hackescher Hof;
      Chamäleon Variété;
      Aedes East Galerie;
      Arndt & Partner Galerie;
      Fahrradstation; Oxymoron;
      Hackesches Hof-Theater
21   Fraueninfothek;
      Café Seidenfaden
22   Police Station
23   Atlas Reisewelt
24   ADM Mitfahrzentrale
25   World Time Clock
26   Alte Nationalgalerie
27   Pergamon Museum
28   Bodemuseum
32   Bruno Winkler Boats
33   Ministry of the Environment
34   Reichstag
35   Federal Press Office
37   Kilroy Travel
39   Neues Museum
40   Altes Museum
41   Stern und Kreis Boats
43   Hungary House; Ungarn Tours
44   Hekticket
45   TV Tower; Telecafé
46   Post Office
47   Marienkirche
48   Neptune Fountain
49   Polish Cultural Institute
52   Berliner Dom
54   Zeughaus
55   Neue Wache
56   Humboldt Universität; Mensa
57   State Library
58   Canadian; Belgian and
      Dutch Embassies
61   UK Embassy
62   Berlin Story
64   US Embassy
65   Future French Embassy
66   Wall Victims' Memorial
67   Brandenburg Gate;
      BTM Tourist Office
68   Future American Embassy
69   Future Academy of Arts
70   Future UK Embassy
72   Polish Embassy
73   Russian Embassy
76   Healthland
77   Deutsche Guggenheim;
      Dresdner Bank
78   Old Royal Library

80   Crown Princesses' Palace;
      Opernpalais
81   Crown Princes' Palace; Museum
      of German History (temporary)
82   Schlossbrücke
83   Berliner Water Taxis
84   Palace of the Republic
85   Rotes Rathaus
86   Courts of Justice
87   Franciscan Abbey Ruin
88   Podewil Culture Centre; Café
      Podewil; Tanzwerkstatt Berlin
90   Stern und Kreis Boats
91   Parochialkirche
92   Mint; Palais Schwerin
93   Altes Stadthaus
94   Hanfmuseum
98   Nikolaikirche
99   Knoblauchhaus;
      Historische Weinstuben
100   Ephraim-Palais
101   Berlin City Library
102   Ribbeckhaus; Centre for
      Berlin Studies
103   Neue Marstall
104   State Council Building; Bike City
105   Friedrichwerdersche Kirche;
      Schinkelmuseum
106   St Hedwig Cathedral
108   H&M Clothing;
      French Embassy
109   Stasi – Die Ausstellung
110   Hungarian Consulate
111   Site of Holocaust Memorial
112   Gate Sauna
114   American Express
117   Französischer Dom;
      Hugenottenmuseum
119   Schiller Statue
121   Police Station
122   Märkisches Museum; City
      Bears; Köllnischer Park
125   Otto-Nagel-Haus
127   Museum of Childhood &
      Adolescence
128   Czech Centre; Čedok Travel
130   Deutscher Dom;
      German History Exhibit
133   Czech Consulate
134   Hitler's New Chancellery
135   Site of Hitler's Bunker
137   Infobox
138   Martin-Gropius-Bau
139   Topography of Terror; Former
      Gestapo Headquarters; Wall
140   Abgeordnetenhaus
      (City Parliament)
141   Finance Ministry;
      former Air Force Ministry
142   Thomas Cook
144   Former Checkpoint Charlie
146   Haus am Checkpoint Charlie

MAP LEGEND

CITY ROUTES

Freeway .... Freeway	--------- .... Unsealed Road
Highway .... Primary Road	--→---- .... One Way Street
Road ..... Secondary Road	.... Pedestrian Street
Street .... Street	⊓⊓⊓⊓⊓ ..... Stepped Street
Lane .... Lane	⊃)= ⊂ .... Tunnel
...... On/Off Ramp	========... .... Footbridge

HYDROGRAPHY

.... River, Creek	⊂⊃ ⊂⊃ .. Dry Lake; Salt Lake
●–●–●... Canal	° ⌒ ... Spring; Rapids
⬭ .... Lake	⑤ ⊣⊦⤙ .... Waterfalls

REGIONAL ROUTES

=== ... Tollway, Freeway	
.... Primary Road	
.... Secondary Road	
.... Minor Road	

BOUNDARIES

▬ ▪ ▬ ▪ ...... International	
— ▪ — ▪ .... State	
— — .... Disputed	
▬▬■▬ ...... Fortified Wall	

TRANSPORT ROUTES & STATIONS

⊢––O .... Train	––––⬚ .... Ferry
⊢––⑤ .... S-Bahn	– – – ....Walking Trail
═──Ⓤ .... U-Bahn	. . . . Walking Tour
⊢–⊹–⊹ .. Underground Train	▬▬ .... Path
▬▬▬...Tramway	▬▬▬ ...... Pier or Jetty

AREA FEATURES

▬▬... Building	.... Market	⋔ .... Beach	.... Campus
✿ .... Park, Gardens	⬭ ..... Sports Ground	.... Cemetery	.... Plaza

POPULATION SYMBOLS

✪ **CAPITAL** .... National Capital	⊙ **CITY** .... City	● Village .... Village
◉ **CAPITAL** .... State Capital	⊙ **Town** .... Town	.... Urban Area

MAP SYMBOLS

■ .... Place to Stay	▼ .... Place to Eat	● .... Point of Interest

✕ .... Airport	▣ ...... Embassy, Consulate	⋔ .... Museum	⊡ ..... Swimming Pool
▣ . Archaeological Site	⚘ .... Fountain	▣ .... Parking	⊠ .... Synagogue
⊖ .... Bank	⊕ .... Golf Course	★ ...... Police Station	⊠ .... Telephone
▣ .... Bus Terminal	⊕ .... Hospital	▣ .... Post Office	▣ .... Theatre
▣ ... Castle, Chateau	⊠ ...... Internet Cafe	▣ .... Pub or Bar	▣ .... Tomb
▣ .. Cathedral, Church	⚲ .... Monument	⊠ ... Shopping Centre	❶ . Tourist Information
▣ .... Cinema	☪ .... Mosque	▥ ...... Stately Home	⌕ .... Zoo

Note: not all symbols displayed above appear in this book

LONELY PLANET OFFICES

Australia
Locked Bag 1, Footscray, Victoria 3011
☎ 03 8379 8000 fax 03 8379 8111
email: talk2us@lonelyplanet.com.au

USA
150 Linden St, Oakland, CA 94607
☎ 510 893 8555 TOLL FREE: 800 275 5555
fax 510 893 8572
email: info@lonelyplanet.com

UK
10a Spring Place, London NW5 3BH
☎ 020 7428 4800 fax 020 7428 4828
email: go@lonelyplanet.co.uk

France
1 rue du Dahomey, 75011 Paris
☎ 01 55 25 33 00 fax 01 55 25 33 01
email: bip@lonelyplanet.fr
www.lonelyplanet.fr

World Wide Web: www.lonelyplanet.com *or* AOL keyword: lp
Lonely Planet Images: lpi@lonelyplanet.com.au